DAVID'S QUESTION

"What Is Man?"

[PSALM 8]

RUDOLF STEINER, ANTHROPOSOPHY AND THE HOLY SCRIPTURES

An Anthroposophical Commentary on the Bible

TERMS AND PHRASES : VOLUME 2

DAVID'S QUESTION

"What Is Man?"

[PSALM 8]

EDWARD REAUGH SMITH

ANTHROPOSOPHIC PRESS

Copyright © Edward Reaugh Smith 2001

Published by Anthroposophic Press
PO Box 799, Great Barrington, MA 01230
www.anthropress.org

Library of Congress Cataloging-in-Publication Data

Smith, Edward Reaugh.
    David's question : "what is man?" (psalm 8) / Edward Reaugh Smith.
        p. cm. -- (Rudolf Steiner, anthroposophy and the Holy Scriptures ; v. 2.)
Includes bibliographical references and index.
    ISBN 0-88010-500-3
 1. Anthroposophy.   I. Title.
    BP595 .S59 2001
    299'.935--dc21   2001004222

Excerpts from *Catching the Light* by Arthur Zajonc, Oxford University Press paperback edition, 1995. Copyright © 1993 Bantam Books. Reprinted by permission of Bantam Books, a division of Random House, Inc.

Excerpts from *Electromagnetism and the Sacred* by Lawrence Fagg. Copyright © 1999 Lawrence W. Fagg. Reprinted by permission of the Continuum International Publishing Company, Inc.

Excerpts from *The Temple of Man* by R. A. Schwaller de Lubicz, published by Inner Traditions International, Rochester, VT 05767. Translation copyright © 1998 Inner Traditions International.

Excerpts from *The Egyptian Miracle* by R. A. Schwaller de Lubicz, published by Inner Traditions International, Rochester, VT 05767. English translation copyright © 1985 Inner Traditions International.

10 9 8 7 6 5 4 3 2 1

Printed in the United States of America

CONTENTS

TITLE THOUGHT

If ultimately there is only one reality,
then neither religion nor science is fulfilled
until they become one on a higher plane
than either now occupies.

ACKNOWLEDGMENTS

Without the warm encouragement, advice and assistance of Mary, Chris and Michael at the Press since the early days of my anthroposophical studies, this book surely could not have come about. How beautifully coincidental their parallel to the high spiritual trinity of Mary/Christopher/Michael.

Will's helpful suggestions and meticulous editing of the manuscript protect me from much embarrassment in both form and substance.

The many persons in this country and abroad who have spoken highly of THE BURNING BUSH *have encouraged me greatly in the preparation of this sequel.*

But it is Jo Anne, whose companionship and love are always there, who has sacrificed the most to make this book possible.

PREFACE

THIS VOLUME IS THE SEQUEL to *The Burning Bush,* the first volume in a series envisioned as a complete Bible commentary based upon the "anthroposophical" understanding given to humanity by Rudolf Steiner during the first quarter of the twentieth century.

While this volume has a vital connection with *The Burning Bush,* it can nevertheless stand alone and be profitably considered without necessarily having first absorbed the contents of its predecessor. The thesis of *The Burning Bush,* fairly stated in the first sentence of its General Introduction, is that "the parable of the Prodigal Son (Lk 15,11-32) is an allegory [about the human soul] in which Christ crystallizes the full Bible message." The thesis of the present volume is best approximated by the title thought on p. vi: science and religion, which were one in ancient times, must again become one if either is to be fulfilled. And it is the work of Rudolf Steiner, probably more than any other, that points to powerful forces of mutual attraction within these two paradigms, so often at odds historically—forces suppressed by each discipline as traditionally practiced, even by those who conscientiously profess to be both religious and scientific.

Steiner called his work "anthroposophy"[1] and also, more apropos for our present purposes, "spiritual science." The very phrase suggests the marriage of two polarities in human evolution.

Those familiar with the first volume will notice some changes in format and style in this volume. My general approach here, as in the earlier volume, is to include essays on what I see to be key "Words and

---

1. Anthroposophy is a combination of the Greek root words *anthropos* and *sophia.* The latter, with a capital, is defined in our dictionaries as "wisdom," and given a feminine attribute. The Sophia is personified as the feminine "Wisdom" in the first nine chapters of Proverbs. Our common suffix "sophy" derives from it and means "knowledge or thought," as in "philosophy," "theosophy," and the like.

Anthropos should be distinguished from *homo,* a Latin word referring to a two-legged primate. We should think of *homo* as referring to the body, and *anthropos* as referring to what sets the human being above the animal. It represents the higher aspect, the soul, or the soul and the spirit, of the human being. Thus, "anthroposophy" is the wisdom of the soul of the human being.

Phrases." However, the practice of capitalizing these phrases in the text and placing them in quotes, as was done in the first volume, is generally discontinued here, except where reference is made to the title of an essay itself. It served its purpose there, as an introductory work, but could become more disruptive than helpful if carried over into this and future volumes.

In the text the references in bold having a Roman numeral followed by a hyphen and an Arabic numeral (I-4, e.g.) refer to the Charts and Tabulations, which present key ideas of anthroposophy. The Roman numeral refers to the volume number where the chart first appears. There are only a few new charts for this volume but there are many references to ones from *The Burning Bush*. Due to space considerations, not all of those charts are included here, but the most important and most frequently cited ones are reproduced in the appendix. Readers who do not have access to *The Burning Bush* can find all of the charts at my website, *www.bibleandanthroposophy.com.*

The Bibliography in Volume One is a research tool by itself, listing chronologically and by lecture location all Steiner titles available in the English language, insofar as I was able to identify them at the time. The Bibliography in this volume lists only works that are cited in this volume or were not included in the first volume.

Readers who have a copy of the original edition of *The Burning Bush* should note that a revised edition is now in print. The substantive changes in it are quite limited. Those who do not have access to a revised copy can see the nature of the changes in the Preface to the Revised Edition in the website identified above.

Shortly after publication of *The Burning Bush*, upon the helpful recommendation and advice of friends and associates, this larger project was expanded to include the publication of smaller books written in a more popular style, focusing upon limited portions of the larger volumes. Two of these "little books," derived from *The Burning Bush*, have been published to date: *The Incredible Births of Jesus*, summarizing "The Nativity" essay, and *The Disciple Whom Jesus Loved*, focusing largely upon the "Peter, James and John" and "Egypt" essays. Where relevant, these little books are cited in this volume.

Since this book attempts to relate both science and theology on what it deems a higher level than either now occupies, the word *science* appears frequently. By definition, *science* means the state of knowing. Since the thrust of this work is that there are critically important areas where *science* fails to know, or "knows" things that are not real or true in the deepest sense, I have been tempted to put the word in quotes. But I have not done so. Unless the context clearly indicates otherwise, the term *science* as used herein refers broadly to the pertinent domains of learning exclusive of what can be known through, and in contradistinction from, the *spiritual science* (or anthroposophy) advanced by Rudolf Steiner.

The policy of avoiding sexist writing followed in the first volume continues in this one with these addenda. **First**, the title of this book and the last essay would seem to visibly violate this principle. Quotation marks are used to emphasize the historical prominence of the phrase as it is. Happily, several modern translations have gotten away from the male implications of the patriarchal versions.[2] The problem is that they are neither well enough known nor sufficiently uniform to convey precisely this passage, with all it entails, in the eighth Psalm. Therefore, I feel that too much is lost in focusing on the subject matter if the traditional language is not used in the title.

The **second** addendum is to comment on the use of the traditional "Father-Son" language within the doctrinal Trinity. The term "Creator God" is sometimes used instead of "Father." But because Christ spoke in terms of the "Father," even if metaphorically, it is difficult in all cases to break away from Gospel language. Even those translations that translate Ps 8,4 in the sex-free "human" mode uniformly use Christ's reference to the Father.

Those bothered by these concessions to tradition should take note, however, of the clear stand to the contrary taken with respect to the asexual nature of the Creator God and the Christ, and thus the Holy Trinity, in the essay entitled "Darkness."

Finally, as this volume was essentially ready for printing I received the newly published *The Fourth Dimension/Sacred Geometry, Alchemy, and Mathematics* (FD), AP, 2001, including a 1905 five-lecture cycle and other items by Steiner not previously published in English. My brief inspection of this work suggests its relevance to topics covered in this volume.

---

2. These include the New Revised Standard Version (NRSV), Revised English Bible (REB), New American Bible (NAB), New Jerusalem Bible (NJB) and Contemporary English Version (CEV). But just within these, the variations include "human beings," "a human being" and "humans," with quite a variety of syntax.

THE QUESTION

THE NOBLE KING ANFORTAS, grievously afflicted, could only be healed if his nephew Parzival asked the right question. Advised early in his adventures not to ask *too many questions*, Parzival failed to ask the question. The king suffered on until at last Parzival, tearful and concerned, asked that question, *"Uncle, what is it that troubles you?"* Then he who raised Lazarus healed the king.

Thus Wolfram von Eschenbach (ca. 1170–ca. 1220), in his wondrously allegorical epic *Parzival* (PARZ), suggests the title of this book.

That Anfortas symbolized humanity since its Fall (Gen 3) is made clear by the circumstance that, being periodically exposed to the Grail, he could not die in spite of his longing for death—the curse divinely imposed upon both Cain and Job (Gen 4,13-16; Job 2,6).[1]

---

1. Those who want will find numerous other clues. The inability of the human soul to die is, of course, the title thesis of Vol. 1, *The Burning Bush.* The bush, though burned, is not consumed (Ex 3,2-3; Is 6,13). But the parallels go on and on. For instance:

   (a) Anfortas had three noble siblings (Trevrizent, Repanse de Schoye and Schoysiane; cf. Job's three "friends"). It was said of them that, though rich, they lived in sorrow, and one had even chosen poverty. The three bodies of the human being (physical, etheric and astral; see I-9, also "Three Bodies" in The Burning Bush) are indicated.

   (b) The kingdom (castle and surrounding region) of Anfortas was known as Munsalvaesche. One can hardly fail to see in it the meaning, "the world's salvation" (mundus = world; salvare = to save). And it was a place not to be found by those that seek it per se (Mt 11,12; Lk 16,16), but only by those who "chance upon it unawares" (cf. it comes like a thief in the night; Job 24,13-14; Joel 2,9; Mt 24,43; Lk 12,39; 1 Th 5,2; 2 Pet 3,10; Rev 3,3; 16,15).

   (c) Parzival had been given twelve pieces of advice at the start of his journeys, only one of which was "Don't ask too many questions." These suggest the twelvefold zodiacal influences so clearly shown in the Bible starting with the instructions to Abraham to look to the stars and his descendants would be like them (Gen 15,5). His descendants were thus twelvefold through both Isaac and Ishmael. Christ patterned his disciples accordingly, and the sevenfold nature of creation in Revelation resolves into the twelvefold pattern of the Holy City.

   (d) Parzival was given a priceless bejeweled sword before he first approached Anfortas. The sword was said to bring a magic spell and to give great power—it was to be a sign to him to ask the question. His failure to do so greatly extended the king's suffering. The "sword" symbolizes the powerful word of God (Mt 10,34; Eph 6,17; Heb 4,12; Rev 1,16; 2,12,16; 19,15,21).

   (e) The return of Parzival, when he asked the right question, was anticipated as his "second coming" and brought about the healing of the king.

For others, see Stein, *The Ninth Century and the Holy Grail* (NCHG).

There are *many questions,* but the deepest question of the human soul, and *the one* it fails to ask, is *"What is man?"* For to ask it earnestly is to let the one who raised Lazarus heal all its suffering. The question is the basis (i.e., self-knowledge: "he came to himself"; Lk 15,17) of the Prodigal Son's (humanity's) return.

Four times in scripture the question is asked (see the Chapter End Note).

But as we begin our quest, we immediately notice that the setting is different in each of these passages.

In Job, probably the most ancient, the question clearly arises out of the normal human condition.

We then notice that each Psalm passage includes both "man" and "the son of man" in its question. But the second line (the "son of man" clause) in each instance merely restates the first line in different words—the ever-present parallelism in the Psalms.[2] The context in Ps 144 is very brief. It speaks only of the brevity of human life in a single short sentence, and even then with parallelism. Missing in it is the mystical nature that

---

2. "Parallelism," everywhere recognized as the most persistent poetic characteristic of the Psalms, means that the second line (and third if there is one) of a verse is related in some way to the first. It can be synonymous or antithetical, but more frequently it is related in some other more subtle way. See 4 NIB 652, 16 AB xxxiii and INTPN (Psalms), p. 5. Since three of the four passages use "son of man" in the second line, a phrase that has intrigued Judeo-Christian scholars through the centuries, it would be inappropriate to say that it merely restates the meaning of the first line. It is theologically treated in 6 ABD 137 et seq. But it derives its true meaning from the ancient mysteries, and can be best understood today in an anthroposophical light. Steiner shows its meaning in a number of lectures: *The Gospel of St. John* (GSJ), Lect. 6, p. 105; *The Gospel of St. John* (GOSPSJ), Lect. 5, p. 47 and Lect. 6, p. 61; *The Gospel of St. Luke* (GSL), Lect. 10, p. 194; *The Gospel of St. Matthew* (GSMt), Lect. 11, pp. 188 et seq.; *Background to the Gospel of St. Mark* (BKM), Lect. 6, pp. 111-113; *The "Son of God" and the "Son of Man"* (SGSM), single lecture; and *The Gospel of St. Mark* (GSMk), Introduction (by Stewart C. Easton) p. xiii and Lect. 9, pp. 174-175. See also Andrew Welburn's *The Beginnings of Christianity* (BC), Chap. 9, pp. 145-163, and Sergei O. Prokofieff's *Eternal Individuality* (EI), Chap. 12, pp. 206-207. That the phrase's meaning derives from the ancient mysteries is also strongly indicated by the *Rule of the Community* discovered as part of the Dead Sea Scrolls; see *The Dead Sea Scrolls: Rule of the Community* (RULE), p. 58, described as Col. III, line 13, "(It is) for the Master to instruct and teach all the Sons of Light concerning the nature of all the sons of man." At the risk of oversimplifying, anthroposophy shows that the "son of man" is the perfected human Ego (on Earth) as the "son" of its heavenly archetype and of the lower three bodies; Jesus of Nazareth, by the time he hung on the Cross, was the first earthly "son of man" through having been indwelt for three years by the Christ. The distinction, however, between the "son of man" and the "son of God," is that the former is the perfected earthly human Ego while the latter is the Christ.

characterizes the "son of man" phrase in the Gospels and the influential Book of Enoch (Enoch I). That mystical nature also seems absent in Ps 8, for while it does speak of the dominion given by God over other creatures, only earthly creatures are listed.

But the Hebrews passage clearly brings the Christ into the formula. Whatever reference Paul may have had to the "man" portion of the parallelism—and in this there is, perhaps, still the faint hint of melding the two together—without a doubt Paul spoke of the Christ as being "for a little while lower than the angels" (vss 7 and 9). And this must necessarily be the case also because the dominion given him was not limited to earthly creatures but included also the heavenly, though Paul notes that humanity is not yet able to see all things that are subject to him (vs 8). That Paul included heavenly creatures also as being under the dominion of Christ is fully in keeping with his "letters."[3] This then gives special effect to his saying that Christ was, for a little while, made lower than the angels—the lowest of the nine levels of the hierarchies (see the footnote just cited).

We saw in the "I AM" essay of *The Burning Bush* that there is both a higher and a lower "I Am," the normal human and the Christ, and that the end to human evolution is that these will become one. The question "What is man?" will not be answered except in seeing both the existence of these two and the necessity of their union in the evolution of human consciousness. This is the great mystery that Paul refers to in Eph 1,9-10: "For he has made known to us in all wisdom and insight the mystery of his will, according to his purpose which he set forth in Christ as a plan for the fullness of time, to unite all things in him, things in heaven and things on earth."

My mother never would read a book without reading the last page first. If it did not end right she would not read it. I think God did the same with his creation. But as normal human beings we have been denied that vision. The last essay in this book has the book's own title.

---

3. In Phil 2,9-10 we read, "Therefore God has highly exalted him and bestowed on him the name which is above every name, that at the name of Jesus every knee should bow, in heaven and on earth and under the earth"; and in Col 1,15-16, "He is ... the first-born of all creation; for in him all things were created, in heaven and on earth, visible and invisible, whether thrones or dominions or principalities or authorities" all are spiritual beings of the hierarchies, see I-6, and also the discussion of the word "Name" in the "I Am" essay, in *The Burning Bush*.

But the nature of our question is such that to read the end first serves no purpose. We must work our way through several of the most basic biblical terms and scientific quandaries before gaining entrance to the final contemplation. Like both Cain and Job, as the Prodigal Son we must travel from Alpha to Omega, seeking the Unity of all.

CHAPTER END NOTE

All four quotations are from the Revised Standard Version (emphasis mine).

Ps 8,3-8:

> ³ When I look at thy heavens, the work
> of thy fingers, the moon and the stars which thou has
> established;
>
> ⁴ **what is man** that thou art mindful of him,
> And the **son of man** that thou dost care for him?
>
> ⁵ Yet thou has made him little less than God,
> And dost crown him with glory and honor.
>
> ⁶ Thou hast given him dominion over the works of thy hands;
> thou hast put all things under his feet,
>
> ⁷ all sheep and oxen, and also the beasts of the field,
>
> ⁸ the birds of the air, and the fish of the sea,
> whatever passes along the paths of the sea.

Job 7,17-21:

> ¹⁷ "**What is man**, that thou dost make so much of him,
> and that thou dost set thy mind upon him,

^{18} dost visit him every morning, and test him every moment?

^{19} **How long** wilt thou not look away from me,
Nor let me alone till I swallow my spittle?

^{20} If I sin, what do I do to thee, thou watcher of men?
Why hast thou made me thy mark?
Why have I become a burden to thee?

^{21} Why dost thou not pardon my transgression
and take away my iniquity?
For now I shall lie in the earth;
Thou wilt seek me, but I shall not be."

Ps 144,3-4:

^{3} O Lord, **what is man** that thou dost regard him,
Or the **son of man** that thou dost think of him?

^{4} Man is like a breath, his days are like a passing shadow.

Heb 2,5-9:

^{5} For it was not to angels that God subjected the world
to come, of which we are speaking.

^{6} It has been testified somewhere,
"**What is man** that thou art mindful of him,
or the **son of man**, that thou carest for him?

^{7} Thou didst make him for a little while lower than the angels,
thou hast crowned him with glory and honor,

^{8} putting everything in subjection under his feet."
Now in putting everything in subjection to him,
he left nothing outside his control. As it is,
we do not yet see everything in subjection to him.

[9] But we see Jesus, who for a little while was made lower than the angels, crowned with glory and honor because of the suffering of death, so that by the grace of God he might taste death for every one.

EVOLUTION

The Last Shall Be First and the First Shall Be Last

WAS THERE A PATTERN ON THE MOUNTAIN?

When Jesus' disciples asked him whose sin had caused the man to be born blind (Jn 9,1-3), the man or his parents, Jesus answered neither.[1] The debate on evolution that has raged through the nineteenth and twentieth centuries and into the twenty-first demands the same answer, excepting only that it be "none of these," for the debate's contentions are essentially threefold, namely, that the human being

1. evolved from the lower kingdoms without divine involvement;
2. evolved from the lower kingdoms with divine involvement;
3. did not evolve but was specially created by God in six days just a few thousand years ago.

The problem is that the question posed by the debate is based upon a false premise, namely, that a human being is something that can be perceived by the senses as we know them. And since our senses perceive only the mineral kingdom, the debate rages over whether or not the human being came into existence (either with or without divine involvement[2]) by the progression from one mineral state to another.

The true premise must be sought by first answering the question, What is the human being? That was the Psalmist's question.[3] And it is the question that must control the debate. To say the human being is made up of nothing but minerals means Darwinism (or neo-Darwinism as the case may be) wins the debate. But the problem with that is no one has ever shown how "nothing but minerals" could produce anything but an aggregation of minerals. Even more, no one has ever shown how minerals came into existence in the first place—the creation of matter. The start is

---

1. The meaning of Jesus' answer is discussed at p. 145 in *The Burning Bush*.
2. While the terms "divine" and "intellegent" are not synonymous, in this discussion "divine involvement" is deemed to include the currently popular standard "intelligent design."
3. See the End Note to "The Question" above.

always with existing matter. Even the "big bang" theory, which is only a theory, starts there.[4]

A central thesis of this book, and of the series of which it is a part, is that the human being is neither the result nor the sum total of an aggregation of minerals but is rather a state of consciousness merely clothed for a time, sojourning if you will, in the mineral kingdom.[5] Consider what differentiates the four kingdoms, mineral, plant, animal and human. The mineral kingdom standing alone is dead, from an earthly standpoint. The plant kingdom rises above the mineral kingdom with the addition of life. The animal kingdom rises above the plant kingdom with the addition of sensate consciousness. The human kingdom rises above the animal kingdom with the addition of self-consciousness or self-awareness, called the "I Am," biblically speaking. The "I Am" is the name that "no one knows except him who receives it" (Rev 2,17; 19,12-13; 3,12), for, as Rudolf Steiner first pointed out, no one can speak that name except the one to whom it is given; this cannot be said of any other name. The depth of its meaning is the subject of the "I Am" essay in *The Burning Bush*. John identifies the Christ as the "I Am" in his Gospel, and specifically equates that name to him in Rev 3,12 where the Christ reveals it to John as "my own new name." Moreover, the same Christ is clearly the Alpha and Omega, the first and the last in Second Isaiah's prophecy (Is 44,6; 48,12), as is shown in the next essay. But it is equally clear from the above passages in the Apocalypse that the same name is given to the human being when perfected as "a son of man" (as in the Christ-perfected Jesus of Nazareth, Rev, 1,17; see fn 2 in "The Question" and *Christianity as Mystical Fact* [CMF], Chap. 8, pp. 128–129). At the very time in human evolution when self-awareness began to emerge out of tribal consciousness, it confronted Moses on Mount Sinai in the form of a burning bush. But it was not a normal bush as we know it. Philo described it as a bush "entirely enveloped ... by the abundant flame ... [but] it nevertheless remained whole without being consumed, like some impassible essence, and not as if it were itself the natural fuel for fire, but rather as if it were taking the fire for its own fuel."[6] Its name was given as

---

4. As will be seen in this book, I reject that theory as a universal cop-out.

5. Volume one, *The Burning Bush*, began by offering as a major premise that the parable of the Prodigal Son is an allegory of the journey of the human soul that crystallizes the full Bible message.

6. This Philo passage, commenting upon Ex 3, is the epigraph in *The Burning Bush* (at p. viii).

"the I Am." It was the Christ speaking to Moses,[7] and it is clear from that and the rest of the Bible that it applies both to the human being and to the Christ, and that the two must be joined together as one. While we, as human beings, say "I am," we still ask who we are, and only when the higher "I Am" of Christ lives fully in us will we attain to the ultimate consciousness of being that constitutes the human as a god, that is, a spiritual being (Jn 10,34; Ps 82,6).

The spiritual reality of the first and the last (the Alpha and Omega) found expression also in Prov 25,6-7 (as also in its larger context Prov 25,1-14), and then in Christ's aphorism that the "first will be last, and the last first" (Mk 10,31; Mt 19,30; 20,26; Lk 13,30). I showed in *The Disciple Whom Jesus Loved* (as well as in the essay in *The Burning Bush* from which it was taken, "Peter, James and John") that these synoptic passages are Christ's reference to the relationship between Zebedee John ("the first who became last") and the one who would become the Evangelist John ("the last who became first"). But the principle is not limited by that instance, and can be seen to have dramatic application to the evolution of the four kingdoms. It is the shibboleth to understanding the true nature of human evolution.

A most intriguing illustration of its applicability has come to light in recent scientific research on embryonic stem cells, which exist only early in the embryonic process before they turn into more specialized cells. Ethical issues aside, by preserving these cells in their undifferentiated state, before they specialize in (metamorphose into) a particular human organ, it appears they can be used to replace terminally diseased human organs of all types. This is a most dramatic illustration of the "As Above, So Below" principle—the fractal discussed later in this volume. What holds back until the time is right[8] replaces phenomena that commit to specialized form at an earlier stage. This is what explains the evolutionary relationship of the human kingdom to the three lower ones. Humanity waited until the times of specialization—the descent of the animal kingdom—were over before descending into mineral form, though vestiges of all animals remain in human nature (which is the meaning of Noah's taking a pair of all animals

---

7. Paul recognizes that the descending Christ was active in Old Testament times (1 Cor 10,4) as does Evangelist John (Jn 12,41, as discussed in *The Burning Bush*, as well as Jn 1,3).
8. The concept of the "right time" is certainly biblical; see Mk 1,15; Rom 5,6; Gal 4,4; Eph 1,10; cf. 1 Pet 1,20. In the stem cell it can also be seen to be biological.

into the ark, the post-Atlantean human body [see Gen 6,19–7,3]; it is also implicit in the "wild beasts" in Christ's temptation experience [Mk 1,13][9]).

Nowhere have I found these principles, as they apply to human evolution, more ably expressed than in Hermann Poppelbaum's *Man and Animal* (MAA), published in 1931. Poppelbaum was already a capable biological scientist when he had a fateful meeting with Rudolf Steiner in 1921 and a whole new world conception opened to him. A portion of his expression of it follows:

> During the Azoic era the solid mineral matter of the earth is separated off for the first time. But it can only be taken up by those beings who are most backward in evolution; hastening ahead of the others, they "embody" themselves in the new substantiality. Thus the minerals appear as the first solidified kingdom on the earth. The remaining kingdoms, though already existent in rich variety and even at this stage divided into plant and animal and differentiated into types [he is here elaborating Gen 1,9-25, all of which existed in etheric form before taking on substantiality beginning with Gen 2,4b], still resist solidification. Their archetypes have remained behind hitherto in the more plastic elementary kingdoms; now, as they begin little by little to incorporate the solid elements, they take form as those organisms which belong to the great order of invertebrates. These were previously *already* differentiated as to their essential being, and their separation into types was an accomplished fact before the mineralization of their bodily form set in ["according to their kind"—Gen 1,11,12,21,24,25]. *And here we have the answer to one of the great riddles of paleontology:—the plasticity of the ancestral forms and the lack of true intermediate forms able to relate the chief types in the geological records.* The ancestral forms did indeed exist in bodily shape,—but they were of the finer substantiality which Rudolf Steiner has described as belonging to pre-earthly conditions, composed of the elements of warmth, air and water, *without as yet having absorbed any solid matter.* This supplies the reason for that mutability which has up to now completely baffled research. At the same time, we see why no impressions nor remains of them could be left in the earth's crust.... The germs of the future human body are among those forms which resist densification. (pp. 56-57)

---

9. See the discussion of the three temptations in *The Burning Bush*, pp. 434-436.

Poppelbaum goes on through the various geologic ages describing the evolution of the Earth and its inhabiting kingdoms. But running as a thread through it all is the plasticity that exists in the succeeding stages until those stages take on materiality. Thereupon they become imprisoned in their form, and what takes place in that form thereafter is a higher specialization and imprisonment. The animal is thus far more efficient in its speciality than the human being. But the human being remained plastic until the last, unspecialized, and could thus, at the "right time," take on materiality in a form that would permit it to receive self-awareness, "the I Am." "*Time and time again*," Poppelbaum says, "*on the long path of evolution it has been this quality of remaining plastic which has made steady advance possible for man.*" The human being is the "stem cell" of earthly evolution. It did not evolve from any "specialized cell" (any already-materialized lower kingdom), but had its own independent origin, still reflected in the mystery of embryology, which mirrors the heavenly bodies.

Teilhard de Chardin, in *The Phenomenon of Man* (PHEN), expresses the same thing.

> [I]t is the characteristic of minerals (as of so many other organisms that have become incurably fixed) to have chosen a road which closed them prematurely in upon themselves. By their innate structure the molecules are unfitted for growth. (p. 69)

> *In the world, nothing could ever burst forth as final across the different thresholds successively traversed by evolution (however critical they be) which has not already existed in an obscure and primordial way.* (p. 71)

> Nothing is so delicate and fugitive by its very nature as a beginning. As long as a zoological group is young, its characters remain indeterminate, its structure precarious and its dimensions scant. It is composed of relatively few individual units, and these change rapidly.... What, then, will be the effect of time on this area of weakness? Inevitably to destroy all vestiges of it. Beginnings have an irritating but essential fragility.... (pp. 120-121)

Returning to Poppelbaum's MAA (pp. 65-66; fns mine):

Man alone continues to abide in those parts of the earth in which he can still remain plastic, until at last for him too the hour has come. He makes his geological appearance in the later Atlantean epoch (glacial drifts), and has … from the beginning all the essential human characteristics together with signs of a developed culture. The fossil remains which the paleontologist finds today are not indeed those of men of the highest races (who carried on the Atlantean civilization) they belong to side branches; even Neanderthal man, as Rudolf Steiner has expressly shown, is not a direct ancestor of the civilized humanity of today. Years after Rudolf Steiner, contemporary research has arrived at the same conclusion, and has placed Neanderthal man on a side branch of the genealogical tree. The culture and life of the Atlantean, even his speech and his manners, have been described by Rudolf Steiner in his book, "Atlantis and Lemuria."[10] In this book he depicts the wonderfully high culture of the true "primeval man" of which Natural Science, with its "cavemen," the contemporaries of mammoth and cave bear, knows only the degenerate descendants. [Here he quotes from that book.]

With the Atlantean epoch begins the history and pre-history of man. This was the time, first of the oracle and later in the post-Atlantean epoch, of the mystery centers; from which all civilization comes forth. The post-Atlantean sub-epochs, of which ours is the fifth, have it as their task to develop, from the original clairvoyance of man, clear objective consciousness, and from the tribe-bound will of early times to evolve the free activity of self-conscious individuality.[11]

In the reluctance, so to speak, of Atlantean (Tertiary) man to proceed to mineralization, we perceive the secret of the absence of older traces of man in the geological record, and of their sudden appearance in the Diluvial (Glacial) periods. This solves the darkest problem of evolution, one which has presented extraordinary difficulties to Natural Science and provided the opponents of the theory of evolution with a welcome argument.

---

10. If this book has been translated to English, I am unaware of what its title is and whether it is in the bibliography in *The Burning Bush* under another title.
11. The gradual transition from tribal to individual consciousness, anticipated in the "I Am" appearance in Ex 3, is finally reflected in the sixth-century prophesies of Jeremiah and Ezekiel that the old proverb, "The fathers have eaten sour grapes, and the children's teeth are set on edge," would no longer apply but that only the soul that sins will die; Jer 31,29-30 and Ezek 18,1-4.

In the later Atlantean Epoch then, when the descending spiritual and soul powers of man united with the ascending physical vehicle, the spiritual and the physical processes of evolution come into contact. The human "I" is now received as a kernel into the matured sheath of the body.[12] Before this the bodily development was only a kind of shadow of the soul and spiritual kingdom; now the two halves have united to form a single process.

Here Poppelbaum gives us the following diagram illustrating the descending human being and the ascending physical form (p. 67):

Geologic Time Per I-5[13]

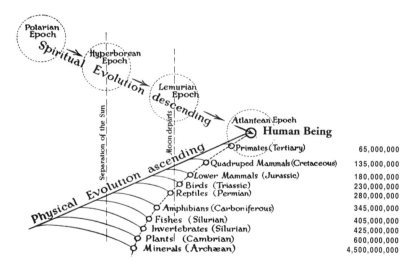

We have here the most graphic portrayal of the principle "the first shall be last, and the last shall be first." The first (earthly being) in the spiritual world was the human being, who came last into materiality, while the first into materiality (the mineral kingdom) will be the last ultimately

12. See the diagram in the "Naked" essay at pp. 402-403 of *The Burning Bush* and the related chart I-35.
13. Neither Steiner nor modern science necessarily agree with all these durations, but they suffice for purposes of the present illustration.

redeemed (spiritualized) from the material world (cf. Rom 8,19-23). In no true sense can the human being be said to have evolved from any of the lower kingdoms. The converging lines in Poppelbaum's diagram result from the active agency of the descending "I Am," being at one and the same time both the germinal human soul and the descending Christ (the "image" and "likeness"[14]). While all of the three lower kingdoms are in some way reflected in the human being's makeup,[15] both physical and sensate, those elements remained plastic in the human so as not to predominate or entrap, but to be mastered and purified by the human being over time as it seeks on Earth the perfection of its own "I Am," its merging with and into the higher "I Am" of Christ.

Kranich, a paleontologist and biologist as well as anthroposophist, shows in his *Thinking Beyond Darwin* (TBD) how the Goethean idea of the archetypal form must be applied, and how it emerges from the workings of the soul, the "I Am." He threads the process through the transitions from class to class, from fish to amphibian, from amphibian to reptile, from reptile to mammal, and from mammal to human. The "I Am" is always there in the course of physical evolution, pulling the form forward until the time is right for the "I Am" to enter. Kranich's work is highly cognate to Poppelbaum's, and in fact he says near the end, "I could conclude our considerations at this point with the reference to Poppelbaum and Kipp, were it not for several new aspects that have emerged in the foregoing discussion" (relative to the "main trunk of vertebrate phylogeny").[16]

With the beginning of the critical analysis of the Bible and the rise of Darwinism in the nineteenth century, Christendom has been torn asunder on the issue of the origin of the human being. "Progressives," Christians as well as others, and scientists have accepted its descent from the ape,[17] while fundamentalists and anti-intellectuals have insisted on the

---

14. The idea inheres that one is patterned after the other, but which (the "image" or the "likeness") dominates has never been clear. See the discussion at 1 NIB 345 pointing out that the "image-likeness" order in Gen 1,26 reverses as "likeness-image" in Gen 5,3.

15. Obviously the mineral kingdom is found in the incarnated human being, but the higher animal and plant kingdoms were specifically taken into the post-Atlantean human body by Noah, as prescribed (described) in Gen 6,19-22.

16. Unfortunately, all of the works of Kipp cited by Kranich are in German, untranslated into English as far as I know.

17. The idea of the slow evolutionary development of the human being is at least tacitly accepted by these, as also are the ideas of scientists about evolutionary biology. *(continued on following page)*

doctrine of creationism.[18] So the battle in the Scopes trial early in this century rages even today in school systems across the country. It would appear that we are at a most critical fork in the road both in our attempt to understand evolution and in our hope of reconciling the widely divergent views of it in science and religion.

Classical Darwinism is essentially dead, even among scientists, relying as it does upon the concepts of natural selection and survival of the fittest. But scientists in general ascribe to neo-Darwinism, which includes at least one additional element, the idea of adaptability. Unless otherwise indicated, I use the term "Darwinism" to include both.

Charles Darwin and those who have labored in his camp have performed an important and noble task for humanity. They began to look at phenomena and were willing to break with outmoded religious dogma where the two appeared in conflict. That their conclusions may have been in error does not detract from the major step forward they took on behalf of humanity.

That said, Darwinism seems to have been completely and effectively refuted. The foremost spokesman in this development is probably Phillip E. Johnson, a Berkeley law professor and an obviously conservative Christian who nevertheless disdains what he calls "creation-science," the "young-earth, six-day special creation." *The Wall Street Journal*, August 16, 1999 (p. A14), published his article "The Church of Darwin," a succinct torpedo against Darwinism. But his real contribution is his *Darwin on Trial* (1st ed. 1991, 2nd ed. 1993) in which he systematically demolishes the various arguments science has put forward in both paleontology and molecular biology.[19]

---

17. *(continued from previous page)* Descent from the animal kingdom seems clearly to be implicitly accepted, while couched in more theological language which clearly has the divine hand being involved in the process. Illustrative are the recent works by Korsmeyer, *Evolution & Eden* (EVED), and Edwards, *The God of Evolution* (GODEV).

18. "Creationism" is variously understood. I suspect most people take it to indicate the fundamentalist idea of a "young-earth, six-day special creation," and for that reason that is the way I use it here. Philip E. Johnson, near the beginning of his *Darwin on Trial*, wisely defines his terms and does so differently from mine. He coins the above phrase "young-earth, six-day special creation," and calls it "creation-science," while including in his definition of "creationism" the belief that evolution is controlled by a supernatural, divine hand. "Darwinism" he defines as "fully naturalistic evolution, involving chance mechanisms guided by natural selection" without any supernatural involvement, and with that definition I am comfortable. All three of these terms are defined, slightly differently, by WNWCD.

19. His later books, *Reason in the Balance, The Case Against Naturalism in Science, Law & Education* (1995) and *Defeating Darwinism by Opening Minds* (1997), while incorporating his various points of attack from *Darwin on Trial* and containing some meritorious arguments, *(continued on following page)*

What Johnson accomplishes is the annihilation of the materialistic (naturalistic) idea of evolution free from divine guidance. He is not alone in recognizing that scientists speak out of both sides of their mouth on the subject. Among themselves, there is almost universal recognition that the problems with their theories are immense and so far unsolved, while to the public they hold to the validity of their theories. The fatal defect in their position is that they exclude, in their deductive approach, any possibility of supernatural involvement, saying that since it cannot be measured or detected by their methods it must not be considered. They are flipping a two-headed coin and calling "heads." The poverty of the scientific position, at least the paleontological part after almost a century and a half of fossil research and analysis, becomes obvious by evaluating the concluding words of Ian Tattersall's, "Where Are We?" in his *The Fossil Trail* (1995).[20] And Roger Lewin's *Bones of Contention* (1987) depicts the powerful preconceptions and individual motivations that have littered the "scientific" findings and interpretations from the first. One begins to question the use of the term "science" as it relates to evolution. Speculation and hypotheses are rampant and inherent, and inductive reasoning, and certainly intuitive insight, are completely absent.

In all fields, whether it be spiritual "wineskins" or the breeding practices of elk (from the bull's standpoint), the old must be destroyed before the new can take its place. As this reality applies to the understanding of evolution, both Darwinism and creationism are the old. Johnson has destroyed them both (disdaining as he does what he calls "creation-science"). But the conservative Christian views that he would put in their place are, in the final analysis, little different from those from which Darwin's clan rightly rebelled. Johnson admits to having no "theory of evolution" to replace the one he shoots down,[21] aside from the fact that he passionately (and accurately) believes that the supernatural has a hand in

---

19. *(continued from previous page)* take on too much of a distinctive flavor of advocacy for social and religious views of the conservative or right-wing political establishment to be of equal merit with their forebear. While Johnson advocates philosophical rather than political means of implementing his ideas, these later writings seem couched in language calculated to play into political activity.

20. Tattersall is head of the anthropology department at the American Museum of Natural History.

21. See, for instance, his *Reason in the Balance* (RIB), p. 12, where he admits feeling no obligation to offer his own theory and says, "It is better to admit ignorance than to have confidence in an explanation that is not true."

the process. But having destroyed the old without giving us anything new, he leaves us in the situation where "the last state ... is worse than the first" (see Mt 12,45 and Lk 11,26). If we revert to pre-Darwinian religious understanding without rising to a higher perception of evolution, we will sink back into ways that are worse now, because of the needs of our age, than when Darwin challenged them in the nineteenth century.

One can investigate the libraries of both evolutionary science and theology without finding any significant reference to the intuitive revelations of Rudolf Steiner. But if the understandings of evolution imperative for our age are to be had, they must begin to move toward what this early twentieth-century prophet disclosed.

Steiner himself, at least in the works so far translated into English, could only give the guidelines to be followed, though these were extensive. The seeds of a broader understanding were sown in Vol. 1, and are carried forward in the balance of this book. And I have already mentioned the powerful anthroposophical writings of Poppelbaum and Kranich on the specific subject of evolution that demand now to be considered.

Norman Macbeth's *Darwin Retried: an appeal to reason* (1971, with 1978 Foreword) (DR) is similar in nature to Johnson's *Darwin on Trial* (DOT). One commentator calls it "elegantly impudent" in disassembling the various pillars upon which Darwinism rests. And had Johnson not come along, it could have stood in for his work, although it could not address, as Johnson has, those features of molecular biology that have been more recently advanced. It is well worth studying in connection with Johnson's work. But what is most intriguing about Macbeth's book is not what it says, but what it doesn't say. For Macbeth was an anthroposophist, elegantly qualified to go beyond and provide what Johnson could not (or at least didn't) provide, but for some reason chose not to do so. Perhaps he thought the time was not yet ripe. Macbeth belches pungent rhetoric out of the retort of his natural talent and strong liberal education forged by years at O'Melveny & Myers, a prominent Los Angeles law firm. In 1959, "living in Switzerland as a semi-invalid largely retired from the practice of law," he began to study biological evolution, which led eventually to *Darwin Retried: an appeal to reason*.[22]

---

22. In addition to *Darwin Retried: an appeal to reason*, he also seems to have written the similar-sounding *Darwin Retried* (pub. 1973) and was the subject of a 1982 interview by the magazine *Towards* published as *Darwinism: A Time for Funerals* (pub. 1985). The 1973 *Darwin Retried* is out of print and unavailable except for library or private sources. I have not had access to it.

I learned about Macbeth from an anthroposophic friend who had followed him at O'Melveny & Myers. What then amazed me, after reading his book, is my discovery that he had translated Vol. 3 of Guenther Wachsmuth's writings on evolution from the 1953 German edition into English in 1961. Wachsmuth was one of the circle of Steiner's closest disciples and a member of the original executive committee of the Anthroposophic Society formed by Steiner. Wachsmuth's three-volume work comprises Vol. 1, *Earth and Man*; Vol. 2, *The Evolution of the Earth*; and Vol. 3, *The Evolution of Mankind* (EVM). Several years earlier I had borrowed Vol. 3 from the Rudolf Steiner Library (Ghent, NY), and now I finally see that Macbeth translated it—obviously while recuperating in Switzerland, perhaps at one of anthroposophy's Arlesheim Clinics near Dornach.

Unfortunately, Vol. 3 is out of print (though still available from that library) and Vols. 1 and 2 have never been translated. While it is beyond the scope of this essay, anyone seriously interested in understanding the evolution of the various kingdoms on Earth should study this book. That Macbeth ignored it in attacking Darwinism himself suggests his thinking—first he had to demonstrate the invalidity of Darwinism itself, and trying to go beyond and show the deep insights of anthroposophy reflected in Wachsmuth's work would have jeopardized the important first step.

Maybe Macbeth's lawyer instinct also told him there were weaknesses in Wachsmuth—and probably that is true. But times march on. The interval has given us Johnson's devastating attack on Darwinism. The scientists' position, Johnson says, is invulnerable, but only because it both starts and ends with the premise of a wholly naturalistic evolution, unguided by any divine hand; it calls the toss but uses a two-headed coin. He properly asserts that the solution to the evolutionary puzzle must come from a source that is itself vulnerable to further testing—in short, he is urging the Goethean method of letting the phenomena speak as long as possible before entering judgment, a form of plasticity or waiting if you please. Only he stops short of observing all the phenomena.

Teilhard's beautiful articulations above combine with Steiner's revelations to unravel the mystery of why no connecting link has been found between archaeology's various earlier humanoids and homo sapiens. Fossilized evidence in the rocks of time is left only by species that have hardened into crusty or bony structures. But while the spiritual plan for bones is laid first, they necessarily come into mineral existence last. Something of the relationship between the spiritual foundation and the mineral-physical condition is discussed in *The Burning Bush* where it speaks of the three supersensible deeds of the descending Christ.[23] The first, which laid the foundation for the human being's upright skeletal stance, occurred in the primordial Lemurian Epoch.

While cellular life surely began during the recapitulation of ancient Sun in the Hyperborean Epoch (the Earth's second Great Epoch; see I-1), the early animal forms could begin to take shape even in bony structure only as the Earth increasingly mineralized, as Poppelbaum shows. The highly fluid condition of earthly existence permitted the wide dissemination of this fossil evidence. But it was during the later Lemurian and early Atlantean Epochs that the human being increasingly took on mineralized form, divided into sexes, and eventually, by mid-Atlantean time, stood upright with skull shaped like the dome of the heavens.

The brain with its two "tablets of stone" (2 Cor 3,3; Ex 24,12), mineralized substance in left and right brain with its *twelve* pairs of nerves (see I-20), could then begin to develop, lifted as it is toward and reflecting the heavens.

Early human migrations from Atlantis, preceding those of Noah but long after the ape's appearance, resulted in the older hominoid skeletons nearest to homo sapiens, but the primary skeletal evidence for the evolution of the human being has to lie on the bottom of the Atlantic Ocean in the submerged continent of Atlantis.[24] These human skeletons developed far later than those of the animal kingdom, which was gradually

23. See its charts I-76 and I-50, both based upon Steiner's lectures. These three supersensible deeds made possible the development first of upright skeletal stance, then speech, and then thinking, respectively. Only the fourth deed, Golgotha, occurred in the sense world of Earth.
24. However, even there skeletal evidence is not likely according to Steiner. In *Wonders of the World* (WW), Lect. 6, pp. 112-113, Steiner said:

Atlantean men were so formed that they did not have skeletons such as men have today. The human body has become more solid; it was much softer in Atlantean times. For this reason it was incapable of preservation, and the geology, the paleontology, of today will be hard put to it to find any trace of the real Atlantean man. But a geology, a paleontology, of quite a different kind *has* preserved the Atlantean man for us!... To burrow in the earth is quite absurd; in the earth we shall never find traces of prehistoric man which are anything but decadent.

He goes on to indicate that spiritual geology has preserved these early remains for us in Greek mythology and in the Akashic (see the essay "Akashic" in *The Burning Bush*).

20   DAVID'S QUESTION, "WHAT IS MAN?"

expelled, species by species, from the spiritual world as the human being developed there in its descending mode.

In the case of every species, however, including the human being, it is as Teilhard has said: its earliest earthly existence was too fragile to imprint itself in the rocks of time. Even the animal skeletons that survived give us only a degenerated form of their earliest earthly presence. Poppelbaum's work graphically displays this phenomenon, the degeneration of each animal species as it becomes more and more specialized and efficient. Only the human being is unspecialized, able to adapt on Earth to its changing needs. Animals are condemned from the first to their defective, though highly efficient, forms.

The development of the unique human skull, so that a large brain and intellect could emerge, is shown later, particularly in the essay "What is Man?" Only this brief sketch is possible here, but it points to the profound insight that a deeper immersion into anthroposophy can reveal.

In its millennial edition (January 1, 2000), *The Wall Street Journal* included a special section of articles deemed appropriate for reflection and contemplation on that symbolically pivotal date. One of those, by Peter Waldman, was entitled "Unsolved Mysteries/A look at four questions that we may never answer" (p. R57). While significant, the fourth question, "Will War End?", seems out of character with the first three, which are basic to this book's quest. They are:

1. How did the universe start?
2. How did life begin?
3. What is consciousness?

That such a sophisticated publication as *The Wall Street Journal* is willing to admit, in spite of all that science and religion have given us to date, that humanity may never be able to answer these most basic questions, is itself a commentary upon the state of recognized science and religion today. Anthroposophy is unwilling to make that admission. The high level of consciousness attained by Rudolf Steiner, possible over time for all human souls, has revealed insight into these mysteries beyond anything science and religion have thus far given us. That the path to this insight is demanding, and that so few have found it, does not negate its existence (cf. Mt 7,13-14). Perhaps only Steiner himself has actually experienced the answers, and this in a realm to which earthly language fails to conform. But from his own experience and intuition of the higher spiritual world he has struggled to express, in human concepts and words that all can understand who devote themselves to the study, both the pathway to this experience and the answers to these fundamental questions. It is the demanding task of this book to set out, as far as my limited and inadequate capabilities permit, these concepts as I have been able to grasp them.

So we return to our beginning, "Was there a pattern on the mountain?" What is the meaning of the Lord's instruction to Moses to make the temple according to the pattern he was shown on the mountain (Heb 8,5; Ex 25,40)? While the human body is the earthly temple for the sojourning soul, it's higher counterpart, the resurrection body, must surely be what was seen on the mountain (Jn 2,19,21; Rev 11,1-2). It was patterned in the spiritual world (Heb 8,5; 9,24), whence the "I Am" descended, forming its bodies from that archetype. No builder starts until the architect has handed down the pattern—that comes first. Then the builder creates accordingly.

Science and Darwinism are right in espousing the principle of evolution, but wrong in directing it from animal to human and in giving up on the literal truth of the biblical creation account. The truth is, the human came first, though descending into minerality last, and all animal species are a by-product of that human descent. Fundamentalists and anti-intellectuals are right in denying human descent from apes, but wrong in rejecting human evolution (descent) and in degrading the biblical creation account by rejecting so much God-given phenomena. They are right in saying the biblical account is literally true, but wrong in their myopic understanding of that truth.

One sensitive to the content of *The Burning Bush* will see in it the reconciliation of these two antagonistic positions. And the concepts presented in the present volume should lead the student to even deeper understanding of the reality of evolution and of the literal accuracy of the Bible when its language is more deeply understood in its proper literary character.

CREATION
AND
APOCALYPSE

CONTENTS

GENERAL COMMENTS

THE NOAH LEGEND handed down by Moses pictured the lower king-doms (animal, plant and mineral) as being contained within the ark, the physical body of the human being, as Atlantis sank into the ocean bearing its name.[1] The rise of sea levels relative to surviving land masses about ten to twelve thousand years ago is now well documented scientifically, and can be explained by melting polar caps, condensing ancient mists,[2] the submergence of some continents such as Atlantis through earthquake and

---

1. Gen 6,19–7,3; see the discussion of these in *The Burning Bush*, pp. 241, 280, 467 and 667. We saw there that these were not two different accounts of the same thing; rather they described different aspects in human development. The taking of both male and female in Gen 6 corresponds with the fact that when the androgynous human being was divided into male and female (Gen 2,18-25), the etheric body of the male became female and of the female became male, thus the principle of sexual duality within each of us. The Gen 7 version, on the other hand, portrayed the sevenfold nature of the organs of both the etheric and astral bodies; see **I-21** (Figure 13) and **I-86**, respectively portraying the astral and etheric bodies and their relationships to the seven planets (the "seven stars" of Rev 1,16,20; 2,1; and 3,1).

2. See the discussion of the meaning of "Nephilim" in *The Burning Bush*, pp. 20 and 465, with reference to Gen 6,1-4. Shortly after *The Burning Bush* was published I received a letter from a reader in North Dakota who could not find the term "Nephilim" in Gen 6,4. Upon examination I did indeed find, and report to him, that four translations in my library (*King James* [KJV], *New King James* [NKJV], *Amplified Bible* [AMPB] and *Living Bible* [LB]) did not use that word but substituted instead the word "giants." *(continued on following page)*

volcanic activity, and the upward thrusting of other continents and islands. That a people living on Atlantis during these events would describe the inundation of their known world as "the earth" (Gen 7,17-24) is quite understandable. It was their "earth."

Whether or not the Individuality who lived in Moses was the same who lived in Paul, as I have surmised,[3] Paul's description of the redeemed human being as the liberator of the rest of "groaning" creation (Rom 8,19-23) certainly corresponds with the understanding that the human being was both the first and the last in the creative scheme, an "image" in that sense of the Alpha and Omega, the Christ. The awesomeness of this recognition helps us, along with the Psalmist, to properly frame the question, "What is man?"

We have seen in the "Evolution" essay how both science and religion have fastened their star to purely materialistic concepts of creation, whether or not claiming divine guidance. If we are to gain a true perspective of the reality of both creation and apocalypse, the beginning and the end, the first and the last, we must leave that materialist mode and see in the biblical account a description of how things came from the spiritual world into material existence and how they will leave it. Genesis and

---

2. *(continued from previous page)* The other nine all used "Nephilim" which seems clearly to be preferred, for it relates to the word "cloud" or "mist," as an investigation into its etymology in any good dictionary suggests. The Greek combining form *nepho* seems relevant, and the Hebrew *nfl* means "fallen ones," i.e., fallen angels, though something between angels and human beings is probably implied in the Gen 6,1-4 passage. Nevertheless, the huge size of the "mist-being" before it condensed into later human form is suggested. In my response to the reader in North Dakota, I added:

One of the most complex, yet important, parts of the book is the Appendix to "Three Bodies," which gives a new explanation of Genesis 4 and 5, the relationships of which have baffled theologians considerably. This passage about the Nephilim follows immediately upon those chapters as a sort of mortar between Atlantis and post-Atlantis (the Noah transition), but in doing so it looks back to an early stage in the Lemurian and Atlantean Epochs that led eventually up to the "flood." The indicated "Appendix" material, though complex, tells of how, in these early stages, the gods (Elohim) joined with the human to create the offspring in the preceding chapters of Genesis.

3. See *The Burning Bush*, "Pillars on the Journey," pp. 540-544. What is said there may give stirring new insight into the significance of Paul's statement that upon his conversion he went first into Arabia (Gal 1,17). The complete lack of archaeological evidence of occupation of the Sinai peninsula during the time of Moses and the wilderness years has led many scholars to believe that Mount Sinai is in northwest Arabia, the vicinity of Moses' initiation by his Midianite father-in-law, Ex 18–19 (see "Mt. Sinai—in Arabia?", *Bible Review*, Vol. XVI, No. 2, April 2000, pp. 32-39, 52).

Revelation are telling this story, but in a manner that can only be disclosed by the Spirit of Truth speaking through the intuition of its prophets.

As a part of the general cultural development of humanity, the seventeenth and eighteenth centuries ushered in what is called the historical-critical method, a paradigm shift in the approach to scriptural study and interpretation. While its roots in regard to the Gospels really go back to Origen and his recognition of the differences in the four Gospels,[4] the documentary hypotheses of both the Old and New Testaments are the brainchild of this later cultural development in both the Jewish and Christian traditions.[5] Early in the twentieth century, Steiner lamented the immense application of human efforts in this approach, for his works show that the spiritual truth represented in the scriptural accounts is completely obscured by it.

We will likely neither comprehend the phrase "Alpha and Omega" nor approach a meaningful answer to the title question "What is man?" unless we familiarize ourselves with the *fractal*, a term coined only late in the twentieth century. MWCD defines it:

> Any of various ... curves or shapes for which any suitably chosen part is similar in shape to a given larger or smaller part when magnified or reduced to the same size.

Later we will see it illustrated far more fully in the "Fire" essay. But for now we might think of it simply as a pattern that remains constant whether magnified or reduced, whether applied in a higher dimension or lower. In Gen 1,26 we are told that the Elohim desire to pattern the human being after themselves ("in our image, after our likeness"). The fractal that portrays the human being is the same that portrays its creators and its own creatures. A fractal is without beginning or end.[6] We cannot

---

4. See Dungan, *A History of the Synoptic Problem*, NY, Doubleday, 1999 (part of the *Anchor Bible Reference Library* [ABRL]).
5. With respect to the Pentateuch, see Holladay, "Contemporary Methods of Reading the Bible," 1 NIB 125 at 128 ("The Historical Paradigm"). For a recognition of some of the problems that have recently been recognized with this approach, see Blenkinsopp, "Two Centuries of Pentateuchal Scholarship," in *The Pentateuch*, Chap. 1, NY, Doubleday, 1992 (part of ABRL).
6. Compare Heb 7,1-3, which speaks of the "avatar" character of Melchizedek. See the discussion of the "avatar" nature in connection with Heb 7,3 in the "Spiritual Economy" essay in *The Burning Bush*, pp. 94-96.

understand either the human being or creation itself without seeing in it the application of this principle. Hermes expressed it in his aphorism, "As above, so below; as below, so above."

Scripture, to be holy, must be of the same character, true at infinitely different levels or dimensions. Christ's parables have this holy character, none more so than the one we call the "parable" of the Prodigal Son, where its higher meaning is expressed by allegory. It is of the same fractal as the entire canon, portraying the creation, descent and reascent of the human being. A fractal can be observed as truth at countless different levels, depending upon the level from which seen. For this reason the Bible has always given reassurance of truth to persons at infinitely different levels of comprehension and at different periods of human development. But in order to do so it speaks in pictures reflecting, but transcending, time and space: pictures that can not be appropriated exclusively to any one time frame, but that ultimately eliminate time and space as a factor.

In the final analysis, the "written word" is a form of "graven image" proscribed by the second commandment (Ex 20,4). It relates to the second set of tablets graven by Moses (Ex 34) because the hardness of the people's hearts would not accommodate the message on the first (Ex 32), reflected by the mineralized tablets that constituted the human cerebrum. It was for the same reason, the hardness of their hearts, that Moses in that "second law" (literally "Deuteronomy"; Deut 24,1-4) allowed divorce to occur (Mt 19,7-8; Mk 10,2-6). It is this aspect of the written word that so troubled Paul (the same Individuality as Moses?), who expressed it so well in 2 Cor 3. Theologians generally agree that none of the Bible was actually written by Moses, and this is in keeping with the second commandment. But as humanity evolved and entered that age described by Isaiah at the Seraphim's command (Is 6, 9-11), the age of "the valley of the shadow of death" (Ps 23,4; Lk 1,79; cf. Ezek 37), it was necessary to write down what had previously been only the more fluidly expressive spoken word. No wonder some of the things in Paul's letters have wrung so contrary to human conscience in later ages, things such as slavery, the subordination of women, and the expulsion from church fellowship based upon judgment of the local congregation.[7]

What could more powerfully show the written word to be a "graven

---

7. The full implication of Mt 7,1 ("Judge not, that you be not judged") has perhaps yet to be realized in religious belief and practice. *(continued on following page)*

image" within Ex 20,4 than the fact that Jesus Christ himself wrote not
a single word for posterity. His only act of writing was in a medium that
the elements would quickly destroy (Jn 8,6,8),[8] and the one Gospel that
mentions it does not tell us what he wrote, doubtless because of John's
deep understanding of what was important to pass on. Not only did
Christ not write anything, but providence had it that no image of his
mineral-physical body was preserved for posterity by the art of his day, as
was done for other prominent persons. The fact that he was the most
exalted human being who ever lived yet left neither physical likeness nor
writing is a circumstance whose significance cannot be overemphasized.

But the written word became a practical necessity even for sacred purposes, commencing at approximately the time of First Isaiah (Is 1–39).
However, if the Bible was to present the deepest and most critical spiritual realities for humanity's guidance, it had to present the archetypal
image (image-ination) in all its magnitude, and to do so in a manner that
would be meaningful at all times during the human being's evolutionary
passage through the "valley of the shadow"—when God's face was "hidden" through the densification and materialization process. Hence the
biblical narrative was given in allegorical mode, utilizing sufficient historical phenomena but always as the servant of the higher spiritual reality.
When the time is right, and the soul has sufficiently developed to receive
it ("I have yet many things to say to you, but you cannot bear them now,"
Jn 16,12), the higher truth will be revealed by the Holy Spirit to those
whose karma (the higher law) permit its recognition. The Holy Spirit
"will teach you all things and bring to your remembrance all that I have

---

7. *(continued from previous page)* Today, in a time when the realities of evolution, involving as
it does transitions through karmic connections and multiple incarnations, are unrecognized,
judgments made today about matters such as homosexuality and abortion may ride hard upon
the judging souls in their own future development. These are raging current issues in the heart
and soul of humanity, not to be minimized, but neither Mt 7,1 nor 2 Cor 3 can be shelved in
their consideration. For what was right and proper at one stage of humanity's journey is not
necessarily right at another, witness the slavery issue upon which surely all religions must now
agree. And the ancient caste system of India was right in its time, but neither it nor race or sex
discriminations are proper in our time.

8. Literally, from the Greek, he wrote "in the earth" (KJV/NIV-INT). Virtually all versions
have expressed it "on the ground," the only exceptions in my library aside from KJV/NIV-INT
being LB, which, although notorious for taking liberties for evangelical purposes, nevertheless
comes closer to the meaning in this case by translating it "in the dust." But in all cases, the
writing medium was calculated to be obscured quickly by the elements, if not by human
scuffling.

said to you" (Jn 14,26). It "will guide you into all the truth" and "declare to you the things that are to come. [It] will glorify me, for [it] will take what is mine and declare it to you. All that the Father has is mine; therefore I said that [it] will take what is mine and declare it to you" (Jn 16,13-15). At that time it will be seen that the higher truth was there in the Bible all along—and the Bible is "holy" writing in that respect alone.

Nevertheless, the prophecy was given that the Holy Spirit would come like a "thief in the night" and would not be detected by those not awake (Mt 24,43; Lk 12,39; Rev 3,3). It would not be sufficient merely to speak of Jesus as "Lord, Lord" (Mt 7,22-23) nor to darken the doors of the church or temple (Jer 7,4) on every occasion, for the "temple" of the Lord is not, nor has it ever been, either a structure or an organization other than the higher components of the human being developed by its Ego out of the lower (cf. 2 Sam 7,4-17; Zech 6,12-15; Mal 3,1; Mt 26,61; Mk 14,58; 15,29; Jn 2,19; Acts 6,14; Rev 11,1). The particular task during Earth evolution is the transformation (perfection or purification; Mt 5,48; Mal 3,2) of the astral body into *manas* (manna) or Spirit Self (see I-9).

Let us consider the claim of the Lord to be the "Alpha and Omega." The phrase appears only in the works of two great biblical seers, he who is called Second Isaiah and he who calls himself John (Lazarus/John as shown in *The Burning Bush*, and more completely in *The Disciple Whom Jesus Loved*). They are as follows:[9]

Is 41,4: Who has performed and done this, calling the generations from the beginning? I, the Lord, the first, and with the last; I am He.

Is 44,6: Thus says the Lord, the King of Israel and his Redeemer, the Lord of hosts: "I am the first and I am the last; besides me there is no god."

Is 48,12: Hearken to me, O Jacob, and Israel, whom I called! I am He, I am the first, and I am the last.

---

9. Rev 1, 17–18 reads as follows:

Rev 1,17-18: [17] When I saw him, I fell at his feet as though dead. But he laid his right hand upon me, saying, "Fear not, I am the first and the last, [18] and the living one; I died, and behold I am alive for evermore, and I have the keys of Death and Hades.

This passage seems to refer not primarily to the Christ but to the human being who has been initiated to the highest degree, perfected as "a son of man." See the discussion of Rev 1,17 in "Evolution" and of the "son of man" in fn 2 of "The Question"; also *The Apocalypse of St. John* (ASJ), Lect. 2 and *The Apocalypse of Saint John* (ApSJn), Chap. 1, esp. p. 21.

Rev 1,8: "I am the Alpha and the Omega," says the Lord God, who is and who was and who is to come, the Almighty.

Rev 21,6: And he said to me, "It is done! I am the Alpha and the Omega, the beginning and the end. To the thirsty I will give from the fountain of the water of life without payment."

Rev 22,13: "I am the Alpha and the Omega, the first and the last, the beginning and the end."

The Bible story is itself fractal, part of the larger Alpha and Omega, subsumed under but not coextensive with it, for as we shall see, the Prologue of John's Gospel (Jn 1,1-18) excepted, the creation account (Gen 1–3) does not start at the real beginning, nor does the Revelation account take us to the ultimate end, of humanity's spiritual evolution. To some extent this is reflected by the Bible's own indications that as a "writing" it will cease to be of further use at a certain point in that evolution (Jer 31,31-34; Heb 10,16-17; 2 Cor 3).

Among the initiates of ancient Greece, the guiding spiritual powers prepared the Western soil upon which the seeds of Christianity were later to be sown. In a sense, this ancient wisdom culminated in Plato. Through his student Aristotle and Aristotle's student Alexander, Greek influence flowered in Alexandria. Providentially, it was reborn in Philo of Alexandria (ca. 20 B.C.-A.D. 50), and, through him, influenced the writers of the New Testament.[10] Lazarus/John began his Gospel with the heart of this wisdom, the Logos, equating it to the creative Word of God, to the Christ. It was this Word, which long preceded the events in Gen 1, that was truly "In the beginning." It was this Word, the Christ, that was meant when the human being much later, experiencing its own breath, uttered the primeval sound expressed by the Greek letter "Alpha" (see *Alphabet* [ALPH]) and that the same Lazarus/John expressed in his Apocalypse. In *The Influence of Spiritual Beings Upon Man* (ISBM), Lect. 5, p. 86, Steiner says, "… what is active last was always there first; for that which pressed into matter as 'Word' was there the first of all."

The very name of our own "alphabet" is taken from the first two letters of the Greek alphabet, "alpha-beta." But one can hardly appreciate the meaning of "Alpha and Omega" by simply identifying them as the first and last letters of the Greek alphabet, thus symbolizing "the beginning

---

10. See "Egypt" in *The Burning Bush.*

and the end," anymore than if our own A and Z were substituted. Their meaning goes back to the time suggested by Gen 11,1 when "the whole earth had one language and few words."[11]

Together, Alpha and Omega imply something quite important to humanity, as shown in *The Principle of Spiritual Economy* (SE), Lect. 10, "The God of the Alpha and the God of the Omega," (pp. 137-138):

> Regardless of whether you regress or progress, whether you seek God in the Alpha or in the Omega, you will be able to find Him. What is important is that you find Him with your own heightened human power. Those forces necessary to find the God of the Alpha are the primal forces of a human being. However, the forces necessary to find the God of the Omega must be acquired here on earth by striving human beings themselves. It makes a difference whether one goes back to Alpha or forward to Omega. He who is content with finding God and just wants to get into the spiritual world has the choice of going forward or backward. However, the individual who is concerned that humanity leave the earth in a heightened state must point the way to Omega—as did Zarathustra.[12]

Omega implies the fully completed journey of the Prodigal Son, humanity, to the pigpen and back (Lk 15,11-32). It means the parabola has returned to the higher spirit world whence creation entered its first primeval state in preparation for the commencement of Ancient Saturn.[13] At Omega the human being takes its place in the heavenly pantheon. That the journey is then complete and that all is in oneness is suggested by the fact that only the first and last creatures, the Word (Christ) who emerged first (Jn 1,1), and Spirit Man (see I-9 and Mt 13,33) who will come last, will have dwelt in the depths of the mineral-physical state, there tasted Death, and returned to the highest spiritual sphere. There the last sheep will have returned to the fold (Lk 15,3-7; Mt 18,10-14). Steiner often spoke of the human being as the work, the fulfillment, of

---

11. See I-77.
12. This is the Zarathustra that Steiner shows is the leader of the second post-Atlantean Cultural Era, the prehistoric Ancient Persian. His was the Individuality that incarnated many times between then and the birth of Jesus, and that, when the time was right, incarnated in the Solomon Jesus child of Bethlehem. See "The Nativity" in *The Burning Bush* as well as *The Incredible Births of Jesus.*
13. See I-1.

the hierarchies. Then, in the highest sense, is the first last and the last first, the Alpha and Omega, the full joinder of the higher and lower "I Am," the fulfillment through the unity of all things in heaven and Earth (Eph 1,3-10). Then the question "What is man?" will have its full answer.

How is it that the Christ identifies himself as the Alpha and the Omega, and yet this is the symbol of humanity's journey out and back? This relates to the identification of the beginning and the end to the "I Am."[14] According to *The Festivals and their Meaning* (FM), Lect. 2, pp. 38-39, it was said in a legend, referring to the human entelechy, "I am He who is and who was and who is to come."[15] Steiner identifies this as that (in the burning "Bush"[16]) "which passes through all incarnations, the power of ever-evolving man who descends out of the light into the darkness and out of the darkness ascends into the light."

While similar, the statement is not identical to Rev 1,8, "I am the Alpha and the Omega," for the Word existed before the commencement of the human being's creation on Ancient Saturn, even before the hierarchies, and the human Ego did not come into being until Earth evolution (see I-35). As indicated above, the Christ, as the Word, has always been in all creation. This mystery would seem to lie at the base of Paul's statement in Gal 1,16 that the Christ was revealed not *to* but *in* him. In any event, I made it clear in Vol. 1 (*The Burning Bush*) that the Christ must be voluntarily taken in as the governing force of one's existence if one is to attain to the ascent. Doing that serves to conditionally join one's own Ego or "I Am" to that of the Christ so that in effect, *ab initio*, one's own existence becomes eternal, having no beginning nor end, in oneness with the Word, the Christ.

Save only that he reverses Steiner's usage of Individuality and Personality, Teilhard de Chardin leads us to see essentially the same thing as Steiner—that the human Ego, without loss of its own eternal Individuality, merges in love into the greater All, which is essentially the Christ.[17]

---

14. See "I AM" in *The Burning Bush*.

15. Compare this with the various translations of Ex 3,14 as given in fn 1 of the "I AM" essay in *The Burning Bush*. As indicated in that essay, the better interpretation, announced first by Rudolf Steiner, which has not been adopted in any translation to date so far as I know, is simply, "I Am the I Am." It was the Christ speaking to Moses through Yahweh at the point in human evolution when the transition from group soul to individual soul was in the bud.

16. See the essay "Bush" in *The Burning Bush*.

17. See *The Phenomenon of Man* (PHEN), Book 4, Chap. 2, Sec. 1 ("The Convergence of the Person and the Omega Point").

THE CREATION—GENESIS 1–3

Our objective in discussing the "creation" here is not to look in detail at substantive content nor apply exegesis in the normal sense. Rather it is to reform our entire approach to understanding what the biblical message of creation says—to provide an adequate conceptual framework, one that will enable in us a more truthful imagination of what took, and is still taking, place in humanity's journey. It is only such a framework that can then be fleshed out by the several most profound biblical terms that follow. So steeped has humanity become in the various prevailing modes of interpretation, and in the conflicts that rage between them, that the essence of these most sacred biblical terms and concepts has fled the awareness of today's religions.[18]

One who reflects deeply upon the most sacred and profound human writings must surely see that the spiritual path leading to life will not be one quickly or easily discerned by those in positions of worldly authority, including not only the voices of "scientific authority" but also those pronouncing rules and interpretations from pulpits, seminaries, chairs or councils of institutionalized religion, the modern Sanhedrins. In essence, the path to the spiritual world will never be apparent to the majority, else prophecy would always have been superfluous. All those in power have to do to kill the prophets is ostracize them as a *cult*, as Rome did the early Christians. The deepest writings have always declared that few would find the path (Mt 7,13-14), the key of David (Rev 3,7), the stone the builders rejected (Mt 21,42; Mk 12,10; Lk 20,17; Acts 4,11; 1 Pet 2,7), the pearl of great price (Mt 13,45-46), the Rosetta stone, the chosen Cinderella whom alone the glass slipper fits. And that philosophers' stone, if you will, is so elusive precisely because it cannot be easily described in so many words, especially those reduced to writing, codified, graven in matter. It is rather more like the wind's origin that lies beyond our perception (Jn 3,6-8), like what causes the prophet in one age to throw aside the graven images (writings) of an earlier age (Mt 5,21-47; Mt 12,1-8; Mk 2,23-28; Lk 6,1-5).

During most of the second millennium, the time was not right for the

---

18. See Brueggemann, *Theology of the Old Testament* (TOT), esp. Chaps. 1 and 2, for an excellent discussion of these "prevailing," and clearly conflicting, "modes of interpretation"; see also Birch, et al., *A Theological Introduction to the Old Testament* (TIOT).

highest initiates to reveal, in any broad sense, what they had perceived in the spiritual worlds. Muffled voices came from the mystic and even the devout medium, but it was not until the prophet, Rudolf Steiner, began to lecture at the opening of the twentieth century that the time and messenger were both right to disclose in comprehendible images what is experienced by the soul in the highest spiritual worlds. I have already written at some length why the time was then right.[19] What now needs to happen is for humanity to see if the glass slipper fits these revelations. When that is done, passages of scripture that have long confounded theological pundits will come brilliantly into the light.

Only since the beginning of the present Cultural Era[20] with the Renaissance has humanity begun to direct its attention to a meaning applicable to our time, and only during more recent centuries to an increasingly critical analysis of these sacred accounts. And thus far that analysis has been able to see only form of, and not substance in, the ancient account, both canonical and pagan (but including also a large portion of the pseudepigraphal and apocryphal writings).

Probably the highest of the initiates, prior to Steiner, was one who lived before the Renaissance, Christian Rosenkreutz, known to modern scholarship only by errant legend.[21] In spite of the fact historians know little of Christian Rosenkreutz, he must have planted spiritual seeds in

---

19. See the discussions of the current age of the Archangel Michael in *The Incredible Births of Jesus* (IBJ), *The Disciple Whom Jesus Loved* (DWJL) and *The Burning Bush* (BB). These show that such age began in 1879 and will last until approximately 2233.

20. The Cultural Era of the Consciousness Soul (see I-9, I-19, I-24 and I-25).

21. Rudolf Steiner often indicated that the substance of his own lectures and writings was what Rosenkreutz had given his own intimate disciples in the thirteenth and fourteenth centuries, teachings that disappeared before the emergence of what scholars know as Rosicrucianism. What now needs to be known about this high initiate can be gathered from Steiner's works reflected in the following sources: *Rosicrucian Christianity* (ROSC); *Esoteric Christianity and the Mission of Christian Rosenkreutz* (ECMCR); *The Mission of Christian Rosenkreutz* (MCR); *Rosicrucian Wisdom: An Introduction* (RWI); *Rosicrucian Esotericism* (RE); *The Chymical Wedding of Christian Rosenkreutz* (CWCR); *Rosicrucianism and Modern Initiation* (RMI); *A Christian Rosenkreutz Anthology* (CRA) and *The Secret Stream: Christian Rosenkreutz and Rosicrucianism* (SSCRR), most of which are listed in the bibliography of *The Burning Bush*. In addition, in 1982 the Steiner Book Centre published Steven Roboz's compilation of references to Christian Rosenkreutz from the works of Rudolf Steiner, *Christian Rosenkreutz; From the Works of Rudolf Steiner* (CRRS). While Roboz disclaims exhaustiveness, in its twenty pages is a most extensive compilation.

The exalted nature of the soul (Individuality) of Christian Rosenkreutz is shown in *The Burning Bush*, "Pillars on the Journey," p. 543.

human evolution on the cusp of the Cultural Age of the Consciousness Soul that was to begin with the Renaissance ("rebirth") in 1414. Something of divine insight (intelligence) visited those outstanding personalities who marked the birth of the Consciousness Soul. The famous sculpture by Michelangelo of Moses portrays him with the stub of two horns just above the hairline of his forehead. These were symbols of the ancient spiritual vision ("fading splendor") he still retained, whereby the ancient brain, in what must henceforth be developed in the pituitary gland (lotus flower, Job 40,21-22), received divine communication.[22, 23]

22. As human evolution progressed, the etheric and astral bodies, which to begin with extended far beyond the slowly forming mineral-physical body, drew gradually within the confines of that body. It is through these more spiritual bodies that the human being is able to perceive in the spiritual worlds (see *The Burning Bush*, "Overview," pp. 21-22, and ""Mysteries," p. 335). As these bodies, particularly the etheric body, became confined more and more within the mineral-physical body, intelligence gradually increased but the ability to perceive (intuit) in the spiritual world diminished. This is reflected in the scriptures by the reference to God's "hiding his face," or words of similar import (see scriptures cited in *The Burning Bush*, "Mysteries," p. 354). Moses' "fading splendor" (2 Cor 3,7-11) was simply a recognition of the reality of what was happening within humanity, though Moses had greater atavistic clairvoyance than his contemporaries and further, had been initiated into the mysteries of both Ancient Egypt and Midian. It is the mineral-physical body of the human being that is the "veil of the temple" that was "rent" by the Resurrection of Christ, as the "first fruits" of the return journey of the Prodigal Son back into the spiritual world. According to Steiner, the "two men in dazzling apparel" who appeared to Mary Magdalene at the tomb on the first Easter morning were the etheric and astral bodies of Jesus freed from their mineral-physical "veil" (Jn 20,12; *The Gospel of St. John* [GSJ], p. 187; see also Lk 24,4).

23. Regarding the development of the pituitary gland, see *The Burning Bush* (BB), "Second Coming," particularly pp. 225-243, as well as the additional discussion of the "lotus flowers" (Job 40,21-22) at pp. 332 and 428 (a portion of the BB text is incorporated near the end of the "Blood" essay herein). Those readers with an original version of BB should note that the revised version corrects a minor error on p. 225 in reversing the locations of the pineal and pituitary glands; the pineal is at the top of the head in I-21 while the pituitary is the one "between the eyes" or at the "forehead," as in the case of Moses' "horns." *(continued on following page)*

Probably no one thing was more responsible for launching the historical search and the documentary hypothesis, as they apply to the Old Testament, than the notice taken of the apparent difference between the creation story in Gen 1–2,4a (the seven "days" of creation) and that in Gen 2,4b–3,24 (the descent of the lower kingdoms, sexual division of the human being, and temptation and Fall in the Garden of Eden). They have been taken to be two different interpretations or traditions of the same events, and thus perversions or modifications of what Moses originally taught. To modern sensate comprehension, this development is

---

23. *(continued from previous page)* Chart I-21 correctly identifies the numbered "petals" of these *seven* flowers (also known as "chakras" in the Orient or "wheels" in the Bible; see fn 17 in "Blood") to their respective organs. It is noteworthy that in his discussion of the development of the seven lotus flowers in *How to Know Higher Worlds* (HKHW), Chap. 6 ("Some Effects of Initiation"), pp. 108-150, he specifies at first only the lower six, leaving out the 8-petalled pineal gland that relates to the dim (mineral) consciousness of Ancient Saturn. The reason for this is that only the lower six of these lotus flowers can be consciously developed, and then the seventh, the 8-petalled flower of the pineal gland will appear of its own accord (see paragraph numbered "7" at pp. 111-112); it is the original eight within the 16-petalled flower at the larynx (the "rod of iron"; see Rev 2,27; 12,5 and 19,15, discussed in the "Blood" essay herein).

The initiate René Schwaller de Lubicz, Egyptologist *par excellence*, quite independently of Steiner and with no apparent connection to anthroposophy as such, said in his *The Temple In Man* (TIMN), a preliminary outline of his massive magnum opus, *The Temple Of Man* (TOMN), at p. 107:

> The head is the container of the spiritual being, where the blood, built up in the body, comes to be *spiritualized* in order to nourish the nervous flux and prepare the "ferments" of the blood and the "seed."

Immediately following in his fn 11, he discusses the epiphysis (the pineal gland), being apparently the "seed," in which sense it relates back to what was planted in human evolution in Ancient Saturn. One has to think of the concluding sentence in Isaiah's seminal vision (Is 6,1-13), "The holy seed is its stump" (Is 6,13c), that reaches out beyond contemporary human imagination.

We cannot really comprehend the meaning of the biblical "forehead" (Ex 28,38; Lev 13,41-43; Num 24,17; 1 Sam 17,49; 2 Ch 26,16-23; Is 48,4; Jer 48,45; Ezek 3,4-11; 9,3-8 and Rev 7,3; 9,4; 13,16; 14,9; 17,5; 20,4 and 22,4) absent these considerations. The "forehead" is the center of the divine intelligence the administration of which is committed to the Archangel Michael.

The "forehead" organ, the pituitary 2-petalled "lotus flower," can be developed only under the guidance of the Archangel Michael, who for the first time since Christ's blood fell into the Earth came into his primary leadership or regency of humanity in 1879. It is critical that humanity progress in the development of this divine intelligence in the forehead during that current regency that will run only until about A.D. 2233, or three hundred fifty-four years; see the Epilogue in *The Incredible Births of Jesus* and also I-19 on pp. 574-575 of the *revised* edition of BB.

understandable, but it is not spiritually accurate according to the insights given by Rudolf Steiner, which indicate only a single account of creation, in the order set out in Genesis 1 through 3—and not two separate stories of the same creation.

Steiner gives one simple approach to solving this puzzle in the question and answer period following his lecture of January 19, 1905, *The Idea of God* (TIG):

> The division of Creation into two parts can be understood if we learn to distinguish the human being without any sex ... i.e., the spiritual astral man.... Then a revolution took place: the sexless spiritual man became a physical bi-sexual being, and for this reason it is necessary to speak of a double Creation.

This original androgynous human being is what Christ meant in his comment about divorce when, referring to Gen 1,27 and 5,1-2, he said, "Have you not read that he who made them *from the beginning* made them male and female ... " (Mt 19,4; Mk 10,6; italics mine). This primeval unity is what lies behind the oneness ("one flesh") of marriage, the event in the fallen state that symbolizes the prior unity to be regained in the reascent of humanity back into the spiritual world whence it came.[24]

We shall briefly explore how this division came about. But let us first note that, once biblical scholars "discovered" this seeming discrepancy in the two accounts, it became fashionable for them to then find other "parallel or duplicate accounts." A concise listing of what it apparently considers the most significant of these can be found (at p. 8) in the "Introduction to the Pentateuch" in the NJB, as follows:

---

24. This future "oneness" of the flesh is what is meant by that passage in the so-called "little apocalypse" passages (Mt 24,19; Mk 13,17; Lk 21,23) that speak of the misfortune of "those who are with child ... and give suck in those days." See the discussion of these in *The Burning Bush* at pp. 186 and 189-192 (190-192 in orig. ed.). This lack of awareness, perhaps more than anything else, suggests that humanity does not know enough yet to make proper, critical judgment with respect to those born with homosexual tendencies (cf. Mt 7,1, "Judge not, that you be not judged").

Accounts

Story	First	Subsequent
Creation	Gen 1–2,4a	Gen 2,4b–3,24
Cain/Kenan genealogies	Gen 4,17 et seq.	Gen 5,12-17
Flood	Two Interwoven in Gen 6–8	
Covenant with Abraham	Gen 15	Gen 17
Dismissals of Hagar	Gen 16	Gen 21
Misfortunes of patriarchal wife	Gen 12,10-20	Gen 20; 26,1-11
Stories about Joseph and bros.	Interwoven in Gen	
Calling of Moses	Ex 3,1–4,17	Ex 6,2–7,7
Water miracles at Meribah	Ex 17,1-7	Num 20,1-13
Decalogue texts	Ex 20,1-17	Deut 5,6-21
Liturgical calendars	Ex 23,14-19	Ex 34,18-23; Lev 23; Deut 16, 1-16

While the last two examples seem clearly to stem from different elaborations of the same event, many if not all of the others can be seen to be not duplicates but either consecutive events or continuations in which the second account gives a meaning not fully spelled out in the first. Though any superficial reading would immediately suggest that Gen 5 duplicates Gen 4, I show at length in *The Burning Bush* how this is not the case.[25] We saw at the first of this essay that there was a reason, in the "flood"

---

25. See there the Appendix to "Three Bodies" at pp. 459-473.

story (Gen 6–8), for the difference between the animal accounts (Gen 6,19-22 and Gen 7,1-3).[26] And it was shown in *The Burning Bush* that a different purpose was served by the three accounts of patriarchal wife misfortune.[27]

One who sees the Bible's creation account in the light of anthroposophy must surely come away with a renewed sense of respect and awe for its precise spiritual accuracy. And the same growing realization applies to the rest of the canon. Anthroposophy is thus virtually a resurrection of the power to believe in the Bible story literally, when its allegorical meaning is shown by Steiner's direct spiritual perception, offering hope for reconciliation between those who hold to its literal truth and those who spurn it because it flies in the face of sensate comprehension. It may be unreasonable to expect this immediate result, but persons of reasonable and unprejudiced intellect and goodwill must begin to see the spiritual realities expressed. And when this is done, the foundation will be laid for Christianity to begin to appeal to those of other ancient religious persuasions who rightly see the materialistic limitations and absence of intuition that have pervaded biblical interpretation for the last two millennia, especially since the seventeenth century. Until then, Christian doctrinal "evangelism" in our time is probably more harmful than helpful, at least for a major segment of humanity.

In looking at the creation accounts it will now be helpful to incorporate the "Overview" from Vol. 1, *The Burning Bush*. Ideally, the serious student will then carefully inspect the contents of *Outline of Esoteric Science* (OES).[28] And my own experience suggests that comprehension will be difficult without the aid of the "Charts and Tabulations" in Vol. 1,

---

26. Whenever the various "flood" myths of different world cultures are considered, it is well to take into account what was said about floods in the "Second Coming" essay in *The Burning Bush*, at pp. 236-239, particularly in the scholarly confusion between the Noah account that related to the transition from the Atlantean Epoch to the post-Atlantean and the Gilgamish Epic that related to the transition from the Ancient Persian Cultural Era to the Chaldo-Egyptian (see fn 7, p. 239, in that essay). The "fading splendor" of Moses himself may have caused his spiritual vision to be fuzzy on the place where the Noah expedition landed, placing it on Ararat (Gen 8,4) in the Ancient Persian vicinity instead of in the region of Ireland. Moreover, the etymology of Ararat, of Assyrian origin, shows it to mean simply "mountainous country" (see 1 AB 351), a description that could have expressed the feeling of those on Noah's expedition upon sighting land jutting out of the sea.
27. See *The Burning Bush*, item 7 (p. 430) in the listing in "Three Bodies," as well as the discussion of these events in "Egypt," pp. 530-531.
28. Also helpful are *Cosmic Memory* (CM) and *Evolution in the Aspect of Realities* (EAR).

particularly the earlier items. In other words, some basic anthroposophical knowledge must be assimilated to be able to comprehend the true story of the creation as set forth in Genesis. It may be objected that the study is demanding, but no real effort in this regard, however seemingly fruitless, will be lost to the soul.

As critical analysis began to observe the apparent duplication of accounts, it saw support in the two different names for God in the Genesis account, and from that derived the first two so-called documents, the older Yahwist (Y) account in Gen 2,4b–3,24 and the later Elohist (E) in Gen 1–2,4a. But there is no support for a hypothesis of two documents, for the God referred to in the two accounts is different. And an understanding of this also eliminates the duality in the calling of Moses listed above. To understand this the student should look again at "I AM" and "Bush" in *The Burning Bush*. It is absolutely essential that one learn what Paul gave to Dionysius the Areopagite about the hierarchies and their positions and functions between the Trinity and humanity. They are summarized in I-6, and their activities are extensively detailed in the OES account of creation.

We are not, in the Genesis 1–3 creation account, dealing at any time directly with God the Father, for creation and the evolution of the human being were far advanced from the time when the Word went out during the Ancient Saturn evolutionary Condition of Consciousness. Already, by Gen 1,1-2, three Conditions of Consciousness had come and gone in the creative process, those represented by Saturday, Sunday and Monday (the Old Saturn, Sun and Moon "planetary" evolutions), as well as the first two Evolutionary Epochs of Earth evolution. See I-1 through I-3. The physical, etheric and astral human bodies already had their foundations laid (I-14).

Not the Father God acting directly, but rather the plural (seven; e.g., see "our" in Gen 1,26) Elohim (see I-6) are involved. They reflect the will of the Father and serve as his agents, but they are the hierarchy in charge at this relatively late stage of creation (see I-16). Steiner appropriately labels them "Spirits of Form," for they take up the matter of lack of form in Gen 1,2 in order to carry out the formative process.

Then in proper sequence each formation that took place among the earthly creatures in Gen 1 is said to be "according to its kind" (Gen 1,11,12,21,24,25), by which is meant that physical form was given to all its creatures which were to harden prematurely (due to failures in earlier Conditions of Consciousness)—they were thus not the forerunners of the human being but rather the by-products of the higher evolution of humans, who came first into spiritual being but last into hardened form, an archetypal instance of the reverberating scriptural phrase, "the last will be first, and the first last." But as of Gen 2,4b-5, as clearly stated there, none of those things created were yet actually reduced to mineral-physical form. All were still etheric, though the order of their later appearance in mineral-physical form is basically as set out in Gen 1.

For the reduction to mineral-physical form to take place on Earth, the Moon had first to separate from the Earth, an event that occurred during the Lemurian Epoch. At that time, the Elohim who had been the formative agents withdrew from the Earth. All but the Eloha Yahweh went to the more spiritualized Sun (the Sun sphere[29]) whereas Yahweh sacrificially went to the more proximate region to the Earth, the Moon (the Moon sphere), from which he could direct the formative process. It is this Eloha Yahweh who becomes the singular "LORD God" in the translations available today. Thus, he first appears alone in Gen 2,4b to carry on the process of densification into mineral-physical form.

When the Deuteronomist reduced Moses' laws to writing, of prime importance to Israel was the *Shema* (Deut 6,4), "Hear, O Israel: The Lord our God is one Lord." It had to be thus, for Israel was "chosen" by Yahweh to create the form of receptacle, through the pure blood line, that would serve as the human vehicle of the incarnating Christ at the "right time."[30] Yahweh was thus necessarily a jealous God. But he was still a hierarchical agent of the Father and the Word, Christ, who reigned supreme over all. When Christ spoke of his Father, he spoke not of the divine spiritual servant Yahweh, but of the one Father from whom the creative Word went out at the very beginning. The Bible is witness to the existence, otherwise seemingly contrary to Deut 6,4, of numerous "gods" between the Father (or the Trinity) and the human being (see Mt 26,53, the "twelve legions of angels," and the related discussion in *The Burning Bush*, pp. 220-221).

---

29. The Sun sphere is the sphere whose extent is defined by the Sun as though it orbited around the Earth. And reference to the other planetary bodies of our solar system (including the Moon), also means the sphere prescribed in like manner by its orbit around the Earth. That the other planets and the Sun orbit around the Earth from the Earth's perspective, cannot be doubted. And that they orbit around it in spiritual reality since the blood of the creator, the Word, fell upon it and became one with the Earth's etheric being must surely now be recognized.

30. The "right time" is a clear theme in the kerygma; Acts 2,23; 1 Pet 1,20; Rom 5,6; Gal 4,4; Eph 1,10; Mk 1,15.

Indeed, even human beings are recognized as an incipient "gods" by both the Psalmist and Christ (Jn 10,33-36; Ps 82,6) and thus are, though as yet unperfected, the tenth rank in the hierarchies (see I-18).

It is noteworthy that Steiner gave only one lecture cycle specifically on Genesis, and that it was devoted almost entirely to the first chapter, the seven days of creation. This is not to say that he did not extensively touch upon other parts of Genesis in his other lectures and writings, particularly upon the account of the Fall, but his Genesis cycle of ten lectures, given in Munich from August 17 through 26, 1910, dealt with Genesis 1 almost exclusively.

As one would expect, so much is telescoped within Genesis 1 that any ten lectures purporting to cover it must do so with immense conceptual complexities. Indeed, my personal experience suggests that this cycle is one of the most difficult to comprehend of any given by Steiner. It must be taken as only laying the seed for further investigation by those who have to a great extent mastered, through a process of gradually dawning awareness, the fundamentals of spiritual science. How little did I comprehend in my first or second reading. Notably, this cycle was not given until all of his basic books[31] had been written, and a significant portion of his lectures upon the Gospels was already in place, as indicated by the chronological bibliography in Vol. 1. It is almost as though he realized that it would take time for this to seep down into the understanding of his followers. The most complete basis for understanding is in the complex creation portions of *Outline of Esoteric Science* (OES), but it is written in a way that requires the student's own recognition of how it relates to the Bible, for there are very few specific references to highly relevant scripture.

What anthroposophy had to say about the biblical creation accounts, along with the nativity accounts, John's Apocalypse, and a far more complete picture of karma and reincarnation, was a strong motivation behind my decision to attempt a comprehensive reduction of Steiner's teachings to show traditional Christendom their applicability to the Bible itself.

---

31. In addition to the nineteenth-century foundational writing, *Intuitive Thinking as a Spiritual Path* (ITSP), in chronological order the following twentieth-century writings are generally included in Steiner's basic books: *Christianity as Mystical Fact* (CMF), *How to Know Higher Worlds* (HKHW), *Theosophy* (THSY), and *Outline of Esoteric Science* (OES). All of these are new translations, all but two of which (CMF and THSY) have different titles from those cited in Vol. 1, *The Burning Bush* (ITSP is the former PSA; HKHW the former KHW; and OES the former OS).

And no section has presented, in that regard, a greater challenge than the very beginning of the Bible, Genesis 1.

What we are here about is to set out a more easily comprehendible imagination of the progressive "days" of creation and the succeeding Fall expressed by the Bible's first chapters. To do so, we must take note of the Hebrew word for day, *yom* (e.g., *Yom Kippur* means "*Day* of Atonement"). Steiner, discussing the deep and primeval meaning of specific Hebrew words used in Genesis, tells us (GEN, Lect. 4, p.57) that *yom* meant not a day as we know it, but an aeon, which was a being, a living spiritual entity (see 1 Brit 119, "aeon"; also WNWCD and MWCD). This is clearly in keeping with what we are told in Gen 2,4a about these "days" after they had all been described: "*These are the generations of the heavens and the earth when they were created*" (Gen 2,4a). In Latin this is reflected by the primeval connection between *deus* and *dies*—god and day, *dies* being the expression of the *deus* in its descending adjustment to the mode of time.[32] What we are here dealing with is the level of the hierarchy immediately below the Elohim, namely, the Archai, or Spirits of Personality (Principalities, or Primal Beings; see I-6). Immediately subordinate to the Elohim, they were their helpers in the creative process. And just as there were seven Elohim, so also were there seven Archai, or "days," described in that process. Collectively, they are the *Yamin* ("days"). Thus, the Elohim, in Gen 1,1, call to their service their immediate subordinates, the Archai, who are really spirits of time as their Greek name clearly implies, along with the idea of ancientness or originality— almost certainly corresponding with Daniel's "Ancient of Days" (Dan 7,9,13,22).[33] These gods work successively over distinctively different

---

32. Contemplate this in light of the mythical Greek god Kronos (or Cronus, etymological ancestor of our "chronology"), associated with Saturn. Kronos was overthrown by Zeus, or Thor, Jupiter representing then the next step in the condensation of the Earth. See I-17.

33. This phrase, appearing in the canon only in Dan 7,9,13,22, has an inherently electrifying effect. But sadly, with the progress of postmodern biblical interpretation and translation, particularly in the last half of the twentieth century, the magic has largely disappeared where the phrase "Ancient of Days" has been changed to "Ancient One" or words of similar import (see, for instance, NRSV, NAB and AB using "Ancient One," REB using "Ancient in Years," and NJB using "one most venerable"). See the comment in 23 AB 206 indicating that the Aramaic words (in the Masoretic Text; both 23 AB 3 and 7 NIB 19 point out that Daniel 2,4b–7,28 are in Aramaic while the rest of the book is in Hebrew) are *'attiq yomin*, but saying that "the word *yomin* could be dropped after *'attiq*, which then by itself came to mean 'old'." Similarly, 7 NIB 103 says "The description of the 'Ancient of Days' (NIV; 'Ancient One,' NRSV) is fanciful and impressive, suggesting an old man with great authority...." *(continued on following page)*

and succeeding eons (aeons). The seven Archangels assume successive regencies, each of approximately three hundred fifty-four years.[34] The time periods of the Archai were much longer, especially before the parabolic slowing of events (cf. the mirror-image reversal, the turning around of the parabola, in Mt 24,22 telling of the shortening of days during the reascent of humanity) with the establishment of measurable time in Gen 1,14—after which the smaller divisions of time came under the domain of the servants of the Archai, namely, the Archangels (GEN, Lect. 5, p. 70), though they work closely together, for the Archangels are also Folk-Spirits. When one begins to understand the importance of these time periods, then the ascendancy of the Archangel of the Sun, Michael, in 1879, takes on resplendence of meaning and significance for our own period. Michael, the custodian of the heavenly intelligence before casting Lucifer down to Earth (Rev 12,7-9), has now, in his first regency after the coming of Christ (Rev 12,10), to lead us, in the face of that castdown "deceiver," into that divine spiritual knowledge of which Steiner is

---

33. *(continued from previous page)* I suggest that the element of "fancy" is in the newer translations which are the fruit of Christendom's having lost the significance in the modern era (i.e., since the sixteenth century) of the various levels of the hierarchies (I-6). There, just below the Elohim we find their agents, the Archai. They are the ones in charge of the *yomin*, the "days" of creation. They are indeed "ancient" in the sense that the "days" (i.e., the "ages," "aeons" or "generations") began under their domain. Their very name, Archai, means "ancient," so that the true meaning of Daniel's phrase is "the Archai of the days of creation." All higher ranks among the hierarchies existed and were active prior to that stage, so the Archai are the most ancient within the hierarchies to deal directly with the "days" of creation.

The only Old Testament references in the Protestant Bible (the Septuagint, or Jewish Hellenistic "Bible") to named Archangels are at Daniel 8,16 and 9,21 (Gabriel), and 10,13,21 and 12,1 (Michael). Prior to both of these there are references to "thrones" (Dan 7,9) and "dominions" (Dan 7,27; also in the singular, 4,3,22,34; 6,26; 7,6,12,14,26,27; as well as later in 11,3,4,5). For what it is worth, it is sobering to note the relationship between the hierarchical (spiritual) beings called "Thrones, Dominions and Archai." Note from I-6 their positions in the ranks of the hierarchies. Then, if we may assume for present purposes the validity of I-7, note the relationship it indicates of these three ranks to each other and to the Father God. If one then rereads Dan 7, the higher Thrones came first, upon which the Archai were seated (7,9). The "one like a son of man" (Dan 7,13; the same phrase that refers to the Christ-perfected human soul in Rev 1,13) was presented before the Archai and given Dominion (7,14). Then later in Daniel's chronology, the Archangels appear who, according to I-7, have a special relationship with the Son (Christ) and the Exusiai (Elohim), but it is the Archangel Michael who stands with the Spirit of Truth within the third hierarchy (Dan 10,21).

34. In chart I-19 in the original edition of *The Burning Bush* (pp. 574-575), I expressed confusion over the correct length of these periods. The matter was cleared up in the revised editon and in *The Incredible Births of Jesus* in its "Epilogue" dealing with the current regency of the Archangel Michael (p. 88). A more complete clarification is given in fn 7 in the "Light" essay herein.

the foremost prophet and servant since Christian Rosenkreutz hundreds of years ago.

Steiner says in the first and last lectures of the *Genesis* (GEN) cycle (Lects. 1 and 10, pp. 13 and 114) that Gen 1,1 is set at the point in Earth evolution when the Sun and the Earth were about to separate. We must bear in mind that three prior Conditions of Consciousness had come and gone, namely, Old Saturn, Sun and Moon (see I-1). During these primal Conditions, the spiritual origins of the human being's three bodies had been laid down (I-14), which would be transformed into a higher state in the Earth Condition of Consciousness.

What was now to take place during the seven "days?" Let us defer what was taking place in the human being at these progressive stages until we have looked at what was taking place in the lower kingdoms. Here we need to look at Lects. 2 and 3. Inasmuch as the lower (earthly) form is always patterned after the higher (spiritual) form (see "As Above, So Below"), we must recognize that when the Elohim assumed their rulership of Earth creation (see I-16), they brought with them a remembrance of the stages of development from the three prior Conditions of Consciousness.

In *Genesis* (GEN), Lect. 3 ("The Seven Days of Creation"), Steiner makes what must at first blush be taken as a startling revelation. He mentions the characterization of the event of the first day, "Let there be light," and then says:

> [This] allude[s] to an event which we can see as the recapitulation at a higher level of an earlier stage of evolution…. In fact all that is narrated in the Bible of the six or seven "days" of creation is a reawakening of previous conditions, not in the same but in a new form.
>
> … [W]hat kind of reality are we to attribute to the account of what happened in the course of these six or seven "days"? It will be clearer if we put the question in this way. Could an ordinary eye, in fact could any organs of sense such as we have today have followed what we are told took place during the six days of creation? No, they could not. For the events there described really took place in the sphere of elementary existence, so that a certain degree of clairvoyant knowledge, clairvoyant perception, would have been needed for their observation. The truth is that the Bible tells us of the origin of the sensible out of the supersensible, and that the events with which it opens are supersensible events, even if they are only one stage higher than the

ordinary physical events which proceeded from them and are familiar to us. In all our descriptions of the six days' work of creation we are in the domain of clairvoyant perception. What had existed at an earlier time now came forth in etheric, in elementary form. [See I-2, third tier, which shows that we are now in the "Physical-Etheric" Condition of Form, which is, even in the "etheric," lower than the Conditions of earlier planetary existence. For instance, our three bodies have their Egos in the higher three states, the higher and lower spiritual and astral, as indicated in I-89.] We must get a firm grasp of that, otherwise we shall be all at sea over the true meaning of the impressive words of Genesis. (pp. 34-35)

If we ask where in I-1 these seven "days" of "etheric" creation appear we may well scratch our heads in perplexity. For we know that the Sun separated from the mineral-physical Earth in Hyperborea and the Moon in Lemuria, and yet we are told of the creation of both of them in the fourth day (Gen 1,14-19), in the very midst of the series of the six-day creation—and all the while Steiner is telling us that nothing thus perceptible to our senses occurred in any of the seven "days." On this critical concept, we need the additional perspective given in I-2. Let us direct our attention first to the three progressive Elementary Kingdom Life Conditions in the second tier of I-2. Since mineral-physical heat first appeared during the Polarian Epoch, air in the Hyperborean, and water in the Lemurian, and since the Sun, Moon and planets ("stars") all appeared on the fourth day, it would seem we must assume that all seven "days" occurred prior to the Physical-Etheric state of the Present Mineral Kingdom of our Earth evolution. At least they occurred prior to the descent from the etheric into the physical during that Epoch. Based on this assumption, all the events of the seven "days" were prefigured into the spiritual, astral and/or etheric worlds during the three Elementary Kingdom Conditions of Life and the first three Conditions of Form (Arupa, Rupa and Astral) of the fourth Condition of Life (the Present Mineral Kingdom) of Earth evolution. The character of the Elementary Kingdoms and the meanings of the Arupa and Rupa Conditions of Form are generally described in I-4.

The pre-physical Conditions of the fire, air and water elements had their origin during the prior three Conditions of Consciousness and are in place in Gen 1,2, in the memory-like contemplation of the Elohim. But these are all undifferentiated, commingled, in a state of confusion, "without form" and, so far as sensate perception is concerned, "void." What then occurs during the first "day"?

Steiner discusses this in Lect. 3. But the easiest way to comprehend it is probably by referring to the following chart (from I-22) of the four ethers and elements (see "The Four Elements" herein) and how they come about by fission. In the "first day," the fire and air ethers were differentiated—separated. This fission caused, in the contemplation of the Elohim, light to arise as air descended. In the "second day," the Elohim

<u>Saturn</u>	<u>Sun</u>	<u>Moon</u>	<u>Earth</u>
			Life
			/
		Sound	
		/	\
	Light		Light
	/	\	/
Warmth (Fire)		Warmth	
	\	/	\
	Air		Air
		\	/
		Water	
			\ Earth

differentiated the air from the water so that there was a spiritual firmament dividing the waters. The "first day" corresponds with Ancient Saturn, the "second day" with Ancient Sun. When we come to the spiritual recapitulation of Ancient Moon, we have the "third day," when life appears in the form of plants. We are told (pp. 42, 117-118) that the "after its kind" language pertains to the group souls of the lower kingdoms. Thus, in the "third day" we are dealing with the group soul or Ego of the plant kingdom (see I-11). It was not yet possible in the "third day" for there to be animals, for the Moon had first to separate. This happened in the "fourth day," and in the "fifth day" we are told that the animals appeared "after their kind," or, in other words, the group souls or Egos of the various animal species. There were, as yet, no plants or animals, for the contemplation of the Elohim was simply that these would come in the mineral-physical Condition of Form "after their kind," or, in other words, in keeping with their group souls or Egos in their respective supersensible worlds (**I-11**).

When we come to the "sixth day," we change from "the Elohim created," as though already determined from prior Conditions of Consciousness, to "Let us make man." For the first time we are dealing with a new format or image, that of the higher Elohim themselves—as a reflection of the Father. In other words, instead of the "Ego" of the lower kingdoms, we are dealing with the "I Am" of the creative Word itself, the Christ.

We then have the period of cosmic rest (*pralaya*) between the supersensible and the sensate worlds. Then, in Gen 2,4b we are told, in accordance with the above scenario, that Yahweh, who now had gone with the Moon (i.e., contracted *his* spherical volume from the Sun sphere down to that of the Moon sphere) in the Moon's separation from the Earth during the Lemurian Epoch, began to act and "made the earth and the heavens, when no plant of the field was yet in the earth and no herb of the field had yet sprung up."[35] The time had come for the etheric to become mineralized in the physical existence. With the coming of the "dust" of Earth came also the "breath of life" (Gen 2,7) reflective of the fourth stage of the ethers and elements (again see the **I-22** chart above).

Let us pause here to conceptualize by analogy what has been said thus far about the "days" of creation. We know that before anything manufactured by the human being can actually take shape or form it must first be formed as an image in the human's mind. Take the case of a building. First an architect must create a conceptual design. For that, many steps ("days") must fall in place before it is time to bring the concepts into their mineral-physical existence. They exist as physical form only in the mind of the architect at first and then on plans and specifications. But the space where the building is to go is still completely "without form and void." Then a contractor is hired, who first assembles the materials and finally begins to assemble them into a structure. At the outset of construction, it is difficult to visualize what it will eventually become.

---

35. In deference to entrenched custom, the masculine gender pronoun is being used to refer to Yahweh. In the Appendix to "Three Bodies" in *The Burning Bush*, I explained how Yahweh's nature was feminine, not masculine.

Finally, over a period of time, involving many stages and subcontractors, it becomes a habitable structure and the resident for whom it was intended, the "I Am," can move in (cf. Heb 10,5, "but a body thou hast prepared for me"). Over time, the building wears out, even if regularly replenished by repair. At some point, it disintegrates sufficiently that, if not destroyed by an owner, it stands empty as a mere shell or skeleton as it goes back to the elements.

This is just one of limitless examples of how our sensate phenomena here on Earth reflect heavenly patterns. See "As Above, So Below." They are part of the fractal nature of creation. In the example, we see that the architect performs on the building what the Elohim as a group performed in the seven "days." The contractor hired to bring the building structure into existence is the Eloha Yahweh, working from his home on the Moon (the Moon sphere). Yahweh (the contractor) is the "one god" of the on-site artisans, but what he is doing reflects what was done by the group of Elohim (the architect), and what they did reflected the desires of the owner to be (Christ, or the "I Am"). With this picture, let us return to where we left off in Gen 2,7, where the human being had just received the "breath of life."

That human was still in a most primitive condition, gross in form, without bones, androgynous (male and female, undifferentiated sexually, and reproducing innocently from itself[36]). As yet, no descending Ego had penetrated the human body on Earth. And while the account in the Garden has this human being created first, as indeed was the case in the spiritual world, the descent into the mineral-physical was prefigured by

---

36. An interesting study can be made of the essentially synonymous and interchangeable biblical terms "worm" and "maggot." The Old Testament Hebrew term *rimma* or *rimmah* is so translated, as is the Greek term *skolhx* in the New Testament (Mk 9,44,46,48). The worm or maggot can be a symbol for one or more of the following four phenomena:

1. Putrification of the mineral-physical state, the flesh;
2. Preparation of the soil (see 6 ABD 1151 on the earthworm and this "forty"-year process);
3. Regeneration of severed anterior or posterior portions; and
4. Reproduction by an androgynous creature.

Conventional theology seems to focus on only #1, or occasionally on #2, as above. I suggest it is well to consider all four of these phenomena worthy of consideration for deeper insight, especially in passages such as Is 66,24 and Mk 9,44,46,48 when seen in the light of anthroposophy. All four, putrification, preparation, regeneration and reproduction, are part of the cycle (cf. Jas 3,6) presented in *The Burning Bush*.

the earlier "days" of creation so that in fact, as our geology confirms, the lower kingdoms all hardened into the mineral state before the human being. It would be a long time before any human skeleton would be hard enough to leave traces in the rocks of time.

The higher human being, in perceiving the group souls of the various animal species which were thus created "out of their kind," recognized the nature of each one and was thus able to give it its proper "name" according to the character of its group soul.[37] And being of higher origin, the human being was given dominion over these on Earth. But with this passage (Gen 2,19), we jump ahead of ourselves.

The human being, the crown of creation, actually came into spiritual being first, but descended last. Thus is a long, complex and heretofore mystifying process clarified and epitomized (see "Evolution").

What then was happening in the spiritual worlds in regard to the development of the human being during the six days? Steiner shows us in Lect. 8. To picture this, it is well to have at hand charts I-9 and I-22. Observing the former, we see that the human being comprises six components from the physical up through the soul (lower Ego), leaving the spirit (higher Ego) of the threefold human being aside as something to be developed through the Christ-element. According to Steiner, development during the six days proceeded as follows:

1st day (Gen 1,3-5): The Sentient Soul is developed out of the light ether ("Let there be light").

2nd day (Gen 1,6-8): The Intellectual or Mind Soul is developed out of the sound or chemical ether (the waters are separated).

3rd day (Gen 1,9-13): The Consciousness or Spiritual Soul is developed out of the *life* ether (the *living* plants are brought into etheric being).

4th day (Gen 1,14-19): The astral body is prepared along with the "astral" world's Sun, Moon and star (planet) physical (but not yet mineralized) form(s).

---

37. The Ego, or soul, of each group of animals dwelt, and was to be recognized by the human Ego, in the astral world (see I-11). We can only begin to understand the "instinctive" actions of animals when we can understand that their group soul dwells in the astral world whence they are guided.

5th day (Gen 1,20-25): The etheric body is prepared along with the as yet unmineralized form(s), first of the animals that were to dwell in the fluid air or water, and then of those that were to dwell on land ("earth").

6th day (Gen 1,26-27): The as yet unmineralized form (phantom) of the human physical body was prepared by the Spirits of Form, the Elohim.

Then on the **7th day** the Elohim rested, which is to say that there was a timeless "time" of cosmic rest when all such activity ceased before being brought back into its enhanced state of existence in accordance with what had taken place during the first six days. Thus came first the necessary mineral-physical condition of the Sun, Moon and stars over a vast period of time. To visualize this it might be helpful to review I-27. Then think something like this: In order to bring the astral and etheric conditions and their physical form(s) into a mineralized state, a vast globe occupying what is now all that would fall within the orbit of Saturn consisted first of the finest mineral elements in a high state of activity generating heat, thus bringing back in its advanced state what came spiritually into being on Old Saturn. Gradually this condenses into a smaller sphere within the orbit of Jupiter, comprising heat and denser air, the Earth's reprise of Ancient Sun. Still further condensation brings it within the orbit of Mars so that we have what may be described as a sphere of warm "mist" (Gen 2,6; cf. also the "Nephilim" of Gen 6,4).[38] As this condenses further the conditions begin to appear in which crystallization (Rev 4,6) can begin, from which eventually the primitive plants, sea life and land beasts (Rev 4,7) descend into primeval mineral-physical being.

Only then could the life be "breathed" into the human being on Earth (Gen 2,7), and as yet in a most primitive, gross and malleable form. But the human soul (Ego) still dwells in the "Garden" where grow the "tree of knowledge" and the "tree of life."[39] In other words, it still dwells in the bosom of the gods that (as agents of the Christ) created it, as detailed in *Outline of Esoteric Science* (OES).

---

38. See fn 2.
39. Compare the proverbial apple tree in the Garden with that in Song of Solomon (Song of Songs), Song 8,5. See its discussion under "Dusting off the Ancient Song" in *The Disciple Whom Jesus Loved*.

Let us therefore postulate that the descent of the full fourfold human being can be portrayed by the progressive infusion into it of the four elements (see "The Four Elements") in the following scriptural descriptions:

Element	4-Fold Component	Scripture
Fire (Warmth)	Ego	Gen 1,26–2,6
Air	Astral	Gen 2,7-9
Water	Etheric	Gen 2,10-16[40]
Earth (Solid)	Physical	Gen 2,17–3,24

Thus, the "image" of the Elohim is the Ego "likeness," the "I Am" which Yahweh-Eloha introduced to Moses in Ex 3,14.[41] The astral body is the "air" that was breathed into the human being, the "air" still containing also the "dust" yet to be formed by further condensation of the elements. The etheric body is the rivers of water that go out of Eden, "watering the trees" there (cf. Ezek 47,1-12). Finally, the solidity is represented by the "hardness" indicated by the word "Adam" in Gen 3,17.[42] Of course, these boundaries cannot, in reality, be so precise. For instance, we must know that sensate awareness, the Sentient Soul, commenced with the "taste" of the fruit and the opening of the "eyes" in Gen 3,6-7.[43] And the condensation of all elements was indiscriminately gradual. But

---

40. One who observes the paragraph structure in modern Bibles (as compared, for instance, to the KJV) might wonder if I have ended the etheric and begun the physical stages one verse too soon, as though the etheric went through verse 17 and the physical started with verse 18. The transition of the human soul from the etheric realm into the three human bodies began during the Lemurian Epoch and continued through the Atlantean. It is only as the Ego (the soul) progresses into the mineral-physical body that it begins to experience death; see I-2 and I-35. Verse 17 anticipates this, so I've included it within the physical component.

41. See the essay "I AM" in *The Burning Bush.*

42. On the name "Adam," see the Chapter End Note.

43. Something in the nature of smell may have existed even earlier. In I-23, the generally acknowledged five senses are seen to have had their earthly beginnings in the following order:

Smell	Gen 2,7	Relates to "breathing"
Taste	Gen 3,6	"Ate" the fruit
Sight	Gen 3,7	"Eyes ... were opened"
Touch	Gen 3,7	"Knew" their nakedness
Hearing	Gen 3,8	"Heard the sound ... of God walking"

this is the portrayal in three short chapters of a vast panorama of evolutionary development of earthly existence out of the spiritual world.

Much more has been said about the so-called "first creation account" than will be said at this time about the "second," the account of the Fall of humanity. The second is spread so profusely throughout Steiner's work that it will be often encountered, whereas the lecture cycle *Genesis* (GEN) and the book *Outline of Esoteric Science* (OES) stand as primary beacons for the first.

To conclude the creation discussion, I will speak generally about the Fall account (Gen 3). While the human being still dwelled as an innocent and androgynous being in the Garden, spiritually fed by the gods, the Yahweh-Eloha commenced to bring into physical earthly existence the other living creatures (Gen 2,19), according to their group soul kind in the spiritual world, as recognized there ("named") by the human.[44] For the human to progress to the next level, that of dwelling on Earth in accordance with the will of the gods, the division into sexes had to occur, but for this, a period of cosmic rest was necessary. Presumably this occurred between Lemuria and Atlantis, a "deep sleep" (Gen 2,21), from which the separate male and female arose in the next awakening of activity—but the Ego remained only in the etheric state, not yet embodied in the still quite gelatinous three bodies on Earth. The Ego had not yet descended and did not yet experience reproduction, which, though physical, thus remained innocent. The Ego was not to penetrate the outer astral body until approximately the last third of Lemuria and the first third of Atlantis (see I-35 and the essay "Naked" in *The Burning Bush*). Adam and Eve were "naked" in the sense that the Ego was not yet clothed with any of the three bodies, but they "were not ashamed" because, being unconnected with these bodies, they had not experienced the sexual act even though it may have taken place animalistically by what had descended. In other words, what occurred in Genesis 3 must be seen as involving the three bodies, which were on Earth, and the Ego, which was still undescended though in the process of doing so.

Meanwhile, in heaven (i.e., the astral world[45]) the germinal Ego-seed was encountering a fallen Archangel (see I-32) called "Lucifer," literally

---

44. See the significance of "name" in *The Burning Bush*, p. 248, and the discussion there of the philosophical conflict between nominalism and realism.
45. For the spiritual locus of the "astral" world, see I-33 in *The Burning Bush*, at pp. 604-605.

"light-bringer," who desired to bring experiential knowledge to humanity prematurely, before it was ready (i.e., capable of responsible judgment) and before this was desired by the higher spiritual powers.[46] The decision by the human being to follow Lucifer was an animalistic one (made by its astral body, over which it has as yet no control) and thus innocent, without experience or knowledge, but it resulted in the gaining of experience. However, it brought about an infection of the astral body, which progressively over time infected first the etheric and then the physical bodies also so that they began to experience pain, toil and death, the divine cures for the astral, etheric and physical bodies, respectively (Gen 3,16-19).[47] The process of karma and reincarnation commenced with that of death and is to continue until earthly death is no more (see I-2). Excellent highly relevant short cycles of one or two lectures are *The Concepts of Original Sin and Grace* (OSG) and *The Origin of Suffering; The Origin of Evil, Illness and Death* (OSOE).

Ironically, Lucifer desired to bring knowledge to humanity to keep it from descending further and experiencing what was intended by the higher gods, rather like a hovering parent who tries to shield a child from the rough experiences necessary for its proper development. The net effect has been an overshoot in the opposite direction. By virtue of the Luciferic influence and premature experience, what humanity did experience came as maya, deception about its true spiritual nature. Because it has acted without knowledge of the true spiritual nature of things on Earth, the human being has descended into hardness (Adam, Gen 3,17) beyond that originally envisioned by the Elohim. The overshoot plays into the hands of Ahriman, originally perceived by Zarathustra in the prehistoric Ancient Persian Cultural Age. Esoterically, Lucifer is known as the "Devil" and Ahriman as "Satan," though our modern translations do not properly differentiate the polarity of their domains. We shall see a reflection of their respective natures in Luke's version of the two crucified thieves (Lk 23,39-43), for at Christ's crucifixion Lucifer himself repented (though many of his Luciferic spirits remain unconverted and still menace human beings to this day), while Ahriman did not. Chart I-32 is helpful in understanding the relationship between these two

---

46. What the higher spiritual powers desired for the human Ego at this point is more fully described in the "Blood" essay.
47. See references to Gen 3,16-19 in the "Index of Scriptures Cited" in Vol. 1, as well as chart I-37.

"fallen" spiritual beings and their "legions."[48] The words of the repentant thief are an earthly reflection of the higher spiritual reality seen by Paul's "beloved" physician, Luke.

One who studies Steiner's works extensively will come upon statements that can, to some extent, raise serious question. An example is the time periods involved in the creation account. The one thing he made clear, which must be obvious to any serious and realistic observer, is that vast periods of time and timelessness are covered in the six days of creation and their implementation into the mineral world, not to mention what came thereafter. Steiner made various and seemingly inconsistent statements about the time factor. Some exploration of these can be found in Dankmar Bosse's 1993 article "How Old is the Earth?" in the *Journal of Anthroposophic Medicine*, Vol. 11, No. 1, Spring 1994. Probably the best that can be said is that one should approach with caution any statement in terms of years that goes back beyond our post-Atlantean Epoch, or the end of the last great ice age.

For a while this bothered me. However, if one realizes that Steiner's insights were into the spiritual world where there is no element of time, then one can begin to sense its immateriality so long as the events are fairly described in reasonable sequence, though sequence too fades as unity approaches with the spiritualization of matter. To perceive the nature of timelessness or eternity, it may be helpful to look at Goethe's idea of the "archetypal plant." If one sets out to describe a rose, one will likely give a picture of it at a given point in its development. But that is no more a rose than the skin on one's face is the person. To even get close to a description of the rose, one would have to observe it in its complete life cycle from seed to sprout to stem to flower and back to seed again, and then one would only describe its manifestation. The rose is a being in lower devachan whose manifestation is simply "after its kind." In the spiritual world all stages are collapsed into the essence, just as one's life on Earth is later collapsed there in keeping with timelessness or eternity, which prevails.

And so, for now, I leave the reader with what is given above, suggesting that Steiner's original work stands knocking for the seeker who wills to open the door.

---

48. There is also an excellent research tool available from the Rudolf Steiner Library by the title *Lucifer and Ahriman as Referred to in Writings & Lectures of Rudolf Steiner, in Chronological Order.* It is in typewritten form and does not indicate the compiler's name or date of compilation.

THE APOCALYPSE

One who diligently searches all that eminent scholarship has previously offered in explanation of St. John's Apocalypse must come away feeling that its deep truths have surely eluded detection. To that seeker, Steiner's gift can be a verdant, self-revealing oasis of authenticity. In withdrawing the veil from the biblical mysteries, never did Steiner more forcefully confirm to me his spiritual authority than when he spoke on St. John's Apocalypse. In this, surely he came fully within the spirit of the ancient test of prophecy (Deut 18,22; 1 Cor 14). For the book of Revelation, he is for us the Pharoah's Joseph and Nebuchadnezzar's Daniel, a spiritual interpreter par excellence for our own time.

Steiner's primary cycle on the Apocalypse is *The Apocalypse of St. John* (ASJ) comprising twelve lectures (June, 1908, Nuremberg). Other cycles on it include:

> *On Apocalyptic Writings, with special reference to the Apocalypse of St. John* (AWASJ; 3 Lects., Oct. 1904, Berlin)
>
> *The Apocalypse* (APOC; 2 Lects., Mar. 1905, Cologne)
>
> *Reading the Pictures of the Apocalypse* (RPA; 4 Lects., Apr.-May 1907, Munich, and 12 Lects., May 1909, Kristiania)
>
> *Occult Seals and Columns* (OSC; 1 Lect., May 1907, Munich)
>
> *The Book of Revelation and the work of the priest* (REVP; 18 Lects., Sept. 5-22, 1924, Dornach)[49]

Much has been written about Revelation. Aside from its baffling imagery, questions of authorship and purpose have been foremost. Whether or not Evangelist John, whoever he was, was its author has been widely

---

49. These lectures were given by Steiner in the last month in which his physical condition permitted him to lecture. They were given privately to the priests of the Christian Community, a denomination that arose among European clergy who were attracted to his insights and came to him for guidance in forming a compatible new ritual. While he had an affinity with this group, he never changed his position that anthroposophy was not itself a religion. Rather it was spiritual intuition that was available for the spiritual enrichment and perfection of all human souls and the proper guidance of humanity's institutions. His position was rather well expressed by the title given the two-lecture cycle, *Christianity Began as a Religion but is Greater than all Religions* (CBRel; March 17, 1907, Munich and May 13, 1908, Berlin).

debated without consensus. Substantively, it has generally been seen primarily as having had a contemporary, reassuring purpose in the face of persecution. Rome was seen as the chief villain it was directed against and consequently as a primary source of its inspiration.

Just as anthroposophy's explanation obviates the increasingly burdensome baggage of the documentary hypothesis of the creation account, so also does its explanation of the Apocalypse erase the probability that contemporary events prompted it or aid significantly in its interpretation.[50] And just as questions about the authorship of the John Gospel are cogently resolved in favor of Lazarus/John, so also is authorship of the Bible's concluding book clearly attributable to him. When the character of Lazarus/John's high vision is understood, as well as his activities, locale and longevity, the accuracy of the tradition of identical authorship can be seen to override the various critical analyses to the contrary. See *The Disciple Whom Jesus Loved* (DWJL), which is based in large part upon the essays "Peter, James and John" and "Egypt" in *The Burning Bush*. Evangelist John's Revelation can no more be attributed to persecution of himself or others than the "cup" that Christ prayed to have removed from himself in Gethsemane was his Crucifixion. On the latter, see the discussion about this "cup" in Appendix Two of DWJL.

Steiner opened his APOC cycle by saying, "In common with every great religion Christianity has had its secret doctrine.... The Christian secret doctrine is none other than the Apocalypse." We have already seen, particularly in regard to karma and reincarnation, how it was necessary that for two millennia Christianity develop within the capacity of

---

50. A careful study will reveal that there was no basis for any reasonable expectation of serious persecution by Christian converts at the time of John's Apocalypse. That he was on Patmos by virtue of conflict between the new faith and the state, or that his preeminence might have brought exemplary punishment upon him, can hardly be denied. But the threat of *undesired* martyrdom during this time is grossly overblown. The almost universal assignment of the threat of persecution as the primary stimulant of the Apocalypse can be seen, in the light of anthroposophy, as due only to the total lack of deeper insight and the susceptibility of the uninitiated to be misled by the seemingly bizarre nature of apocalyptic writing. By definition, apocalypse discloses. It uncovers what is hidden. It is the opposite of the apocryphal that hides. The Apocalypse is translated as "revelation," and is hidden only to those unable to understand the meaning of its language. Until Steiner, no true prophet had come forward to show us in modern terminology what that meaning has always been. That meaning, true to the character of all scripture, is as valid for us today as it was in John's time, for it has no connection whatsoever to outer circumstances other than as they reflect our individual and collective karma.

humanity of that age (cf. Jn 16,12).[51] Consequently, the exoteric teaching denied reincarnation, while the few initiates who had the esoteric teaching understood it. Those who sought, however feebly, to bring forward the knowledge of the mysteries were disposed of by the Church as heretics, as in the case of Julian the Apostate.[52] In the long run, these things had to come about. But we are in the age now where new Michaelic understanding (divine intelligence) must be engendered.

Just as critical biblical analysis in recent centuries has had its limitations in comprehending the creation account, so also has its comprehension been limited for Revelation. However, the last part of the twentieth century has seen a few rays of encouraging light, summarized in 5 ABD 704 under the caption "Relation to Other Ancient Literature" under the broader "Book of Revelation." These new approaches are said to be "a major breakthrough in the scholarly study" of the book, and not "primarily allegories invented to comment on current affairs." The referenced works date primarily in the 1970s, the earliest being in 1966, but seem to feed off of and relate to a much earlier work by one Gunkel (see 5 Brit 570) in 1895, further stimulated by the twentieth-century discoveries at Ugarit. Gunkel had shown that important aspects of Revelation should "be understood in comparison with ancient Mesopotamian mythic literature." While embryonic and recognized as helping give rise to "form criticism," this particular aspect of Gunkel's work notably appeared in the midst of the critically important spiritual time that gave rise to anthroposophy itself.

On the matter of authorship, Steiner is unequivocal: Lazarus/John is the one who experienced and (presumably also) wrote the Apocalypse. There is something mystically providential about this. Only two persons were explicitly initiated by Christ, namely, Lazarus/John (Jn 11) and Paul (Acts 9,1-9; Gal 1,12). The divine authority of the New Testament seems marvelously enhanced when it can be seen that the vast majority of its contents, all but the first two Gospels and the letters of James, Peter and Jude, were written by or under the influence of these two.[53]

---

51. See "Karma and Reincarnation" in *The Burning Bush*.
52. Steiner did not indicate that Julian understood the "Mystery of Golgotha" or that he acted properly in his retributive actions against Christians, only that he had some understanding of the ancient mysteries and desired to go back to them. What was needed was an understanding of the relationship of the "Mystery of Golgotha" to those former mystery traditions. Neither Julian nor the developing Church in his time understood that.
53. See *The Disciple Whom Jesus Loved*, pp. xiii–xiv.

Steiner's most important contribution on the content and structure of the Revelation may well be the schematic in chart I-1, drawn by him during the lectures and reproduced in the back of the fourth edition of ASJ (1977, and perhaps also earlier editions). For not until Revelation as a whole is seen as expressing primarily the ascending part of the parabola of the Prodigal Son's journey from the Garden to the Holy City can its deeper message be even remotely comprehended. Parenthetically, it should be noted that Steiner's chart contained the explanatory statement, quoted from lecture ten therein, that the scheme "related to the full reality not even like the inner framework of a house to the complete building, but only like the outer scaffolding . . . that has to be taken down when the building is complete." In a sense, perhaps this expresses the spiritual reality that all we know as "time," expressed by the chart, will be collapsed into "timelessness" when its goal is accomplished. It is like the stages of a rose's cycle, or the lives of an Individuality (cf. Jas 3,6)[54]: any given part or life has no significance other than as a part of a more comprehensive whole. But to get there, one has to progress from Alpha all the way to Omega, over a vast individual and collective evolutionary expanse.

In REVP, Steiner says that to the ancients the sound "Alpha" was expressive of awe or surprise at the creation of spiritual fire on Old Saturn, while "Omega" expressed what would not be reached until Vulcan (see the first tier, Conditions of Consciousness, in I-1). We have seen that Genesis 1 commences long after Old Saturn, and we shall see that Revelation essentially ends at the Jupiter Condition of Consciousness. Thus, the Christ, the "Alpha and Omega," which we are to take into ourselves

---

54. The best literal translation of the Greek in Jas 3,6, *trochos geneseos*, is "wheel of birth" or "wheel of origin," as recognized by RSV, NRSV, AMPB and Barc; cf. AB, NJB, NACB, KJV, NKJV, REB, NEB and INTPN where the same meaning is implicit (as in AB ["cycle of life"; see its excellent discussion at 37A AB 260], NJB ["whole wheel of creation"], KJV and NKJV ["course of nature"], REB ["whole course of our existence"], NEB ["wheel of our existence"], and INTPN, *First and Second Peter, James, and Jude*, p. 118 ["wheel of becoming"]); while more conservative translations struggle to avoid the obvious karmic implications of the language by words suggesting that it applies only to the speaker's lifetime (as in NIV ["the whole course of his life"], CEV ["entire life"], LB ["whole lives," not lit.], NAB ["entire course of our lives"], and PMEB ["whole of life"]). The Greek *trochos* in the Septuagint (LXX), Ps 77,18, is normally translated as "whirlwind," a term whose progressive evolutionary, karmic implications become crystal clear in the "Fire" essay, an observation that enhances the element of fire in this James passage (3,5-6). The karmic meaning of the passage is discussed in *The Burning Bush*, pp. 112, 155 and 166.

as our own higher "I Am" (see "I AM," especially as it incorporates Rev 2,17; 3,12 and 19,12), actually reaches out beyond both ends of our biblical story. But it is only during the middle part of the biblical span that anything like the written word of the Bible is required. At each extreme, there is a direct perception of the spiritual world which superannuates the written word's function.

In ASJ, Lect. 3, Steiner tells us how Lazarus/John's spiritual perceptions in the Apocalypse rose progressively from the fruits of one stage of initiation to another. We are pointed to four different levels in the evolution of human souls, each represented by the divine creative number of seven stages (Prov 9,1), successively represented by the letters, seals, trumpets and bowls. These four levels are identical to the levels experienced by the human Individuality (entelechy) in its long journey between lives, (see I-33):

Etheric World—where it experiences the Seven Letters

Astral World—where it experiences the Seven Seals

Lower Devachan—where it experiences the Seven Trumpets

Higher Devachan—where it experiences the Seven Bowls of Wrath

In his seminal pronouncement (Is 6,9-13), Isaiah obediently reveals humanity's loss in ancient clairvoyance and laments the great duration of the deprivation (vss 11-13). His announcement corresponds to the three stages of initiation that progressively have been lost and must be regained (vss 9-10). It is the progressive manifestation in human evolution of the "fading splendor" of which Paul spoke in regard to Moses' condition half a millennium before Isaiah (2 Cor 3). Steiner refers to these stages in ascending order as Imagination, Inspiration and Intuition (touched upon in I-31 and I-27), which correspond with Isaiah (6,9-10) as follows:

Seeing	Imagination (Image-ing)
Hearing	Inspiration
Understanding	Intuition

And this corresponds with the successive Apocalyptic perceptions as follows:

Seeing	Seals
Hearing	Trumpets
Understanding	Bowls of Wrath

The "letters" to the Angels of the seven churches are perceptions from the spiritual elevation where the etheric world borders on the higher astral world. Immediately after the etheric perceptions expressed in the "letters," Lazarus/John is told to "Come up hither and I will show you ..." (Rev 4,1). At that first level of initiation he "sees" what is covered by the seven "seals." Then at the next level he "hears" what is revealed by the seven "trumpets," and finally he experiences so as to "understand with the heart"[55] (intuit) the seven "bowls." Eventually, after all the sevens are thus perceived, he is carried "away to a great, high mountain" (Rev 21,10) from which he can observe the "holy city" with its zodiacal "twelves."

In the course of the ASJ cycle we see the evolutionary development of humanity through these various spiritual levels. The seven "letters" to the seven respective Asian churches (Rev 2–3) express characteristics in them that are expressive of the seven Cultural Ages, from Ancient Indian to the seventh Cultural Age of the fifth, or post-Atlantean, Evolutionary Epoch (see I-1). The seven "seals" (Rev 5,1–8,1) then express what is to be unsealed in the succeeding sixth Evolutionary Epoch, and the "trumpets" (Rev 8,2–11,15) what is to be experienced in the seventh Evolutionary Epoch of the Physical Condition of Form of the Mineral Kingdom of the Earth Condition of Consciousness. As chart I-1 shows, at the sounding of the "last trumpet" humanity moves out of the "Physical" Condition of Form and into the "More Perfect Astral." It is this time to which Paul refers in 1 Cor 15,52 (also 1 Th 4,16-17).

The "bowls of wrath" (Rev 16) are experienced in the astral world because the human being no longer has a mineral-physical body, so that one who is preoccupied with the importance of the physical body (as our current civilization clearly is, including those who look for a return of Christ in the physical body or the reassembly of human bodies atom by atom) will experience great anguish in the absence of such a body. Those who have not come to recognize and apply anthroposophical truth will then face a grim, and progressively worsening, state of existence.

---

55. The involvement of one's heart in rising to this level of understanding is described in "Second Coming," *The Burning Bush*, pp. 227-234.

After being forewarned, "This calls for wisdom," we are presented in Rev 13,18 with the mysterious "number of the beast, [which] is a human number, its number is six hundred and sixty-six." In ASJ, Lect. 11, Steiner addresses this number 666, identifying it in a most cogent and insightful way with Sorath, "the Sun-demon, the adversary of the Lamb" (and thus of the Sun-prince Michael, Rev 12,7). For the details of his interpretation, see ASJ. For now, suffice to say that he is the beast with two horns (Rev 13,11) that appears at the end of the *sixth* Age of the last Evolutionary Epoch of the last Condition of Form of the Mineral Condition of Life of the Earth Condition of Consciousness. For when the *seventh* Age has ended, the 666 will roll over and end the Mineral Condition of Life (see I-1).

The number 666 appears in Revelation prior to the "bowls" because it has also an earlier application as a "human number" if we assign one six (6) to each of the last three Evolutionary Epochs of the Physical Condition of Form, starting in our own post-Atlantean Epoch in which the birth of Christ occurred. Then the number 666 is representative of the time immediately before the blowing of the "last trumpet," after which we move into the astral realm (again see I-1).

In both of these applications, we are dealing with a system of numbers based upon seven, the divine number of creation and wisdom (Prov 9,1). It would equate with our modern system based upon the number ten if we consider that on the odometer of an automobile the number 999 corresponds to 666, and is indicative of the imminent move up to another level. The "beast" to which this lower level applies is the human being who has not by then taken into itself as its own higher "I Am" the Christ in the development of its Spirit Self (manas or manna, see I-9), the primary goal of the Earth Condition of Consciousness. The apocalyptic "one hundred and forty-four thousand" who have his "name written on their foreheads,"[56] and who alone can "hear" and "learn" the new "song" being sung in that heaven (see Rev 14,1-5; also Rev 7,4, and Song of Songs [Song]) have developed this "condition" and are those who will implant "love" into the Jupiter Condition of Consciousness in the same way that "wisdom" was implanted in the Earth during the Old Moon Condition.

The number 144,000 is a symbolic number, being the ultimate zodiacal

---

56. See fn 44 on the significance of the "name"; the "I AM" essay in *The Burning Bush* on the "I Am" as the "name" of Christ; and fn 23 on the meaning and biblical significance of the "forehead."

number twelve squared,[57] times one thousand. It merely means those
who have attained to Spirit Self level during Earth evolution. They will
have attained to the consciousness that exists in the higher spiritual world
represented by the twelves of the zodiac ("the ordinances of the heavens,"
Job 38,33). In ASJ, Lect. 12, Steiner touches upon the condition of those
not among that number when the Jupiter Condition of Consciousness
arises like the phoenix from the ashes of Earth evolution. In doing so he
looks beyond the end of what we are told in Revelation, just as he began
before the book of Genesis. Likewise, the Prologue of John's Gospel goes
back beyond Gen 1,1, and Paul, in Rom 8,19-23, sees beyond the time
described in Rev 22. Steiner says (p. 218), "Jupiter will be quite differently formed, it will be a 'new earth'; soil, air, water, and every being will
be different. It will be impossible for beings who have only gained the
Earth consciousness to live a normal life; they will be backward beings."
But he goes on to tell us that, even on Jupiter and the later Venus,
redemption of the lower creation will still be possible because of the
immense power of the redeemed. This is not to say that all will be
redeemed, but merely that the possibility still exists up until the Vulcan

---

57. Emphasis upon the zodiacal number twelve, and the fact that it is squared, can be found
encrypted also in Rev 21. There, between vss 12 and 21 the number twelve can be found twelve
times as follows:

Verse	Item Described
12	gates
12	angels
12	tribes
14	foundations
14	names
14	apostles
16	city length
16	city breadth
16	city height
19-20	jewels
21	gates
21	pearls

Furthermore, vs 17 says that within the city the wall measured 144 cubits. We can then again
see twelve squared in Rev 22, where, in verse 2, we are told of the "tree of life with its twelve
kinds of fruit, yielding its fruit each month." The Moon circles the Earth monthly, covering,
from the Earth's perspective, the zodiac monthly; thus within the year the "tree of life" gives
twelve kinds of fruit (zodiacal influences) twelve times each year (allowing for a year of twelve
lunar months).

Condition. It is this to which Paul refers in Rom 8,19-23, for none of the "creation" he speaks of there could otherwise be among the 144,000 during the Earth Condition of Consciousness.

But there is an even stronger esoteric indication of the symbolic nature and meaning of the 144,000. It relates to fire and the fire ether (I-22). To most fully appreciate what is said here, the essay entitled "Fire," which follows below, must be considered. We see there the deep esoteric meaning of the symbols of the phoenix and the pyramid, both involving fire; the pyramid (tetrahedron), according to Plato, is the original "element and seed" of fire and even today can be seen as etymologically deriving from it. And we can see the connection of the golden mean (or ratio, symbolized by *phi*) to the pyramid and to fire, and thus to the symbols both of the phoenix and the zodiacal Cancer (the crab; see I-81). With these things in mind, the Imagination thus given reveals that 144,000 can be seen not only as the point where the sevens of time become the twelves of zodiacal timeless space but also as occurring at the point of fire, i.e., of *phi*. For the first multiple of twelve that appears in the Fibonacci series, which portrays *phi*, is 144.[58] And the "thousand" terminology merely magnifies the importance of the number. Not only is twelve squared, 144, the first multiple of twelve that occurs in the Fibonacci series, but 144 is the twelfth Fibonacci number in the series, and the intersection of the twelve multiple and the Fibonacci series recurs only on each subsequent twelfth Fibonacci number.

From this, it can be seen that the point at which fire and fire ether first touch is at the point where the sevens of creation touch the timeless space of the zodiacal number twelve. But since both time and space are vehicles for anything to exist in form, as in our earthly creation, the fullness of

---

58. The sequence starts with one and moves as follows:

$$
\begin{array}{rrll}
1. & 1 & & = & 1 \\
2. & 0 & + \ 1 & = & 1 \\
3. & 1 & + \ 1 & = & 2 \\
4. & 1 & + \ 2 & = & 3 \\
5. & 2 & + \ 3 & = & 5 \\
6. & 3 & + \ 5 & = & 8 \\
7. & 5 & + \ 8 & = & 13 \\
8. & 8 & + \ 13 & = & 21 \\
9. & 13 & + \ 21 & = & 34 \\
10. & 21 & + \ 34 & = & 55 \\
11. & 34 & + \ 55 & = & 89 \\
12. & 55 & + \ 89 & = & 144 \\
\end{array}
$$

twelve squared, or 144, is the point where both the sevens and twelves touch the timelessness and spacelessness of eternity.

In *Karmic Relationships*, Vol. 1 (KR-1), Lect. 1 (p. 23), Steiner, in speaking of how the geometrical concept that a straight line eventually returns to itself is illustrative of spiritual truths, said:

> Once more then, we may say: To deal with the plant-nature and with the *etheric nature in man, we must go to the very limits of the ether.* But if we wish to explain the animal nature, and the astral in man, we must go right outside all that there is in space. We must go for a walk, in time—beyond all that is contemporaneous; we must move forward in time. And now we come to the human kingdom. (Emphasis mine.)

If we look at Chart I-1, we see that the ultimate (seventh) Condition of Life before Earth evolution ends is the human kingdom. If we look again at I-22, we can then start with the lowest point on the triangular "tree of life" depicted there, the element earth, and move upward through the elements and kingdoms (Conditions of Life) to the human:

Element	Ether	Kingdom
Earth	Life	Mineral
Water	Chemical/Sound	Plant
Air	Light	Animal
Fire	Fire	Human

And we see emerging in Rev 14,10,18 the prospective element of fire. But not until Rev 20,9 is it said that "fire came down from heaven," and then we are told that all matter was burned, came to an end at the point of fire, the "second death," the death of the etheric body (Rev 20,14-15). The human being, moving down through the etheric world to incarnation first became matter at the point of fire, and it is at that point that the human being leaves forever the world of matter. The point of fire, which represents the human Ego (see the text at fn 40), is the "first and last" stage of the mineral-physical human being. Here the 144,000 are the "sons of man" (Rev 1,13-16), "the first and the last" (vs 17), knowing death no more (vs 18). All else disintegrates in fire (Rev 20,14-15; 2 Pet 3,7). Moving upward from fire, through the light and chemical/sound ethers, the 144,000 come to and pass through the life ether (Rev 20,12).

The "tree of life" (I-22; Gen 3,24) points them upward (see I-87; the "Key of David," Rev 3,7).

Within the Holy City, the New Jerusalem (Rev 21), we are told in verse 17 that its wall is 144 cubits, "a measure of a man, which is of an angel." This interpretation is directly from the Greek interlinear portion of KJV/NIV-INT, and seems to give a more appropriate picture than most modern translations. It points to the 144 as being descriptive of the human being itself, not merely humanity's devised method of measuring. This concept is supported by the reference to the angel, for angels didn't devise the cubit or other earthly standards of measurement. Rather, the meaning seems clearly to be that by this point, the human being has attained the level of 144, the Jupiter Condition of Consciousness, the level the angels had attained at the commencement of the Earth Condition of Consciousness—as reflected in I-15.

This awareness that here the biblical account stretches out further, both before and after, than the Bible otherwise indicates, again comes down to the vision of those two alone who, as earlier shown, were personally initiated by Christ, namely, Lazarus/John and Paul. They knew more nearly the parameters of the true "Alpha and Omega," as also Isaiah would appear to have known. However, when the "law" is written upon the hearts of all (Jer 31,33; Heb 10,16), these things will be known by those who are sufficiently "perfected" (Mt 5,48).[59]

Those who do not attain the twelvehood of the zodiacal state of consciousness during Earth evolution will gradually, through their allegiance to materiality, the "beast," take upon themselves, their "foreheads," the "mark of the beast."[60] Steiner tells us that in our time, the fifth Cultural Age of the post-Atlantean Epoch, the human being is able to deceive others by

---

59. That the "law" they speak of is the higher karmic law rather than the writings of the Torah, see the discussions of Mt 5,17 in *The Burning Bush* (see its Index of Scriptures Cited).

60. The phrase "mark of the beast" is most significant in that it relates so pointedly to the "forehead" (on which, see fn 22). This ominous phrase pervades Revelation by virtue of its application primarily to the future evolution of humanity (see Rev 13,16-18; 14,9,11; 16,2; 19,20 and 20,4). The meaning of "forehead" as shown in fn 22 should be carried with it throughout the Bible, as in Ex 28,38; Num 24,17; 1 Sam 17,49; 2 Ch 26,16-23; Is 48,4; Jer 48,45; Ezek 3,4-11; 9,3-8; Rev 7,3; 9,4; 13,16; 14,19; 17,5; 20,4 and 22,4. How prophetic then becomes the blood of the "lamb" on the forehead in the Exodus account, reflective of the eternal spiritual reality that the human being can only be saved by the blood of Christ the "lamb of God" on the forehead (the divine intelligence) that blocks out the "mark of the beast" emerging there. When the "I AM" essay in *The Burning Bush* is taken to heart along with the "Blood" essay that follows herein, the power of these observations can become overwhelming.

outward appearance and word. But the time will come, in the Age of Phil-adelphia (Rev 3,7-13; see I-25), when those who do not have the "name" of Christ, the "I Am," written upon their foreheads will commence to have the "mark of the beast" there. As human evolution progresses, the outward appearance will begin to reveal the inner character of the human being in the next Cultural Era, when deception will no longer be possible. It should be sobering to realize, however, that by failing to take into the self the knowledge offered by anthroposophy, including that of karma and reincarnation, something priceless is lost which will be detrimental in the individual's future evolutionary development (indicated by the parable of the talents). The failure to recognize these spiritual truths when presented is abetted by the influence of the beast of materiality, Ahriman. While Steiner characterizes the beast in Rev 13,18 (whose number is 666) as "Sorath," the "Sun-demon," it must be assumed, it would seem, that he is either one and the same as, or closely allied with, the Ahriman whom Zarathustra in Ancient Persia saw as the opponent of the then Sun-Spirit, Christ, the Ahura Mazdao or Ormuzd, or "Great Aura" of the Sun. (For Ahriman, see the "Overview" in *The Burning Bush*, as well as 12 Brit 934-936, "Zoroaster" and "Zoroastrianism.") Lucifer, the serpent in Genesis 3, was thrown down from heaven to tempt humans on Earth (Gen 3,14) at the time of the Fall. Through his deception about the real nature of cre-ation, he plays into the hands of Ahriman, the beast of materiality or of those who see mineral-physical existence as reflecting that reality. Lucifer himself repented as Christ hung upon the Cross, but his legions continue to deceive. Nevertheless, because of Lucifer's conversion, it is not he who is referred to as the beast, but Ahriman, the "sun-demon." Lucifer was a fallen spiritual being, but Ahriman was also a spiritual being who had fallen from one higher hierarchical rank (see I-32), thus having much greater power. Michael, the prince of the Sun, fights against this beast. The account of Michael's battle against the dragon (Rev 12,7-17), as is typical of scripture, is applicable to various battles fought by Michael, the Sun-prince, in the heavens. It also applied to the battle with Lucifer when the latter was thrown down. More recently, it applied to the throwing down of the two-horned beast (Rev 13,11) in the nineteenth century in the decades just before Michael's reign on Earth began in 1879 (see *The Archangel Michael* [ARCHM], Lect. 7). Materiality began to rear its uniquely ugly head during such time in particular reference to the human Consciousness Soul.

However, the beast that the "Sun-demon" aggrandizes (Rev 13,12) and makes the Earth's inhabitants worship is the beast "with ten horns and seven heads" (Rev 13,1). In ASJ, Lects. 9 and 10, Steiner shows us how this "beast" is the human being who fails to take the higher "I Am," the "name" of Christ, into its being. In these excellent lectures Steiner indicates that in the language of the mysteries the term "head" refers to what is in the formative and creative etheric body while "horn" is what arises in the physical body that develops out of an etheric head. The human being's organs are "horns" that have arisen in the physical body because of the prior activity of the etheric heads. In other words, "physical organs ... are really densified etheric organs" (Lect. 9). In Lect. 10, Steiner shows at considerable length how the "ten horns and seven heads" describes us as human beings today in our present physical-etheric constitution. Near the end of the lecture he summarizes as follows:

> If we regard the outer human form as the condensed part of the etheric, we have in the fourth Atlantean age the four horns in addition to the four group soul heads [he has explained these four as being the four group souls described in Rev 4,7]. Now, however, in the last three ages of Atlantis something twofold begins to develop physically. [Obviously the etheric preceded the physical development in this regard; furthermore we need to remember that every human being is now both male and female, the etheric body of a male being female and that of the female being male.] At each stage where a group soul head was to develop, a double physical, male and female, was formed. In the first four stages you find man formed with four heads, the condensed etheric with four horns. We now have three more heads which are invisible because the external human form absorbs them. These three are only perceptible to clairvoyant vision, three etheric heads, the principal human heads, and in between them two others which are like shadows beside each, like double shadows. Thus when the Atlantean Flood burst, we have seven race or group soul heads, of which the last three always appear in such a way that they have their physical part in a double form, as male and female. From this you see that at the end of the Atlantean epoch the entire group soul nature of man— although the later portion remains invisible—has seven heads and ten horns. The horns of the first four heads are not separated into male and female, but only the last three.

The last paragraph of the lecture goes on to explain that the human being who is able to take the higher "I Am" into its being during Earth evolution will be able to overcome sexuality, whereas the hardened ones who have stressed the "flesh" or material aspects of existence will keep the full component of sexual nature and will appear, at the time of "666" (Rev 13,18) as the beast with the seven heads and ten horns. The 666 is actually the Sun-demon, but the "human number" refers to the hardened and still sexually divided human beings who are served by that "beast"; these are the humans who have the "mark of the beast."[61]

In the "Lord of Karma" essay, item 5 in the discussion of the "little apocalypse" (Mt 25,31-46; Mk 13,26-27; Lk 21,36) took special note of "the misfortune of being with child in those days" (Mt 24,19; Mk 13,17; Lk 21,23). That discussion is most enlightening on the necessity of humanity's evolution now moving to the state where the male and female elements again become one within the human being, as they were in the beginning (Gen 1,27; Mt 19,4; Mk 10,6), before their separation in Gen 2,18-24. The joinder together in marriage at our present stage is only symbolic of what must happen within each human being in times to come.

In this regard alone, that aspect of materiality reflected by our modern preoccupation with sex must surely be seen as an ominous development. One can even see the recognition of this in Paul's emphasis upon the celibate state, not to mention the imposition (prematurely?) upon the clergy in the Roman Catholic faith.

Rev 11,3 refers to "two witnesses," and what follows clearly identifies them as Elijah and Moses. We have already seen in the "Peter, James and John" essay the extent to which Lazarus/John carried the Elijah being within him down as far as his Consciousness Soul. It is hard, from an anthroposophical standpoint, not to extend something of the same character into the relationship between the Moses being and Paul. Moses gave Israel its law. Christ revised that so as to bring it in keeping with, and thus to fulfill (Mt 5,17-48), the higher karmic law, of which Paul says the law of Moses is but a "shadow" (Heb 10,1). Paul dwells with greatest emphasis upon the consequence of this, especially in Romans and Galatians, but

---

61. On a somewhat smaller scale, but one ominous for our immediate time, there are also anthroposophical indications that Ahriman himself, whether or not recognizable as such, will incarnate in human form at or shortly after the expiration of the third cycle of 666 years from the turning point of time. These three cycles of 666 years (3 X 666) equal the year 1998. It is not difficult to see how much humanity is in the materialistic grip of Ahriman in our time.

then in a most exalted way in Hebrews. Some respected anthroposophists have previously come to the conclusion that the Individuality of Moses and Paul is one. Given the karmic law that "each individual who accomplishes something in the service of the Guiding Powers of the world must, after a certain time, perform a similar deed in consequence of it, but in such a way now that it appears like the opposite pole of the first," Paul would be the obvious personality of the Christian era to embody the Moses Individuality, a la the Steiner/Aristotle thread (see "Pillars on the Journey" in *The Burning Bush*). And given that the majority of the New Testament comes from these two "witnesses"[62] who "stand before the Lord of the earth" (Rev 11,4) in their "written word," we may well ponder that it is so if we are to judge the trees by their fruit.

With no more than what has been attempted in this essay, one should begin to comprehend the majestic sweep of the Bible from Genesis 1 to Revelation 22—and more than that to see that even within it are indications, in the works of Christ's two special initiates, Lazarus/John and Paul, that the Alpha goes back further than Genesis 1 and the Omega stretches beyond Revelation 22—and that those upon whose forehead his "name," the "I Am," is written shall become a part of that timelessness called eternity from which they came.

CHAPTER END NOTE

In *The Burning Bush*, the name "Adam" is associated with hardness and thus with the first human beings to stand upright with skeletal bones. The passage in Gen 3,17 (referring to Adam) is there identified to that stage of human evolution (see pp. 19, 111, 429 and 466). The tendency in most modern translations is to speak of "man," rather than "Adam," prior to the passage in Gen 3,17. This certainly lends itself to what Steiner said about the stage when the human being was first able to stand upright. It must be recognized, however, that there is great difficulty in dissociating the name "Adam" from the solids of which the human being was formed. While I am

---

62. If the Moses/Paul Individuality was one witness, the other was the Elijah/John the Baptist Individuality that penetrated down as far as the Consciousness Soul of Lazarus/John (see *The Disciple Whom Jesus Loved*). It was Lazarus/John who gave us the testimony of the "two witnesses" in Rev 11 long after Paul's death.

not trained in Hebrew, it is clear that two different terms are used in the creation account (Gen 2,4b–3,24), which, though seemingly similar, do not fully coincide in meaning. One of these is *ha-ʿadam* and the other is *ʿadam*. The former has in it the definite article, while the latter does not (on this see also 1 AB 18, Note 22). Moreover, *ha-ʿadam* seems to have a direct derivative relationship to the term used for "ground" or "earth," namely, *ha-ʿdama*, as, for instance, in Gen 2,5d ("no man [*ʿadam*] to till the *ground* [*ha-ʿdama*]").

The term *ʿadam* without the definite article appears only four times in the creation story, in Gen 2,5,20 and 3,17,21. Some translations use the name "Adam" in Gen 2,20, but none that I know of use it in Gen 2,5— a quite interesting observation if one thinks about it. The tendency has been to translate *ha-ʿadam* as "man" or some other terminology indicating a state prior to sexual differentiation.

Perhaps the definitive work on the meaning of these terms is Phyllis Trible's *God and the Rhetoric of Sexuality* (GRS). *The New Interpreter's Bible* on Genesis commends her work highly and relies on it in the interpretation of the creation story (see 1 NIB 324-325, and its fn 5). Working from the Hebrew itself, she makes a powerful case for interpreting the human being as non-sexual (asexual) in Gen 2 prior to the sexual differentiation that takes place in Gen 2,21-24. There (in vs 23) she points out, quite significantly, that the Hebrew term translated "woman" is *ʿissa* and that translated "man" is *ʿis*.

Those who hold, according to tradition, to the male nature of the Trinity and hierarchical spirits, and to the subordination of female to male in the creative process (and since), would do well to consider the powerful indications in Trible's work that these positions are contrary to what is indicated by the Hebrew language used in the biblical creation account.

Initially Trible interpreted *ha-ʿadam* as androgynous prior to this differentiation into male and female, but by the time of GRS she had changed her position since *"androgyny* assumes sexuality, whereas the earth creature [the prior human being] is sexually undifferentiated" (see p. 141, fn 17). In *The Burning Bush*, I also expressed the pre-separation state as androgynous (see, for instance, p. 19). For our present purposes, we need not discuss whether any reproduction prior to this time of sexual differentiation was by asexual division or androgynous procreation.

THE FOUR ELEMENTS [1]

I

BEFORE MODERN "SCIENCE" relegated them to the archaism of ancient Greece, the four elements, fire, air, water and earth, were part of the common knowledge of the West. Today they are generally seen only as a part of the history of humanity's advance in "scientific" knowledge. We are told how the Greeks came, between approximately the sixth and fourth centuries B.C., to conceive of these as the basic four elements. But in truth that knowledge preexisted the Greeks, going back to the Egyptians and Mesopotamians and even before. [2]

When science speaks of elements today, it is speaking of their proliferation as identified by chemistry or atomic physics. [3] And having little use for the ancient concept of the four basic elements, it looks condescendingly upon them as an anachronism from the past.

That Steiner accepted them as fundamental and basic is beyond question, and he did so for reasons of which modern science is oblivious. It will help to remember that in ancient times the priests in the mysteries were the sole source of humanity's knowledge of both science and religion, which were one and the same. With the fading of the ancient clairvoyance, the resulting decadence in the mysteries, and the eventual institutionalization of religion, religious matters were preempted by the Church. Consequently, both science and religion have historically accepted their mutually exclusive domains, thus spoiling the deeper conclusions of, and precluding the higher reality from, both. Only when the two have again become one can the deeper realities for which they search be found. Indeed, the two cannot be separated. Ultimate reality cannot be thus divided; see Mt 12,25; Mk 3,24; Lk 11,17. Both need to

---

1. This essay was called "Elements/Four" in Vol. 1.
2. The existence of that earlier knowledge is explored in the Chapter End Note.
3. See 14 Brit 339 at 364-365, "Atoms: Their Structure, Properties and Component Particles; Isotopes; Table 3 entitled, 'Abundances of the Isotopes'," and 15 Brit 916 at 925, "Chemical Elements; Geochemical distribution of the elements; Terrestrial distribution; Table 3 entitled, 'Abundances of the Elements in Different Geochemical Materials'."

recognize anew the same archetype with its amazingly fresh and expanded parameters.

Even while he pointed to fundamental errors in widely accepted scientific assumptions, most of which, as we shall see, prevail to this day, Steiner repeatedly stated that science had given humanity many marvelous inventions. Today we know that these have exploded beyond imagination in areas of commercial utility, medical discovery and the like. Doubtless they will continue to do so. Steiner was no Luddite. He lauded these accomplishments and their human value up to the point at which they begin to serve unworthy purposes. But, sensitive to the demands of Christ's earthly mission, he saw something badly amiss in the prevalent morality of his time. Today it is probably even more aggravated. Pervasive inequity among human beings has persisted with the materialism of our age, even in the midst of great religiosity (1 Jn 3,17; Mt 25,31-46). The increase in human intellect and skill has not been balanced by an increase in sensitivity to, and sacrificial concern for, human suffering and need. Privilege rather than sacrifice is still valued, contrary to Christ's example and the ultimate meaning of his Crucifixion.

Anthroposophy is like a marriage counselor dealing with obstinate spouses, science (husband) and religion (wife). Only by bringing them into oneness can they be fruitful. Just as much in *The Burning Bush* may have seemed to stand conventional theology (religion) on its head, in the essays that follow anthroposophy seems to stand science on its head. Not an end in itself, this results from the basic tenet in all Steiner's work that all phenomena should be permitted to speak for themselves. They are, after all, what are given from the spiritual world to humanity. The thinking and reasoning capacity that has evolved in the human being is necessary and natural. But it has been permitted, in one sense, to overshoot its bounds, racing ahead of what patient and open observation will reveal. The latter was the great verity behind Goethe's approach to human existence. Doctrines, dogmas, principles, laws, and the like that are not in accord with phenomena have been set forth by both science and religion, and when propounded have become so widely accepted that it is deemed heresy to seriously question them.

If all phenomena were permitted to speak for themselves, there would be no inconsistencies between science and religion, or indeed between any of the human disciplines. The challenge to humanity is to accurately observe, realistically interpret and courageously accept and apply its message.

II

The classical four elements are part of that phenomena. Understanding them and their provenance is a necessary first step in demonstrating what has been said above. In the course of this book, we shall see that the four elements, classically and esoterically called *fire, air, water* and *earth*, are synonymous with the more common and exoteric terms *warmth, gas, liquid* and *solid*, and we shall also see that they interact and interpenetrate or indwell one another while at the same time being individually archetypal in character. This entire essay is really just an introduction to the elements, since the rest of the book will deal with them both individually and in their interrelationships. A fundamental truth in the teaching of ancient wisdom is that the four elements, in ways quite new to modern thought, are in fact the building blocks of creation and the basis for all that is perceived by the senses in earthly existence. In the course of this book we will see how this is true inasmuch as these elements relate directly to the four, and only four, etheric states—the states the Prodigal Son (humanity) must traverse to reenter the spiritual world.

The four elements are reflected in I-22, partially reproduced in the Creation essay, at p. 45 herein. They have their counterparts also in the four Conditions of Consciousness of humanity's evolution (I-1), Old Saturn, Old Sun, Old Moon and Earth; the fourfold human being (I-9, I-14); the four ethers; and many other fourfold profiles (including those in I-72 and I-73). The sevenfold nature of the four elements and their four related ethers is set out (in declining density) below:

Solid (Earth)

    Watery

        Gaseous

            Warmth (comprising both Fire and Fire ether)

                Light (ether)

                    Chemical/Sound (ether)

                        Life (ether)

One notes there are three classifications on each side of fire, the midpoint at which heaven and Earth touch each other.

In its descent from the highest regions of the spiritual world to redeem creation, the Christ Spirit had necessarily to follow the same path as the Prodigal Son into the flesh[4]—starting from the highest heaven. The distance of Christ's journey downward is suggested when Paul says he is "far above all rule and authority and power and dominion, and above every name that is named, not only in this age but also in that which is to come" (Eph 1,21; see I-6 and I-18). That Christ had first come from that position is indicated by Paul's saying that "though he was in the form of God, [he] did not count equality with God a thing to be grasped, but emptied himself, taking the form of a servant, being born in the likeness of men" (Phil 2,6-7) and that "he had to be made like his brethren in every respect, so that he might become a merciful and faithful high priest ... to make expiation for the sins of the people" (Heb 2,17). He had to become flesh just as we did in order to take human karma upon himself (see "Forgiven Sins" and "Lord of Karma" in *The Burning Bush*).

Thus, leaving higher devachan (spirit world), his Spirit descended through lower devachan, then the astral world, then the etheric (sometimes called the "elemental world"), and finally into the world of the four elements themselves, fire, air, water and earth (heat, gas, fluid and solid). The four elements as they are known from antiquity are the earthly reflection ("shadow" or "image" in biblical imagery) of the four stages of the etheric world, as shown in I-22. It is at once apparent that even the descent through the etheric world was thus a fourfold journey, from life ether to chemical/sound ether, thence to light ether, and thence to fire ether. As the descent continued from there, the fire ether manifested in earthly fire (molecular activity), then molecular air separated from light, and so on.

The above scenario is given only to demonstrate the relatively late stage at which the four elements come into being, that of Earth evolution itself.

---

4. Consider again how even the three temptations of Christ (Mt 4,1-11; Lk 4,1-13) reveal this to us. See #17 in "Three Bodies" at p. 434 in *The Burning Bush*.

III

In section I we looked at how our study of the elements should be approached. Section II dealt more pointedly with the fourfold nature of the elements as the fundamental and integral building blocks of matter by, from and reflecting spirit. In this middle section we will look for what, if anything, the Bible says on the matter.

While historians have concluded, with myopic vision as indicated above, that knowledge of the four elements reaches back only so far as the sixth century B.C., the Bible itself suggests otherwise. Except for the middle and later period prophets, scholars date the earliest writings of most of the Old Testament books before the sixth century B.C., namely, the ninth through the seventh centuries. Even then they reflected what had been handed down orally from earlier times, especially from priests within the ancient mysteries of Israel, its ancestors and neighbors.[5] Steiner also indicates that knowledge of the four elements came from primeval times. In the anthology *Nature Spirits* (NATS), Lect 3, April 9, 1909, he calls it the "primeval divine teaching."

Several early sacred writings, both canonical and extra-canonical, refer to the *elements*, and these are generally considered to mean the classical four elements, fire, air, water and earth.[6] We will defer until section IV Paul's use of the term in Galatians and Colossians.

Without calling them *elements*, many passages of the canon name or describe them so that there can be no question of the writers' consciousness that these were the building blocks of all creation. In the Creation essay I showed that the first three elements, fire, air and water were etherically present in Gen 1,1-2, and that all four, including earth, came into sensibly perceptible form in Gen 2,4b et seq.

---

5. For instance, Elijah's initiation into the Mithraic mysteries from prehistoric Ancient Persia is shown in *The Burning Bush*, pp. 346-347 ("Mysteries"); see also the more elaborate account in "Widow's Son" in the same volume. And Moses was initiated into the Mysteries of both Egypt and Midian, as also indicated in Vol. 1. Moreover, Jacob, Moses and Jonah are all shown to have taken the "Three Days' Journey" of initiation.

6. See 2 Pet 3,10,12 (when "the elements will be dissolved [or "will melt"] with fire"); Wisdom 7,17 and 19,18-21; 4 Macc 12,13. See OTP2, p. 557; The Pastor of Hermas, Chap. 13 ("For the world also is kept together by means of four elements"). See 2 NICENE-1, p. 17; Tertullian I, Chap. 3 (showing that the elements themselves were not divine, and citing "the enlightened view of Plato"). See 3 NICENE-1, p. 131; and Philo, "Noah's Work as a Planter," 28,120, "On Dreams—Book 1," 3,16 et seq., "On the Eternity of the World," 21,107-110, and "Concerning the World," 10 and 11.

And one can hardly miss seeing that Yahweh's control over the four elements is the essential aspect of the account of Elijah's contest with the prophets of Baal on Mt. Carmel, 1 K 18–19. It opens with the need of *water* in the form of rain (18,1). Dramatically it then incorporates the element of *earth* in the form of stones, altar, wood and bull (18,32-33). The element of *water* is then made to drench all these (18,33-35). Then *fire*, that critical element that joins heaven and Earth, enters the picture and prophetically consumes all the other elements (18,38) and those (here the prophets of Baal) who fail to adapt themselves to the God of *fire* (18,40). Chapter 18 ends with *air* in the form of wind that brings with it *water* in the form of "a great rain" (18,45). Chapter 19 returns to the other three elements, *earth* in the form of a cave (19,9), *air* in the form of "a great and strong wind" (19,11), and *fire* (19,12).

Job 38,24-25 speaks of the wind, earth, rain and thunderbolt (fire). Proverbs 30,4 speaks of heaven, wind, waters and earth.[7] Then verse 19 speaks of sky (air), rock, seas and "the way of a man with a maiden" (fire). Psalms 104,3-5 speaks of waters, wind, fire and earth, while Psalms 135,7 says earth, lightnings (fire), rain and wind.

The four elements are abundantly in evidence in Revelation. Revelation 11,4-6, speaking of the two witnesses who appeared with Christ on the Mount of Transfiguration, Moses and Elijah, reiterates the elements of fire, air (sky), water (rain) and earth. (Note its later reference to their initiation in the three-and-a-half-day "temple sleep" of the ancient Mysteries, Rev 11,7-12.)

But to appreciate more fully the evidence in Revelation, certain preliminary observations are needed. We will speak of the "four corners of the earth" and the "four winds," neither of which is exclusively the domain of Revelation but both of which are used here in a manner that casts light upon their usage elsewhere.

Obviously the Earth is a sphere, which has no "corners" geometrically

---

7. "Heaven" and "fire" are sometimes used synonymously by those who specify the four elements; see Philo, "On Dreams, That They Are God-Sent," Book 1, Chap. III, v. 16, which reads:

> Accordingly, we find that the four elements in the world are the earth, and the water, and the air, and the heaven, of which, even if some are difficult to find, they are still not classed in the utterly undiscoverable portion.

As we shall see early in the "Fire" essay, the Greek word *empyrios*, the source of our "empyreal" (adj.) and "empyrean" (noun), meant both fire (*pyr*) and heaven.

speaking.[8] What meanings can be given to the term? Notice that the Bible speaks of the four directions of a map, east, west, north and south (Gen 28,14; 1 K 7,25; 1 Ch 9,24; 2 Ch 4,4; Ps 107,3). These can be thought of as corners, but as such they are only an image or recapitulation, so to speak, of what the term "corners" means in the larger perspective of humanity's evolution, namely, the four Conditions of Consciousness upon which are based the four elements and the four components of the human being (physical, astral and etheric bodies plus Ego). The last of these four Conditions, that of Earth evolution itself, is the crowning event of the four, and thus can be looked upon as the one "corner" where the "cornerstone" is to be placed. It is Earth evolution when the Ego, the "I Am," enters the picture. The higher "I Am" that must become ensouled in each human being is the Christ, who during Earth evolution has been made "head of the corner" (Mt 21,42; Mk 12,10; Lk 20,17; Acts 4,11; 1 Pet 2,7; cf. Ps 118,22).

That the phrase "four corners" has a meaning tied to the entire evolution of the human being seems evident from Rev 4,7. It speaks of a lion, an ox, the face of a man, and an eagle. These represent, respectively, the zodiacal symbols Leo, Taurus, Aquarius and Scorpio (see "Peter, James and John" in *The Burning Bush*, pp. 516-518, and *The Disciple Whom Jesus Loved* [DWJL], p. 34, showing that the eagle is the higher name for the scorpion). The charts (I-18 and I-19 for example) in *The Burning Bush* show that these four animals are spaced at ninety degree intervals from each other, thus constituting the "four corners" of the creative cycle of the heavens.[9]

In considering the "four winds," we need first to remember that the term interpreted as "wind" in the Bible can mean wind as we know it or it can mean "spirit." We learn this elementary point in the second verse

---

8. Later essays herein show how Copernicus merely rediscovered the globular nature of the Earth, based upon Kepler's "stealing the sacred vessels" from the temples of Egyptian culture, that was part of the clairvoyant knowledge of humanity in ancient times. Pythagoras, who is thought to have studied the Mysteries in other regions, knew of the globular nature of the Earth. He, and the Ptolemies who followed almost a half millennium later, must be seen as the end, rather than the beginning of this ancient knowledge that was to disappear during the later Roman period, only to emerge again after the Renaissance. "Corners" then could not have referred to the solid Earth itself, but to the four representatives of the twelve heavenly influences involved in its creation.

9. Early Christian iconography applied these four ancient symbols to the four canonical Gospels, see I-62.

of the Bible (Gen 1,2) where the Hebrew word used for "spirit" (*ruah*) of God primarily means "wind"; see 1 AB 5 and 1 NIB 343. And the close relationship between the concepts is utilized by Jesus in John 3,7-9 where, in the RSV, there is a footnote stating, "The same Greek word means both *wind* and *spirit*." That word is *pneuma*.[10] But while *pneuma* can mean wind in either a material or spiritual sense, another Greek word, *anemos*, means wind in a material sense only. The term "four winds" is found in both the Old and New Testaments, but in the Old Testament it is almost always part of the phrase "four winds of heaven," or has similar meaning (Jer 49,36; Ezek 37,9; Dan 7,2; 8,8; 11,4; Zech 2,6; 6,5[11]), clearly suggesting a spiritual nature. In the New Testament, the Greek word used for *wind* in the phrase "four winds" is *anemos*. In Matthew 24,31 the Old Testament usage is carried forward in the phrase, "from the four winds, from one end of heaven to the other," while Mark 13,27 says, "from the four winds, from the ends of the earth to the ends of heaven." But in both of these "little apocalypse" passages God is sending out his angels to gather in the elect, clearly suggesting the connection of the spiritual with the material element of wind. In Revelation 7,1 the "four winds" are tied in with "four spirits" and "four corners":

> After this I saw *four angels* standing at the *four corners* of the earth, holding back the *four winds* of the earth, that no wind might blow on earth or sea or against any tree.

So, when Revelation speaks of the "four angels" (see also Rev 7,2; 9,14-15; and Rev 20,8 speaks again of the "four corners") we are quite warranted in seeing in them the four spirits (i.e., hierarchies) that are primarily related to the four Conditions of Consciousness in humanity's evolution (see **I-16**):[12]

---

10. Jn 3,8 uses the Greek word *pneuma* (blast, wind), while Jn 3,5,6,8 also use *pneumatos* (air, an *element*).

11. The reader can hardly fail to note the similarity in vision between the four horses in Zech 6,1-5 and the so-called "four horses of the apocalypse" in Rev 6,1-8, which deals with the opening of the first four seals (the revelation by Christ in the sixth Evolutionary Epoch of what is "sealed" in the first four Cultural Eras of our own post-Atlantean Epoch; see *The Burning Bush*, p. 395, "Trumpets").

12. Interestingly, the four can be seen as the ones Paul identifies in Eph 1,21, even if not in the same order, e.g., rule (Thrones), authority (Exusiai), power (Dynamis) and dominion (Kyriotetes); see **I-6**.

Exusiai (Elohim, Gen 1,1)	Earth
Dynamis	Ancient Moon
Dominions	Ancient Sun
Thrones	Ancient Saturn

The term "four corners" and "corners" are often used in the canon.[13] Notably, "corners" appears in some translations of Job 37,3, the chapter immediately preceding the list of the four elements (Job 38,24-25 above).[14] Important non-canonical books also speak of the "four winds." Perhaps most notable is Enoch 76,1-4, which speaks of the "twelve gates" that open from the four corners of heaven from which the winds come. These "twelve gates" bear a strong resemblance to those in Revelation 21,12 and to the clearly spiritual influences of the zodiac as reflected in the twelve tribes and twelve apostles. From the Old Testament pseudepigrapha, the book of Jubilees speaks of "the angels of the spirit of the winds" as one of "all of the spirits which minister before him" created by God on the first day (Jub 2,2). Included in that group are "all of the spirits of his creatures which are in heaven and on earth." This "heaven" fits well with I-11 which shows that the locus of the Ego of the three lower

---

13. Thus, in RSV, "four corners of (or upon) the earth," Is 11,12; Acts 10,11; Rev 7,1; 20,8, or "four corners (of something else)," Ex 25,26; 27,2,4; 37,3,13; 38,2,5; Deut 22,12; 1 K 7,30,34; Job 1,19; Ezek 7,2; 43,20; 45,19; 46,21,22; Acts 11,5, or simply "corners," Ex 26,23,24; 36,28,29; Num 15,38; 2 Ch 26,15; Is 41,9; Jer 9,26; 25,23; 49,32; Ezek 41,22; Zech 9,15; Mt 6,5 as in text above.

14. These translations include 15 AB, RSV and NRSV. However, by far the most common translation of the Hebrew term in Job 37,3 renders it not "corners" but "ends" of the Earth, while one (NJB) says "extremities" and another (CEV, not literal) says "across the sky." Surprisingly, none of the sources in my library discuss the translation of the relevant Hebrew word (which I, with some hesitation, transliterate as either *tdts* or *trts* [e.g., *taw aleph daleth/ resh? sadhe*], depending upon whether the second consonant is *daleth* or the closely resembling *resh*—the second letter is the non-consonant *aleph*). While I have located the Hebrew word in *Hebrew and English Lexicon* (HEL) at pp. 1061 and 357, I am unable to see that it gives a definition. What I do find, however, is that the Hebrew word translated as "corners" in the three versions of Job 37,3 above is identical to the Hebrew word often, if not generally, so translated in three other verses I tested, namely, Is 11,12 and 41,9 and Ezek 7,2; thus cf. KJV, NKJV, RSV, NRSV, NIV, NJB, REB, NAB and AMPB. While "corner" means the point at which two sides of a polygon meet, most of us probably think of it as referring to such a point in a rectangle, as suggested by NIV's translating it in Is 11,12 as four "quarters" rather than four "corners."

kingdoms (animal, plant and mineral "creatures") is in the astral, and lower and higher spiritual, realms, respectively.[15]

In Revelation 8,1 Christ opens the seventh seal and the angels, after a period of silence in heaven,[16] begin blowing the first six trumpets. The seventh Evolutionary Epoch of the Physical Condition of Form is underway. The dissolution of the elements is beginning. We are told that first a third of the Earth and then a third of the waters were destroyed. See *The Burning Bush*, p. 395, "The Trumpets," for a tabulation showing the progression of human evolution as revealed in St. John's Apocalypse.

But it is in Revelation 16, following the blowing of "the last trumpet" (1 Cor 15,51-52; 1 Th 4,16; Mt 24,31; Mk 13,27), that we come to the pouring out of the seven bowls of wrath. While the "bowls of wrath" are events that precede the final lake of fire in Revelation 20, they depict what the mineral world and humanity face when the time for surrendering the mineral-physical body has come. The four elements then come into focus as they are successively volatilized. We are told that the first angel poured out his bowl on the *earth* (vs 2), the third upon the *rivers and waters* (vs. 4), the fourth on the sun in order that it would scorch men with *fire* (vs 8), and finally the seventh into the *air* (vs 17) to complete the elimination of the four earthly elements. The order of the elimination of the elements corresponds with that in I-22 except for the reversal of fire and air. However, the Greek word used here for "air" is neither *pneuma* nor *anemos,* but *aera*, which means a condition of great thinness or height, as in "thin as air" or "high in the air." One seems justified in seeing here the stage between the lower etheric and higher spiritual realms. This seems to be particularly true when one observes that Paul uses exactly the same Greek word (*aera*) for "air" in 1 Th 4,17 where he speaks of "the voice of the

---

15. In his *The Old Testament Pseudepigrapha* (OTP, Vols. 1 and 2), Charlesworth and the scholars engaged with him in its production estimated the date of 1 Enoch (herein called Enoch), which they see as a composite, as during the period of the first two centuries B.C. while they date Jubilees in the second century B.C. According to their analysis, and probably also the more widely held view, the book of Enoch was very influential in the Church for the first three centuries of our era. It was recognized in the canonical book of Jude (Jude 1,14) as well as in the writings known as the New Testament Apocrypha and those of many of the Church Fathers, including Justin Martyr, Irenaeus, Origen and Clement of Alexandria.

16. The clause "there was silence in heaven for about half an hour" (RSV) is John's way of referring to the period of rest, sometimes called "sleep," "deep sleep" or (in the Orient) *pralaya*, that separates one evolutionary condition, epoch or age from another (see I-1 and I-2). These periods are mentioned or described in *The Burning Bush*, with particular reference to Gen 2,21, at pp. 19, 208, 429 and 467-468. See particularly the discussion at pp. 208-209.

archangel [Michael] and with the sound of the trumpet" and then says that whether alive or dead we will "meet the Lord in the air [*aera*]." Recall that the last trumpet is when the Earth and humanity pass into the More Perfect Astral Condition of Form of the Mineral Kingdom (see I-1 and "Trumpets," p. 395 of *The Burning Bush*). In other words, it is when our Physical Condition of Form has come to an end. The Bowls of Wrath that are then to follow are for those who have not perfected, become the master (lord of), their astral bodies (i.e., have not come to the manna condition, what is called *manas* or Spirit Self in I-9). They will then suffer the conditions specified in Revelation 16.

A particularly intriguing biblical indication of the four elements can be found in Proverbs 30 and the first verse of Proverbs 31. In *The Christ Impulse and the Development of Ego Consciousness* (CIDE), Lect. 4, p. 74, Steiner spoke of the Individuality (Ego) of the ancient Zarathustra (see "The Nativity" essay in *The Burning Bush*, as well as *The Incredible Births of Jesus* [IBJ], showing this Individuality as the Ego of the Solomon Jesus child in Matthew's Gospel): "The ancient Hebrews called the ego of this ancestor Itiel." He went on to say that they called his other bodies as follows:

Astral body	Lemuel
Etheric body	Ben Jake
Physical body	Agur

Typically, Steiner did not say these names were in the Bible. But they are. And where might we find them? In the very chapter of Proverbs that names (Prov 30,4 and 30,19) the four elements. Proverbs 30,1 reads (my emphasis), "The words of *Agur* son of *Jakeh* of Massa [fn: Or *the oracle*]. The man says to *Ithiel*, to *Ithiel* and Ucal." Proverbs 31,1 then reads (my emphasis), "The words of *Lemuel*, king of Massa [fn: Or *King Lemuel, the oracle*], which his mother taught him."

The obscurity of these names in theological sources fits well with Steiner's assertion that they came from "the secret doctrine of the ancient Hebrews." So also does the fact that the second century A.D. Septuagint (the LXX), the translation of the Hebrew Bible into Greek for Jews in the dispersion, does not use any proper names here (see 4 Interp 947). In fact the indications are that the names are of Arabic origin (4 Interp 947 and

5 NIB 251) rather than Hebrew, and this conclusion would lend itself well to the Persian background of Zarathustra. For the obscurity of the terms in general, see:

Agur	1 ABD 100
Ithiel	3 ABD 581
Jakeh	3 ABD 615
Lemuel	4 ABD 277

The association of these four names in juxtaposition with mention of the four elements seems too much for coincidence. The appearance here of the esoteric indication of the fourfold being of the ancestral Zarathustra strongly suggests that the four elements are indeed being identified in this passage.

Before our last peek into the New Testament, let us look at certain provocatively obscure passages that seem to be related, but in a way that has thus far apparently escaped scholarly detection. The Chapter End Note to this essay concludes with a discussion centering on the peerless Egyptologist René Schwaller de Lubicz. It is he above all who is cited as a reference by Peter Tompkins in his more recent *Secrets of the Great Pyramid* (SGP). Schwaller's culminating work, the massive *The Temple Of Man* (TOMN), expounds on the profound insights of the Egyptian mind, and its understanding of human evolution, in the Temple of Luxor. At p. 901 he writes about the "waters above" (cf. Gen 1,7). The paragraph preceding the one in point commences, "It is said that men are born from the tears of the eye of Ra, that is, from the salty waters of Nun [cf. Ex 33,11], the primordial chaos." To give adequate context, the full paragraph in point is quoted below (with the focal sentences italicized and certain words in bold):

As for specificity, that is, the coloring or animating particularity, when it is carried in the waters above, it is called Hat-hor, the house of Hor or Her (Horus), and its appearance is that of the eye of Ra (the visible sun). It is an unguent, triple in nature, issued from the fourth that remains below. *This aspect is represented by the "boxes for cloths" and the "four calves," those who suckle milk, the first of which is* **black***, the second* **white***, the third* **red***, and the fourth* **spotted***. These are*

*the four "elements" as well as the four phases, because the elements of
this philosophy are in reality phases of the becoming.*

The first thing to keep in mind is that Moses was initiated into these
ancient Egyptian Mysteries and thus would have their content in his
consciousness. Previously (in fn 11), attention was called to the relationship between the four horses in Zech 6,1-5 and in Rev 6,1-8. The colors
of the four animals in both passages are essentially identical with those
in the quoted paragraph above. Schwaller tells us these animals represent
the four elements in the Egyptian mind. Note that in Zechariah the
fourth color is called "speckled gray" (RSV, but a footnote indicates the
Hebrew word is uncertain) while in Revelation it is called "pale." But
this whole thing throws considerable potential light upon a passage that
has befuddled Bible scholars (and me too) from the first, namely, the
uniquely-bred sheep and goats that Jacob "earned" as pay from his
father-in-law Laban. Aside from the "black lambs," the Moses myth
indicates that Jacob was to get those animals that were "spotted and
speckled" (including also those later called "striped" or "mottled"); see
Gen 30,32-39 and 31,8-12. It is these "spotted, etc.," that are the fourth
and final category in all these listings. In the fourfold human being (I-
9), the Ego is the one that came last (Ex 3,14, "I Am the I Am"). Jacob
is the one through whom Abraham is to establish his twelvefold dynasty
in the pattern of the twelvefold heaven above (Gen 15,5 and 17,18-21).
It is he, rather than Ishmael (who also fathers a great twelvefold lineage)
through whom the higher "I Am" is to come in fulfillment of the covenant. The four elements and the four earthly kingdoms and the fourfold
human being must be seen in a basic and fundamental relationship; and
the Ego that dwells in the human being, Jacob's "spotted" animals in the
myth, must be seen as the strongest of the lot (Gen 30,41-42). This
strength (stronger animals) reflects the Ego, the "I Am"—"the *God* of
Abraham, Isaac and Jacob"; see "I Am" as well as #26 in "Three Bodies,"
both in *The Burning Bush.*

Finally, perhaps nowhere does the Bible present the four elements
more forcefully than in the Prologue of John's Gospel. The three higher
ethers, life, sound (word) and light are all present in verses 1-4 ("In the
beginning was the *Word,* ... In him was *life,* and the *life* was the *light* of
men"). In Jn 14,6, Jesus calls these "the way [light], the truth [word] and
the life." The relationship of these to the more solid three elements (earth,

water and air) is shown in **I-22**. The element of fire is reflected in the fact that he was before John (Jn 1,15), just as he was before Abraham ("Before Abraham was, [was the] I am"; Jn 8,58). The "I Am" is the Ego that came only with the element of fire (see "Fire" and "Blood").

In the light of all the above, one can see the four elements profusely demonstrated in the Bible.

IV

We cannot leave biblical examples without considering what Paul was saying in Galatians 4,3,9 and Colossians 2,8,20 when he spoke pejoratively of "the elemental spirits of the universe" (RSV). What relationship, if any, do these have to the four elements? The matter has long intrigued biblical scholars and has been the subject of considerable writing.

In order to consider the matter properly, we need to look at the Greek words used and how they have been translated in Galatians 4,3,9, Colossians 2,8,20 and Hebrews 5,12:

Scripture	Greek Word(s)	Translation	
Gal 4,3	*stoicheia tou kosmou*	RSV	elemental spirits of the universe
		NRSV	elemental spirits of the universe [or fn–the rudiments of the universe]
		KJV	elements of the world
		NIV	basic principles of the world
		NJB	elemental principles of this world
Gal 4,9	*stoicheia*	RSV	elemental spirits
		NRSV	elemental spirits [or fn–rudiments]
		KJV	elements
		NIV	principles
		NJB	elements

Col 2,8	*stoicheia tou kosmou*	RSV	elemental spirits of the universe
		NRSV	elemental spirits of the universe [or fn –the rudiments of the world]
		KJV	rudiments of the world
		NIV	basic principles of this world
		NJB	based on the principles of this world
Col 2,20	*stoicheion tou kosmou*	RSV	elemental spirits of the universe
		NRSV	elemental spirits of the universe [or fn—the rudiments of the world]
		KJV	rudiments of the world
		NIV	basic principles of this world
		NJB	principles of this world
Heb 5,12	*stoicheia tes arches ton logion tou theou*	RSV	first principles of God's word
		NRSV	basic elements of the oracles of God
		KJV	first principles of the oracles of God
		NIV	elementary truths of God's word
		NJB	elements of the principles of God's sayings

Martyn, quoting others, says there are four major possibilities for the meaning of *stoicheia:*[17]

1. The elements, or fundamental principles, of learning
2. The four classical elements, earth, water, air and fire

---

17. Aside from what Steiner had to say, the finest exposition on the subject up to its time was the very recent work by Martyn in his 1997 Anchor Bible volume on Galatians (see 33A AB 393 et seq., Comment #41 entitled "Christ and the Elements of the Cosmos"). See also 2 ABD 444, "Element, Elemental Spirit." To Martyn's fine analysis should be added those in the recently published (2000) NIB, Vol. XI, on Galations and Ephesians, which cite Martyn's work as support for their conclusions. The commentary at 11 NIB 565-568 is excellent, however, in going further, appearing to recognize that Paul was speaking of spiritual beings, whether good or evil, related to the classical elements, but inferior to the supreme power of the Christ Spirit.

3. Elementary spirits of the type associated with pagan religions

4. Heavenly bodies, especially of a demonic or hostile nature to human beings

The diversity in translation boils down simply to the question whether "spirits" and "principles" are the same thing. Neither, of course, accurately nor adequately describes the four classical elements. It isn't normally satisfying today simply to say that a tangible solid (e.g., earth) is either spirit or principle. Only the KJV speaks simply of the "elements," though one wonders why it changes to the not fully synonymous "rudiments" in Colossians. But for now the initial observation begs the question whether spirits and principles are one and the same, which comes close to resurrecting the Middle Ages debate between realism and nominalism.

The *Greek-English Lexicon* (GEL) lists five relevant possible meanings for *stoicheia*:

1. A simple sound of speech, as the first component of the syllable (cf. phonetics)

2. The four classical elements, earth, water, air and fire

3. The elements of proof

4. Elementary or fundamental principles

5. Stars or planets, with Galatians 4,3 and Colossians 2,8 cited as meaning a sign of the zodiac

Martyn comes to the reasonable conclusion that one must have "a strong reason to read" the Greek, including its reference to the cosmos or universe (*kosmou*), as meaning anything other than the classical four elements. He goes on to discuss the polarities involved in creation, and suggests that Paul incorporates these into his meaning, exemplified by his doing away with the polarities or distinctions between circumcision and uncircumcision, Jew and Gentile, or Law and Not-Law. And he has an intriguing discussion, based upon Philo and other Greek philosophers with whom Paul was familiar, of the division of the elements into pairs. This comes strikingly close to the divisions involved in the descent of the four elements from their related four ethers (see **I-22** and its discussion in the Creation essay). But Martyn's discussion does not show an understanding of the ethers, so it fails to take them into account.

Martyn's treatment of the subject, from the standpoint of insight available to traditional theological thinking, is admirable. But I think he errs in a very important point. He thinks that in some fashion or other the Law is one of the elements Paul refers to, being a part of, or perhaps even identical with, what enslaved the people and was of beggarly nature. (See and compare what is said in the recently published 11 NIB 565-568, as discussed in fn 17 above.)

So often the mere existence of an accumulation of scholarly writings and widely divergent views upon a particular passage of scripture can be seen to betray a lack of insight into the true nature of things. When anthroposophical light is thrown upon it, then the meaning becomes clear. Many instances of this were shown in *The Burning Bush*, and the major objective of this larger work is to point up the extent to which this is true with the entire understanding of the Bible. Paul's *stoicheia* in Galatians 4,3,9 and Colossians 2,8,20 seems clearly to be such an instance.

Let us see what Steiner had to say on the matter. He often spoke of the *elemental beings* or *elemental spirits*,[18] but I know of only one instance when he specifically identified these spirits with what Paul was speaking of. In his discussion of the Easter festival, *The Festivals and Their Meaning* (FM), p. 132-133 (Lect. on April 2, 1920), he said:

---

18. Instances include two recent anthologies, *Nature Spirits* (NATS) and *World Ether/ Elemental Beings/Kingdoms of Nature* (WEEB) and a number of other titles. References to elemental beings or spirits pervade Steiner's works, but so vast is their applicability that it is bewildering to attempt to bring them into any form of comprehensive organization. These two anthologies help the student cope with this problem. NATS is a collection of twelve carefully selected lectures dealing primarily, though far from exhaustively, with elemental spirits. Without a doubt WEEB is the most ambitious and organized effort to educate the student on what Steiner had to say about elemental spirits. The Steiner bibliography in WEEB on this topic is substantial and is followed by some helpful charts on the activities of the various elemental spirits. The following list of works are among those from my own reading:

ARCHM	*The Archangel Michael* (p. 216)
BG	*The Occult Significance of the Bhagavad Gita*, Lects. 4 (pp. 54-56) and 9 (p. 127)
CHS	*Christ and the Human Soul*, Lect. 1 (p. 16)
CSW	*Christ and the Spiritual World/The Search for the Holy Grail*, Lects. 2, 4 and 6
CY	*The Cycle of the Year*, Lect. 3 (pp. 39-51)
ELW	*The East in the Light of the West*, Chap. 3 (p. 40)
FM	*The Festivals and their Meaning*, Lects. 4-2-20 (132-133) and 6-7-08 (pp. 296-305)
FSC	*The Four Sacrifices of Christ* (p. 14)
HCMF	*How Can Mankind Find the Christ Again?* Lect. 4 (p. 56) *(continued)*

This was what Paul was continually emphasizing to those of his hearers who were able to understand it: that the old spiritual vision brings no approach to Christ, that with this old vision one can only mistake some elemental being for the Christ. Therefore Paul exerted all his power to bring men out of the habit of looking to the spirits of the air and of earth [editorial fn refers to Gal 4,3,9].

Indirectly he spoke of it at other times in reference to the sibyls. These, he said, were tied in with the forces of the elements and the elemental spirits, and were the influences that the Hebrew prophets and Paul strove so hard to overcome, those of atavistic clairvoyance. See *Christ and the Spiritual World/The Search for the Holy Grail* (CSW), esp. Lect. 4, pp. 82-83, and Lect. 6, p. 130, but also Lect. 2, pp. 44-45 and 48-49; see also *The Four Sacrifices of Christ* (FSC), p. 14. Some evidence of the sibylline influence was preserved in the Sibylline Oracles; see 6 ABD 2, "Sibylline Oracles," and 14 Brit 835, "Biblical Literature, The Pseudepigraphal Writings, Apocalyptic and Eschatological Works."

---

18. (*Continued from previous page*)

ISBM	*The Influence of Spiritual Beings Upon Man*, Lects. 1, 8, 9 and 10
JTC	*From Jesus to Christ*, Lect. 9 (pp. 154-155)
KM	*The Karma of Materialism*, Lects. 6 (p. 96) and 8 (p. 123)
KR-2	*Karmic Relationships, Vol. 2*, Lect.13 (p. 208)
KR-3	*Karmic Relationships, Vol. 3*, Lect. 6 (pp. 87-90)
KR-4	*Karmic Relationships, Vol. 4*, Lects. 3 (pp. 48-49) and 4 (pp. 58-61)
LAI	*Luciferic and Ahrimanic Influences/Influences of the Dead*
LBDR	*Life Between Death & Rebirth*, Lect. 2-16-13 (p. 196)
MK	*Manifestations of Karma*, Lects. 2 (p. 50) and 7 (p. 157)
MM	*Macrocosm and Microcosm*, Lects. 6 and 7
MSCW	*Man as Symphony of the Creative Word*, Lects. 7, 8 and 9
MSF	*Michaelmas and the Soul-Forces of Man*, Lect. 2
MWS	*Man and the World of Stars*, Lect. 5
REVP	*The Book of Revelation and the work of the priest*, Lect 17 (9-21-24)
RPA	*Reading the Pictures of the Apocalypse*, Lect. 3 (p. 40)
RCE	*The Reappearance of Christ in the Etheric*, Lects. 10 and 11
SHPW	*The Spiritual Hierarchies and the Physical World/Reality and Illusion*, Part 1, Lect. 2
SIS	*The Search for the New Isis, Divine Sophia*, Lect. 3 (p. 31)
SMRC	*The Sermon on the Mount and the Return of Christ* (pp. 7-8)
ST	*Secrets of the Threshold*, Lect. 3 (p. 38)
TFP	*True and False Paths in Spiritual Investigation*, Lects. 7, 8 and 9
THSY	*Theosophy*, p. 132 (p. 152 of 1994 ed.)
TR	*Theosophy of the Rosicrucian*, Lects. 2 (p. 20) and 4 (p. 46)
WH	*World History in the Light of Anthroposophy*, Lects. 2 (pp. 24-27, 33-34) and 4 (64-65)
WSK	*A Way of Self Knowledge/The Threshold of the Spiritual World* (Part 2, Chap. 5)

Steiner seems clearly to have rejected the idea that Paul was speaking only of "principles." He opens Chapter 3, *The East in the Light of the West*, with the following paragraph:

> Our attention has been called to the fact that to human beings at a certain stage of evolution, the external phenomena of warmth, air, water, etc., become living and permeated with spirit, and it has been said that this stage may be designated as that of "penetration into the world of Spirits of the Elements." I would ask those who have been students of Spiritual Sciences for some time to note the words carefully, and to realize that they are used, not in an approximate, but in an exact sense. "Spirits of the Elements" was the expression I used, and not "Elementary Spirits."

Implicitly he is adopting the idea of "elemental" and not "elementary." The distinction is that the former applies to what is an element of something while the latter, when distinguished from "elemental" as in Steiner's statement, means "first principles." But if we go beyond these semantics to the content of his vast revelations on the subject, there can be no doubt that the only translation that comports with them is that found in the RSV (or the NRSV if the footnote is omitted), namely, "elemental spirits." He uses the phrase "elemental spirits" and "elemental beings" interchangeably.

The student can gain a substantial beginning by contemplating charts I-12, I-47 and I-51, in conjunction with I-22, and the cited works from which they are derived. Even these, however, hardly give one an adequate concept of the scope of the topic. Perhaps the best tool for this is the Table of Contents to the WEEB anthology. All that can be afforded here is the broadest form of summary.

V

All phenomena derive from a pattern in the spiritual world. We will see this in the following essay, "As Above, So Below." The Hierarchies (I-6), as agents of the creative word of God, the Logos or Christ Spirit, by their sacrifices have brought all phenomena into being. And it can be said that the objective of this immense spiritual panorama is the development of the perfected human being, Spirit Man (I-9), and that all phenomena, including human beings as we know them historically, are mere by-products of that process, the as yet uncompleted journey of the Prodigal Son. This journey ultimately requires the redemption of all the kingdoms (human, animal, plant and mineral) as we know them (see I-1; Eph 1,9-10 and Rom 8,19-23).

But just as there are multitudes of spiritual beings above the human being, so also are there spirits at a lower level. While in a sense the hierarchies are the spirits behind the elements, when Steiner uses the term "elemental spirits" or "elemental beings" he is speaking of beings lower than human. These are the "nature spirits," those invisible to human sight that dwell and are active within the four elements. He calls them "messengers" of the hierarchies; see *The Spiritual Hierarchies and Their Reflection in the Physical World* (SH), Lect. 2, p. 20 and *The Book of Revelation and the work of the priest* (REVP), Lect. 17.

We have seen that there are good and bad spiritual beings above the human level. In general we think of the hierarchies (I-6), the "heavenly host," as "good" and those spiritual beings who have "fallen" (those who in general we call Luciferic or Ahrimanic; see I-32) as bad. But just as there are multitudes of good and bad spirits above the human level, so also are there good ("very useful") and bad (Ahrimanically and Luciferically influenced) elemental spirits. The form and manner of their creation is multifarious, many coming from the evolution of the lower kingdoms but many also coming from the activities of the human kingdom. WEEB gives probably the most extensive outline and discussion of these. While elemental beings are "messengers" of the hierarchies, they have no Egos (see I-12) and so are subject to influence by those many levels of beings with Egos. They are like tools to be used. As Paul says (Gal 4,8), they are not "gods" themselves (but instruments of the "gods," including human beings). In the essay "Forgiven Sins" in *The Burning Bush*, I say (p. 107), "Every sin, however slight, actually generates evil spiritual beings (e.g., demons) or food for such evil beings, and generates a karmic burden upon humankind." "Demons" are only one class so created or fed. All materialization is the result of the use by Ahriman of elemental spirits. The Fall described in Genesis 3 resulted from the false leadership of the serpent (Lucifer), who led humanity into the materialization process of Ahriman. The fact that we have materially sensible bodies today is a result of this process (see the end of I-23). All material (mineral-physical) existence is a result of this process. Elemental beings are thus instruments used by the hierarchies to bring about the movements of the material bodies of our solar system and the universe. Just as our visible physical bodies are only a manifestation of our spiritual being, so also the visible bodies of the Sun, Moon, planets and outer stars are only the manifestation of spiritual beings. The influence of these beings comes not primarily from the physical but from the far larger sphere of their full spiritual being. Thus Paul could criticize the worship of the elements in the sky as well as those on Earth (Gal 4,10).

Moses himself was able to see the Lord in the elements, as on Mt. Sinai, but the Incarnated Christ came to fulfill, by superseding, the Mosaic law by a higher law (Mt 5; Jude 1,9). The Hebrew prophets rightly condemned reliance upon mediums, stargazers and the like.[19] Mediums surrender their own consciousness (Ego) to spiritual beings and are thus susceptible to error because they can be used by bad spirits, both higher and lower than human. Stargazers, including most of modern astrology, do not perceive the true nature of the influence of the spiritual beings represented by either our solar bodies or the zodiac. When the Bible is seen for what it sets out in the light of anthroposophy, humanity will come to a new reverence for the spiritual beings represented by these visible objects. But a new clairvoyance, replacing the ancient (atavistic), whereby full Ego-consciousness is retained when one enters the spiritual domain must be the goal of human evolution. The prophets foresaw this (Jer 31,31-34), and the Christ has made it possible, but humanity has yet to come to an understanding of the meaning of the Mystery of Golgotha. The mission of anthroposophy is to assist in ushering that understanding into the minds and hearts of human beings in the days ahead.

There seems to be a sense among an important segment of humanity today that we are indeed creating much of the evil that exists in the world. When we come to understand more fully the elementary spirits that both Paul and Steiner talked about, Paul but briefly (as was so typical of his flashes of revelation) and Steiner so extensively, we will see that our germs, epidemics, natural disasters and the like are to so great an extent the result of human failures over time in the moral sphere. By our enslavement to materialization and the comforts and eases that we all tend so much to seek we are still "slaves to the elemental spirits of the universe"

---

19. Lev 19,31; Deut 18,9-22; 1 Sam 28,3,7-9; 2 K 21,6; 23,24; 2 Ch 33,6; Is 2,6; 8,19; 19,3; 47,12-13.

against which Paul preached (Gal 4,3-9). And through this enslavement we are increasing the burden we shall all have to overcome in this and future incarnations as we learn more and more the meaning of the Crucifixion and Resurrection of Christ as the "first fruits" among humanity and have the will to follow his example of sacrifice to the end.

The mission of anthroposophy today is to bring a sufficient portion of humanity into the intellectual recognition of these truths (the "divine intelligence" administered by the Archangel Michael[20]) and to stimulate its courage in the face of immense inertia and false understanding and piety, especially among the religious community. For while our knowledge will pass away (1 Cor 13,8-10), nevertheless while we are incarnated here on Earth it must be a tool for our hearts and wills, to bring about the high moral deeds that will overcome evil by our sacrificial good (Rom 12,21).

In conclusion, we return to the question of what Paul was saying when he spoke of "the elemental spirits of the universe" (RSV). Clearly he did not just mean the four elements; equally clearly he did not just mean fundamental or rudimentary principles. He was speaking of actual beings who lived and worked in the four elements, beings who in ancient times were recognized by human beings and who left their imprint in legendary accounts. Steiner generally classifies them among the four elements as "gnomes, undines, sylphs and salamanders" (see I-12). But just as the higher spiritual beings withdrew their face from human recognition over time as the ancient clairvoyance grew dim and disappeared (the "fading splendor" of 2 Cor 3,7,13), so also did the last traces of human recognition of the these lower spirits, the "nature spirits," fade completely away by around the twelfth and thirteenth centuries of our era. One can still imagine their presence by immersing oneself in the sounds of Grieg's Peer Gynt Suite (his "trolls" are one and the same as Steiner's "gnomes"). Nevertheless, while Paul was not referring to the four elements himself, he was implicitly recognizing them as the fields of activity of their respective

---

20. That our present time, from 1879 to about 2322, is the first regency of the Archangel Michael since the time of Christ (the prior one being during the period of the Greek philosophers who prepared the way for the spreading by Paul of Christianity within the Greek-speaking world), see the Epilogue in *The Incredible Births of Jesus* (IBJ) and the section entitled "Background" in *The Disciple Whom Jesus Loved* (DWJL), pp. 11-13. These indicate that Michael can only in his present regency bring the divine intelligence down to Earth, for in his Greek regency the blood of Christ had not yet been spilled so as to infuse the etheric Earth.

indwelling subhuman spirits. In doing so, he was fully within the intend-
ment of all the other biblical expressions of the four elements as the four
seminal stages in the evolution of mineral-physical creation out of the
etheric and spiritual worlds.

CHAPTER END NOTE

We are told that the Greek philosopher Thales (ca. 624-546 B.C.) concluded that water was the essence of all matter, thus the single basic element. If Thales ever reduced his teaching to writing, none survives, nor
is the substance of his teaching based upon the writing of any contemporary source. We are further told that in the next two centuries, Greek philosophers concluded that Thales was wrong in attributing all matter to
water; rather it was seen to derive from the four basic elements listed
above.[21]

Historians of science have thus deduced, based upon those later writings alone, that the ancient knowledge of the four elements was first born
between the sixth and fourth centuries B.C. I suggest that this is not the
case, but rather that this ancient knowledge was primordial in human
evolution, and that what Thales taught expressed what was developing,
among all peoples of that time, in humanity's long, slow transition from
its ancient clairvoyance and blood-related memory to its grappling with
the intellectual handling of observed phenomena.[22] It was the gradual,
evolutionary transition from the Garden to the laboratory. Something
was gained (intellectual analysis and reasoning) at the price of something
being lost (memory and understanding). This is what Isaiah had said only
shortly before, at the commencement of the Cultural Age of Aries, the
"Lamb" (Is 6,9-10):

---

21. See 11 Brit 670, "Thales of Miletus" and 27 Brit 32-42 at p. 34, "Science, The History of."
22. It was inherent, for instance, in the Mosaic myth handed down from even earlier times. See
the discussion of the infusion of the four elements in the creative process in the text of the
Creation essay between fns 39 and 41. There the fourfold nature of the water element, Gen
2,10-14, essential for all chemical processes, could well equate to Thales' focus upon that stage
in the condensation of the elements. In a very real sense, water does embody all the four
elements, from fire (warmth) to earth (solid). For even the solid is contained within the water,
which becomes a solid when enough of the fire element (warmth) is removed from it. We shall
nevertheless see in this volume the distinct characteristics and integrity of each element.

[9] And [the Lord] said, "Go and say to this people: 'Hear and hear, but do not understand; see and see, but do not perceive.' [10] Make the heart of this people fat, and their ears heavy, and shut their eyes; lest they see with their eyes, and hear with their ears, and understand with their hearts, and turn and be healed."[23]

According to modern scholarship, it was essentially at the time of Isaiah (i.e., "First Isaiah") that the oral teachings of Moses, which even earlier had come from the "fading [primordial] splendor" (2 Cor 3), were first reduced to writing. And what was said of Moses? It was said, according to the Mosaic myth, that he was called Moses because he came out of the water (Ex 2,10).

The full significance of this, as an expression of human understanding of that time, can probably best be seen in what, in its present written form, is known as *The Apocalypse of Adam*, whose roots must surely lie with this particular phase of the evolution of the human mind/soul (consciousness). It was first discovered among the Coptic manuscripts in the gnostic library found at Nag Hammadi in 1945. Its expressions relate to those of this particular era, though its extant written form is dated to early in the first century B.C.[24] It purports to describe the coming of humanity's great "Illuminator" in fourteen stages. The first thirteen accounts

---

23. As I've often emphasized, the seminal nature of this prophecy for the evolution of the human soul is demonstrated by the fact that it is quoted in all four Gospels, the book of Acts and Paul's letter to the Romans (see Mt 13,14-15; Mk 4,12; Lk 8,10; Jn 12,39-41; Acts 28,26-27; Rom 11,8). Christians seem generally to have assumed that the loss of spiritual perception Isaiah prophesied in this passage was lifted for them by their professing Christ. Perhaps this assumption is based upon the Acts and Romans passages, where Paul cites it in preaching to the Jews, the inference being that it applies only to the Jews for in speaking to them Paul may have emphasized its applicability to them by reference to Isaiah's commission to "go and say *to this people* ..." But none of the Gospel passages justify this distinction, for in the synoptics Jesus is telling those close to him why he is speaking in parables to others who have not had the special instruction; and in John's Gospel this passage is quoted with general reference to all. Moreover, from the standpoint of the evolution of human consciousness, the same things were happening in other cultures as were happening among the Jews.

24. See Welburn's commentary on it entitled *The Book With Fourteen Seals* (BFS). Other scholars have dated these manuscripts themselves to as early as the first century A.D., though all recognize that its sources are Jewish, rather than Christian, apocalyptic tradition that may have come from earlier times. In its written (as distinguished from earlier mythic) form, its first appearance was probably in the Greek language sometime during or after the first century A.D. See 1 ABD 66; Robinson, *The Nag Hammadi Library* (NHL), at p. 256; Charlesworth, *The Old Testament Pseudepigrapha*, Vol. 1 (OTP1), at p. 708.

(incarnations) conclude with the statement, akin to that said of Moses, "And thus he came on the water." The fourteenth, according to Welburn, is the Christ, who is described as having been chosen by God "from all the aeons ... out of an alien air, out of a great Aeon."[25]

We shall see the relationship of these four elements one to another as this volume proceeds. For now it is well to observe that as the senses (the instrument of the astral body) developed, the human being was able to perceive in the mineral world what had previously been known in the spiritual world.[26] The five senses we normally recognize came progressively, as Genesis shows us.[27] But water was the first element that could be perceived by all five of the senses, for fire (warmth) and air could not be perceived by the sense of sight. As the first fully sensually perceivable element it may thus have been noted by Thales in his effort to express these matters to the human intellect. This does not mean that he did not understand the prior states out of which "matter" was born, but merely that he did not fasten upon them the point at which all human senses were able to observe it. It was only shortly after Thales that Heraclitus (ca. 540-480 B.C.) spoke of the logos and of fire as the essential material uniting all things, and of a hidden connection between all things.[28]

The evidence strongly suggests either that Thales himself comprehended the finer elements from which the fully tangible water element derived, or that he was not a sufficient peg upon which to date ancient human understanding of the elements. The very existence of the pyramids, whose "name" according to Plato means fire, and whose construction and purpose still baffle modern humanity, suggests human

---

25. See the discussion of the meaning of "aeon" at pp. 211-212 in *The Burning Bush*.

26. See the discussion of the philosophical debate between "realism" and "nominalism" at pp. 248-249 in *The Burning Bush*. The preexisting spiritual reality implied by the "name" of a creature is shown in Gen 2,19-20; see the text related to fn 43 in the Creation essay.

27. In I-23, p. 590, in *The Burning Bush*, the following sequence of the usual five senses is identified in Gen 2–3 as follows:

Smell	Gen 2,7	Relates to "breathing"
Taste	Gen 3,6	"Ate" the fruit
Sight	Gen 3,7	"Eyes ... were opened"
Touch	Gen 3,7	"Knew" their nakedness
Hearing	Gen 3,8	"Heard the sound ... of God walking"

28. See 5 Brit 860, "Heracleitus"; also Steiner's discussion of Heraclitus in *Christianity as Mystical Fact* (CMF).

understanding of the character of the most basic element, fire, at least two millennia before Thales. Indeed the very mysterious phenomenon of the Great Pyramid of Giza (among others), built so soon after the commencement of writing, itself suggests the fading of an ancient memory and intuited knowledge commensurate with the gradual increase of intellect.[29]

In fastening upon Thales' identification of water as the basic element and thus the point from which knowledge of the four elements commenced, our historians of science have overlooked far more compelling evidence to the contrary. Solon (ca. 640-559 B.C.) was a slightly older contemporary of Thales. And Plato, in *Timaeus*, quoting Critias' statement to Socrates, says of Solon that "he was the wisest of men and the noblest of poets." He then recounts how Solon had gone to Egypt and there communed with the priests "who were most skillful ... about antiquity," and who, after Solon had related the Greek understanding of the origins of things, said to him, "O Solon, Solon, you Hellenes are never anything but children, and there is not an old man among you ... there is no old opinion handed down among you by ancient tradition, nor any science which is hoary with age." Clearly in ancient Egypt and earlier prehistoric times, science and religion were one. How they could be so, and how such marvelous things were done then that are beyond modern understanding, can only be understood in the light that spiritual beings were guiding humanity then. This guidance, originally innate with every human, devolved in the Atlantean Epoch upon the priests as evolution progressed. In chapter three of *The Spiritual Guidance of Man* (SGM), Steiner tells of how the earliest Cultural Ages of the post-Atlantean Epoch were guided by higher, more fully evolved spiritual beings than the later, diminishing right down to the time of the Greco-Roman, the Cultural Age of Aries, the Lamb, when humanity was left to fend for itself, and the Christ incarnated. It was then, and in this very *Timaeus*, that Plato lays out so extensively the activity of the four elements, starting with fire, which he equates to the pyramidal form and thus Egyptian science.

---

29. The "fading splendor" of Moses that Paul spoke of (2 Cor 3) was implicit throughout the Old Testament in the recurring lament that God was "hiding his face"; see the passages discussed in the essay entitled "Mysteries" in *The Burning Bush*, pp. 354-356.

Surely no Egyptologist has penetrated the ancient Egyptian mind so deeply and thoroughly as René Schwaller de Lubicz.[30] The inherence of the knowledge of the four elements in ancient Egypt is shown in *The Egyptian Miracle* (EM), Chap. 6 ("Elements and Triangles"), and is profusely shown in the large work *The Temple Of Man* (TOMN). Schwaller starts chapter twenty-three ("The Architectonics of the Pharaonic Temple") as follows:

> The master builder said to the disciple:
>
> "You come from the earth, it has nourished you, and you will return to the earth. This element holds and keeps the other elements.
>
> "Know that everything that, of itself, diffuses outward without form needs a receptacle. Thus, Air retains the Fire of the Universe, and Water retains Air, as Earth is the vase that holds Water and gives it form. Thus, Earth is the container of All. I speak to you of the earth upon which you tread, the gross image of the spermatic Earth of which you are made.
>
> "Always see, in the lower things that your senses reveal to you, the image of the things that your spirit alone can conceive when your senses are closed to the world of transitory appearances."

We shall see how well this is elaborated by Steiner and anthroposophy in the essays that follow.

Schwaller (1887-1961), though Germanic, gives no indication of having been associated in any formal way with either Steiner or anthroposophy, nor even of having been exposed to it. However, his writings seem fully compatible with, and even illustrative of, the reality of anthroposophical understanding. And clearly they show that there existed in ancient Egypt a far deeper comprehension of the four elements and of the

---

30. His magnum opus, a monumental work, is *The Temple Of Man* (TOMN). As an early outline for TOMN, he wrote *The Temple In Man* (TIMN). His other books include *The Egyptian Miracle* (EM), *Esoterism & Symbol* (ESOTS), *Nature Word* (NW), *Sacred Science* (SAC) and *Symbol and the Symbolic* (SYMB). See also Vandenbroeck's book about Schwaller entitled *Al-Kemi* (AL-KEMI); one immediately sees in that phonetic title the word alchemy, and indeed it furnishes the etymology of the latter, for "kemi" means "Egypt," and "al" is the Arabic prefix attached to it. Thus, the esoteric knowledge of the true alchemists (the spiritual ones, not the metal-seeking charlatans history speaks of) comes from ancient knowledge generally lost by the Greco-Roman Cultural Age.

nature of creation and evolution than science of today enjoys, even if what existed then was more a matter of direct perception than intellectual knowledge. Humanity (the Prodigal Son) today (in the fifth post-Atlantean Cultural Age) retraces its experience in the Egyptian Cultural Age (the third post-Atlantean) in its parabolic journey back to the spiritual world whence it all began. Guided now by the Christ, the highest spiritual being, we must regain, and in the process transform, these ancient insights.

The ancient Egyptian knowledge of the fire element, encapsulated in the pyramid, will be more fully explored in the "Fire" essay below.

AS ABOVE, SO BELOW

RINGING DOWN TO US from the ancient mysteries, this phrase declares that nothing has ever existed in all of creation that was not first prefigured in the patterns of the spiritual world. All phenomena are but shadows of higher reality. Not even so much as a fleeting thought comes into being otherwise. Until this insight is absorbed into the very fabric of the soul, ascribing all creation to the Word of God, to Christ, while ultimately correct (Jn 1,3; 1 Cor 8,6; Col 1,16; Heb 1,2), reveals no depth of comprehension.

"As Above, So Below" is an abridgement of the longer expression, "That which is above is like to that which is below, and that which is below is like to that which is above." The *Corpus Hermeticum* of Hermes Trismegistus began with these words.[1] In keeping with the practices of the mysteries, it was not reduced to writing until much later, but clearly it purports to reflect what came down from the Egyptian Hermes of far earlier times. Steiner tells us that Hermes was the seminal, spiritually perceptive personality of the Chaldo-Egyptian Cultural Age, for which destiny the astral body of the prehistoric Zarathustra had been imparted to him.[2]

The substance of fundamentalism in religious persuasions is that it professes to take its sacred organic writings (e.g., the Bible, Torah or Quran) literally. Moreover, in doing so it places upon such words its own interpretation to the exclusion of all other. While interpretation normally requires going outside the bounds of a word itself, the fundamentalist asserts that anything outside the bounds of the literal word, as so interpreted, is subject to error and thus not to be considered. It is interesting, in passing, that Steiner also insists that the Bible is literally true word for

---

1. See 25 Brit 79, "Occultism."
2. See text related to fn 4, p. 38, *The Burning Bush.*

word. However, he points out that we have no translations today that are accurate, word for word.[3] And even then we must first understand what the words mean before we ascribe literal truth to them. A metaphor or allegory can be just as "literally" true as pedestrian prose. And then there is the fact that the nature of scripture is to have different levels of meaning, the higher almost always throwing quite different, and more resplendent, light than the lower.

The irony of all this is that, at least in the case of Christians, Jews and Muslims, what we call literalism actually blinks at those parts of their scripture that gnaw away its very foundations. Consider the second commandment given to Moses on Mount Sinai:

"You shall not make for yourself a graven image, or any likeness of anything that is in heaven above." (Ex 20,4; Deut 5,8)

In "Blood" we will see how the commandment, "Thou shall not kill" (Ex 20,13; Deut 5,17) is to change in meaning over time as human consciousness evolves. In his highest teachings, those from the spiritual *mountain* (Mt 5,21-48), Christ himself demonstrated this convincingly. The same could be said with respect to essentially all the commandments of Moses, including specifically this one about graven images.[4] Moses was an initiate of the ancient mysteries (of both Egypt and Midian). Initiates taught and governed, but did not write. We have seen that the commandments that were *graven* (cf. Ex 32,16) upon the "tables of stone" were perceptions in the mineralized brain of Moses, and that these were not even given to the people until much later when they were in the Plains of

---

3. This defect is not cured by the profusion of translations that have occurred during the twentieth century, because it relates to the earliest extant manuscripts upon which our available translations are based. See, for instance, the discussion in "Akashic" (*The Burning Bush*, pp. 300-304) of Christ's answer when he was asked by Pilate whether he was a king sent from God (Mt 27,11; Mk 15,2; Lk 23,3 et al.). Other significant examples discussed in *The Burning Bush* include, for instance, Gen 15,5; Ex 3,14 and Mt 18,19-20 (see its Index of Scriptures Cited).

4. See the editorial footnote on this passage on p. 33 of *Redemption of Thinking* (RT). A completely supersensible concept of the spiritual is required. In the text, Steiner had quoted Augustine's recognition that nothing in the earth, sea, winds, Sun, Moon or stars sufficed (cf. Ps 139,7-10), and then asserted that the Divine could not be found in anything to be observed with the senses. All sensibly perceptible objects, though reflecting the spiritual, are themselves deception.

Moab.[5] Even then they were probably not written down, as we know it, for centuries (cf. Ex 24,4a).

Ask yourself what the Bible means by the fact that Moses, seeing the disinclination of the people to spirituality, was unable to deliver to them the message written by the hand of God, thus breaking it at the foot of the *mountain* (Ex 32,19). These first tablets were the revelation to Moses of divine insight (Ex 31,18 and 32,15-16). When he saw the people were not yet ready for this, he had to write it into his memory so as to deliver it to them (orally) much later on the Plains of Moab (Ex 34,27-28) in what would eventually become the "second law," or Deuteronomy.

In the preceding footnote, we saw that the giving of the law by God was *threefold*. If we look back and consider it carefully, we can see that the first giving was in the mental *perception* of it by Moses, a function of the astral body; the second was in his committing it to *memory*, a function of the etheric body; and the third was in the stone tablets written

---

5. Deut 5,28; see 5 AB 1 and 2 ABD 168. In the "Blood" essay below, Steiner speaks extensively of the blood as a "tablet." But another significant body "tablet" is the human brain. It is well to reflect upon the meaning of the progression of instruction Moses received from God on Mount Sinai. The first instruction there was not written down (by God) at all (Ex 19,1–24,11). Then Moses went back up on the *mountain* and the Lord gave him the "tables of stone" with the law written on them. These are the tables that Moses broke at the foot of the *mountain* when he saw the idolatry of the people (Ex 24,12–33,23). Moses had been instructed to put these two tables of "testimony" in the "ark" (Ex 25,16), which he could not do after he broke them. So, the Lord told Moses to cut two tables of stone for the Lord to write upon back on the *mountain*. And these two tables of stone (testimony) he finally put in the "ark" (Ex 34,1–40,21). We see here a *threefold* giving of the law to Moses, yet its substance, repeated in the "law" handed down in Deuteronomy (literally, the "second law") was not given by Moses to the people until much later in the plains of Moab (Deut 5,28). While the later giving is termed the "second law," the phrase may hark back to the second set of "stone tablets" Moses brought down from the *mountain*. It was this second set of stone tablets that Paul referred to in 2 Cor 3,7-18; and we should also consider his deep meaning in discussing this matter in Heb 9,1-5 (which he only hints at for later instruction; see *The Burning Bush*, pp. 226 et seq.).

We saw briefly in the Overview of *The Burning Bush* (p. 21) that the "ark" is the human body, metaphorically speaking. Anthroposophy shows us that the two "stone tablets" were the increasingly mineralized and highly evolved right and left sides of the human brain; see Tomberg, *Anthroposophical Studies of the Old Testament* (ASOT), pp. 116-117, also cf. Steiner, *The Human Being in Body, Soul and Spirit* (HBBSS), Lects. 2–5. As this instrument solidified, and human intellect increased, ancient clairvoyance diminished, what Paul called Moses' "fading splendor" (2 Cor 3,7-13; also cf. Deut 5,22-27 with Is 6,9-10 in the light of the "Fire" essay below). What at one time did not have to be written down then had to be reduced to writing.

Paul, Origen and others have also recognized the allegorical nature of Moses' traditions (cf. Gal 4,24).

by the "finger of God," its implantation in the physical body ("ark") of the people. This can be an awesome recognition.[6]

That the "tablets of stone" were not external to the human brain is made clear by the meaning of the "finger of God" that wrote them (Ex 31,18). The phrase "finger of God" is used sparingly, but significantly, in both the Old and New Testaments, and can be seen especially in the light of Philo's teachings, to be something other than the cutting of ordinary rock such as is done on tombstones.[7]

How clearly Paul points out the fact that the written word itself becomes a *graven image* when Christ is understood in the human heart. Paul's words clearly show an evolving human consciousness in understanding what was given to Moses on the *mountain*. See 2 Cor 3; also Jer 31,33 and Jn 16,12.

That "the Word of God" is higher than the words of the Bible need hardly be pointed out (Jn 1,1), and that "the law" of God is higher than the words of the Torah Paul also makes clear (Heb 10,1). That the second commandment, against making any "likeness of anything that is in heaven above," applies to "the Word of God" seems eminently clear. To claim the written word, the Bible itself, as "the Word of God" must be

---

6. It had not yet occurred to me at the time the original edition of *The Burning Bush* (BB) was published, so it was not among the biblical illustrations of the three human bodies in the essay there entitled "Three Bodies." But the list there was merely illustrative. No claim was made that it was exhaustive—obviously it was not. See p. x in the rev. ed. of BB for additions.

7. The only other scriptural usages are in Ex 8,19 (where the magicians of Egypt said to Pharoah that Moses' ability to create gnats by striking the dust of the Earth with his rod was brought about by the finger of God); Deut 9,10 (where Moses is recounting the Exodus 31,18 experience to the people); and Lk 11,20 (where Luke, in his "divided household" response to the people said, "But if it is by the finger of God that I cast out demons, then the kingdom of God has come upon you"). But since Jesus is the very image of God, the passage in Jn 8,6,8 is also in point (where, in the incident of the woman caught in adultery, he bent down and wrote in the ground, or as some translations more appropriately say, in the dust; a medium reminiscent of the passage in Ex 8,19 above). These other usages consistently show a spiritual action quite different in nature from the tombstone type of engraving.

The powerful influence of Philo on the New Testament writers is shown in the "Egypt" essay in *The Burning Bush*, particularly at pp. 522, 532-539. What he has to say about the "finger of God" in Ex 32,16 is instructive. At PHILO, p. 261, he interprets the meaning in Ex 32,16 in the light of Ex 8,19, and at p. 290, speaking of the "writing of God engraven on the tables," he points out that the ten commandments are divided into two equal groups of five, the first five being different from the second, one being rational and the other irrational. How better could he have described the left (rational) and right (more spiritual, which he characterizes as "irrational") sides of the human brain?

seen as blasphemy.[8] As much as we cherish it, we cannot lose sight of the essential point. Even the Bible has the mark of Ahriman (Satan) impressed upon it, not upon its essential message (for it tells us these things itself), but rather upon the vehicle by which it had to be delivered to humanity due to the hardened and materialized condition of humanity in the post-Atlantean Epoch.[9]

Certain facts from the time of Christ stand out. His foremost enemies, the Scribes, Pharisees and Sadducees, were literalists, fundamentalists of the written word in his day. It is the hallmark of that mind-set, while speaking always as though the contrary were true, to reject the reception of radical new spiritual light, and to see things in a materialistic way—to speak, for instance, of a second coming of Christ in a physical body. How can we fail to see this as a recurring phenomenon in our own time?

Is it not also eminently significant that Christ left us not a single written word in his own hand? We are told only that on one occasion he "wrote with his finger on the ground" (Jn 8,6). And in a day when likenesses of prominent figures were preserved for posterity by Greek and Roman alike, we have not so much as a single replica in clay or paint of his holy "likeness." One could say that he simply conducted his ministry in such manner as not to invite this. But indeed is not this the point, if not the fact that it was ordained in the spiritual world itself that there should be no such production by or about the Christ himself?

---

8. The phrases "Word of God" and "word of the Lord" appear hundreds of times in the Old Testament. See 6 ABD 961, but this article shows that these are not talking about printed matter. Consider Jn 1,1-3 ("In the beginning was the Word, ...").

9. In his cycle *The Influences of Lucifer and Ahriman* (LA), Lects. 1 and 3, Steiner discusses the dangers involved in the way the Bible is read in our time. Absent the insights of spiritual science, such dangers are immense, and any real understanding of the Christ almost impossible. Illusion is rampant. In Lect. 1 he says, "I shall merely put before you the deeper fact, namely that no true understanding of Christ can be reached by the simple, easy-going perusal of the Gospels beloved by most religious denominations and sects today." The wisdom present "at the time of the Mystery of Golgotha and for a few centuries afterwards... has now disappeared, and what sects and denominations find in the Gospels does not lead men to the real Christ for Whom we seek through spiritual science, but to an illusory picture, at most to a sublimated hallucination of Christ. The Gospels cannot lead to the real Christ unless they are illumined by spiritual science.... The people who do most to prepare for the incarnation of Ahriman are those who constantly preach: 'All that is required is to read the Gospels word-for-word— nothing more than that!' ... A good deal of what is spreading in external Christianity today is a preparation for Ahriman's incarnation. And in many things which arrogantly claim to represent true belief, we should recognize the preparation for Ahriman's work."

It is true that the Word became flesh and dwelt among us (Jn 1,14), but as *flesh and blood* alone Jesus of Nazareth was maya (Mt 16,17; see also Jn 3,6). Steiner explicitly says so in *Background to the Gospel of St. Mark* (BKM), Lect. 12, p. 209. He is not saying what some gnostics expressed, namely, that there never was a physical Incarnation, but rather that the mineral-physical body per se of Jesus was maya just as is the mineral-physical body of every other human being.

I have deemed it appropriate to digress into the above thoughts in regard to the phrase "As Above, So Below." For when one opens the mind to its full implications, by going to phenomena themselves, what is revealed to us outside the words of the Bible, if we but observe, will lead us to truths within the Bible far deeper than could otherwise be imagined from a mere reading of the words of translations as they have come down to us in our day, hidden as they are beneath the veneer of modern materialistic understanding.

While recognizing that all creation has come from "the Word of God," the Christ, Paul demonstrates over and over again that it has all come about by virtue of that creative principle expressed in the ancient mysteries, "As Above, So Below." Certain words have always been keys to this principle, such as "copy," "shadow," "pattern" and "image" (or "likeness"). The following are examples (my emphasis):

Heb 8,5: They serve *a copy and shadow of the heavenly sanctuary*; for when Moses was about to erect the tent, he was instructed by God, saying, "See that you *make everything according to the pattern which was shown you on the mountain.*"

[It is very important that we understand the meaning of *mountain* in spiritual writings. It is universally recognized by the enlightened as meaning the condition in which one has an experience beyond or above that of the world of the senses. The metaphor is so apt that even in common parlance we understand this to be the meaning of the phrase *mountaintop experience*. It is not necessary to be on a physical mountain in order to be *on the mountain* in a spiritual sense. Physical location is irrelevant. It is entirely possible that all references to Mount Sinai or Horeb in the Bible were only spiritual events that did not take place on a physical mountain, though this is not necessarily the case as we shall see. This truth can help, however, when one considers the difficulty in locating the

mountain from the biblical description of it. The same can be said for
the term "wilderness," especially in view of the lack of archaeological evidence to support the Bible's description of the wanderings in the wilderness. The term wilderness means in the loneliness or desolation of the
soul.[10] The importance of this passage in Heb 8 cannot be overemphasized, for it deals with the matter of the "temple." In the Gospels Christ
spoke of raising the temple after three days, where he is clearly referring
to the temple of the body (Jn 2,21), the purified astral, etheric and physical bodies that Paul immediately thereafter calls "manna," the "rod that
budded" and "tablets," respectively (Heb 9,4).[11]]

Ex 25,9,40: [9] According to all that I show you concerning the pattern
of the tabernacle, and all of its furniture, *so you shall make it.* [40] And
see that you make them after the pattern for them, which is being
shown you on the mountain.

Acts 7,44: "Our fathers had the *tent* of witness in the wilderness, even
as he who spoke to Moses directed him *to make it, according to the pattern that he had seen."*

Heb 9,23-24: [23] Thus it was necessary for *the copies of the heavenly
things* to be purified with these rites, but the heavenly things themselves with better sacrifices than these. [24] For Christ has entered, not
into a sanctuary made with hands, *a copy of the true one,* but into heav-
en itself, now to appear in the presence of God on our behalf.

Heb 10,1: For since *the law* has but *a shadow of the good things to come
instead of the true form of these realities,* it can never, by the same sacrifices which are continually offered year after year, make perfect those
who draw near.

---

10. See fn 15 in "I AM," in *The Burning Bush.*
11. Here it will help to review what was said about Mt 13,33 in *The Burning Bush,* pp. 420-
423 ("Three Bodies"); also what is said there about Heb 9 on p. 226 ("Second Coming") and
361 ("Mysteries"). Matthew's version of the three loaves finds its counterpart in Lk 13,20-21,
and also in 11,5-8, explained in *The Burning Bush* at pp. 113 (fn 5), 438 and 540. In these
references we see that manna is the purified astral body. One might almost say that the theme
of Hebrews is purification (see Heb 1,3 and 9,13-14,22-23).

Col 2,16-17: [16] Therefore let no one pass judgment on you in questions of food and drink or with regard to a festival or a new moon or a sabbath. [17] These are *only a shadow of what is to come; but the substance belongs to Christ.*

Gen 1,26-27: [26] Then God said, *"Let us make man in our image, after our likeness...."* [27] So *God created man in his own image, in the image of God he created him.*

Heb 11,3: By faith we understand that the world was created by the word of God, *so that what is seen was made out of things which do not appear.*

Mt 6,10b: "Thy will be done, *on earth as it is in heaven."*

Job 38,33: "Do you know the *ordinances of the heavens?* Can you establish *their rule on the earth?"*

Gen 1,11,12,21,24,25: [11] And God said, "Let the earth put forth vegetation, plants yielding seed, and fruit trees bearing fruit in which is their seed, *each according to its kind.* [12] The earth brought forth vegetation, plants yielding seed *according to their own kinds*, and trees bearing fruit in which is their seed, *each according to its kind....* [21] So God created the great sea monsters and every living creature that moves, with which the waters swarm, *according to their kinds*, and every winged bird *according to its kind....* [24] And God said, "Let the earth bring forth living creatures *according to their kinds*: cattle and creeping things and beasts of the earth *according to their kinds...."* [25] And God made the beasts of the earth *according to their kinds*, and the cattle *according to their kinds*, and everything that creeps upon the ground *according to its kind.*

Prov 27,19: As in water face answers to face, so the mind of man *reflects* the man.

Ex 31,1-5: [1] The Lord said to Moses, [2] "See, I have *called by name Bezalel* the son of Uri ... [3] and I have filled him with the Spirit of God, with ability and intelligence, with knowledge and all craftsmanship, [4] to devise artistic designs, to work in gold, silver, and bronze, [5] in cutting stones for setting, and in carving wood, for work in every craft."[12]

Job 8,8-10: [8] For inquire, I pray you, of bygone ages ... [9] for we are but of yesterday, and know nothing, for *our days on earth are a shadow.* [10] Will they not teach you, and tell you, and utter words out of their understanding?

Hos 14,7a: They shall return and dwell *beneath my shadow.*

We cannot begin to exhaust the proof of this maxim "As Above, So Below" in this essay. All that follows in this volume tends to corroborate it. However, the reader should note in particular the discussion of "fractals" in the Creation essay as well as in "Fire" below. In the latter, we explore Plato's "fairest mean," the geometrical progression, particularly the "fairest" one of all, which the Greeks called *phi*.[13] Plato speaks of this mean in connection with the very process of creation itself. We have seen in "The Four Elements," fire, air, water and earth, their progenitive, etheric counterparts, and we shall see in the essays that follow how each element relates to the one adjoining it in the creative process. We then begin to see that all phenomena our senses observe descend into materiality from the etheric border of the spiritual world in accordance with this mean. As we shall later see, Steiner shows us that each state tends to "give a picture of" its neighboring state and then in turn to be itself reflected by its neighbor on the other side. When we see this, Hermes' ancient words, "That which is above is like to that which is below, and that which is below is like to that which is above," can hardly fail to impress themselves upon us anew.

---

12. *Bezalel* is also mentioned in Ex 35,30; 36,1,2; 37,1; 38,22; 1 Ch 2,20 and 2 Ch 1,5. In all of these he is carrying out the commission given Moses in Ex 25,9,40 above. The significance of these passages for our purpose is found in the meaning of the "name"—"Bezalel." We are told in 1 ABD 717 that it means "in the shadow of God." In accord is PHILO, p. 61, "Allegorical Interpretation, III, Para. XXXI. (95-96).

13. The wondrous mysteries of *phi* seem endless. It is represented by the ratio 1.618 to 1 and finds application in the most prolific way in the phenomena of nature, as well as in the human body. The Great Pyramid of Giza reflects its truths. *Phi* is the twenty-first letter in the Greek alphabet, concluding the third series of the creative number seven. Steiner equates the twenty-four letters of the Greek alphabet to the "twenty-four elders" in Rev 4,4,10; 5,8; 11,16 and 19,4 (see I-1 and *The Apocalypse of St. John* [ASJ], Lect. 5, p. 101). What is known as the "Fibonacci series" reflects the unique geometric progression of *phi*.

This maxim so pervades anthroposophical insight that we must banish any thought of capturing all Steiner said about it. In his most thorough work about the creative process, *An Outline of Esoteric Science* (OES), he said that the whole of anthroposophy (spiritual or esoteric science) must spring from the following two thoughts (Chap. 1, p. 19):

> ... that behind the visible world there is an invisible one, a world that is temporarily concealed, at least as far as our senses and sense-bound thinking are concerned [and] second ... that by developing human capacities that lie dormant in us, it is possible to enter this hidden world.

So we must content ourselves with only a few illustrations.

In Chapter 3 of the same work (OES), Steiner speaks of the progressive phenomena of human feeling, thought and wisdom, and shows how these relate to successive phases in the spirit world. In their most important aspects, they represent the culmination of a fivefold sequence of experiences: First a departure from what had previously been one's base or "home," so to speak (leaving home is a prevalent theme in both the Old and New Testaments). Then a feeling of being in a new experience, as though adrift on the waters. Next some sort of trouble arises, a "storm or tempest." For better or worse it is resolved so that one has clarity of mind (thought). Finally, from the entire experience one sees the light (wisdom). These are the first five stages in the spirit world. One should study them in I-33. Not only do these comport with life's experience, but they are the sequence of biblical revelation. The pattern is first to leave shore (land, or home), launched upon water, whereupon a storm arises that is finally resolved (warmth or thought) and leads to a new and lasting experience (wisdom or light). In reality it is the entire picture of the Bible, the Prodigal Son's journey. The elements are all there even though water itself is not part of that story; the son leaves home and is adrift. Numerous Bible stories portray the entire scenario. Most notable, perhaps, are the book of Jonah (Jon), Christ's stilling of the winds and waves (Mt 8,23-27; Mk 4,36-41; Lk 8,22-25), and Paul's final journey (Acts 27-28).[14]

The point of this is that what is experienced on Earth is but a *shadow* or reflection of what the soul experiences between lives in the spirit world.

---

14. See also Ex 1–2,10; 14–15; 1–20; Mt 14,24-33; Mk 6,47-52; Jn 6,16-21; Gen 32–33; 6–8; 2,7–3,24; Rev 8–9 and 16; Jn 21.

It is the essential pattern of all life, and one can even see it in the normal pattern of a given human life from beginning to end.

The term *shadow* appears frequently and with significant meaning in esoteric writings, including the Bible. We find it in no less than three of Paul's writings cited above (Heb 8,5; 10,1 and Col 2,17) as well as those of Job (Job 8,9) and Hosea (Hos 14,7). One can also gain significant insight from its usage in others.[15]

One of Plato's most widely known passages is his cave parable (*Republic*, Book VII). Human beings are pictured as prisoners chained in an underground cave with a fire above and behind them. All they can see are the *shadows* of one another on the opposite wall of the cave. The account is a magnificent allegorical portrayal of the human soul incarcerated in its bodies. In his best selling book *Shadows of the Mind* (SHAD), the scientifically minded Penrose, after recognizing *phi* (in the so-called Fibonacci series) in the human brain, concludes with the refreshing hint that we must return to the realities of Platonic insight.

Similarly, in his *Theosophy* (THSY), p. 123,[16] Steiner says, "Thought as it appears in human beings is only a shadowy image or phantom of its real being. A thought appearing by means of a human brain corresponds to a being in the country of spirit beings as a shadow on the wall corresponds to the actual object casting the shadow." He says the same thing in *An Outline of Esoteric Science*, p. 93.[17]

Other Steiner usages of *shadow* include (by no means exhaustively) *Man and the World of Stars* (MWS), p. 51, and *Theosophy of the Rosicrucian* (TR), p. 45. In the latter, he says:

> When the faculties of the seer develop, he often makes a striking discovery. When he stands in the sunlight, his body holds up the light and casts a *shadow*; very often he will discover the spirit for the first time when he looks into this *shadow*. The body holds up the light but not the spirit; and in the *shadow* that is cast by the body the spirit can be discovered. That is why more primitive peoples who have always possessed some measure of clairvoyance, have also called the soul, the "shadow." (Emphasis mine)

---

15. See, for instance, Judg 9,36; Ps 17,8; 36,7; 57,1; 63,7; 91,1; 102,11; Song 2,3; Is 49,2; 51,16; Ezek 31,6,12,17 and Acts 5,15.
16. Page 102 of the former edition.
17. Page 78 of *Occult Science, An Outline* (OS).

Examples of such "primitive peoples" are the Native Americans whose myths are typified by those of the Oglala Sioux in the western Dakotas. They speak often in similar terms of the *shadow*. See, for instance, *Lakota Myth* (LAKM), p. 210, which speaks of Skan, the fourth of the "superior Gods," who bears a remarkable resemblance to the Elohim, especially Yahweh-Eloha (I-16). It says there, "The shadow of each thing shall be its spirit and shall be with it always."

Let us see how this insight can clarify a certain passage of scripture (2 K 20,1-11; see also Is 38) that has remained obscure to theologians to this day. In addition to "shadow," one should be aware of two other terms, "third day" and "figs." Briefly speaking, "third day" means the time when something spiritually important will happen (see the discussion of Jn 2,1 in *The Burning Bush*, p. 140). "Figs" often refers to initiation into the ancient mysteries. We often read the phrase "under the tree." For now, the reader can best think of it in connection with Christ's cursing of the fig tree (Mt 21,18-22; Mk 11,12-14,20-24). Without understanding what was meant, this story has also been a puzzle to theologians until this very day. What is meant by it is that Christ was bringing in a new method of initiation. The old method of the "Three Days' Journey" (see *The Burning Bush*) was passing away, never again to produce fruit (Jn 1,45-51 and Lk 13,6-9). The story of Buddha gaining enlightenment "under the bodhi tree" is illustrative of this point in the Bible. When one reaches the level of spiritual insight represented by having attained enlightenment "under the tree," one can go back in his or her "house" (soul) and see the karma there from prior incarnations. For instance, the "illness" in one's life normally stems from this.

The passage from Second Kings reads (RSV; emphasis mine):

[1] In those days Hezekiah became sick and was at the point of death. And Isaiah the prophet the son of Amoz came to him, and said to him, "Thus says the Lord, 'Set your house in order; for you shall die, you shall not recover.'" [2] Then Hezekiah turned his face to the wall, and prayed to the Lord, saying, [3] "Remember now, O Lord, I beseech thee, how I have walked before thee in faithfulness and with a whole heart, and have done what is good in thy sight." And Hezekiah wept bitterly. [4] And before Isaiah had gone out of the middle court, the word of the Lord came to him: [5] "Turn back, and say to Hezekiah the prince of my people, Thus says the Lord, the God of David your

father: I have heard your prayer, I have seen your tears; behold I will
heal you; on the *third day* you shall go up to the house of the Lord.
[6] And I will add fifteen years to your life. I will deliver you and this
city out of the hand of the king of Assyria, and I will defend this city
for my own sake and for my servant David's sake." [7] And Isaiah said,
"Bring a cake of *figs*. And let them take and lay it on the boil, that he
may recover."

[8] And Hezekiah said to Isaiah, "What shall be the sign that the
Lord will heal me, and that I shall go up to the house of the Lord on
the *third day*?" [9] And Isaiah said, "This is the sign to you from the
Lord, that the Lord will do the thing that he has promised: shall the
shadow go forward ten steps, or go back ten steps?" [10] And Hezekiah
answered, "It is an easy thing for the *shadow* to lengthen ten steps;
rather let the *shadow* go back ten steps." [11] And Isaiah the prophet
cried to the Lord; and he brought the *shadow* back ten steps, by
which the sun had declined on the dial of Ahaz.

In this light, one is warranted in seeing that Hezekiah was enabled by
the spiritual guidance of Isaiah to look back into his own karmic past and
there to foresee what faced him still.[18] In the verses that immediately follow, it is said that all that was in the "house" of Hezekiah was revealed,
meaning all of his karmic picture or "destiny." With this insight, one can
certainly have spiritual "peace and security" all of one's days (2 K 20,19;
Is 39,8). We have to note also that on the *third day* Hezekiah was "to go
up to the house of the Lord." This can in no way mean only that he was
to go into an earthly temple, but rather that his soul should be raised to
a plane of high spiritual perception. The juxtaposition of his "going up"
to the *third day* cannot be overemphasized. When Abraham was to offer
up Isaac it is said, "On the *third day* Abraham lifted up his eyes and saw
the place afar off" (Gen 22,4, emphasis added). Before Moses' first

---

18. Much has been made in recent times about the psychological benefits of "past life
regression." That some apparent cures may have been effected is not hard to understand. But
these could have come about in spite of the fact that there is error in the karmic picture. Steiner
condemned hypnosis in no uncertain terms, requiring as it does the surrendering of one's own
Ego-control to another, saying that the only proper way to gain certain insight into one's karma
is through the spiritual path of initiation open to humanity since the time of Christ. It is a path
of highest moral development, outlined in his *How to Know Higher Worlds* (HKHW). Prior to
the time of Christ, this path was that of the "Three Days' Journey" that took place "under the
tree" (cf. Jon 4,6).

encounter on the mountain, we read, "On the morning of the *third day* there were thunders and lightnings, and a thick cloud upon the mountain" (Ex 19,11,16, emphasis added). Over and over again in the Gospels of Matthew and Luke, Jesus tells his disciples that he will be raised on the third day (and one has to stretch meanings in order to call thirty-six hours three days). It was after "three days" that Jesus multiplied the loaves and fishes (Mt 15,32; Mk 8,2). The significance of the third day is massively demonstrated throughout the Bible. One should never minimize the spiritual significance attached to it.

Naturally when we begin in our minds to apply the "As Above, So Below" principle to the created world, we think of various objects or phenomena we observe with our senses. Let us think, however, of what is the most important of all creatures. It is the human being who is created in the image of the Elohim (Gen 1,26), who themselves are created (fractal-like) in the image of the Father. Every living human being, in each of its three bodies and soul (Ego), is the reflection of polarities, rhythms, forces and forms that preceded it in the spiritual world. All of these are built up in the spiritual world as the soul travels from incarnation to incarnation, and they reflect the unresolved karma built up over the eons by that soul in its earthly lives.[19] We are the result of what we have been (i.e., "stored up in heaven," Mt 6,20) and the cause of what we will be (i.e., "talents"; Mt 25,14-30; Lk 19,12-28; also Mt 13,12; 25,29; Mk 4,25; Lk 8,18).

For what is said here, it would be well to review **I-20** and **I-21**. We shall see in "Blood" a powerful illustration of how the higher worlds work in formation of our earthly life substance. Reflect upon the passage from Ps 139 quoted near the end of "Blood":

> For thou didst form my inward parts, ... Thy eyes beheld my unformed substance; in thy book were written, every one of them, the days that were formed for me, when as yet there was none of them.

At how many different times and in how many different ways Steiner poured forth this process would be hard to say.[20] The student should reread

---

19. This "being" was identified in *The Burning Bush*, p. 427, as what Steiner calls "the Lesser Guardian of the Threshold, described in Job 40. Steiner calls it an "astral being," and we see that it lies under the "lotus" (Job 40,21-22), which is identified with the astral body (see **I-14** [nerve organs] and **I-21** Fig. 13).
20. See for instance, *The Burning Bush*, p. 112, fn 4 (fn 3 in rev. ed.).

"The Overview of Karma and Reincarnation" in *The Burning Bush*, pp.
110-127. But that karma and reincarnation apply specifically and elegantly
to the human soul is also brought out at considerable length in *Philosophy,
Cosmology & Religion* (PCR), Lect. 6, and in *The Threshold of the Spiritual
World*, Chap. 5.[21] In these passages, one sees that not only do we create on
Earth the "spectral being" we meet in the spiritual world in our journey
between lives, but in the long process of returning from the spiritual world
to Earth, in conjunction with the hierarchies we build up our new three
bodies (the "three [new] loaves for a friend ... on a journey" in Lk 11,5-6)
designed to address a portion of our unresolved karma (the "spectral being"
of the Lesser Guardian of the Threshold, the Behemoth of Job 40,15-24).[22]
And upon Earth our three bodies are a direct reflection of what was stored
up in the heavenly book (see "Akashic" in *The Burning Bush*; also Ps
139,16). Steiner tells us that the Seraphim, Cherubim and Thrones (the
highest hierarchy; see I-6) actually experience in advance what we will live
out in our next life (*Karmic Relationships*, Vol. 7, Lect. 3, p. 42).

We cannot understand how it is that we have free will, yet our actions
are known beforehand in the spiritual world. This seeming paradox can
only be understood when the nature of clairvoyance is grasped. We know
that Christ told his disciples on many occasions precisely what their
actions would be in the future, which they at the time denied but later
carried out (cf. Ps 94,8-11). And even our hindsight is blurred. Historians
who search in libraries or interview sensate eyewitnesses cannot give us a
real understanding of history. For that only the seer suffices who perceives
those individualities and impulses in the spiritual world that are reflected
in earthly occurrences (see Steiner's *Occult History*, esp. Lect. 1). In the
most manifold ways the life we live on Earth is a reflection of the spiritual
world and the unbending principle "As Above, So Below."

---

21. This title constitutes the second half of *A Way of Self Knowledge/The Threshold of the
Spiritual World* (WSK).
22. The Egyptologist nonpareil, René Schwaller de Lubicz, in *Esoterism & Symbol* (ESOTS), p.
54, says:

> Fixed in a material form, the seed is the part which retains acquired consciousness.
> Conversely, we may say: it is the indestructible and immutable fixed part of a thing
> which represents the seed of continuations in the cycle of cosmic genesis, and attracts to
> itself the next radiation in order to make a new individual.

Here Schwaller says in a footnote, "This is the meaning of the Egyptian *ka*." WNWCD defines
"ka" thus: "in ancient Egyptian religion, the soul, regarded as dwelling in a person's body or in
an image." Surely "ka" is etymologically cognate to "karma." See WNWCD "karma."

We have spoken, and will often speak, of the forces of the planets (the "seven stars"; Rev 1,16,20; 2,1; 3,1) and the zodiac ("twelve stars"; Rev 12,1). These are spiritual beings. What we see in the heavens with our eyes are like the bodies we carry as human beings. Our bodies are not our being, our "I Am." No more so are the planets and stars we see the spiritual beings or forces they represent. Between lives we dwell with and are conscious of these beings. But in the process of descending we lose that consciousness. In PCR, Lect. 6, p. 91, Steiner tells of what we perceive of these beings at a certain point in our descent back into earthly bodies:

> At a certain point of pre-natal existence, man begins to say to himself: Along with my own being I have seen other spiritual-divine beings around me. Now it appears to me as if these divine beings are beginning to cease to show their complete form to me. It now seems to me as if they were assuming an external figurativeness in which they envelop themselves. It appears to me as if they were becoming starlike—like stars I learnt to know through physical sight when I was last on earth. They are not yet stars, but spirit beings which seem to be on their way to star-existence.

Earlier in the same lecture he had shown how our Ego-being was spread over the vastness of the universe and how these planetary forces, as they applied to our specific karmic being, were to become our bodily organs (see I-21) just as the spiritual beings were to become (for our earthly perception) planets or stars.

The awesome vastness of the principle "As Above, So Below" begins to dawn on our awareness as these things sink into our consciousness. No longer need we merely say that all things were created by God (or Christ; Jn 1,3), for we shall gain some new insight into the spiritual beings and processes whereby God brings this about.

Someone will say, how can we attribute our earthly being to this karmic principle when we know that each of us is born with countless hereditary features that come from earthly ancestors? All of our genes come from them. If we are to become spiritually mature, we must learn the limits of heredity (let alone those of genetic manipulation). When the spiritual laws of karma and reincarnation are understood, we see that earthly heredity is a mere tool to be used, not one to dominate us. The choice of parents by the incarnating soul makes this clear. There are no perfect matches of earthly parents and karmic needs, but the incarnating soul, in conjunction with the hierarchies, works for many generations to prepare the most appropriate parents available through whom to enter earthly birth. One can even see a similarity here between the individual human soul and the incarnating Christ.[23] Only the weak soul remains constrained by heredity during earthly life. It has chosen those limitations only as tools to work with to address its karma. Christ stressed the spiritual blessing of leaving home (father and mother; Mt 19,29; Mk 10,29-30; Lk 18,29-30; cf. Gen 12,1) and the spiritual failure in loving father and mother more than him (Mt 10,37; Lk 14,26; cf. Mt 12,48 and Mk 3,33, especially as discussed in *The Burning Bush*, p. 482). This certainly does not nullify our obligation to honor our parents throughout our lifetime. Rather it indicates that we are to let our own eternal "I Am" take over its own destiny. Our nature is such that we are to shed our heredity in seven-year stages from the time of our birth so that by middle age heredity per se has ceased to be a factor in our lives (fn 19 in "The Nativity" in *The Burning Bush*; also *The Gospel of St. Luke*, Lect. 7). The "I Am" must overcome its hereditary restraints if it is to be worthy of the higher "I Am" of Christ.[24]

In *The Gospel of St. John in Relation to the Other Gospels* (Jn-Rel), Lect. 7, pp. 122-125, Steiner speaks of how the soul that fails to understand that physical processes are psycho-spiritual and subjects itself to the constraints of heredity will grow weaker and weaker over time, more enslaved to these limitations (again consider the meaning of the biblical "talents"). It is a mistake to overestimate the power of spirit in our time, for spirit like all else must grow in strength, but it is critical to nourish the spiritual aspect so that the material realm can be overcome. It is this that constitutes following the higher "I Am" of Christ.

We must come to recognize whence we have come and how our own eternal souls are themselves the cause of what we call our heredity. Only by the Ego's working back through the astral body to the etheric and eventually to the physical can these be redeemed from the Luciferic and Ahrimanic forces set in motion in the Garden; only then will our resurrection be complete (Mt 13,33; Lk 20,35).

So many are the angles from which to illustrate the reality of the maxim

---

23. See "The Nativity" in *The Burning Bush*; also *The Incredible Births of Jesus*.
24. See the discussion of Jn 2,4 ("O Woman, what have you to do with me?", more correctly rendered, "What have I to do with you?") at pp. 141-142 of *The Burning Bush*.

"As Above, So Below" that it would be easier to list the works of Steiner that have no bearing on it (if any exist) than to cite those that do. In closing, let me stress how the principle applies to the Bible account itself. It would be well to review the discussion of the significance of a "name," and the change in human consciousness represented by the ancient debate between nominalism and realism (see *The Burning Bush*, pp. 248-249). Our loss of this consciousness is nowhere more evident than in the manner in which we so often interpret the Bible. Speaking particularly of John's Gospel, Steiner said (*The Gospel of St. John* [GSJ], Lect. 4, p. 71):

> All names and designations in ancient times in a certain sense are very real—yet at the same time they are used in a profoundly symbolical manner. This is often the source of tremendous errors made in two directions. From a superficial point of view, many say that according to such an interpretation a great deal is meant symbolically, but with such an explanation in which everything has only a symbolical meaning, they wish to have nothing to do, since historical, biblical events then disappear. On the other hand, those who understand nothing at all of the historical events may say:—"This is only meant symbolically." Those, however, who say such things, understand nothing of the Gospel. The historical reality is not denied because of a symbolic explanation, but it must be emphasized that the esoteric explanation includes both, the interpretation of the facts as historical and the symbolic meaning which we ascribe to them.... Therefore in almost all of the events and allusions, we shall see that John ... really has a supersensible perception; he sees at one and the same time the outer events and the manifestation of deep spiritual truths.

We must begin to see that almost everything in the Bible is there to reflect a higher reality than the mere earthly meaning of its words. Paul saw this aspect of "the law" (Heb 10,1 and Gal 4,21-26). It is a cruel irony by which Christendom so often tends to read the rest of the Bible otherwise. What is there would never have been written had its lower meaning been primary. Always we must seek the higher understanding that it reflects.

But we must not stop with the Bible. The same discipline must be applied to all phenomena. We must learn to observe every creature we meet, every event we experience, every thought we think or feeling we sense, in contemplation of its spiritual origin—for all phenomena is but the shadow of a higher reality.

FIRE

CONTENTS

TWO CONCEPTS, *blood* and *fire*, perhaps more than any others, pervade the Bible from start to finish. They are not unrelated. We examine *blood* in the penultimate essay. The *fire* concept is expressed in such terms as flaming, fiery, burning, lightning, or the like, or even by heat, smoke or smoldering. We saw in the Creation essay how fire is found in the second verse of Genesis in the concept of warmth (as in the brooding of a mother hen on the nest).[1] And just as we found there a deeper meaning extending beyond common understanding into the etheric world, so must we

---

1. That the spirit-action in Gen 1,2 implies warmth (*fire*) has long been recognized. *(continued)*

explore the meaning of the concept as it surfaces again and again in the biblical account.

The Trysting Place (Where Heaven and Earth Meet)

Fire's deeper meaning is pointed to by the fact, which cannot be overemphasized, that it is so frequently the medium of communication between Earth and heaven. The ancient Greeks still understood this, for their word *empyrios* (i.e., "in fire"; *en* = in, *pyr* = fire) is the source of our own *empyreal*.[2] The "flaming sword" divides the two (Gen 3,24). Fire was present at Noah's altar (Gen 8,20), at the first covenant with Abraham (Gen 15,17-18), at the tendered sacrifice of Isaac (Gen 22), in the call of Moses through the evolutionary appearance of the "I Am" in the burning bush (Ex 3), in the pillar that led Moses and the people in the wilderness (Ex 13,21-22), in the revelation to Moses on Mt. Sinai (Ex 19,18 et al.), in the recurring theme of altar sacrifice, in the lifting of Elijah and Elisha to heaven (2 K 2,11 and 6,17), in the destruction of earthly matter (Job 1,16; 2 Pet 3; Rev 20), in the communication of the Lord's voice (Ps 29,7; Jer 23,29; Rev 4),

---

1. *(continued from previous page)* Commentators and translators have used such words as "brooding upon" or "hovering over" (WNWCD defines the verb "brood" primarily as brooding eggs or offspring, and includes "hovering" as a synonym); see 1 Interp 466; NKJV ("hovering over"); NIV ("hovering over"); AMPB ("moving [hovering, brooding] over"); REB ("hovered over"); LB ("brooding over"). Clearly the element of warmth is inherent in the "brooding over an egg" concept.

Philo specifically recognizes the presence of a "third element" in Gen 1,2, saying, "But the spirit of God is spoken of in one manner as being air flowing upon the earth, bringing a *third element* in addition to water," and elaborating on it later he says, "It is here, as is the case in an operation effected by *fire* ..."; PHILO, pp. 153-154 ("On the Giants"), emphasis mine.

Ante-Nicene Fathers also spoke in terms of "brooding, hovering or wafting." See 3 NICENE-1, p. 392 (Tertullian "Against Marcion") and 5 NICENE-1, p. 77 (Hippolytus "The Refutation of All Heresies").

Quite significant, whether or not deemed heretical by later church authorities (joining, if so, such exalted company as Origen and many others), is the passage in "Excerpts of Theodotus," 8 NICENE-1, p. 44, describing the spirit-action in Gen 1,2, as "the twofold fire,—that which lays hold of what is visible, and that which lays hold of what is invisible." We will more fully appreciate this dual, intermediary nature of *fire* as the essay progresses.

But most telling among these early spokespersons is what Hippolytus says in "Discourse on the Holy Theophany," in discussing Gen 1,2: "This is the Spirit that at the beginning 'moved upon the face of the waters .... This is the Spirit that was given to the apostles in the form of *fiery* tongues'" (emphasis mine); 5 NICENE-1, p. 237.

2. WNWCD defines *empyreal* as "of the empyrean; heavenly; sublime," and *empyrean* as "1 the highest heaven; specif. *a)* among the ancients, the sphere of pure light or fire *b)* among Christian poets, the abode of God 2 the sky; the celestial vault; firmament."

in the purification and testing of his servants (Is 6,6; Dan 3; Mal 3,2-3), in the higher baptism (Mt 3,11), in the descent of the Holy Spirit (Acts 2,3), in the appearance of the Lord (2 Th 1,7), in visions of future times, what we call "apocalypse" (Ezek 1; Rev 1,14 and 19,12), and countless others. It reverberates through the highly influential book of Enoch.

"I came to cast fire"

But most inescapably it is thrown down before us by Christ when he says, "I came to cast fire upon the earth" (Lk 12,49). Or, as the Greek more emphatically states (9 NIB 266), "Fire I came to cast on the earth!" And then he says, "and would it were already kindled." The Gospel of Thomas phrases it (Saying 10), "I have thrown fire on the world and, behold, I am guarding it until it is ablaze"; then later (Saying 80), "Whoever is close to me is close to the fire."

He was no arsonist. What does he mean?

The resolution of this question is the key to bringing religion and science back into the union that existed in ancient times: times that preceded "religion" or "science" as we understand them, for their common meaning today veils higher reality than they reveal. Religion literally means to reconnect what is severed, thus ceasing to exist when accomplished; see *The Festivals and Their Meaning* (FM), pp. 207-208, 213-214 (April 13, 1908, Berlin). Science means knowledge, but can we call something science which is not calculated to reveal higher truth?

Neither religion nor science as they are practiced today comprehend Christ's meaning here, save only superficially. Religion sees it simply as some form of ardor, however characterized, as in "on fire for God," while science sees it merely as molecular action. To a great extent this situation has prevailed from the time of Christ till now, though more especially since the beginning of our Cultural Era with the Renaissance, and even more during the last two centuries of evangelistic fervor and "scientific progress." I do not say for one minute that nothing good has come from these superficial concepts in times past, nor that nothing good will come from their application in the future. The point is rather that the time is here when science and religion will work, and in some ways already are working, against that very thing they strive for unless redirected by a higher, divine intelligence. New insight is becoming increasingly imperative for salvation of the human and the lower kingdoms.

The rest of this volume takes up what Steiner, a trained scientist as well as a consummate, disciplined "intuitant," has to say "scientifically" about fire (heat), light and the human being as a cosmic creation. When these are understood according to their true nature, the spiritual will be revealed within them, what religion has thus far failed to reconnect, to re-ligate, with. More and more it will be seen that there is no difference between real science and the divine intelligence sought by true religion. The truth is that the failure of each of them, science and religion, to perceive truly, is the complement of the other, for if either were righted the other would fall in place also. The same revelation that solves one would solve the other. The scales would fall from *both* eyes at essentially the same time.

Understanding what Christ meant by the fire he came to cast upon the Earth seems a proper first step.

The Inadequate Understanding by Theology

What does modern Christian theology say? In the canon only Luke gives us this passage (12,49), and it is followed (vss 51-53) by a common Gospel theme that families will be divided (Mt 10,34-36; Lk 21,16), but this cannot itself be what he meant by his stated mission. Steiner has told us that the best and oldest extant manuscripts upon which our Bibles are based are themselves not the same as the original versions (see "Akashic" in *The Burning Bush*, pp. 300-304), and that even when faithful to the earliest versions do not always accurately report, in terminology intelligible to the modern mind, the events upon which they were based for they were written in the mode and idiom of the ancient mysteries (see *From Jesus to Christ* [JTC], Lect. 4, pp. 73-74 and "Mysteries" in *The Burning Bush*). To get to the original versions and events, true intuition is essential. We saw an instance of how Steiner was corroborated on this in our discussion of the so-called "Secret Gospel of Mark" (see "Peter, James and John" and "Egypt" in *The Burning Bush;* see also *The Disciple Whom Jesus Loved*). And our scholars, in their struggle with the documentary hypotheses, have figuratively cut and pasted the Gospels to the point of obliterating narrative. But if we take the passage as it is written, there is still no warrant for equating the fire that Christ wanted to cast with the family conflicts the passage seems to suggest. That such division may have been a consequence is not the same as saying that the fire Christ desired was

conflict between loved ones. The reader would do well to go back to the
first "sign" in John's Gospel, and what Steiner had to say about it
(Christ's statement to his mother at the Cana wedding) as told in *The
Burning Bush* (p. 141). Christ came to change the direction of humanity
from blood relationship to the brotherhood of all, breaking down the primacy of old alliances such as family, tribe, nation and race, even extending to brotherhood with the lower kingdoms. He recognized that salvific
necessity would create conflict. But the fire he wanted to cast was not the
conflict but rather the phenomenon that would divide because some were
more ready for truth than others. Though in his perfect knowledge Christ
could see that divisions would come (just as he told Peter of his denials),
he himself prayed for unity. And Paul epitomized the higher Christ-like
vision in seeing the eventual unity of all (Eph 1,9-10).

Nor is enthusiasm the fire in question, for one can be enthusiastic for
or against the truth. The truth itself is more closely related to the fire in
question than is enthusiasm per se. If enthusiasm is added, however, in
the form of involvement to knowledge of the truth (gnosis) and desire to
follow it, one comes much closer to comprehending the fire Christ came
to cast.

If theology says that in practice Christianity divides families, it neither
endorses nor encourages that in its practical urging, nor should it. But
theology has also attempted to equate two other concepts to the fire in
question, namely, *baptism* and *judgment*, and with or as a part of judgment the element also of *purification*. The first of these, baptism, has been
enshrined in Christian doctrine as a sacrament and cause célèbre whose
mechanics have been the subject of bitter internecine controversy within
Christendom's own family.[3] What is practiced relates in some way to
water,[4] though lip service is given to the idea that fire is in some way
involved, reverting to the idea of inner enthusiasm so as again to beg the
question.

---

3. As a boy I was baptized by immersion in my mother's church, which rejected the validity of
any other method. My father belonged to a nearby congregation that accepted baptism by
sprinkling. Both parents had been raised in these respective congregations. Soon my mother
decided that she and I should join our family together in my father's church, and this was done.
But as this was being contemplated, I was much disturbed by my barber who told me that my
father was going to hell because he was not properly baptized.
4. See the discussion of "baptism" at 1 ABD 583. It is all subsumed under the definition, "A
rite of incorporation employing water as a symbol of religious purification."

The idea that this fire meant baptism seems based on the Baptist's statement that, in contradistinction to his own practice of water immersion, Christ would baptize with fire (Mt 3,11), as well as on Christ's own statement (Lk 12,50) that he still had a baptism to go through. Obviously this latter baptism had nothing to do with the sacramental practice that has since prevailed, nor can it merely mean that he would receive the Holy Spirit (cf. Jn 1,33), for he had already become one with that at his baptism in the Jordan. And it begs the question to equate that Holy Spirit baptism with fire based upon the Pentecostal experience, for we have yet to explore the meaning of the tongues of fire on that occasion (Acts 2,3). Nor again can that baptism have anything to do in Christ's case with judgment or purification, for Christendom has always properly insisted that he was beyond the need of these. Surely the baptism that he spoke of in verse fifty had reference to the entire sweep of his passage from the material body into the resurrection body, an event that mandates the passage through what only the ancients and the initiates knew to be fire. This passage was encompassed in the Crucifixion that Paul preached. Christ, as the first fruits, had to go the way that humanity itself would have to tread over the ages that were to follow.

The practice of baptism at the time of Christ, which even then was not a new procedure, having been practiced as we now know by the Essenes and others of an earlier time, served a very important function that cannot be served today. The etheric body in human beings has drawn progressively more and more into the confines of the physical body. It is this evolutionary process that over the ages has caused us to lose our conscious presence with the spiritual world (what the Bible sometimes calls God's "hiding his face"). At the same time it has brought brain thinking more and more into being.[5] Steiner tells us that by the time of Christ the etheric body had so entered

---

5. Abraham is properly referred to in knowledgeable circles as the father of arithmetic. (The earlier works of pharaonic Egypt reveal astounding apprehension of numbers, but, as we see later herein, they were perceived not as numbers per se but rather as divine principles, and not through brain thinking so much as through revelation.) He fathered both Arab and Jew through his two sons, Ishmael and Isaac, through each of whom the number twelve appeared; Ishmael fathered twelve sons as did Isaac's son, Jacob. The basis for arithmetic and for the twelvefold nature of biblical revelation is established in Gen 15,5:

And he brought him outside and said, "Look toward heaven, and number the stars, if you are able to number them." Then he said to him, "So shall your descendants be."

(continued on following page)

into the veil of the mineral-physical body (for brain thinking) that people
were no longer able to remember what they had come from in primordial
times. Even in the early church, baptism was only a symbol, but it was a
symbol of something that had actually taken place in a few of those who
had been immersed in the water, as in the case of John's baptism. For these
few were held under water long enough to experience something akin to
what sometimes happens to drowning persons—their lives flashed before
them. In this case the etheric body was separated sufficiently from the physical body (as could then still happen with some people, though not enough
to bring death) that it was able to perceive the past whence it had come. It
was a *remembrance* (Eccles 1,11) of ancient times and of the spiritual world.
It brought about the certain knowledge of the existence of that relationship,
and consequently also a change in the way one thought. When John
admonished repentance, he was saying, "Change your way of thinking." It
was not so much a matter of remorse for past misdeeds as a recognition of
them and of the pathway that was now to be opened for humanity's
redemption. Related to this baptism with its change in one's way of thinking was the idea of purification and judgment. Even in that day, only some
were able to have this experience of remembrance, but it was known and

---

5. *(continued from previous page)* The "stars" here are what humans have looked overhead to see
from ancient times, the twelve animals composing what we call the zodiac. Here God is telling
Abraham both that his descendants will be influenced by these twelve heavenly forces from the
beginning to the end of their journey and that he must learn to deal with the earthly
phenomena of number. Immediately after this anointing of Abraham, God established his first
covenant with him through the agency of fire (Gen 15,17-18), and then God tells him that
everything between the river of Egypt (see "Egypt" in *The Burning Bush*, meaning the
backward looking clairvoyance that had to be overcome) and "the great river, the river
Euphrates," would be his—the entire gamut of insight.

In the western myth of Prometheus, the name "Prometheus" means "forethinker," while
his brother, Epimetheus, means "backward looking," the same as Egypt, into the clairvoyance
of even more ancient times when we dwelt consciously with spiritual beings. That Abraham
was to bring humanity into the domain of looking forward is ordained here by the name of the
river Euphrates, which means "good mind" (see the etymology of the cognate term "euphrasy"
from the Greek *eu* [well] and *phren* [mind]). Notably, this river is the final one of the four rivers
in Gen 2,10-14, and it is the river crossed by Jacob, the immediate father of the twelve tribes,
at a critical juncture of his life (Gen 31,21). The ancestry of the fathers of this people had been
"east" (a term related to the ancient clairvoyance) of that river (Josh 24,2). But this Prometheus
was the one who stole fire from heaven and brought it down to Earth, and the myth tells what
then had to happen to Prometheus before he could return (see *The Burning Bush*, p. 241). It
is a story of the evolution, both past and future, of humanity that Christendom still fails to
comprehend. It is but another instance of things once known, then forgot, that must still be
recovered in the transformation humanity is slowly undergoing.

became the basis for the symbolic act of baptism. This was the baptism of John. Such baptism accomplishes nothing of this sort today, though the symbol remains as a sacramental relic in virtually all Christian doctrine and ritual. Better that it be looked at as a symbol of belief in the true fire of the Christ baptism, once the nature of this fire comes to be recognized.[6]

But the baptism that Christ brought was one of actual death to the physical world and birth into the world of fire, the etheric and higher worlds. Paul preached Christ and him crucified (1 Cor 1,23; 2,2), for death in the physical world is essential to life in the higher worlds. For Christ, it was brought about in one lifetime, but to accomplish this even the Christ had to have an earthly body more advanced than any other, one that he and his legions had prepared even from the time of Adam (Heb 10,5 ["When Christ came into the world, he said, '... a body hast thou prepared for me'"]; see "The Nativity" in *The Burning Bush* as well as *The Incredible Births of Jesus*). For the rest of humanity it would take more, but the pathway to the future was opened by Christ, and it was the pathway of fire. Only through that fire could the Prodigal Son return home to the spiritual world.

Paul himself appears to have minimized water baptism in his ministry. True, he had himself been baptized, but this appears to have been at the hands of an Essene community in Damascus, a community we now know had practiced baptism in its initiatory rites before the time of Christ. And Christ had been baptized, but for different reasons than others. While Paul admitted to baptizing one household with water, he appears not to have done so otherwise (1 Cor 1,16-17). Instead he preaches baptism into Christ's death (Rom 6,4).

Just as division was a foreseeable consequence of this fire, so also is judgment; neither however is its equivalent, its meaning nor its synonym. The subject of judgment is rather fully addressed in my essay "Lord of Karma" in *The Burning Bush*, where the basis for understanding its relationship to fire is laid down. Nor is baptism as understood and practiced in Christendom to date the equivalent of the fire Christ came to cast upon the Earth. It can only become such an equivalent when the nature of that fire is understood—then passed through. In other words, the baptism of Christ can be

---

6. Steiner's most complete discussion of baptism is probably that found in Lects. 6 and 7 of the 1909 cycle delivered in Kassel (Germany) entitled, *The Gospel of St. John And Its Relation to the Other Gospels* (Jn-Rel).

explained by fire, but fire cannot be explained by baptism as we have known it within the beliefs and practices of Christendom to date.

So an understanding of fire eludes Christendom, for it is not enthusiasm, division, baptism, judgment nor purification, though each of these can and normally does have some consequential relationship to it.

The Inadequate Understanding by Science

But "science" can claim no better understanding of this fire, for it is not identical to molecular activity nor confined thereto. Steiner was accomplished in both science and mathematics, I in neither. What he did was to express the scientific and mathematical in words and pictures that spoke to both those who were professionals and those who were lay persons in these fields. It is beyond the scope of these final essays in this volume to attempt a complete presentation of his illustrations. Rather I hope to look at a sufficient portion to let both professional and lay person see where science is going awry in its search for the path to higher knowledge. In its explorations, science hopes to find the answers to such things as life and where, if at all, it exists in other parts of our universe. In its search, it has limited itself to what can be observed by the physical senses, aided by instruments such as microscope or telescope, or predicated upon theories developed from these inspections of matter. Staggering amounts are spent in an effort to explore space, but what is found there is measured only in material earthly terms. Anthroposophy shows that answers to the deeper questions science seeks will not be found in these realms. Investigation must go beyond mineral-physical existence. The laboratories we have are not equipped for such an investigation.

Goetheanism

And yet, the Bible tells us, as does anthroposophy, that what we call creation does indeed reflect the higher realms (Ps 19; Rom 1,19-20), those beyond our senses, measuring instruments, or even our mathematics. Steiner saw in the works of Goethe an even higher perception than academia has ascribed to him. While Steiner knew that his own insights went beyond those of Goethe, he lauded the latter as one who had observed phenomena in a much more penetrating way than science to date has done; and Goethe was no mathematician, nor has history (aside from Steiner) accorded him much due for his scientific findings, which he himself felt were his most significant works. Steiner called the physical structure housing anthroposophy's world center, in Dornach, Switzerland, the *Goetheanum*, and often referred to his own method of observing phenomena as *Goetheanism*.

The difference between this Goetheanism and the methods secular science has applied comes down to the matter of two things: one, the proper observation of phenomena, and two, the willingness to defer formulating laws or principles from it until it has spoken fully. Science impatiently makes observations, from which it postulates rules, only to find out later that it either wrongly observed in the first place or wrongly formulated in the second.[7] Consequently, in almost every field of secular science there has been a junking, time after time after time, of laws or formulations that had earlier been spoken of as "science." To the extent that any postulate is warranted, to have any validity it must first be a proper observation of all the phenomena on the subject that has been made available to our senses.

In what have been labeled his "scientific lectures," those upon which this essay and those following in this volume are based, Steiner limited his illustration to things that could be observed by his audiences with their senses. However, those who had been exposed to many aspects of his teachings knew, in their own minds and hearts, that he knew what he presented to be certain reality because of his ability to perceive with organs the rest of us have yet to develop in our own spiritual journey through the ages. Like Steiner, I will only use here those illustrations that can be observed by the reader's senses when properly applied to the phenomena.

The Biblical Meaning of "Fire" in the Light of Anthroposophy

With this, we turn our attention to what Steiner said about fire. It is to be found primarily in his cycle of fourteen lectures given to teachers in the original Waldorf School in Stuttgart, Germany, in March, 1920,

---

7. It seems harsh to attribute "impatience" to scientists who seem to work so long and hard gathering data, and who seem to have such brilliant analytical minds in then drawing conclusions and postulating laws or rules based upon them. But the impatience is involved in other ways. In some cases, it may take a broader span of time than one life to make proper observation of phenomena. In others, pertinent phenomena fall outside the realm of investigation simply because of errors compounded in scientific knowledge from much earlier times. Laws that have such revered names as Copernican and Newtonian have come to be seen as modified by later scientists such as Einstein, and his Theory of Relativity will suffer the same fate in time.

called *Warmth Course* (WC).[8] What we are about is to discover the real *nature* of heat, for only then can its biblical meaning be understood, and only from that understanding will science progress into an understanding, literally the science, of life.

Steiner often speaks of "the heat being," and it is well that we utilize this if we are to come to understand heat's nature. We grant to science the fact that this being manifests in the mineral-physical world through molecular activity. For science, the nature of heat begins and ends with that. But this assumption is no more valid than that you and I, in our essential nature, are no more than the chemicals that compose our mineral-physical bodies. On this point, surely the spiritual approach must prevail, and even "scientists" will generally admit this.

THE PRIMORDIAL CONDITIONS OF FIRE

We must go back to the conditions that existed at the beginning of Earth evolution. Recall that three prior evolutions had come and gone, Old Saturn, Old Sun and Old Moon. The spiritual beings in charge of Earth evolution, the Elohim of Gen 1 (see **I-16**), recalled the experience of these earlier conditions and recapitulated them at a new and different level closer to the material realm but not yet there. All was in an etheric condition. That is, what came to be known as the four ethers were combined in a massive spherical condition too subtle to yet constitute materiality, so as to be "void" and without form (Gen 1,2). We saw in the earlier essay "Creation and Apocalypse" ("the Creation essay") how in the first day the heat ether was separated from the light ether, creating "light"; in the second, the sound ether was separated from the light ether so that there was a division of the waters; and so on through the third day when the life ether appeared. All of this is portrayed by **I-22**, partially reproduced in the Creation essay. If we again inspect that chart, we will see that all three higher ethers have been divided between their etheric condition and their corresponding descendant condition, e.g., light ether was separated from air, sound (or chemical) ether from water, and life ether from the solid condition (earth).

---

8. Aside from what has been said about fire or warmth in prior essays in this volume, other Steiner works that deal with the subject include *The World of the Senses and the World of the Spirit* (WSWS), Lect. 6, p. 87; *The Principle of Spiritual Economy* (SE), Lect. 7, p. 94; *An Occult Physiology* (OP), Lect. 7, p. 143 and Lect. 8, pp. 200-203; *Occult Seals and Columns* (OSC), p. 3; and *What Has Astronomy to Say about the Origin of the World?* (WHA), pp. 16-21.

But we notice that one ether, the fire ether, has not been permanently separated from its material manifestation during Earth evolution. We then realize that in the three Conditions of Consciousness preceding Earth evolution (Old Saturn, Sun and Moon) similar conditions existed with respect to the higher ethers. The respective ethers came into existence with these successive prior Conditions or evolutions, but in such a way that what had been merely fire ether on Saturn becomes life ether/solids (or life and earth) during Earth evolution. And, during Saturn evolution, as in Earth's earliest stage, it was not divided. During Sun evolution, light ether came into being, but again, it was not divided into light ether and air. Similarly on Old Moon, sound (chemical) ether arose, but was not divided into its etheric condition and water. In the "days" of creation, as given in Gen 1, these prior Conditions are brought back into existence at the inception of Earth evolution, but still only in their etheric form so that not only had no solids, fluids or gases been created, but neither had any molecules come into material form so as to have heat as our science describes it. Up through Gen 2,4a, no matter yet existed in Earth evolution in spite of the long spiritual activity that preceded it.

We said in the Creation essay that on the first day the Elohim separated the light ether from the fire ether so that there was "light." But there was yet no air (gas) separate and apart from its related ether. The same goes for the other ethers and their related elements. What this means is that in the most primeval period of Earth evolution, the nature of light, sound and life were different from the way they are now. They were like fire and fire ether are today in the sense that the spirit still dwelled within what was to become material upon later division. Fire is the only one of the four elements where spirit and matter remain in touch. *This is why fire is nearly always present in the Bible when the earthly apprehends the heavenly.* They can only meet at the state where the unmaterialized etheric condition of fire dwells. It can help to comprehend this if we look at what emerges wherever fire appears here on Earth. As a result of the high degree of molecular activity that generates combustion, we have emerging both light and air (gas, usually at least partially in the form of smoke). As we shall show in the "Light" essay, we cannot see the light, but we can see things when it falls upon them and we therefore *indirectly* perceive the etheric condition of light. Thus, looking at I-22, we see that in fact one moves from fire into a division of light and air.[9] The spiritual beings dwell in the etheric light (and higher ethers), but they only touch the material realm at the point of fire—as "tongues of fire" (Acts 2,3) if you will; they do not enter the material element of molecular action. We saw in "The Four Elements" how their lower agents, the "elemental beings" of which Paul spoke, do enter the material realms (Gal 4,3,9; Col 2,8,20).

THE PHENOMENA OF HEAT—HEAT AND THE OTHER ELEMENTS

Steiner shows us that our eyes and our ears, the organ systems by which we perceive what is revealed by light and sound, were created in the etheric world by these respective ethers. The impingement of light ether upon the etheric body created a wound that, in the healing process, became an eye. Thus, our eyes were created by the light for the light. The same with our ears and sound. The situation is different when we come to the action of the fire ether and our ability to perceive heat. We have no organ for that. Rather our entire body is the organ that detects heat, just as molecular heat pervades our body and the etheric heat regulates our body temperature (at approx. 98.6 degrees Fahrenheit regardless of surrounding temperature).

And yet our sense of heat is subjective. Our whole life is bound up with the fact that we have no zero or heat reference point within us. If we immerse our right hand in hot water and our left in cold, then put both of them in temperate water, the right hand will say the water is cool while the left hand will say it is warm. There is, of course, molecular heat in every object that is above what we call "absolute zero" (minus 459.67 degrees Fahrenheit). Earthly life absolutely cannot exist for an instant at such temperature; instant death would result.

---

9. It is just the recognition of these spiritual realities that opens the door to a further insight into scripture. We first have a hint of it in Gen 8,20-22, where the smell (gas) of the offering, brought about by the fire on the altar of Noah, brings about both light (the ability to see the rainbow in Gen 9,13) and the material blessing of farming by reversal of that part of the curse of Cain (Gen 4,12; 8,22 and 9,3; archaeologists confirm that farming began about ten thousand years ago, the time frame for Noah). The phenomenon is repeated more obviously in Gen 15,17-18 where, in the darkness, there appeared "a smoking fire pot and a flaming torch," but then especially in that multitude of Old Testament passages that speak of the delivery of the people of Israel from bondage. The seminal passage is Ex 13,21-22. God leads his people "by day in a pillar of cloud ... and by night in a pillar of fire." During the day, the less spiritual time, there is light by which the mineral-physical world can be seen—figuratively "smoke"—while during the night, the more spiritual time, Moses receives direction from the etheric world of light through the connecting point of fire.

This brings us to an observation that should point the direction for our examination of the nature of the heat being. For instance, how long can a human being remain alive on Earth as access to the four elements is successively removed? It stands to reason that those closest to the spiritual world are the most necessary while those furthest from it are the least. Or to put it another way, we can survive longer without those furthest from, than we can without those nearest to, the spiritual world. Thus, when fire (heat) is removed, death occurs instantly. One can survive for a matter of seconds or minutes without air, for a short number of days without water, and for a rather lengthy number of days without solid food (earth).

However useful science's own concepts of heat have been in working with the mineral-physical world, and they have been that, they will never lead into an understanding of the higher plant, animal and human kingdoms, and actually impede those investigations. What it knows in these realms is only about their mineral-physical content. Life and soul itself are, and will remain, ever more mysterious the deeper they penetrate into the mineral-physical.

It is noteworthy that science has fashioned its most widely used measurement of heat, the centigrade system, on a basis from zero to one hundred degrees, to reflect the condition of the most basic fluid element, water, in its fluid condition. Below zero it becomes a solid, while above one hundred it becomes a gas. We cannot begin to understand the nature of the heat being until we begin to see what happens to it, the heat being, at these points of transition. Steiner leads us into a provocatively insightful discussion of these. I shall attempt to give below a portion of the picture he presents.[10]

---

10. The content from here to the section called "Fire, the Spiral and the One Hundred Forty-Four Thousand" leans heavily upon the actual text called *Warmth Course* (WC) as Steiner delivered it in 1920 to the faculty at the first Waldorf School in Stuttgart. It seemed to me that clarity and accuracy would best be afforded by following his presentation closely. While condensed as far as feasible, I have attempted a precis, a summary, using not only the substance but often the mode of expression, adopting an exact word or phrase and often substantial portions of paragraphs or even entire paragraphs or series of paragraphs as he presented them, or nearly so. The distracting effect of proper editorial markings identifying all quotations, or their omission, would have outweighed, in my judgment, any benefit to be derived from them. Often my own contributions or paraphrases will be identifiable by the context. The student who desires more should have little difficulty following the progress of my presentation by comparing it with the WC text itself. Specific biblical analogies or references, when they occasionally appear, are mine. Any quotation marks used are merely to emphasize that they are Steiner's direct words.

If we apply constant heat to any solid, its temperature will:

a. rise constantly until melting commences,
b. remain constant until fully melted,
c. rise constantly until evaporation commences,
d. remain constant until fully evaporated, and
e. commence rising constantly as gas thereafter.

Thus on a graph the heat applied can be represented by an ascending diagonal line that is uninterrupted in its rise, while a line representing temperature is interrupted and stays at one point during the periods when the substance changes from one state to another by melting or evaporating.

What happens to the heat during the times of transition from one state to another? It falls outside the realm of the line drawn for temperature. In other words, we cannot grasp what happens to the heat applied by representing the temperature as an ordinary geometrical line. Even if we extend the graph to three dimensions, we get the same result. The heat condition, insofar as it is revealed by temperature, cannot be expressed in three-dimensional space. The heat applied disappears. Science says that the heat that has disappeared is used in converting from one state to another, but pays no attention to the significance of this.

Steiner tells us that there is a relationship between science's ignoring this fact and its ignoring of another heat-related phenomenon. All solids, fluids and gases expand when heated. Physics textbooks, in calculating the expansion in area and volume of metals when heated, leave out the terms in the equations that involve the second and third powers (the squares and cubes) of the coefficient of expansion of the metal multiplied by the squares or cubes of the temperature change. This is done because coefficients of expansion are very small fractions, which makes their second or third powers extremely small, so terms involving them are considered insignificant in practical physics. But Steiner says that the more important things are obscured by leaving out calculations that seem insignificant or that cannot be handled adequately, for these second and third powers of temperature are related to the disappearance of heat from three-dimensional space.

How can this fail to grip the attention of anyone interested in spiritual matters—fire (heat) simply disappears from the radar screen of matter, only to again reappear? Surely there must be some connection with what Christ came to cast upon the Earth.

The disappearance of heat is a "sign"—a sign or phenomenon whose meaning science and theology have ignored. All creation gives us signs (Ps 19, Rom 1,19-20). Even in his day, Christ said, "You know how to interpret the appearance of the sky, but you cannot interpret the signs of the times...."[11] We are told in Gen 1,14 that the "lights in the firmament of the heavens" are to "be for signs," yet science and religion ignore them still. The disappearance of heat is a sign in our quest for the meaning of things and of our own being. The disappearance of the very thing (fire) that Christ came to cast upon the Earth cannot be ignored.

Steiner pointed out that the physicist Sir William Crookes concluded that temperature changes had to do essentially with a kind of fourth dimension in space, but that "the relativists, with Einstein at their head, feel obliged when they go outside of three-dimensional space to consider time as the fourth dimension." The problem with this is that time only applies in three-dimensional space perception. Movement of a three-dimensional object from one spot to another involves time. It can occupy space only in time. But to understand what happens to the heat during these transitional periods, we need another dimension and it is not time. We must go out of space altogether.

Now let's look at another aspect. All solids, fluids and gases expand when heated, with one partial exception.[12] Solids and liquids expand consistently at rates governed by their individual substance, whereas all gases have the same coefficient of expansion. Consequently, regarding expansion from heat, the property of solids is *individualization* whereas that of gases is *unity*. This first came to human reflection in cosmic terms. The Greeks called all that was solid earth and all that was liquid water. The influence of the Earth within the cosmos created solids and the Sun influenced gas. The loss of this awareness necessitated our attention to the way atoms and molecules are arranged in a body so that the ability to bring about change had to be ascribed to these poor, merely reflective, creatures.

---

11. Mt 16,3; in vs 4 Jesus goes on to say, "No sign shall be given ... except the sign of Jonah." That sign was the "Three Days' Journey" (see *The Burning Bush*), a reference to the ancient initiation rite of the temple, the raising of Lazarus (see "Peter, James and John" in *The Burning Bush;* also *The Disciple Whom Jesus Loved*), and finally the raising of the temple of Jesus' body. And in the larger dimension, the "three days" can be seen to refer to the three Conditions of Consciousness still to be traversed by humanity after Earth evolution comes to an end (see I-1).

12. The exception is water. Between zero and four degrees centigrade (thirty-two and thirty-nine plus degrees Fahrenheit) water contracts when heated, but above four degrees C it expands with further heating.

Consider, for instance, these characteristics:

a. A solid holds its form without application of any external pressure.

b. A liquid requires pressure on the sides and bottom to contain it, whereby it then provides a horizontal upper surface.

c. A gas, if it is to be contained, must be enclosed by pressure on all sides.

Liquid is an intermediate condition between the solid and gas states, which are polar opposites in the sense that the solid has within it what must be applied from the outside to give form to the gas. It is thus self-evident that form is related in some way to changes in the heat state.

Profound spiritual truths are illustrated by these two simple statements of Steiner, that we must go out of space to understand what happens to heat during transitional periods, and that form is related in some way to changes in the heat state. What Steiner called "Imagination" (image-ination) is related to the type of "seeing" whose loss Isaiah lamented (Is 6,9-10)—people who "see and see but do not perceive"; likewise, even earlier, David (Ps 19,1-4). Paul spoke similarly in Rom 1,20-21, saying of the ancients that "his invisible nature ... his eternal power and deity, has been clearly perceived in the things that have been made ... but they became futile in their thinking and their senseless minds were darkened." But the nature of Christ's fire revealed in these two simple observations by Steiner has not been perceived by modern scientists or theologians of any stripe to my knowledge.

Consider first that, very simply stated, increasing heat causes matter to expand and rise while reducing heat causes matter to condense and fall. Heat causes matter to change elemental form, but in the process of that change disappears from space for the duration of the transition. Consider the course of the human soul (Ego) in the cycle of reincarnation (see the Overview in "Karma and Reincarnation" in *The Burning Bush*), how it too leaves space. While on Earth it either uses or misuses its "talents," but its treasures are stored up in heaven (Mt 25,14-30; 13,12 and 6,19-20; Lk 19,12-28). At death it leaves space, but returns again in a different form (entirely different person) that reflects its prior uses or misuses of opportunity. If one approached the fire Christ cast during the prior earthly life, then upon return the soul has risen to a higher state; conversely, if one moved away from that fire the soul falls under karmic burden. We have in these simple observations of heat phenomena a portrayal of the ancient hermetic principle, "As Above, So Below; As Below, So Above." When we begin to Imagine (see) higher things out of earthly ones, to see in natural phenomena higher spiritual reality, we begin to reclaim and transform an ancient aptitude about which Paul and the prophets spoke.

Perhaps with this early digression, the reader's own initiative will now be stimulated to recognize similar pictures of the higher world. By proper "seeing" of earthly things (Is 6,9-10), one can begin to draw one's own picture of what the higher reality must be like. It is all bound up in the proper "seeing," for all earthly phenomena are mere images of the spiritual world. The very next statement by Steiner seems to lend itself readily to what has just been said.

Gaseous bodies can interpenetrate each other; solids cannot. The volume of gas and the pressure exerted upon it are inversely proportional. Volume and pressure changes both relate to heat and both are mechanical facts that can be observed. But the being of heat, the third power in the equation, remains unknown for ordinary physics, for some of it appears to be lost in the process, and we are obliged to go out of three-dimensional space. Physics can explain the phenomena only in terms of three-dimensional space, thus assuring it will pass over the real nature of heat. This is the point where science must, as Steiner says, "cross the Rubicon" to reach a higher view of the world. And I might add, that it is also the point at which theology must do so to understand the meaning of fire in the Bible.

Since the nineteenth century, physics has had the mechanical theory of heat which postulates that heat and mechanical effects are mutually convertible, given a loss of heat in the process. But this leaves out the part of the transaction that occurs outside three-dimensional space. When I write, there is a conversion of heat into work, but to say that the two are mutually convertible leaves out the part that the non-three-dimensional part of me plays in the process. Consider the senses. We perceive light with the eye and sound with the ear, but heat and pressure only with our entire organism. We have no organs to directly perceive magnetism and electricity, but can only perceive them through their effects.

Our words represent ideas that are the residues of what our sense organs have provided us. But there is another side of our soul nature in our Will, and we are asleep in regard to that. We are not aware of what happens between our consciousness and the delicate processes of our arm moving. But something is there whose existence cannot be denied simply because we do not perceive it.

How silly, you say, to make this comparison. Of course, we can't perceive the inner processes that translate our Will into the movement of our arm. Why exasperate us with this comparison? Because if we are unable to consider this, we are shut out at the very gate of deeper insight. To even conceive of it, let alone to eventually perceive it, would then be out of the question. The Seraphim's *flaming* sword is there to guard against it. If we are to know the true nature of fire (heat), and then of light, and then to seriously address the question "What is man?" we must let phenomena such as this speak to us. That we sleep through the inner processes that execute our Will is highly significant. What does it mean? Let us continue.

When Steiner arrived at the newly organized Waldorf School at Stuttgart in late December 1919, he was asked by the teachers there, as part of their preparation, to lecture on the subject of light. As always, he accommodated them, so the first of the three lecture cycles that have been called his "scientific courses" was on this subject. Because of the depth of his genius and spiritual insight, he could speak spontaneously on so profound a subject with no more preparation than this. The ten lectures constituting the *Light Course* occurred between December 23, 1919, and January 3, 1920. They were followed two months later, upon his return, by the fourteen lectures of the *Warmth Course* (March 1-14). The third course, which he warned them not to call an "Astronomy Course," has in fact been called that. He entitled it "The Relation of the diverse branches of Natural Science to Astronomy" (eighteen lectures January 1-18, 1921).[13]

Because fire is closer to our mineral-physical existence than light (see I-22), we have reversed the order of these first two subjects. But at the outset of the *Light Course* Steiner presented something essential for an understanding of both, which he then could refer to but briefly at this point in the *Warmth Course*. We must consider it carefully.

---

13. This lecture series was not in print at the time Vol. 1 was published, nor is it yet. A more legible copy was provided me by the Rudolf Steiner Library than the one in the former bibliography. The earlier one was described in that bibliography as an "unpublished English typescript (U.E.T.), and given the abbreviation ARNS, representing the title *Astronomy: The Relation of the Diverse Branches of Natural Science to Astronomy*. The title given by its translator, Rick Mansell, to the copy in the current bibliography is *Rudolf Steiner on Astronomy*. Because the original title and abbreviation were in line with Steiner's desires, they are retained for reference purposes. Both titles are described in the current bibliography listing under the abbreviation ARNS.

Three things, he said, must be understood before actually reaching nature, namely, arithmetic, geometry and kinematics. The first two we immediately recognize. The third, *kinematics,* is defined as "the branch of mechanics that deals with motion in the abstract, without reference to the force or mass" (WNWCD). Steiner called it simply "the science of movement," but emphasized that it was still very remote from what we call the *real* phenomena of nature.

To illustrate he draws two identical parallelograms with corners a-b-c-d and diagonal a-b, as follows:

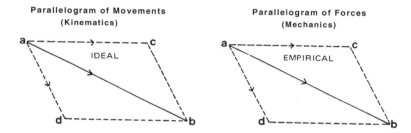

One need not observe any process in outer nature to simply think the first one (movements), by which the diagonal is actually formed of the movements of the other two sides, but having thought it out one may then observe and find that it corresponds with nature. The second one (forces), however, cannot be thought out in the same way, for here one must first actually *measure* the force. We can reach movements but not forces with mental activity. Forces must be measured in the outer world. One is by reasoning, the other is empirical.

Mechanics has to do with forces, not mere movements. It is thus already a natural science. Arithmetic, geometry and kinematics are not yet natural sciences in the proper sense. Mechanics is the first of the natural sciences, and to reach it we must go beyond mere ideas and mental pictures. Science does not envision this distinction clearly, and so, equipped with arithmetic, geometry and kinematics, enhanced with a bit of mechanics, it tries to work out a mechanics of molecules and atoms, and to imagine that what is called matter is to be thus subdivided. Then, in terms of this molecular mechanics scientists try to conceive the phenomena of nature. The existence of molecules and atoms is not to be denied, and many marvelous discoveries can be had based on them, but they will never lead to a knowledge of nature, only to the mechanical workings of the lowest rung, the mineral kingdom. The plant, animal and human kingdoms will always lie beyond the grasp of such a science, for it can only understand the mineral kingdom that also dwells in these other kingdoms. And so it is with microscope, telescope and space programs. They are declaring the wonders, but in language that passes us by (Ps 19,1-4; Is 6,9-10; Rom 1,20-21).

What still presumes to call itself science is at pains to express everything in mechanical terms. But it will have to take the *leap* from what is not alive in nature to what is; from kinematics to mechanics and then from external, inorganic nature into those realms that are not accessible to calculation, where every attempted calculation breaks asunder and every potential is dissolved away. Calculation ceases where we want to understand what is alive.

To help us bridge the gap, Steiner writes down a certain familiar formula:

ps = m times v^2 / 2, where p =force; s = length of path; m =mass; v = velocity

We immediately see from the equation that the bigger the mass, the bigger the force must be. But notice that on the right-hand side we have mass, which is the very thing we can never reach kinematically (theoretically or ideally). We can only get to know it by outer observation.

Or is there yet a bridge between the kinematical and the mechanical? Physics today cannot find the transition, and the consequences of this failure are immense. It has no real human science, no real physiology. It does not know the human being. When I write v^2 I have only something calculated as spatial movement—only the kinetic. When I write *m* on the other hand, I must first ask, "Is there anything in me myself to correspond also to this?"

The answer is yes, but the first step is to make yourself conscious of this. Press with your finger against something. Mass thus reveals itself through pressure. Try to exert pressure on some part of your body, and then go on making it ever more intense. At length you will lose consciousness from it. The loss of consciousness that you experience with a pressure stronger than you can endure is taking place partially and on a small scale whenever you come into any kind of contact with an effect of pressure from some mass. Our consciousness is dimmed at once. If this only happens to a slight degree we can still bear it, but if to a great extent we can bear it no longer. What underlies it is the same in either case.

When we write down *m* (mass), we are writing down what in nature, if it does unite with our consciousness, eliminates it. That is to say, it puts us partially to sleep. When we write down the above formula we must admit that our human experience contains the *m* no less than the *v*, but our normal consciousness does not enable us to seize the *m*. It at once sucks out, withdraws from us, the force of consciousness. Here you have the real relationship to the human being. To understand what is in nature, you must bring in the states of consciousness.

But while we cannot live with consciousness in all that is implied in the letter *m*, we do live in it after all with our full human nature. We live in it above all with our Will.

Steiner demonstrates this through Archimedes' principle, the law of buoyancy, whereby every body immersed in a liquid becomes as much lighter as the weight of the liquid it displaces. In a sense it withdraws itself from the downward pressure of weight. This is of great importance in the human constitution. The brain weighs about 1250 grams, or 2.76 pounds. However, it swims in cerebral fluid and displaces a weight of about 1230 grams, or 2.71 pounds, which leaves it actually weighing only 20 grams, or .044 pounds.

What does this signify? With our intelligence we live not in forces that pull downward but on the contrary, in forces that pull upward—a force of buoyancy. This applies, however, only to our brain (and the spinal cord), for the remaining portions of our body are only slightly in this condition. Taken as a whole their tendency is downward. Our Will, above all, lives in the downward pull. It has to unite with pressure. Precisely this deprives the rest of our body of consciousness and makes it all the time asleep.[14] This indeed is the essential feature of the phenomenon of Will. As a conscious phenomenon it is blotted out, extinguished, because in

---

14. One can never contemplate too deeply the significance of the threesome Peter and the two sons of Zebedee sleeping three times while Christ prayed for their consciousness over the event of Crucifixion (Mt 26,40-45; Mk 14,37-41; Lk 22,45-46). Unlike Evangelist John (and later Paul), who was initiated by Christ into a higher level of consciousness, these were not yet to that point. That the body of matter (mass) must eventually be overcome by human consciousness (i.e., be crucified) seems clearly to be implied. And the element of threefoldness (three slept three times) suggests that not only the physical body, but all three bodies, must eventually be crucified (Mt 13,33). These three also slept through the spiritual dialogue with Moses and Elijah at the Transfiguration of Jesus (see Lk 9,30-32). See the essay "Peter, James and John" as well as "Three Bodies" in *The Burning Bush*; also *The Disciple Whom Jesus Loved.*

fact the Will unites with the downward force of gravity or weight. Never could Intelligence arise if our soul's life were bound only to downward tending matter. Only a tiny portion of it, amounting to the twenty grams' pressure, manages to filter through to the Intelligence. Hence our Intelligence is to some extent permeated by Will.

With these thoughts, borrowed from his earlier lectures on light, Steiner differentiated between the mere kinematics applied by science and mass. Kinematics involves only time and space and can only be surveyed there because all persons on Earth are *within* time and space. If space were within us, it would matter not where we were, but we stand *within* time and space. Not so with mass, for it is *within* us, thus falling into a different category from time and space. Because we take it up into our being, we are not conscious of it. The processes of our Will are largely dependent upon processes of mass inside us, but we are unconscious—asleep—as to them.

Hold these thoughts on the nature of mass and its relationship to consciousness ever in mind. With this concept in place, we can now move into some important phenomena that point the way to an understanding of fire (heat).

Temperature changes correspond externally to a form. We are experiencing the dissolution and reestablishment of form. The gas dissolves form for us and the solid establishes form. And we experience this in a very interesting way. Liquid is the transitional state between solid and gaseous form. Surface inheres within the solid nature, relates in liquid to the center of the Earth (a liquid's upper surface being perpendicular to the Earth's radius at that point), and is completely absent in the gas nature. The solid thus encompasses within itself what in the case of water resides in its relationship with the whole Earth, while gas enters into no relationship with the Earth at all in terms of surface form. Thus, we have the ancient Greek perception of earth-water-air.

When a solid reaches its melting point, it loses its individuality.[15] Water behaves peculiarly between zero and four degrees centigrade—the exception noted earlier to the general rule of expansion as temperature increases. Within this four-degree range it expands as temperature is lowered. Why? Steiner says it is because there it begins to struggle against the transition to an entirely different sphere. This relates to the phenomenon

---

15. It becomes self-less (Rom 6,6; Phil 2,3; 2 Tim 3,2; 2 Cor 12,20; Gal 5,20).

that heat disappears during the melting.[16] Analogously, our bodily reality disappears for us when we rise to the sphere Steiner calls Imagination (a form of spiritual seeing unrelated to sensate sight).

We return to the general principle: fluid solidifies when brought below its melting point. In the case of water, this occurs at and below zero degrees centigrade. But remarkably, pressure applied to its solid condition can again liquefy it. Steiner illustrated this by hanging a weight upon a wire stretched across the top of a chunk of ice. It melts its way through the ice. But instead of falling in two, the ice rejoins behind the wire in the same manner that the air (gas) rejoins behind itself if you wave a pencil through it.

When different molten metals are mixed, they form an alloy; that is, they combine without chemical action so that each retains its individual character in the mixture. Steiner then demonstrates by experiment that when so alloyed, however, the melting point of the mixture is lower than that of any of its constituent metals. He leaves us to draw our own inferences from this. But it seems clear that in giving up something of their separate individualities through the process of mixing, the metals move back closer to the liquid condition of form, for less heat is then required to reduce them again to fluid. And this is true even though in the solid state, as an alloy, they may be made stronger than they were as separate metals.

What force lies behind solidification (crystallization)? Consider how solid earthly bodies behave when not connected with the Earth mass. When their support is removed, they fall in a line perpendicular to the surface of the Earth. As such, in toto they represent what is real in fluid bodies that seek an upper surface through the same force.

What is the significance of this? Solids thus give a picture of what is materially present in liquid—a direct image as it were. Water is always evaporating. Its lines of escape go off in all directions. Thus the surface tendency of water gives us a picture, an image, of what gas is as a material reality. Here we have a phenomenon in nature that clearly demonstrates the hermetic principle "As Above, So Below." Or, to use the biblical metaphor, the lower is created "in the image" of the higher. It is important to recognize that this principle both pervades the realm of materiality and

---

16. Does this struggle not also portray the spiritual event of the soul's struggle as it leaves its heavenly dwelling to enter again into earthly life through the birth canal? It leaves the region of the etheric fire and falls again into the earthly condition of matter, crossing again the watery (fluid) stage of the mythical river Lethe, meaning oblivion or loss of consciousness or memory.

does not stop at its threshold—where it meets the realm of nonmateriality. Nothing could be clearer than the fact that this is pronounced very early in the book of Genesis (Gen 1,26-27; also the earlier "according to its kind" passages, Gen 1,11,12,21,24,25).

We discover that in every state of aggregation downward (or upward if you like) from the solid, pictures of the preceding state develop. Thinking thus,

> *In solids we have the images of the fluid state*
>
> *In fluids we have the images of the gaseous state*
>
> *In gases we have the images of the warmth (fire) state*

we have taken an important step giving us a picture of the nature of heat itself. But we must observe it rightly. Normal physics gets nowhere with it. While best observed in the gaseous condition, the being of heat does penetrate the liquid and solid states through the process of cooling.

The wire that was passed through the ice, and the pencil through the air, illustrated a similar thing, namely, that both solid and gas have in them a similar process, a "closing up," though acting in different realms. Thus, in states of materiality, however attenuated, there is a cohesive tendency, an attraction or coagulation, that seems to be countered only by an increase in heat.

What happens to corporeality, however, when carried through the melting and boiling points? Fundamentally, solid bodies possess form, liquids require a container in order to form their own surface, and gases must be completely enclosed by pressure on all sides. What is active in the liquid surface (called gravity) that is within solids to give form? Recall that upon evaporation the liquid surface ceases, and that all gases have the same coefficient of expansion as material emancipated from the Earth— thus lacking individuality.[17]

Solids have somehow taken up gravity for their form-building, but when falling freely portray what underlies the surface tendencies of liquids. We here on Earth can thus say that we perceive what is surface-

---

17. In this shared coefficient as well as in the fact, recognized earlier, that gases interpenetrate each other (like most liquids), fire (heat) has caused matter to approach more nearly a state of unity or oneness. The etheric fire that Christ desired to cast upon the Earth is at a stage even higher, characterized by greater unity. Christ prayed for unity (Jn 17,11) and Paul recognized it as the mystery of God's will set forth by Christ (Eph 1,9-10).

forming in water and call it gravity. If we lived on a fluid cosmic body (as the Earth once was), it would have to be above the surface, thus having the same relationship to the gaseous as we now have to fluids, meaning that we would not perceive gravity. Gravity can only be perceived by beings living on a solid planet. (This was illustrated by his discussion of Archimedes' principle and the brain.) And beings who lived on a gaseous planet would regard as normal something the opposite of gravity, a striving in all directions from the center—negative in respect to gravity—having passed thereto through what Steiner calls a kind of "nullpoint."[18]

And we've seen that applying heat to a gas raises its diffusing tendency, so this warmth being does the same thing that a negative gravity would do. It manifests like negative gravity.

But earthly form is dissolved in passing from solid to fluid such that the form is imposed by the general influence of the Earth—it becomes a liquid surface. But when divided into small particles, form is thus spherical—the synthesis of all polyhedral[19] (crystal) shapes. Thus the passage from solid to gas goes through the sphere. If a tetrahedron (four-sided solid)[20] becomes a gas, it is as though a glove were turned inside out,

---

18. We must remember that human evolution during its Earth Condition of Consciousness, in recapitulating in mineral-physical form during the first three Evolutionary Epochs what it went through during the first three Conditions of Consciousness (Ancient Saturn, Sun and Moon), actually went through these successive states of fire, then gas and then fluid, taking up its acquaintance with gravity and learning to stand upright as Adam (hard or bony, in Gen 3,17; on this point see fn 40 (in the Creation essay) and the Chapter End Note in the Creation essay) during the fourth Epoch, the Atlantean, when the human descent finally placed it more completely upon the ground (solid) rather than the fluid. The four elements were then fully represented in the human body, along with the progressive decline in consciousness they represented. See I-1 and the Creation essay. The four elements were, of course, present much earlier in Earth evolution in the lower three kingdoms (mineral, plant and animal) than in the human, even though the human kingdom is the original and older one from which they all fell away and descended into materiality. The progressively lower states of consciousness in these lower kingdoms, compared with the human, is recognized by all.
19. A "polyhedron" is a many-sided solid geometric form, derived from the Greek roots, *poly* meaning "many," and *hedron* meaning "side."
20. Note the progression: one side = sphere; two sides = cone; three sides = cylinder; and four sides = tetrahedron or three-sided pyramid. The tetrahedron is thus the least condensed solid geometrical body with entirely flat sides, escaping the curvature of the gravity-forming liquid state. It represents the first fully solid crystal form. What is particularly fascinating about this is the "eye" at the top of the pyramid on the back of our dollar bill. The perception of the new secular order implied by the Latin words is accompanied by symbolism that doubtless escapes modern Americans. It would seem to be the etheric vision of the cyclopean eye that sees into the creative nature of the pyramid, which, as we shall see later in this essay, means "fire."

passing through the sphere so that what was positive or solid before becomes negative. Within the filled space outside, there is a hollow tetrahedral hole—a negative tetrahedron. Every polyhedral body goes over into its negative only by passing through the sphere like through a null-point—a null sphere. The fluid is intermediate between the formed and the formless.

What happens to our Earth under the warmth being of our solar system, the Sun? During the time we are not exposed to the Sun, when the Earth is left to itself, it strives toward form, whereas under the influence of the Sun there is a continual dissolving, a Will to overcome form. We thus, both daily and seasonally, vacillate in the cosmos between two conditions. Contemplate the significance of the fact that the Sun is both a creative and a destructive force to our earthly existence. It creates life, then destroys it.[21] Is there meaning in this simple observation? Is it a giant agent of even higher powers that both create and crucify, in purposeful, rhythmic evolution toward an ever moving goal?

This thought leads to another. While science has observed astronomical phenomena enough to see that at least in a certain sense cosmic creation takes place out of fiery circumstances, Steiner has shown us clearly how our solar system came into being during the Old Saturn Condition of Consciousness through an original state of fire, an immense sphere, composed only of etheric heat. One can see this from the "Overview," in connection with I-27, in *The Burning Bush*. Understandably the Bible collapses the more remote aspects of our materiality, telling us that physically we both came from "dust" and shall return thereto (Gen 2,7; Eccles 3,20 and 12,7), but in its broader spectrum that we came from fire (Gen 1,2; Ezek 1,4-5; Jn 1,1-3) and physically shall again return through it (2 Pet 3,1-13 and Rev). In fact the Bible, science and Steiner all tell us this. Long before these "science lectures" that Steiner gave (1919-1921), and in the very middle of the time that he was concentrating on the Bible

---

21. Consider what was said earlier about the total absence of heat at "absolute zero" where all molecular action ceases (or is at least "nontransferable"). No such condition actually exists on Earth. Some heat (fire) is found in everything (Ps 19,6, "there is nothing hid from its heat"). Yet we've seen that where enough fire exists, matter eventually ceases to exist, passing from the material to the immaterial; thus fire destroys (i.e., crucifies) matter. The fire Christ came to cast (Lk 12,49) will eventually bring this about, and the Sun portrays it in its destructive aspect. Later in this essay, we see what Steiner says about the interior of the Sun being the opposite of matter.

(1908-1914), in a single lecture in Berlin (March 16, 1911) entitled *What Has Astronomy to Say about the Origin of the World?* (WHA), he made these remarks:

> Within natural scientific thinking, research and experimenting it is clearly shown how it is correct in general to say that we can change nature forces into one another, that we can, for instance, change heat into work, or, if we have done a certain work, change this back into heat. But it is only correct with a very important limitation.... Some heat is always lost, so in all processes of nature where heat-energy is transformed into movement, we have to reckon with a *loss of heat*, as is certainly the case with a steam-engine.... But as in the transformation a remnant of heat always remains, it is not hard to see that ultimately the final condition of our evolution—material evolution—is the transformation of the total movement-energy, and of all other kinds of nature processes, into heat. That is the final condition which must come about. Everything else in nature-processes must finally be transformed into heat because always a remnant of heat remains over.... Thus the resulting heat will become greater and greater, till the final result must be that all movement will be transformed into heat. Then we should have universal chaos consisting only of heat which can no longer be transformed back again.... Everything that streams to us from the sun tends eventually to "pass over into a universal death by heat." That is the famous "Claudius' death by heat".... And here, for anyone who understands cognition, a piece of knowledge is given which is quite incontrovertible, and against which physically no objection can be brought. Our material universe is striving towards this heat-death in which everything in nature will some day be burned.

The Claudius Steiner mentioned lived from A.D. 129 to 199, and is also known as Galen of Pergamum.[22] His "heat death" still retains validity to this day based upon the principle of entropy.[23]

---

22. See 5 Brit 82.
23. See 25 Brit 825 and 841, "Physical Science, Principles of; Entropy and Disorder"; and "Physics."

But here science has a problem, for its conclusion is that there will be a "heat death" since it is impossible in a closed system to transform all heat into mechanical energy. The very solidification process is nature's attempt to attain a closed system, but the closed system never fully arises because the system is not left to itself, but is worked upon by its whole environment. There is always a tendency at various points for a closed system to arise, but a counter tendency appears at once. This alters the abstract thinking of physics. A closed system is always striving to arise, but the constitution of the cosmos prevents it.

Here science falls by the wayside, while both the Bible and Steiner confirm that a new state arises for humanity. Ecclesiastes says that while the dust returns to Earth as it was, "the spirit returns to God who gave it" (Eccles 12,7), and both 2 Peter and John's Apocalypse tell us that "a new heavens and a new earth" come into being after the elements have been dissolved by fire (2 Pet 3,13; Rev 21). The etheric and astral states are entered.

With these thoughts in mind, let us return to where we said that each state of aggregation gives a picture of its neighbor, in solids the image of the fluid, in fluids the image of the gaseous, and in gases the image of fire. Today we speak of two forms of energy, mechanical (solid bodies) and acoustical (sound waves). They can be placed in their respective spheres and tabulated as follows:

X

Warmth

Gaseous   — Acoustical

Fluid

Solid   — Mechanical

Just as fluid was left out in moving from solid to gaseous, so also warmth is left out to arrive at X. We must find something lying on the far side of the warmth being just as the sound world lies this side of it.

Sound manifests in gases through waves (condensations and rarefactions). But gases themselves condense and rarefy with temperature change. If we pass over fluids and seek to find in gases what corresponds to form in solids, we must look for it in condensation and rarefaction. If we then pass over warmth to postulate the region next above it, we have the following tabulation:

$\underline{X}$	Becoming material—Becoming spiritual
Heat	
Gas	Negative Form—Condensation and Rarefaction
Fluids	
Solids	Form

By analogy, I must look in $\underline{X}$ for something corresponding to but beyond condensation and rarefaction, passing over heat just as fluid was passed over below it. So long as condensation and rarefaction are present, so is matter. But if we rarefy enough, we finally pass entirely out of the material realm, becoming spiritual. Thus, we are obliged to think of $\underline{X}$ as a realm of materiality and non-materiality if we are to be consistent in our extension from the realms below it.

Heat thus leads to a condition where matter itself ceases to be. It stands between two strongly contrasted regions, essentially different from each other, the spiritual and the material. This is completely in accord with the Bible's use of fire when there is communication from one world to the other, the spiritual to the earthly.

Here the reader might find it worthwhile to meditate on the meaning of the allegorical story of the three noble creatures thrown by Nebuchadnezzar into the fiery furnace in the third chapter of Daniel. See its discussion in "Three Bodies" in *The Burning Bush*, p. 432. Of special significance is the appearance of the fourth who emerged from the fire (Dan 3,24-25). It is the same "I Am" that Moses saw in the burning bush (Ex 3,1-6,13-14).

HEAT AND THE OTHER ETHERS

Most readers will likely find this section, a fourth of the essay in length and its architectural center, becoming progressively the most tedious. It should help to bear this in mind and to analogize it to the image of the parabolas depicting the Great Epochs of Earth evolution and the Cultural Eras of the post-Atlantean Epoch (see the diagrams in "Christ, the J-Curve and the Right Time" below). All these centers represent the slowest point, and perhaps the most vital, of the entire journey. Without it, we falter at the gates of our inquiry "What Is Man?". How apt we hear the message to the angel of the church in Thyatira, the fourth church, the Greco-Roman

Cultural Era (see those diagrams below), "He who conquers and who keeps my works until the end, I will give him power over the nations" (Rev 2,26).

When we have arrived at X, the etheric realm of light adjoining and still playing into the fire (warmth) that we perceive with our senses, we have, in one respect, perhaps gone as far as necessary to cover our topic of fire.[24] However, to stop here, though it would greatly shorten our endeavor, would leave us little better off than when we started. It is like saying that one can understand the human foot by looking only at the foot and not the entire human organism. An amputated foot is not like a foot still part of that organism. Nor is the leaf of an annual plant (one that starts anew each year from seed) comprehendible save as a part of the entire life cycle of the plant. When Steiner was a mere twenty-two years of age (in 1883), he published his *Goethean Science* (GS) in which he set out Goethe's theory of metamorphosis (see GS, Chap. II, pp. 16-23). There Steiner discusses Goethe's concept of the archetypal plant (*Urpflanze*). It might be thought of as the plant kingdom's equivalent of the human kingdom's "man" in Gen 2,4b–3,16 before it materialized into an "Adam" in Gen 3,17. We are talking about these kingdoms in the etheric world, the world that finally produces all material existence, the world of Gen 1 and 2. It helps to conceive of the idea if we think of the various stages of the annual plant, starting at any point. Let us start with the seed. From there we move, to use lay terminology, through germination into stem, then leaf, bud, flower and finally back to seed. One cannot adequately describe the plant at any one stage. At best, it can only be understood as the entire cycle, as though we eliminated time or sequence and had before our vision the entirety of the plant cycle. Even here we would not have Goethe's archetypal plant (*Urpflanze*) but merely one of its many species. The archetypal plant is the first etheric state of the plant kingdom, just as the pre-Adam human being of Gen 1–2 is the first etheric state of the human kingdom.

But the etheric world does not stop with the fire ether. The etheric world that is interposed between the higher astral and spiritual worlds and our physical world is fourfold, the earthly ancestor of the four elements, so that in ascending order we have the fire ether, light ether, chemical or sound ether, and finally life ether (see I-22). And then from

---

24. This statement ("we have gone as far as necessary") does not apply to the last part of this essay called, "Fire, the Spiral and the One Hundred Forty-Four Thousand."

the ether world we enter these higher worlds. No part of the cycle can be adequately comprehended without considering the entire cycle. So in order to lay an adequate groundwork for understanding the biblical cry "What is man?" we must go on beyond the X realm. Now observe the color spectrum, red through violet, as follows:

Infrared

    <   Red

       Orange

         Yellow

           Green

             Blue

               Indigo

                 Violet >

                   Ultraviolet

It does not break off at the red but becomes warmer and warmer until there is no light but only heat (infrared). On the other side similarly, when we no longer have light there is only chemical action (ultraviolet). Both are effects manifesting in matter.

Goethe's theory was that there were not seven colors, but twelve, in circular form. When the circle was made sufficiently large, the portion visible to an outside observer became practically a straight line in such manner that only the lower seven colors were visible, with the extremes fading out into Darkness. The color opposite the green was peach-blossom, the color of human skin.[25] See the diagram below:

---

25. No idea of race superiority should be gathered from this, but rather that peach-blossom was the archetypal color of human skin before differentiation brought about genetically due to geographical and cultural differences in tribal exposure to the Sun. That skin coloration is today a genetic matter is clear (19 Brit 703), but that it results from a pigment called *melanin* is also clear. "In fair-skinned persons the epidermis, or outermost layer of the skin, contains little of the pigment; in the dark-skinned races epidermal deposits of melanin are heavy. On exposure to sunlight, human epidermis undergoes gradual tanning with increases in the melanin content, which helps to protect underlying tissues from injurious sun rays" (16 Brit 588).

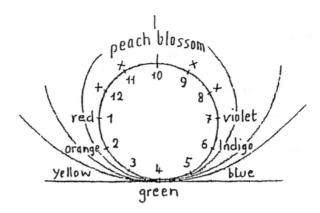

Is there not a precise analogy and parallel between the heat and light phenomena, as presented above? Human senses detect only a middle band of materiality in the one case, or colors, in the other. And do not both present us with the divine numbers seven and twelve? For we gauge our material sound waves, an earthly reflection of the long separated sound (or chemical) ether, on a normal scale of seven notes and a chromatic (meaning color) scale of twelve. Did we not perceive the sound ether (the Word of God?) in the garden during the Fall (Gen 3,10), even as it was being separated from us in our descending materiality?

But we cannot stop at either X or solid bodies, for these do not close up the circle of which our materiality is but a sensate band. Steiner goes on.

It is not difficult to see that we can go beyond X to a Y and a Z realm, just as in the light spectrum we move from green to blue, blue to violet and then to ultraviolet. And to be consistent, we can then postulate a realm $\underline{U}$ below the solid on the basis that it must in like manner as above give us a picture (image) of the solid realm. Thus:

Z	
Y	
X	Materialization — Dematerialization
Heat region	
Gaseous bodies	Rarefaction—Condensation
Fluid bodies	
Solid bodies	Form
$\underline{U}$	

To that end, let us go back momentarily to the fluid. Its enclosed surface level shows its relationship to the entire Earth. The gravity thus active in it is a force akin to the creation of the form of solids. In the $\underline{U}$ realm we must find something that happens similarly to the form-building in the world of solids that would parallel the picturing of the fluid world by solids—an action that foreshadows the various formations of the solid world.

According to Steiner, the $\underline{U}$ realm is that of *polarization*. Under the influence of the form-building force, something appears in the $\underline{U}$ realm that creates form in the realm of solids just as gravity forms only the surface in the fluid realm. It is what he calls polarization figures. One can study the normal texts (e.g., 9 Brit 556, "polarization," and 26 Brit 474, "Radiation ... Wave aspects of light") and find polarization "explained" by the wave theory of light. While there is a certain practical utility in this approach, Steiner denies the reality of the wave theory, as we shall see more fully in the "Light" essay below. Arthur Zajonc, professor of physics at Amherst College and also a prominent anthroposophist, in his *Catching the Light, The Entwined History of Light and Mind* (CLT), tells us that Augustin Fresnel explained polarization through his theory that light waves were transverse in contrast to the longitudinal compressions and rarefactions of sound waves (pp. 116-118). But Zajonc says that more recently science has discovered problems with this theory of polarization that simply have not yet been solved (pp. 311-316). It would seem that the existing state of perplexity on the matter vindicates the assertion by Steiner early in the twentieth century. He said that while nineteenth-century physics (still maintained in common textbooks) determined (based upon an erroneous wave theory) that light itself gives rise to the phenomenon of polarization, in reality it only makes the phenomenon visible. This is consistent with the present state of perplexity among those who have delved into it most deeply, as indicated by Zajonc's book. To comprehend polarization figures, Steiner says, one must seek an entirely different source than the light itself, for what is taking place has nothing to do with it. It simply penetrates and makes visible what is going on there as a foreshadowing of the solid form.

Returning to the so-called spectrum, we saw that beyond the infrared and the ultraviolet we passed into infinity—to the point Goethe saw as being peach-blossom in color. So also do the $\underline{X}$, $\underline{Y}$ and $\underline{Z}$ realms pass into infinity in one direction while at the opposite end the $\underline{U}$ realm passes into infinity in the other. But before we depict it as Steiner seemed to suggest, let us, as he also suggested, consider the rainbow. A remarkable thing about the rainbow is that it is never just one bow. There is always a second, even when it is not very obvious. The two belong together. Their meaning as phenomenon is missed unless they are considered as components of a single picture. And the imperative for understanding the picture is to give due consideration to the fact that the second rainbow always reverses its colors from those of the first. They head off in different directions, the ultraviolet escaping from the top of one and the bottom of the other. Nature presents us this picture as an integral portion of the entire universe—and we must so comprehend it. The second rainbow converts the phenomenon into a closed system so to speak. It is as though the first rainbow has run around to the other side of a transparent sphere and shown itself to us again, albeit more weakly and with its colors appearing thus reversed. But if the sevens become twelves, there is still the hint of the peach-blossom falling in between the two in the invisible portion of the sphere.

Science is still bewitched by what it calls "rays of light." As a practical matter, light manifests in ways, i.e., optical laws, that seem to work in accordance with the existence of rays, and yet their nature otherwise remains a total mystery—for they seem to behave with effect, and manifest, in a material world without themselves having any materiality. But using drawings of these putative rays, science explains how the rainbow comes into existence by primary and then secondary reflections within millions of individual raindrops so that seeing the rainbow depends on where one stands in relation it. Excellent illustrations are given in 9 Brit 906, "rainbow," and in CLT, pp. 169 and 176, and they complement one another for fuller understanding.

Zajonc's book gives an excellent portrayal of how human beings of all walks have been fascinated from primeval times by the rainbow. And the Bible student must surely recall its first appearance to Noah (Gen 9,13-17). Less memorable but equally remarkable are its appearances in Revelation. At that early stage of insight when to John's clairvoyance the four corners of the twelvefold zodiacal heavens appeared (Rev 4,7) and the crystallization of the waters began (Rev 4,6), a rainbow had appeared (Rev 4,3) in the midst of the twenty-four elders (reflective of twelve[26]).

---

26. Recall that the "twenty-four elders" mentioned in Rev 4,4,10; 5,8; 11,16; 19,4 et al. were explained in **I-1** in *The Burning Bush* as beings having a unique relationship to the twenty-four Conditions of Life that preceded our present one.

And it was only then that the "seven torches of fire" appeared that presaged the descent of the human being into materiality. We have the seven colors that appear to the senses, but hidden from the senses are the five others, including the peach-blossom of archetypal human skin.

We come again to the rainbow in Rev 10,1, between the blowing of the sixth and seventh trumpets (see "Trumpet[s]" in *The Burning Bush*), the final age before humanity will leave the Physical Condition of Form. It speaks of the seven thunders, but the days are approaching when it will speak of the "twelve stars" (Rev 12,1) and then all of the twelvefoldness of the "new heaven and new earth" (Rev 21–22).

The rainbow and the so-called spectrum present seven colors to our senses, but just as the biblical sevens become twelves, so also is the mystic rainbow twelvefold, with peach-blossom on the far side still hidden from our earthly perception.

And so Steiner carries our illustration to completion, and from his lecture his hearers have given us the following completed diagram, but at the point corresponding to the peach-blossom we find the human being:

What do we find corresponding to the colors of the twelvefold spectrum in the states of aggregation? Nothing less than the whole of nature, which we saw disappearing at both ends of the visible and coming together in the human being on the far side. The human being takes up what comes from both sides and is placed there at that point.[27]

---

27. This point seems clearly to be what is esoterically called the soul's "midnight hour" or "cosmic midnight." It is discussed in the Overview in "Karma and Reincarnation" at p. 118, as well as in I-33 at page 605, in *The Burning Bush*. And the parable of the friend who arrives at midnight seeking three loaves of bread is best seen as portraying this point (Lk 11,5-8).

The form-giving forces come from below, from the ultra-U realm so to speak, and these, in the outer world, also give the human being its mental images. Insofar as form is incorporated within the human being, it does not belong to the sphere of consciousness. In embryo and infant, form is very plastic and related to formative forces. With advancing age formative forces withdraw progressively in proportion to the increase in conscious mental activity, even to the point that from and after death, in the discarnate state, these forces reveal themselves when form is completely dissolved.

What then comes from the top, the infrared realm? We know that physiologically we go through a certain interaction with outer nature to produce warmth, i.e., movement, voluntary and involuntary, which is a reflection of Will, both conscious and unconscious. Thus, just as the formative outer objects are akin to mental activity, so is heat related to our Will. We experience it in our Will.

We see form in solid bodies, but what brings about the form is not there. Just as the soul-spiritual element is not within a corpse but has been in it, so is what determines form not within the object. If I perceive heat in nature, I experience the same thing that is active in me as Will. In the thinking and willing human, we have what meets us in outer nature as form and heat respectively. Of course, thinking and Will, form and heat, have all possible intermediate stages where they interpenetrate one another just as the realms of aggregation and colors do.

Both form and heat, in meeting within the human, must do so by disappearing from space. Nature shows us that when we think of her in relation to the human being, we must leave her.

But what does this mean mathematically? A linear series representing in sequence the states of aggregation may be considered as positive. Then what works into the human, both form and heat, must be put down as negative. Mental image in the human is related to outer world form as negative to positive. Photography gives an earthly representation of this.

Matter is characterized by the human as pressure effects. We saw this earlier as it related to our consciousness. Thus ideas about form (matter) must come into the picture as the opposite of pressure, namely, *suction*. Mental activity is suction. On the other hand, when positive outer heat enters the human, it is "sucked up," disappearing from space as a counter-image manifesting as Will. Debits remain debits although they are credits elsewhere. Human nature must be thought of as what continually sucks up and destroys matter.

Steiner observed that unfortunately modern physics had not in his day developed the concept of negative matter. After his death, science has developed experimentally the concept of antimatter (1 Brit 455). Though there certainly appears to be some relationship in concept, science still seems to me to deal with it only in the realm of matter (what can be observed through instrumentation). Will and thought phenomena have to be given negative values in relation to heat phenomena and form-giving forces.[28]

Steiner demonstrated to his audience by experiment (placing different substances in the path of light to see what type of effect each blocks) that heat effects arise in the red portion of the spectrum, chemical (e.g., phosphorescence) in the violet, and light in the central portion. Under earthly conditions, a spectrum can only be presented as an image. The one we get is the well-known linear one formed from the circular one by making the circle larger and larger so that the peach-blossom disappears, with violet fading off to infinity on one side and red on the other. The forces that make the circle larger, and the line thus straight, are forces of form, including magnetic forces. And since these are everywhere active on Earth and within the spectrum it is necessary to represent it in a straight line, thus:

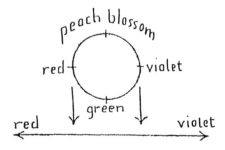

We must link this thought with another, portrayed as follows:

Materializing, dematerializing; dark, light	
Heat	
Rarefying, densifying	
Liquid	
Solid form	

---

28. In regard to these matters, the reader might refer also to charts **I-40**, **I-80** and **I-82** in *The Burning Bush.*

The denser matter is, the less light can pass through, and vice versa. Thus, dematerialization will appear as brightness and materialization as darkness. The light realm is just above that of heat. But we've seen that each realm gives a picture of the one above and is pictured by the one below. And recall also that there is a mutual interpenetration of qualities. This takes on a particular form in the heat realm. There dematerialization works down into heat from above, while the materialization tendency works up into it from below (see arrows in the diagram).

Heat is thus conceived of as involving a living weaving—as against the concept of the mechanical theory of heat involving atoms and molecules in a closed space colliding with each other. Heat is indeed motion, but in the sense that there is a tendency to create material existence and then let it disappear again.[29] This is why we need heat in our organism, simply to change continuously the spatial into the nonspatial. Heat is what makes it possible for me to deal with things in space while forming ideas outside of space. Thus within me there is intensive motion continually alternating between pressure effects and suction effects, pictured below:

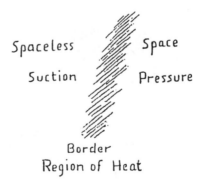

Thus, heat must be conceived as intensive motion, as an alternation between spatial pressure and spaceless suction, but in such a way that neither pressure nor suction is spatially manifested. To comprehend it, we must entirely leave the material world and with it three-dimensional space.

---

29. Steiner is here expressing heat phenomena in language almost identical to that science would use many decades later in describing certain light phenomena. In the "Light" essay below, see the discussion from Fagg, pp. 51-54, who speaks (on p. 52) of "evanescent pairs of particles ... that materialize for a brief instant and then vanish." On p. 54 he speaks of such particles that "emerge ... and then vanish as long as they do not stay around long enough for us to observe them."

It is a vortex continually manifesting in such a way that what appears physically is annihilated by what appears as the spiritual—a continuous interplay—a sucking up of what is in space by the entity that is not. Such is the figurative Imagination.

Another widely applied "scientific" conceptual term is called the "heat conduction principle." It is of practical utility. But Steiner says it does not exist in fact, nor is it in keeping with the more important phenomena, for what happens in what we call heat conduction is not "conduction" in any proper sense. He compares it to placing a row of boys on a metal rod that is heated at one end. As the rod becomes hot the boys cry out, first one, then the next, and so on. But it would never occur to us to say that what we heard from the first boy was conducted to the second, the third, and so on. When physicists apply heat and perceive it moving down the rod, they are really observing how the body of the rod reacts, one part after another, to the warmth being, just as the boys standing on the rod yell out. You cannot say the yells are "conducted."

Returning to the prior discussion, the heat, light and chemical effects in the spectrum can be initially portrayed in the following line:

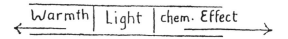

But if we want to construct a picture of this spectrum, we must not think of light, heat and chemical effects as stretched out in a straight line, but rather as shown in the following diagram:

Thus, it is not possible to remain in the plane of light effects if we wish to symbolize either the heat or chemical effects. We have to move out of this plane, leaving only the light effects in it. But if we reserved the positive sign for heat and the negative for chemical effects, we cannot use either of these for light effects. We have to use *imaginary numbers*. In essence, these involve the square root of a negative number.[30]

30. See 8 Brit 826-827, "number system" and 14 Brit 72 at 75, "Arithmetic…Complex numbers".

When the positive and negative factors of the warmth (red) and chemical (violet) bands are considered, it is easy to see that the color circle with the peach-blossom above cannot be thought of as being closed up in a circle in one plane. We here begin to see the development of the *spiral*. Steiner was able, in answer to a question posed by one of his hearers, to relate this discussion of spirals to what he called, even in his day, *superimaginary* (hypercomplex) numbers.[31] We shall explore the immense significance of the spiral in understanding fire later in this essay. Steiner went on to suggest the following correspondences between the fourfold human being and mathematics:

Physical = Positive numbers (+)

Etheric = Negative numbers (-)

Astral = Imaginary numbers

Ego = Superimaginary numbers (also called hypercomplex)

One who has the organ to perceive these things finds something highly remarkable here. The same sort of difficulty that meets one in considering superimaginary numbers also meets one when the attempt is made to apply the science of the inorganic to the phenomena of life. It cannot be done with these concepts of the inorganic. It is necessary for us to recognize how the purely mathematical leads up to the problem of life. With the facilities at hand today we can handle the phenomena of light, heat and chemical action, but we cannot handle what is evidently connected with these, namely, the closing off of the spectrum, which cannot be expressed by the same kind of formulae. The matter requires that we see as the most essential aspect not the quantitative mechanical change from one energy to another, but rather a truly qualitative transformation (cf. 1 Cor 15, esp. vs. 51, "we shall all be changed"). Such things as characterizing heat as a bombardment or collision between molecules and atoms or between these and the walls of a vessel would not have arisen if it had been seen that, even when we calculate,

---

31. See 13 Brit 252 at 255, "Algebra ... Quaternions and hypercomplex numbers." An editorial footnote to Steiner's lecture at this point (p. 150; 195) states,

"Superimaginary (hypercomplex) numbers ..." P. A. M. Dirac introduced superimaginary numbers into atomic physics for access to a deeper understanding of the electron. This step, in conjunction with the concepts of the quantum theory and the theory of relativity, created the possibility to think "anti-matter" within the thought forms of atomic physics. This "anti-matter" is capable of destroying matter.

we must take into account the qualitative differences between various forms of energy. Otherwise, we have but a one-sided mathematics in physics.

Thus, it seems fairly certain that a relationship must exist between heat, light and chemical effects, on the one hand, and the X, Y and Z realms, on the other.

Gas manifests in its material configuration what heat is doing. From this interplay, we should also be able to conceive of the difference between the X realm and the gaseous. Consider that light does not relate in the same way to gas as does heat. Temperature changes in air space when heat passes through, but not when light passes through.

As we've seen, fluidity stands between gas and solid, heat between X and gas. Also the solid realm gives a picture of the fluid, fluid a picture of the gaseous, and gaseous a picture of heat. We can thus say that the X realm can be a picture of heat, while heat is itself pictured in the gaseous. So in the gaseous realm we have, as it were, *pictures of pictures* of the X realm. These pictures of pictures are really present when light passes through air. We are not dealing with a direct picturing but rather the light has an independent status in the air. Look at the diagram:

z	Life
y	Chemical effects
x	Light
	Heat
	Gaseous realm
	Fluid
	Solid
U	

If we extend this train of thought we can identify Y with chemical effects and Z with life effects (see I-22). Just as there is a certain independence between the light realm and the gaseous, so also would such independence exist in the interplay between chemical and fluid. Indeed, in order to call forth chemical action, solutions are always necessary; and in these solutions chemical action is related to the fluid as light is to air. We then would expect to find the Z realm associated with the solid. Formerly, we knew solid bodies only as forms, but now we can come to conceive of things that are very real in our lives:

X in gas is simply light-filled gas,

Y in fluid is fluidity in which chemical processes are going on, and

Z in solid matter is life effects acting in solids.

But there is no such thing as life effects in solid bodies. We know that under earthly conditions a certain degree of fluidity is necessary for life. However misdirected their programs might otherwise be, our scientists hope to find fluid conditions on other heavenly bodies so that life might exist there. Under earthly conditions life effects are not present in the purely solid state. But these earthly conditions force us to establish the hypothesis that such a condition is not beyond the realm of possibility, for the order in which we have been able to think of these things necessarily leads to this.

This leads us to see that in the earthly domain, solids, fluids and gases in their supplementary relations to light, chemical action, and life phenomena represent something that has died out. Heat stands as if set off by itself in a certain way (i.e., it is the one etheric condition still intertwined with its material manifestation, as depicted in I-22). The other relationships above are not directly expressed under earthly conditions. This might help us to live with the circumstance, which we shall encounter in the next essay, that science has not yet been able to connect light directly with any material character. Sound is produced under earthly conditions by waves in the material gas. But not so with light. So-called light waves are only a faulty hypothesis that has some utility in practice, but conclusively fails in other experiments.

The relationships that can exist in the earthly domain point to something that was once there but is there no longer. They force us to bring *time* concepts into the picture. A human corpse forces us to this. The form of the human body would never have arisen without the soul-spiritual element.[32] The corpse forces us to say that what is there has been abandoned by something. This is no different from saying that the earthly solid has been abandoned by life, the earthly fluid by the emanations of the chemical effects, the earthly gaseous by the emanations of the

---

32. This alone reveals the insanity of any thought of cloning a human being. It seems as bereft of spiritual justification as the suggestion made by an Iowa State math professor that we should just blow up the Moon in order to solve our climatic catastrophes, though other professors completely repudiate the idea (see *People*, June 24, 1991, p. 84).

light effects. And just as we look back from the corpse to life, so we look from the solid bodies of the Earth back to a former physical condition, when the solid was bound up with the living.[33]

At that time the Earth was not solid as we now understand the solid condition, no more than the corpse of today was a corpse five days ago. Solids were not found in an independent state anywhere on the Earth and only occurred bound to the living. Fluid existed only bound to chemical effects, and gases only bound to light effects. Earlier we saw these separations ("fissions") taking place in the etheric world in the "creations" of Gen 1. So we are forced by physics to admit a previous period of time when realms now torn apart on the Earth existed together. The realms of the gaseous, fluid and solid are now found on one side (of the "tree of life"; Gen 3,22-24; I-22), and on the other are the realms of light, chemical effects and life. Earlier they were within each other.

Heat (fire) had an intermediate position, not sharing such kinship of material and more etheric natures, but participating in both the material and the etheric, and being the condition of equilibrium between the two—ether and matter at the same time. By its dual nature we find everywhere in heat a difference in level, an observation without which we cannot understand or arrive at anything in the realm of heat phenomena. But this fact alone points up the significance of fire in scripture as the only medium in which the spiritual and material worlds can meet—and the reason why Christ came to cast it upon the Earth, for humanity (and all creation; Rom 8,19-23) must pass through that sphere in its eventual transformation back into spiritual being. This is what the book of Revelation is disclosing, and the reason it is still not comprehended to this day.

Here we come to something much more fundamental and important than the so-called "second law of thermodynamics,"[34] for the latter really tears a certain realm of phenomena out of its proper connection, a realm that is bound up with other phenomena and essentially and profoundly

---

33. Anyone who doubts this, that at one point life ether and archetypal solids were bound up together but have since separated, or that the other three ethers were also at one time bound up with their present earthly (material) counterparts, should read Teilhard de Chardin's powerful classic *The Phenomenon of Man* (PHEN), especially the chapter entitled "The Advent of Life." Teilhard was almost a generation behind Steiner, but the circumstances indicate that their work, though so very closely related in their amazingly cognate disclosures, was never in any formal sense coordinated and that they were not aware of each other.

34. This "law" states that whenever heat is changed into mechanical work some heat remains unchanged.

modified by them. If you will only see that the gas/light, fluid/chemical and solid/life relationships were once one, then you can also come to think of the two polarically opposed portions of the heat realm, namely, ether and ponderable matter, as originally united. Heat was then completely different from heat as we think of it now (e.g., Old Saturn, or its primal earthly recapitulation in Gen 1,2). We can come to see that physical phenomena today are limited in their meaning by *time*; physics is not eternal, something Bible students, of all people, should grasp.

Inasmuch as not all heat can be converted into mechanical work—some heat always remains as heat in the conversion—all energy must finally change into heat and the Earth come to a heat death (as we have seen, with the Bible in accord). But the same principle applies also at higher levels. For we can show likewise that when we produce light from heat not all of the heat reappears as light. Some gas (e.g., smoke, etc.) results. It is similar with the relationship between light and chemical phenomena. But this leads us to imagine the whole cosmic spectrum as bent around into a circle. It runs down here on this side, but then runs back up on the other. Thus even if the heat death actually occurs on one side, on the other side something occurs to reestablish the equilibrium, and that something opposes the world's death with universal creation, as in the case of "a new heaven and a new earth" (2 Pet 3,13; Rev 21,1; Is 65,17 and 66,22).

We must symbolize the world process with a circle. Then we can include within it what lies in our various realms. But even then we cannot think of it as a circle in a single plane, but rather as a spiral, for we have not yet, for instance, included the acoustic phenomena in these realms, and they do not lie in the same plane as the fluid but rather in the gaseous. Here Steiner gives us the following diagram in which he adds the interrelationship involved in sound or tone effects:

z	Life effects
y	Chemical effects
x	Light realm
	Warmth
x'	Gaseous
y'	Fluid
z'	Solid
	U

We must conceive, however, that it is impossible for us to think that this working of one realm into another is limited, for instance, to the activity of heat in the gaseous realm. All realms work within each other, calling forth certain effects in this or that field of action. So we can say that although chemical effects work primarily in the fluid medium (since they have an inner kinship to it), we must also picture the working of chemical effects in the gaseous element. This clarifies what was, for me at least, the confusing labeling of the one etheric condition as the dual chemical and/ or sound ether. It can also help to point to one of scripture's more profound disclosures, where the human word will be effective not just in the gaseous (sound) realm but also in the denser fluid realm, the lowest in which life now exists on Earth.[35]

By "chemical effects" we should not think only of chemical processes, but rather of something that comes to clear manifestation in the blue-violet portion of the spectrum and is penetrated with an inner spiritual element (e.g., photochemical processes, such as fluorescence and phosphorescence). Here we have them revealing themselves somewhat independently in relation to material existence. Just as light acts independently within the gaseous, so also does its next higher ether realm act within the gaseous. We are really dealing with the chemical effects as they interpenetrate the material realm—something that to begin with has nothing to do with ponderable matter but interpenetrates it—the fluid first because of its inner relationship, but then the next element, the gaseous. In the fluid element, the chemical effect seizes upon matter.

Let us assume, however, that in the gaseous realm the action does not reach the point where the chemical effect lays hold of matter itself. Rather let us assume that it works on matter from the outside only, remaining a bit more removed from it than is possible in the fluid realm. Then something reveals itself as a side effect of the chemical effects more strongly in the gaseous realm than in the fluid. The imponderable has a certain independence here from the material carrier. In chemical processes proper,

---

35. Looking ahead to our discussion in "Blood," we encounter Steiner's statement (and drawing of the phallic appearance of the air stream that produces the human voice) that the larynx will evolve into the instrument of human reproduction (cf. Mt 24,19; Mk 13,17; Lk 23,29, where one will not want to be "with child" at that *time*), and its relationship to the "rod of iron" (Rev 2,27; 12,5 and 19,15) by which the higher "I Am" shall govern, when the mouth will be truly a "sharp sword" like the "Word" of God—when the human will reproduce by the word in the image of its creator.

the imponderable lays hold strongly of the material. In the gaseous realm, however, we come upon domains where there is not such a strong connection, where the imponderable does not remain within matter. This is the case in the acoustical domain, with the effects of tone. While in chemical-material processes we have a complete immersion of the imponderable in matter, in tone we have a persistence, a self-preservation, of the imponderable in gaseous matter. This leads us to the point where we have to say that there must be a reason why in fluids the imponderable seizes directly on the material, while in tone effects arising in the gaseous realm the imponderable is less able to do this.

It is the difference between solids and gases, what tends to form as opposed to what tends to escape form. Forces of the Earth (solids) are involved in fluids when the imponderable chemical ether lays hold of matter. But the reverse force in the gaseous realm tends to overcome the Earth, removing the imponderable from the Earth. This is the peculiarity of the tone (sound) world, the world of the Word. It is this that gives the particular characteristics to the physics of tone or acoustics. What lives in us as a *subjective* experience of the world of tone is far, far removed from the physics of acoustics. This is due to the fact that the tone element preserves its individuality. It reveals its origin to us, showing itself to be determined from the periphery of the universe, while chemical processes active in fluid matter show themselves to be determined from the center of the Earth.

Considered correctly, in chemical processes we have to do with a certain relationship between $\underline{Y}$ and fluid, and in the activity of tone we have to do with a certain relationship between $\underline{Y}$ and gas, as in the diagram above. Here we see the chemical realm, which lies just above the light realm, playing into two adjoining realms in the material world (fluid and gas). Now let us consider whether the same thing applies in the case of the light realm. Does it also play into two material realms? Yes, but in a slightly modified way. For the material realms that it plays into are warmth (fire) and gas, and warmth is a composite of both ponderable and imponderable—the meeting place between the two. So what might we expect?

When we move from earthly forces (gravity) that manifest in form to those resulting in liquid surfaces, we come to a sphere. In other words, gravity applies to both solids and liquids. But how must we picture the situation where we move outside the sphere? We must imagine the opposite condition. In the drawing on the left we have solids filled with matter, while on the right we have space filled with negative matter, i.e., space emptied out. We must consider that an emptying of space is possible. And we must also consider that countless such empty spaces are

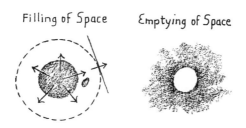

Filling of Space   Emptying of Space

involved in our universe. We can readily conceive, as Steiner assures us is true, that it would not be possible to have a separation of continents from bodies of water, or the difference between north and south poles, if there were only one such hollow empty space in the Earth's environment. Rather, these "matterless" spaces must work in from various directions. What the ancients designated as planets were primarily empty spaces. The bodies we call planets merely circumscribe by their orbits the spheres of their respective empty spaces that are the "planets" of ancient reference. Now, contrary to what our "scientists" tell us, Steiner says that if they were able to actually observe the interior of the Sun, they would find it emptied of matter. Only the spheres radiating out from its surface contain gaseous matter. We may picture the Sun as being a sphere entirely emptied of matter, as is the case with all the radiant stars in the sky.

Now all of these empty spaces, be they the empty planetary spheres or the more concentrated, so to speak, emptiness of the Sun and outer stars, produce the exact opposite of gravity, namely, suction. This suction works in upon the Earth. Indeed there is an interaction of the suction of all planets with each other. But they all revolve around the Sun because of its greater power of suction. And beyond the solar system, the more subtle influences upon Earth evolution come from the suction of these outer empty spaces of the stars.

The earliest theory suggesting the existence of the mind-boggling, so-called "black holes" in our universe seems to have come from Karl Schwarzschild in 1916 (2 Brit 255, "black hole" and 10 Brit 548, "Schwarzschild, Karl"). I'm not aware that Steiner ever discussed the black hole phenomenon. But it would seem implicit in his imagination of the Sun, the outer stars and the empty planetary spheres. Our scientists speak of the black hole as originating from the gravitational inward collapse of a massive star, as though the matter within the star somehow is exhausted. They come to the idea of suction, but perhaps not in the right way. The black hole is, indeed, the polar opposite of the star. The star gives out light and heat, while the black hole pulls them in. The star represents the presence of spiritual beings too exalted to exist in matter, e.g., the Elohim of our Sun. The "black hole" represents an imaginary point totally devoid of spirit where matter has presumably collapsed with unimaginable and destructive concentration upon itself.

These black hole comments are mine, an inferred hypothesis not to my knowledge articulated by Steiner, but merely offered for the reader's contemplation.

The suction effect of space is obvious to all today because of air travel. Pressurized cabins are the norm. At an altitude of 30,000 feet, air will explode outward through a sudden hole in the side of an airliner, violently thrusting matter through it. What is pressure on the inside of the wall is suction on the outside. And at that elevation, truly empty space is not yet reached.

Air travel was a thing of the future in Steiner's time. But he did say that the mutual interaction between the earthly and the cosmic is due to the suction-like effect of emptied spaces, while in the formative forces there are pressure effects. Suction and pressure are polar opposites, just as are spirit and matter. How wonderful this concept becomes when we consider the unspeakable spiritual level of the Christ and the statement in John's Gospel, "And I, when I am lifted up from the earth, will draw all men to myself" (Jn 12,32). His "lifting up" on the Cross is only an earthly image (involving Death) of his Ascension in the spirit into heaven. As the spiritual Sun, he then draws the spirits of human beings to him just as the Sun draws the planets into their orbit around it.

And who can fail to see in these polar opposites what is so familiar in John's Gospel: "That which is born of the flesh is flesh, and that which is born of the Spirit is spirit.... The wind blows where it wills, and you hear the sound of it, but you do not know whence it comes or whither it goes" (Jn 3,6,8). Christ is here (vs 8) speaking of the gaseous realm (air), but he then does what Steiner does, saying that it is a picture of the spirit world: "so it is with every one who is born of the Spirit." The elements are signs and symbols that *picture*.

The atoms and molecules that scientists speak of are only the materialized, fractal, dwarf-like expression (images) of these extraterrestrial, cosmic interactions.

Steiner carries us still further. There is a force in the left drawing (below) that fills space with matter. In the right, we still have the same force but there it is spread out in such a way that it must ultimately come to the condition where there is an emptying of space. And a region must exist between them where space is torn apart, so to speak.

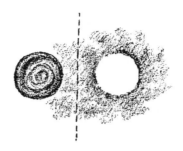

When we go from the ponderable into the imponderable, space is torn apart. And something enters through the tear that was not there before. Something nonspatial, namely, lightning, enters through the tear. Space is torn apart where the lightning flash appears. The lightning fills the space intensively, but not dimensionally, erupting like the blood from a cut. Always, Steiner says, when light appears accompanied by heat space is torn apart, revealing what dwells within it. In the flash of lightning, we see the inner content of space.

Contemplate here how the first hierarchy, the highest, manifests in Earth evolution. See **I-29**. There, with supporting reference from Steiner's lectures, we find the Seraphim manifesting in lightning and fire, the Cherubim in clouds and air, and the Thrones in solid matter (hence their name). The point where the Seraphim's "flaming sword," i.e., lightning (the imponderable that produces both fire and light), meets the Cherubim in the air (ponderable matter) is where the tree of life (the imponderable) and the tree of knowledge (the ponderable) were divided when humanity descended into materiality, i.e., was driven from the garden (Gen 3,22-24). It is there that the spatial becomes the nonspatial, and vice versa. In Steiner's words, space is "torn apart." We might say instead that "the veil [of matter] is rent" (Mt 27,51; Mk 15,38; Heb 10,19-20; Ex 26,31-35; Heb 9,3,8).

So when we ascend from the ponderable to the imponderable, passing
through the realm of heat, the heat wells out in the transition from the
pressure effects of ponderable matter to the suction effects of imponderable spirit. Small wonder that such massive heat radiates from the point
of transition at the surface of the Sun.

If our proud science of today is to move to a higher level, to what
Steiner calls spiritual science, so that it can come closer to understanding the mysteries of our existence, it must begin to apply these concepts
to such areas as what it now calls the "conduction" of heat, the hearing
of sound, the cause of disease, and countless other domains where spirit
manifests in the presence of materiality. Only by moving through these
points will we learn how "the heavens declare his righteousness" (Ps
50,6), and only so will science and religion again become one, as they
once were, but now transformed at a higher level. We are talking here
not about a hike, but about a long journey. But a start must be made.
A change in the way of thinking (what John the Baptist called "repentance") is necessary. But by undertaking this journey and moving
through these levels, humanity will evolve new organs of perception
opening to it more and more of the divine intelligence administered by
the Archangel Michael (Dan 10,13-14,21; Rev 12,7-9; see also *The
Incredible Births of Jesus*, Epilogue citing the book of Enoch at pp. 86-
88).

Then we will come to know and understand what Christ meant when
he said he had come to cast fire upon the Earth.

Fire, The Spiral and the One Hundred Forty-Four Thousand

"This is how the world began—as a coil.... The first people came up
from the middle and walked around in a spiral." So began an article in
People for January 22, 1996 (p. 63), about a sixty-one-year-old Navajo
woman who wove such designs in her baskets. "A relative of her grand-
mother's taught [her] to weave the tales of supernatural beings" when she
was eleven. Now, a century after the last embers of Indian conflict have
died out, many people are looking more thoughtfully at the ancient sha-
manistic legends of Native Americans. Even here, in this statement from
a simple Navajo basketweaver we come upon a deep truth, known of old,
but, not unlike the Copernican rediscovery of the spherical shape of our
Earth and the heliocentric nature of our solar system, only now beginning

to flicker back into human consciousness after millennia of lost consciousness surrounding the Incarnation of Christ.

FIRE AND *PHI*

Before Aristotle and later Arabism[36] laid a more secular "scientific" slant on earthly phenomena, Plato had summarized his gleanings about creation from the ancient mysteries in a work called *Timaeus.* The threads from this work are clearly to be seen in the later writings of Philo, Clement of Alexandria, Origen and other Church Fathers, but especially in the Logos that opens John's Gospel as well as in the teachings of Paul on the hierarchies as finally reduced from oral tradition to writing by Pseudo-Dionysius (PSEUD), who wrote in the name of Paul's Athenian convert, Dionysius the Areopagite (Acts 17,34).[37] It is well that we start with Plato's words in our search for the relationship of *fire,* the *spiral* and the *one hundred forty-four thousand*; thus we read (emphasis and footnotes added):

Now that which is created is of necessity corporeal, and also visible and tangible. And nothing is visible where there is no fire, or tangible which has no solidity, and nothing is solid without earth. Wherefore also God in the beginning of creation made the body of the universe to consist of fire and earth. But two things cannot be rightly put together without a third; there must be some bond of union between them. *And the fairest bond is that which makes the most complete fusion of itself and the things which it combines; and proportion is best adapted to effect such a union. For whenever in any three numbers, whether cube or square, there is a mean, which is to the last*

---

36. During 1924, the last year of Steiner's life, he gave a series of lectures that have been published in eight volumes entitled *Karmic Relationships,* Vols. 1-8. In every one of these he speaks of the Arabian cultural influence that emanated through Europe from the eighth and ninth century court of one Haroun al Raschid of Baghdad (see 5 Brit 731, "Harun ar-Rashid"), calling it "Arabism." He carefully distinguished it from Aristotelianism much as Saint Thomas Aquinas did in his battle against that influence several centuries later. While Aristotle directed human thinking toward earthly phenomena and is thus the putative founder of scientific thinking, it is Arabism that focused that thinking upon the purely materialistic approach that has enthralled scientists to this day. The depth of the distinction between Aristotelianism and this materialist approach to science can best be appreciated in the light of my concluding essay in *The Burning Bush* entitled "Pillars on the Journey."

37. That Paul was strongly influenced by Philo, see the essay "Egypt" in *The Burning Bush,* esp. pp. 533-535.

*term what the first term is to it; and again, when the mean is to the first
term as the last term is to the mean—then the mean becoming first and
last, and the first and last becoming means, they will all of them of necessity come to be the same, and having become the same with one another will be all one.*[38] If the universal frame had been created a
surface only and having no depth, a single mean would have sufficed
to bind together itself and the other terms; but now, as the world
must be solid, and solid bodies are always compacted not by one
mean but by two, God placed water and air in the mean between fire
and earth, and made them to have the same proportion so far as was
possible (as fire is to air so is air to water, and as air is to water so is
water to earth); and thus he bound and put together a visible and
tangible heaven. And for these reasons, and out of such elements
which are in number four, the body of the world was created, and it
was harmonized by proportion, and therefore has the spirit of
friendship; and having been reconciled to itself, it was indissoluble
by the hand of any other than the framer.[39] (31b-32c; 7 GB 448)

Literally, this "fairest bond" language describes any geometric progression. Simple cell division (one, two, four, eight, …) is an example. However, there is considerable acceptance of the idea that the highest example
of this "fairest bond" is what has come to be called the "golden mean,"
designated by the Greek letter *phi*. As we shall see, its character and meaning were also known and applied by the Egyptians much earlier. Later in
Timaeus (62a; 7 GB 462), Plato says:

And we must not forget that the original figure of fire (that is, the
pyramid), more than any other form, has a dividing power which cuts
our bodies into small pieces, and thus naturally produces that affection
which we call heat; and hence the origin of the name" [fire, or *phi*].

Paul similarly identifies this *phi* or fire in Heb 4,12 when he says, "For

38. Note the presence here of Johannine and Pauline expressions, the Alpha and Omega of
Revelation (as also "the first and last" in Second Isaiah) and divine "oneness" of all; Rev 1,8;
1,17-18; 21,6 and 22,13; Is 41,4; 44,6 and 48,12; Jn 17,20-26 and Eph 1,9-10.
39. This accords with the anthroposophical insight that Earth evolution both began and will
end with fire, as expressed in Gen 1,2 (the etheric fire or warmth there indicated as a
recapitulation of Ancient Saturn's condition in the original "fireball" of the Earth Condition
of Consciousness; see *The Burning Bush*, p. 18); 2 Pet 3,10; Rev 20,14 and 21,8.

the word of God is living and active, sharper than any two-edged sword, piercing to the division of soul and spirit...." The pyramid Plato speaks of here is a tetrahedron, the three-sided pyramid that, with its base, has a total of four sides, the least condensed of any solid geometrical body with entirely flat sides (see fn 20 above). But as we shall see, the Egyptians enshrined *phi* and other secrets in their four-sided pyramids also, and these forms still thus take a name meaning fire.

But what is meant by *phi*?

Normally it is given a geometric definition. It can be stated most simply as a geometric progression where *A* is to *B* as *B* is to *A* plus *B*.[40] If, applying such progression, the line *XZ* below is divided at *Y* so as to form segments *A* and *B*, and *A* is given a value of one, then *B* will have a value of

1.618, and *XZ* (the sum of *A* and *B*) will have a value of 2.618. We can at once determine that the ratio 1/1.618 equals .618, while the ratio 1.618/2.618 also equals .618. And we could continue on ad infinitum showing these ratios between two successive numbers of the series. The place where *Y* bisects *XZ* is known as the "golden section" and segment *B* as the "golden mean" or words of similar import. Kepler (1571-1630) apotheosized it as a divine proportion as follows:

> Geometry has two great treasures: one is the theorem of Pythagoras; the other, the division of a line into extreme and mean ratio. The first we may compare to a measure of gold; the second we may name a precious jewel.[41]

It is the mean 1.618 (segment *B* above) that is known as *phi* for it both cuts and builds, as shall be amply demonstrated herein, as "the fairest bond" among the fair, the most divine building block. It is also mathematically stated as: one plus the square root of five divided by two; or (1 + 2.236) / 2 = 1.618. It is portrayed in the following figure,[42] where we can already see a relationship to the circle beginning to emerge:

---

40. See Robert Lawlor's essay "Ancient Temple Architecture" in *Homage to Pythagoras* (HP), p. 87.
41. Quoted as the head note for Chapter 2, "The Divine Proportion," by H. E. Huntley in his book *The Divine Proportion* (DP).
42. Figure used by Matila Ghyka, *The Geometry of Art and Life* (GAL), Chap. 2, "The Golden Section, Figure 1.

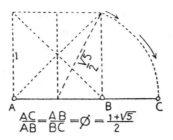

$$\frac{AC}{AB} = \frac{AB}{BC} = \emptyset = \frac{1+\sqrt{5}}{2}$$

PHI, THE GNOMON AND THE SPIRAL

This brings us to the *gnomon* and what is called "gnomonic growth." Gnomon is a Greek word meaning "one who knows,"[43] and in its geometric usage seems to be defined in most dictionaries as "the part of a parallelogram remaining after a similar smaller parallelogram has been taken from one of its corners" (WNWCD; another definition is the column or pin of a sundial the shadow of which indicates the time of day—thus relating the gnomon to time, or creation). This definition can be seen in the following figures:[44]

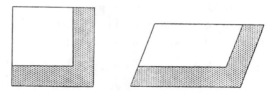

However, geometers, who have long been fascinated with gnomons, have defined the concept more broadly according to a definition that reminds us of "fractal." Huntley, echoing Hero of Alexandria (first century A.D.), says, "A gnomon is a portion of a figure which has been added to another figure so that the whole is of the same shape as the smaller figure. Hero of Alexandria showed that in any triangle *ABC* [see figure below], triangle *ABD* is a gnomon to triangle *BCD* if angle *CBD* equals angle *A*":

---

43. The reader might perhaps muse not only on the obvious relationship with the Greek word *gnosis* (divine knowledge the gnostics could only seek) but also upon the remarkable similarity to those elemental beings known as "gnomes" (see **I-12** and "The Four Elements").
44. From Thompson, *On Growth and Form* (OGF), p. 760.

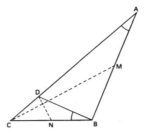

Now let us look at an elegant example of gnomonic addition, illustrated in the following figure.[45] We begin with the smallest rectangle (indicated by *e* at the lower right-hand corner),

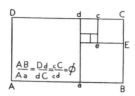

whose sides are in the golden mean (*phi*) proportion. By adding a square (the gnomon) to the longest side, a larger *phi* rectangle is created; by adding another square gnomon in like manner to the new rectangle, another larger *phi* rectangle is created, and so on. We could also start with the largest rectangle (*ABDC*) and go in the opposite direction by subtracting the square gnomon.

Now, if we draw through the same corner of each corresponding square in this figure we have another elegant form, a spiral (below)[46]

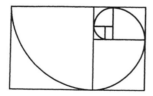

In fact this spiral is a member of a family of spirals called equiangular or logarithmic spirals. Ghyka (GAL, pp. 91-92) explains that "the logarithmic

45. GAL, Chap. 2, Figure 7.
46. From Carolan, *The Spiral Calendar* (SCAL), p. 31, Fig. 3-4.

spiral is the only plane curve in which two arcs are always 'similar' to each other, varying in dimension but not in shape (in the same spiral), and this property is extended to the surfaces determined by the vector radii limiting the arcs.... Every logarithmic spiral is directly connected to a characteristic geometric series or progression." The spiral above is of particular interest to us, for reasons that will become clear below, because it exhibits a *phi* progression.

The figure below (from DP, p. 171) demonstrates the logarithmic spiral of *phi* on the Pythagorean "golden triangle," an isosceles triangle *ABC* with base angles 72 degrees and apex angle 36 degrees. This triangle is inherent in the pentagon, being formed by drawing two diagonals from the same apex and connecting the base. In fact *phi* appears in many of the pentagon's proportions.

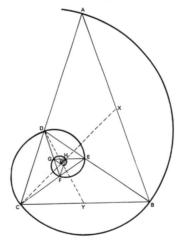

It is also well to know that *phi* gnomonic growth is popularly identified with the so-called Fibonacci ratio, named after a medieval Italian mathematician Leonardo Pisano, or Leonardo of Pisa, originally named Leonardo Fibonacci (see 7 Brit 279, "Leonardo Pisano"). In 1202 he wrote *Liber abaci* ("Book of the Abacus"), including the following problem from which his famous sequence is derived:

> A certain man put a pair of rabbits in a place surrounded on all sides by a wall. How many pairs of rabbits can be produced from that pair in a year if it is supposed that every month each pair begets a new pair which from the second month on becomes productive?

The resulting number sequence is 1, 1, 2, 3, 5, 8, 13, 21, 34, 55, 89, 144, ... After the first few numbers, the ratio between succeeding numbers ad infinitum becomes ever closer to the golden mean, *phi*, or 1.618. In truth Fibonacci had merely happened upon the divine ratio given earthly expression in the Bible under the hermetic concept "As Above, So Below." If we plot this sequence as the (Cartesian) coordinates on a graph, we get the same spiral produced by the gnomonic growth figure above. Carolyn illustrates this with a golden spiral (see figure) that has radii in the *phi* proportion at right angles.[47]

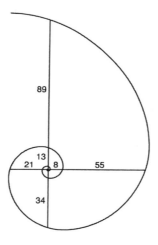

Though we have barely scratched the surface of the endless mathematical relationships to be found in *phi*,[48] these should suffice for us to move on to see its presence in creation. We can at once see that gnomonic growth is identical with the *fractal* nature of creation that we saw in the Creation essay and again in "As Above, So Below." We shall see below examples demonstrating this growth perhaps even more profoundly. The importance of the concept cannot be overemphasized.

This gnomonic growth ("As Above, So Below") according to the golden mean (or section) impresses itself as the dominant feature in nature's creation in time (and space). In GAL (p. 91), Ghyka writes, "A certain pref-

---

47. SCAL, Chap. 3, p. 32.

48. The student will find numerous excellent works on the subject. Those I have used herein include DP, GAL, HP, OGF, SCAL, *The Curves of Life* (CURV), *Elliott Wave Principle* (EWP) and the works of Peter Tompkins and René Schwaller de Lubicz more fully discussed later herein.

erence for pentagonal symmetry, a symmetry connected with the Golden Section and unknown in inanimate systems, seems to exist in the animal reign as well as in botany." We note the implied relationship above between the gnomon (the post of the sundial) and time. Time, as seasons, days and years, was planted into the etheric creative process back in Gen 1,14. Then an even larger frame of time reference was laid by "the stars" (the twelve zodiacal periods) in Gen 1,16. The symbol of transition from one era of time to another has been signified from ancient days by the zodiacal symbol of Cancer, the Crab, depicted by two separated but intertwining logarithmic spirals of precisely this gnomonic configuration (see I-81).

As in geometry any effort to identify all instances where this *phi* spiral occurs in the created world we know is doomed to failure simply because it shows up ever again in places newly investigated. It is found in the phylotaxis of plants (the helical or spiral form of leaf arrangement on the stem), pine and fir cones, the pattern of seeds in the sunflower, the trunk of the palm tree,[49] animal horns (as in the case of the Ram, the zodiacal symbol of Aries, the Cultural Era of the coming of Christ, the Lamb of God, the Creative Word; Jn 1,1-3 and I-19), the spiral form of galaxies, water running out of a drain, breaking ocean waves, or hurricanes (see "The Whirlwind" below), the dimensions of ancient temples, the Parthenon, the Great Pyramid, the most pleasing classical art, the human body (including the internal dimensions of its vertical stature, its countenance,[50] its pentagonal dimension of head and limbs as well as digits, its outer ear, the helical microscopic spiral in its DNA,[51] and the tiny microtubules in the human brain[52]), and on and on.

In *The Kingdom of Childhood* (KC), Lect. 5, Steiner spoke of the amazing nature of the theorem of Pythagoras, where "if I have a right-angled triangle here (see left diagram on following page) the area of the square of the hypotenuse is equal to the sum of the other two areas, the two squares on the other two sides."

---

49. See Penrose, *Shadows of the Mind* (SHAD), Chap. 7, p. 361, listing palm tree trunks in his discussion of Fibonacci numbers in the human brain. The symbol of the palm tree is examined later in this essay.

50. See GAL, Chap. 6, Plates XXXVI and XXXVII.

51. See Prechter, *Elliott Wave Principle* (EWP), Chap. 3, p. 96.

52. SHAD, *supra*, p. 361. In this best-selling, microbiological, rainbow-like search for how human consciousness arises in connection with the brain, Penrose seems to finally jump off at this mystical point and suggest then in his final chapter the Platonic nature of creation and human consciousness.

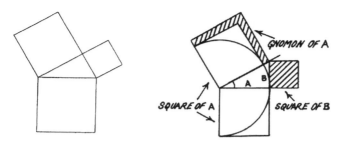

This figure can also be used to demonstrate another example related to gnomonic growth (see right digram).[53]

One must marvel upon seeing that this diagramed theorem of Pythagoras is itself a fractal that when extended in diminishing scale grows both the logarithmic spiral of the Ram's horn and an outline of the human brain. It is illustrated by Hans Lauwerier in his *Fractals* (FRAC), Chap. 4, p. 70, in the following computer-drawn figure:

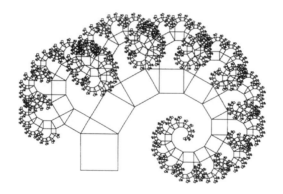

Interestingly, he terms it "a lopsided Pythagoras tree," and we may well see in it an expression of the "tree of knowledge" spawned by the descent of the human being and its separation from the "tree of life," (the Fall; Gen 3,22-24 frequently discussed in this connection in *The Burning Bush*).

CHRIST, THE J-CURVE AND THE RIGHT TIME

In order to have an adequate basis for understanding where we stand in the human evolutionary process, we must digress to review some of what has

---

53. In HP, p. 61; also Schwaller de Lubicz, HOMN, Vol. 1, pp. 144 and 193.

been said in this larger work. My "General Introduction" to *The Burning Bush* began by pointing out how Christ summarized the entire Bible story, from humanity's start in the spiritual world until its return thereto, in Luke's parable of the Prodigal Son (Lk 15,11-32). Throughout *The Burning Bush* I tried to bring out a theme that underlaid all of Steiner's teachings, namely, that the human being, and all creation as its incident, descended gradually over very long evolutionary stages from the spiritual world in a process of solidification from the rarest form of matter into its present highly densified condition, and that the escape from this condition and reascent back into the spiritual world is taking place now, also over very long evolutionary periods, made possible by the Incarnation of Christ at just the "right time," when humanity had reached a point beyond which it could not go and hope ever to be able to reascend into its original home.[54]

Take note of the schematics portrayed in I-1 and I-2. The position of Earth evolution is detailed as the fourth Condition of Consciousness with three preceding and three to follow, all as a part of the long human journey. In order to portray the mineral-physical stage of Earth evolution (i.e., the Physical Condition of Form in the Mineral Condition of Life), we must drop down on those charts to the two lower series of seven stages, called Evolutionary Epochs and Cultural Ages, respectively. We are at present in the fifth Great (or Evolutionary) Epoch, called the post-Atlantean. Within it, we are in the fifth Cultural Age, called European. Each such Age corresponds with the period of a zodiacal sign of 2,160 years (one-twelfth of the period of 25,920 years it takes the Sun to go through all twelve signs).[55] The Noah account is the Bible's description of the passage from the Atlantean

---

54. See, for instance, *The Burning Bush* pp. 1, 34-35, 220-223, 254, 283-285, 532-533, 540-542 and 550; also I-81 and I-87. Our theologians have missed the immense significance of what was meant by "right time," a clear New Testament concept relating precisely to this evolutionary scenario; see Mk 1,15; Rom 5,6; Gal 4,4; Eph 1,10 and 1 Pet 1,20.

55. Until the student is well advanced in the study of anthroposophy, it would be well not to try to extend the 2,160 year period to Epochs or Conditions (of Form, Life or Consciousness) prior to the present post-Atlantean Epoch (called the "European or "Aryan"), or certainly not further back than the Atlantean Epoch in any event. An excellent article on the problems of extending it further back is Dankmar Bosse's "How Old is the Earth?", *Journal of Anthroposophic Medicine*, Vol. 11, #1, Spring 1994, pp. 50-56. Certainly the separation of the Sun and Moon from Earth (see I-2 and I-27) would be essential for any measurement of time as we conceive of it (cf. Gen 1,14; even there still only in the etheric state). There is probably a close analogy between what was said in "The Nativity" (in *The Burning Bush*) about biblical generations prior to Abraham not being measured by single lives but by the duration of the lengthy blood-related memory of ancient times. *(continued on following page)*

Epoch to our present post-Atlantean Epoch. It occurred about the time the last great ice age ended, with the melting ice and the condensing mists. ("Nephilim" in Gen 6,4 means "mist people," *nephos* being "cloud" in Greek). The condensation of the enveloping mists permits the first appearance of a "rainbow" in Gen 9,13, as the Sun could begin to be seen. Archaeology shows us that the first appearance of civilization in the rest of the Earth begins as life on Atlantis was becoming more hazardous up to and through its final cataclysmic submergence around ten to twelve thousand years ago. Atlanteans emigrated both to the east and west, but the dominant cultural influence was that of Noah, or the one known as "Manu" who founded the Ancient Indian culture of the first Cultural Age.[56]

It helps to visualize the evolutionary process in the form of a parabola.[57] The Great Evolutionary Epochs would appear on it as follows;

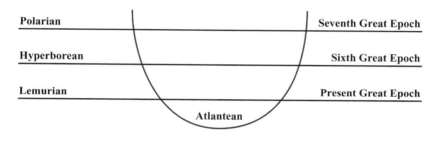

55. *(continued from previous page)* Far longer periods probably comprised the earlier equivalents to the Cultural Ages of the post-Atlantean Epoch, and it is not unreasonable to contemplate that the "time" line was progressively more and more elongated as we look up the ladder from Age to Epoch to the respective Conditions of Form, then Life, then Consciousness (see I-1 and I-2).

56. The east and west migration from Atlantis suggests that, with the probable exception of the Eskimo in Alaska, the American Indians came from Atlantis rather than having migrated across an earlier land mass where the Bering Straits now are. One of the most complete archaeological excavations on the North American continent is the Lubbock Lake Site, Lubbock, Texas. The first presence of humans at the site was about 10,000 B.C., corresponding with the first evidence of civilizations from the migration eastward.

57. There are four types of conic sections, namely, circle, ellipse, parabola and hyperbola. All four can be seen in the figures below (from 19 Brit 903, "Geometry," and 23 Brit 568, "Mathematics, The History of"). As these references indicate, the circle is an ellipse produced by a section perpendicular to the axis; the parabola by a cutting plane parallel to a slope of the cone; the ellipse by a section that completely cuts one cone; and a hyperbola by a plane cutting both upper and lower cones. The ellipse is said to have an eccentricity less than unity; the hyperbola an eccentricity greater than unity; and the parabola an eccentricity of unity. The ellipse has two inner focal points, the parabola one. But the parabola may be thought of as an elongated ellipse with its center and one focus and vertex all coinciding at infinity. Kepler showed us that our planets move in ellipses. *(continued on following page)*

and the Cultural Eras of the present Great Epoch as follows:

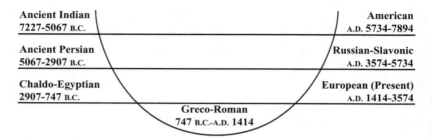

Ancient Indian 7227-5067 B.C.	**American** A.D. 5734-7894
Ancient Persian 5067-2907 B.C.	**Russian-Slavonic** A.D. 3574-5734
Chaldo-Egyptian 2907-747 B.C.	**European (Present)** A.D. 1414-3574
	Greco-Roman 747 B.C.-A.D. 1414

The point of greatest density among the Great Evolutionary Epochs would seem to be the Atlantean, the lowest point on the curve. However, Steiner has indicated that there is a lag in effect. In economic language it is called a "J-Curve," where an impulse calculated to bring a change of direction actually causes an increase in the original direction for a time before the reverse sets in. It is a reflection of what happens with the influence of our heavenly bodies. For instance, the Sun reaches its winter solstice around December 21. Theoretically, days should begin then to warm, but actually they keep getting colder till winter is more than half gone. The same is true with the summer solstice around June 21, when things should begin to cool down, but they don't until the summer is over half gone. We shall see this is true of the influence of zodiacal signs also. The deepest point of human incarnation (densification) has come in our present Great Epoch, the post-Atlantean by reason of this type of lag.

---

57. *(continued from previous page)* We should think of the journey of the Prodigal Son as a parabola that is really just one end of an ellipse with the other end, as indicated, in the infinity of the highest heaven. Then we have not only the evolutionary cycle of humanity completed, but also the cycle of life (Jas 3,6 and I-33) as the smaller fractal.

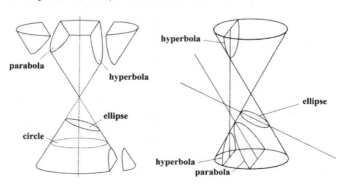

And since this lag throws the deepest point into our present Cultural Era, we see the same phenomenon when we break our post-Atlantean Epoch down into its seven Cultural Eras. The low point on the parabola of the post-Atlantean Epoch came in the Greco-Roman Era. That was the "right time." And just as there was a further densification from the Atlantean to the post-Atlantean, so also does the J-Curve effect show a further densification from the Greco-Roman Era to our present Era. We are approximately the same distance into our present Era as was the "right time" of Christ's Incarnation in the Greco-Roman. The J-Curve must soon swing rapidly in the opposite direction, at least for that portion of humanity that is to come within the *one hundred forty-four thousand* (Rev 7,4; 14,1,3; 6,11; 7,9).

This J-Curve phenomenon is yet another corroboration of what was said in *The Burning Bush* (pp. 133-136), that reincarnation was not to be taught in exoteric Christianity for two thousand years (see also the Epilogue in *The Incredible Births of Jesus*). The greatest of all impulses on Earth, the Christ Event, could change the overall downward direction of humanity only as its power could be assimilated into and appropriated by the broader human consciousness as the latter moved from Ram to Pisces, from the Cultural Age of the Lamb of God to the Cultural Age of the fishes (see I-19). We will see this more fully when we get to the "feedings" of the "four thousand" and the "five thousand," metaphors for the fourth and fifth Cultural Ages, respectively.[58] The widespread appearance of "sign of the fish" bumper stickers in our day may well be a spontaneous, though unwitting, manifestation of the arrival of the appropriate time in Pisces (the heavenly "sign-of-the-fish") for humanity to recognize the reality and grace in the higher "law" of the Father God, the law of karma (see the many citations and discussions of Mt 5,17 in *The Burning Bush*).

The J-Curve effect also applies in the relation of the zodiacal signs to the Cultural Eras on Earth. Chart I-19 shows that there is a time lag of twelve hundred years (actually 1,199) from the Zodiacal Ages to the Cultural Ages.[59] If we study that chart, we can see a clear connection between Cultural Ages and their respective symbols. The two most obvious, of course, are the Ages of Taurus and Aries. Figures of the bull prevailed

58. See Mt 14,13-21; 15,32-39; 16,5-12; Mk 6,32-44; 8,1-10; 8,13-21; Lk 9,10-17; Jn 6,1-14; 1 K 17,8-16; 2 K 4,42-44. See also *The Disciple Whom Jesus Loved*, p. 9.

during the Chaldo-Egyptian Era. All Bible students will be aware of this and of the findings of archaeology that overwhelmingly support it. And the relationship of Aries to the Era of Christ, the Lamb of God, is beyond question. The historical age goes back only to the Chaldo-Egyptian, but Steiner has revealed the nature of the two earlier Ages and they fit precisely with their zodiacal symbols. Ancient India represents a complete break (the Noah break) from Atlantis, and the intertwined spirals of Cancer (the Crab) mean precisely that (see I-81). The Ancient Persian is the age of the first Zarathustra, he who saw the Ahura Mazda, the descending Christ, in the Sun sphere. He saw a duality of light and darkness, characterizing the latter domain as that of Angra Mainyu (Ahriman).[60] This duality bears a relationship to the later twin falsities of Lucifer ("light-bearer") and Ahriman (see I-32). Clearly, the idea of the Twins, Gemini, is apparent. Christ's mission on Earth was forward-looking (Promethean). Its ubiquitous fish symbolism (probably none more powerfully symbolic than Jn 21) meant that it was looking ahead to what would come into the consciousness of human beings in the present Cultural Age of Pisces (A.D. 1414-3574). Again we note the "feedings" of the five thousand and the four thousand (the fourth and fifth being the Cultural Age of Christ and our present Cultural Age, respectively).[61] Christ's words in Jn 16,12 ("I have yet many things to say to you, but you cannot bear them now") are a different way of saying the same thing. Human consciousness had yet to evolve further.

Let us return to the parabola above that portrays the seven Cultural Eras. If we visualize that on a Cartesian chart where the vertical coordinates represent spiritual progress (densification/rarefication) and the horizontal coordinates the passage of time, we can see that spiritual progress was very slow in the Greco-Roman Era, slower than at any time before or since. Who could argue that in fact this has been the case. The many centuries that slid off into the "dark ages" of medieval Europe can hardly be

---

59. The revised edition of *The Burning Bush* clarifies the confusion expressed in the original edition (Chart I-19) regarding the length of the archangelic periods, and also cites Steiner's *The Spiritual Hierarchies and the Physical World* (SHPW), Lect. 7, showing a special relationship of the Archai to Venus.
60. See 12 Brit 934-936, "Zoroaster" and "Zoroastrianism," noting however that the real origin of these things was much earlier than there indicated, being in the Ancient Persian prehistoric Cultural Era.
61. See fn 58.

compared with those since the Renaissance. And who can but marvel at the acceleration of pace in the twentieth century? Unfortunately, evil and materiality have veiled the second coming from human vision (see *The Burning Bush*). In many respects, however, we must see in this a replay of the Greco-Roman Era and the conditions that prevailed at the time of Christ. In that Era humanity did not recognize the Christ in the physical body. Now Christ has come in the etheric body and humanity again fails to recognize. It has not prepared itself, and the Christ has returned in the way he said he would, as a "thief in the night."[62]

This speeding up of spiritual development, the end of the J-Curve effect, must now take hold, for it would seem that this is what Christ spoke of in his so-called "Little Apocalypse" passage: "And if those days had not been shortened, no human being would be saved; but for the sake of the elect those days will be shortened" (Mt 24,22). These words pertain more to the later Cultural Eras, when human beings will give up their sexuality and begin to reproduce through the larynx by their "word," in the image of the Father ("Alas for those who are with child and for those who give suck in those days"; Mt 24,19 and Lk 21,23; 23,29). However, the tendency toward this begins by a sharp upturn in the parabola as we can see above.

THE TRANSFIGURATION OF EGYPT

Now this brings us to the reason for these several pages of digression, which is to help us come to appreciate the relationship of our Era to the Chaldo-Egyptian. We can see from the parabola that we are to retrace the same evolutionary, spiritual stratum as that traversed during the earlier Era of the Pharoah with its pyramids, Sphinx and glorification of the mineral-physical body by mummification and elaborate entombment, the age when the "I Am" was first identified to Moses during the descent, and when Moses and the priesthood of the ancient mysteries still had clairvoyance. But in retracing all these, we are charged not with merely regaining what was lost but with transforming all of it into a higher state.

---

62. Mt 24,43-44; Lk 12,39-40; 1 Th 5,2-3; 2 Pet 3,10. Most notable is Rev 3,3, for it is said to the angel of the church in Sardis, the fifth church, meaning the fifth Cultural Era, our own. In Rev 16,15, the same phenomena repeats again, fractal-like, near the end of the sixth Great Epoch (see I-25; also "Trumpets" in *The Burning Bush*, p. 395, and the Apocalypse portion of the Creation essay herein).

We seek not the clairvoyance and mystic power belonging to the guidance by external spiritual beings and atavisms, but the manas (manna) state of Spirit Self, the purified astral body, when the "I Am" has gained complete control over it. We need not give up acquired intelligence and hard-won experience, going back to near perfect memory (including past lives). Rather we need to bring to what we have acquired over the ages the new clairvoyance and sight into the spiritual world. To get there, we need a new understanding of "the straight and narrow path" described in the Sermon on the Mount (Mt 7,13-14). It is a path revealed to us by the modern prophet, Rudolf Steiner.

I attempted in the "Egypt" essay (in *The Burning Bush*) to address essential aspects of this. But a fuller appreciation of what we face in our Era is essential if we are to comprehend the meaning of the fire that Christ came to cast upon the Earth. Only by raising our consciousness into that etheric fire will we recognize the Christ's second coming, already upon us.

Steiner indicated that mathematics represents something existing in the spiritual world. Geometrical forms, for instance, are not things we perceive with our senses. We discover them by what he calls "pure thinking," that is thinking in the lowest realm of the spiritual world. But our thinking is not what creates the forms, for they were always there to be discovered. It is, therefore, entirely appropriate that these spiritual world creatures be contemplated for the truths they can reveal to us of the activity of the higher dimensions. It was in Egypt that these things came to be known. We honor Pythagoras as their founder, but Pythagoras was initiated into the mysteries of the Egyptian temple.[63] And even those insights were presented to him during a time when the more glorious insights were fading (cf. 2 Cor 3,7,13). Built into the Great Pyramid, the Sphinx and the temples was the reflection of spiritual realities long since faded away. These must be regained with the even greater splendor that

---

63. In TOMN, Chap. 7, at p. 207, we find the following:

   The Egyptians have often affirmed that they knew the law of number. We also cannot deny that they jealously kept secret this key of knowledge. Hippolytus said, "Pythagoras learned number and measure from the Egyptians; and being struck by the plausible and difficult to communicate wisdom of the Egyptian priests, in a desire to emulate them, also prescribed the law of silence" [cf. 5 NICENE-1, pp. 81-82]. It is therefore absolutely not in the texts that we must look for this law of measure, but rather in the monuments themselves.

awaits humanity's development of the purified astral body. The new clairvoyance will come through a loosened etheric body, but a purified astral body is the doorway to it. The manna of old, the Chaldo-Egyptian clairvoyance (Ex 16,31; Rev 2,17) must be regained and transformed now in our present Cultural Era (Rev 3,1-7; Jn 6,31,49; 1 Cor 10,3; Heb 9,4). Christ said, "You will know the truth, and the truth will make you free" (Jn 8,32). Emancipation of the etheric body from the veil of the physical is the "freedom" that will make direct perception of the truth possible. Steiner, with this direct perception, has brought us that "truth" so that by earnestly pursuing it we can also become "free."

Steiner aside, I know of no modern student who has penetrated so deeply into the consciousness of the Egyptian mind and soul as René Schwaller de Lubicz. Some four centuries ago Kepler acknowledged reaching back into that consciousness ("I have stolen the golden chalice of the Egyptians") in divining his third law of planetary movements.[64] But today's Egyptologists, as well as its scientists and theologians, tend to think of human consciousness and intelligence in that ancient time as resting on the same essential mind and soul foundation, cultural environment and experience aside, as they do today. At great length Steiner has shown us that this is not so. Vol. 1, *The Burning Bush*, makes this point throughout (see I-24). In his excellent *Secrets of the Great Pyramid* (SGP), Peter Tompkins cites Schwaller de Lubicz repeatedly on most critically important points. To read Schwaller's work is to transport oneself back in time to a consciousness far different from today's, to a time when signs and symbols were themselves a language, archetypal in nature. It might be well to contemplate that the biblical assertion "the whole earth had one language and few words" (Gen 11,1) fell between the time of Noah (when human evolution moved from Atlantis to other continents) and that of Abraham (almost midway into the Chaldo-Egyptian Cultural Era; see I-19). Moses came later in this same time frame, and Paul refers to his soul consciousness as one of "fading splendor" (2 Cor 3,7,13), that phenomenon in human evolution that Isaiah was later commanded to announce (Is 6,9-13) in terms that ring loudly through the New Testament. In the light of that phenomenon, the command to the angel of the fifth church (our own Cultural Era) to "Awake" for he "will come like a thief" sounds loud and clear, and the haunting

---

64. Id., Vol., 1, Chap. 9, p. 274.

sound of Isaiah as the Chaldo-Egyptian Cultural Era came to a close (see I-19 and I-25) rings down to us as the angel of our "church" closes its message to us: "He who has an ear, let him hear" (Rev 3,6).[65]

Schwaller, like Steiner, requires a type of disciplined contemplation that has not proved very inviting to modern materialistic thinking in either science or religion. But it offers a means of piercing the veil of matter and permitting a higher view of reality where both domains become one.

Our tendency, when we see the marvels of geometric analysis relating to *phi*, is to think of *phi* in mathematical terms. But Schwaller sets us right on this, saying, "The golden section is not a product of mathematical imagination, but the natural principle of the laws of equilibrium."[66] And earlier, "The golden number, or sacred number (designated by the symbol ϕ), is to be regarded as a creative or separating power; it is the power that *provokes* the scission, and consequently is not derived arithmetically from the root of 5, because the *power five* is not a cause but a result of this function *phi*."[67] And since *phi* expresses itself outwardly in phenomena, in ways that are the most pleasing of all, we must conclude that it is a primal creative law, not caused but merely observed mathematically. When Schwaller speaks of it as a "creative or separating power" he sounds like Paul, in Hebrews 4,12: "The word of God is living and active, sharper than any two-edged sword, piercing to the division of soul and spirit, of joints and marrow," the same two-edged sword of Rev 1,16.

We don't have the luxury of dwelling long on Schwaller. But before moving on, there is a further mathematical expression of higher reality that he reveals to us by his interpretation of the figure of a royal mummy in the tomb of Rameses IX in the Valley of the Kings at Thebes. It portrays the Egyptian king as the hypotenuse of a sacred 3-4-5 triangle

---

65. It is notable that Isaiah's message (Is 6,9-13) came at almost precisely the end of the third Cultural Era and the beginning of the fourth (i.e., 747 B.C.), when the prophets began to write their messages. Isaiah's "call vision" came "in the year that King Uzziah died" (Is 6,1). Uzziah died in 742 B.C. (see 6 ABD 777; 5 Interp 161). Accordingly, we note that his call for those with ears to hear is not given in any one of the first three Cultural Eras (Rev 2,1-17), which had already ended, but it is sounded in each of those that follow (Rev 2,29 and 3,6,13,22). Very few were able to hear it in the fourth (Jn 16,12; Heb 9,5b). It is important that more of us "awake" in the fifth. But the call will still ring out in the sixth and seventh.
66. TOMN, Vol. 2, p. 814; *The Temple In Man* (TIMN), Chap. 1, p. 42; *Nature Word* (NW), Part II, p. 147.
67. TOMN, Vol. 1, Chap. 5, p. 89.

formed by a snake. As shown below, the king has his arms raised above the head the length of one royal cubit.[68] One of the expressions of *phi* in the human body is that the navel in an adult is the golden section dividing

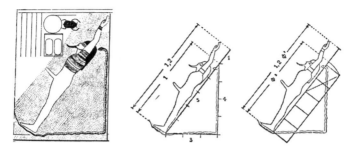

the body height so that the upper portion is one and the lower is *phi* or 1.618. Since one plus *phi* equals *phi* squared,[69] it follows that the total height is *phi* squared. On p. 103 of EM, Schwaller says:

The figure of Ramses IX, representing the King, obtains the value *Five* as diagonal, as hypotenuse of the sacred triangle. Thus it is that this figure reveals a function that measures the cycle, namely the height of the King, worth 5 plus one cubit (or theoretically, plus one-fifth his height), which, in conjunction with the Golden Section, gives the numbers

ϕ^2 squared plus its fifth part or 2.618 / 5 X 6 = 3.1416.

This is the value of the coefficient *Pi*, equal to 1.2 ϕ squared, or 12 ϕ squared for a diameter of ten, being 31.416....

"Thus twelve royal Men measure the cycle of heaven."

The function ϕ resides in the original impulse of becoming, and the Golden Mean yields functionally the *only real* value for the *cyclical* co-efficient, being itself a cyclical number. Our *rational* calculations of *Pi*, based on the average of inscribed and circumscribed polygons, attempt to define a curve by straight lines and lead to infinite absurdity.

---

68. Illustration from *The Egyptian Miracle* (EM), Part 1, Chap. 7, p. 102. See also TOMN, Vol. 1, Chap. 10, p. 279; Vol. 2, Chap. 37, pp. 842, 844; and Plates 62 and 63; also SGP, Chap. 15, p. 194, "a figure whose geometric significance has never been understood."
69. Thus, since *phi* is 1.618, we see that 1 + 1.618 = 1.618 X 1.618 = 2.618.

We simply must contemplate how the Lord, the Word of God (Jn 1,1-3), the twelve, and the circle, are portrayed in this beautiful expression of the relationship of *phi* (1.618...) and *pi* (3.1416...). We've already discussed the relationship of the creative fire of *phi* to the Word. But let us look at a few passages indicating how the Bible expresses these same things:

> **Gen 15,5:** And he brought him outside and said, "Look toward heaven, and number the stars. If you are able to count them," he added, "so shall your offspring be."[70]

Thus his descendants through both Ishmael and Isaac's son Jacob were twelvefold, as were those Christ later chose to follow him (see Is 13,10, "the stars of the heavens and their constellations," and Is 40,12, "[He] has ... marked off the heavens with a span").

> **Job 26,10:** He has described a circle upon the face of the waters at the boundary between light and darkness.

> **Prov 8,27:** When he established the heavens, I was there, when he drew a circle on the face of the deep....

> **Job 38,33:** Do you know the ordinances of the heavens? Can you establish their rule on the earth?

The Book of Enoch also speaks of "the entire law of the stars" (Enoch 80,7). See also Ps 19,1-7a; 119,89; 123,1 and 148,3-6. Then in Rev 22,1-2, we are told that the "water of life ... flow[s] from ... the Lamb through the middle of the street of the city" and that on each "side of the river, the tree of life [stands] with its twelve kinds of fruit...." It seems significant

---

70. To more clearly give effect to the original intent, I have revised the punctuation from the normal translations, which in the RSV reads:

> And he brought him outside and said, "Look toward heaven, and number the stars, if you are able to number them." Then he said to him, "So shall your descendants be."

According to Steiner the rendering that his descendants would be as numerous as the stars is not in keeping with the original intent, which was that Abraham's descendants would reflect the twelve spiritual influences of the star patterns, the zodiac (cf. Rev 12,l). See *The Gospels* (GOSP), p. 22; *The EGO, The God Within and The God of External Revelation* (EGO), Lect. 2, p. 52; *The Gospel of St. Matthew* (GSMt), Lect. 4, p. 77 and Lect. 11, p. 195; also **I-20** and Prokofieff's *Eternal Individuality* (EI), fn 304, p. 310.

that the living water flowing from the Lamb, the *Golden Mean*, is described as flowing in the "middle of the street of the city," for the "mean" is always in the middle.

We have already, in discussing gnomonic growth, seen something of the emergence of the circle. Schwaller speaks of the derivation of this as "the throne of the world and the royal pharaonic throne, symbolized by a square divided into four, that is, 1 and 3 making 4, with one fourth being added to the four others to make the gnomon of 4 to 5," and then he draws in the arc of one quadrant of the circle (top figures below).[71] Tompkins then shows us (bottom figures below) how the Great Pyramid depicts the sphere of our Earth, being designed to incorporate not only *pi* (3.1416…) but also

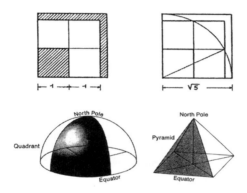

the golden mean, *phi* (1.618…).[72] Said Tompkins, "With the Pyramid, the ancient Egyptians had not only squared the circle but effectively cubed the sphere.[73] And the corners of the edifice "are accurately oriented to the four cardinal points of the compass" (5 Brit 288, "Giza, Pyramids of"). Astronomical, astrological and geophysical aspects of this pyramid are so astoundingly precise that, considering that its sarcophagi contained no human remains, Tompkins and others have concluded that the Great Pyramid was built to preserve esoteric insights of the ancient initiates and to serve as a temple of initiation.[74] The sarcophagi would

---

71. TOMN, Vol. 1, Chap. 5, p. 94.
72. *Phi* is enshrined in the Great Pyramid by giving its faces a slope height (i.e., its height apparent to the observer, not the angular length from base to peak) equal to 1.618 times half its base, so that the pyramid's vertical height is the square root of 1.618 times half its base.
73. SGP, Chap. 15, pp. 189-200.
74. Id., Chap. 20.

then have been used as coffins for the ancient "temple sleep" (see "Three Days' Journey" in *The Burning Bush*; also the raising of Lazarus, Jn 11).

It must dawn on one who studies the works of Schwaller de Lubicz that the immensity of the marvels of ancient Egypt have not yet been fathomed in our time, nor shall they be so long as our quest remains only in the realm of matter.[75] The importance of this realization cannot be over-emphasized when we contemplate Steiner's revelation that we must both retraverse (i.e., reassimilate) and transform all that we came through on our descent.

With that we come to the significance of certain terms and concepts as they relate to the Bible, namely, the *phoenix*, the *palm* and the *one hundred forty-four thousand*.

THE PHOENIX AND THE PALM TREE

Steiner spoke often of the Egyptian myth of Osiris (Osiris, Isis, Horus and Typhon), and to a lesser extent of the significance of the Sphinx.[76] Though I've read only a fraction of his works, I have no recollection of

---

75. The works of Schwaller upon which I base this statement are EM, *Esoterism and Symbol* (ESOTS), NW, *Sacred Science* (SAC), *Symbol and Symbolic* (SYMB), TIMN and the magnificent TOMN. In addition is the third-party writing about Schwaller's work by Andre VandenBroeck, *Al-Kemi* (AL-KEMI). The Al-Kemi, according to its author, means Pharaonic Egypt, and comes from a Pharaonic hieroglyph for the Black Land, the Nile valley. It is thus not surprising to see this also as the etymological source of *alchemy* (see WNWCD). And the work of Peter Tompkins, *Secrets of the Great Pyramid* (SGP), relying so heavily upon Schwaller, has also been considered.

76. See *Egyptian Myths and Mysteries* (EMM) at pp. 59, 70, 73, 77, 86-90, 94, 124-126 and 144 (for the Osiris myth) and at pp. 33,85,98 and 125-128 (for the Sphinx). The Sphinx represented the perception of the ancient initiates of the four human types still in their etheric condition during Lemuria; those whose physical nature predominated were the Bull, the etheric the Lion, the astral the Eagle, and the Ego the Face of a Man—the four apocalyptic creatures (Rev 4,7; Ezek 1,10), represented by the "four corners" of the zodiac (Taurus, Leo, Scorpio [scorpion/Eagle] and Aquarius, each ninety degrees apart; see I-19). The Sphinx has a bull-form, lion body, eagle wings and human face (EMM, p. 85).

Noting their presence in Ezekiel, something is very eerie. The "ineffable name of God" was the Tetragrammaton, the four Hebrew letters *yod-he-vau-he*, or YHVH, that we call Yahweh. If one transliterates these four Hebrew letters into the Greek, they become KEZE, and if one reads them in the Hebrew manner from right to left (noting, however, that KEZE already represents the Hebrew practice), one gets *EZEK* which, if the "iel" relating to a god is dropped, gives us the name of the prophet who first saw and wrote of the four animals. As we've seen, Yahweh was the leader of the Elohim whom Steiner calls Spirits of Form. Ezekiel spoke of these four creatures as having "the form of men" and coming forth out of "the midst of the fire" (1,4-5).

his mentioning the phoenix myth, but certainly the truths it reflects are manifoldly expressed there. However the phoenix myth is widely attested, and we will examine it.[77]

Starting with modern Bible literature, we read in 5 ABD 363, "Phoenix (Bird and Poem)":

> In the ancient world, the phoenix was a bird whose symbolic power proved international and durable. Although its long history, including occurrences in Egypt, Greece, and Rome, exhibits significant and interesting variety, several constant factors define the boundaries and establish the identity of the phoenix: bird of the sun, an immensely long life, the capacity for self-renewal or self-regeneration after its death, and a sign of the human soul and its destiny.

The account then traces the Egyptian version back as early as 2500 B.C. "to the Heliopolitan mythology of Atum/Re ... [a] creation account [which] portrays the emergence of land and life from the primeval waters," at least back to the time of "the origin of the inhabited world." It is hard to escape the comparison of this beginning with that of the beginning of reincarnation in humanity's evolution in Lemuria, as related in the Gen 3 creation myth of Moses, himself an Egyptian initiate (see I-2). It is hard not to notice the similarity in sound between "Atum" and "Adam," or even between "Atum" and "Aum" (see the discussion of "Aum/I Am" at pp. 268-270 in *The Burning Bush*).

The first paragraph under "phoenix" in 9 Brit 393 reads:

> In ancient Egypt and in classical antiquity, a fabulous bird associated with the worship of the sun. The Egyptian phoenix was said to be as large as an eagle, with brilliant scarlet and gold plumage and a melodious cry. Only one phoenix existed at any time, and it was very long-lived—no ancient authority gave it a life span of less than 500 years. As its end approached, the phoenix fashioned a nest of aromatic boughs and spices, set it on fire, and was consumed in the flames. From the pyre miraculously sprang a new phoenix, which after em-

---

77. *The Chiron Dictionary of Greek & Roman Mythology* (CDGRM) lists three phoenix myths, but we are concerned only with the third about the mythical bird. The other two relate to a king of Phoenicia and a king of the Dolopians, respectively.

balming its father's ashes in an egg of myrrh, flew with the ashes to Heliopolis ("City of the Sun") in Egypt, where it deposited them on the altar in the temple of the Egyptian god of the sun, Re. A variant of the story made the dying phoenix fly to Heliopolis and immolate itself in the altar fire, from which the young phoenix then rose.... Probably the phoenix story originated in the Orient and was assimilated to Egyptian sun worship by the priests of Heliopolis. The adaptation of the myth to an Egyptian environment helped to bring about the connection between the phoenix and the palm tree (also called *phoinix* in Greek), which was long associated with sun worship in Egypt.

There is something very significant in this particular description—the "nest of aromatic boughs and spices" that is "set on fire, and ... consumed in the flames" from whose "pyre miraculously sprang a new phoenix, which after embalming its father's ashes in an egg of myrrh, flew to ... Egypt." Or, in the other version, it immolates itself in an "altar fire, from which the young phoenix" arises. We will see below the significance of the palm tree.

Surely we must see that Matthew's Gospel incorporates this myth in regard to the Zarathustra Individuality reborn as the Solomon Jesus child (see "The Nativity" in *The Burning Bush*). The spiritual students of Zarathustrianism, the magi (wise men) of Mt 2,1 bring the infant child gifts of gold, frankincense and myrrh (Mt 2,11). Gold has always been recognized as the metal of the Sun.[78] Myrrh is "a fragrant, bitter-tasting gum resin exuded from ... plants of Arabia and East Africa, used in making incense, perfume, etc." (WNWCD). Frankincense is a combination of two root words, "frank" and "incense," the first being an archaic term

---

78. *Foundations of Esotericism* (FE), Chap. 26, pp. 206-207; also I-27 at p. 598 in *The Burning Bush*. It is also well to reflect upon the fact that the Sun beings, the Elohim of Gen 1, are the Spirits of Form in charge of Earth evolution (I-16), and that their creative fire is reflected in the *golden mean* so prevalent in earthly matter. As Steiner said in *The Gospel of Saint John* (GSJ), Lects. 4 and 5, pp. 74-75 and 82, the "fulness" in Jn 1,16 means the light of all the Elohim, Yahweh from the Moon and the other six from the Sun. The Greek word is *pleroma* or *pleromatas*. According to *The Greek-English Lexicon* (GEL), p. 1420, both mean "that which fills, complement." Christ represents the full complement of all seven Elohim. The term is found not only in John's Gospel but also in Paul's letters: Eph 1,10,23; 3,19; 4,13; Col 1,19; 2,9. In the New Testament the Elohim are called by their Greek name, *exusiai*, which is there translated "authorities" (see I-9 and I-16).

meaning "free in giving; generous," and the second, deriving from a root meaning "to burn." It is a gum or resin substance producing a pleasant odor when burned (WNWCD; see also 4 ABD 940, "myrrh," and 2 ABD, "frankincense"). Not only are these three symbols of the phoenix myth grouped together as gifts from the Zarathustrian magi, but immediately after their appearance the parents of the Solomon Jesus child are told to take him into Egypt (Mt 2,13-15). It is this Individuality, the Zarathustrian Ego, that emerges in Luke's Gospel in the twelve-year-old Jesus of Nazareth who is the "suffering servant" of Second Isaiah, surrendering itself for the entry of the Christ Spirit at the Baptism.[79] Then at the end of his Gospel, as do all the Evangelists, Matthew gives the equivalent of the ancient bird's self-immolation in the "altar fire from which the new phoenix rises."

WNWCD says that the phoenix is "a beautiful, lone bird which lives in the Arabian desert for 500 or 600 years and then sets itself on fire, rising renewed from the ashes to start another long life: a symbol of immortality." RHCD calls it, "a unique mythological bird of great beauty fabled to live 500 or 600 years, to burn itself to death, and to rise from its ashes in the freshness of youth, and live through another life cycle."

The Encyclopedia Britannica tells us, "A mosaic at Antioch represents the Phoenix—the solar bird who died and resurrected from its own ashes and who was its own father and son at the same time—with sunrays encircling its head" (24 Brit 713, "Mystery Religions; Religious Art and Iconography; Mosaics").

The time cycle of the phoenix is of interest. It coincides very closely with the average cycle of reincarnation, according to Steiner.[80] And just as the majority of that time period is spent on an Individuality's journey between death and rebirth (see I-33), we note that the life of the phoenix also illustrates the path of the soul (the Ego, "I Am," or Individuality) between lives rather than during an earthly life. Aside from the relatively short time of its purification in the astral world, the soul's sojourn in spiritland (devachan) in the company of the heavenly host must be described as incredibly beautiful (like the bird) in comparison

---

79. See *The Burning Bush*, p. 60 (citing Ps 2,7; Mt 3,17; Mk 1,11 and Lk 3,22) regarding the entry at Baptism, and *The Burning Bush*, p. 348 regarding the "suffering servant" passages of Is 40-48, and *The Incredible Births of Jesus*, "From Jesus of Nazareth to Jesus Christ," pp. 72-73.
80. See *The Burning Bush*, "Karma and Reincarnation," p. 159.

with life on Earth. The fashioning of a nest as its pyre (fire) portrays what the Ego does as it approaches physical birth, selecting appropriate parents and circumstances in accord with its destiny, then entering the birth canal through the narrow isthmus where the etheric fire meets the earthly fire in a newly born human body. But the fire itself must rage during the entirety of the earthly life and perhaps even through the "purifying fire" of the ensuing astral world before birth into spiritland is again accomplished. Time itself is not a major factor for the fire, for the life of the bird is measured by the period in spiritland. This reversal of the normal way of looking at the myth also takes into account the nature of the bird as an allegorical symbol relating to the more spiritual nature, whereas the ashes more properly reflect the flesh of earthly life. That the bird is both its own father and son (parent and child) tells us that the earthly life fashions the soul's life in spiritland, while the latter in turn fashions the next earthly life, all as a part of the karmic cycle leading to "perfection," the gold as a symbol of the Sun (or Heliopolis, the City of the Sun; cf. Rev. 21,15,18,21,23). Anthroposophy does not adopt the Oriental cyclical view of ever repeating lives, but rather the Western linear view of progress toward such perfection (Mt 5,48), but in this it lays the basis for reconciliation between the religions of East and West, for Christianity had Eastern parents and was born on the border between the two.

Notably, even in later times (ca. A.D. 1600), a constellation (Phoenix) visible in the southern hemisphere was named for the mythical bird; see 28 Brit 225, "Stars and Star Clusters."

Early Christendom also accepted the myth as a symbol of human resurrection. Surely Paul must have been among those from whom it came. The author of The First Epistle of Clement is probably the one Paul calls his "fellow worker" in Phil 4,3.[81] Chapter XXV of the letter reads:

---

81. According to the commentary on Phil 4,3 in 11 Interp 108, "Clement was the name of a Roman Christian, the author of an epistle which still survives—the earliest Christian document outside the New Testament." Barclay also speaks of this in his commentary (Barc). The Introductory Note to that letter at 1 NICENE-1, p. 1, indicates a probability that Paul's Clement was the author of the letter. Well he could have been, for Clement of Rome (A.D. 30-100) would have been old enough to have served with Paul at Philippi in A.D. 57. And if Luke's use of "Phoenix" in Acts 27,12 is as I surmise in the later text, then these two companions of Paul are both early witnesses to the spiritual reality of the phoenix myth.

THE PHOENIX: AN EMBLEM OF OUR RESURRECTION.

Let us consider that wonderful sign [of the resurrection] which takes place in Eastern lands, that is, in Arabia and the countries round about. There is a certain bird which is called a phoenix. This is the only one of its kind, and lives five hundred years. And when the time of its dissolution draws near that it must die, it builds itself a nest of frankincense, and myrrh, and other spices, into which, when the time is fulfilled, it enters and dies. But as the flesh decays a certain kind of worm[82] is produced, which, being nourished by the juices of the dead bird, brings forth feathers. Then, when it has acquired strength, it takes up that nest in which are the bones of its parent, and bearing these it passes from the land of Arabia into Egypt, to the city called Heliopolis. And, in open day, flying in the sight of all men, it places them on the altar of the sun, and having done this, hastens back to its former abode. The priests then inspect the registers of the dates, and find that it has returned exactly as the five hundredth year was completed. (1 NICENE-1, p. 12)

There is an editorial footnote at the end which reads, "This fable respecting the phoenix is mentioned by Herodotus (ii,73) and by Pliny (Nat. Hist., x,2), and is used as above by Tertullian (145-220 A.D.) (De Resurr., sec. 13) and by others of the Fathers."

Tertullian's "On the Resurrection of the Flesh," Chap. XIII (3 NICENE-1, p. 554), reads as follows:

FROM OUR AUTHOR'S VIEW OF A VERSE IN THE NINETY-SECOND PSALM, THE PHOENIX IS MADE A SYMBOL OF THE RESURRECTION OF OUR BODIES.

If, however, all nature but faintly figures our resurrection; if creation affords no sign precisely like it, inasmuch as its several phenomena can hardly be said to die so much as to come to an end, nor again be deemed to be reanimated, but only re-formed; then take a most complete and unassailable symbol of our hope, for it shall be an animated being, and subject alike to life and death. I refer to the bird which is

---

82. See the discussion of the word "worm" in fn 36 of the Creation essay.

peculiar to the East, famous for its singularity, marvelous from its posthumous life, which renews its life in a voluntary death; its dying day is its birthday, for on it it departs and returns; once more a phoenix where just now there was none; once more himself, but just now out of existence; another, yet the same. What can be more express and more significant for our subject; or to what other thing can such a phenomenon bear witness? God even in His own Scripture says: "*The righteous* shall flourish like the phoenix;" [here editorial fn 1 below the quote] that is, shall flourish or revive, from death, from the grave—to teach you to believe that a bodily substance may be recovered even from the fire. Our Lord has declared that we are "better than many sparrows:" well, if not better than many a phoenix too, it were no great thing. But must men die once for all,[83] while birds in Arabia are sure of a resurrection?

Fn 1 reads, omitting its rendering in Greek letters, which is then translated, "Ps 92,12—'like a palm tree' (A.V.). We have here a characteristic way of Tertullian's quoting a scripture which has even the least bearing on his subject."

The above-quoted 5 ABD 363 article, at p. 365, after quoting several Egyptian texts on the phoenix, then says:

> Several Christian texts contain copious references to the phoenix. Two invite discussion, for they demonstrate how Christians adopted and utilized a pagan symbol as a vehicle for expressing new religious content. The first is the 3d-century C.E. poem of Lactantius, *De ave phoenice.*

After giving a one sentence summary and a brief comment upon the above, it then cites "A coptic Christian text dating to the first half of the 6th century C.E., the *Sermon on Maria.*" The Lactantius text, summarized in one sentence, is actually three pages long. And while the ABD summary clearly supports my above interpretation of the phoenix as being in spiritland during its five-hundred-plus-year "life," the longer text (entitled "The Phoenix" in 7 NICENE-1, pp. 324-326) makes that

---

83. See the discussion of Heb 9,27 in the essay, "Karma and Reincarnation," at *The Burning Bush,* p. 129.

clear beyond any shadow of a doubt. Not only so, but it contains the informative statement, "Then she [the phoenix] chooses a lofty palm, with top reaching to the heavens, which has the pleasing name of phoenix from the bird...." It is from this that she begins to build her nest.

The picture I gather from this is that the high palm tree reaching to heaven is the beginning of the descent into birth, the archetypal heavenly tree that has its roots in the womb, for the text goes on, "Afterwards she builds for herself either a nest or a tomb, for she perishes that she may live; yet she produces herself." The point here is the light Lactantius sheds on the meaning of the "palm tree" in Ps 92,12, which Tertullian was interpreting (above) as the phoenix. While ABD attributes "The Phoenix" to Lactantius, and it is placed with the latter's works in 7 NICENE-1, ABD subcaptions the writing, "By an Uncertain Author. Attributed to Lactantius." While the account may have been reduced to writing by Lactantius (A.D. 260-330), the substance of the legend must have been much earlier, for it is more likely to have influenced Tertullian (A.D. 145-220) than the reverse.

So what, if anything, are we to make of the one biblical usage of "Phoenix," in Acts 27,12, "And because the harbor was not suitable to winter in, the majority advised to put to sea from there, on the chance that somehow they could reach Phoenix, a harbor of Crete, looking northeast and southeast [fn—or "southwest and northwest"], and winter there"? Here again we encounter the palm tree. In 5 ABD 365, "Phoenix (Place)," we are told that the harbor of Phoenix is near the west end of Crete's south shore (in accord, see *Oxford Bible Atlas*, NY, Oxford University Press, 1962). Consistent with Luke's handling of the entirety of Acts, this passage utilizes actual geographic locations, and presumably gives something of an accurate description of the event. But this does not mean that the factual elements were not selected in order to tell a deeper spiritual story, namely, a pattern of events tracking the character of the soul's journey in spiritland as given by Steiner [see I-33, especially as it is discussed in the essay, "As Above, So Below"]. Significantly, the 5 ABD 365 discussion says, "The Greek designates both the date palm (from which the harbor name probably arose) and the mythical bird of Egypt [citation omitted] for the common origin of these."

Given the clear meaning of the ancient phoenix myth, and the mythical connection between the phoenix and the palm tree, it would seem wise to keep this connection in mind when the Bible speaks of the "palm tree."[84]

The plausibility of the suggestion that Luke, in designating specifically the Cretan harbor of Phoenix, intended the deeper meaning of the spiritual harbor mythically symbolized by the ancient phoenix is greatly enhanced by another consideration. Recall, review and reflect upon what has been said elsewhere in this work with regard to Luke's treatment of the parable on the levirate law in Lk 20,27-40. There (see the essay "Bush" and Point #5 under the essay "Karma and Reincarnation," both in *The Burning Bush*) Luke chose "the burning bush," to illustrate that "the dead are raised," while distinguishing that state from the state of "resurrection" on the ground that only those who have reached the state of perfection such that "they cannot die anymore" have attained to the latter. Fire is the passageway back and forth between earthly and heavenly life for those who are merely "raised from the dead." They are so "raised" that they may dwell in the state of the phoenix until returning again as it does. It is significant that of the Evangelists, only Luke makes this point crystal clear and that he and Clement were both with Paul.

It seems quite notable that near the end of Acts Luke writes (in Acts 28,11) that "after three months" of "wintering" they set out in a ship

---

84. Let us look at three significant instances. In Ex 15,27 the Israelites had just crossed the Red Sea and come to their second camp, at Elim, the first with potable water, "where there were *twelve* springs of water and *seventy palm trees*" (emphasis added); and they encamped there by the water (cf. Ps 1,3). The presence of both seven and twelve must surely be highly significant. Compare the passage about Anna in Lk 2,36-37 and what is said about it in "The Nativity" in *The Burning Bush* as well as in *The Incredible Births of Jesus*. The seventy palm trees suggest many evolutionary incarnations, which fits the Apocalypse that moves from sevens to twelves.

The synoptic Gospels all record Christ Jesus' triumphal entry into Jerusalem, with Matthew and Mark both saying that the crowds threw "branches" in his path. Evangelist John (Lazarus/John) alone identifies those as "palm branches," suggesting his recognition of all the incarnations that had gone into preparing the body of this Lamb of God, as well as all of the incarnations that would be required for the perfection of those who follow him. Clearly Jesus of Nazareth, was the servant *branch* from the root of Jesse that necessitated such preparation (see Is 11,1; 4,2; Zech 3,8; 6,12; Jer 23,5; 33,15).

The same Evangelist John, in Rev 7,9, speaks of those who have already risen to the spiritual stature of the *one hundred forty-four thousand* (Rev 7,4). Yet while they constituted "a great multitude," their full number will not be attained until after the seven trumpets have sounded (Rev 14,1), at the end of the Mineral-Physical Condition of Form; see I-1 and "Trumpet(s)" at p. 395 in *The Burning Bush*. And John says of these that they have "palm branches in their hands." One sees here the end of their incarnations, as expressed by Luke to the Sadducees (Lk 20,36).

described as "a ship of Alexandria, with the Twin Brothers as figurehead." Twins are a zodiacal sign (Gemini). Considering the close philosophical and theological relationship between Paul and Philo, in speaking of Alexandria (Philo's home) is Luke not saying that the "Twin Brothers," in a spiritual sense, are Paul and Philo? In "Egypt" (in *The Burning Bush*) we saw the relationship of Philo not only to Paul but to all the Evangelists— and even the otherwise enigmatic statement by Photius "that Philo became a Christian" (quoted in a footnote to Eusebius in 1 NICENE-3, p. 117).

THE ONE HUNDRED FORTY-FOUR THOUSAND

This intriguing number (Rev 7,4; 14,1,3; 6,11; 7,9) has fascinated Christendom from the first, and I have found no other commentary or theological writing that plumbs its meaning to any depth. Only in connection with fire does it seem to have much depth. In the Creation essay[85] we saw this relationship as the point in the creative *phi* spiral where the *sevens* of creation first meet the *twelves* of the spiritual world (and only on each subsequent *twelfth* Fibonacci number thereafter).

But we could not yet, in the Creation essay, adequately appreciate its significance. We had first to reflect more deeply upon a few facets of the many-splendored *phi*. It is an unutterable principle, a divine law no less. The gnomon of the golden mean seems to be one with the Word that both creates and destroys (cf. Jn 17,10-11; Eph 1,9-10). Look back at the figures portraying it. Moving in one direction it enhances, giving the growth of creation; in the other it shrinks or reduces into eventual immateriality. It is the "two-edged sword" (Rev 1,16; 2,12; Heb 4,12), the "law" that must be fulfilled (Mt 5,17-18). It is the image of the first and the last, the Alpha and the Omega. It is not a human device. Humans have only observed that part of it revealed to them. None has yet encompassed or fathomed it fully. It is not the "golden calf" (Taurus; Ps 50,9; Ex 32), but the "sign" (Aries) of the higher Lamb.

Lazarus/John's vision on Patmos did not give him a number to be understood by human reckoning. The *one hundred forty-four thousand* is not there a number but a symbol. Neither the sevens of creation (Prov 9,1) nor the twelves of the zodiacal heavens (Gen 15,5) can alone give

---

85. See its fn 58 and related text.

birth to it. The leaven of *phi* (cf. Mt 13,33) must enter and work its way through both. Only when twelve has reached its own square (when the twelve tribes have become the "twelve apostles of the Lamb"; Rev 21) in the *one hundred forty-four* (Rev 21,17) do *phi* and twelve meet at the gates of the Holy City, the end of Earth evolution and the opening of the Jupiter Condition of Consciousness (see I-1). And the twain only meet again with every succeeding twelfth *phi* number (see the Creation essay) picturing, it would seem, the conclusion of succeeding Conditions of Consciousness (Venus, Vulcan, etc.). With this insight countless Old Testament passages can be seen as prophetic signs of precisely this meaning that comes to fruition as the Bible ends in the Apocalypse of St. John. (See "The Whirlwind" below.)

Now that we have studied the principle of gnomonic growth and the nature of the logarithmic spiral that appears over and over in the phenomena of matter, we begin to see that all creation came from fire (*phi*). But with the number *one hundred forty-four* we also begin to see that creation ends with fire, the point where the Earth moves from the Mineral-Physical Condition of Form to the More Perfect Astral Condition (see I-1), following the blast from the seventh trumpet (Rev 11,15 and 14,1; 1 Cor 15,52; 1 Th 4,16; see also the essay "Trumpet[s]" in *The Burning Bush*). This previously mysterious number is then said to be also the "man's measure" in the Holy City who has attained the status previously held only by an "angel" (Rev 21,17; Lk 20,36). And it is there stated in "cubits," a term that has itself baffled theologians and Egyptologists alike (6 ABD 899-890, "Weights and Measures"). Rather than a measure objectively defined, it seems better to comprehend it as a measure innately unique to every human being,[86] generally considered to be the length of the forearm. Only thus does it fit with the "I Am," the "name … which no one knows but himself" (Rev 19,12-13; 2,17 and 3,12), for the "I Am" only applies to the one who speaks or thinks it. No one else can know it.

THE WHIRLWIND

Having now, for the first time, a new and deeper understanding of the *one hundred forty-four thousand*, we must take a new look at the meaning

---

86. See fn 68 and related text; also Deut 3,11, "the cubit of a man."

of the *whirlwind*, for inherent in both terms we see the spiral of the fire ether.

The prophetic signs in the Old Testament can be found in those passages that utilize words composed of the Hebrew letters (consonants) *gll* or *glgl*. The Hebrew letters *g* and *l*, *gimel* and *lamed*, are the third and *twelfth* letters in the Hebrew alphabet. Both three and twelve are readily recognized as prevalent and meaningful in scripture. Moreover, these letters are often interpreted according to their number in the alphabet. In this light, the potential significance of the juxtaposition of two *twelfth* letters becomes immediately apparent, as in *l* x *l* or twelve times twelve giving us the number *one hundred forty-four* (and this even though the *lamed* is also used as numeral thirty). So frequently do these appear in Old Testament passages that we cannot list them all. But the names by which they appear become familiar, as in Gilgal (Deut 11,30; Josh 4,19,20; 5,9,10; 9,6; 10,6,7,9,15,43; 14,6; 15,7; Judg 2,1; 3,19; 1 Sam 7,16; 10,8; 11,14,15; 13,4,7,8,12,15; 15,12,21,33; 2 Sam 19,15,40; 2 K 2,1; 4,38; Hos 4,15; 9,15; 12,11; Amos 4,4; 5,5; Mic 6,5), Geliloth (Josh 18,17) and especially Galilee (see 2 ABD 879; also Is 9,1; Mt 26,69; 28,7,10,16; Mk 16,7; Jn 2,1-11; 21); probably also cognate in Gilead (Gen 31,21,23,25; Num 26,29,30; 32,1,26,29,39,40; et al.), Galeed (Gen 31,47,48) and in the significant epic of Gilgamish.

To appreciate the meaning of ancient names, we need also to consider the meaning of the letters they comprise; in these cases, as indicated, *g* and *l*. This was of greater significance in the older Hebrew than the later Greek, but the latter still reflects it somewhat. We've noted these letters' placement third and twelfth in the Hebrew alphabet; and the same in the Greek (when it is seen that originally *lambda*, now the eleventh letter, was also twelfth (GEL, p. 1021). In both languages the first letter, *aleph* (Heb) and *alpha* (Gk), stands for the original unity. One can hardly fail to see such terms as our "all" and the Allah of Islam as carrying this concept even into our own time. And we use the term "alpha" to designate the beginning of anything or the brightest star in a constellation. Again, the second letter, *beth* (Heb) and *beta* (Gk), indicates that one has a position *in* a place. It has usually been interpreted as "house," and this is not wrong, but is merely an application of the more overriding concept that finds expression even today in our use of the term "beta." It indicates that there is no longer unity, but the first step away from it, implying duality by the preposition *in*. Then we come to the third letter, *gimel* (Heb) and *gamma* (Gk), which means three. We see it also in our prefix "gamo-" relating to marriage and reproduction of a third, also in our term "gamete" relating to cells that can combine to make a new individual. This "gam" can also be seen as a matter of emphasis in the term "Gilgamish." That mythical epic has been compared closely with the Mosaic myth in Genesis, and it points toward the evolving consciousness of the human soul (see 2 ABD 1024; also *The Burning Bush*, pp. 544, fn 4, 237, and 239, fn 7). This "ish" then means, as in our language, "pertaining to" (WNWCD indicates that either Gilgamish or Gilgamesh is correct).

When we come to the twelfth letter, *lambda* (now the eleventh in Gk) and *lamed* (Heb), we are dealing with something that points in a *direction*, one might even say a "sign": a preposition indicating "toward" but not denoting motion (see HEL 510). Yet when, as in *gll*, they are found together they indicate something in a curvature as we see below. But one must surely contemplate that there is a relationship between this letter twelve and the similarly sounding *Lamb*, the zodiacal Aries, or the Lamb of God. In this connection, see the tabulation in I-18. This contemplation is then enriched when we remember, as Isaiah foretold (Is 9,1; Mt 4,14-15), that he was to come from GaLiLee and be known as a "GaLiLean."

The oldest manuscripts available to our scholars are dated many centuries after the originals from which they were copied, and even the originals were first written, in most of these passages, centuries after the events that had come down to them by oral transmission of tradition. As critical scholarship has often suggested, and Steiner certainly confirms, faithfulness to the original meaning is compromised in these instances by the "fading splendor" phenomenon, the dimming spiritual consciousness of the later scribes causing them to give vulgar or mundane meanings to the pictorial metaphors (Imaginations) of the traditions handed down as all ancient myths were.

If one examines these words in a Hebrew dictionary (e.g., HEL), it can be seen that they not only embody the concept of "circle," as our modern translators have given them to us (e.g., Josh 5,9, where "rolled" becomes the basis for the name "Gilgal" and suggests that the twelve stones in Josh 4 were placed in a heap or "circle"; see 2 ABD 1022), but also the concept of "waves" (Job 38,11; Is 51,15; Jer 5,22 et al.) and "whirlwinds" (Ps 77,18; see the note on this verse [there called vs 19] at 17 AB 232). The note at 17 AB 232 just cited in reference to Ps 77,18 is highly informative on our point. It indicates that the *galgal* there translated "dome of heaven" is usually translated "whirlwind." Steiner often said that the human brain (see the gnomonic figure of the Ram and human brain above in the section "*Phi,* the Gnomon and the Spiral"), with its twelve pairs of nerves, reflected the firmament or "dome of heaven." The note in question goes on to say that the Hebrew *gulgolet* (and the Akkadian *gulgullu*), obviously related to Golgotha, means "skull, a container shaped like a human skull." Here we ponder, realizing that it can fairly be stated that the central mission of Rudolf Steiner was to bring to humanity a deeper understanding of what he termed "the mystery of Golgotha."

The Bible student will immediately think of the whirlwind that carried Elijah and his fiery chariot into heaven (2 K 2,1,11). Actually the *gll/glgl* term is not used there, the KJV having selected "whirlwind" undoubtedly because the event took place at "Gilgal" (2 K 2,1); see 11 AB 31. But many other Old Testament passages do translate the term as "whirl-wind(s)" (Is 5,28), or "hurricane" (Ps 83,15), or "whirling dust" (Is 17,13).

In the text enumeration above of examples where the golden mean *(phi)* manifests, we saw all of these in the form of ocean waves, galaxies, hurricanes and the human brain. And we now see in the text above that this *phi* reaches a culmination with the number twelve in its square, the apocalyptic *one hundred forty-four*.

Now it was at Gilgal that Joshua commanded that twelve men be selected, one from each tribe, to "take twelve stones … out of the midst of the Jordan" (Josh 4) and the interpreters agree that they must have been placed in a "circle" because of the term Gilgal (see 2 ABD 1022), which can also mean spiral (as in the case of the whirlwind). And then twice the question is asked, "What do these stones mean?" (Josh 4,6,21), for the commandment itself was given "that this may be a sign among you" (Josh 4,6).

And just as the sign, the phenomenon, manifested in the disappearance of heat is missed by our scientists, so also do our theologians miss the sig-nificance of the spiral of stones in Josh 4 that comes to fruition in St. John's Apocalypse in the meaning of the *one hundred forty-four thousand* of the redeemed and the *one hundred forty-four* as the dimension of the Holy City. At the time of Joshua, the spiral in the parabola of human evo-lution was still downward, toward the "right time" of Christ's Incarna-tion. Perhaps this densification is indicated here by twelve "stones," as compared with the twelve precious stones in Rev 21,19-20 and the twelve pearls in vs 21. Meaning can then be seen in the creative sevens (Prov 9,1) associated with bringing down the walls of Jericho immediately thereafter (Josh 6), especially as it involved repeated circles (seven times seven) and the imagery of trumpets so visible in the reascent in Rev 8–11 and the "last trumpet" of 1 Cor 15,52 (also 1 Th 4,16). That archaeology has cast substantial doubt on the physical destruction depicted in Josh 6 and 8 having taken place at Jericho and Ai strongly suggests the higher prophetic meaning of these passages (see *Archaeology of the Land of the Bible*, ABRL, p. 331; 3 ABD 736-737 and 2 NIB 615-616).

This understanding seems further strengthened by the meaning of the name *Jericho*, namely, *City of Palm Trees*. Its identification as such in the last chapter of Deuteronomy (Deut 34,3; see also 1 ABD 1052) is given at the very time that Moses, from the summits of Mounts Nebo and Pisgah, was shown Jericho and the promised land and told he could not lead the people over there. And then Joshua is handed the leadership (Deut 34,9), and it is said that no prophet like Moses has arisen since, "whom the Lord knew face to face" (vss 10-12). There Deuteronomy ends, and the book of Joshua begins, and we come to the passages about the stones and the walls of Jericho.

Just as Moses killed the Egyptian to start the exodus (Ex 2,12), now Joshua brings down the walls of Jericho to start the conquest of the promised land. The meaning of Moses' killing the Egyptian is that he was to kill the capacity in his people that characterized the ancient clairvoyance of the Egyptians. They were to transform that into the hardening of the human brain for intellectual thinking (the two tablets of stone being the two mineralized sides of the human brain with its twelve pairs of cranial nerves).[87] Moses was the last to carry this ability of "seeing God face to face." That quality could not be carried over into the earthly promised land.

And now we see the same pattern emerging at the outset of Joshua's campaign with the bringing down of the walls of Jericho. We've seen above that the palm tree was essentially involved with the phoenix myth, the ancient symbol of reincarnation. Now we see that Joshua was to bring the walls of this knowledge (the City of Palms) down. Human consciousness of this spiritual reality was to be darkened until the time was right for

---

87. See the threefold giving of the law to Moses (Ex 19–40,21) as an additional scriptural example of the "Three Bodies" at p. x in the "Preface to the Revised Edition" of *The Burning Bush*.

it to reemerge in the fifth Cultural Era of the Consciousness Soul (i.e., the "five thousand"), the 2,160-year era of the *fishes* (Pisces) that commenced with the Renaissance (ca. A.D. 1414; see I-19 and I-25). But evolution of consciousness is gradual. What started with the Gilgal experience of Joshua might be said to have been brought to a conclusion in the Gilgal experience of Elijah and the whirlwind. We then soon have Isaiah being instructed by the Lord to tell the people they would no longer see, hear or understand (in the spiritual realm) for a long period of time (Is 6,9-13). But the later prophets consoled them with the assurance that they would again someday regain higher vision (e.g., Jer 31,31-34). The Christ had to incarnate at the "right time," in the midst of a people "who sit in darkness and in the shadow of death" (Lk 1,79; Is 9,2). What came to pass slowly before Christ had then to reverse itself slowly thereafter.

There is probably no more fitting point upon which to close our consideration of the whirlwind than we find in the book of Job. The story of Job is the story of the evolution of the human soul, the "I Am," the "burning bush" (see "Three Bodies" in *The Burning Bush*, pp. 423-429). We must not miss the relationship between Cain and Job, for both reflect the soul of every human being exposed to the "original sin" metaphorically described in Gen 3. It is said of each of them that they cannot die (Gen 4,12-15; Job 2,6). If Gen 4 is to be more deeply understood, it must be seen as positing in each human soul the Cain element, as more fully shown in "Appendix to 'Three Bodies'" in *The Burning Bush* (pp. 459-473). The book of Job, including both its prose prologue and epilogue as well as its lengthy poem, is an elaboration of the soul's journey imposed upon its Cain element.

Within the full gamut of prevailing theology, there does not yet seem to be any recognition of this. But what is widely recognized is the point at which Job first becomes aware of the Lord's response, the *whirlwind* (Job 38,1; and then 40,6). And what theologians have noted is that there is wide diversity of judgment as to how the Lord's cosmic response is to be understood (see Brueggemann's *The Theology of the Old Testament* (TOT), pp. 390-391; 4 NIB 595; INTPN, Job, p. 225). This is a normal result where meaning is hidden and deeper understanding is lacking. But what we then notice is how consistently the prophets speak of the whirlwind as the place where we meet the Lord (see Is 29,6; Jer 4,13; Ezek 10,2,6,13 ["whirling wheels"]; Dan 11,40; Amos 1,14; Nah 1,3; Zech 9,14). Is 29,6 says, "you will be visited by the Lord ... with whirlwind ...

and the flame of a devouring fire." Ezek 10,6 speaks of taking "fire from between the whirling wheels, from between the cherubim" (cf. Gen 3,24 with its cherubim and flaming sword guarding the way to the tree of life). In Amos 1,14 the Lord says "I will kindle a fire ... in the day of the whirlwind." Nah 1,3 says that the way of the Lord is in the whirlwind. Zech 9,14 reads (emphasis mine), "Then the Lord will appear over them, and his arrow go forth like *lightning*; the Lord God will sound the *trumpet*, and march forth in the *whirlwinds* of the south."

So we see that when the Bible speaks of trumpets, one hundred forty-four, or a whirlwind, it is talking about the point that joins heaven and Earth, the point where we pass from the material sphere into the etheric, the point of fire and fire ether, the New Jerusalem. However, during Earth evolution (the Earth Condition of Consciousness, see I-1), it is the point the elevated soul attains where it perceives in the etheric world, and there meets the risen Christ in the second coming. It is in our present Cultural Age that this long awaited event begins (see "Second Coming" in *The Burning Bush*).

Conclusion

"I came to cast fire upon the earth." What lurking power implied! Are we, in this day of exploding discovery, to be denied new insights? Must we not aspire to move beyond the long "seeing but see not, hearing but hear not" (Is 6,10) age, veiled with matter, to apprehend higher meanings than the simplistic ones of the past? We have taken a long walk through territory new to and uncharted by prevailing orthodoxy. But what magnificent new vision it affords! Let us not fail to seize it through lack of diligence and courage. For only those who enter into that etheric fire while on Earth will ever see the Christ in the Earth, he who waits for us there even now.[88] The way is neither short nor easy. But he who waits there has bidden us take it.[89]

---

88. See "Second Coming" in *The Burning Bush*.
89. Consider Mt 7,13-14; 23,37-39; Lk 13,34-35; Rev 3,20.

LIGHT

CONTENTS

Introduction

THOSE WHO WERE BLESSED to witness, on the *mountain*, the Ascension of Christ heard "two men" in "white robes" say that Jesus would "come in the same way as you saw him go into heaven" (Acts 1,10-11). These are the same "two men" who appeared "in dazzling apparel" to the women at the tomb (Lk 24,4; Jn 20,12). In *The Burning Bush* we saw that these "two men" were the etheric and astral bodies of Jesus (pp. 414, 447 and 449).

Through these bodies, remaining in the etheric and astral domains of the Earth, these followers were enabled to "see" and "hear" a spiritual event of great moment.[1] A window into spiritual reality was briefly opened to them, as witnesses, for the day when this could be more fully understood. That day, only now beginning to dawn, can evolve into full understanding only when "cities lie waste without inhabitant, and houses without men, and the land is utterly desolate" (Is 6,9-12).[2] The Earth is already dying as the Prodigal Son begins the long return journey home. The Gospel accounts of the Resurrection appearances, the forty days, and the Ascension can be reconciled and understood only in the light of Koenig's divine perception set out in *The Burning Bush* (p. 506). We saw there in the "Second Coming" and "Lord of Karma" essays how the Christ, who had "gone to the Father" (Jn 14,28; 16,10,28 and 20,17) in those early days, was returning to reveal himself again through those "bodies," that is, "in the same way as you saw him go into heaven" (Acts 1,11). The "fish" that were partaken after the Resurrection were of the same character as those in the divine "feedings," symbols (signs; see Jn 6,14) of the Age of the Fish (i.e., two fish, Jn 6,9, the sign of Pisces), our present Cultural Era that began with the Renaissance, when the human spiritual soul would begin to "see" the Christ returned in the etheric world.[3]

In the last essay, we saw what it meant that Christ "came to cast fire upon the earth" (Lk 12,49). We cannot begin to understand the meaning of light until we grasp firmly the organizational structure of creation, the four ethers and their earthly counterparts, the four elements, expressed

---

1. We need to recognize that all three bodies, even the physical when perfected and entirely freed from its mineral content (as has occurred thus far only in Jesus of Nazareth through the indwelling of the Christ Spirit), exist not only in the etheric but also the astral and higher worlds (Mt 13,33). That this is so is indicated by what took place as these human bodies descended in the earliest Epochs of Earth evolution—see *Outline of Esoteric Science* (OES), Chap. 4, pp. 199-200—for the reascension traverses the same supersensible regions as the descent. That even the mineral-free physical body of Jesus could later be "seen" and "touched" by his close followers (Jn 20,14-29; 21,1-22; Mt 28,9-10; Mk 16,9-19; Lk 24,13-51; Acts 1,3-9; 1 Cor 15,4-8) further demonstrates this spiritual reality.

2. The Bible's apocalyptic writings are not what theology typically ascribes to them but are instead visions similar to this seminal one of Isaiah. A consistent thread runs through them all that defies comprehension by the mind set upon the historical or contemporary scene or the material world.

3. See I-19, particularly the chart showing the dates of the "Astrological Ages"; also the Epilogue in *The Incredible Births of Jesus*, about the age of the Archangel Michael that began in 1879. See especially the discussion of these feedings in *The Disciple Whom Jesus Loved*, p. 9.

not only in classical Greek but also in the Old Testament, condescendingly disregarded in the scientific revolution of the last few centuries.

From a human standpoint, no more arrogant statement has ever been uttered than the one from Christ's lips in John's Gospel, "I am the way, and the truth, and the life; no one comes to the Father but by me" (Jn 14,6). Until it can be considered in the light of this organizational structure of creation, schematized in the chart reproduced in the Creation essay from I-22, it cannot be understood as the one and only return path of the Prodigal Son in its reascent to the Father. The same creative scheme is set out in the life, word and light expressed in the prologue of John's Gospel (see its discussion in *The Burning Bush*, pp. 438, 448 and 533). Every human soul, and indeed all creation (Eph 1,9-10; Rom 8,19-23), must traverse it to escape the eventual abyss.

Ironically, that period in human spiritual evolution in the eighteenth century that is known as "the Enlightenment" coincided with the rise of the documentary hypothesis of the Old Testament (1 Interp 134; 1 NIB 107) and the increasing certainty that the first three chapters of Genesis present not a single, sequential story of creation, but two different accounts, the second one (Gen 2,4b–3) being the earlier (the so-called Yahwist, or "J," account) and the first (Gen 1,1–2,4a, the so-called Elohist, or "E," account) being the later. By recent decades this understanding became almost universally accepted among Christian scholars, though major cracks in the dike are certainly now appearing.[4] The Creation essay above shows how the documentary hypothesis fails to comprehend the nature of the creative process through the etheric conditions into the material.

And nowhere is the lack of understanding more significant than in the case of Gen 1,3-5:

[3] And God said, "Let there be light"; and there was light. [4] And God saw that the light was good; and God separated the light from the darkness. [5] God called the light Day, and the darkness he called Night. And there was evening and there was morning, one day.

Recall what was said in the Creation essay about the first six days of creation. Nothing that we would today recognize as matter came into existence during those six days. The fission between light and darkness in the

---

4. See fn 5 in the Creation essay; see also Gnuse's "Redefining the Elohist?", 119 *Journal of Biblical Literature*, No. 2, p. 201 (Summer 2000).

first day was in the contemplation of the Elohim, the Spirits of Form. The fire and light ethers were separated, thus creating the physical form of air (gas). But recall the difference between the spiritual *physical* principle and its condition when in the mineral-physical state. The physical principles of form exist even before they are filled with matter (see fn 1). So the eye, had it existed during the "first day" of creation could not have beheld anything, not even the dome of heaven, illumined by light, for atmosphere is matter. Matter enters the creative process of Earth evolution commencing with Gen 2,4b.

As every scientist knows, light itself is not visible to our physical eye until it falls upon matter in either solid, liquid or atmospheric (gaseous) form. And even then the light itself is not visible, but only the matter it illuminates.

To then comprehend the transition from the purely etheric, form-creating conditions of Gen 1 to the materializing conditions of Gen 2, we must go back to what was said in the "Fire" essay (in its section called "Heat and the Other Ethers"). In the tabulations there, heat is shown between the higher realm of "materializing, dematerializing; dark, light" and the lower gaseous realm of "rarefying, densifying." And it was said, against the mechanical theory, that "heat is indeed motion, but in the sense that there is a tendency to create material existence and then let it disappear again.... It is a vortex continually manifesting in such a way that what appears physically is annihilated by what appears as the spiritual—a continuous interplay—a sucking up of what is in space by the entity that is not."

Later in the same section of that essay we were led by our observations to see that before the separations ("fissions") taking place in the etheric world in the "creations" of Genesis 1, the realms of the gaseous, fluid and solid, now existing only in matter, were then in union with their related etheric condition. While still in this etheric union, as we saw in the Creation essay, Gen 1,3-5 tells of the creation of the sentient soul (the portion of the human soul that would later relate to the sense body in perceiving physical light; see I-9). When the actual separation of the light ether from its related gaseous condition took place, air was breathed into the living sentient soul as described in Gen 2,7.[5]

---

5. This primordial condition of the union of all states of matter with their etheric state must surely someday come to be seen as the higher meaning of the "living water" (Song 4,15; Jer 2,13; 17,13; Zech 14,8; Jn 4,10-11; 7,38), namely, the condition when earthly water shall again be fused with (evanesced into) its etheric (life) nature (the chemical/sound ether) on the return journey of the Prodigal Son. This is the journey envisioned *(continued on following page)*

And today science has come to the point of recognizing that, just as heat is a continual interplay between what is in space and what is not, something of the same character is to be found in what we know as light. Lawrence W. Fagg, in his recent *Electromagnetism and the Sacred* (EMS), tells us that the "virtual photon," a phenomenon shown by quantum theory to exist though it cannot be observed, is the workhorse of all electromagnetism that pervades all material existence. Related to the virtual photon is what he calls a "virtual particle," an electron-positron pair that emerges as mass and then disappears from observation. In language similar to what Steiner used to describe the nature of heat, Fagg says (p. 53), "It is as if the particle pairs 'borrow' energy in the form of mass [from Einstein's famous formula] from the vacuum but must pass it back quickly, and the more the mass-energy that is 'borrowed,' the more quickly it must be paid back." We shall look more fully at this later, noting for now only that science has recently come to conclusions in relation to light that articulate quite precisely what Steiner said early in the century, namely, that light is the realm characterized by "materializing, dematerializing."

If we stand in awe of the nature of light, we are in good company. In 1951, a mere four years before his death at seventy-six years of age, Einstein said, "All the fifty years of conscious brooding have brought me no closer to the answer to the question, 'What are light quanta?' Of course today every rascal thinks he knows the answer, but he is deluding himself."[6]

There has never been a time when the human soul did not intuit the divinity of light. The canon pervasively reflects this archetype from Gen 1,3 ("Let there be light") to Rev 22,5 ("they need no light of lamp or sun, for the Lord God will be their light"). Not until the thirteenth century

---

5. *(continued from previous page)* by Christ's (otherwise most arrogant) statement in Jn 14,6, "I am the way [light ether], and the truth [the living word—from the chemical/sound ether; cf. the "living oracles" in Acts 7,38 and Heb 10,1, discussed in *The Burning Bush*, p. 150], and the life [life ether, originally joined with solid matter]; no one comes to the Father but by me" (see the discussion of Jn 14,6 in *The Burning Bush* at pp. 324 and 438-9 [#22]). The Old Testament is the story of the "fissions" in humanity's descent. The New Testament is that of the "fusions" made possible by Christ's blood on the return journey of humanity, the Prodigal Son (Eph 1,9-10; Rom 8,19-23). Chart I-22 is the schematic. Evangelist John's Revelation is the portrayal of the sevenfold and twelvefold paths of that return.

6. Quoted by Arthur Zajonc in his *Catching the Light* (CLT) at pp. ix and 279, where he gives credit to Emil Wolf's "Einstein's Researches on the Nature of Light," *Optics News*, vol. 5, no.1 (Winter 1979), pp. 24-39.

did Christendom, and the human soul in general, begin to look critically at the nature of light. It started with Robert Grosseteste (1175-1253), prominent English bishop and first chancellor of Oxford. In his *Catching the Light* (CLT), subtitled *The Entwined History of Light and Mind*, Arthur Zajonc (pronounced "zionce," sounding remarkably like "science"), Amherst physics professor and prominent anthroposophist, says that according to Grosseteste, "Light ... was the first form of corporeality, and from it all else followed" (p. 53). And, along with Christian tradition from the first, Grosseteste accepted the reality of the hierarchies (see I-6) and the ages that the Archangels respectively administer in human development (CLT, p. 220). According to that tradition, lost in Christendom after the sixteenth century, the light of *divine intelligence* is administered by the Archangel Michael. According to Steiner, Michael's current regency of approximately 350 years began in 1879, his prior regency having been before the Incarnation of Christ and encompassing the age of the Greek sages Heraclitus, Socrates, Plato and Aristotle as well as the spreading of Greek civilization so instrumental in preparing for the spread of Christianity.[7]

Happily, today there is at least a minority in each camp, theologians on one side and scientists on the other, that is reaching out as though to bring the two historically separated disciplines more nearly into union. Perhaps nothing is more indicative of the onset in 1879 (or thereabouts) of the new age of the Archangel Michael than the difference in nature and consequence between Vatican I (1869-1870) and Vatican II (1962-1965). During the life of Rudolf Steiner it would have been hard to imagine greater mutual antagonism than existed between his anthroposophy and the Jesuits. Yet Teilhard de Chardin (1881-1955), only twenty years Steiner's junior and ordained a Jesuit priest in 1911, began his paleontological missions to China in 1923 that led eventually to his magnificent *The Phenomenon of Man* (PHEN). The three quotes from it in the "Evolution" essay above splendidly articulate anthroposophical principles. It

---

7. These respective archangelic "ages" are discussed in the original version of *The Burning Bush*, in chart I-19, where I assumed that all seven such ages or regencies "fit" within each 2,160 year cultural (or zodiacal) age. This erroneous assumption was corrected in the recently revised edition, as also herein and in the Epilogue of *The Incredible Births of Jesus* (IBJ) which sets out more fully the scriptural basis for the Archangel Michael as the regent of light, i.e., the divine intelligence, and circumstances showing the reality of 1879, or thereabouts, as the inception of his current dominion over human evolution.

is no surprise that his superiors not only frustrated his own teaching efforts but prohibited his publication of this priceless work. He could only avoid violating his vow of obedience by arranging for its posthumous publication in 1955. He was followed by another freethinking Jesuit priest, Karl Rahner (1904-1984). Since Vatican II, a new spirit of ecumenism in biblical study and outreach seems clearly to be emanating from a significant segment of Roman Catholicism. It has been matched in this impulse by a significant segment of Protestantism, and both have opened active dialogue with other religions in recognition of the common bond of all human beings.[8]

It is just this phenomenon that gives me (traditionally a Methodist) such joy in finding recent writings by Catholic authors upon which to carry forward the discussion on light. I refer, for example, to *The Numinous Universe* (NU) by Daniel Liderbach, associate professor in the department of religious studies at Canisius College in Buffalo, a Jesuit institution, and to Lawrence W. Fagg's previously cited *Electromagnetism*

---

8. Such ecumenism has been resisted, of course, by the more conservative in each camp. One must wonder if this ecumenical spirit within Roman Catholicism will continue. That the liberalizing spirit of Vatican II is threatened as the prospect of a new papal election approaches may be suggested by the following snippet appearing on the front page of *The Wall Street Journal* of September 6, 2000:

> **The Vatican declared** that efforts to depict all religions as equal are wrong, forcefully restating that the Catholic Church is the one true church. The document says some theologians bend too far toward pluralism.

The "one true church" concept is based primarily on Mt 16,18, "And I tell you, you are Peter, and on this rock I will build my church." This is increasingly recognized as being ecclesiastical dogma contrary to the deeper meaning, namely, that Christ was referring to the human capacity of recognizing the Christ, indeed manifested on that occasion by Peter's revelation, but focusing not on Peter himself but rather on the human capacity he there displayed; see *The Burning Bush*, p. 480, also 8 NIB 344. Moreover, while New Testament writers later spoke of the organizational church, Christ himself reportedly spoke of the church (*ekklesia*) in only two verses of the Bible, Mt 16,18 and 18,17. But apparently most Christian scholars today (at least outside of Roman Catholicism) doubt that these words (in Mt 16) were actually spoken by Jesus; see 8 NIB 344. And there seems to be a general reluctance to interpret the "church" (*ekklesia*) in Mt 18,17 as applying other than to a local congregation or community; see 8 NIB 378 and 26 AB 220-221; and Barc, *Matthew*, Vol. 2 (1975), p. 187, says, "It is not possible that Jesus said this in its present form." Whether or not this passage was ever spoken by the Christ, the general weakness of Matthew's Gospel on such matters as this is indicated by what Steiner said about Jerome's spiritually inept translation from the original Hebrew, which he illustrated in regard particularly to the passage in Mt 27,11, "Thou sayest it," spoken in reply to Pilate's question, "Are you the King of the Jews?" (see *The Burning Bush*, pp. 300-304).

and the Sacred (EMS). Fagg is Research Professor in Nuclear Physics (retired) at The Catholic University of America in Washington, D.C., with a master's degree in religion from George Washington University. Liderbach, while not himself a physicist or mathematician, collaborated with his colleagues who were, in producing his book, and one of them, James J. Ruddick, himself a physicist and priest, wrote the book's Foreword. Before focusing on anthroposophy's special contribution, I shall be looking at the respective approaches to science and religion, relating to light, taken by these two excellent works.

Coinciding with the commencement of the new regency of the Archangel Michael, the last half of the nineteenth century brought to the Western world new impulses, or at least a heightening of those with their seeds as far back as the Renaissance, in both religion and science. And the progressively greater explosion in both fields as the twentieth century unfolded must not obscure the significance of the dramatic changes that gave birth to them in the last half of the nineteenth.

The theological underpinnings of religion were beginning to reflect a new consciousness across a broad spectrum, from the new appreciation of ancient Oriental religions introduced by H. P. Blavatsky, to "the peak in nineteenth-century German scholarship and genius as far as the text of the New Testament was concerned,"[9] to the two-source hypothesis (i.e., Mark and Q) of Holtzmann and Weiss (from which later sprang Streeter's four-source hypothesis) as a solution to the "synoptic problem,"[10] to the abolition of the evil of slavery and eventually of feminine subservience in America (both condoned by Paul as recognized conditions of humanity in his day; Eph 5,22-24; 6,5-8; Col 3,18,22). Later, the deeply religious Edgar Cayce would initiate a new and unorthodox form of spiritual investigation in America, while in Europe Rudolf Steiner broke away from the Theosophical Society (as it then existed) to reveal Christ-centered spiritual insights of such depth and radical newness that

9. David Laird Dungan, *A History of the Synoptic Problem* (part of the ABRL), NY, Doubleday, 1999, p. 293.

10. The extent to which the two source hypothesis came to life by reason of political circumstances in Germany is skillfully presented by Dungan, *Ibid.* pp. 326-329. It suited the purposes of Protestantism to exalt Mark over Matthew since the latter (Mt 16,18-19) was the source of the Roman Catholic Church's claim of papal succession of apostolic authority. Ironically, perhaps as evidence of the ecumenism within twentieth century Catholicism, even prominent Catholic scholars have joined the bandwagon of the four source hypothesis.

they can only be absorbed into human consciousness during the unfolding divine guidance of a Michealic regency. What the Enlightenment did to the Genesis creation account, the nineteenth century did to the Gospel accounts, namely, enucleated them with documentary hypotheses. While anthroposophy shows the error in both cases, the phenomena themselves demonstrate a departure from prior orthodoxy.

Modern Scientific View

When Steiner, having already laid the foundations in his work on Goethean science, began to reveal his spiritual insights at the beginning of the twentieth century, scientific thinking was in the midst of a revolution. Scientists were breaking the chrysalis of Newtonian physics and developing dramatic new theories now identified as electromagnetism, quantum mechanics, and special and general relativity. Among the array of physicists and mathematicians taking part in this development, certain names stand out. Thanks to Michael Faraday's discovery of electromagnetic induction in 1831, James Clerk Maxwell published, in 1873, on the very threshold of the new Michaelic age, his *Treatise on Electricity and Magnetism* (said to "rank with Newton's *Principia* as one of the most important works in the history of science");[11] Max Planck introduced quantum theory in 1900; Einstein pronounced his theories of special and general relativity in 1905 and 1916, respectively; and then Heisenberg his uncertainty (or indeterminancy) principle in June 1925 (published in 1927), shortly after Steiner's death.

Most of my readers will likely be as unqualified as I to understand the mathematical formulations, and much of the discussion, behind these scientific discoveries and their subsequent elaborations by hosts of other highly qualified persons. Fortunately, however, qualified scientists with distinctly, if quite varied, religio-spiritual interests have provided us lay readers with writings that make it possible for us to enter meaningfully into the dialogue on the nature of light. From what may well be a far wider bibliography of such works, I have chosen four, all directly or indirectly cited above, namely, Einstein, *Relativity* (REL); Liderbach, *The Numinous Universe* (NU); Fagg, *Electromagnetism and the Sacred* (EMS); and Zajonc, *Catching the Light* (CLT). It is quite infeasible to relate here

11. Fagg, *Ibid.* p. 40, citing Richtmeyer and Kennard, *Introduction to Modern Physics*, 46-49.

more than certain points developed in these respective works, and thus to be completely true to all that each sets out. Each is a splendid reference in and of itself and is commended to the student (particularly those like myself without extensive scientific background) who desires to contemplate even more fully the subject at hand.[12]

EINSTEIN

The first of these, Einstein, a naturally devout Jew with an almost archetypal childlike openness for new revelation, writes with characteristic ingenuousness in the Preface (1916):

> The present book is intended, as far as possible, to give an exact insight into the theory of Relativity to those readers who, from a general scientific and philosophical point of view, are interested in the theory, but who are not conversant with the mathematical apparatus of theoretical physics. The work presumes a standard of education corresponding to that of a university matriculation examination, and, despite the shortness of the book, a fair amount of patience and force of will on the part of the reader. The author has spared himself no pains in his endeavor to present the main ideas in the simplest and most intelligible form, and on the whole, in the sequence and connection in which they actually originated.

With this standard, some university graduates may occasionally wonder about the validity of their own university "matriculation." But they must surely be impressed with the degree to which Einstein has stooped to articulate, in the simplest possible terms, the complexities of his theories. Aside from highly recommending it, I shall not make primary reference to it below since it is inherent in the three other works cited.

LIDERBACH – THE SPIRITUAL APPEAL TO SCIENTISTS

Daniel Liderbach is described in his book only as a theologian and associate professor of religion at Canisius College, a Jesuit school, but I

---

12. For those students with greater background in mathematics who desire to read more deeply into these matters, I can cite the following works assembled eclectically in my own abortive efforts to dig more deeply into areas for which I am not yet qualified: Heisenberg, *The Physical Principles of the Quantum Theory* (PPQT); Pauling and Wilson, *Introduction to Quantum Mechanics* (IQM); Born, *Einstein's Theory of Relativity* (ETR).

infer he may also be a priest since the copyright is in the name of the Society of Jesus (Jesuit). He is the only one of my group not a physicist. Nevertheless, he seems to have done a remarkable job in penetrating the domain so as to present it to lay persons in understandable concepts, at least insofar as illustrating the thesis he sets forth. In his Preface he acknowledges "the considerable assistance of academic colleagues trained in … physics and the philosophy of science." One of these physicists, James J. Ruddick, S.J., wrote the Foreword in which he pointed out two narrow areas in which Liderbach, as a theologian, may have erred in relatively insignificant peripheral points. But Ruddick makes the point, Liderbach's own thesis, "that Bohr, Born, Schroedinger, Heisenberg, and the others were open to a possibility that the world was vastly different from what they had previously thought." From this he extrapolates, again as does Liderbach and implicitly the other authors I cite above, that similar openness is demanded of those who would seek the kingdom of God, "a willingness to risk being faced with new and quite different challenges."

It would take us too far afield to look at the many aspects of Einstein's *Relativity* that Liderbach presented. As Zajonc says in CLT, "Of the many rich veins we might follow into Einstein's theory of relativity, none glitters more brightly than light" (p. 256). But since Liderbach's treatment of light is incidental to his elaboration on the nature of "relativity," let us look only at some examples of the latter that serve our present purpose of taking a fresh look at light. The radical openness demanded by relativity is certainly key to that purpose. And the deep mystery that light still presents to both science and religion points to the need for a radically new and different dimension of perception and comprehension.

Special and general relativity are conceptually related, the latter going beyond the limits of the former. As Liderbach puts it, "Special relativity restricts its concerns to the relationship between the motion of physical occurrences and the motion of those who observe occurrences. The more general theory is concerned … with all motion … all possible frames of reference" (p. 41).

To introduce special relativity, he quotes Einstein's example of a stone dropped from the window of a uniformly moving railway carriage. What is the trajectory of the stone as it falls to the earth? The answer is that it has no "independently existing trajectory, but only a trajectory relative to a particular body of reference." To the one who drops the stone from the window and watches it fall, it falls in a straight line. To a pedestrian standing somewhere on the railway embankment, it falls in a parabolic curve. Each trajectory is equally valid judged from its own perspective or frame of reference.

To introduce general relativity, Liderbach adapts Einstein's illustration of an empty chest suspended somewhere in empty space (Chap. 20) to the more common experiential case of "a person riding in an elevator within an extraordinarily tall building" (p. 42). When the car is at rest, the person feels the effect of gravity and notes its pull upon a key dropped to the floor. If the car then ascends, the person notes an increase in gravity and a more rapid descent of the key, i.e., the floor comes up to meet it. When the car descends, the person's gravitational pull (relative to the elevator car) decreases and the key falls more slowly, i.e., the floor runs away from it as it falls. If then the cable breaks, both the person and the key float in the car, and without knowledge of anything outside the car it could be interpreted as being motionless.

The seed for both theories was planted when Einstein was only sixteen years old. The thought came to him, what if he could run at the speed of light? Would light then stand still? With all the marvelous and startling insights he gave humanity, at the end of his life light was still the big question mark, though the speed of light was the basis, the measuring stick, of his formulas. Everything was relative except the speed of light. Neither space nor time had any independent validity, only space-time, a continuum in which everything without exception exists. Energy became mass. Einstein developed two postulates. The first had the effect of making the idea of ether (matter) unnecessary for the transmission of light. The second was that the speed of light in a vacuum is constant and is independent of its source, the observer and the observer's motion. This flew in the face of both common sense and the general laws of physics as they previously existed, but it has been confirmed. Thus, the movement of the source of light does not affect the speed at which it travels in front or behind such movement relative to a fixed observation point. In other words, it does not travel faster when emitted in the direction its source is moving, nor slower when emitted in the direction away from which its source is moving, than it does when emitted from a stationary source.

Again under the general theory of relativity, there is an equivalency of all reference frames. Space is curved, and the shortest distance between two points is a curved line, an arc. The common sense rules of Euclidean geometry have to be suspended. A triangle, which we know has interior angles totaling 180 degrees, has more than that when traced upon a sphere. Liderbach gives the example of a triangle formed on the Earth's sphere by dropping two of its sides from the north pole to the equator. They would each make right angles (90 degrees) with the equator, so that the interior angles would total 180 degrees plus the arbitrary angle between the sides at the pole.

This is the simplest of illustrations, but in its way it typifies how relativity has shaken the foundations of common sense and classical physics and cosmology.

Liderbach reverses the chronology of their inception and takes up quantum physics following relativity. Much of the ground he covers there is covered by both Fagg and Zajonc, both of whom, particularly Zajonc, are directed more specifically toward light. What Liderbach crystallizes from his discussion are "enigmatic presences" within the physical world "that elude the range ... the senses can grasp" (pp. 68 and 107). He calls them "quantum occurrences [that] challenge ... common-sense." We will sample these later with Fagg and Zajonc. For now, we consider his conclusion "that the Presence of the kingdom is at least plausible for Christian believers who are sympathetic to physical science," for that "kingdom is not more extraordinary than [those] of relativity and quantum physics." Since his thesis (of openness by scientists to the presence of the Kingdom), as thesis, is unique among the quoted authors, and is quite well conceived and expressed, let us also look at its broader implications.

As we look at these scientific revelations that have emerged from the womb of human awareness since the last half of the nineteenth century, consider how they demonstrate what the Bible reveals from the very first—fission—a term we tend to associate with nuclear physics but which means simply "separation" or "division." It is the characteristic phenomenon of the Old Testament and the growth process, though it must finally reach fruition in its counterpart—fusion—where things come together again (Eph 1,9-10; Rom 8,19-23). Together they are the outgoing and return of the Prodigal Son. Our willingness to leave the old and move into the new is the very substance of Noah's departure from Atlantis (Gen 6-10), Abraham's departure from Ur (Gen 12,1-4), Jacob's departure from Haran (Gen 31-32, though Jacob's journeys show two such departures which, taken together, represent an outgoing and a return, Gen 28-32), and on and on.

A primarily New Testament version of the same spiritual phenomenon of "fission" is that of "homelessness." To follow the Christ one must leave the security of the past, of "home," and move into the uncertain terrain of the future (Mt 8,19-22; 19,27-29; Mk 10,28-30; Lk 9,57-62; 17,31; 18,28-30). Churches today are internally rent by social issues of this nature. Slavish devotion to church doctrine has proven unwise in the history of Christendom. Even going back only as far as Galileo, the Church's cosmology has had to be modified. During the twentieth century all but the most conservative have seen the necessity of accommodating the idea of evolution (though anthroposophy shows that the scientific idea of evolution, a necessary first step, is one hundred eighty degrees off course, for the lower kingdoms descended from the human and not the human from the lower). Martyrs imprisoned, tortured or burned at the stake by the Church, or otherwise anathematized in times past have been rehabilitated officially or unofficially. Origen, the first real Christian theologian, anathematized for his belief in the preexistence of the soul (which the Church, excepting perhaps only the Mormons, still does not recognize), immediately comes to mind. And it is only a short step from preexistence to the idea of reincarnation which the Church must surely someday recognize, or at least consider, as new organs of human consciousness evolve. Teilhard de Chardin, whose works were proscribed by superiors during his life, is today admired in many circles. Examples could go on and on. It is in the nature of things.

The sword Liderbach uses, "enigmatic presences" in the physical world, is effectively wielded, but it is two-edged and cuts also in another direction. He certainly seems to endorse the idea that there are new ways to experience the Kingdom of God in the world. He even suggests putting aside "the interpretations already learned and the consequent personal security" and accepting the "challenge to adopt a new world-view" (p. 119). Then in his next, and penultimate, chapter he endorses Darwinism right along with Homer, Einstein and Bach. It is, of course, now no risk within Christendom, even Catholicism, to accept the idea of evolution. One doesn't now become "homeless" thereby. It would be another thing, in our day, for theologians to recognize the evolution of the human soul and bodies, through multiple lives on Earth, as the journey of the Prodigal Son, the crown of creation and fountainhead from which sprang the lower three kingdoms rather than the reverse. Liderbach calls "openness" a necessary "heuristic" (an aid to discovering or understanding) for the Kingdom of God. Perhaps it is this characteristic of childhood, implied in Mt 19,14 ("for to such belongs the kingdom of heaven"; also Mk 10,14-15; Lk 18,16-17; Mt 18,3-4), that is most necessary in our day. It is a heuristic needed as much by theologians in their own outlook as in their preachments to science, a heuristic needed both in religion and science if they are to become as one, as eventually they must.

FAGG — LIGHT AS ELECTROMAGNETISM

We now move more particularly toward the subject of light with Lawrence W. Fagg's recent *Electromagnetism and the Sacred* (EMS). Just as Einstein, in his *Relativity*, wrote "in the simplest and most intelligible form" he could, so also Fagg, thankfully for the benefit of most of us, has "avoided using any mathematical equations" except for Einstein's famous one ($E = mc^2$, or energy equals mass times the speed of light squared).[13]

At times he speaks of light and of electromagnetic radiation as being synonymous, e.g., "light (which is electromagnetic radiation)" (pp. 11, 43, 67, 99, 105 and 124). Fortunately, however, in the final analysis he confesses that there is a difference between electromagnetism as light and God's "immanence" as light (pp. 22-23, 109 and 130). He goes right to the threshold that science makes possible, yet recognizes there is still something beyond. It is that force beyond that now beckons us.

For most of us, the term electromagnetism probably elicits an image of a simple electromagnet of the type discovered by Michael Faraday in 1831.[14] Electromagnetism is defined either as "magnetism produced by an electric current" or as "the branch of physics that deals with electricity and magnetism."[15] Most of us also know that light in a vacuum travels at the speed of approximately 186,000 miles per second, the upper limit of velocity in what we know as creation.[16] Einstein's *Relativity*

---

13. David Bodanis' recent book, $E = mc^2$, subtitled "A Biography of the World's Most Famous Equation," is highly recommended as not only a highly readable account of the personalities and principles that underlay the famous formula, but also an aid to the lay person in understanding the mysterious way that its energy becomes mass or its mass becomes energy.

14. WNWCD defines "electromagnet" as "a soft iron core surrounded by a coil of wire, that temporarily becomes a magnet when an electric current flows through the wire."

15. *Ibid.* "electromagnetism."

16. A cryptic front page notice in *The Wall Street Journal* for July 20, 2000, said, "The [186,000 mps] speed of light was surpassed in Princeton experiments that passed a laser beam through cesium vapor, according to a Nature article." For now, we merely note this in passing.

calls it "a limiting velocity, which can neither be reached nor exceeded by any real body" (p. 41). Writing in 1916, he also said that "we have experience of such rapid motions only in the case of electrons and ions" (p. 49).[17]

Mystery abounds in the study of light to this day. "Light—that convenient legacy of the mystical tradition of both Eastern and Western Christian versions—behaves for quantum scientists sometimes as a particle and sometimes as a wave."[18] It seems generally accepted now, since more precise knowledge is not yet available, that light behaves at one and the same time according to two different theories which, according to common sense, are mutually exclusive of each other. One such theory is that light is composed of particles (i.e., mass) that move through space, while the other theory is that it is mass-less and thus moves through space in transverse waves (up and down rather than longitudinal as in the case of sound waves produced by vibrating mass).

Apparently among scientists there is a rather widespread tendency to equate electromagnetism to light, and vice versa. Even Zajonc, when speaking of Faraday's discovery, says, "The impact of Faraday's discovery both practically *and for our understanding of light* is so great that we must pause to examine it. For in attempting to understand what appears to be a purely electrical effect, the foundations were inadvertently set *for a new understanding of light*," (p. 130, emphasis mine). Zajonc's work wends its way, however, to some distinctions not so clearly made by others, as we shall see. And while Fagg ultimately admits that electromagnetism is not God's ultimate "immanence," he draws no clear line of demarcation between them. One wonders if there is a way to really distinguish this exaltation of electromagnetism from Spinoza's pantheistic equating of God to the entirety of what can be observed in nature (creation).[19] Is the

---

17. WNWCD defines an "ion" as "an electrically charged atom or group of atoms, the electrical charge of which results when a neutral atom or group of atoms loses or gains one or more electrons during chemical reactions, by the action of certain forms of radiant energy, etc.: the loss of electrons results in a positively charged ion (*cation*), the gain of electrons in a negatively charged ion (*anion*)."

18. Catherine L. Albanese, "The Subtle Energies of Spirit: Explorations in Metaphysical and New Age Spirituality," *Journal of American Academy of Religion*, Vol. 67, No. 2, June 1999, p. 310.

19. See Dungan's discussion of Spinoza's *Theological-Political Treatise* in his *A History of the Synoptic Problem*, *supra*, Chap. 16, "Baruch Spinoza and the Political Agenda of Modern Historical-Critical Interpretation."

Whole simply the sum of its parts? The study of light challenges us with this question.

Science, if Fagg's work is any indication, regards electromagnetic phenomena, apparently more or less in its entirety, as moving with the speed of light. He refers to "alternating electric and magnetic fields in an electromagnetic wave [as] moving at the speed of light" (Fig. 2, p. 42). He portrays (Fig. 3, p. 42) the spectrum of electromagnetic radiation by both wavelength and frequency, complementary quotients from dividing the speed of light. And then he says, "The whole spectrum of radiations—radio waves, [microwaves], infrared, visible, ultraviolet, x-rays, and γ-rays—[are] all electromagnetic radiations moving at the speed of light. Indeed the generic name for all these radiations has become light.... Maxwell's work, therefore, not only unified electricity and magnetism but also incorporated the disciplines of light and optics into the realm of electromagnetism."

Neither my study of the cited works, nor my research through *Britannica*, has yielded any discussion of the speed of magnetism as a separate phenomenon. Yet Rodney Collin (1909-1956), most prominent disciple of the Russian mystic and mathematician P. D. Ouspensky, indicates that magnetic influences travel at about four hundred miles per second, one five-hundredth the speed of light. And he cites as the basis for this conclusion tests of solar magnetism measured by the delay in sunspot change and its effect on the magnetism of the Earth's atmosphere.[20] I am unable to reconcile this anomalous information, and cite it only as a curiosity for some wiser reader to resolve.

The reader should not infer, even for a moment, my disapproval of Fagg's work. It has been for me, in fact, of immense educational value, and I surmise most others without extensive backgrounds in mathematics and physics, especially nuclear physics, will also benefit greatly from studying it.

Before considering Fagg's work, however, let us look at the recognized unit, or quantum, the smallest possible unit, of light measurement—the *photon*. It has apparently taken almost a century for this measurement to be adequately developed (if it is). A good discussion of this development can be found in Zajonc, Chapter 11 entitled "Least Light: A Contemporary View." He indicates that Planck and Einstein

---

20. See Collin, *The Theory of Celestial Influence* (TCI), pp. 43-44, 102 and 122.

"were the first to posit the existence of an elementary quantum of light, suggesting light was not infinitely divisible, and so possessed a least part" (p. 293). The name "photon" was then first used by an American chemist, G. N. Lewis, in 1926. Einstein seems to have suggested the use of a "beamsplitter" early on, but not until the 1980s was a sufficiently elegant test devised (by a French group in 1986) to adequately demonstrate the possibility of such a quantum (photon). Zajonc describes it thus (fn mine):

> Although technically somewhat difficult, it is conceptually supremely simple. One passes the suspected photon into an optical instrument that divides light, sending half one way and half another way. If at some point the light is no longer divisible, then we have reached the level of the photon, or "atom" (from the Greek, meaning indivisible)[21] of light. The optical device that divides light in half is a half-silvered mirror, or "beamsplitter." When light falls on it, half the light is transmitted and half reflected. Imagine a single, atomlike photon striking the beamsplitter. What will happen? If it is truly indivisible, then it will go one way or the other but *not* both. This is called "anticorrelation." If, on the other hand, the light can be divided, both branches will have light, half will go one way and half the other. This is the test.
>
> In contrast to an atomic theory of light, the wave theory conceives of light as infinitely divisible; there is no lower limit to how weak the light's intensity can be. Therefore the beamsplitter will *always* divide the light, transmitting half one way and reflecting the other half. The beamsplitter is, therefore, a litmus test for light: wave or particle.

---

21. Surely there must be an archetypal relationship between adam (hard) and atom (indivisible) from which these two Greek sources arose. Can one not sense the presence of both meanings in the first appearance of Adam as a human male in the canon at Gen 3,17? (See the Chapter End Note in the Creation essay.) Schwaller de Lubicz equates the Greek adam to the ancient Egyptian Atum in *The Temple of Man* (TOMN), p. 968. That ancient meaning of Atum, beautifully mystical but beyond the scope of our present discussion, can be studied in TOMN by reference to its index under the designations "Atum" or "Atum-Ra." It would be well for Bible students, in evaluating the meaning of Adam in Gen 3,17, to bear in mind that Moses was trained (i.e., initiated) in the mysteries of Egypt (Ex 2,10; Acts 7,22, as well as those of Midian, Ex 2,15b-20). And Plato tells us that the deepest insights of ancient Greek wisdom paled by comparison with their sources in Egypt.

As he explains, single-photon sources of light are not normal, but in recent years two have been devised that, when properly used, pass the single-photon litmus test. The anticorrelation is always there. Chalk up one for the particle theory, but don't relax your cortex yet. Hold the thought until we can more fully examine the Janus character of light as both particle and wave. In reference to knowing light (and harmony), Schwaller de Lubicz, characterizes it as "having a sense of the simultaneity of opposites … in us."[22] Does light, as science itself now recognizes, demonstrate this presence of mutually exclusive opposites at one and the same time?

But let us first digress to understand more of electromagnetism as Fagg has simplified it for us.

Early in "Fire" we reproduced from Steiner's *Light Course* (LC) two parallelograms, one of movements (kinetics) and one of forces (mechanics), and later discussed the relationship of force to mass (matter). Still later we saw that there were forces at the etheric and higher levels that were involved in the creative process but as yet not recognized by science. In the discussion below, we deal with forces that are recognized by science, but in connection with the force in light science comes up against puzzles that it has yet to solve. At this or some comparable point science must come eventually to grips with the reality that to advance beyond knowledge of the mineral kingdom it must leave its instruments behind and look to revelation made possible only by newly developed (evolved) organs of human perception. Perhaps in its study of light science is at that threshold Steiner described when he said that science must continue in its study of the material world until it reaches the point of absurdity, or, in other words, paints itself into a corner. It can look only so far into the minuteness, on the one hand, or the magnitude, on the other, of material creation. There, in ever so many patterns it could have seen analogy to the spiritual world whence it came ("As Above, So Below"), but it must reach its own limitations and turn back upon itself, the "point of recognition" by the Prodigal Son (Lk 15,17). There are glimmers of hope in that direction. The works cited herein seem to fall in that category.

---

22. TOMN, p. 28.

Early in the century, Steiner wrote a book entitled *Riddles of Philosophy* (RP; there were three later editions, 1914, 1918 and 1923). In one of these editions, he recognized Einstein's relativity. Of it, to conclude the penultimate chapter of Part II, he said (p. 444, fn mine):

> Insofar as man considers himself within the world of natural things and events, he will find it impossible to escape the conclusions of this theory of relativity. But if he does not want to lose himself in mere relativities, in what may be called an impotence of his inner life, if he wants to experience his own entity, he must not seek what is "substantial in itself" in the realm of *nature*[23] but in *transcending nature*, in the realm of the spirit.
>
> It will not be possible to evade the theory of relativity for the physical world, but precisely this fact will drive us to a knowledge of the spirit. What is significant about the theory of relativity is the fact that it proves the necessity of a science of the spirit that is to be sought in spiritual ways, independent of the observation of *nature*. That the theory of relativity forces us to think in this way constitutes its value within the development of world conception.

Nature shows itself to us in the world of matter. Even its forces have thus far manifested themselves to our senses and thinking only in the world of matter. We could not feel the rush of wind if air had no mass. As beautiful as that world is as an *image* of the higher (Jn 3,8), we must recognize that the world of nature, the world of matter, is the pigpen in the parable of the Prodigal Son. In spite of the billions of years back to the birth of our material universe, we must recognize that all matter (and forces manifesting through matter) is the menopausal child of the creative process.[24] Relativity shows us that these billions of years, in and of themselves, do not independently exist. Unspeakably earlier in the creative process, far, far rarer than anything our senses or instruments

---

23. "He is not here!" Mt 28,6a; Mk 16,6b; Lk 24,5b.
24. In *The Burning Bush* (BB) I try to relate this reality, which, insofar as it is possible to reach back to such beginnings, is set out schematically in chart I-1. But to grasp these early processes more fully and adequately, the student must study (contemplate, not just read) the critical anthroposophical foundational book *An Outline of Esoteric Science*, formerly *Occult Science* (OS) as it is cited in BB.

can detect or our thinking conceive, the initial creative force went out from the Father God (to borrow from the concept of the Trinity). John calls this "the Word" (the Christ) from which all matter and all lesser forces eventually came (Jn 1,1-3). But to come to our "point of recognition" we must examine "nature."

Science recognizes "four forces of nature," and Fagg sets them out as nuclear, electromagnetic, weak and gravity. The nuclear and weak forces are "short-range" while electromagnetic and gravity forces are "long-range," each characterization indicating the expanse over which they are effective. Thus the nuclear and weak might be said to be microscopic and the other two telescopic, so to speak. Ranked by their relative strength, from greatest to least, they are nuclear, electromagnetic, weak and gravitational. The gravitational force is only attractive while the electromagnetic can be repulsive or attractive. Both long-range forces are inversely proportional to the square of the distance between two bodies and thus never die out to exactly zero. In this there is a hint of a pattern of diminution pointing in the direction of the spiritual world—but to cross that threshold is to pass through what Steiner calls the "null point" where the photograph becomes the negative, the higher mirror image (Gen 1,26-27). Einstein showed that there could be no space without mass and vice versa, but on the other side of the null point we leave space (as well as time) behind. We shall look more fully at this concept in the final essay.

Having listed the forces, Fagg asks, "How is the force transmitted?" and answers by saying "by the exchange of ... particles [called] bosons." Further, "except for the fleeting existence of the bosons discharging their function as force messengers, the totality of the known matter in the cosmos is made up of a variety of particles" ranging from "the most elementary, such as quarks and electrons, to the more complex, such as protons and neutrons, to the still more complex, such as atoms and molecules."[25] He then gives us the most helpful table below (p. 30):

---

25. Liderbach also mentions "hadrons" (pp. 98-99), a subnuclear particle made up of quarks (per WNWCD). It may be an alternative classification to part of what Fagg gives. Hadrons seem to be identified with the concept of "spin." Interestingly, the Hebrew word *gll (or glgl)*, the base of many biblical terms, such as Gilgal (Deut 11,30; Josh 5,9-10), has a similar meaning (see the section called "The Whirlwind" in the "Fire" essay).

Table 1

BUILDING BLOCKS OF MATTER

Quarks

Up	Charm	Top
Down	Strange	Bottom

Leptons

Electron	Muon	Tauon
Electron	Muon	Tauon
neutrino	neutrino	neutrino

Force Carriers (Bosons)

Nuclear—8 Gluons

Electromagnetic—Photon

Weak—W^+, W^-, Z^0

Gravity—Graviton

As indicated in "Fire," forces cannot be seen. And all of the above "building blocks" are far too minute to ever have been seen by the human eye, even through the most powerful microscope. Fagg makes the interesting observation that "all matter" is composed of *twelve* "indivisible particles," being the above six quarks and six leptons. Each lepton has a corresponding neutrino that is far lighter than its partner. Further, "Each of the quarks and leptons has a corresponding antiparticle (not listed in table 1) that is in general identical to the particle, except that it has an electric charge opposite to that of the particle" (p. 31). The best known is the one corresponding to the electron, which is known as a "positron" since it has a positive charge compared to the negative of the electron. For perspective, the tauon is far smaller; theoretically it may be on the order of one ten-millionth the mass of the electron. These twelve building blocks, together with their antiparticles, compose "the complete list of particles that are the irreducible ingredients of the ... material universe" as far as is known by science today (p. 32). The only force carriers (bosons) that have any mass are the threefold group associated with the weak force (p. 34 and

WNWCD, "photon"). Noting that "nothing that has mass when at rest can move at the speed of light," and that the photon (the force carrier for electromagnetism) has no mass *at rest*, Fagg points out that the photon nevertheless has "an effective mass by virtue of its energy of motion through the use of Einstein's well-known equation linking mass and energy, $E = mc^2$" (p. 34).

According to my understanding of anthroposophy, I am unable to go along with Fagg on the widely held big bang theory of creation, arrived at by a science that has not yet taken anthroposophical insights into account. This detracts little, however, from my admiration for his work otherwise.

Here Fagg sets out, as do the other sources, an account of the history and personalities involved in the development of electromagnetic science down to the present time. The names I've mentioned above are included in his account, along with others particularly significant in the century's more recent developments. The story of the development of electromagnetism from the very first has read like a pantheon of genius for which all creation should be grateful, even if insights of this science only carry us to the threshold of a higher realm of knowledge, the crossing of which must await the gift of true intuition (the basis of anthroposophy, according to its founder and the understanding of its adherents).

During the latter part of the twentieth century, the nature of the photon as it relates to electromagnetism has been further refined so that now one speaks of "real" photons and "virtual" photons. Inasmuch as Fagg (in line with scientific thinking) tends to equate electromagnetism and light, and an inspection of Fagg's Table 1 above shows us that our discussion of electromagnetism must relate to the photon, we now approach the critical questions, for our purposes, presented by his most helpful exposition. At this point it is well, considering my lay status in regard to nuclear physics, that I surrender enough originality of expression to avoid error by quoting liberally from Fagg's exposition at pp. 51-54 (fns mine):

> QED [quantum electrodynamics] tells us that the electromagnetic force is transmitted by photons. These "carrier" photons are very transient and are actually unobservable; in the parlance of the trade they are called "virtual" photons.
>
> This is the hidden mode of existence for photons. In contrast, the photons that help us see light and color and vivify the world around

us are called "real" photons. While virtual photons are continually being produced and exchanged between any bodies that interact via the electromagnetic force, real photons are generally produced in two ways.... Using the word "virtual" to specify the force-carrying photons is perhaps unfortunate because it tends to imply that they do not exist, when indeed they do. Just because we cannot observe them does not mean they are not there. They are there and are a vital part of [QED] calculations; and if they are not included in these calculations, we do not get the right answer—that is, the answer that agrees with experimental observations.

Note that from the Goethean standpoint, science here departs from observation in fact to observation only through kinetics or calculation. Recall Steiner's twin parallelograms of kinematics (ideal) versus mechanics (empirical) set out in the "Fire" essay. It seems that Einstein, that paradigm of open-minded genius, to the end of his days was also troubled by this aspect of quantum mechanics. Is this not already the cusp of the chasm or null point between nature and the spiritual world? Steiner indicated that Einstein's relativity would be a catalyst toward ultimate human penetration of the spiritual world. Perhaps the symbiotic twins of quantum theory and relativity, both born out of science's quest for an understanding of light at the outset of the new age of the Archangel Michael, Christ's faithful and majestic regent of light, will jointly serve as that catalyst. Fagg continues:

> Another vital part of QED calculations that also involves unobservable phenomena has to do with the nature of the vacuum. If we had a perfect vacuum pump that could pump every single molecule of gas out of a sealed container, then we might reasonably suppose that the volume of the container had been reduced to a completely dormant space of nothing. But this is not true. The vacuum is alive with evanescent pairs of particles, mostly electrons and positrons, that materialize for a brief instant and then vanish.[26]

---

26. The "hidden energy" in a vacuum is also meaningfully discussed by Zajonc, *ibid.*, at pp. 327-328, where he also links it in a special way with "darkness." In this and other phenomena of light that violate "common sense," there is a place for the activity of the hierarchies. The reader might find comfort here in contemplating what is said about them in I-29.

The reader will recall Steiner's characterization in the "Fire" essay above of the realm of light as that of materialization-dematerialization, and this decades before science began to use the same language for light. But science is still on this side of the null point, and the Cherubim with the Seraphim's flaming sword (Gen 3,24) prevents its going further until it leaves the mineral kingdom and seeks the mysteries of the higher three kingdoms. Fagg goes on:

How can this be? This seems to fly in the face of the time-tested law of the conservation of energy. That is, if we use Einstein's famous formula, $E = mc^2$, we see that the masses of the electron and positron are really a form of energy and the conservation law is violated.

This, however, is where quantum theory comes in to tell us that under certain circumstances this apparent violation is possible. At the core of the quantum theory is what is known as the Heisenberg uncertainty principle, which essentially states that two complementary quantities describing the state of a particle cannot simultaneously be measured with ultimate accuracy. In other words, nature has imposed an objective limit on how precisely we see what is going on with a particle. For example, it is impossible to determine at the same time and with perfect accuracy both the position and momentum, or velocity, of the particle.

Another version of the uncertainty principle tells us that there is also a limit to how precisely we can simultaneously measure both the energy of a particle and the duration of time that it has that energy.[27] This does not mean, however, that below this limit, particles, which are not too massive or too long-lasting, cannot exist for a very short time, only that it is impossible for us to observe and measure them.

Thus, the law of conservation of energy applies to energy and mass we can observe, so that pairs of electrons and positrons can emerge out of the vacuum and then vanish as long as they do not stay around long enough for us to observe them. It is as if the particle pairs "borrow" energy in the form of mass from the vacuum but must pay it back

27. I assume this is the same as, or closely related to, what Liderbach (p. 76) describes in discussing the so-called "complementarity" principle. Waves and particles are "complementary concepts" and to measure one is to alter the identity of the other, so that they cannot be simultaneously measured. It would seem that the "duration" of a particle and the length or frequency of a wave must be essentially the same thing.

quickly, and the more the mass-energy that is "borrowed," the more quickly it must be paid back (Harrison [*Masks of the Universe*], 126).

Nevertheless, the question immediately arises: if we can't observe them, how do we know they are there? This again is where QED comes in. For without accounting for the brief presence of such electron-positron pairs in the calculations we make to predict the results of an experiment, we do not get the right, experimentally verified answer, just as in the case of the virtual photons. The presence of both the virtual photons and the virtual particle pairs tell us, therefore, that nature, and indeed space itself, is electrically alive.

In fact, the great majority of space occupied by all earthly objects is impregnated with an astronomical number of such essentially nonmaterial phenomena in a constant flurry of activity. All things that appear to be solid or liquid or to have substance consist principally of this vibrant space. This can be understood by considering, for example, a carbon atom in your pencil where some 99.97 percent of its mass is concentrated in the nucleus at its center, which occupies roughly one-trillionth of the volume of the atom as a whole. The remainder of the volume is occupied by six electrons (of very low mass) and trillions of virtual photons transmitting the electromagnetic force that keeps them in their orbits. Hence, we and all apparently material earthly objects are a part of a vast ocean of essentially nonmaterial space energized by an innumerable multitude of virtual electrodynamic phenomena.

In any case, with the inclusion of these virtual phenomena in calculations on a host of electrodynamic phenomena, QED yields incredibly accurate answers, answers that agree with experiments to better than one part in ten billion. Indeed, QED is by far the most accurate theory in all of physics. It is a case where humans have come as close as they may in a long time to describing accurately an aspect of nature. In Richard Feynman's words, "But so far, we have found nothing wrong with the theory of [QED]. It is therefore, I would say, the jewel of physics—our proudest possession" (Feynman, *Q.E.D.*, 8).

Jesus told the Pharisees and Sadducees they knew how to interpret the appearance of the sky in regard to the weather, but did not know how to "interpret the signs of the times" (Mt 16,3). "Signs" are what phenomena give us as *images* of higher reality. The significance of the first sign in

John's Gospel (Jn 2,1-11, the wedding at Cana) is explained in *The Burning Bush*, pp. 137-142). There we see that one cannot be satisfied with superficiality. We need to ask ourselves whether, in the light of the revelations of QED above, the theologian should perceive any "sign" in what the nuclear physicist has demonstrated? (The open mind Liderbach urges upon the scientific-minded seems here also advisable for the theologian.) It seems fairly clear that in Christ's time neither the "theologians" nor his own followers apprehended the meaning of the sign of Jonah (Mt 12,39; Lk 11,29). Nor do theologians today adequately apprehend its meaning, for they still miss the meaning of the raising of Lazarus, a "sign of Jonah" (see "Peter, James and John" in *The Burning Bush*, also *The Disciple Whom Jesus Loved*). If Christendom is to rise to the spiritual demands upon it in this new age of Michael, that insight must soon be attained.

But what about the new "signs of the times" presented by these scientific developments of the twentieth century? What is the meaning of this phenomenon at the lowest subatomic level, this coming into existence and then withdrawing again of matter before its nature can be fully defined (materialization-dematerialization)? Do we not see at this subatomic level of observable creation the analogue to the human soul, the "burning bush," the "I Am," crossing back and forth over the null point between incarnation and the discarnate state in the process of its perfection (Mt 5,48), its own coming to the light? As Job (the Prodigal Son) approached the two guardians of the threshold, before being restored to the fullness of God's presence, we read that "the Lord answered Job out of the whirlwind" (Job 38,1), that is, out of the spiral (the Hebrew *gll* or *glgl*[28]), the fire ether, and said to him (Job 38,19-21, emphasis mine):

> *Where is the way to the dwelling of light*,
> and where is the *place of darkness*,
> that you may take it to its territory
> and that you may discern the paths to its home?
> You know, for you were born then,
> And the number of your days is great!

What is seen in any given life is only a part of the karmic being and cannot be fully measured by any earthly standard of measurement or judgment.

---

28. See the section called "The Whirlwind" in the "Fire" essay.

It is the Behemoth that can only be found under the lotus tree[29] and that cannot be taken by hooks or pierced in his nose with a snare: the lower guardian of the threshold (Job 40,15-24). The Heisenberg principle of uncertainty, or indeterminancy, is reflected in this passage, for certainly the minutest part "cannot be taken by hooks or pierced in its nose with a snare."

Or, if we would look further, do we not apprehend from the structure of our minutest part that we and all that we observe with our senses are far less than one percent mass and the rest is empty space—and in this are we not of the same nature in our minutest part, as well as our whole, as is the expanse of universe we look out upon? Our Sun is but one of one hundred billion stars in our Milky Way galaxy, and our galaxy is itself like a star in the galaxy of the known universe. Moreover, to account for gravitational effects, there must be unaccounted for mass (or alternately suction) in the intergalactic spaces, not unlike the activity discussed above in a vacuum. In the composition of our mineral-physical bodies as well as in all we look out upon, we are but a fractal within the universal design that reaches to the limit of perception both macroscopically and microscopically. In our "likeness" we are part and parcel of the "image" of the Elohim, the Spirits of Form (Gen 1,26; see also I-6).

And relativity suggests that, from the standpoint of light, all of these lives are collapsed into the one Behemoth (karmic being) so that time as an independent phenomenon does not exist and what came after is the same as what came before ("the last will be first, and the first last"; Mt 19,30; 20,16; Mk 10,31; Lk 13,30; see also the "Alpha" and "Omega" discussions in the Creation essay). When we have reached the state of being one with Christ, it shall be so. And all creation is one and one is all, a part of a living unity (Eph 1,9-10; Rom 8,19-23).

Before leaving Fagg's presentation, it remains only to say that he demonstrates over and over that electromagnetic interaction, which he calls EMI, the phenomenon involved in all of his presentation above, is the most pervasive phenomenon in the material realm and is the most complete analogue to God's immanence that is available in the physical realm. He bases this on four similarities (p. 105): 1. Both are ubiquitous and all-pervasive in our world. 2. Both reach from the most subtle and sensitive to the most powerful and awesome experiences. 3. They both relate to,

---

29. Job 40,21-22; the lotus is the ancient symbol of the organs of the human astral body (see I-21). See fns 22 and 23 and their related text in the Creation essay.

and are normally identified with, light, and extend far beyond what we can sense. 4. Both are constant in their nature. While in the final analysis EMI is not God or God's immanence, it is "the primal physical mechanism provided by God for us to have access to that immanence" (p. 109).

ZAJONC — SCIENCE FRUSTRATED: "FOR ALL PRACTICAL PURPOSES"

As he nears the conclusion of *Catching the Light*, Zajonc discusses the contemporary view of light (Chap. 11) pointing out quandaries that still exist. He speaks of an archetypal instance of wave-particle duality being the interference that a single photon imposes upon its own image. It travels only one path, not two, yet in interfering with its own image it acts as though it were not a particle but a wave traveling two paths instead of one. As Zajonc says, "The implications ... are fundamental," constituting "an archetypal phenomenon" for which we "lack the ideas with which to see it rightly" (p. 299). And he makes the apt observation:

> Goethe was right. Try though we may to split light into fundamental atomic pieces, it remains whole to the end.... Perhaps for light, at least, the most fundamental feature is not to be found in smallness, but rather in wholeness, its incorrigible capacity to be one and many, particle and wave, a single thing with the universe inside.

Zajonc then discusses further instances where common-sense solutions to light phenomena just don't exist. He details such an instance involving tests of "twin photons" differently polarized. He says that "only four attributes are used to define light formally; they are polarization, wavelength, direction and intensity." Yet he shows that each is ambiguous, so that "there is no truly unambiguous attribute of light!" (p. 314).

I cannot help but relate this to the Christ, who identified himself with light, yet left neither artistic nor narrative record of his physical appearance on Earth. One has to think how very unique this is for any historically significant person, but it is also of the nature of light, and seems to have been divinely ordained so that, upon reflection, humanity would realize that it was not his mineral-physical being that has any importance for our understanding of his first presence, his Resurrection, or his coming again.

Perhaps the most amazing aspect of light phenomena is what is called "non-locality." Fagg does not discuss it in elaborating his thesis. Liderbach gives an excellent abbreviated illustration at pp. 103-104 where he also gives it the name "action-at-a-distance." Zajonc gives the most extensive discussion in the section of his Chapter 11 called "Entangled Light" (pp. 307-320). It seems intrinsically cognate to Heisenberg's "uncertainty principle" discovered shortly after Steiner's death in 1925, but these more amazing implications had to await fuller development during the last quarter of the twentieth century. The experiment through which it emerged is known as EPR, an acronym taken from Einstein, Podolsky and Rosen, who first performed it in 1935. Its implications so befuddled Einstein in his own views of rationality that he apparently balked at its revelation till the end of his days (1955). Zajonc dates the more recent developments to the period from 1975, when John Bell "proved his famous theorems" enabling physicists to successfully perform Einstein's 1935 EPR experiment.[30] What is it that is so amazing about "non-locality?" It is the seeming ability of one photon at one location to communicate with another photon (its twin) at another location in such manner that the latter seems to take on the previously different character of the former, and to do so instantaneously. Thus, an examination of the photon in New York instantly changes the character of the photon in London, to borrow the geographic settings from Liderbach's example. As Zajonc says (p. 309), there is no "noninvasive, to use medical terminology" way to test these delicate quantum objects, for in the very testing they are "disturbed so violently" that they change character in one's hands. There is something in this subatomic world that can only be described as "holistic." Light is "holy," and like the God who spoke to Moses (the higher "I Am," the Christ—through the Eloha Yahweh), it cannot be fully observed by normal human modes of perception yet evolved.

Zajonc first illustrates this phenomenon by describing EPR laboratory experiments in which twin photons are distinguished from one another only by the characteristic of polarization. Distant actions on one twin immediately affected the polarization of the other. There was thus "*no local, realistic* way of understanding polarization correlations!" As previously noted, "only four attributes are used to define light formally ... polarization, wavelength, direction, and intensity." The dual

---

30. Zajonc had the opportunity of co-organizing a workshop at Amherst College featuring John Bell shortly before the latter's untimely death in 1990. Along with Einstein, Bell emphasized over and over that orthodox quantum mechanics was not good enough and would someday be superseded because "It carries in itself the seeds of its own destruction" (p. 308).

path phenomena made "direction" ambiguous, and other experiments have shown wavelength and intensity to also be ambiguous; again, "there is no truly unambiguous attribute of light!" (P. 314).

To carry astonishment to an even higher level, Zajonc indicates that the EPR experiment has been performed with matter, including electrons or other atomic particles. Nor does it stop there, for it goes on up through experiments with atoms that show similar interference effects to massless photons. And a few experiments have similarly been conducted with "many-particle" subjects, where the "entangled states do not always diminish with increased numbers of particles."

Zajonc is himself attracted to a view advanced by the physicist David Bohm that is not yet widely accepted, nor has any method of proving it been yet devised. It is called "quantum potential" and postulates a source of energy within all elementary particles that does not push or pull (i.e., attract or repel) other particles but rather "informs" their motion (p. 318). If true, it would solve some of the puzzles of quantum mechanics including non-locality, but as yet it remains only an unproven and unpopular theory.

Zajonc concludes his "entangled light" section with a concept of wholeness or unity that, while he does not cite it, brings to mind the unity of Paul's most exalted passages in Eph 1,9-10 and Rom 8,19-23. And he immediately follows it with a section called "The Place of Light" predicated upon Job's ancient question, "Where is the way to the dwelling of light?" (Job 38,19a). According to 4 NIB 603, nowhere else does the Bible speak of the dwelling place of light. And the "Date and Provenance" of the book of Job, according to the discussion in 4 NIB 325, has been uniquely difficult to establish and shows at p. 328 that the book is probably not of Israelite origin. See also 3 ABD 858, "Job, Book of." Few things seem more clear in anthroposophical light than that theology today still has no adequate comprehension of the meaning of this ancient book (see *The Burning Bush*, esp. pp. 423-429).

This question, the dwelling place of light, was posed as one that led back to the earliest beginnings, the answer to which, still evading us today, will make it possible to "discern the paths to its home" (Job 38,20b). That it could have been asked so long ago sobers us. Perhaps it came from the day when structures were built in Egypt whose construction is still a mystery to modern Egyptology, a day when the light of Ra still pervaded all, or perhaps even from the prehistoric time when the Ancient Persian Zarathustra "saw" Ahura Mazda in the Sun. The Bible indicates that it was still earlier, saying that Job should know for he was born in the days when light still dwelled in its pre-earthly abode (4 NIB 603). Anthroposophy shows that Job is each of us, and each of us is Job, for among other things the nature of Job is the same as that inherited by each of us from Cain, who, like Job, was unable to die (Gen 4,11-16; Job 2,6; cf. Ex 3,2-3).

I think scientists today would not quarrel with Goethe's statement that the eye was formed by the light for the light. And probably they would also not quarrel with Steiner's statement that our eye kills the light that enters it, or stated differently, that the photon dies when it falls upon the retina. But neither are we unaccustomed to the idea that death is a precondition to transformation. Considering the holistic nature of light, there is much to meditate insofar as light reaching the eye is concerned. But let us hold that thought until we look at what Steiner had to say. Zajonc concludes the scientific portion of his book by indicating that there is extreme frustration on the part of some physicists who are unable to accept the "bad" state of affairs, and that perhaps quantum theory does indeed carry the seeds of its own destruction in spite of its incredible accuracy in predicting consequences. The foremost response of physicists to the metaphysical implications of light is what Zajonc calls FAPP, "for all practical purposes" (p. 315). It seems to relate back to what he said earlier: "The majority of physicists by far simply do not concern themselves with the meaning of their quantum calculations. Nor do they trouble themselves about the implications of archetypal quantum experiments. Science is not, they say, concerned with truth or meaning, but only with prediction and control; it is an instrument. Nineteenth-century scientific arrogance here changes to twentieth-century cynicism" (p. 301).

Theologians must ask themselves if this is not also paralleled in seminaries and pulpits through patterned necessities that append to each of these areas of modern responsibility. Is it not FAPP easier to follow paths more or less widely recognized than to seriously search for truth in a new paradigm, outside their acceptably defined (orthodox and non-heretical) bounds? Is not heresy, as it has always been, a necessary way station on the road to truth?

In any presentation of a major field of study, which light certainly is, focus cannot rest on more than a few salient approaches calculated to develop its thesis. Each of the three writers above, Liderbach, Fagg and Zajonc—although not Nobel Prize winners nor mantled by the recognized stature of those scientific geniuses, both cited and uncited, who have brought relativity and quantum theory to its current posture of acceptability—brings into the equation a well-developed understanding of the scientific aspect together with an intense desire to connect that with what I might call the soul aspect. They have in common significant orientations in the science of modern physics and matters of the soul and a powerful impulse to amalgamate them. Liderbach and Fagg are Roman Catholic, Zajonc an anthroposophist.

As could be expected, my own views vary at least a little from each of them, though I have obviously found much in each to admire and put forth. As an anthroposophist, I cannot share any enthusiasm for the scientifically popular big bang theory adopted clearly by Fagg and maybe implicitly by Liderbach. My views are probably closest to those of Zajonc, though I do not know of specific statements by him on either evolution or the big bang and do not hereby imply his position. It is now time to look at what Rudolf Steiner had to say about light.

Rudolf Steiner

As a man of towering intellect, it should seem fairly obvious, upon adequate inspection, that Rudolf Steiner could have been recognized as a salient genius in any human discipline he may have chosen to follow. Instead, following his soul's transcending demand, he embarked at the turn of the twentieth century upon a rigorous, lonely, and emotionally and physically excruciating spiritual path. The nature of that path can perhaps best be understood in the light of a little book that first appeared a few years earlier (in 1877),[31] on the very threshold of the new age of the Archangel Michael (which began in 1879) so extensively perceived and expounded by Steiner. *Flatland* is an incredibly clever caricature of the society of that day, yet timeless in application and certainly pertinent in our own. Abbott, an educator, set his story in Euclidean terminology and humanized its elements. One group lives and perceives in the domain of the point, another in that of the line, then the plane, then the three-dimensional figure, and so on up. The dialogue between those who perceive in different geometric domains brings out the ever-present conflict

---

31. Edwin Abbott Abbott, *Flatland* (Fld), Princeton, NJ, Princeton University Press (1991). The second and revised edition is dated 1884 but its Preface seems clearly to identify the original as having been seven years earlier.

where attempts are made to communicate between human beings who perceive in different dimensions. Steiner claimed to have perceived in what he called the "supersensible" world, dimensions many levels higher than those indwelt by (at least almost all of) the rest of us.[32] A relatively small, but nevertheless numerically significant number of people with the necessary soul disposition and intellectual capacity have sufficiently investigated his works over the last century to have formed deep conviction in the validity of his claim. I am one of those, as is Zajonc. Neither my career nor my present circumstances, unlike most scientists, theologians and clergy, constrain me in any way from expressing my convictions freely. My writings are an effort to do so in relation to the meaning of the Bible.

Of the many initiatives begun by Steiner, probably none is so well known as Waldorf Schools. The initial Waldorf School was founded by Steiner in Stuttgart, Germany, at the request of an industrialist for the purpose of educating the children of his employees according to the principles of child development unique to anthroposophy. Anthroposophy is not taught to the child, nor even to the teachers (though some study it), but anthroposophical insights into child development are applied in Waldorf education, which has become highly sought by many who have no interest in anthroposophy as such.[33]

From 1900 to 1925 Steiner wrote thirty or forty books and gave over 6,000 lectures all over greater Europe, from the Balkans to Great Britain to Scandinavia. The Waldorf system did not commence until after World War I. Quite a number of Steiner's lectures were to train teachers for this

---

32. Steiner's perception was direct and in full consciousness, like that of a prophet, not a medium, a critically important distinction not only for evaluating him but for what it implies for human evolution. While the Old Testament proscribed mediums for the Hebrew people (Lev 19,31; Deut 18,9-22; 1 Sam 28,3,7-9; 2 K 21,6; 23,24; 2 Ch 33,6; Is 2,6; 8,19; 19,3; 47,12-13), it apotheosized the prophetic nature of Joseph, Solomon and the other prophets, though according to Christ seldom during their lives (Mt 5,12; 23,37; Lk 6,23; 13,34; 16,31), and it recognized that this power would again come to humanity in a future day (Jer 31,33-34; Joel 2,28). The Hebrews' much-heralded "end of prophecy" bespoke the condition of humanity, the Prodigal Son, as it entered the "far country" in its evolution, the "right time" for the Incarnation of Christ, the parabolic "valley of the shadow," the "darkness," (Lk 1,79; Is 9,2; Ps 23). The time for new vision in humanity would be long after that (Is 6,11-13), but its arrival could be heralded, as indicated, by prophets who would again arise. Rudolf Steiner should be evaluated as the foremost of these in our age, the prophet of the new age of Archangel Michael.
33. Waldorf education is mentioned not to endorse any form of private versus public education, about which there is much debate, but rather to indicate the desirability of incorporating anthroposophical insights into the educational process.

school at Stuttgart. Over the years of his lectures, he typically lectured on a Christ-centered Christmas topic at or near Christmas. One would have expected this to be his focus on the occasion in question. His ten-lecture cycle to which attention is now directed commenced in Stuttgart on December 23, 1919 and went through January 3, 1920. It is entitled *Light Course* (LC) and is the first of three cycles that have been called his "scientific courses" (though other cycles also deal with scientific matters to some extent or other).[34] The other two are the *Warmth Course* (WC), the main basis for the "Fire" essay above, and what is called the "Astronomy Course" in spite of his insistence that it was to be called *Astronomy: The Relation of the Diverse Branches of Natural Science to Astronomy* (ARNS), the basis for the final essay in this volume.

Steiner's Light Course

INTRODUCTION

Some indication of his genius is indicated by the fact that he did not know this course was desired by the teachers until his arrival at Stuttgart shortly before. In the first paragraph of his lecture he says, "On this occasion as you must also realize, I was only told that this lecture-course was hoped-for after my arrival here. What I can therefore give during these days will be no more than an episode." He admonished his hearers also that his remarks were directed to them as teachers of children, not for direct material for their lessons "but as a fundamental trend and tendency in Science, which should permeate your teaching." Moreover, the reader should remember that relativity and quantum theory, while broached by then, were still in their infancy and not nearly so well developed as they are today. Among other things, Heisenberg's uncertainty principle post-dated Steiner's death in 1925; Einstein's test, later known as EPR, from which "non-locality" came into scientific awareness, was not till 1935, and the bulk of the refinements developed by the litany of scientific geniuses of the twentieth century, upon which the works of Liderbach, Fagg and Zajonc rely so extensively, were then still in the future.

---

34. Some indication, however, of how apropos a cycle on light is at Christmas is set out in *The Incredible Births of Jesus* under the caption "Christmas Day" at pp. 31-32. The date of December 25 was eventually chosen in the fourth century as the day of Christ's birth because it was then thought that it was the date of the winter solstice, the day the Sun was born each year, i.e., when it started its six-month march toward its exaltation (high point) in the Northern Hemisphere.

Immediately Steiner told his audience that he had been invited in the nineties "to speak on Goethe's work in Science" (having become, by then, perhaps its foremost authority by having edited those works for the Goethean archives in Weimar). He explained that he had confined his remarks at that time to the organic sciences,

> For to carry Goethe's world-conception into our physical and chemical ideas was, as yet quite impossible. Through all that lives and works in the Physics and Chemistry of today, our scientists are fated in regard, whatever takes its start from Goethe in this realm, as being almost unintelligible from their point of view. Thus, I opined [in the nineties, before either the Planck or Einstein pronouncements], we shall have to wait till physicists and chemists will have witnessed—by their own researches—a kind of "reductio ad absurdum" of the existing theoretic structure of their Science. Then and then only will Goethe's outlook come into its own, also in this domain.

This foresight, so typical of his recurring prescience, ran like water off the sophisticated back of modern science in his day, and runs off theologians still in our own. Perhaps it will not come in my lifetime, but the day must surely come in the not too distant future when this prophet is recognized for the exalted spirit that he was (i.e., is), herald and servant of the Archangel Michael and of the returning Christ.

Between scientists and theologians, the scientists seem to have been the first to begin humbling themselves in the light of twentieth-century discoveries in relativity and quantum theory. Liderbach points this out about them. Only the more open-minded theologians have seen that perhaps religion also is in need of a drastic revision in approach and understanding. As the work of Liderbach the theologian seems to suggest in its focus upon the scientific minded, that self-recognition has not yet widely dawned in the theological camp.

The "reductio ad absurdum" is already somewhat recognized in science by the FAPP ("for all practical purposes") approach. Those who refuse to rest with this have still to come up with a theoretical (i.e., kinetic) alternative, having not as yet embraced the ancient four elements and their related etheric conditions as the basis of creation (I-22). The Prodigal is still studying the situation in the pigpen, but hopefully with a dawning awareness that there is a higher and better dwelling.

Every scientific work cited above recognizes that the twentieth century witnessed the death of common sense in the subatomic realm. Only the mysterious quantum theory, far beyond the reach of direct human observation and experience, has been able to reconcile the emerging phenomena, and some have gagged on it while the rest have suffered indigestion. Einstein, the century's most celebrated physicist, died still alienated by the answers of quantum theory and mystified by his life's study of light. And how far can we be from that "reductio ad absurdum" when Richard Feynman (1918-1991), brilliant corecipient of the 1965 Nobel Prize in physics for the final formulation of the QED (quantum electrodynamics) theory, said that its phenomena are "impossible, *absolutely* impossible, to explain in any classical way"?[35]

One thing seems clear to all. Light has never revealed itself to human senses except in its capacity as revealer, and in that capacity it still has concealed its deeper nature from observation. As Zajonc has shown us, even those four characteristics that have been used to describe it are ambiguous and indefinite. It seems to have a character that exists only in the unity of all creation. How very like the Christ ("I have come as light into the world," Jn 12,46), the most adored and consequential individual who ever lived, who has attracted the desire and devotion of a wide swath of humanity who yet quarrel and disagree among themselves on who he was or what he accomplished save in general and humanly ambiguous terms. John says of him as light, "The light shines in the darkness and the darkness has not *understood* it" (Jn 1,5).[36]

As the works cited above suggest, science has reached the point in its work with light, where matter touches upon non-matter, where it can calculate but not explain. It hasn't yet given in to the idea that it must come

---

35. R. P. Feynman, R. B. Leighton, and M. Sands, *The Feynman Lectures on Quantum Physics*, vol. 3 (Addison-Wesley, 1965), p. 1-1.

36. The italicized part is Steiner's, but not his alone. Clearly the Greek admits this interpretation rather than "has not *overcome* it," as most modern translations prefer. While the latter interpretation can hardly be said to be wrong as an expression of truth (i.e., it has not been extinguished by darkness), the higher meaning must surely be that those of us (Christendom and essentially all humanity thus far in its evolution) who remain in darkness (mineral-physical embodiment is the "veiling" of truth by matter) have not yet understood it. As twentieth-century developments have shown, at least in its study of light science is coming slowly to this recognition. It has yet to dawn on any appreciable segment of Christendom. The older King James Version, as well as its revision (NKJV), and such others as the New International Version (NIV), accord with Steiner's translation.

to the still further region that it might call, for want of a better term, "non-force," where it cannot even calculate. If it is to move from its fascination with the mineral kingdom into gnosis (divine knowledge; "science") of the higher plant, animal and human kingdoms, it must "leave home,"[37] for to date it knows only the mineral aspect of these higher kingdoms. Knowledge of them does not lie in the world of matter and force (as we know force), but rather in the etheric, astral and spiritual realms, respectively. These realms can only be known through what may properly be called "spiritual science." It is this study that Steiner propounds and brings. Let us look at a part of the light "episode" he gave impromptu to the Waldorf teachers in 1919-1920.

THE PHENOMENON OF COLOR

Note should be taken of two things. First, the *Light Course* (LC) is presented here by paraphrasing and condensing Steiner's lectures in the same manner used for the *Warmth Course* (WC) in the "Fire" essay as set out there in footnote 10.

Second, pages 134-138 in the "Fire" essay present a discussion expressly taken from the first part of the *Light Course* which had been given before the *Warmth Course*. The discussion deals with the difference between the ideal and the empirical and is graphically demonstrated by two parallelograms, one of movements (kinematics; the "ideal") and one of forces (mechanics; the "empirical"). The *Light Course* actually opened with that discussion, which is equally applicable to both "Fire" and "Light." The reader must have what was said there freshly in mind before going on.

The final thought there borrowed from LC dealt with how the human brain is immersed in cerebral fluid so that, under Archimedes' principle over ninety-eight percent of its weight is displaced, leaving it weighing only about seven-tenths of an ounce (19.6 grams). Only the brain (and spinal cord) is so buoyed in the body; consequently it is largely relieved of the pressure, the downward pull, of matter. Our intelligence lives in this buoyed condition, but our Will has to unite with body matter that deprives it of consciousness, puts it to sleep—the essential phenomenon of Will.

This buoyancy permits our brain, to a very high degree, to bring our etheric body into play, whereas in the rest of the body it is overwhelmed

---

37. See the earlier discussion of "homeless" in the Liderbach section; Mt 8,19-22; 19,27-29; Mk 10,28-30; Lk 9,57-62; 17,31; 18,28-30.

by matter. Our forces of consciousness unite with what comes to meet us in the light. Because of the light we also perceive color. Like the positive and negative of electricity and magnetism, color has polar qualities. At one pole are yellow and its kindred colors, orange and red. At the other pole is blue and its kindred colors, indigo and violet and some of the lesser shades of green (i.e., where only six colors are listed, green is kindred to blue, and indigo is omitted; this tends to classify green with the blue end of the spectrum, whereas if a full seven are listed it is the middle one).

Steiner agreed with Goethe that *color is among the most significant phenomena of all nature* and should be studied accordingly. He demonstrates what Goethe called the *ur-phenomenon* of color by an experiment.

First he establishes a light projection through a small circular opening in an otherwise opaque object so that a cylinder of light is projected on the opposite wall (Figure 1):

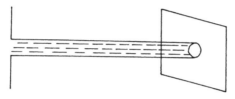

FIGURE 1

Then he places a water prism in the path of light with the wider portion of the prism on top (Figure 2):

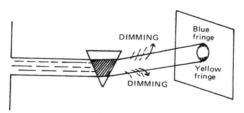

FIGURE 2

The patch of light is deflected upward and at its upper edge is a bluish-greenish light while on the lower edge is reddish-yellow. This is the phenomenon. Then Steiner does the experiment again with a far narrower cylinder of light. This time the circle of light is completely filled with colors, all those of the rainbow in their proper order. We are told to hold to the simple phenomenon, the pure and simple fact. Then once more he inserts the larger aperture (Figure 2) and asks that we observe. The cylinder of light goes through the prism of water and there is thus an interpenetration of the light with the water. The light somehow has the power to make its way through to the other side, but in the process is deflected upward. Something deflects our cylinder of light upward.

When you see the light through clear unclouded water, you see it in a greater brightness than when the water is cloudy, for then the light is weakened. This is stated simply as a fact. In some respect, every material medium is dim, even the prism of clear water. It always dims the light to some extent. Inside the prism, we have a working-together of matter and light; a dimming of the light arises here. What is it that comes about by a dimming of the light? Not only is it dimmed but it is also deflected, both brought about by matter.

But if what is deflected upward is light, then what is dim is deflected upward too. Their joint product is beamed upward. Here we are dealing with the interaction of two things: the brightly shining light, itself deflected, and the sending into it of the darkening effect deflected in the same direction as the light is. Here in the upward region the bright light is infused and irradiated with dimness, and by this means the dark or bluish colors are produced, while further down they are light or yellowish.

On top the dimming or darkening tends to go *into* the light; down below, the working of the light is such that the deflection of it works in an opposite direction to the deflection of the dimming, darkening effect. What is the result? Above, the dimming and light are deflected so as to work together, while below the dimming works back into the light but is overwhelmed as it were by the light so that the latter predominates.

We may thus say: upward the darkening runs into the light and there the blue shades of color arise; downward the light outdoes and overwhelms the darkness and there the yellow shades of color arise. In Figure 2, the working of the darkness or dimming is shown by arrows going out of the stream of light on both sides so that the arrows on the upper side exit upward while those on the downward side exit downward. This helps to see where, in terms of direction of the deflected beam, they work together on the upper side and in opposition on the lower side.

While Steiner stated it as above, it might be simpler to think of it in the traditional way that the light is simply slowed down more in having to pass through the wider upper portion of the prism. But that is not the way he presents it, and would appear to be contrary to the spiritual way of seeing it. Lest we scoff at this, let it be said that Steiner's (and Goethe's) version is at least as much in keeping with the observable phenomena as is the traditional scientific view, and when followed further can be seen to be the correct one.

Thus by adhering to the plain facts and simply taking what is given, purely from what is seen we have the possibility of understanding why yellowish colors on the one hand and bluish colors on the other make their appearance. Downward, the darkness and the light are interacting in a different way than upward.

Colors therefore arise where dark and light work together. It is the same type of phenomenon, for instance, as the way the human etheric body is inserted into the muscles and into the eyes. It is inserted into a muscle in such a way as to blend with the functions of the muscle; this is not so when it is inserted into the eye. In the isolated eye, it remains comparatively independent. Consequently, the astral body can come into very intimate union with the portion of the etheric body that is in the eye. While the astral body is inserted into both muscle and eye, it is inserted in a different way in each. It is so inserted into the muscle that it goes through the same space as the physical bodily part and is by no means independent. It is inserted into the eye such that it works independently, though the space is filled by both in both cases. It is but half the truth to say that our astral body is there in our physical body. We must ask *how* it is in it. Ingredients can interpenetrate each other and still be independent. So too, you can unite light and dark to get grey; then they interpenetrate as do the astral body and muscle. Or on the other hand light and dark can so interpenetrate as to retain their several independence as is the case with the astral body and the physical organization in the eye. In the one instance, grey arises; in the other, color.[38]

---

38. At the end of the next lecture, Steiner performs an experiment to illustrate this grey phenomenon further. He uses a disc mounted on a wheel and painted with the colors of the rainbow. One sees the seven distinct colors. He rotates it fairly rapidly. One no longer sees the colors, but rather a uniform grey. So he asks, "Why do the seven colors appear to us in grey?" Modern physics [spoken in 1919, but still true today] says what was already said about it in Goethe's time: the eye puts the seven colors together again, which must once more give white. But Goethe saw no white. All that you ever get is grey, he said. The modern text-books do indeed admit this. However, to make it white after all, they advise you to put a black circle in the middle of the disc, so that the grey may appear white by contrast. A pretty way of doing things! Some people load the dice of "fortune," but the physicists do so with "nature" by correcting her to their liking. This is being done with quite a number of the fundamental facts.

When some of Steiner's audience expressed difficulty in comprehend-ing what he had given, he told them they would understand it better by and by, for he would have to go more into the phenomena of light and color. It was, he said, the real piece de resistance in relation to the rest of physics. It would not be found, he said, in the textbooks, and it remains so to this day. His objective was to explain the interplay of light and dark-ness as well as the polarity of color. He assigned the difficulty his hearers were having to their hankering after a kinetical treatment of light and color, a mental habit instilled by the "strange" education one is made to go through (as against the type, for instance, given in the Waldorf Schools, whose initial faculty were his audience). People tend to restrict their thinking to the arithmetical, spatially formal and kinematical, and when called upon to think in terms of *quality* they get stuck because of the unnatural direction pursued by modern science (little seems to have changed in this respect).

Steiner explains how Goethe was also told by the physicists that when you let colorless light go through a prism it is analyzed and split up into its seven component colors. Goethe borrowed some apparatus to examine for himself and came up with some surprising phenomenal contradictions to that theory. For when he let the light pass through the prism, the only place where he could see any color at all was at some edge or border line (as above). The phenomena just was not as described to him. He saw that it is not that the light is split up. In point of fact he saw that the colors occur not because the light is split up but because the image projected through the aperture has edges where the light adjoins the dark. For there is darkness outside the circular patch of light, while it is relatively light within it. The colors thus, to begin with, make their appearance purely and simply as phe-nomena at the border between light and dark. This, and this alone, is the primary phenomenon. We are no longer seeing the original phenomenon when by reducing the circle in size we get a continuous sequence of colors. The latter phenomenon only arises when we take so small a circle that the colors extend inward from the edges to the middle. In both instances, the colors arise at the borders where light and dark flow together.

I wonder how many of my readers had the same reaction when they were introduced to this phenomenon in their introductory physics study of the so-called light spectrum. I couldn't understand, if light comprised seven colors as we were told, why we still saw regular light in the middle when all seven colors were present. If they represented the fullness, the *pleroma* (as in the case of the Elohim in Jn 1,16), as indicated, then why did we still see the light as well? It didn't really make sense, but it was never explained—because it conflicted with the (kinetic, ideal) scientific theory.

The point, says Steiner (a la Goethe), is not to bring in theories but to confine ourselves to the given facts. In these phenomena, not only are the colors at the edges, but the entire cone of light is also laterally displaced.

Next Steiner puts two prisms together, one positioned the same as before and the other placed on top of it as in Figure 3:

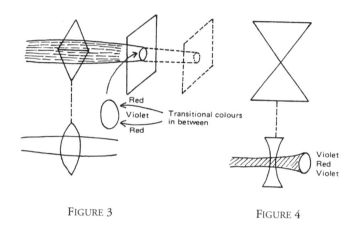

FIGURE 3   FIGURE 4

When the stream of light is made to pass through the central part, as in Figure 3, it is pushed together, reduced in size, and the red is on the outside with the violet in the middle.

Steiner then substitutes a convex lens (which is the same as the two prisms with their surfaces curved instead of plane) and the effect is generally the same. If the light passed through an ordinary plate of glass or water, the cylinder of light would just go through and a simple picture of it on the screen would be the outcome (only slightly dimmed for the passage depending upon the clarity of the glass or water). Not so if a lens is used.

He then sets up a concave lens (or prism setting) as in Figure 4. Here the circle is considerably enlarged but violet and bluish colors appear at the upper and lower edge with red in the middle—just the opposite of what it was before—again with the intermediate colors.

What do we see from these phenomena? How can it be that the light is thrust apart (in the latter experiment)? It can only be through the fact that it has less matter to go through in the middle and more at the edges, so that it passes through more easily in the middle retaining more of its force after passing through. The facts are the facts. What is seen has nothing to do with the light. It is simply brought about by the light's going through the slit. And if one says that the light moves in this or that direction, that again has nothing to do with the light as such, for if the source of light is moved upward, the light that falls on the slit would move thus and so, which again would not concern the light as such. People have formed a habit of drawing lines into the light, and from this habit they have gradually come to talk of "light rays." In fact, says Steiner, we never have to do with light rays; what we have to do with is a cone of light due to the aperture through which we caused the light to pass.[39]

FAULTY HYPOTHESES—LIGHT RAYS AND REFRACTIONS

The truth is that where we have to do simply with images or pictures, physicists speak of all manner of other things—light rays etc. The "light rays" have become the very basis of materialistic thinking in this domain. Suppose I have a vessel (Figure 6) filled with water. On its bottom is a coin. The eye is as shown in the figures. Before the water is placed in the vessel, I look at the coin as in Figure 5. Such is the simple fact, but if I now begin explaining, "There is a ray of light proceeding from the object to the eye," I am already fancying all kinds of things that are not given.

39. In his attack upon the widespread use of the phrase "ray of light," Steiner is getting to a point that requires a degree of contemplation. In this instance, he speaks of a "cone" of light, but suppose the geometric figure was not a cone but a parallelogram of light that we might call a beam, tube, rectangle or the like. Even the eminent anthroposophic scientist, Arthur Zajonc speaks of "light rays," e.g., CLT, p. 176, discussing the formation of the rainbow through the raindrop. The only real distinction between a "ray" and a "cone" seems to be that the latter expresses the geometric shape of the light in a multiple dimension that has area whereas "ray" would seem to imply simply a line. The distinction may seem too semantic for practical purposes, and the "ray" usage will be hard to drop, witness Zajonc above. Even the poet might speak of "rays" of light streaming through a window or the clouds when it might have been better simply to speak of the light so streaming. Steiner is probably right, when one comes to understand the nature of light. It is simply there when not blocked by matter (deep darkness). And perhaps also it is well to think in terms of distinguishing between "physical light" that illuminates objects and spiritual light (light ether) that penetrates them so that, for instance, the "spiritual sun" can be seen by the mystic at "midnight," through the mass of the Earth. It may be too early to draw the battle line with "science" on the use of "ray" terminology for light, holding that for an advanced course, so to speak, while trying to understand the nature of light, which science admits still escapes it. Still, I think it would be well to remember what Steiner has said about the terminology.

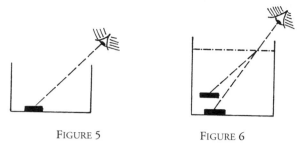

FIGURE 5   FIGURE 6

Now fill the vessel with water. A peculiar thing happens. I see the object lifted to some extent, along also with the whole bottom of the vessel. When there was no water I could look straight to the bottom; between it and my eye was only air. Now my sight line impinges on the water, which does not let my force of sight go through as easily as the air does. It offers stronger resistance. It is as though it is more difficult for me to see through the water than through the air. Hence I must shorten the distance through which the force has to travel and so I myself draw the object upward. I shorten the distance the force has to work. If I could fill the vessel with a gas thinner than air (Figure 7), the object would be correspondingly lowered, since I would then encounter less resistance—so I would push it downward.

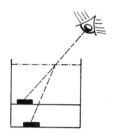

FIGURE 7

Instead of simply noting this fact, physicists will say that the ray is "refracted" in this direction. And then they go on to say a very curious thing. The eye, they say, having received information by this ray of light, produces it on and outward in the same straight line and so projects the object there. They want to leave the whole matter of resistance and sighting force of the eye out and to ascribe everything to the light alone, just as they say of the prism experiment that it is not the prism at all for the seven colors are there in the light all the time. Yet as we saw, the colors are really caused by what arises in the prism. This wedge of dimness is the cause. The colors are not due to the light as such.

We must be clear that we ourselves are being active with our eye. Finding increased resistance in the water, we are obliged to shorten the line of sight. The physicists, on the other hand, speak of rays of light being sent out and refracted. And now the beauty of it! The light, they say, reaches the eye by a bent and broken path, and then the eye projects the picture outward. So after all they end by attributing this activity to the eye: "The eye projects ..." Only they then present us with a merely kinetical conception, remote from the given realities. It is at such points that you see most distinctly how abstract everything is made in our conventional physics. Thus in the first place they divest the eye of any kind of activity of its own. Yet in the last resort the eye is said to project what it receives. Surely we ought to begin with the activity of the eye from the very outset. We must be clear that the eye is an *active* organism.

THE EYE AND INNER LIGHT

Let us now consider the nature of the human eye. Steiner draws a cross-section of it in Figure 8:

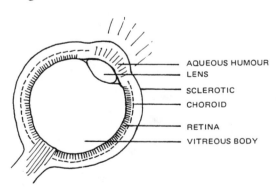

AQUEOUS HUMOUR
LENS
SCLEROTIC
CHOROID
RETINA
VITREOUS BODY

FIGURE 8

The spherical eyeball is seated in a bony cavity with a number of skins enveloping the inner portion. Outside these skins there is connective and fatty tissue. The first integument (covering) proper is the so-called *sclerotic*, of which the transparent portion is the cornea. The sclerotic is sinewy—

of bony or cartilaginous consistency. A second layer is the so-called *choroid*, containing blood vessels. The third layer is the *retina*, which is continued into the *optic nerve* as you go farther into the skull. Thus there are three integuments of the eye. And now behind the cornea, which itself is embedded in the ciliary muscle, is a kind of *lens*. Between the cornea and the lens is the so-called *aqueous humor*. Thus light entering the eye first passes through the cornea, then the aqueous humor and then the lens, which is inherently movable by means of the ciliary muscles, and then comes to what is commonly known as the *vitreous humor* which fills the entire space of the eye. The sequence of light's passage inward is thus as follows:

1.   Cornea
2.   Aqueous humor
3.   Lens
4.   Vitreous humor
5.   Retina
6.   Optic Nerve
7.   Brain

Now the eye reveals very remarkable features. The aqueous humor is very like any ordinary liquid from the outer world. Here therefore, the human body is quite a piece of the outer world. The lens too is to a high degree "objective" and unalive. Not so when we go on inward to the vitreous humor. It is not like any external fluid. In it there is decided vitality—life. Truth is, the farther back we go into the eye, the more life we find. Tracing the comparative development of the eye, the tissue of the outer parts, the aqueous humor and lens are formed from neighboring organs, not from within outward, while the vitreous humor grows from within outward to meet them. This is the noteworthy thing. In fact the outer light is at work bringing about that transformation whereby the aqueous humor and lens originate, to which the living being then reacts from within, thrusting outward a more living, vital organ in the vitreous humor. Notably in the eye, formations whose development is stimulated from without meet others stimulated from within in a very striking way.

Another thing about the eye is scarcely less remarkable. The retina is really the expanded optic nerve. The peculiar thing is that at the very point of entry of the optic nerve the eye is insensitive. There it is blind. We may begin by saying that it is surely the nerve which senses the light. Yet it is insensitive to light precisely at its point of entry. Take note of this.

While Steiner does not say so, should it not be of more than passing interest that the process of "seeing," as he outlines it above, is a seven-step procedure (Prov 9,1)? What is thus true with perceiving the light on physical objects must surely also be true of perceiving the spiritual light, or "seeing" as Isaiah speaks of it (Is 6,9-10). Even the structure of the eye carries out the sevenfold fractal nature of creation.

The whole structure and arrangement of the eye is full of wisdom from the side of nature, which you may tell from the following fact. During the day, objects appear sharp and clear. But in the morning when you first awaken you sometimes see the outlines of surrounding objects very indistinctly—with a little halo. To what is this due? It is due to there being two different kinds of things in our eye, namely, the vitreous body and the lens. The lens is formed from without and the vitreous humor from within. While the lens is rather unalive, the vitreous body is full of vitality. In the moment of awakening they are not yet adapted to one another. Each tries to picture the objects in its own way. We thus see again how deeply mobile everything organic is. The one has to adapt itself to the other.

Perhaps no single book presents so complete a panorama of the many-splendored aspects of light as Arthur Zajonc's *Catching the Light* (CLT), appropriately subtitled *The Entwined History of Light and Mind*. He opens Chapter 1 with the pathetic situation of the congenitally blind whose eyes are thereafter surgically made completely healthy as physical organs. Sadly, vision is not restored save with enormous therapeutic effort on the part of the patient, failing which functional blindness continues. What is otherwise developed from the day the infant first squints and opens its eyes can later be retrieved only through the greatest effort and proper education. It is almost Helen Keller-like in difficulty. We recognize in this the same thing brought out in Mark's story of the healing of the blind man (Mk 8,22-25):

> [22] And they came to Bethsaida. And some people brought to him a blind man, and begged him to touch him. [23] And he took the blind man by the hand, and led him out of the village; and when he had spit

on his eyes and laid his hands upon him, he asked him, "Do you see anything?" [24] And he looked up and said, "I see men; but they look like trees, walking." [25] Then again he laid his hands upon his eyes; and he looked intently and was restored, and saw everything clearly.

We miss the significance of the passage if we don't recognize the healing as a *two-step* procedure. First, the eyes were completely healed organically. But vision still did not exist except in some form of unintelligible blur. Only when the inner light was restored by the second step did the man see clearly. John's version of the healing of the man born blind does not bring out two steps quite so clearly, but two are nevertheless there. Christ's action had to be followed by the man going to wash in the pool of Siloam (Jn 9,1-11).

Christ speaks of the eye as providing light: "The eye is the lamp of the body" (Mt 6,22; Lk 11,34). Commenting on Mt 6,22, 8 NIB 210 says, "In contrast to the modern understanding, which regards the eye as a window that lets light into the body, the common understanding in the ancient world was that the eye was like a lamp [citing, among others, Prov 15,30 and Dan 10,6; see also Rev 1,14], an instrument that projects the inner light onto objects so they may be seen." More boldly, 9 NIB 244, commenting on Lk 11,34, implies Christ misunderstood the nature of things in using his metaphor, saying "The verse [34] has often been misinterpreted ... because it assumes an ancient understanding of the eye and sight. We know that the eye responds to light from outside the body, but in antiquity the common understanding in both Greco-Roman and Jewish literature was that the eye emitted light and that sight was possible when the light from within met light from outside."

The unmitigated presumptuousness of these comments nevertheless speaks for most of us in our day who accept without question what is said in our textbooks, theology books and scientific treatises. Yet Einstein said "It seems that the human mind has first to construct forms independently before we can find them in things," and in 1917, after completing *Relativity*, "For the rest of my life I will reflect on what light is!" (both cited as epigraphs in Zajonc, Chap. 10). Zajonc himself writes in Chapter 1:

In my own professional life, I first sought to understand light by means of laboratory research in quantum optics. In laser experiments performed at institutes in Boulder, Amherst, Paris, Hanover, and

Munich, I studied light and the way it touches matter. The more I learned of the quantum theory of light, theoretically and experimentally, the more wonderful light seemed. Even armed with such sophisticated theories, I have no sense of closure regarding our knowledge of light. Far from it, light remains as fundamentally mysterious as ever. In fact, quantum theory has taken the simplistic, mechanistic conceptions of light provided by early science and, on the firm basis of experiment, shown them all to be impossible. In their place, it has framed a new theory of light that every great modern physicist from Albert Einstein to Richard Feynman has struggled to understand—unsuccessfully, as they realized themselves.

Before returning to Steiner's lectures, let us look at what was said by that unsurpassed modern mystic of Egyptology, René Schwaller de Lubicz in his monumental *The Temple of Man* (TOMN), pp. 108-109 ("The Symbol of the Eye"):

The eye is the only nerve that comes to the surface of the body, the only one we can observe in its living function. It blossoms into a sphere filled with a white crystalline liquid. It is sensitive to light, to the *effect of fire*, and it reacts to colors....

The constitution of the eye shows that the "fire" of light must be neutralized by the watery nature of the aqueous humor and the vitreous body, the Amunian aspect of life. The phenomenon of vision is a reaction to the light filtered by the iris; then the "fire," neutralized by the crystalline lens, strikes the complementary rods and cones of the retina. If this *reaction* did not occur, the phenomenon of light would never exist for the intellective optical center of the brain. Functionally, this complete process constitutes the "eye of Ra"; the *reactive* emanation from the retina is the true light. The electromagnetic vibration, or the photons, are the impulsive activity, the active mechanical energy, and the light that we see is the reactive vital energy. The physical and chemical effect of the light only exists through some similar reactive phenomena, but these effects are only visible (to the eye) after this vital genesis. It is thus that the sun, the eye of Ra (and not Aten, the solar disk) emanates an *invisible light* that nourishes the world; this invisible light—the luminous vital energy—makes possible our *intelligence* of the active, visible light, our *knowledge of the light*. This concerns the esotericism of the symbol of the eye. To these explanations is added the symbol of genesis represented by the eye and in which, as in all generation, the amniotic crystalline lens takes part. The myth says that it is from the *tears* of Ra, the salty Water evoked by solar Fire, that human beings were created.

Have we moderns, like Esau, sold our heritage for a mess of pottage (Gen 25,24-34)? Just as we've lost the great insights of the four elements and the four ethers, so also the understanding that there is no light in the human kingdom unless the inner light of the eye joins with the outer light of the Sun (for all that can create physical light comes directly or indirectly from the Sun via the fire).

But let us return to Steiner's next lectures (Lect. 4 et seq.).

THE IMPLICATIONS OF INTERFERENCE

Steiner directs us to look at the "ur-phenomenon" of the theory of color. Goethe would have expressed it, to begin with, by saying that when you look through darkness at something lighter, the light object will appear modified by the darkness in the direction of the light colors, i.e., in the direction of the red and yellow tones. Figure 9 thus shows candle light being seen through a block of dim or cloudy matter. Conversely if I look at a simple black surface through a trough of water which is illumined (Figure 10), blue or violet colors will appear. Thus, in summary: Light through dark appears yellow, while dark through light appears blue.

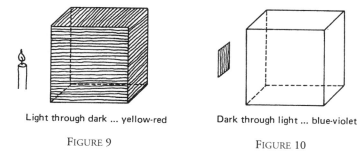

Light through dark ... yellow-red   Dark through light ... blue-violet

FIGURE 9   FIGURE 10

Taking this principle forward Steiner recalls Figure 2 which he reproduces except that this time he places the human eye where the image fell on the wall in Figure 2.

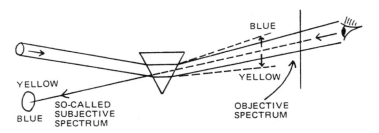

FIGURE 11

What then is seen by the eye? One must hold to what is seen. You see the light, but you see it coming through dark. On the top side you are looking at it through the darkened blue side of the image that previously fell on the wall; you are looking through dark and thus see yellow on top. Conversely, on the bottom side you are looking through the light yellow colors that previously fell on the wall, and thus see blue on the bottom side. And, of course, what you see has been displaced, i.e., "projected," downward by the action of your eye (rather than by refraction) as previously discussed. It is the polarity that matters. If one wants to speak in "learned terms," the image on the screen can be called the "objective" colors and the one seen by looking back through the prism at the light the "subjective" colors. The latter image appears as an inversion of the former.

There has been much intellectual speculation in modern time concerning all these phenomena, beginning with Newton. He came up with the corpuscular theory, but that was seriously shaken by others later, so a wave theory was adopted. At first longitudinal waves, like sound waves, were considered, it being thought that they moved in a very fine substantial medium of "ether," but phenomena were seen as being at variance with this type of waves, so transverse waves were settled upon.

Steiner refers to the experiments of Young and Fresnel and others in connection with this matter, saying that it was Fresnel's work which shook the corpuscular theory. But before getting further to their work, we take note of his Figures 12 and 13 with particular reference to the portion of the screen upon which the two reflected beams of light overlap. There is a lattice-work image upon the screen within this area. How is it explained?

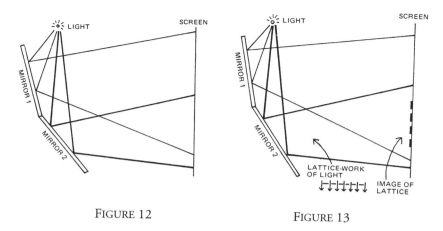

FIGURE 12   FIGURE 13

(Note might be taken that this experiment is one that shook the corpuscular theory.) I here quote directly what Steiner says on the matter:

Now let us try to grasp what happens in reality in this experiment. Suppose that this [stream that hits mirror 1] is the one stream of light. It is thrown by reflection across here, but now the other stream of light [directed toward mirror 2] arrives here and encounters it—the phenomenon is undeniable. The two disturb each other. The one wants to rush on; the other gets in the way and, in consequence, extinguishes the light coming from the other side. In rushing through it extinguishes the light. Here therefore on the screen [where the two reflected streams overlap on the screen] we do not get a lighting-up but in reality darkness is reflected across here. So we here get an element of darkness (Figure 13). But now all this is not at rest—it is in constant movement. What has here been disturbed goes on. Here, so to speak, a hole has arisen in the light. The light rushed through; a hole was made, appearing dark. And as an outcome of this "hole," the next body-of-light will go through all the more easily and alongside the darkness you will have a patch of light so much the lighter. The next thing to happen, one step further on, is that once more a little cylinder of light from above impinges on a light place, again extinguishes the latter, and so evokes another element of darkness. And as the darkness in its turn has thus moved on another step, here once again the light is able to get through more easily. We get the pattern of a lattice, moving on from step to step. Turn by turn, the light from above can get through and extinguishes the other, producing darkness once again, and this moves on from step to step.... When one light rushes into another the light is canceled—turned to darkness.... The velocity of light—nay, altogether what arises here by way of differences in velocity of light—is not of great significance. What I am trying to make clear is what here arises *within the light itself* by means of this apparatus, so that a lattice-work is reflected—light, dark, light, dark, and so on.

Steiner explains how the physicists solve this problem with their theory of transverse waves perpendicular to the direction the light is moving. "When the train of waves arrives here [where the paths of light reflected from the two mirrors overlap on the screen in Figure 13], it may well be that the one infinitesimal particle with its perpendicular vibrations happens to be vibrating downward at the very moment when the other is vibrating upward. Then they will cancel each other out and darkness will arise at this place. Or if the two are vibrating upward at the same moment, light will arise. Thus they explain, by the vibrations of infinitesimal particles, what we were explaining just now by the light itself. I was saying that here we get alternations of light patches and dark. The so-called wave-theory of light explains them on the assumption that light is a wave movement in the ether. If the infinitesimal particles are vibrating so as to reinforce each other, a lighter patch will arise; if contrary to one another, we get a darker patch."[40]

You see from this example that our fundamental way of thought requires us so to explain the phenomena that they themselves are the eventual explanation. They must contain their own explanation. Please

40. This interference phenomenon was apparently first discovered by Thomas Young in 1803. He characterized the interference as the result of waves intermittently canceling and then reinforcing each other just as intersecting waves of water might do. His theory was soon thereafter independently confirmed, as far as science was concerned, by Augustin Fresnel through a masterful application of the relatively new mathematics of calculus. This *theory* has held the day from then till now. The reader can find a more involved explanation in the Encyclopedia *Britannica* in the discussion of "interference" under the general topic of "Light." Fagg does not discuss interference. Liderbach does so only briefly (pp. 92-93), readily accepting the conventional theory. Zajonc also deals with interference (pp. 110, 115, 178, 298). Even though a leading anthroposophist, he does not directly contradict the standard view, at least initially. Whether he demurred for professional reasons or because Steiner himself did not appear categorically to reject the conventional view or because he simply agreed with it is not indicated. However, while Steiner had tendered a plausible alternative, both he (as we shall see) and Zajonc (pp. 296-301) did point out evidence inconsistent with the wave theory.

set great store by this. Mere spun-out theories and theorizings are to be rejected. Of course the waves might conceivably be there, and it might be that the one swings upward when the other downward so that they cancel each other out. But they have all been invented! What is there, however, without question is this lattice. It is to the light itself that we must look if we desire a genuine and not a spurious explanation.[41]

Steiner also demonstrated phenomena in conflict with the wave-theory explanation of interference. He performed an experiment which he then illustrated in Figures 14, 15 and 16. In Figure 14 the light from a white incandescent solid body passes through a downward pointing prism (wider part at top) so that the light is displaced upward with the blue colors on

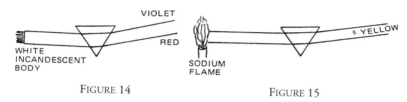

FIGURE 14   FIGURE 15

top and red on bottom. In Figure 15 the light from the solid body is replaced by a sodium flame, i.e., a flame that turns the sodium into a gas. A spectrum of the sodium (as distinguished from sunlight or a glowing solid body) is made from the glowing gas. One place in the spectrum is strongly developed. All the colors are there but the yellow is enhanced and the others stunted—hardly there at all. We get a very narrow bright yellow strip or line. Note that the entire spectrum is there, only the other colors are stunted or atrophied as it were. (The flames from different substances give off different colors.)

But then the remarkable thing comes about when we combine the two experiments as in Figure 16. What happens then is very like what Steiner was showing us in Fresnel's experiment (Figure 13).

---

41. Nick Thomas, who at the time had been General Secretary of the Anthroposophical Society in Great Britain for thirteen years, in his recently published *Science Between Space and Counterspace* (SBSC), 1999 (a highly technical and mathematical presentation of projective geometry referred to in the "Conclusion" to this essay), gives a brief section on interference in his chapter on light. He calls his book an incomplete "work-in-progress," stating that he has not yet dealt with this problem. He does say, however, "This consideration indicates the necessity for this [further work on this problem], but it requires an understanding of how darkness and rhythmicity can become incorporated into light, which in turn depends upon the chemical ether. The same applies to coherence which is also important in connection with interference phenomena."

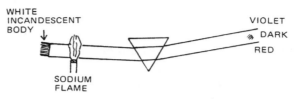

FIGURE 16

In the resulting spectrum you might expect the yellow to appear extra strong, since it is there to begin with and now the yellow of the sodium flame is added to it. But this is not what happens. On the contrary, the yellow of the sodium flame extinguishes the other yellow and you get a dark place where it was. Precisely where you would expect a lighter part you get a darker. Why is it so? It simply depends on the intensity of force that is brought to bear. If the sodium light arising here were self-less enough simply to let the kindred yellow light go through it, it would have to extinguish itself in so doing. This it does not do; it puts itself in the way at the very place where the yellow should be coming through. It is simply there, and though it is yellow itself, its effect is not to intensify but to extinguish. As a real active force, it puts itself in the way, even as any indifferent obstacle might do; it gets in the way. This yellow part of the spectrum is extinguished and a black strip is brought about instead. From this you see again that we need only bear in mind what is actually there. The flowing light itself gives us the explanation.

Finally, Newton's way of explaining things would say that if we have a piece of white—say a luminous strip—and look at it through a prism, it appears in the colors of the rainbow as in Figure 17. Goethe said that this might do in a pinch if light is indeed composed of seven colors. But to carry it a step further, the same people who say light consists of these seven colors allege that darkness is just nothing—the mere absence of light. Yet if we leave a black strip in the middle of the same piece of white paper and look at it through a prism, then too we get a rainbow, only the colors are now reversed (Figure 18), mauve (a delicate purple) in the middle and one side merging into greenish-blue and the other into the yellow colors.

FIGURE 17   FIGURE 18

The order of the colors is different. Based on the analysis theory we ought now to say the black too is analyzable, and would thus be admitting that darkness is more than the mere absence of light, for its analysis would also yield seven colors. That he saw the black band too in seven colors, but in a different order, is what put Goethe off—and shows how needful it is simply to take the phenomena as we find them.

Next, Steiner said, we have to consider the relation of colors to what we call "bodies." As a transition to this problem, he projected a complete spectrum upon the screen, then placed a trough containing a little iodine dissolved in carbon disulfide in the path of the cylinder of light. The middle part of the spectrum was extinguished so that only the violet on one side and the reddish yellow on the other, the two poles of color, were seen. He then indicated the need to see how it comes about that the bodies around us appear colored at all. How, simply by dint of their material existence, so to speak, do they develop such relation to the light that one body looks red, another blue, etc.? Physicists adopt the simple explanation that when full light falls on a body that looks red it is due to that body's swallowing all the other colors and throwing back only the red. Similarly with the other colors. But we must shun these speculative explanations and approach the phenomena by the pure facts.

Here Steiner interjects a background reference. In the seventeenth century a Bologna cobbler doing an alchemical experiment with barytes, a kind of heavy spar, found that it held and then gave off a certain colored light after it had been exposed to light for a while. If one comes across the word "phosphor" or "phosphorus" in the literature of that time, it is not what is called "phosphorus" today but refers to phosphorescent bodies of this kind—bearers of light, phosphores. Stating that this is not the simplest phenomenon Steiner moves on to the following one, "really the simple one."

If you take ordinary paraffin oil and look through it toward a light, the oil appears slightly yellow. If on the other hand you place yourself so as to let the light pass through the oil while you look at it from behind, the oil will seem to be shining with a bluish light—only so long, however, as the light impinges on it. You can do the same experiment with a variety of other bodies (speaking of a liquid here as a "body"). It is most interesting if you make a solution of plant green-chlorophyll (Figure 19). Look toward the light through the solution and it appears green. But if you stand to some extent behind the light, the chlorophyll shines back with a red or reddish light, just as the paraffin shone blue.

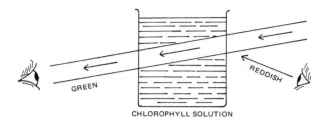

FIGURE 19

There are many bodies with this property. They shine a different way when, so to speak, they of themselves send the light back—when they have somehow come into relation to the light, changing it through their own nature—than when the light goes through them as through a transparent body. When we look at the chlorophyll (or body) from behind, we see the mutual relation between the light and the chlorophyll. When a body shines thus with one kind of light while illumined by another kind of light, we call the phenomenon *fluorescence*. The difference between fluorescence and *phosphorescence* is that the latter is a fluorescence which lasts longer. And now there is a third stage, the body that, as an outcome of whatever it is that the light does with it, appears with a lasting color. Thus, this sequence:

1. Fluorescence
2. Phosphorescence
3. Coloredness-of-bodies

The terminology is found in standard scientific works.[42] The evolution

---

42. For instance, on "phosphorescence," see 9 Brit 395; on "fluorescence," see 13 Brit 543, "Analysis and Measurement, Physical and Chemical, Spectroscopy, Introductory survey of optical spectroscopy, Practical considerations," and 16 Brit 599, "Colour, Physical and chemical causes of colour." The interesting thing in the last Brit reference is how the entire subject of color begins. The statement is as follows: "Aristotle viewed all colour to be the product of a mixture of white and black, and this was the prevailing belief until 1666, when Sir Isaac Newton's prism experiments provided the scientific basis for the understanding of colour. Newton showed that a prism could break up white light into a range of colours which he called the spectrum, and that the recombination of these spectral colours re-created the white light." The first thing that comes to my mind is that Steiner is the same Individuality as Aristotle (see "Pillars on the Journey" in *The Burning Bush*). The second is that Newton merely manifested the "fading splendor" (cf. 2 Cor 3,13) of the ancient knowledge (Aristotle's, for instance) of the truth about color which Steiner attempts to re-establish as in this cycle.

of the ability to detect color, while not our main concern, is nevertheless an interesting cognate.[43]

SPACE/TIME, VELOCITY AND COLOR

Steiner now, by way of getting us into the "pure facts" of the matter, takes up a rather astonishing point. Think of the formula for *velocity*. It is scientifically expressed by dividing s, the distance (or space) the mobile object passes through, by the time t. The formula is thus $v = s/t$. The

---

43. The preceding footnote mentioned Aristotle's belief that all color is the product of black and white. Considering the prism experiments above, where color arises only when light engages darkness, the concept seems archetypal. Just as television was at first only black and white, did human vision not begin with the detection only of light and darkness? Except for those who reject any thought of evolution, the idea is widely accepted, as Goethe said, that the eyes were made by the light for the light. (A similar idea in relation to the ears is found in some translations of Ps 40,6 [quoted by Paul in Heb 10,5]; e.g., in the RSV and NRSV fn, "ears thou hast dug for me" and in NIV, "my ears you have pierced." The variety of translations of the Hebrew suggest the complexity, and variation, in the interpretation of ancient meaning.)

Under "colour blindness," 3 Brit 470 tells us, "In the retina … there are, in human beings, three types of cones, the visual cells that function in the perception of colour." Each absorbs light of a different "wavelength" associated with a particular color, one blue-violet, another green, and the third yellow-red. From an evolutionary standpoint, obviously the retina nerve in the eye may well have evolved gradually over time so as to add color perception bit by bit, even suggesting that perhaps it is not yet fully evolved. In this connection, it is well to consider the chronological development, suggested by scripture, of the so-called "five senses" as set out in I-23 (p. 590 of *The Burning Bush*) and also the evolution of the ear's ability to experience musical intervals as set out in I-79.

Zajonc, in the section of Chap. 2 captioned "The Wine-Dark Sea of Antiquity" (pp. 13-18), shows that the ancient Greeks of Homer's time apparently had no consciousness of the colors blue (as Goethe noted) and green, as we have them today, though by the time of Aristotle, five hundred years later, that consciousness existed. (He also shows that color-blindedness caused by trauma, where no lasting physical injury is otherwise evident, is even today a mystery.) Some might contend otherwise by pointing out that the books attributed to Moses refer to both blue and green, the earliest appearances in the Bible being Gen 1,30 (green) and Ex 25,4 (blue), describing the green plant and blue fabric, respectively. No serious scholar would say that Moses wrote these words. Even the more conservative would say at best that he originated the oral custom behind them. Considering, however, how late the oldest manuscripts are, and the changes that took place during the many centuries between Moses and these manuscripts (see Judith E. Sanderson's "Ancient Texts and Versions of the Old Testament" in 1 NIB 292 et seq.), there is little basis to question the evidence from Homeric Greek literature as to the color blue. And as Zajonc points out, Greek color theorists use the word *chloros* for green. But in Homer's *"Iliad*, honey is *chloros*; in the *Odyssey*, so is the nightingale; in Pindar, the dew is *chloros*; and with Euripides, so are tears and blood! From its use, we can see it means not green but moist and fresh—alive." Clearly this interpretation fits Gen 1,30 better than does our word "green." Gen 1,30 is talking about life, and the plant is the lowest kingdom to have life. Consider also I-83 in *The Burning Bush*.

opinion prevails that what is actually given in real nature in such a case is the distance (*s*) the body passes through and the time (*t*) it takes to do it. Velocity is regarded as being not quite so real but more as a kind of function, a mere quotient. And yet in nature it is not so. Of the three magnitudes—velocity, space and time—velocity is the only one that has reality. The *s* and *t* we only get by splitting up the given totality, the *v*, into two abstract entities. That a moving "body" has this velocity is the one real thing about it. We dismember what is really one into two abstractions (remember the parallelograms at first!—he doesn't say this, but the analogy seems clearly there). The space and time are no realities at all. They are abstractions that we ourselves derive from the velocity. We shall not come to terms with outer reality till we are thoroughly clear on this point. The real thing we have outside us is the velocity and that alone. As to the space and time, we ourselves have first created them by virtue of two abstractions into which the velocity can fall apart for us.

Two observations seem pertinent here. First, it seems clear from the rest of Steiner's lecture cycle on light that he is not necessarily saying that neither space nor time can ever be a phenomenon in itself. Rather, in this particular instance it is our identification with space and time that keeps them from being phenomena outside of us—and phenomena is what is observable on the outside of the observer. Second, Steiner seems to be in accord with Einstein's *Relativity* in saying that space and time are not independent realities.

We can separate ourselves from the velocity, but not from the space and time. With them (*s* and *t*) we are one. Nor should we, without more ado, ascribe to external bodies what we ourselves are one with. We only measure the velocity by means of space and time. The space and time are our own instruments. Here we see sharply the dividing line between the "subjective" (space and time) and the "objective" (velocity) things. It will be good if we will bring this home to ourselves very clearly. The truth will then dawn upon us more and more.

Steiner makes it clear that he is not saying that space and time are within us, but merely that in perceiving the reality outside us we make use of space and time for our perception. They are at one and the same time both inside and outside of us. The point is that we unite with space and time but not with the velocity.

In like manner, we are in one and the same element with the so-called bodies whenever we behold them by means of light. We ought not to ascribe objectivity to light any more than to space and time. We swim in space and time just as the bodies swim in it with their velocities. So too we swim in the light. You will never understand what light is without going into these realities. We with our *etheric* bodies, our life bodies (I-9), swim in the light, or, if you will, the light ether, for the word does not matter in this connection.

In the most manifold ways (as he has shown above) colors arise in and about the light. So also they arise, or subsist, in the so-called bodies. How then do we relate ourselves to the fleeting colors? We are in them with our *astral* body, our sense body (I-9). We are united with the colors with our astral body. When we see colors, we must realize that it is with our astral body that we are united with them. If we would reach any genuine knowledge we have no alternative but to say to ourselves, "The light remains invisible to us. We swim in it." It is the same as with space and time—we ought not to call them objective for we ourselves are swimming in them. So too we should regard light as an element common to us and to the things outside us, while in the colors we have to recognize something that can make its appearance only inasmuch as we through our astral body come into relation to what the light is doing there.

Let us make then the following tabulation of the things that, with our "three bodies" we swim in, and that should thus not be considered as part of the phenomena:

1. We are in *space and time* with our *physical* body.

2. We are in *light* with our *etheric* body.

3. We are in *colors* with our *astral* body.

(Steiner specifically states 2 & 3, but the meaning has to be the same in regard to 1, for in the very act of incarnating into mineral-physical being we have to become one with space and time.)

The spectrum is a phenomenon that takes its course purely within light and its perception must be referred to as an astral relation to light. But we may also have the phenomenon of color in the form of a colored surface. To begin with, we think rather crudely that the color extends beneath the surface also. But this is different from the spectrum in light itself. With the red surface of an apple we have an astral relation, but in that relationship we are separated by the bodily surface. In the spectrum we see colors in light as an astral relationship of a direct kind where nothing is interposed between us and the colors. When on the other hand we see the colors of bodily objects, something is interposed between us and our astral body, and through this something we nonetheless entertain astral relations to what we call bodily colors. These are basic concepts—very important ones—which we shall need to elaborate.

What is being said cannot be got from textbooks, nor from reading Goethe's "theory of color." Goethe died in 1832. What we are seeking is not a Goetheanism of the year 1832 but one for our time—further evolved and developed. Steiner considered the *Fairy Tale*[44] to represent the high-water mark of Goethe's spiritual vision. Something of the pathos of Pisgah (Deut 34) is reflected in Steiner's apotheosis of Goethe (*Autobiography* [AUTO], p. 125, fn mine):

> I often upset those idealists by airing the conviction I gained by intimately studying Goethe's era—the conviction that Western culture had reached a high point, and that the height of that development had not been sustained. Our scientific age, which affects individuals as well as whole cultures, indicates a decline. Before it can progress further, it needs an entirely new spiritual impulse. To continue the spiritual trends followed thus far will lead only to a reversal. Goethe represents the peak of a certain evolution,[45] but its final stage rather than a beginning. He gathers the fruits of development that led up to him, and it culminated in him in its fullest form. Progress cannot, however, continue without far more original sources of spiritual experience than those contained in that development. This was my mood as I wrote the last part of my exposition on Goethe.

The whole way of thinking about the phenomena of physics today reaches hardly any farther back than the sixteenth century. Before then it was radically different. (Recall the earlier footnote about Aristotle's beliefs on color prevailing until the time of Newton.) Today it is extremely difficult for one to find one's way back to the pure facts.

---

44. Goethe's *The Fairy Tale of the Green Snake and the Beautiful Lily* (FTSL).
45. Earlier Steiner had pointed to Goethe as the "last great individual to combine in his soul the full fruits of" the last three six-hundred-year cultural cycles since Christ, i.e., Arabic, Renaissance and Buddhist, the next being the Christ Impulse; *Background to the Gospel of Saint Mark* (BKM), Lect. 9.

Steiner next uses Figure 20 to again illustrate what physics calls the "refraction" of light with the eye's then "projection" of the image to a different (displaced) position. But he now goes on to say that it should be observed that not only is the object (the "lighter part") shifted upward (displaced) by the eye's "projection," but so also are its surrounding darker areas. In other words, the entire complex we are looking at is found to be displaced. Please take this well into account.

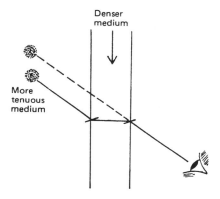

Denser
medium

More
tenuous
medium

FIGURE 20

Physics speaks in a way that abstracts the one light patch from all its surroundings, as though it alone were displaced. Surely this is wrong! In point of fact, what is displaced in these optical phenomena can never be abstractly confined. Thus, in repeating Newton's experiment where the cone of light gets diverted by the prism, it simply is not true that the cone of light alone is diverted. Whatever the cone of light is bordering on— above it and below—is diverted too. We really ought never to speak of rays of light, but only of luminous pictures or spaces of light being diverted. For if the lighter part is shifted, the darker part is shifted too.

But now, what is this "dark?" You must take the dark seriously—as something real. The errors that have crept into modern physics since the sixteenth century were able to creep in only because these things were not observed spiritually at the same time. You will not deny that some light is more intense than other—there can be stronger light and less strong. How is this fact related to darkness? The ordinary physicist of today thinks there is stronger light and less strong, but he will only admit one dark-ness—darkness which is simply there when there is no light (essentially the dictionary definition, absence of light). Yet as untrue as it would be to say that there is only one kind of lightness, just as untrue is it to say that there is only one kind of darkness. Debt is debt and that is all there is to it—to analogize to modern physics' view of darkness—but in reality there are differences in the extent of debt. It is this failure to progress to a qualitative way of thinking that largely prevents our discovering the bridge between the soul-and-spirit on the one hand, and the bodily realm on the other. For just as when a space is filled with light it is always filled with light of a certain intensity, so likewise is it with darkness. We must conceive of a space that is not abstract but is in some specific way filled with light or negatively filled with darkness, in the one case "qualitatively positive" and in the other "qualitatively negative."[46]

How does the positive filling of space differ for our perception from the negative? We need only compare our sensation when surrounded by darkness with that when we awaken from sleep and are surrounded by light, how we unite our subjective experience with the light that floods and surges around us. There is an essential difference between being given up to light-filled space and to a darkness-filled space. The feeling in relation to a light-filled space is that of a kind of in-drawing of the light, as though our soul were sucking in the light. We feel an enrichment when we draw the light into ourselves. How is it then with darkness? Precisely the opposite. We feel the darkness sucking at us. It sucks us out—we have to give something of ourselves to the darkness.[47]

So too must we distinguish between the lighter and the darker colors. There is indeed another occasion in life when, as previously shown, we are somehow sucked out, this time in our consciousness, namely, when we fall asleep. It is like a cessation of consciousness when we move from the lighter colors nearer the darker ones.

And you will recall from that portion of the *Light Course* introduced in the "Fire" essay (in conjunction with the parallelograms of kinetics versus

---

46. The Bible describes the intensity of *darkness* as "great," "thick," "deep" and "outer." See "Darkness."
47. The innate fear of darkness seems to illustrate this. Fear is a negative aspect of the "I Am." We saw in *The Burning Bush* how the higher "I Am" was related to the Christ. John's Gospel certainly brings this out. In John's Gospel the Christ says, "The Father and I are one" (Jn 10,30; 17,11,21). In the fourth chapter of his epistle, John says, "God is love" (1 Jn 4,16), and then, "Perfect love casts out fear" (1 Jn 4,18). Christ is light, and fear is darkness, and the two are like oil and water; they do not mix.

forces) what Steiner said a few days before about the relation of our life of soul to *mass*—how we are put to sleep by mass, how it sucks out our consciousness. We feel something very like this in the absorption of our consciousness by darkness. So we can discern the deep inner kinship between the condition of space when filled with darkness and the filling of space with what we call matter, which is expressed in "mass."

The following statement in Britannica's introductory paragraphs on "Light" (23 Brit 1) caught my attention. "When light energy ceases to move, because it has been absorbed by matter, it is no longer light." In the first three verses of Evangelist John's Gospel prologue, he identifies Christ as the Word by which all things made have been made, and he calls it first life and then light. Christ was both, but in the descending tree of life (I-22), the state closer to matter is the light ether, so that in reality all things have been made by light. While it must first pass through the fire state, when it is thereby absorbed, that is when it ceases to exist, matter takes its place—and that light can be restored only when that matter is dissolved again by fire. There is greater reality in the etheric conditions of fire and light than in their sensate conditions that abut matter. But there is a relationship between their etheric and sensate states.

Thus we shall have to seek the transition from the phenomena of light to the phenomena of material existence. The reader might find it worthwhile to consider again the diagrams from Steiner's *Warmth Course*, reproduced in the "Fire" essay, that show the different states of matter and the ethers and their interrelationship.

DETERMINING THE WHOLE

Something else. There is an immense difference between the way we unite with the light-flooded spaces and the way we unite with the warmth conditions of our immediate environment. Physics since the sixteenth century has quite lost hold of this difference. The distinction is that we share in the *warmth* conditions of our environment with our *physical* body and in the *light* conditions, as we said just now, with our *etheric* body. This proneness to confuse the two has been the bane of physics since the sixteenth century, especially since Newton's influence came to be dominant. On the whole scientists have lost the faculty of focusing attention purely and simply on the given facts.

What is called *gravity* is an example. The fact that material bodies in the neighborhood of other material bodies will under given conditions fall toward them has been conceived entirely in Newton's sense—gravity. Yet ponder how you will, you will never be able to include among the given facts what is understood by the term "force of gravity." If a stone falls to the Earth, the fact is simply that it draws nearer to the Earth. We see it now at one place, now at another, now at a third and so on. If you then say, "The Earth attracts the stone," you in your thoughts are adding something to the given fact. You are no longer purely and simply stating the phenomenon.

People have grown so unaccustomed to stating phenomena purely, yet upon this it all depends. For if we do not state the phenomena purely and simply, but proceed at once to thought-out explanations, we can find manifold explanations of one and the same phenomenon. Suppose for example you have two heavenly bodies. You may then say, "These two bodies attract one another—send some mysterious force out into space and so attract each other" (Figure 21). But you *need not* say this. You can also say, "Here is the one body, here is the other, and here (Figure 22) are a lot of other, tiny bodies—particles of ether, it may be—all around and in between the two heavenly bodies. The tiny particles are bombarding the two big ones on all sides. Now the total area of attack will be bigger outside than in between. Hence the two will approach each other." (Please note, Steiner is *not* saying this is true or is an observable phenomenon. He is simply saying that, as theory or kinetics, it is as valid as Newton's theory of gravity which also, as in the case of any force, cannot be directly observed.)

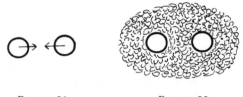

FIGURE 21   FIGURE 22

There are no doubt many other explanations to add to these. It is a classical example of how people fail to look at the real phenomenon but at once add thought-out explanations. What is at the bottom of it all? It saves one the need of doing something else. Adventitious theories relieve one of the need of making one fundamental assumption, from which the people of today seem to be very much averse. For if these two apparently independent bodies approach each other, we cannot but look for some underlying reason (such as gravity) why they do so—some inner reason. Now it is simpler to add in thought some unknown force (such as gravity) than to admit that there is also another way, namely, no longer to think of the (heavenly) bodies as independent of each other. If for example I put my hand to my forehead, I shall not dream of saying that my forehead "attracts" my hand, but I shall say, "It is an inner deed done by the underlying soul-and-spirit." My hand and forehead are not really independent, separate entities, but rather I must regard myself as a single whole. I would have no reality in mind if I were to say, "There is a head, two arms and hands, trunk and two legs." There is nothing complete in that. My task is not merely to describe what I see. I have to ponder the reality of what I see. The mere fact that I see a thing does not make it real.

Steiner here repeats his oft-used illustration of a crystal cube of rock salt, which is in some respect a totality (everything will be so in *some* respect), while a rose, cut from the shrub it grew on is no totality.

The implications of this are far-reaching. Namely, for every phenomenon, we must examine to what extent it is a reality in itself or a mere section of some larger whole. In considering the Sun and Earth and Moon separately, the things you have in mind are not totalities. They are but parts and members of the whole planetary system.

Our scientists have saved themselves the need of contemplating the inherent *life* of the planetary system. The tendency has been to regard as wholes those things in nature that are only parts, and then to construe by mere theories the effects that arise in fact between them. The essential point is that for all that meets us in nature we have to ask, "What is the whole to which this thing belongs?" Things are wholes, of course, only in certain respects. Even the crystal cube of rock salt is a totality only in some respect. Our need is to give up looking at nature in the fragmentary way so prevalent in our time.

Science has conceived the idea of universal, inorganic, lifeless nature since the sixteenth century. There is indeed no such thing, just as in this sense there is no such thing as your bony system without your blood. Lifeless nature is the bony system. It is impossible to study it alone as is done in Newtonian physics to this day. The only really inorganic things are our machines, and even these are only so insofar as they are pieced together from sundry forces of nature. Only the "put-togetherness" of them is inorganic. Whatever else we may call inorganic only exists by abstraction. From this abstraction present-day physics has arisen.

In the phenomena of sound and tone, there is a direct connection between vibrations executed by a body or by the air and our perceptions of tone or sound. Vibrations are going on around us when we hear sounds. But it is a pure play of analogies that leads one to the idea that the same thing applies in the case of light or colors so that some hypothetical ether with its vibrations beats upon our eye to produce a sensation of light. By the application of kinetics or theoretical movement calculations are made that cannot be perceived but are at most assumed theoretically. Of course, in time the assumption that light moved by waves through some tenuous elastic substance called ether fell by the wayside. This came about because of the experiments showing that an electromagnet brought to bear upon a cylinder of light (from which a spectrum was made) affects the phenomenon of light. The old theories were shaken, and many physicists then concluded that light is among the electromagnetic effects—that it is really electromagnetic rays passing through space. (This appears to be Fagg's primary thesis, along with the fact that electromagnetism is ubiquitous in our creation and travels with the speed of light. But to say it is ubiquitous in creation is not to say that it is the Creator, as Fagg concedes, or even that it is light. If it is not light, the Creator, then how can light be said to be an electromagnetic effect? Rather than concede that electromagnetism is not light, Fagg prefers to say that "God is not light" [p. 109]. Fagg's work is marvelous, and was very helpful to me, but one can see that Steiner's work differs markedly from it in spiritual conclusion, while not rejecting its utility in the kingdom of matter. The distinction is not unlike that made by Christ, "Render ... to Caesar the things that are Caesar's, and to God the things that are God's" (Mt 22,21; Mk 12,17; Lk 20,25). If Christ is light, then light is not to be understood in Caesarean terms.)

Now think a moment what has happened. First scientists thought they knew what light was in reality—vibrations in the elastic ether. Then they said, "What we regarded as vibrations of the elastic ether are really vibrations of electromagnetic force." Only they do not know what these are! It is a highly interesting journey that has here been made from the hypothetical search for an unknown to the explanation of this unknown by yet another unknown. The whole assumption is hypothetical.

These things Steiner gave as background to move into other areas he felt necessary for an adequate understanding of the spiritual aspects of light.

He then performs an experiment portrayed in Figure 23 (placing a red glass in front of the left light only, as indicated). He shows that the right shadow is greenish even when looked at through a tube which shuts out the red surroundings from the viewer's vision. But when the red glass is removed the greenish color immediately disappears.

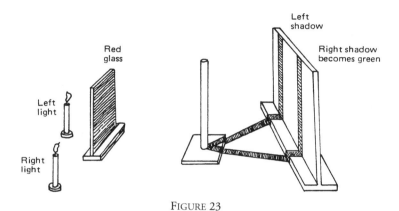

FIGURE 23

(The colors could be reversed by using a green glass, and in the same manner the other complementary colors could have been used for demonstration, e.g., blue-orange or purple-yellow.) The green shadow in Figure 23 is perceived just as one would perceive green for a time by looking first at a red object and then either closing the eyes or looking at a white background. The only difference is that one is spatial and the other temporal. There is a tendency to refer to the green shadow thus created in Figure 23 as "objective" and to the lingering after-effect in the other situation as "subjective." However, such distinction has no foundation in any real fact. For the physical apparatus in Figure 23 is the same, for such purpose, as the apparatus in the eye, recalling what was said earlier about its construction, i.e., the vitreous body, lens, aqueous humor and cornea. It is the same objective phenomenon in both cases. It only remains for a while in the latter instance while the apparatus of the eye is adjusted, i.e., the red plate can be removed more quickly than the comparable component of the eye can adjust. In one case the apparatus is outside the body while in the other it is in the eye. So, Steiner asks, "What difference does it make whether the necessary apparatus is out there or in your frontal cavity?"

This experiment demonstrates that with respect to the phenomena of color in all their aspects, "we are *in* them—not, it is true, with our ordinary body, but certainly with our etheric body and thereby also with the astral part of our being."

And now Steiner goes from light to heat (warmth, or fire). There is a very significant difference between the perception of light and the perception of warmth. You can localize the perception of light clearly and accurately in the physical apparatus of the eye. For warmth the whole of me is, so to speak, the sense organ, it is what my eye is for the light. We are swimming in the warmth element of our environment. What is it that is swimming when you are swimming in the warmth of your environment? He mentions the experiment of putting both hands in a bucket of lukewarm water to test it. Then put your left hand in water as hot as you can bear and your right in water as cold as you can bear. Then put both back into the lukewarm water. The latter will then seem very warm to your right hand and cold to your left, whereas before, it felt lukewarm to both. It is your own warmth that is swimming there. It makes you feel the difference between itself and your environment. It is your own warmth brought about by your own organic process. This is far from being an unconscious thing, for your consciousness indwells it. Inside your skin you are living in this warmth, and from that you converse with the element of warmth in your environment.

So we swim in both the elements of light and warmth. But so too do we swim in the element of air, which we also have within us. We are to a very small extent solid bodies, being over ninety percent a column of water which is a kind of intermediary between the airy and the solid. Our consciousness descends into the airy element even as it enters into the elements of light and warmth. Here again it can "converse"—communicate with what is taking place in our environment of air. It is precisely this "conversation" that finds expression in the phenomena of sound or tone. We live in and with the respective elements of light, warmth or air at different levels of consciousness. Our consciousness dives down into air, and we are thus able to perceive sound. We must have something of the airy element in us in order to be able to so perceive. Through our breathing and the movement of the diaphragm, we raise and lower the level of cerebro-spinal fluid as an image of this rhythmic process. In that my bodily organism partakes in these oscillations of the breathing process, there is an inner differentiation enabling me to perceive and experience the airy element in consciousness. We are thus an organ of vibrations, which in our ear we bring to bear upon what sounds toward us from without. The real process of hearing is, as you see, very far removed from the abstraction commonly presented.

COMPARING THREE SENSE ORGANS

Thus we have these three stages in a human being's relation to the outer world, namely, light, warmth and sound. But there is a remarkable fact about them. It is only with the etheric body that you can live in the element of light. You live in warmth with your whole bodily nature. Further down, the air in which we swim is the external physical matter of air (though it is also within us). Our life of warmth is for our consciousness a kind of midway level. It is portrayed as follows (note how this corresponds with I-22):

Element/Ether	Sense Organ	Domain in which Perceived
Light	Eye	Etheric body and world
Warmth	Whole body	Border of etheric/material
Sound/Air	Ear	Material air

For light we ascend as it were into a higher etheric sphere to live in our consciousness, while we descend into materiality to perceive sound, and come again to terms with the outer world in regard to warmth in the border between them.

Steiner speaks of the psychology of his time (1919) as being in an even sorrier position than physiology and physics, having been only too well disciplined by the churches to stay away from soul and spirit and focus on external apparatus—in a mere collection of words. Psychology speaks of a science of the senses as though there were such a thing as a sense organ in general, without realizing how completely different such organs are.[48]

---

48. The following statement is found in 16 Brit 603 under "Colour, The perception of colour": "Scientists did not know the process by which the eye and brain perceive colour until the early 1960s and even now do not understand all the details."

Steiner traces the historical development of natural science's treatment of sound and light—first of the velocity of sound, then of its sympathetic vibrations, then of its characteristics of intensity, pitch and quality, and then of the nature of its waves assumed to be longitudinal. He notes the special contribution of the Jesuits in this branch of physics, largely because they accepted the idea of keeping the spiritual element out of the study of nature, studying it in purely materialistic ways, the first to do what is today so prevalent.

He reminds us of the prior discussion that outward realities can never be merely spatial, arithmetical, or time-bound (in accord here with Einstein's then new theory of relativity). So we must look at a qualitative study of sound rather than only at the quantitative as physics does. But today there is surrender to the concept that sound is simply vibrations while recognizing that there is *something* within us that transforms these objective phenomena into subjective experiences. To deny light and sound the inner life and being that is experienced in a seemingly subjective way is precisely as it would be if, having you here before me, I looked on all that is before me as merely part of my subjective life, and thus denied to you the experience of inner life and being.

This is so obvious and trite that scientists would naturally not presume they could ever fall into such an obvious mistake. And yet they do. The whole distinction usually made of subjective impression from objective process amounts to this and nothing else. The physicist could, of course, say that he does not enter into what is qualitative and thus he would be candid. But he must not then go on to say that the one is "objective" and the other "subjective," or that the one is the "effect" of the other.

How easily it can be argued that the oscillatory character of sound is evident. Yet we do not understand what is happening in such a case unless we bring it into connection with a more widespread phenomenon. For instance, the sympathetic vibrations obvious in the laboratory actually extend to a wider domain. We see it in the sympathetic going-together of events attuned to one another which are making themselves felt in a highly spiritual realm. Consider the parallel phenomena of much more spiritual nature as when we experience one another's thoughts, or when the same thoughts occur throughout the world more or less simultaneously.

As he did earlier for the human eye, Steiner now gives the successive stages from outer to inner in the human ear as follows:

(a) External auditory canal

(b) Drum (inner end of the canal)

(c) Hammer, anvil and stirrup (minute bones or ossicles behind the drum)

(d) Three semi-circular canals, their planes at right angles to each other according to the three dimensions of space

(e) Cochlea, filled with a kind of fluid

(f) Auditory nerve

So we have the eye as one sense organ and the ear as another. If they are put side by side, science may abstractly elaborate a general physiology of the senses and sensation. But recall what was said about the rhythm of the ascending and descending cerebro-spinal fluid and how it interacts with what is taking place externally in the outer air, enabling us to perceive and experience the airy element in consciousness. Remember too that a thing may look complete and self-contained when outwardly regarded, but we must not therefore take it to be a finished reality. Here again he gives the cut rose as an example, and how we must go on to the totality. *So too for hearing; the ear alone is no reality*, though nearly always so represented. What is transmitted inward must first interact in a certain way with the inner rhythm, manifested in the rise and fall of the cerebro-spinal fluid. But even then we still have not reached the end.

All this that takes its course in rhythm is also fundamental in the human being to what appears in the *larynx and adjoining organs* when we are speaking. For these are inserted into the breathing process to which the rhythmic rise and fall of the cerebro-spinal fluid is also due. In the whole rhythm of breathing you can therefore insert on the one hand your active speaking and on the other hand your hearing. Then you will have a totality. It manifests intelligently in hearing and volitionally in speaking. *To separate the ear and the larynx is thus an abstraction.* You have no real totality, for the two belong together.

Consider what is left of the eye if I first take away the vitreous body, retina, optic nerve and cerebral connection—only the ciliary muscle, lens and aqueous humor, and cornea or outer integument. What is left would be an organ that could never compare with the ear but only with the larynx. It is a metamorphosis not of the ear but of the larynx. For just as the muscles of the larynx take hold of the vocal chords, widening or narrowing the aperture between them, so do the ciliary muscles with the lens. And now if I reinsert the retina, vitreous body and other inward instruments, I shall truly be able to relate to the ear. Thus, at one level in the human body I have the eye. In its more inward parts it is a metamorphosed ear, enveloped from without by a metamorphosed larynx. If we take larynx and ear together as a single whole, we have a metamorphosed eye upon another level.

The ear can be compared only to the part of the eye behind the lens. We can then no longer conceive as parallel, without more ado, all that goes on in the phenomena of sound on the one hand and light on the other. My seeing is fundamentally different from my hearing. *When I am seeing, the same thing happens in my eye as happens when I hear and speak at the same time.* In the eye we have a kind of monologue. The eye always proceeds as you would do if you were listening intently and, to understand what you were hearing, you first repeated it aloud. Etherically we are talking to ourselves when we are seeing. With hearing alone, we have but a single factor of the dual process.

Sound is already in existence, only it is outside of space—not yet in space. The conditions for it to enter space are not given until I (or some agency) make them. The outer air waves (oscillations connected with sounds) can be compared to the vacuum inside a sealed and evacuated jar, and what becomes audible can be compared to what penetrates—the vacuum from outside when the conditions have been created for this to happen. In essence the air waves have no more to do with sound than that; where they are, a process like suction has been produced to draw the sound from its nonspatial realm into the spatial. So the processes of sound have their external image in the observed processes of oscillation.

WHERE WE ARE ASLEEP

Steiner then reviews the discovery and development of electricity; telling how the search for an abstract, single unitary principle applicable to all "forces of nature" led to the idea that electricity traveled in "waves" the same as light was thought to do; and how these ideas about electricity had to be changed, first by giving up the "wave" theory in favor of "radiant matter"(material particles shooting through space attracted by magnetic force), then by giving up any idea that "matter" was involved in favor of the belief that electricity just "flowed." But then came the discovery of the X-ray and then of the radiations of "alpha, beta and gamma rays" from radium in metamorphosis.

The latter "rays" were said to go off in different directions, "beta" to the right, "gamma" straight ahead, and "alpha" to the left. Interestingly, all three had different velocities, that of "beta" rays being about nine-tenths that of light, while that of "alpha" only one-tenth—very striking differences of velocity![49]

Recall that the *real* thing in space is *velocity*, and then think what it signifies that one element moves nine times as fast as the other. Steiner sees the three different velocities as representing how the three different spiritual activities, the normal (the Christ), the Luciferic and the Ahrimanic, work into one another. He indicates that the scientific pathway is thus compelling even physics, though unconsciously, to go into differences of velocity in a way very similar to the way spiritual science has to do for the great all-embracing agencies of cosmic evolution. (Anthroposophy sees the deep truth of these three agencies represented by the three crucified victims on Golgotha's hill in Luke's Gospel, Lk 23,32-33,39-43; see *The Burning Bush* at pp. 117, 332 and 456.)

All these phenomena in the electrical domain have one property in common, namely, their relation to us differs fundamentally from our relation to the phenomena of sound or light or warmth. In light, sound and warmth we ourselves are swimming. The same cannot be said of our relation to the electrical phenomenon. We do not perceive it as a specific quality in the way we perceive light, for instance. Electricity is obliged to reveal itself by means of a phenomenon of light. (It is also interesting in that it moves closer to us through the element of fire.) But light has built in the human being the eye, sound the ear, and warmth the total organ, but for electricity there is nothing analogous. We can perceive it only indirectly.[50]

---

49. Apparently Fagg does not include alpha rays and beta rays among the "spectrum of electromagnetic radiation" (pp. 42-43) as are X-rays and gamma rays. And 26 Brit 472, "Radiation, … Matter rays," says, "Unlike X rays and gamma rays, some high-energy radiations travel at less than the speed of light."

50. While Steiner does not here discuss it, nevertheless we know that if too much electricity enters an earthly organism, it kills it, for we (all such organisms) do not swim in it; it is not part of our fourfold being (I-9). We shall presently see in the text that Steiner points us in this direction regarding electricity. While he does not there discuss the degree to which electrical and chemical impulses are involved in the astral body as, for instance, in synaptic transmissions, nevertheless we know that they are involved, the electrical being far less common than the chemical (see 24 Brit 792, "Nerves and Nervous Systems, … *(continued on following page)*

Remember that we are threefold beings, of thinking, feeling and willing. We are awake in our thinking, dreaming in our feeling, and asleep in our willing (a reality we need to hold in mind as we consider the biblical meaning of "sleep"). And now remember, too, that wherever we write the formula involving *m* for *mass*, we are in fact going beyond mere arithmetic, mere movement, space and time. We are including what is no longer kinematical and corresponds to the consciousness of sleep. We must admit that our experience of light, sound and warmth belongs to a high degree to our sensory and thinking life, especially light. On the other hand, in *mass* we are approaching those forces that develop in us when we are sleeping. And we are going in precisely the same direction when we descend from the realm of light, sound and warmth into that of electrical phenomena. (Charts relevant to the threefold human activities include I-66, I-70 and I-80.[51])

We have no direct experience of the phenomena of our own will (cf. I-40). It is likewise with the electrical phenomena of nature. We only experience what they deliver into the realms of light, sound and warmth. Light, sound and warmth thus relate to our conscious life, while electricity and magnetism relate to our unconscious life of will.

When we go down into the realm of electrical phenomena we are entering the same realm as that of *mass*. When we study electricity and magnetism we are studying matter in all reality. (See again the tree of life in I-22, and the idea of the "flaming sword" of the Seraphim.[52] How

---

50. *(continued from previous page)* Transmission at the Synapse"). Recall from our discussion of Lucifer as the "serpent" in Gen 3 bringing about the infection of the astral body (with its consequent infection then of the lower etheric and physical bodies), the home of the nervous system in the descended human being (and animal). Then see the relationship of these domains, the electrical and chemical, to Lucifer and Ahriman in the sub-physical worlds as set out in I-22 (the full chart reproduced in the appendix). While the sub-physical thus enters us in that way and to that extent, as Steiner says it does so in our sleeping Will and not as part of the elemental physical world in which we "swim."

51. Chart I-66 comes from Tomberg's earliest, and probably his best, work. As indicated elsewhere, Tomberg is a highly controversial figure who, tragically, has occasioned a deep split among anthroposophists from the 1930s to the present time. While I feel his work should not be accepted as the equivalent of Steiner's, neither should it be thrown out altogether if one sufficiently acquainted with Steiner's works sees in it helpful elements compatible with what Steiner himself gave us. The chart cited here seems to fall within the latter circumstance (save only that I have not been able to fully so verify all portions of chart I-7 referred to therein).

52. At first glance, Gen 3,24 seems to imply that the Cherubim have the "flaming sword" in their hands. However, if one reads carefully, it will be seen that translations uniformly show the flaming sword, however described, to be separate and distinct from, and not in the hands of the Cherubim, and the commentaries that address the manner *(continued on following page)*

descriptive this is of lightning, which reveals itself only through light and then fire. See also I-29, I-32 and I-27.)

In concluding his lecture on electricity and magnetism, Steiner says, "In fact our scientists have taken the first step—they only do not yet admit it—towards the overcoming of matter."

And he opens the next (Lect. 10) by saying the last three decades, i.e., 1890-1920, had in fact been revolutionary. Physics had suffered no less a loss than the concept of matter itself in its old form. The entities (like radium) that emit rays of three kinds, to begin with, alpha, beta and gamma, show different properties. Moreover the chemical element itself (radium) in sending out its radiation is transmuted into helium. We have to do no longer with stable and enduring matter but with a complete metamorphosis of phenomena. Electricity has become manifest to some extent, as a form of phenomena in the outer world, but the "ether" refuses to turn up. It was not given to nineteenth-century thinking to penetrate *into* the phenomena. But this is just what physics will require from now on.

What science relied upon most was that it could explain the phenomena so beautifully by means of arithmetic and geometry. But calculations have begun to fail us if applied in the same abstract way as in the old wave theory. Something of the way that theory first began is illustrated by the assumption that it can be proved that the triangle has one hundred eighty degrees as the sum of its three internal angles. The proof of this was based upon drawing parallel lines, one along the longest side and the other touching the opposite vertex. However, what we are taking for granted is that the upper line is truly parallel to the lower one, for this alone enables us to carry out the proof. But in the whole of Euclid's geometry there is no way of proving that the two lines are really parallel.

There is no guarantee that what is going on in the outer world does really work in such a way that we can fully grasp it with the Euclidean geometry that we ourselves think out. Might it not be—the facts alone

---

52. *(continued from previous page)* are fully consistent with this. And the descriptions of the "flaming sword" incorporate the imagination of lightning/fire (see I-29) and/or the characteristics thereof. How impressive it is then to go back to Steiner's *Outline of Esoteric Science* (OES) and see that the highest rank among the hierarchies that sacrificed its own will to commence the formation of the human being was that of the Thrones, while the Cherubim and Seraphim looked down upon them from the highest spiritual domains, remaining, in this sense, in the "garden," not entangled in what was being created in matter (Gen 3,24).

can tell—that the processes outside are governed by quite another geom-etry? He does not here pursue this point to conclusion in the *Light Course*, but it is implied and actually came into the picture in the *Warmth Course* (in "Fire" above), and will be more fully demonstrated in the "Astronomy Course" in the illustration of the Cassini curve where Euclidean geometry fails us in that we have to "go out of space" on the line of the equation that is used (and that is incorporated into the human structure). We look at the "Astronomy Course" in the last essay herein, "What is Man?"

If people once begin to reflect deeply enough in modern science—above all in physics—they will detect what an appallingly blind alley they are in. They will only emerge if they first take the trouble to find out the origin of all our kinetical, arithmetical and geometrical ideas. Whence do we get them? If we now go further and begin applying to what goes on in the outer world the ideas of "scientific" arithmetic and algebra, geometry and kinematics, we are applying ideas gained not from the outer world but spun out of our own inner life. Where then do these come from? Not from our intelligence that we apply when working up the ideas derived from sense perception, but rather from the intelligent part of our will—the volitional part of our soul.

There is an immense difference between the ideas we have as intelligent beings that are derived from our experience in the outer world, and those that are of a geometrical, arithmetical or kinematical nature. These latter arise from the unconscious part of us, from the will part that has its outer organ in the metabolism. And if you now apply these geometrical ideas to the phenomena of light or sound, you are connecting what arises from within you to what you are perceiving from without—yet the two things do not directly belong to one another.

All this elaboration of the outer world by means of these geometrical, mathematical and kinetical thought forms is in point of fact a dreaming about nature. Cool and sober as it may seem, it is a dream—a dreaming while awake. What people fondly believe to be the most exact of sciences is modern humanity's dream of nature.

But it is different when we get into the realm of electricity. For we then connect with what in outer nature is truly equivalent to the will in the human being. It is from this very realm of will that what we possess in our mathematics, geometry and kinematics arises. They are truly akin. And here for our pondering Steiner brings forward again the diagram from the *Warmth Course* as we first saw it in the "Fire" essay above:

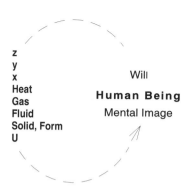

However, human thinking has in our time not yet gone far enough to really think its way into these realms. Humanity today can dream nicely, but it is not yet able to enter with real mathematical perception into that realm of phenomena akin to human will where geometry and arithmetic originate. For this our geometrical and mathematical thinking must in themselves become more saturated with reality.

In recent times (in terms of centuries), physicists have had recourse to a new device, the calculus of probabilities. But this too will come to a point where it no longer works.

Reality today, especially in physics, often compels human beings to admit that with our thinking, our forming of ideas, we no longer fully penetrate into reality; we must begin again from another angle. For it is only when you rise to Intuition, which has its ground in the will, that you come into the region—even of the outer world—where electricity lives and moves. And when you do so you perceive that in these phenomena you are in a way confronted by the very opposite of the phenomena of sound or tone for instance.

Perceptions of sound and those of electricity are at very opposite poles (full chart I-22). When you perceive a sound with your ordinary body, you become aware of the undulations. You draw your etheric and astral bodies together so that they occupy only a portion of your space. You then enjoy what you are to experience of the sound as such in this inward and concentrated etheric-astral part of your being. It is quite different with electricity. With it you expand what you otherwise concentrated, thus driving your etheric and astral bodies out beyond your normal surface in order to perceive electrical phenomena.

Without including the human soul and spirit, it will be quite impossible to gain a true or realistic conception of the phenomena of physics. Ever increasingly we shall be obliged to think this way: the phenomena of sound and light are akin to the conscious element of thinking in ourselves, while those of electricity and magnetism are akin to the subconscious element of will. Warmth is between the two. Even as feeling is intermediate between thinking and willing, so is the outer warmth in nature intermediate between light and sound on the one hand, and electricity and magnetism on the other. As in the spiritual realm we differentiate between the Luciferic, akin to the quality of light, and the Ahrimanic, akin to electricity and magnetism, so also must we understand the structure of nature. Between the two lies what we meet with in the phenomena of warmth.

Sound and Light	Thought	Lucifer
Warmth	Feeling	Christ[53]
Electricity and Magnetism[54]	Will	Ahriman

And so ends Steiner's *Light Course.*

Synthesis/Summation

PRELIMINARY REMARKS

We are at the point of reflection—with our own internal light. Consider where we are in the fractal dimension of human evolution just since the time of First Isaiah.

The most exalted Old Testament revelation, the only appearance in the canon of the lofty Seraphim (I-6), came to Isaiah "in the year that King Uzziah died" (Is 6) about 742 B.C. at the very beginning of the Cultural Age of Aries, the celestial Lamb.[55] First Isaiah was the eponymous founder of the school of prophets whence arose the one called Second Isaiah soon after the commencement of the former regency of the Archangel Michael. It was Michael who brought the later Zarathustra (Zoroaster, the great teacher of the magi), the middle period prophets of Israel

---

53. The Christ seems clearly here implied, though not expressed, by Steiner. Insofar as Earth evolution, the Cosmos of Love, is concerned, his coming to "cast fire upon the earth" (Lk 12,49) seems to correspond fully with this assumption.
54. I-22 relates the four ethers to the subphysical or subsensible realms where the counterparts of light ether, chemical/sound ether and life ether are electricity (Lucifer), magnetism (Ahriman) and a future Third Force (Asuras), respectively.
55. In 747 B.C., see I-19.

(including even Second Isaiah) and Pythagoras to Babylon (Persia). It was Michael who installed the liberator Cyrus on the Persian throne. And it was Michael who introduced the fertile line of philosophers beginning with Heraclitus and Socrates who would prepare the cultural soil for the spreading of Christianity.[56]

Until the time of Steiner Christendom had not, nor has it to this very day, awakened to the meaning of the great commission given First Isaiah (Is 6,9-13). The reader would do well to review its significance.[57] Time after time Steiner referred to the turn of the millennium, the close of a century both of great human turmoil and great material progress, as an enormously important time in human spiritual evolution. Over the last several centuries others of note have also called attention to it, but without the uniquely defining quality of Steiner's vision. What are the fractal dimensions it reflects?

The Cultural Age of the celestial Lamb (Aries; see I-19), foreseen by Moses in the account of the sacrifice by Abraham of his son Isaac (Gen 22,13-14), began in 747 B.C., whereupon Isaiah was immediately visited by the Seraphim. The Christ event on Earth, foretold by both First and Second Isaiah, took place one-third of the way through the Cultural Age of the celestial Lamb. The third millennium of the Christian (or Common) era is beginning as we approach the same one-third point in our present Cultural Age of the Consciousness Soul, the age of the Fishes, Pisces, so significant in the esoteric message of the Gospels. Our present Cultural Age began with the reawakening, literally the "rebirth" or Renaissance, of human consciousness in A.D. 1414 as it emerged from the valley of the shadow into which the Christ Incarnated.[58] As shown early in this essay, the first regency of the Archangel Michael (the leader of the archangels and the administrator of the divine intelligence) since the Christ event, began in 1879 and will run for approximately 354 years. The year A.D. 2000 is nearly one-third of the way through that regency.

The providential coincidence of these things should not be overlooked. Christendom, since the age of "Enlightenment" in the sixteenth century most ironically, has forgotten that the Archangel Michael is associated with the light of divine intelligence. It would be a spiritual tragedy of the most

---

56. The Archangel Michael has been mentioned throughout this essay. See especially fns 3 and 7 and their related text. See also the "Epilogue" in *The Incredible Births of Jesus* (IBJ).
57. See the many references to these verses in the Index of Scriptures Cited in *The Burning Bush*.
58. See "The Valley of the Shadow" in *The Incredible Births of Jesus* (IBJ), pp. 29-31.

awful dimension imaginable if Christendom were to sleep through this time without awakening to the second coming of Christ that is already underway.[59] Michael appears to Daniel "in the third year of Cyrus king of Persia" (Dan 10,1),[60] and we then find the prophecy about this prince of Archangels in Dan 10,13,21, again in Jude 1,9 (wrestling with the legalistic Mosaic law and materialistic mode of understanding still heavy upon Christendom in our own time), and finally fighting against the materialistic deceiver of the world in Rev 12,7. Throughout spiritual history Michael has been associated with the spiritual light of Christ.

Think how Steiner told us, and it was not unique to him, that the thirty years preceding his *Light Course* (in 1919-1920) had shaken the very roots of scientific thinking since the "Enlightenment" days of Newton and the so-called "scientific" revolution. Those early geniuses of the nineteenth and twentieth centuries have been followed by others, but the net result has been, as we have seen, to produce as our millennium turns a condition in which even our most reflective scientists recognize there are forces at work they are unable to identify save by a method (i.e., quantum theory, for instance) that still sticks in their craw, particularly as it applies in the realm of light. In spite of their intellectual genius, materialistically speaking, they simply do not know what light is. Nor do they know how we come by our consciousness of being, on which see, for instance, Penrose's noted *Shadows of the Mind* (SHAD). Yet their work

---

59. See the essay "Second Coming" and its related essay "Lord of Karma" in *The Burning Bush*.
60. If we can put aside the mincemeat that critical biblical analysis has typically made of this marvelously meaningful book (Daniel) and take it as it comes to us, we find that it falls squarely within the early stages of the last pre-Christian age of Michael. As set out in *The Incredible Births of Jesus* (IBJ), at p. 88, that age ran from about 601 to 247 B.C. The Cyrus referred to in the Bible came to the throne of Persia in 559 B.C., though he did not conquer Babylon until 539/538 B.C. Whether the "third year" referred to the earlier or later date is not really important, for in either case, the date clearly fell within the first third of that Michaelic age. Cyrus is referred to in the books of 2 Chronicles (36,22-23), Ezra (1,1-8; 3,7; 5,13-17; 6,3,14), Isaiah (44,28; 45,1) and Daniel (1,21; 6,28; 10,1). Recall from the "I Am" essay in *The Burning Bush*, at pp. 246-247 and 257, that it was the gradually descending Christ who appeared to First Isaiah in Is 6 and who spoke through the Second Isaiah. The latter included the passage where the Lord (Christ) "says of Cyrus, 'He is my shepherd'" (Is 44,28), and then immediately Second Isaiah calls Cyrus the Lord's "anointed" (Is 45,1). I have previously pointed out the importance of one's "name" in ancient times, that it signified the spiritual character of the personality, and that many biblical persons had their names changed as a result of significant spiritual junctures. This leads us to ponder whether it was merely coincidence that the same characterization was given to Cyrus as to Christ, as both derive from the same ancient word (*kurush* in Old Persian [WNWCD], *kores* in Hebrew [ABD] and *kyros* in Greek [WNWCD]).

has been immensely important, for it has brought us, as Steiner said and some of them have also expressed, to the point where a higher intelligence must lead us onward and upward.

Most of our theologians, from ultraliberal to ultraconservative, have not advanced so far, but still wrestle in the arid deserts of either documentary hypotheses or literal, parochial understanding and welter in the same type of moribund, institutionalized scriptural interpretation that afflicted the scribes and Pharisees at the time of Christ. Any thought of reliance upon the intuition of prophets since Christ and the "end of (Old Testament) prophecy" is unthinkable in the solidarity of their ranks. One must have "recognized credentials" to be given credence, credentials bestowed by those of like thinking. The shepherds in our pulpits, trained in such theology, engrossed in daily duties, and constrained by institutionalism, preach and teach within these walls. And while there is a tangible chasm between academic theology and pastoral administration, both suffer from an unwillingness to "leave home" in search of such vast treasures as have been revealed by the unsung, sometimes vilified Rudolf Steiner, courageous, intellectually gifted and spiritually intuitive servant of the Archangel Michael and the Christ.

In what I have just written to open this summation, I make no personal claim to intuition, nor to any divine insight other than, as a result of a lifetime of study of the Bible and whatever unknown karma I represent, having recognized in the works of Rudolf Steiner insights deemed higher than any other I've encountered about the meaning of the entire biblical message. What I have said about pastors applies alike to those whom I have loved and served in churches all my life to this very day, and what I have said about theologians applies to those whom I have admired greatly and still admire. We are told that even Christ chastens those he loves (Rev 3,19), and what parent, or understanding child, would say otherwise?

CONCLUSION

The scientific revolution that began with Newton and the Enlightenment in the sixteenth century brought forward, unconsciously, the ancient concept of the etheric world. Only it was tainted by the idea that, however fine, it was part of the material realm. It had to be, so it was thought, if it was to carry light, for clearly the analogue of sound is carried by waves in the material air. And so light, it was thought, if it is to impinge upon our retinal nerve must itself have some materiality however tenuous. Thus light was alternately, and in more recent times simultaneously, viewed as being particle and/or wave as it traveled swiftly through space. Moreover, light was thought, and still is, to define the outer limits of velocity of matter. Insofar as it applies to matter, that thought is correct to the best of our knowledge.[61] Yet we are met in our investigation with seemingly credible evidence that light is a material particle and thus cannot travel by a transverse wave through other matter; while at the same time we are met with seemingly credible evidence to the exactly opposite conclusion. Thus, we decide that light is at one and the same time both particle and wave while our intelligence otherwise tells us it cannot be so. And we are told that what we call the little photons of light can talk to each other over vast geographical distances and change their performance or relationship to one another, and even their own character, based upon these conversations. We can calculate what their mutual decision is, but there is no way of understanding the meaning of our calculation, or why it is right, except that it simply comes out right.

We are told in John's prologue that the Christ, the creative Word, is our light, and we repeat it with deep religiosity, but we still seek it in the material realm, and it is not there. "He is not here" (Mt 28,6a; Mk 16,6b; Lk 24,5b). We must return again and again to the portrayal of the schematic of the tree of life in I-22 where we see that fire (at once both matter and ether) is the dividing line, the meeting point, between all matter and spirit. We can tell neither the origin nor the destination of the wind because it is the movement of matter created in the image of the light ether. We feel it and we hear it, but we know neither its source nor destination because we know not the light ether that separated from it long ago (Gen 1,3; Jn 3,8 and Job 38,19-20). So also even earlier were the chemical/sound ether and the life ether separated from their earthly counterparts in the descent of humanity and the rest of creation into materiality. Only when Earth evolution (see I-1) has run its course and the holy city of the new Jerusalem, the Jupiter Condition of Consciousness (again, see I-1), has been gained by humanity, eons (ages) hence, will the light ether be again joined with its counterpart, but then in a nonmaterial astral condition. The light, then being within humanity (the one-hundred forty-four thousand discussed in "Fire"), there will no longer be need of Sun nor Moon (Rev 21,23; 22,5).

Let us look at what we rather glibly call the *phenomenon*.

---

61. But see fn 16.

Steiner was totally antagonistic to the Kantian philosophy that there was a limit to human knowledge, claiming instead that any such limit was imposed only by the lack of development of the spiritual potential for human perception. Further, Steiner insisted that there was innate in every human being the potential for unlimited perception. His own horizon, of course, stretched further than his fellows, and that of his fellows he saw as stretching far beyond what they themselves understood with their limited views of the evolution of individual and collective consciousness over the ages.

According to Kantian philosophy there are *phenomena* and there are *noumena*. *Phenomenalism*, is thus the philosophic theory that knowledge is limited to phenomena, either because there is no reality beyond phenomena or because such reality is unknowable (WNWCD). According to this Kantian philosophy, a *phenomenon* is anything that can be observed by the senses, whereas a *noumenon* is "a thing as it is in itself, unable to be known through perception but postulated as the intelligible ground of a phenomenon" (WNWCD). A noumenon is thus a kinetical (theoretical or calculated) postulation—reasoning rather than direct observation.[62]

It is at once apparent that the world of quantum physics is within the world of noumena, not phenomena. The calculation itself might be called a phenomenon; the object of the calculation cannot be. And it seems further apparent that light itself, as distinguished from consciousness of its presence, is in the same noumenal domain. We simply cannot see the light. We see objects only because light illuminates them and we postulate theories about the light. But as John says, the darkness (and as materially incarnated beings we are still within that expression) comprehends not the light (the better meaning of Jn 1,5, rather than that the darkness has not "overcome" the light, though both are permissible translations of the Greek).

Previously in the text I have mentioned in passing my alienation from the big bang theory so widely espoused by science and theology in our day. The position of the "scientists" is in keeping with their "noumenal" (i.e., calculated; not observed) vision of the universe. The position of the theologians is substitutional at best because they (at least most) have no intuitive vision in our day and even abjure its possibility. What an irony, since they profess a revealed religion! Abdicating their rightful domain and

---

62. See also the discussion of these terms, noumenon and phenomenon, in the *Britannica*.

accepting the noumenal pronouncements of the scientists, the general attitude is "Anything is possible with God. If he chose to create the universe
by the mechanism of the big bang, who are we to question it?" Perhaps,
theoretically, the Christ could have entered the three bodies prepared for
the Individuality whose personality we knew as Adolf Hitler, but the
Father God did not act in that way. The bodies prepared for the entry of
the Christ Spirit were those of the most highly qualified human being who
had ever lived, the one who, until his baptism, was properly called Jesus of
Nazareth (Heb 10,5c; see "The Nativity" in *The Burning Bush*, as well as
its popularized version in *The Incredible Births of Jesus*). Shrugging off the
reality that all things were created by the spiritual world through the
agency of light, our theologians, through lack of vision, go along with the
noumena of our scientists to accept the view that the universe as we know
it was created by and through the darkness of materiality so dense that it
was beyond all human comprehension—so dense that it can be described
only in the exponentials of noumenal (mathematical) reasoning.

The whole scenario of this acceptability of the big bang theory is an
analogue to Fagg's de facto recognition of electromagnetism as being
sacred. As can be seen from the complete chart of I-22, electricity and
magnetism are the polar opposites (i.e., mineral counterparts) of the light
ether and the chemical/sound ether (the light and the creative Word of
Jn 1,1-3). It might help us to comprehend the monstrosity of the big
bang theory to look at this unspeakably materialized (dense) origin in
order to compare it with what we know (i.e., what we are told by astronomers with fair plausibility) of the "black holes" that are postulated (i.e.,
noumenal) in our universe. We are told they are matter so densely compacted that even light cannot escape their gravitational pull. I suppose
that the density of the black hole would compare with that of the infinitely infinitesimal speck immediately before the big bang somewhat in
the way that an electron (or perhaps even the tauon neutrino that Fagg
says "may have a mass of the order of one-ten millionth of that of the electron") would compare with the Earth or even perhaps with the Sun
itself—I leave the numerical designation of exponents to the theories of
the mathematicians, scientists and astronomers.

Steiner has shown us, most fully in his *An Outline of Esoteric Science*
(OES), that creation occurred over different conditions of being through
almost incomprehensible cycles of time and timelessness whereby what
was completely spirit at the beginning progressively separated from its

offspring, which became increasingly dense and eventually entered into the state of matter. One who contemplates Steiner's vast disclosures and then the observable phenomena (including the biblical record itself) in a Goethean manner, deferring judgment (noumena) as long as possible, will surely see, it seems to me, that they are completely incompatible with the idea of a big bang.

If we go back to the full chart I-22, we note there were not two, but rather three, forces opposed to the spiritual world, namely, the Luciferic, Ahrimanic and Asuric. The last was an evil power and development so far in the future that Steiner said we need not speak of it in our time, but rather concern ourselves with the first two. The Luciferic is, as its name applies, related to light, but it is misplaced or deceptive light. In that capacity it is called *diabolos*, or "devil." The Ahrimanic goes back to the prehistoric Ahriman of the Ancient Persian Cultural Era (cf. 1 Brit 168, "Ahriman"). This evil force is known as "Satan." See I-32 for a fuller discussion. The balance between Lucifer and Satan is the Christ Spirit, and the three are esoterically depicted in Luke's Gospel by the two thieves and Christ all crucified together (Lk 23,32-43).

Since the big bang theory as we know it today came into existence after Steiner's death, he did not specifically address it. It seems clear to me, however, that one must inevitably infer from his vast works a view of creation diametrically opposed to the big bang. The situation is essentially equivalent to his words on the Darwinism still so widely accepted by scientists today, and again, through lack of insight, also by the theologians, save only the fundamentalists, who adopt their equally fallacious creationism. According to Steiner, Darwin was right in, and to be admired for, his courage in bringing forward the concept of the evolution of the human being, for indeed that is a both a spiritual and a temporal reality. As indicated in the "Evolution" essay, the problem with Darwinism is that its direction is exactly one hundred eighty degrees off course. The human being did not evolve from the animal kingdom or the lower plant and mineral kingdoms, though it has within it all these. Rather, the initial spark of creation had to do with the human being (and the hierarchies themselves), and over the course of evolution the lower three kingdoms, descending prematurely, themselves came into material being as the premature by-products of the descending (evolving) human being. This is, of course, the quintessence of *The Burning Bush* in its effort to bring forth an exposition of the Bible in the light of Steiner's lofty Intuitions.

The big bang theory is analogous to Darwinism, correct in its idea of an evolving universe, but one hundred eighty degrees off course. John's baptism calling for "repentance" has been misunderstood by Christendom almost from the beginning. As Steiner has told us, it means not so much a remorse for past action as a change in the way of thinking—either interpretation is, of course, as in the case of the Jn 1,5b passage above, literally permissible, but the latter carries the deeper meaning associated with the true nature of human evolution and the uniquely pivotal character of the Christ event that was then upon humanity. There is a need for that repentance in both science and theology today, for both in their materialistic approach have need of repentance in the latter sense.

In fn 41, reference was made to British anthroposophist Nick Thomas' book, *Science Between Space and Counterspace* (SBSC). Recall also Steiner's statements earlier that the human unites with space and time but not with velocity, so that for us as space and time beings the real thing is not space and time but velocity. Would that it were feasible for us to look at what Thomas says about velocity. If given that opportunity, most readers would agree it is not feasible, for Thomas shows no mercy whatsoever toward us who are not experts in mathematics, physics and the scientific realm in general and their respective argots. I refer the experts to his book.[63] What is pertinent for our purposes is, first, his demonstration that though an apparent velocity can be associated with light, light does not travel in the way a particle does (and that its apparent velocity will always be judged regardless of the motion of the observer as explained by Einstein's special relativity); and second, his inference that lighted objects come to our consciousness through the two-way action of both outer and inner light (just as the ancients knew it did).

Theologians should have no trouble with the first part, that light does not travel, for it is everywhere. If the Christ is light, that light is ubiquitous in creation. And John's Gospel affirms that Christ is light (Jn 8,12; 9,5 and 1,1-10). True, we humans must wrestle with how to equate Christ as light, on the one hand, with what lights the physical world for us, on the other. For ever since the "first day" when God created light, separating it from darkness (Gen 1,3-5), the light ether and what eventually became gaseous (darkness) were separated, and things are lighted for our observation now only through the agency of fire, whether it be by a match in a dark room or

---

63. See its Chap. 13 on "Light," particularly the section "Light and Time" (pp. 91-93).

matter (gas) igniting as it comes in contact with the Elohim at the outer surface of the Sun. The fact that Thomas "agree[s] with the experimental facts [of the] 'velocity' of light" relates to its mineral-physical character as in Fagg's approach. But his suggestion that it does not travel inheres in the ubiquitous nature of the light ether. The mysteries that plague scientists in their search for the nature of light must surely reflect, in some divine way, the hand of the etheric world of light as it tenderly cares for its creature, the world in which we live. That light photons seem to be at widely separated geographical locations at the same minute instant of time without regard to velocity seems in fact to negate velocity in showing ubiquity.

Remember what Steiner said about the importance of making our evaluations on the basis of the whole rather than its individual parts. A cut rose bloom is not a rose. Gravity may not be the mutual attraction of two bodies for each other any more than we could say that our forehead and our hand are mutually attracted to each other when we put our hand on our forehead. The important thing is to consider what is the whole of which our observed phenomenon is but an integral part. Only then can we speak of reality. And in our fractal universe the whole keeps getting bigger, but by it can the real nature of its parts also be more truly seen.

The reader will long ago have recognized that I purport to speak more as a theologian than as a scientist, though I carry no professionally recognized credentials in either discipline. Clearly there are those in both disciplines who demonstrate the greatest humility of knowledge. Frequently, if not usually, this is characteristic of the most knowledgeable. In our time Einstein is legendary for his openness and his candid admissions of inadequacy. He is an eminent paragon for emulation by all in that regard. A childlike openness and eagerness for new insight is needed by us all—a requisite for entry into the kingdom of heaven (Mt 18,3, though a higher, compatible meaning for this verse is also suggested in *The Burning Bush*, p. 115).

Readers will further recognize that, however much they might also apply to others, my writings are primarily directed to those who are interested in new and deeper insights into the biblical message. These in particular should recognize the passages I will reflect on to close this essay. Light is associated with intelligence, particularly the divine intelligence recognized of old as being Michaelic in character. Its origin is the Christ, the Word (Jn 1,1-10). During the Christ's Incarnation in Jesus of Nazareth, according to John's Gospel he identified himself as the light (Jn 8,12; also 9,5), and he clearly stated that he (for our purposes, the light) "was not of this world" (Jn 8,23; also17,14,16). The concepts are pulled together in *The Burning Bush* in the essay entitled "I AM." We see there the perfect analogue for Steiner's teaching, and that of ancient civilizations, that our vision of any object comes about by the mutual interaction of the outer light and the inner light. Unless by our own spiritual development we reach out with our lower "I Am" toward the Christ so as infuse our own with Christ's higher "I Am," we cannot evolve upward to dwell in the light. The Christ is everywhere available to the soul (the "I Am") who strives in that upward direction ("I stand at the door and knock," Rev 3,20).[64]

---

64. We have seen the mutual relationship of the eye and the light. I suggest that a radical new look needs to be taken at that ancient and well-known translation of Paul's words dealing with the *eye*, namely:

[51] Lo! I tell you a mystery. We shall not all sleep, but we shall all be changed, [52] in *a moment, in the twinkling of an eye*, at the last trumpet." (1 Cor 15; emphasis mine)

This passage, endeared to generations in laying away loved ones, has been understood, along with other eschatological and apocalyptic passages, in a cataclysmic sense. Rather it should be considered in the light of the evolution of the human soul. A review of the essay "Trumpets" in *The Burning Bush*, especially in connection with I-1, shows that Paul is speaking (as in 1 Th 4,16-17) of the end of that distant, future age when the Earth will pass out of its Physical Condition of Form into its More Perfect Astral Condition of Form. The human soul will have evolved through many more ages before then.

The italicized words above seem to demand a fresh look in spite of centuries of interpretation—centuries that did not have the prophetic Intuition Steiner has given us. In the light of his spiritual science, we can now see that the Greek words Paul used bore a quite different meaning—one that is incumbent upon our times to cast in new light.

This traditional interpretation, stems back at least to Tertullian early in the third century (see 3 NICENE-1, pp. 451 and 584). The Greek words translated "in a moment" are *en atomo*, the word translated "twinkling" is *ripe*, and that translated "of an eye" is *ophthalmou*. While *en atomo*, in a derivative way could mean "in a moment," its primary meaning appears to be that which is "uncut" or "indivisible," e.g., see fn 21. Obviously, our "atom" came from it, but the focus was on its indivisibility (until the twentieth century) rather than its smallness, as in the case of "moment." One might also think of it as "wholeness, completeness, soundness or integrity." And while *ripe* has the subordinate meaning "quivering, twinkling light," its primary meaning seems to relate to a different concept variously expressed as "swing or force with which anything is thrown," "the sweep or rush [of the wind]," "gusts of passion," or "rush of fire." The *rip* also seems to relate to "river" and our "riparian" adjective. See GEL for these interpretations.

So instead of "in a moment, in the twinkling of an eye," I suggest something like "in the whole and fire-emblazoned eye." With such an interpretation, we come more into sync with the apocalyptic meaning of the phrase "at the last trumpet." Not only does this take on meaning in what we have called the "inner light" of the eye, but it also prophetically fulfills what Christ spoke about the eye being the light of the body and the whole body being full of light when the eye is "sound" (Mt 6,22; Lk 11,34).

As we stand on the threshold of the third millennium, already well into the first regency of the Archangel of light, Michael, since the time of Christ, each of us, saint and sinner alike, is in a sense still a "man born blind" in need of healing by the Christ. As yet we neither see nor understand the light. At best our vision is like "seeing trees walking" (Mk 8,24; 1 Cor 13,12).

If we are to take the Prodigal Son's first step back to the Father's house, we must first pass through the point of fire. Until then, any real, direct perception and understanding of the nature of light would seem to be only a distant hope (see I-22). What is important for us in our time is to recognize where we are in the greater picture of human evolution.

Light in Perspective

During the course of my work on this essay, in August, 1999 there appeared in the various news media the announcement that scientists studying Australian rocks had just found evidence that primitive forms of life existed 2.7 billion years ago, about a billion years earlier than had been previously thought (cf. I-5 suggesting life as far back, perhaps, as two billion years ago). What we are seeing is another illustration of the typically endless modifications of theory that characterize modern science. Note that the rocks in question were found on a *continent*, Australia. Science does not seem to have even speculated as yet on what might be shown if previous continents, such as Atlantis lying at the bottom of the Atlantic Ocean, were to belch forth their formations, let alone on what formative conditions might have already disappeared eons before even those buried formations came into being. Like an infant fascinated only by what rattles and dances playfully on a string across its crib, science presumes a knowledge of beginnings when the fragile evidence of those beginnings is not even before it but has disappeared from materiality eons before (beautifully expressed in the second quotation from Teilhard de Chardin's, *The Phenomenon of Man*, in the "Evolution" essay herein).

We've had a glimpse in this essay of science peering into the *smallness* of creation, far beyond what can be empirically observed, to what can only be theoretically postulated by a quantum *theory*, and then with results that are baffling and inexplicable. Any knowledgeable reader will have already pondered what science has theorized in its peering into the *largeness* of the universe. From our solar system and its Sun, to the Milky Way galaxy, to the Local Group of galaxies, to the Neighboring Groups and Clusters of galaxies, to the Superclusters of galaxies and on and on, they have found bigness beyond the ability of the human brain to even comprehend, and from that they have mounded theory upon theory, and brought together in one glorious union of "enlightened thinking" the most anti-spiritual theory of all, the big bang.

In truth what science has shown us is that its theories have far outdistanced existing human capacities of direct observation, and are of such nature as to require constant modification. One is tempted, thereby, to adopt the Kantian philosophy that there are limits to human knowledge. Steiner stands opposed to this philosophy, but readily recognizes that there are limits to the knowledge available through the five senses and the thinking that remains bound to them.

The *Britannica* starts its treatment of *"The Cosmos"* with the statement, "If one looks up on a clear night, one sees that the sky is full of stars" (16 Brit 762). The Psalmist noted this during the days of humanity's "fading splendor" (cf. Ps 6,5) as the basis upon which to cry, "What is man that thou art mindful of him?" (Ps 8,3-4a). Within the same general time frame the Seraphim commanded Isaiah to pronounce this loss of seeing, hearing and understanding in the spiritual realm for a period of time such that humanity blocks even the thought of it out, like the amnesic obliteration of memory from the horror of unbearable shock (Is 6,9-13).

The extent to which both science and theology rely upon theory (kinetics) and block out, Kant-like, any reliance upon what Steiner has revealed as Imagination, Inspiration and Intuition (i.e., the spiritual seeing, hearing and understanding [gnosis, or knowing], respectively, that Isaiah spoke about) is but the fascination of an infant humanity jabbing at its string of rattles and fancies.

In *The Burning Bush*, again and again I tried to bring out Steiner's portrayal of the schematic of human evolution, the journey of the Prodigal Son. We would do well to put aside for the time being the larger universe and try to understand the formation of our own solar system within the larger framework. The outer cosmos is given, just as the inner, to confound the human senses and their related theoretical thinking. With all of its discoveries that somewhat deceptively make life "better than it used to be" in the world as we perceive it, science has done its job in bringing humanity to the brink of the chasm beyond which it cannot go without new vision and understanding. It must "repent," which is to say it must change its way of thinking. More discoveries within the physical world and cosmos will inevitably and regularly appear, and more theories, but they will not bring the seeing, hearing and understanding whose loss Isaiah lamented long ago.

The light ether is what will give humanity its first "seeing" of the Christ in the etheric world, just as the light-etheric body, when freed from the mineral-physical body upon death, gives the soul (the "I Am" or Ego) its brief (approximately three-day) panoramic view of the life just passed (see "Second Coming" in *The Burning Bush*, p. 233). As indicated there (*Ibid.*, p. 233), the sixth and seventh Cultural Eras of our post-Atlantean Evolutionary Epoch will bring to humanity the respective perceptions and understanding related to the chemical/sound and life ether aspects of the Christ in his second coming. The etheric world, however, will yield to the higher astral and spiritual worlds in the larger picture, not unlike the way the cosmos unfolds in ever greater stages to our more distant observations. What happens in the larger dimension of the Prodigal Son's journey happens also in the cycle of life (or "wheel of birth"; cf. Jas 3,6) portrayed in I-33. The reader should keep the larger cosmos of human evolution presented by I-1 and I-2 constantly in mind, lest perspective be lost.

The light ether is yet far beyond scientific and theological understanding, but the light ether is itself but one early stepping stone on the long journey of humanity in its return to the heavenly fold whence its journey began. Those who would still block out these understandings are like the creationists who insist that our physical universe, and the fully arrayed human being, all came into existence over a period of one hundred and sixty-eight hours (seven twenty-four hour days as we measure them today).

Humanity will walk that long path. Some will fall by the wayside. The symbolical one hundred forty-four thousand (144,000) are those who will have entered the realm of light by the end of the Earth Condition of Consciousness. Their "I Am's," within the mineral-physical body, will have gained complete control over their astral bodies so that they can enter the holy city, the new Jerusalem, the Jupiter Condition of Consciousness. But only one of the three loaves will have been perfected by that stage so that the mineral-physical human body will have been laid aside forever. The two other loaves will still remain to be perfected (Mt 13,33; Lk 11,5-8).[65]

Just as the amnesic mind is not able to cope with the magnitude of its shock, so also has the human soul not been able to deal with the scope of its journey (Jn 16,12). But with the onset of the regency of the Archangel Michael, the divine intelligence must begin to make its way into human awareness. Recognition is the first step of the return journey (Lk 15,17, "when he came to himself"—he remembered).

The very magnitude of this recognition will force many if not most, unable to cope with it, to go on with their merriment (a la Ecclesiastes) for some time yet. But the more contemplative souls, shocked into this new way of thinking (essentially, for our time, a phenomenon analogous to the repentance and baptism of John), will find themselves, in very important little ways, looking out upon the world in an entirely different way. They become a "new person," to use biblical terminology.

And this brings us to our concluding thought. How are we to interpret the "two paths" (i.e., "gates" or "doors") Christ speaks of in the Sermon on the Mount (Mt 7,13-14; cf. Lk 13,23-24)?

---

65. The goal of Earth evolution, the so-called Cosmos of Love, is for the Ego (the soul or "I Am") to transform the astral body into the manas (manna) state. This is done by the Ego's gaining complete control over, and thus perfecting, the astral body (the body of desire, passion and the like) during its sojourn in the mineral-physical body. By virtue of this, during the Jupiter evolution (the holy city), we will live in the etheric body and the transformed astral body (the manas state), no longer needing to dwell in the mineral-physical. During Jupiter evolution, the Ego must transform the etheric body into the buddhi state so that the etheric body is no longer needed as we pass into the Venus evolution. There we will live only in the manas and buddhi states. During Venus evolution, the Ego will transform the physical body (by that time only fire ether) into the atma state worthy of passing then into the Vulcan Condition, the higher spiritual world. This scenario of perfection of the three bodies (the "three loaves" of Mt 13,33 and Lk 11,5-8) is the mirror image of their creation in Ancient Saturn (physical body), Ancient Sun (etheric body) and Ancient Moon (astral body). It should help to conceptualize the progression from Earth to Venus by realizing that what is the mineral-physical body during Earth evolution was only etheric fire during Ancient Saturn, which fire became etheric air on Ancient Sun, and etheric fluid on Ancient Moon. Thus what appeared on Ancient Saturn is finally perfected on Venus when the original etheric fire (physical body) is transformed into the higher spiritual world whence its journey began. While the initiate of the highest level perceives, and in a state of earthly transformation experiences, these distant goals, even the highest initiate is precluded from gaining them permanently by the higher guardian of the threshold until the rest of the redeemed of all creatures shall evolve thereto (Gen 3,24; Job 41; *The Burning Bush*, pp. 427-428). This is a brief summary of Steiner's *Outline of Esoteric Science* (previously OS) and the larger schematics of *The Burning Bush*.

[13] Enter by the narrow gate; for the gate is wide and the way is easy, that leads to destruction, and those who enter by it are many. [14] For the gate is narrow and the way is hard, that leads to life, and those who find it are few.

Theology sees it as eschatological and hortatorical (see 8 NIB 215-216) and as something of an iteration of Deut 30,19 and Jer 21,8 (the "way of life" or the "way of death"). There is a certain validity in the latter comparison. But both ways of understanding, without more, are inadequate for our time. The "two paths" more appropriately speak of the higher path of initiation as against the more popular path of religion. The latter literally means "to re-ligate" or to seek to join together again what has been severed. The difference between the two is that the one who chooses the path of initiation and pursues it to fulfillment (a "narrow" and "hard" path to say the least) "sees, hears and understands" in the spiritual world what those who choose the wider and easier path of religion will come to see, hear and understand only in much later ages of human evolution. There are, of course, seven levels of initiation. The reader should review again "Mysteries" in *The Burning Bush*. The initiate is the one who enters into and through the mysteries, who raises up the serpent in the wilderness (Jn 3,14; 8,28; 12,34-36; see *The Burning Bush*, p. 332). Christ became the hierophant par excellence by enacting and thus revealing the deepest aspect of the ancient mysteries upon the world stage for all to see. But the world has yet to see its truth revealed in the light ether (Jn1,5). The validity in the "way of life" versus "way of death" versions in the Old Testament is that for those who choose the wider path, though eventually through karmic rectification they have hope, the way of death and gnashing of teeth is amply present in the cycle of life as presented in I-33. The suffering through purification in the astral world is a fractal, for the individual human soul, of the larger journey of the Prodigal Son and the even larger journey of the lower three kingdoms (Rom 8,19-23; Job). This suffering of the individual soul is portrayed, though inaccurately, by the Roman Catholic doctrine of Purgatory; see fn 11 (fn 10 in rev. ed.) in "Karma and Reincarnation" in *The Burning Bush*, p. 130; see also the discussion of Lk 16,19-31, *Ibid.*, pp. 114, 417 and 472. While much remains to be revised in Roman Catholic theology, the vestiges of many true ancient insights were thrown out by Protestantism in the sense of throwing out the baby with the bathwater.

300 DAVID'S QUESTION, "WHAT IS MAN?"

An introduction to the higher path was given by Steiner, both for those who might choose to pursue its strenuous demands and for those who only want to appreciate the path of those who did and of those who taught its ways. See again the "Mysteries" essay.

The important thing for our time is to begin to grasp what is meant when Christ is identified by John, and describes himself in John's Gospel, as "the light" of the world. If that Michaelic dawning can in any way be stimulated in a few by the many words of this essay, it shall have served its purpose.

DARKNESS

FROM THE "LIGHT" ESSAY, we can empirically grasp that darkness, in the present state of creation, is virtually synonymous and coextensive with matter. And we've seen that the descent of the human soul into the darkness of matter during Earth evolution was triggered by the events portrayed by the myth in the third chapter of Genesis, the temptation and Fall from the Garden. Moreover, we have seen that the "veil of the temple," when profoundly understood, is none other than our mineral-physical body, our body of matter—what keeps us from seeing the true light of the human soul and spirit (Heb 10,20; 9,3,8; Mt 27,51; Mk 15,38; Lk 23,45).[1]

Today darkness is generally defined as the absence of light. Yet this understanding, at least from the scientific standpoint, comes about only from phenomena related to matter. Our instruments (whether the physical eye or something humanly contrived) can only observe light when it falls upon matter. Light itself cannot be seen. Even where light is present, it must fall upon matter to be observed, and thus to be phenomena. In other words, we call emptiness darkness, even when infused with light, until the latter falls upon matter. In the mineral-physical realm light remains a mystery to science, acting in ways that defy understanding according to scientific principles. This alone is a "sign" of deep significance.

When we profess faith in the idea that Christ is the *light* of the world (e.g., Jn 1,4-9; 8,12), we do not speak in terms of phenomena. We saw earlier that light dies in the process of becoming matter (I-22), just as it

---

1. Steiner speaks often of this "veil" of the body. See, for instance, *Macrocosm and Microcosm* (MM), Lects. 1 (pp. 13 & 18), 3 (pp. 48, 52, 57 & 62) and 7 (p. 125); *The Gospel of St. John* (GSJ), Lect. 11 (p. 172); *The Gospel of St. John and its Relation to the Other Gospels* (Jn-Rel), Lect. 14 (p. 280); and *The East in the Light of the West* (ELW), Chap. 2 (p. 38). Brown, while not recognizing (or at least expressing) this point, calls these passages "difficult" and points out that there were a number of temple veils with different meanings, thus clouding what any one Evangelist could have meant, in the normal sense, by his reference; see Brown, *An Introduction to the New Testament* (NTINT).

dies upon striking the retina in the creation of the sense of vision.[2] The miracle of Peter's declaration, "You are the Christ" (Mt 16,16), is that he was able in that moment to perceive the true light still clothed in a mineral-physical body.[3]

Putting the matter another way, if darkness is merely the absence of light, why does the Bible use such a variety of adjectives to describe it?[4] The mirror image of the adjectives used to describe darkness is expressed by Isaiah when he prophesied a future event (Is 9,2, emphasis mine):

> The people who walked in darkness have seen a *great* light; those who dwelt in a land of *deep* darkness, on them has light shined.

He speaks not merely of light and darkness, but of great light and deep darkness. The polar relationship between light and darkness is reflected by the countless times they appear together in the same scriptural passage by way of contrast. Yet just as we cannot look directly at the light of the Sun, a light far, far below the *great light* of the Christ, nor can we see the

---

2. It is noteworthy that in a sense the converse is also true. We know that the direct light from the Sun can kill, and certainly kills eyesight that attempts to look directly into it. But on a far grander scale, matter (i.e., flesh) was destroyed when the fullness of the Christ Spirit entered into it. See Appendix One in *The Disciple Whom Jesus Loved* (DWJL), and the light it casts upon Christ's statement, "You are the *salt* of the earth" (Mt 5,13). Cf. also Jn 3,6.

3. The Roman Church has always interpreted Mt 16,18, "And I tell you, you are Peter, and on this rock I will build my church," as indicating that it was the man Simon (whose name was then changed to Peter, the "rock") upon which Christ would build his Church. However, Steiner says Christ meant by this statement that it was this human capacity of cognition, then demonstrated in Peter, upon which he would build his Church. See *The Gospel of St. Matthew* (GSMt), Lect. 11 (p. 194) and 12 (p. 222). See also fn 8 in the "Light" essay.

4. Adjectives used to describe darkness include the following:

great	Gen 15,12; Mt 6,23
dread	Gen 15,12
to be felt	Ex 10,21
thick	Ex 10,22; 20,21; Deut 5,22; 2 Sam 22,10; 1 K 8,12; 2 Ch 6,1; Job 3,6; 23,17; 38,9; Ps 18,9; 97,2; Is 8,22; 60,2; Jer 2,31; Ezek 34,12; Joel 2,2; Zeph 1,15
deep	Job 3,5; 10,21; 12,22; 16,16; 22,13; 24,17; 28,3; 34,22; 38,17; Ps 44,19; Prov 4,19; Is 9,2; Jer 2,6; 13,16; Amos 5,8
utter	Job 20,26; Prov 20,20
outer	Mt 8,12; 22,13; 25,30
present	Eph 6,12
what may be touched	Heb 12,18 (noun form rather than adjective)
blinding	1 Jn 2,11

"least part" of light, the photon—indeed we cannot even begin to approach either of these with our physical eye—so also are both the spiritual light and its polar opposite, spiritual darkness, beyond our present comprehension. Yet we can contemplate their unperceived existence, for scripture clearly points us in that direction, as do the phenomena the spiritual powers have given us, when properly observed. (Cf. Mt 16,3: "You know how to interpret [weather-wise] the appearance of the sky, but you cannot interpret the signs of the times." See also Lk 12,56).

But before we look more deeply at the polarity between light and darkness, let us take the universal phenomenon of color and compare the explanations of science with those of Goethe and Steiner. Why is the cloudless daytime sky blue and the sunset sky red? Science gives this answer, as set out in 11 Brit 397, "sunlight":

> On its path through the atmosphere the solar radiation is absorbed and weakened by various constituents of the atmosphere. It is also scattered by air molecules and dust particles. Short wavelengths of light, such as blue, scatter more easily than do the longer red wavelengths.... The light [when the sun is high overhead] ... encounters less dust and fewer air molecules than it would if the Sun were low on the horizon and its rays had a longer passage through the atmosphere. During this long passage the dominant blue wavelengths of light are scattered and blocked, leaving the longer, unobstructed red wavelengths to reach the Earth and lend their tints to the sky at dawn and dusk.

I find no hint that this has been empirically shown. It bears the clear stamp of the kinetic, theoretical exposition so typical of scientific thought, quickly accepted by an uncritical laity. In contrast, Steiner has shown, by simple, directly observable experiment, why the daytime sky is blue and the sunset sky is red. Look again at the text explaining Figures 9 and 10 in the "Light" essay. When we look through darkness at light, red and yellow tones appear. Thus, when we look through the darkness of the Earth's atmosphere at the light from the Sun, as one does at sunset, red and yellow colors appear. The redness of thin clouds, or their perimeters near but outside the direct path of sunlight at sunset is due to the redness given off by the "refraction" of sunlight, as through the narrower portions of the prism in Figures 2, 3 and 4 in the "Light" essay. Conversely, when we look through light-filled space at darkness, blue colors appear. Thus, during the day when we look into the sky, not being able to look at the light of the Sun itself but rather looking through our nearby atmosphere filled with that light, the darkness of the outer material atmosphere itself is seen as blue.

The ignoring of phenomena such as this (as well as all that was set out in the "Light" essay) by Newtonian science precludes any true grasp of the nature of our biblical terms light and darkness. So a correct assessment of the phenomena is the starting point if we are to have any hope of comprehending these terms. And the phenomena lead us very clearly to an association of darkness with matter. Matter blocks physical light—this is obvious from the phenomenon of the shadow. And that matter blocks human consciousness was demonstrated in a most fundamental way by Steiner's illustration (in the "Light" essay) of the application of pressure to any point on the body.

But as important as this elementary level of understanding is, we cannot stop there if we wish to come to a more complete understanding of darkness. The prologue of John's Gospel sets out the contrast of light and darkness (Jn 1,5), whether the rather obscure Greek word *katelaben*[5] is translated as "understand" or "overcome" (see fn 36 in the "Light" essay).

But if the biblical word "darkness" relates only to matter, we run into a problem in the first chapter of Genesis, for it appears there before the creation of matter (Gen 1,2,4,5,18; see the Creation essay). If we are to reach a deeper understanding, we must turn our attention to some of the most profound concepts that go all the way back to Evangelist's John's "In the beginning." Simply stated, we must recognize darkness as something that, at least if we are to utilize the concept of time, preexisted matter, for we find darkness in the first chapter of Genesis before matter came into being. Our problem is made no easier when we then recognize that in the unity of all things there is no time. We've seen earlier that space and time are neither independent nor eternal realities. Both are themselves phenomenal creations. And within space and time, *polarity* and *rhythm* are everywhere manifest.

If we are to deal adequately with the concept of darkness in its nonmaterial relationship to light, as the various biblical usages now require of us,

---

5. Brown gives the Greek word as *katalambanein*, noting the difficulty of its translations and finding "four tendencies among translators," namely, (a) to grasp, to comprehend; (b) to welcome, receive, accept, appreciate; (c) to overtake, overcome; and (d) to master. See 29 AB 8.

we must go back to "the beginning." And in that venture we cannot leave behind what we have already observed. We must hold fast to the ancient concept of the *image* and then observe how, in the polar/rhythmic, creating and destroying nature of the *fractal*,[6] it is portrayed in the "imaging" characteristics of the four ethers and four elements as they fit into the cycle of life.

Here we must remove our mantle of doctrine in favor of the *image*. Thinking, in a process more military-political than spiritual, became frozen into doctrine and dogma as the reality of Christ's physical presence faded and Christendom joined forces with the powerful arm of the Roman empire. Through that process the doctrine of the Trinity became firmly established (see fn 22 in the "Three Bodies" essay in *The Burning Bush*). That doctrine embodies only the male principle in Father-Son-Holy Spirit terminology. We saw in *The Burning Bush* that the parable of the Prodigal Son is an allegory telling of the descent of the human being into earthly materiality and then its return (ascent) to its heavenly home. It is a parable about a parabola (the pathway of humanity), the image of which we have seen amply demonstrated in the "Fire" essay.

The *descent* of the human being has encompassed, as we have seen, the entirety of creation up to our time, or at least up to the "right time" when the Incarnation occurred. The descent was a process of materialization, of densifying or hardening, the male aspect in the polar/rhythmic nature of creation. What goes in one direction will return in the other—what stands at one extreme will be balanced by what stands at the other—the unity that divides through "fission" will eventually again unite through "fusion." The male (or male principle), standing alone, is like space without time or time without space, a nullity, an impossibility.[7] The only reality is the unity of male and female. Thus, the doctrine of only a male principle occupying the highest spiritual realm must be seen as the false relic of a period of darkening human consciousness. We must courageously rethink, in all humility and reverence, what the *images* of creation have clearly demonstrated to us, namely, the counterbalancing image of the eternal feminine, the coequal of the male principle expressed in the doctrine of the Trinity.

---

6. We've seen the nature of the fractal as one of both creation (enlarging) and destruction (diminishing). The Word of God fits that description. The creation aspect is portrayed in Jn 1,1-3; the destruction aspect in Heb 4,12 (see the discussion of this in I-87 at p. 674 in *The Burning Bush*.
7. Recall the discussion of the phenomenon of velocity in the "Light" essay.

And even in accepting the doctrine of the Trinity, we need to remember that it is just that, only *doctrine*, frozen human thinking, and that Christ himself stressed the unity of himself and what he called the "Father." We must recognize that if the highest divinity were to incarnate during humanity's residence in the mineral-physical body, it had to be done either as a male or a female—there was no other option, hence no exaltation of one sex over the other.[8] But we must see in the incarnation process that both the eternal male and eternal female principles were involved. The presence of the latter in the Nathan Jesus Mary, the real basis for the concept of "the Mother of God," can be seen in *The Incredible Births of Jesus*, as well as in "The Nativity" essay in *The Burning Bush*.

Steiner told us that males have dominated the historical landscape of humanity up to the present time, but that as the human soul evolves in its upward journey on the Prodigal's return, more and more the female (or female principle) will dominate that landscape. See *Karmic Relationships*, Vol. 5, Lect. 7, p. 103.

---

8. Paul's remarks about women (Eph 5,22-23; Col 3,18) and slaves (Eph 6,5; Col 3,22) are misapprehended as spiritual principles. He was merely recognizing legal conditions that existed during that stage of human evolution (see 1 Cor 14,34, "as even the law says"), recognizing that the time for changes in those conditions was still in the future. The favorable reflection of the female in Luke's Gospel (the most directly related to Paul) and of the slave Onesimus in Philemon are more suggestive of his idea of desired relationships. His statements in 1 Cor 11,3-15 can hardly be construed separate and apart from 1 Cor 14,34, which clearly recognizes the law of that day. And his statements about a woman's hair and having to cover her head to pray are hardly recognized by practice even in most fundamentalist churches of our day. His statement in 1 Cor 11,8-12 seems to call upon the literalism of the Gen 2,18-23 myth in legalistic support of what the law already required—and even then he waffles in verses 11-12, concluding not only that neither sex is independent from the other but that "all things are from God" (i.e., both sexes). Paul's letter was addressing a contentious situation, and he was trying to establish some order in line with the prevalent customs of the time. He concludes, in verse 16, by saying, "If any one is disposed to be contentious, *we recognize no other practice, nor do the churches of God*" (emphasis mine).

What is then found in Ephesians, Colossians and 1 Timothy 2,9-15 seems, on the surface to flow from the same rationale. According to Brown, "about 80 percent of critical scholarship holds that Paul did not write Eph[esians]," NTINT, p. 620. But if not Paul, "The writer has been called the supreme interpreter of the apostle ... and 'Paul's best disciple'," Id., p. 620. The same cannot be said for the Pastoral Epistles, which speak of "doctrine" and clearly show a later development of the Church than existed in Paul's clearly authentic letters; see 11 NIB 775-786 and NTINT, Chap. 30 ("about 80 to 90 percent of modern scholars would agree that the Pastorals were written after Paul's lifetime," p. 668). Nor do they present such an exalted Christology as he might have developed in his more reflective and detached setting, as in Hebrews (the overwhelming majority of scholars reject Paul as author, but I hope to present counter arguments in a future volume that they have not, I believe, considered).

Though theologians do not yet generally recognize it, the Bible declares that the human soul is neither male nor female (Gen 1,27; 5,2; Mt 19,4; Mk 10,6).[9] When Jesus responded to the Sadducees' question concerning the woman with the seven brothers as successive husbands (the levirate law matter), he showed that in the spiritual world there is no male/female division (Mt 22,30; Mk 12,25; Lk 20,34-36). And the "mother" of Christ given by Jesus to Evangelist John from the Cross, according to its higher meaning, was the eternal feminine principle that permitted him to write his Gospel (Jn 19,27; see "Who was the Mother of Jesus?" in *The Disciple Whom Jesus Loved*). The Christ Spirit that dwelled within Jesus of Nazareth was neither male nor female. It was the female portion of his unity, however, that would permit Evangelist John to write the Gospel that, more than any other, would point humanity in the direction of its reascent.

If you now rightly ask what relevance this male/female discussion has to the meaning of *darkness*, I will tell you that it refers to the very beginning of creation, to the matter of humanity being made in the *image* of God (Gen 1,26),[10] for all creation reflects ("declares"), fractal-like, the highest Creator God (Ps 50,6; Rom 1,20). We have thus far shown, in examining the meaning of darkness, its relationship to matter. But we cannot stop there. The Bible, as stated above, shows that darkness existed before the creation of matter. While that darkness in Jn 1,5 may or may not have existed before matter, clearly that in Gen 1,2,4-5 did (see the Creation and "Light" essays). And we've previously shown, and the Bible declares, that all matter (e.g., "things seen"; Heb 11,3) is made out of the unseen.

At this point in our quest, we must return to the general definition of darkness as the absence of light. This definition is not patently different from the declaration that in the "first day" light and darkness were separated (Gen 1,4), the darkness having existed *before* light was created (Gen 1,2). Steiner himself, in what I perceive as the highest writing given to humanity outside of the Bible itself, speaks of darkness during the Ancient Saturn Condition of Consciousness as being the absence of light, e.g., "pure spiritual light that is darkness for everything outside" (*An Outline of*

---

9. Only the physical and etheric bodies bear the stamp of gender, and even here one is the opposite of the other.

10. We've seen that it is the plural (the "fullness" of all seven; Jn 1,16) Elohim, the Spirits of Form (see I-6), who speak these words, but in doing so they are themselves an image, a fractal, and acting in the likeness, of the highest Creator God from whom the *Word* went out.

Esoteric Science [OES], Chap. 4, p. 149). Later in the same chapter (p. 159), he speaks of darkness appearing during the Ancient Sun Condition of Consciousness because germinal "human beings who had remained behind at the Saturn stage ... were not able to condense [from "warmth structures"] into air in the right way." This was all before the Earth Condition of Consciousness (Earth evolution) began (see I-1). And this was well before the germinal human soul was endowed with reason or existed in any material state, and preceded by far the conditions mentioned in Gen 1,1 (though not those in Jn 1,1). Our lower kingdoms (mineral, plant and animal) are those that fell behind in the three earlier Conditions of Consciousness (Saturn, Sun and Moon) that preceded the Earth Condition of Consciousness. Yet these lower kingdoms did not come into existence because of their own moral guilt. They are, in fact, what resulted from germinal human souls that did not properly develop (i.e., fell behind) in one or more prior Conditions of Consciousness—sacrificed in the creative process, so to speak, in order to become servants for the benefit of those who did not fall behind, namely, those who are human beings during Earth evolution. Comprehension of this gives greater understanding of Saint Francis of Assisi's referring to all the lower kingdoms as "brothers or sisters," and of Paul's mystical reference to them in Rom 8,19-23.

Darkness is the polar opposite of light. If we are to go back to the very beginning, before the Word went out from the ultimate Creator God, we must follow the *image*, like a prospector seeking the mother lode, all the way back to the point where it merges into that Creator God, losing its own identity in the whole from which it would later come forth.

When the time arrives in any evolutionary development for one stage to be replaced by another, be it concept, mutation or adaptation, the new is normally born through the hard labor of conflict, the dying of the old. Slavery died hard in our country just before the start of the current Michaelic age in 1879. The nineteenth and twentieth centuries have witnessed the struggle for woman suffrage and for full equality of all the downtrodden as against the forces of discrimination, prejudice and bigotry, often associated with religious fundamentalism—present even to this day in some religious persuasions with regard to qualification for priesthood or ministry. The struggle is far from over.

I am certainly not unmindful of the controversy that swirls over any suggestion that the "Father" or "Son" are as much female as male, or over the question of whether the female only came into being after the male.

Nor is there agreement on the meaning of Prov 8,22, which speaks of "wisdom" normally (though not always) thought of as feminine: "The Lord created me at the beginning of his work, the first of his acts of old." Even the Hebrew word "created" is not entirely clear in its translation (see 5 NIB 92). And if "created" is the right translation, some have pointed out that wisdom (the female principle) was brought into existence by the Creator God, presumably the male principle.

Sophia is the Greek word translated as "wisdom." It is of feminine gender, and thus has been used as a feminine name. The nature of the Sophia has been variously viewed within Christendom.[11]

That Steiner spoke sparingly of the mysteries of the Sophia is noted by Prokofieff in the foreword of his book *The Heavenly Sophia and the Being Anthroposophia* (HSBA). He suggests this paucity was because "the unfolding of the mysteries of the Sophia belongs not to our fifth but to the following, sixth, cultural epoch." From what little Steiner gives, however, Prokofieff seems to infer the origin of the feminine Sophia in the fourth period of the Ancient Sun Condition of Consciousness (Part II, Chap. 1). To a certain extent this aspect is reflected in **I-18**.

Another anthroposophist, Robert Powell, leaning heavily upon the works of the highly controversial Valentin Tomberg, posits the existence of a feminine counterpart and coequal of the male Trinity called the Trinosophia. The latter consists of the spiritual beings Mother-Daughter-Holy Soul corresponding to the Trinity's Father-Son-Holy Spirit.[12] Prokofieff attacked this idea in appendix one of his HSBA and in *The Case of Valentin Tomberg* (CVT), p. 129, more vigorously assailed Powell for his position on it.

---

11. One of the most complete books on the Sophia is Thomas Schipflinger's *Sophia-Maria* (SOPH). Schipflinger was ordained a Catholic priest in Innsbruck in 1947 and served as such for many years. A recent article on the female principle in Judaism is Peter Schafer's "Daughter, Sister, Bride, and Mother: Images of the Femininity of God in the Early Kabbala," *Journal of the American Academy of Religion*, June 2000, Vol. 68, No. 2.

The historical tendency to exalt the male over the female is perhaps nowhere more obvious than in those who, based on custom and tradition, view the Trinity as purely male, while at the same time denying the custom and tradition that views wisdom (sophia) as purely female. Presumably this is because history has provided many examples of wise males. But this rationale shows a failure to understand the difference between incarnation in a male physical body and the application by a man of the female principle (by virtue of influence of his higher etheric and astral bodies and Ego).

12. See Powell, *The Most Holy Trinosophia* (MHT), updated by his more recent *The Most Holy Trinosophia And the New Revelation of the Divine Feminine* (MHTNR).

While I take with caution what comes from Tomberg, and on occasion have differed from his conclusions, at other times, particularly in areas where Steiner either did not speak or spoke too sparingly or inconclusively, as apparently on this point, one cannot reject following a particular path simply because it resembles the one taken by Tomberg—particularly if it follows from principles clearly laid down by Steiner. On the particular question we are now considering, namely, at what point the feminine principle first entered into creation or its causative divinity, the application of anthroposophical principles already reflected in this volume (regarding the *image*) seem to lead to a conclusion closer to that of Tomberg/Powell than that reflected by Prokofieff (i.e., the Kyriotetes, or Spirits of Wisdom, during Ancient Sun). And this being the case, the concept of the Trinosophia seems as valid as the *doctrine* of the Trinity. Christ's use of the term "Father" was thus at least partially metaphorical and not determinative on this point any more than the fact that the Christ was incarnated, at that point in history, in a male body. That his last act from that body was to pass on to Evangelist John the "Mother" principle is suggestive of the path that human ascension must take—a path that must lead humanity (and all creation) back to the same heights as those from which the male principle (the Cain principle) has led it.[13]

On this matter, I have as yet read nothing that expresses the matter more to my satisfaction than what I wrote as the "Appendix to 'Three Bodies'" in *The Burning Bush*, pp. 459-473. While it is complex, it is reflective, I believe, of what we are being told in those chapters of the Bible that have heretofore been called "prehistoric," when seen in anthroposophic light. From what is said there, it is clear that, retracing the *image* back to its source, if male and female were originally one, as the Bible indicates (when properly construed), then the Creator God, from whom the Word went out (Jn 1,1), had to have embodied both the male and female principles. If, according to the *pattern on the mountain* (cf. Heb 8,5; Ex 25,40), all things were made by the Word (Jn 1,3), then the Word itself, the Christ Spirit, had to have been androgynous and/or asexual. It was from the androgynous (and/or asexual) "man" in Gen 2, that the hard Adam (Gen 3,17) and Eve, the male and female, emerged from

---

13. Steiner closes his lecture of March 18, 1908, in Munich, entitled *Man and Woman in Light of Spiritual Science* (MWLSS) with this sentence: "The feminine is that element in the world which strives outward in order to be fructified by the eternal elements of life."

unity as metaphorically expressed in Gen 2,18-24. On these matters, see the Chapter End Note to the Creation essay and the excellent work of Phyllis Trible, *God and the Rhetoric of Sexuality*, discussed there.

I have dwelt at length on the male/female question because it seems to me that one cannot properly return to the conditions in Gen 1,1-3,[14] where *darkness* first appears in the Bible, without walking that path.

Having, in any event, found *darkness* present before any matter came into existence, we must grant to it a part in the creative process itself. The pattern of creation, according to the Old Testament, is one of "fission," separation—the archetype for cell division. The first separation in the Bible is that of light from darkness (Gen 1,4). Considering that Gen 1,1-3 is itself in the Lemurian Epoch of Earth evolution, and that creation at that point had progressed downward so far as the etheric world, the world of the four ethers pregnant with their related four elements, we enter upon the schematic so often referred to as the chart from I-22. The upper portion of that chart, the etheric condition, was built up in Gen 1–2,4a, leading to the precipitation therefrom into the mineral-physical conditions of Earth evolution starting with Gen 2,4b.

Darkness must then always be seen as the portion that descends, as the polar opposite of its ascending counterpart, in the creative process of "fission." It is the male (Cain) element, the heavier, so to speak, while the lighter female (Abel) element rises. Every human being is both male and female, if only we could bear that ever in mind. As a male, my creative body, my etheric body, is female—it is my "mother," so to speak. My friends see me only as a man, though in my more spiritual aspect I should be seen as a woman. We must come to recognize our unity with both principles, for when we do we will no longer be able to exalt one sex over the other but will recognize that a part of the Creator God is present in both of these elements within us. The unity of husband and wife is deeply symbolical of this condition. And if one comprehends the parabolic journey of the Prodigal Son, and the necessity of entering upon the upward portion of that journey through the female element, it will no longer be possible for us to say that the wife must be subject to the husband, for it will be counter to the pattern that has been laid before us.

---

14. While as previously indicated, Jn 1,1 goes back further (i.e., to Ancient Saturn) than does Gen 1,1 (to the early Lemurian Epoch of Earth evolution; see I-1), the *darkness* in Jn 1,5 could be deemed to refer only to periods after matter came into being, though it should probably be seen as at least coterminous with light and thus going back as far as Gen 1.

We will then begin to see that when the male (Cain) element predominates, the face of God is hidden (Gen 4,14), and we become more enmeshed in matter, that which we have already seen herein as blocking out the light. It is the veil of our mineral-physical bodies that keeps us from perceiving in the spiritual world. That is the *veil of the temple* that the Christ Spirit rent (Mt 27,51; Mk 15,38; Lk 23,45; cf. Heb 9,8-9), preparing the path as "first fruit" (1 Cor 15,20,23) for each of us.

We are in our mineral-physical condition because of darkness. Just as matter blocks light in the phenomenal, the mineral-physical world, so also does every thought or deed that conflicts with the Christ Spirit either create or feed evil spirits,[15] the spirits of darkness, and block the spiritual light that must fill human souls if they are to follow the upward path. Every such thought or deed that is of darkness creates karmic debt for the soul that produces it, debt that must be eradicated during earthly life however many incarnations that may take, incarnations in mineral-physical bodies. And not only so, but every such thought or deed that is from darkness creates a karmic burden upon all creation, over and above what must be erased by the individual soul, unless and until that soul accepts the Christ, who lifts from the sinner that portion of guilt, taking it upon his own being (see the sequence of essays in *The Burning Bush* starting with "Forgiven Sins" and going through "Lord of Karma").

We then come to see that *darkness* has its own polarity, the *causal darkness* (i.e., sin, the Cain factor) that is itself not yet matter, and the *consequent matter* (the ground saturated with Abel's blood) that produces the earthly phenomena of darkness.

---

15. See "Forgiven Sins," p. 107, in *The Burning Bush*, discussing "objective sins" and "objective karma," the type Christ lifts from the soul of the repentant sinner.

MEDITATION

On Light and Darkness

ALBERT EINSTEIN (1879-1955), whose life epitome reflects the Lord's ancient query to Job (Job 38,19-20, emphasis mine)

[19] "Where is the way to the dwelling of *light*, and where is the place of *darkness*,
[20] that you may take it to its territory and that you may discern the paths to its home?"

bestowed on humanity dramatic new insight into the phenomena of light. Having soared higher than others, he died without finding that dwelling place. Nevertheless, in his willingness to "leave home" in search of truth, he carried us farther than others on this quest. Notably, he was born in the very year that the current age of the Archangel Michael began, the Archangel who administers the divine intelligence.

David Bodanis, seemingly another one of those gems of profound thinking to emerge from the faculty of Oxford University, has written a most delightful and helpful little book entitled

$$E = mc^2$$

A Biography of the World's Most Famous Equation.

Probably more than any other he has opened the door to nonexperts to a degree of comprehension of this terse gem (see fn 13 in the "Light" essay). Its symbols, of course, are fairly well known, namely:

E is for Energy
= means that what is on the left side of it is equal to what is on its right side
m is for mass
c is for the speed of light, which in the formula is squared.

As every schoolchild knows (or thinks it knows), the speed of light is about 186,000 miles per second, or about 670 million miles per hour. When squared, this latter becomes 448.9 quadrillion, or 448,900,000,000,000,000, "square" m.p.h. That distance is a long way by our normal earthly thinking. Yet it is not so enormous when we speak so easily of a "light year," which is 5.88 trillion, or 5,880,000,000,000, miles. In describing our known universe, which seems to be exploding outward at nearly the speed of light (i.e., becoming less dense?), our astronomers speak of distances in terms of billions of light years.[1]

One of the simpler rules of mathematics is that when a multiplier (i.e., c^2 in this instance) is moved from one side of the equation to the other, it becomes a divisor on the other side. Thus, if instead of multiplying the mass (m) by c^2 we move the latter from the right side of the equation to the left, we then divide the energy (E) by the same c^2. Since c^2 is such an enormous number, we immediately see that, moving in one direction, it takes an enormous amount of energy to produce a tiny bit of mass; conversely, when moving in the opposite direction, it only takes a tiny bit of mass to produce an enormous amount of energy.

Sadly, during the twentieth century, or roughly the first third of the current Michaelic Age, the most recognized application of this discovery has been its power to destroy through the agency of the atomic bomb. (In a sense, this could represent the destructive power of the Sun on earthly life.) We have even tried to dramatically enhance this destructive power through what is called the hydrogen bomb, in which an initial atomic explosion (brought about by "fission" of atoms) creates the necessary heat and pressure to start a process of "fusion" of the heavy isotopes of hydrogen. So terrifying is this destructive power that we can only pray it will either be abandoned or turned only into constructive use.

In a way, these discoveries and applications by humanity in the twentieth century are themselves an *image*, or negative, however presumptuous, of the Creator God, perhaps not at all unlike the portrayal in Gen 11,2-9 of the legendary "tower of Babel," archetypal symbol of human arrogance and pride. To preserve our own material being, status and privilege, we will destroy our brother and sister creatures who threaten it.

This is the dark, and spiritually fearsome, side of the meditation.

Let us return to the more constructive, and hopefully higher, path.

Let us think, from what has gone before in this volume, of the nature

---

1. In a stunning schematic called "The Universe Through Time and Space," quasars "rushing away from us at more than 90 percent of the speed of light" are shown as being between 15 and 20 billion light years away, so that the light that is observed from them today, having been generated at that distance that long ago, gives no indication of where (or what) they are today. Each quasar "emits the energy of hundreds of galaxies" of stars. See *Atlas of the World* (AW), at pp. 6-7.

of spiritual activity. We conceive of it in terms of such immense energy and velocity that it disappears beyond the border of the world of matter and that of ether, transcending beyond that into the astral, then the lower devachan (spiritual) and into the higher devachan (spiritual), through the ranks of the nine spiritual hierarchies and finally back into the waiting arms of the Creator God, the ultimate union of all things (Eph 1,9-10). We would simplify this because our minds cannot stretch so far, just as our minds cannot stretch to the vast expanses of our known universe. But if we subscribe to what the Bible tells us, we must see that it is from this non-material realm that all matter came into being, and it is back into this nonmaterial realm that all must return.

And do we not have, in this little equation, the "sign" that points us in this direction?

Think what immense energy came forth to create the imponderable mass of our universe. A tiny example of its magnitude can be grasped in the following passage from Part Three of Bodanis' book (p. 77):

Put a single pound of mass into the "m" slot, and after multiplying by the vast 448,900,000,000,000,000 value of c^2, the equation promises that, in principle, you could get over 10 billion kilowatt hours of energy. This is comparable to a huge power station. That's how a small atomic bomb—with a core small enough to fit in your cupped hands—could heave out enough energy to rip open streets and buried fuel lines; to shatter street after street of brick buildings; to tear open the bodies of tens of thousands of soldiers and children and teachers and bus drivers.

He points out that this bomb works "when less than one percent of the mass inside it gets turned into energy." And we are speaking of one pound, an unimaginable speck in relation to the mass of our solar system alone, itself an unimaginable speck (materially speaking) in the universe.

I have previously suggested herein, based upon Steiner's seemingly very clear Intuition, that, contrary to the kinetic reasoning of science, the interior of stars is not mass but the polar opposite of mass. They are the spiritual forces that generate this immense power within the universe and balance out the known and unknown (such as undiscovered "black holes") matter within it. They are, instead of gravitational forces, forces of suction. In that respect, they are in the *image* of the Creator God who sucks our universe outward in a process of becoming less dense and being drawn into the Creator God itself (cf. Jn 12,32). As the stars themselves sacrifice their power within the universe, they move, along with their children (universal matter) into the Creator God's waiting arms as the universe explodes outward in attenuation.

As humanity moves toward the spiritual, mass is gradually turned into energy under this famous formula, and as humanity ("sons of God") redeems its own material bodies in this manner, it also moves forward in the redemption of its lower servant kingdoms, its little "brothers" and "sisters" (Rom 8,19-23).

In at least one respect there is a similarity between Steiner's revelation about the suction (i.e., negative mass) emanating from the interior of the Sun (and other outer stars) and Einstein's famous equation. No one paid any attention to the latter for a while. They were both expounding at the same time. That only Einstein's theory has been accepted just points to the fact that Einstein has thus far been applied only in the world of matter. But he gave us an *image* pointing to what Steiner has said.

That image, among other things, suggests the immensity of suffering endured by the Creator God (through its Christ aspect) long before the earthly Crucifixion occurred. In fact, the Crucifixion would have been only the tip of a mighty iceberg of suffering.[2] If we conceive, as we should, of the source of the *E* in Einstein's famous equation as being from the energy and velocity of the spiritual world (neither, of course, being measurable or even detectable by human instrumentation), and of the *m* as being the vast mass of our solar system (and even of all the universe) that was brought into existence through that energy and velocity, we begin to think in terms of such unspeakable magnitude that would dwarf our own incomprehensible universe. We then recognize this unspeakable magnitude as the Christ (being one with the Creator God, by whatever name called). For that spiritual power to have "descended" by contraction through the vast globe of created matter into a human body must bring forth contemplation of pain far beyond human comprehension— pain so vast and intense that death by Crucifixion, as horrible as it was, could have been only an earthly reflection of something far greater. The love expressed by John 3,16, "For God so loved the world ...," must be exponentially enlarged by any such contemplation.

---

2. Steiner spoke of the four sacrifices by Christ, only the last of which was in the physical body, and yet all four of which were during the Earth Condition of Consciousness. These may be seen in the charts I-76 and I-50 in *The Burning Bush*, including the references upon which they are based. These are sacrifices that led to the creation of the human being.

BLOOD

"BLOOD!" What word immediately stirs the soul more intuitively, plumbs its instincts more deeply, embraces its gamut more completely, or lures it on more mystically?

Preamble

Because warm blood, like the fire it nurtures, is, in a very real sense, where heaven and earth meet—the agent of the soul, the patron of the heart, the altar upon which the soul and the Christ are wed—we dare not deal with it too lightly and miss its immense significance. We would be presumptuous to believe we here lay bare all of its wonderful mysteries. But Rudolf Steiner has made available such a wealth of insight on the subject that we must not be remiss in our undertaking out of the desire for an unjustifiable brevity. So let us here pause and reflect deeply.

A road map is needed for this meditative journey to help us anticipate its unfolding scenery.

CONTENTS

Opening Remarks

Only three chapters precede the first appearance of *blood* in the Bible and only three follow its last, and it pervades the pages in between, appearing in forty of the sixty-six books of the Protestant Bible. In this respect, it keeps company with a relatively small host of highly significant terms, some of which either have or will be noted.[1] It seems most notable that among these the term *iron* appears in the same first and last chapters as does its cognate blood. It is a remarkable coincidence that it is in the *fourth* chapter of Genesis where both of these terms first appear, and their close spiritual and physical relationship is indicated by the fact that the *fourth* step in the separation of the Sun, Moon and planets from each other as outlined by Steiner (see I-27) was when the planet Mars initially deposited iron within the Earth's mineral substance.

In 1963 I had what is commonly known as a "near death experience." A pervasive divine light and an ineffably tangible love enveloped me. I remained in the hospital for three more weeks and underwent subsequent exploratory surgery eleven days later. But for many days after regaining consciousness from the first surgery I kept hearing a particular hymn. It was August in Texas, and the air conditioning system remained on at all times. Not detectable by others in the room, its rhythm kept

1. These observations are taken from *Nelson's Complete Concordance of the RSV*, 2d Ed., Thomas Nelson Pub., Nashville, 1984.

carrying this hymn into my consciousness. I even asked my wife where the music was coming from.[2] There were five quatrains, with the chorus echoing the third and fourth lines on each one, but I kept hearing over and over again only the first verse and its chorus. The poem in its entirety is as follows:

> There is a fountain filled with blood
> Drawn from Immanuel's veins;
> And sinners, plunged beneath that flood,
> Lose all their guilty stains.
>
> The dying thief rejoiced to see
> That fountain in his day;
> And there may I, though vile as he,
> Wash all my sins away.
>
> Dear dying Lamb, Thy precious blood
> Shall never lose its power,
> Till all the ransomed Church of God
> Be saved, to sin no more.
>
> E'er since, by faith, I saw the stream
> Thy flowing wounds supply,
> Redeeming love has been my theme,
> And shall be till I die.
>
> Then in a nobler, sweeter song,
> I'll sing Thy power to save,
> When this poor lisping, stammering tongue
> Lies silent in the grave.

The hymn was much more popular in my earlier years than in the decades since. But its awesome and mystical impact stayed with me over the years.

---

2. Upon investigation I found that its lyrics were composed in the eighteenth century by William Cowper (pronounced Cooper), 3 Brit 698, in England, and it was set to an early American melody by Lowell Mason, 7 Brit 913, in the nineteenth century.

This essay focuses what Steiner had to say on the subject of blood upon its biblical meaning. What we seek is a fuller understanding of how it is truly the blood of Christ that works the salvation of creation.[3]

Topical List of Scriptures Using the Term "Blood"

Before bringing Steiner's insights to bear on the subject, it is well to note that there appears to be an evolutionary development of the meaning of blood within the Bible itself—a transition all the way from punishments related to the spilling of blood to the blood's saving agency. The following categories are noted (all scriptural uses are found under one of these categories, as shown in the Chapter End Note):

1. The shedding of another human's blood where it is:
   (a) Culpable
   (b) Innocent or inadvertent

2. The express indication that a creature's life is in its blood (whether or not the eating of its blood is prohibited)

3. The prohibition of the eating of blood, while not stating that a creature's life is in its blood

4. The turning of an object into blood

5. The effecting of salvation and/or life preservation through animal blood

6. The ritual of animal sacrifice as an atonement for sin, peace offering, ordination of priests, etc.

---

3. Anthroposophy shows that no individual can selfishly attain to eventual personal (egotistic) salvation so long as any element of creation remains unredeemed. Those who have perfected their own souls and bodies through full payment of their karmic debt are nevertheless unable to enter the highest heavenly sphere if others of God's creatures remain below. It is the deeper meaning of the parable of the ninety and nine (Lk 15,3-7; Mt 18,10-14). The process of entry into the spiritual worlds is portrayed in the book of Job by the two monsters, the Behemoth and the Leviathan. The Behemoth (Job 40,15-24) is one's own karmic beast. In esoteric or anthroposophic terms, it is *the lower guardian of the threshold*. Purification of that beast permits the soul to sojourn in the lower spiritual world. However, entry into the higher spiritual world is barred by *the higher guardian of the threshold*, called the Leviathan in Job 41 (for a description of these worlds, see I-33). One must return ever and again as a Christlike servant (even if only in the spiritual world, as in the case of the Buddha) until all of God's creation has entered the fold. Only then is the higher spiritual world open to any soul (Eph 1,9-10). While Steiner spoke on many occasions of these guardians of the threshold, his most basic and complete portrayal is in the basic book *How to Know Higher Worlds* (HKHW), Chaps. 10 and 11; see also *Outline of Esoteric Science* (OES), Chap. 5, esp. pp. 357-375.

7. The genital discharge of blood through childbirth (parturition), normal menstruation or longer emission[4]
8. The sanctity of human blood
9. The transition away from sacrificing (spilling the blood) of animals
10. Blood as the basis for covenant
11. Becoming drunk on human blood, or the wantonness of having shed it
12. The blood of Christ (ignoring the prophetic aspect of the Old Testament sacrifice of lambs)

    (a) As a sacrament of remembrance

    (b) As the agency of human salvation
13. Blood as a factor in health, sickness or healing
14. Blood as a factor in ancestral inheritance or the birth process
15. The eating, other than sacramentally, of Christ's blood as a necessity of salvation
16. Human blood unable physically, i.e., while still in the flesh, to inherit the Kingdom of God
17. Other significant usage
18. Miscellaneous usages of lesser significance

For detail on these categories, see the Chapter End Note.

---

4. We should not impute impurity from genital discharge only to women. The entirety of Lev 15 deals with genital discharge, vss 1-18 pertaining to male and vss 19-33 to female discharges. Even most fundamentalists today would ignore these requirements, as with much of the rest of the Mosaic law. But the importance in ancient times is suggested by the fact that Jacob Milgrom's 3 AB (*Leviticus 1–16*) devotes 107 pages to Lev 15 alone. At the outset, Milgrom remarks (p. 905):

> One would have expected this chapter to have been joined to chap. 12 [impurity from childbirth] because both deal with genital discharges.... However, the sequence of chaps. 12–15 seems to have been determined according to the duration and complexity of the purification process, in descending order.

Surely the impurity of all genital discharges is a Mosaic recognition of the taint of original sin from Gen 3, for only thereafter did human reproduction require genital discharge of both sexes for childbirth, the pain of childbirth being one of the three healing consequences of sin prescribed in Gen 3,16-19. That male discharge is also impure shows that the pain inflicted by Gen 3,16 is not limited to women. Pain became known among all human beings, male and female, from that point on.

Various Steiner Insights and Biblical Reflections

There is general agreement that the *teachings* of Christ were not new, that their substance had been proclaimed by others before him, excepting perhaps only his teachings about his own sacrifice (and even that was seen by [Second] Isaiah; probably also by Moses [Gen 22,13]). It was his *deed* rather than his *words* that was new, unique and a "once for all" event (Heb 7,27; 9,12,28; 10,10,12-14; Rom 6,10; 1 Pet 3,18). It is that alone, his shed blood, which works the salvation of humanity and eventually of all creation.

But while there is literal similarity between many of Christ's teachings and those of his predecessors, he brought new and different meaning into the words of the old teachings. The six "you have heard, but I say unto you" passages of Mt 5,21-47 spring immediately to mind. But it is particularly Christ's interpretation of Lev 19,18 ("you shall love your neighbor as yourself") in Lk 10,27b and its ensuing "good Samaritan" parable (Lk 10,29-37) that focuses most clearly on this point.

Steiner says that such universal love really commenced in the teachings of the Buddha half a millennium before. It is significant that the source of these teachings, the purified astral body (*Nirmanakaya*) of the Buddha, became the astral body of the Nathan Jesus Child of Luke's Gospel (see "The Nativity" in *The Burning Bush* as well as *The Incredible Births of Jesus*). Those teachings were the seed of the human conscience, for conscience had not evolved in the human soul before that time.[5]

---

5. The word "conscience" is found only in the New Testament (Acts 23,1; 24,16; Rom 2,15; 9,1; 13,5; 1 Cor 8,7,10,12; 10,25,27-29; 2 Cor 1,12; 4,2; 5,11; 1 Tim 1,5,19; 3,9; 4,2; 2 Tim 1,3; Tit 1,15; Heb 9,9,14; 10,22; 13,18; 1 Pet 3,16,21), not in the Old. While the word "conscience" has been used in some modern translations of 1 Sam 25,31, the meaning is not precise, for there was no Hebrew word for conscience in the pertinent era; see 1 ABD 1129. Steiner made this assertion well before these modern translations. He tells us that it was by Siddhartha Gautama, the Buddha (ca. 563-483 B.C.), who planted in humanity the impulse of compassion and love from which conscience grows; see his lecture in Stuttgart on November 14, 1909, entitled *The Gospels* (GOSP). Frequently he showed that there was no concept of conscience in Greek thinking at the time of Aeschylus (ca. 525-456 B.C.), but that it had appeared there by the time of Euripides (ca. 480-406 B.C.); see *The Spiritual Foundation of Morality* (SFM), Lect. 3, p. 65, esp. fn 47; *Metamorphoses of the Soul*, Vol. 2 (MS-2), Lect. 8 (May 5, 1910); and *At the Gates of Spiritual Science* (AGSS), Lect. 8, p. 69. In *The Younger Generation* (YG), Lect. 5, pp. 60-61, he shows that what might have later been interpolated back to be the result of conscience in ancient times was really what came to the soul in those earlier times from the outside, not from the inner nature—it was akin to "the law" of the Old Testament, rather than the "freedom from the law" of the New. In these writings Steiner made it clear, however, that while "conscience" was thus planted seminally in humanity a few centuries before Christ, it was the Christ Event that made its growth in humanity really possible.

For our purposes, what is really at stake in the "good Samaritan" teaching of Jesus is that the time of blood-based love, upon which humanity had thus far been nurtured from primeval time, and upon which Lev 19,18 was historically based in theory and practice (see 28A AB 879 and 880-881, on Luke's Gospel), had ended (or that it would end with the falling of his blood into the Earth). This was one of the teachings also of Mt 5,43-47 (loving one's enemy) and of Jn 2,1-11 (the wedding at Cana, see pp. 137-142 of *The Burning Bush*). That it pointedly involved a historically disdained Samaritan, meaning one of mixed blood, as in the case of the woman at the well (Jn 4,7-42), is indicative of this also. Cana, in Galilee north of Samaria, was also an area of mixed blood, a necessity for the scriptural setting of the wedding (*The Gospel of John and its Relation to the Other Gospels* [Jn-Rel], Lect 9, p. 161; see the meaning of "Galilee" in "The Whirlwind" section of the "Fire" essay). It was because of this that Christ admonished his followers that those who do not "hate" their fathers and mothers and follow him (otherwise an odious spiritual concept) are not worthy of him (Lk 14,26; Mt 10,37; *The Gospel of Saint John* [GSJ], Lect. 4, pp. 69-70). What was here indicated is the earthly establishment of the clear demarcation line between the spiritual validity of the historical group soul (i.e., blood-based love) and the newly christened "I Am" of the individual Christ-inspired Ego whose love billows out henceforth to those of mixed blood, even to the entirety of humanity and creation.

It is particularly critical that we become aware of the current regency of the Archangel Michael over the *divine intelligence* on Earth,[6] the first since the time of Christ (his last having been when the enlightening Greek influence was spread by Aristotle's pupil Alexander across the world in preparation for the coming of Christ; see I-19). The barriers of group thinking and loving that have historically existed in clan, race, creed (including religion or political or other group affiliation) and nationality, must be broken down during this Michaelic regency. The individual Ego (I Am), through Christ-enabled love and concern, must reach beyond any such selective grouping. These various divisions and separations of humanity are, for our time, what the blood-related division between Pharisee and Samaritan was in the time of Jesus.

---

6. The current regency of the Archangel Michael began, according to Steiner, in 1879 and will run until approximately the year 2233; see the Appendix in *The Incredible Births of Jesus* as well as the discussion of the archangelic ages in I-19 in the revised edition of *The Burning Bush*.

The central thread running as underlying substance through all of the blood scriptures from beginning to end is expressed in category #2 above, **"The life is in the *blood*."**

Somewhere fairly early in my Bible-teaching career it came to me, and I thus expounded, that this scripture was based simply upon the observation from time immemorial that when enough blood had drained out of one's body there was no life left. My experience is that one can search the Bible commentaries for any other explanation and find nothing much more profound than this. An animal that died other than through the spilling of its blood was, according to the scriptures, still deemed to have its life within it until the blood was spilled out. Until then, it could not, for that reason, be eaten by God's people.

It is urgent that in this Michaelic era the new intuited light of anthroposophical insight (whether or not so called) illumine human understanding, for the old concepts are inadequate to lead humanity to the point of recognizing the Christ in his second coming. In that event, so different from the days when he walked on the Earth, he will never be observed in a tangible physical body (Mt 24,23-28; Lk 17,22-24; Acts 1,11). Rather this second coming commenced early in the twentieth century in the etheric world where the Christ could be perceived by those who had developed the necessary spiritual organs (Mt 25,1-13; Lk 12,35-40). Those who are to tread the upward path to the Kingdom must increasingly perceive his presence there in the centuries ahead. See "Second Coming" in *The Burning Bush*.

Before we look at some of the finer things Steiner had to say about blood, we need to get the biblical picture firmly in mind. Blood makes its first appearance in Gen 4,10. The immediately preceding chapter spoke of the infection of the human being's three bodies or "members" (first the astral, and then consequentially the etheric and physical in turn) in the so-called fall (the Fall).[7] We are there told that the consequence to these bodies is as follows:

Astral Body	Pain (Gen 3,16)
Etheric Body	Toil (Gen 3,17)
Physical Body	Death, i.e., "dust" (Gen 3,19)

---

7. For a more extensive explanation of the three bodies, see the essay "Three Bodies" in *The Burning Bush*. See also I-9; many other charts in that volume also relate to this subject.

Prior to the spilling of Abel's blood no mention is made of the blood of any animal, not even with respect to the offering Abel had previously made to God (Gen 4,4). No mention is there made of an altar, and none is thereafter made until Noah brings an offering to the altar in Gen 8,20, whereupon God reverses his curse upon the ground and the raising of plants is ordained. The events up through Gen 4 may be considered to have occurred generally in Lemuria and in the periods up to the middle of the Atlantean Epoch; the events from Seth to Noah[8] during the last half of Atlantis; and the events from the Noah transition on during the current post-Atlantean Epoch.

From I-27, we see that during the Earth Condition of Consciousness, the Sun, Moon and planets have separated out from the original Earth mass in the following order: Saturn, Jupiter, Sun, Mars, Moon, Venus and Mercury. We may take it for now that Saturn separated during the Polarian Epoch, the Sun during the Hyperborean, and the Moon during the Lemurian (see I-2). That leaves Mars to have made its iron deposits within the present Earth mass either late in the Hyperborean or early in the Lemurian. In either event, the iron necessary for warm red blood was first deposited relatively shortly before the Moon separated. We shall see that such latter event was necessary for the development of the higher vertebrates and warm blood.

Noah's sacrifice of animals symbolized the opening of post-Atlantean culture to agriculture—a step made possible by the spilling of blood (Gen 8,20-22).

While it is difficult for us in the present stage of human evolution to accept, anthroposophy shows us that spiritual progress is possible only through pain, toil and death. That is the teaching of the Old Testament as early as Gen 3, and the essential meaning of the Crucifixion. Christ as the first born, or first fruit, endured it, shedding his unique and salvific blood whereby a human soul's objective karma was taken upon his shoulders to the extent such human being accepts his sacrificial offering (see "Forgiven Sins" in *The Burning Bush*). Revelation shows us that each individual who would attain to the resurrection must eventually drink that "cup"—there it is in the form of "eating a scroll" that has been "unsealed"

---

8. For why I start here with Seth (in Gen 5) rather than with Cain (in Gen 4), see the "Appendix to 'Three Bodies'" in *The Burning Bush*.

(Rev 10,8-10).[9] The "stomach" represents the mineral-physical body, while the "mouth" (cf. Rev 1,16) represents the ascending power of the new organ of human reproduction, the larynx, from which the human being's creative *word* will someday issue. This will be when one will not want to be "with child" (Mt 24,19; Lk 23,29), that is, when humans who have evolved spiritually through assimilation of the etheric blood of Christ (see the discussion below of the etherization of the blood) will have passed beyond the time of sexual reproduction as we know it now.

In the complex fourth chapter ("Cosmic Evolution and the Human Being") of his deeply profound book *An Outline of Esoteric Science* (OES), Steiner shows us that the human being was created from the time of Old Saturn by the progressive sacrifice by the hierarchies, and that only by such sacrifice did they themselves advance (see also I-6 and I-35). Under the eternal law reflected by Hermes' saying "As Above, So Below," it is also only thus that the human being (in the *image* of its creators) will attain to spiritual advancement. From this it can be seen that the life of luxury and ease so worshiped in our day as the attainment of success is a disguised spiritual burden, even a curse, ominous and with devastating consequence. The scriptures are replete with similar warning (e.g., Mt 13,22; 19,23-24; 25,31-46; Mk 10,23-25; Lk 6,24; 16,19-31; 18,24-25; Jas 5,1-6; 1 Jn 3,17; 1 Tim 6,6-10). The depth of their meaning is still hidden to many of the outwardly devout by the veil of conventional belief, which finds it hard to give up the view held by so many in Old Testament times that riches are an indication of blessing, or righteousness no less (cf. Gen 13,2; 26,12-13; 1 Sam 2,7; Job 42,10-17; Prov 10,4,22). It is hard not to notice the political tendencies of the rich, many of whom are of fundamentalist Christian persuasion and yet very active in support of governmental policies that favor (i.e., preserve or enhance the privileges of) the rich as against the poor. It is not my purpose here to characterize conservative political positions as either good or bad (for the liberal can be equally so), save as they relate to the matter of wealth—for the love of it has been characterized as "the root of all evils" (1 Tim 6,10). Social conflict, as Steiner suggests, is destined to rage until human souls are sufficiently advanced to structure their institutions along the threefold lines of the human being's own bodily nature (see I-88).

---

9. The lower meaning of "cup" is used here, the one that relates to the necessity of the crucifixion of the "flesh" not only of Christ but of every soul that would attain to eventual salvation. For the higher meaning, see the discussion of Mk 10,39 in *The Disciple Whom Jesus Loved*, pp. 35-36, esp. fn 39.

For reasons that shall become apparent, the Bible requires blood sacrifice as expiation for all sin. Blood sacrifice as spelled out in the Old Testament must be seen, in the light of New Testament development, as prophetic of what was to come. It is otherwise difficult for us today to understand how the sacrifice of an animal by spilling its blood erased human sins. But that was the recurring format given for God's covenant as expressed in the "law" (e.g., Heb 9,6-26).

The mechanics by which the blood of the animal cleansed human sins is expressed, as indicated for instance by 1 ABD 761 ("blood"), in Lev 17,11, "For the life of the flesh is in the blood; and I have given it for you upon the altar to make atonement for your souls; for it is the blood that makes atonement, by reason of the life." The theory advanced in 1 ABD 761 is that "by placing a hand on the animal sinners passed their essence on to it," so that the subsequent shedding of its blood, which took the life of the animal, brought the sinner back to life. One can note the preliminary requirement of such a placing of the hands in numerous passages giving the procedure for animal sacrifice, e.g., Ex 29,10,15,19; Lev 1,4; 3,2,8,13; 4,4,15,24,29. The validity of this ancient understanding is attested by the anointing of the head of Jesus, the Lamb of God, in Mt 26,1-13 and Mk 14,1-9. The blood sacrifice of this "lamb" thereafter removed the sins of the world (see "Forgiven Sins" in *The Burning Bush*; also Rev 5,6,9,12).

The equation "blood equals life" was more ancient than the Hebrews, undoubtedly going back to the clairvoyant knowledge of prehistoric time. Moreover, we are told (1 ABD 761) that the two (blood and life) are "attested as lexical pairs in ... Ugaritic and Akkadian poetry," which antedates that found in Hebrew. This primal understanding appears also to have existed among the Native Americans (see, for instance, *Lakota Myth* [LAKM], p. 207). Undoubtedly, the pagan practice of human sacrifice derived from such knowledge as the ancient mystery wisdom became decadent. Abraham's willingness to shed the blood of his only son, Isaac, reflected his tradition, but the (descending) Christ Spirit, acting through its angels, prophetically, profoundly and symbolically delivered "a ram [i.e., lamb] caught in a thicket by its horns," Gen 22,11-14.[10]

How deeply and marvelously esoteric is the prophecy here laid down. And as the "law" thereafter developed, Hebrews, with their God's approval,

10. See the esoteric meaning of "horns" in the discussion of Rev 13,1 in "The Apocalypse" section of the Creation essay herein.

abhorred human sacrifice. Nevertheless, the spilling of human blood remained ambiguously approved under the law for numerous offenses. Even the commandment "Thou shall not kill" (Ex 20,13; Deut 5,17) was more honored in the breach than otherwise by Old Testament law, and seemed, like that of loving one's neighbor (Lev 19,18), to have initially had a quite limited scope. Few commandments extend as near the outer limits of creation as "Thou shall not kill." Anthroposophy shows us that our senses function only by killing what enters the human body from the outside. Light is killed to create sight, sound to create hearing, the constitution of what is ingested to conform it to human metabolism. In time, humanity will cease to kill animals for food (let alone for sport, which is already abhorrent to the more spiritually sensitive), thereafter even plants, and finally even the physical sound and light waves for sense (as we see in Revelation when even the Sun will no longer be needed for light). In other words, as with all written (graven) images, evolution will eventually change the meaning of "Thou shall not kill," and those most sensitive souls will yearn always to move onward to the next stage. Those who most understand the Christ of our time already sense these latent tendencies in their attitude of reverence for all things—such attitude perhaps reflecting the presence in them of the astral body of Saint Francis of Assisi (who had the astral body of Christ; see I-74 and the essay "Spiritual Economy" in *The Burning Bush*).

It would be easier for us to simply skip over the term *blood* because of its complexity, and I might have been tempted to do so if an increased understanding of its spiritual significance were not so vital. Steiner's works are a cornucopia of references to it.[11]

---

11. Aside from his three works that are more fully discussed in the following sections of this essay, and without any claim of exhaustiveness, examples of other Steiner references include GSJ, Lects. 3,4,5,6,7 and 9; Jn-Rel, Lects. 5,10,11,12,13 and 14; *The Gospel of St. Luke* (GSL), Lect. 10; *The Gospel of St. Mark* (GSMk), Lects. 2 and 8; *The Influence of Spiritual Beings Upon Man* (ISBM), Lects. 1 and 4; *The Gospel of St. John* (GOSPSJ), Lects. 4, 7 and 8; AGSS, Lects. 9 and 10; *The Archangel Michael* (ARCHM, an anthology), Part One, Lect. 7; Part Two, Lects. 1 and 2; *The Mystery of Golgotha* (MYSTG), Lect. 1; *The Bridge Between Universal Spirituality and the Physical Constitution of Man* (BBUS), Lect. 1; *Christmas: A Contemplation out of the Wisdom of Life/Vitaesophia* (CCWL), Lect. 1; *The Human Heart* (HUHT); *Manifestations of Karma* (MK), Lect. 5; *Man in the Light of Occultism, Theosophy and Philosophy* (MLO), Lect. 9; *The Mysteries, a Poem by Goethe* (MYST), Lect. 1; *The Origin of Suffering/The Origin of Evil, Illness and Death* (OSOE), Lect. 1; *The Riddle of Humanity* (RH), Lect. 4; *Supersensible Knowledge* (SKN), Lect. 2; *Study of Man* (SM), Lects. 2 and 13. See also the following non-Steiner references: 1 ABD 761, "Blood"; 16 Brit 377 et seq., "Circulation and Circulatory Systems"; 15 Brit 125 et seq., "Blood"; and 28 Brit 669 et seq., "Tissues and Fluids."

Let us look first at the prehistoric knowledge, later reflected in the Old Testament, that "the life is in the blood" and consider how it relates to Steiner's assertions that the blood is the material manifestation of the Ego. We saw above how what was animal sacrifice in the Old Testament gradually and prophetically matured into the sacrifice of Christ as the Lamb of God in the New Testament. Christ, as the higher Ego ("I Am") to be taken in by the human being, tells us, "*I am* ... the life" (Jn 11,25 and 14,6, emphasis mine). He makes clear that his blood is given for us, and other New Testament writers cited above assert that our salvation is through the agency of that blood. In such sense, the life is in the blood in the New Testament's Mystery of Golgotha—the transformation, as it were, of the sacrifice from the animal level to the human through Christ's deed (Heb).

In contemplating the vicarious atonement from the shedding of animal blood (Lev 17,11), it is helpful to reflect upon the origin of warm-blooded creatures (mammals and birds). Let us reflect upon the interconnectedness of a number of phenomena. Only two kinds of animals were acceptable as sacrifice, "animals" (by which is meant only certain mammals) and "birds." Gen 8,20; Lev 1. What is the significance of this limitation for our purposes? It represents the only two types of animals that have warm blood. What is the significance of warm blood? It contains the element of fire, both spiritual fire (fire ether) and its materialized counterpart, fire as we know it, the only point at which the spiritual world and material world come in contact (see the essay "Fire"). What is necessary for blood to be "warm," i.e., to contain fire? Oxygen! What is necessary in the blood stream in order to carry oxygen? Red blood cells. What is the essential mineral component from which red blood cells are made? Iron. What was necessary for warm-blooded animals to arise? Two interconnected constructs had to be developed: the sympathetic nervous system, requiring the evolutionary emergence of a spinal column as exists in the vertebrates (chordates), along with a source of the mineral iron. Let us look at these in order.

The development of the former is given in *Supersensible Knowledge*, (SKN), Lect. 2, esp. pp. 35-38, which appropriates as its title Mephistopheles' statement to Goethe's Faust when his signature was required to be made with his blood—*blood is a very special fluid*[12]—a statement

---

12. Goethe's *Faust*, The First Part, line 1740.

that echoes through Steiner's lectures over and over again. The step-by-step explanation given there can be condensed for our purposes to the point of saying that when evolution had reached the stage of the spinal column found in vertebrates, the interrelationship of the three bodies (physical, etheric and astral) converted certain prior body fluids to "what we call blood." Inasmuch as fluids constituting a sort of blood exist in lower animals, he is here (by saying "what we call") incorporating the concept of warm blood. That, of course, is not limited to humans but extends to mammals and birds. Human development was still, at this point, in the nonmineral, or supersensible, world. But the birds and mammals that came first to materialization carried this human characteristic to embodiment as the premature, i.e., failed, representatives of humanity. They are not human, but progressed further than other animals toward the human state in the supersensible world before failing and thus falling into materialization. The more sophisticated development of the brain (higher nervous system) and other organs which are essential to house *on Earth* the individual Ego had to develop further in the supersensible world. But the element of warm blood that was an integral part of the eventual vehicle of that Ego first existed on Earth in these prematurely descended birds and mammals. Those classes of the animal kingdom which had descended earlier (i.e., fishes, reptiles and the like) did not have it.

The external factor that made the oxygen-carrying capacity possible was the placement of iron in the Earth's mineral composition. This came about when Mars separated from the Earth and in the process (such cosmic bodies still being of unsolidified mass) passed through the Earth leaving the iron element within it. See I-27; ISBM, Lect. 3, pp. 44-45; and *The Gospel of St. John* (GOSPSJ), Lect. 4.[13] While an early version of this manuscript was being written, in early August 1996 a team of NASA scientists made big news (see *Wall Street Journal,* August 8, 1996, p. B7) in announcing evidence that life had existed eons ago on Mars. Their proof was that a meteor from Mars, discovered in Antarctica in 1984, appears to contain the fossilized remains of microorganisms—"what they concluded were chemical, mineral and structural signs of a bacteria-like life form." All of a sudden, the news media projected this into evidence that life like that on Earth existed elsewhere in

---

13. Note that this is a different lecture cycle on John's Gospel than the more noted GSJ.

the heavens. What scientists have not yet considered is that this evidence is as consistent with Steiner's intuitive revelations above as it is with any prior independent existence of life on Mars. In other words, it tends to show not that life ever existed independently on Mars, but rather that what Rudolf Steiner told us at the beginning of the twentieth century was true. For he said then that when the Mars mass separated from the larger unsolidified Earth mass (which until then still contained the Mars-Moon-Earth substance), it passed through the Earth (I-27). In doing so, not only did it leave behind significant portions of its iron element but also took with it the cell life, probably even then moribund or dead, that had originated in the remaining mother mass of Earth evolution's condensation.

It is the confluence of these essentially contemporaneous evolutionary events, making the emergence of *warm* blood possible, that makes the appearance of both blood and iron for the first time in the same chapter of the Bible so remarkable (Gen 4).

Steiner shows clearly (see BBUS, Lect. 1) what we already sense, that the four elements find their home base in the fourfold human being as follows:

1. Solid organism   Physical body
2. Fluid organism   Etheric body
3. Aeriform organism   Astral body
4. Warmth organism   Ego

We humans have always marveled at the instinct of animals, at how perfectly it functions, and how we must think out responses that in them seem innate. We have settled for the idea that these instincts are simply "God-given." While that is certainly true in a sense, we must come to a new understanding of how it is so, for the source of the animal's instinct is the same as our more deliberate human action, namely, the Ego. But, you say, the animal has no Ego—the latter is what sets the human above the animal (cf. I-10). That is only partially true. Members of all of the four kingdoms (mineral, plant, animal and human) have Egos, the difference between them being the locus of that Ego (see I-11). In the case of the animal, the Ego is not within the physical body but is in the astral world. Moreover, it is not an individual Ego, as has, over time, evolved in the human being. Rather it is a group Ego, which accounts for the similarity of instinct within each animal species, there being a group Ego for each species. What is implicit in this is, at least in the warm-blooded animals, that the group Ego acts primarily through the blood.

Another component had to go with the iron to make blood warm, to house its fire and Ego. That component was oxygen. Actually, it came before the iron. It appears in Gen 2,7, where God "breathed" life into the human being. We saw that process in the Creation essay (see its treatment of Gen 2,7). In GOSPSJ, Lect. 4, Steiner said, "Air is the body of Jehovah [i.e., the Yahweh-Eloha] just as flesh is the body of man." This a beautiful thought, that life came into the human being when Yahweh breathed his body into it (as it then existed on the Earth, in primeval condition; review what was said in the Creation essay). But I must confess to having wrestled greatly with Steiner's statement that air was the body of Yahweh (one of the Elohim, Exusiai or Spirits of Form). We can easily see from I-6 that the Elohim are four hierarchical ranks above the human being. Saying that the body of the Elohim is air suggests that they are just two ranks higher, the gas element being only two steps higher, in the materialization (evolutionary) process, than the solid (Earth) that equates to the mineral-physical body. How could Steiner have said this?

Actually the two sentences he spoke just before this were: "Occult Science looks upon all matter only as the expression of spirit. We breathe in and out not air alone, we breathe in the spirit it contains." Finally it came to me what he was saying (and this is typical of how one must sometimes wrestle to find the meaning in his statements). The spirit component of air is light. See I-22 and consider what we have been saying about it. The Elohim represented the light (their home was our Sun sphere). If we start with solids (i.e., our mineral-physical body) in the I-22 chart moving first upward to the left to fire and then upward to the right, the fourth step is that of light. But Steiner didn't say the light was Yahweh's body, rather it was the air. And Gen 2,7 didn't say Yahweh breathed in light, but rather what gives earthly life to physical bodies, namely, air. How do we get from the more spiritual light to air and thus make sense of Steiner's statement? Recall that it was the sacrifice of their own Ego by the Elohim at the beginning of Earth evolution that made the human Ego possible (see I-16 and I-35). In fact, as these charts show, all four kingdoms (mineral, plant, animal and human; or solids, fluids, gases and fire) came into earthly being through the sacrifice of the four hierarchical ranks from the Thrones down to the Exusiai (see I-6 for ranks).

Here let us jump to something Steiner said in a somewhat different context but quite to our present point. He said a human skull is itself evidence of reincarnation, evidence not only that it had once been *inhabited* by a human soul but also that it had been *formed* by that soul for its habitation.[14] The point for our present discussion is simply that the life and the skull had once been one—much like all the four elements and their related ethers had once been one before they were separated in the creative process. A human skull is quite unique to the soul that inhabited it. And because that soul formed it and lived in it before departing, there is something of that soul in it in a manner of speaking. And just as the human Ego resulted from the sacrifice of the Elohim who no longer dwell in it in quite the same way, and as that human skull resulted from the human soul as indicated, so also does air represent, in the world of matter, what came from the lowest component of Yahweh-Eloha, the light which had previously existed in union with the air before their separation in the "first day" (Gen 1,3-4). It is the body of Yahweh in that sense.

So when the necessary preliminary conditions existed, Yahweh "breathed" into the human being and it became a living soul (Gen 2,7). This happened as a process over thousands of years whereby it became a breather of air, a source of warmth. Human beings, in their ancestral Old Moon stage of evolution, breathed warmth (fire) but on Earth they have advanced one stage to air, which is the body of Yahweh, just as the flesh is the form of manifestation of the present human being's lowest (and oldest) body. The spirits which the human being breathed in and out as fire on Old Moon included those spirits who advanced and those who remained behind in their development during the course of Old Moon. The former are the Archangels as agents of the Elohim (especially the Archangel Michael as the special agent of Yahweh-Eloha), and the latter are what Steiner, in this context, called the Fire-Spirits, also known as "Luciferic" spirits.[15]

---

14. See the discussion of this in Lect. 6 of *Occult Physiology* (OP), "The Blood as Manifestation and Instrument of the Human Ego," below.

15. The student who wants to read Steiner's portrayal of these events should see GOSPSJ, Lect. 4, and AGSS, Lects. 9 and 10. It should, however, be remembered that these were early lectures (1907 and 1906, respectively), and that it was not until shortly before Steiner's death that he relented to having any of his lectures made public, and even then not to the extent finally approved by the governing body of the Anthroposophical Society after his death. He never had the opportunity to edit them, as he had always hoped. *(Continued on following page)*

On Earth the Elohim worked on the human being from without, from the Sun and the Moon, while the Fire-Spirits worked on it from within, living in the human being's blood in the element of warmth. There they act as opponents of Yahweh. Yahweh sought to hold humanity together by love in small groups, but in that way they would never have become independent beings. The Fire-Spirits brought art and science (cf. Gen 4,21-22). Yahweh placed the human being in a paradise of love, but then the Fire-Spirit, the serpent (pictured as breathing fire) opened that being's eyes to what still remained from Old Moon.[16] The ancient clairvoyance that all human beings had at one time, which is now an atavism when it appears naturally in an undeveloped state, symbolizes this fire-breathing serpent.[17] The imagery of this being is found in many biblical passages.[18] And Moses' lifting up of the serpent in the wilderness (Num 21,8-9; Jn 3,14-15; cf. 2 K 18,4) cannot be understood except in this context. Of it, Steiner says, in GOSPSJ, Lect. 4:

---

15. *(continued from previous page)* Consequently, so many things that could have been made clearer were left as they had come from his lips, extemporaneously when not impromptu. In reading GOSPSJ, for instance, one's inclination is to say at this point that it was the spirits of the Elohim that the human being breathed in and out on the Old Moon and again in its recapitulation in Gen 2,7—this is how I first read it, before making the distinction in the text above (between light and air). Upon reflection, however, it had to be the Archangels as agents of the Elohim (see I-7). In the lecture, Steiner calls the Luciferic spirits "Fire-Spirits." From I-6, it can be seen that the Archangels were the Spirits of Fire. Here we must distinguish, however, between the Archangels who developed properly on Old Moon and those, such as Lucifer, who there fell behind (see I-32).

16. Recall that Old Moon evolution is called the "planet" (see I-4) of Wisdom, while Earth evolution is called the "planet" of Love. Actually, Wisdom is primarily related to the Old Sun, when the Spirits of Wisdom (Kyriotetes, or Dominions) were the ruling hierarchy (see I-6 and I-16). However, it was by combining their action with that of the next hierarchy during Old Moon that caused Old Moon to be referred to as the Cosmos of Wisdom; see OES, Chap. 4, under "Moon," at pp. 191-193. See also I-53, where "Love" is called "Morality," and I-42, where it is called "Strength."

17. The atavistic clairvoyance must die out, but must be regained, so to speak, by the development of the fire that Christ came to cast. This fire is associated, in spiritual development, with what are known in esotericism as the "lotus flowers, chakras, or wheels" (see Figure 13 in I-21). They are expressed as "lotus plants" or "lotus trees" in Job 40,21-22, and as "wheels" in Ezek 1,16-21; 3,13; 10,2-19 and 11,22 and Dan 7,9. The development of these spiritual centers is discussed by Steiner in *How to Know Higher Worlds* (HKHW), Chap. 6. They are related to what, in the Orient, is sometimes called the "kundalini fire."

18. See, for instance, Deut 8,15; 2 Sam 22,9; Job 41,19-21; Ps 18,8,15; Is 6,6 and 33,11; also cf. Rev 12,15.

The further course of the evolution of humanity proceeded under the influence of Lucifer, who brings freedom and wisdom to man. Under the guidance of the God Jehovah men were to be led together through the principle of blood-brotherhood. The fact that man has become a free citizen of the Earth—this he owes to Lucifer. Jehovah placed men in the Paradise of Love; then there appeared the Fire-spirit, the Serpent, in the form which man once possessed when he still breathed fire, and opened men's eyes to what still remained from the Old Moon. This Luciferic influence was perceived as a temptation. But those who were instructed in the occult schools did not look upon this enlightenment as wrong; the great Initiates have not cast the Serpent down but, like Moses in the wilderness, they have raised it.

This explanation also suggests a deeper meaning for Christ's "Today you will be with me in Paradise" (Lk 23,43), for it symbolized the heavenly conversion of Lucifer (see *The Burning Bush*, pp. 117 and 332). The "tree of knowledge" was the wisdom that was implanted in evolution on Old Moon, while the "tree of life" was the blood-love from Yahweh (Gen 3,22-24). Love gradually spread from smaller to larger groups (e.g., the Samaritans), but the human being's spiritual struggle to expand this still goes on. Steiner points out that in the esoteric (occult) schools, Christ was called the true Lucifer (light-bearer).

The capacity to breathe signifies the acquisition of the individual human spirit. The Ego entered humanity with the air it breathed, the air that made blood warmth possible. If we speak of an Ego common to all men (the Christ "I Am"), it also has a common body, the air. Not without reason did the ancients call this universal Ego *Atma–Atman*, the breath (see I-9).

How marvelously it all fits together! And yet, we are hardly ever finished with new insights and revelations. In the assortment of Steiner citations listed above, as well as in countless other places in his works, they seem to come without end.

The human Ego that existed in the blood carried with it the memory of all that was related to such blood. During the group soul ages, being overwhelmingly strong at the outset and diminishing ever so slowly over time, human memory was carried through the blood of inheritance as a feature of the collectivity of Yahweh's nature (being to bring together instead of, as per Lucifer, to separate). What was of the blood was the basis of love, which initially extended no further than the blood. The ages of the putatively individual, prehistoric patriarchs reflects many generations, each extending from the eponymous founder as long as the blood continued unabated in that line. This accounts for the seemingly long lives, especially prior to Abraham (e.g., see Gen 5). One felt oneself to be "one" with the founder because memory included what had occurred during all the lives starting therefrom in the unmixed blood line. But it was a requisite for the continuity of the blood memory, or group Ego, that marriage be within the family, i.e., endogamous as against exogamous. Hence it is that the Bible emphasizes this in the early patriarchal times: Gen 20,12 and 24,1-4,24; see also Gen 11,27-30; 27,46–28,3; and cf. Gen 36,2. We may picture the "Mogen David-like" opposite pointing triangles (I-87) with one pointing downward coming from above, the more ancient times, and containing the diminishing practice of "endogamy," with the Roman period being where the two touch, representing the "turning point of time," and the upward pointing triangle, coming from below upward and containing the increasing practice of "exogamy." This illustrates the necessity for blood ties to lose their strength. The coming of Christ signified the time when blood-related love had to start being transformed into an ever-increasing love for all humanity and creation.

The Hebraic mantra-like reference to "Abraham, Isaac and Jacob" was a reflection of the group soul memory that related back within the blood of the Hebrew people, albeit diminishing over time. It was this Abraham, Isaac and Jacob consciousness, embodying the whole line of Hebrew consciousness that was felt to be of the divine nature of Yahweh.[19] Its identification with the "I Am" commenced with the revelation

---

19. Over and over Steiner stressed this in one way or another. We need to remember that it was the Elohim who sacrificed their Ego to human beings during Earth evolution (I-35), and how better expressed than "breathed into his nostrils the breath of life" (Gen 2,7), the universal Ego, the *Atman*, becoming in that primordial epoch the undescended, germinal human Ego. In *From Jesus to Christ* (JTC), Lect. 5, p. 94, Steiner said, "What the Hebrew valued as his Ego was in a certain sense also the Divine Ego." Speaking of Abraham, Isaac and Jacob, Steiner said, "It was for the purpose of bringing to the ego all that could be given to the natural being of man through the organization of the blood that the Hebrew people were chosen.... The ego, bound to the blood, had to be conveyed to the physical organization through the blood of the ancient Hebrew people, and this could come about only through the medium of heredity" (*The Gospel of St. Mark* [GSMk], Lect. 8, pp. 150-151). In *The Gospel of St. John* (GOSPSJ), Lect. 4, Steiner says, "In the beginning each human individual did not possess his own Ego. The same Jehovah-force, the Ego-force, the same Ego worked in all who were related by blood, who preserved the same blood through endogamy."

to Moses (Ex 3,6,14) in the long progression from group Ego to individual Ego.[20]

With the increase of exogamy came a decrease of the heritage derived from a remote past. Clairvoyance is associated with the etheric body, and the etheric body derives from the maternal element while the physical derives from the paternal. Inheritance by consanguinity perpetuated itself from etheric body to etheric body, giving clairvoyance and its related wisdom. But as blood became more mixed, the handing down of this ancient wisdom diminished. Human blood became increasingly incapable of bearing the old wisdom but instead became the bearer of egotism. Thus the blood lost its power of uniting humans in love. The blood that flowed from Christ represented the egoism in human nature which had to be sacrificed.

The Hebrew people were chosen to bring to the Ego all that could be given to the natural human being through the blood. Human intellectuality is bound to its physical organization. Other peoples had to allow what comes from without, from initiation, whereas what could come through blood was to be given through the Hebrew people. And this could come only through the medium of heredity. That this physical vessel, the ancient Jewish people, was a gift of God to humanity is indicated by Abraham's willingness to sacrifice his son—whereby his son was received back as a gift of God (Heb 11,19).

We shall see more fully later something of the connection of the human being's body with the cosmos, but for now we note the tabulation in *Man in the Light of Occultism, Theosophy and Philosophy* (MLO), Lect. 9, p. 173, of how human movements are related to the planets as follows:

Movement into upright posture	Saturn
Movement of thinking	Jupiter
Movement of speaking	Mars
Movement of the blood	Sun
Movement of the breath	Mercury
Movement of the glands	Venus
Movement of reproduction	Moon

---

20. This transition was also reflected in the "Forgiven Sins" essay in *The Burning Bush*. There, at p. 101, the passages from Jer 31,27-34 and Ezek 18 are cited as indicative of the growing awareness of individual, for what had in earlier times been group, responsibility.

Christ's descent to Incarnation brought him into the Sun sphere, whence he was seen as the Ahura Mazda, or Great Aura, by Zarathustra in the Ancient Persian era—he from whose instruction came the magi (Mt 2,1). It is thus significant that he who represents the highest "I Am" made his sojourn on the "planet" (the Sun sphere) that inspires the life or movement of the blood.

We have now explored at least a sampling of what comes from the Steiner works listed above. But we have yet to consider the deep connections revealed in *Occult Physiology* (OP), *The World of the Senses and the World of the Spirit* (WSWS) and *The Reappearance of Christ in the Etheric* (RCE). We will now turn our attention in greater detail, out of necessity and thus in spite of their length and involvement, to these. They move progressively to the point from which we can begin to comprehend how Christ's blood is indeed the effective agent of human salvation. Both OP and WSWS involve new and unique perspectives on how human physiology evolved out of, and its relationship to, the spiritual world, and the peculiar and crowning nature of blood in this development. In each of these cycles, a summary of the entire series seems essential to an adequate comprehension of its blood factor. It is noteworthy that both of these cycles were given virtually in the middle (1911) of the period (roughly 1908-1914) in which Steiner gave the bulk of his lectures most directly related to the Bible. He must surely have seen them as inseparable from the others if a deeper understanding of Holy Scripture was to be had. We shall here attempt to honor that astounding vision.

Three Major Steiner Works:

In fn 10 of the "Fire" essay, I indicated that my summary of critical segments of Steiner's *Warmth Course* would lean heavily on the actual text of that lecture cycle, without indicating what was exact quote and what was not. I adopted the same approach in the "Light" essay, and am doing so again for the following three works.

AN OCCULT PHYSIOLOGY (OP)
Eight Lectures at Prague, March 20-28, 1911

1. The Being of Man

This cycle of lectures forms a whole, and no single part of any one lecture should be torn from its context and judged separately.

The human brain and spinal column can be differentiated into what is encased in the skull and the stalk or cord within the spinal canal. The fact that the animals closest to the human being have a brain and spinal cord does not prove that, in their deeper significance, they have the same task in both human and animal.

Goethe and others accurately observed that the brain looks like a transformed spinal cord. Steiner describes the mutations in the bone structures that account for this, so that the skull bones are in a certain respect reshaped vertebrae. Thus, the brain can be imagined as a differentiated spinal cord.

Which of the two, skull or vertebra, is younger? The one that shows the derived form cannot be. Rather it is the one with the original form. The spinal cord is at the original stage and is thus younger. The brain is at the second stage. The forces that built the brain are thus older forces.

When such a reformation of an organ takes place, the question arises whether the evolutionary process is progressive or retrogressive. Which is the case with the present spinal cord? If it is in a regressive stage, then it will not evolve into a brain as the brain did under the guidance of the former forces. Obviously, the former forces were progressive, for the brain actually developed. Observation discloses that the present spinal cord is in a retrogressive stage, for it proceeds downward to a point that indicates a conclusion.

The higher soul activities requiring reflection have the brain as their instrument while the more unconscious activities are directed by the spinal cord. Waking day consciousness is quite different from the chaotic phenomena of dream life, yet clearly both require our brain. In many other places Steiner shows that dream life has changed dramatically over the course of human evolution.[21] Steiner indicates that his esoteric investigation shows that there is, inside the brain, a mysterious spinal cord that

---

21. The farther back one goes, the greater is the degree of true spiritual perception during sleep. During the Atlantean period, there was still great communication between the spiritual world and human beings during their sleep, due to the fact that the etheric body was then still largely outside the physical and joined with the astral body and Ego during sleep; see GSJ, Lect. 8, p. 127 While obviously the change was gradual, post-Atlantean dreams have become progressively less reliable and more chaotic. During Old Testament times, dreams could still be the avenue of communication with the spiritual world, as the scriptures tell us. And significant communications still occurred that way for exalted Individualities during the New Testament period; that this is the meaning of Nicodemus coming *by night* in Jn 3,2, see Jn-Rel, Lect. 10, pp. 195-196, and GSJ, Lect. 5, pp. 90-91, and Lect. 6, p. 95. *(continued on following page)*

is the instrument of the dream life. It reveals what the brain once was, and the fact that we dream indicates that the brain has passed through a spinal cord stage; for the wide awake life of day is related to dream life in the same way that the perfected brain at the second stage of its evolution is related to the ancient spinal cord.

2. Human Duality

The human being comprises a duality. Initially, everything protectively enclosed within the bony structure of the brain and spinal column may be considered as a functional unit as against everything outside of them.

Leaving the brain and spinal column aside, the human being's three most important organ systems are the digestive, lymph and circulatory.

If we start with the circulatory system, we see that the heart is divided into two smaller upper chambers (atria) and two lower ones (ventricles), and that analogously it serves a duality in that its major circulation is to the lower organs and its smaller circulation is to the upper organs including the brain, while in both it carries away from the heart "red" blood and back to it "blue" blood.

The brain is inserted into the upper circulation while three particular organs of the digestive system are inserted into the lower, namely, the spleen, liver and gall bladder. A duality is presented in comparing the functions of the upper and lower in this regard. In the upper there is a working over of impressions received from the outer world. The blood flowing through it is transformed and sent back to the heart in this process. Is this in any way comparable to what occurs in the spleen, liver and

---

21. *(continued from previous page)* But today, dream life is anything but a reliable indicator of truth, and gives a jumbled picture of perceptions that normally relate only in chaotic ways to our waking life. The student who desires to read what Steiner said about the evolution of human dream life may find the following references helpful: for the ancient in contrast to the modern, GSJ, Lects. 3 (pp. 45-46), 8 (p. 127) and 9 (p. 138-139); *The Teachings of Christ the Resurrected* (TCR), Lect. 1, p. 3; and *The Festivals and Their Meaning* (FM), p. 183 (Lect. Apr. 13, 1922); for the Old Testament period, ARCHM, pp. 119-120 (Lect. Nov. 22, 1919) and p. 182 (Nov. 30, 1919); for the modern state, *The Occult Significance of the Bhagavad Gita* (BG), Lect. 3; BBUS, Lect. 1, (pp. 20-27); *The Mystery of the Trinity/The Mission of the Spirit* (MT), pp. 128-129 (Lect. Aug. 30, 1922); and MK, Lect. 6 (pp. 134-135); and for the path to regain a dream-state reflecting spiritual reality, AGSS, Lect. 12 (pp. 108-109), and Novalis, *Hymns to the Night/Spiritual* Songs (HNSS) in its entirety (for the exalted Individuality of Novalis, see *The Burning Bush*, p. 543).

gall bladder in transforming the blood that flows from the lower system back to the heart? Indeed. These three lower organs transform the nutritive substances coming in from the outside world in a manner comparable to how the brain transforms the impressions flowing in through its related senses. Both systems present a transformed outer world to the human organism.

We shall see later that these three lower organs are the compressed microcosmic offspring of three planetary forces within our solar system. Holding this understanding in our minds, it is as though the blood exposes itself like a tablet to the impressions of the outer world in the upper organism and then, in the lower organism, this compressed outer planetary world acts upon the blood from the other side of the tablet. We then have a pictorial scheme of the exterior and interior of the human organism.

Earlier I referred to I-27 showing the order in which the planets separated out from the original mass during the Earth Condition of Consciousness. Ignoring the Sun, which represents the central heart, the order was Saturn, Jupiter, Mars, Moon, Venus and Mercury, the respective orbits shrinking as the Earth mass condensed (if we assign to the Moon its related Earth orbit). Now, if we examine the flow of the blood through the lower circulation we find that it follows the same order in flowing through or engaging the three organs, spleen, liver and gallbladder. Chart I-86 reflects that scheme insofar as these three organs are concerned (though it deals with a different duality insofar as what is taken in through the lungs is counterposed to the three lower organs—we shall get to that later). We shall see more fully under Lects. 4 and 5 below the individual correspondences that esotericism from of old has clairvoyantly assigned between the planetary forces and the human being's seven related organs.

A significant difference exists between what comes into the human organism from the upper circulation and what from the lower. The former relates to the conscious realm and the latter to the subconscious, in that the human being normally perceives the former but not the latter.

For now let us first note in I-14 the following correspondences:[22]

---

22. From a totally different perspective not presently relevant, another profile that excludes both the Ego and the nerve organs is given in I-86.

Physical body and organs working purely mechanically	Physical body
Gland organs	Etheric body
Nerve organs	Astral body
Blood (circulatory) system	Ego

The human being's blood everywhere presses upon its nervous system. And just as the nerve organs thus enter into relationship with the blood system, so do the inner soul facilities of the human's astral body enter into relationship with its Ego. Thus, in the same way that the nerve organs are the instrumentality and manifestation of the astral body, so also is the blood system the instrumentality and manifestation of the Ego.

At this point, we might plead with Steiner to let us rest from our contemplations. But he moves on in order to show us what happens physiologically when a human being is ready to move out into the spiritual world beyond its own Ego. In oversimplification, what happens between such human being's above nerve organ/blood system and astral body/Ego correspondences when steps are taken to move spiritually upward from the Ego stage to the "manna" or Spirit Self stage (see I-9)? I repeat, this is an oversimplification, and thus speaks only physiologically, with respect to what happens along the way when the spiritual path set out in *How to Know Higher Worlds* (HKHW) is tread (cf. Mt 7,14).

To illustrate, Steiner uses the sense of vision. Outer impressions act upon the eye, affecting the optic nerve and thus the astral body. So at the moment when the nerves and the blood interact, the parallel process takes place on the other side of the blood "tablet," and the astral body and the Ego (particularly the Sentient Soul, see I-9) mutually interact. We may use here the metaphor that when the nerve activity comes into contact with the blood the former inscribes itself in the blood, the instrument of the Ego, as on a tablet. The Ego then experiences the outer world as a result, sensing itself as independent thereof.

Next, Steiner points out that if the human being is artificially put in a condition so that the activity of the nerve is severed from the blood circulation, then they no longer act upon one another. This can be brought about when, for instance, a nerve is cut. No impression can be made (unless perhaps by external electric shock) upon the nerve, nor is the human being able to experience anything through the nerve.

But, and this is the point, there is another way of affecting the nerve in such a way that it cannot act upon the blood in this respect. This is done when a person practices the type of rigorous inner concentration discussed in HKHW to the extent that complete control over the nerve is gained, drawing it back from the course of the blood, from all external impressions and from all that the outside world brings about in the Ego. The person then has something in the soul that can have originated only in the consciousness and is the content of consciousness, and that makes a special demand upon the nerve and separates its activity then and there from its connection with the activity of the blood. Consequently whereas the nervous system had previously written its action upon the tablet of the blood, it now permits what it contains within itself as a working force to return into itself, and does not permit it to reach the blood. It is, therefore, possible purely through processes of inner concentration, to separate the blood system from the nervous system, and thereby to cause what, pictorially expressed, would otherwise have flowed into the Ego, to course back again into the nervous system.

One who does this through inward exertion of the soul has an entirely different sort of inner experience. One does not then live in the ordinary Ego nor say "I" in the same sense as before in ordinary consciousness. It is as if one had quite consciously lifted a portion of the real being out of oneself, as if something not ordinarily seen, which is supersensible and works in upon the nerves, now impresses itself neither upon the blood tablet nor upon the ordinary Ego. One feels oneself in another Ego, another self, which before this could at best be merely divined. One feels a supersensible world uplifted within. A world has opened of which the person previously had no intimation, for everything flows back again into the nervous system without going through the blood/Ego connection.

Physiologically, this is the move to the higher being, the Spirit Self (manas or manna) state, insofar as it can be experienced during the Earth Condition of Consciousness.

3. Cooperation in the Human Duality

A person who, through exertion of the soul, is able to experience the inner condition just described has become in a certain sense clairvoyant, feeling as if a higher order of being were towering up in his or her soul life. Thus we may say that the clairvoyant human being learns, through advanced power of observation, to know the spiritual world—that spiritual world with which the human being is indeed connected and which to a certain extent comes to meet one through the nervous system, even though in normal life this occurs by the indirect road of the sense impressions. In ordinary consciousness the human being knows nothing about this spiritual world, but it nevertheless actually inscribes itself upon the tablet of our blood, hence upon our Ego. In other words, we may say that underlying everything surrounding us externally in the world of sense there lies a spiritual world, so that we see as though through a veil woven by the sense impressions. In our normal consciousness, which is compassed by the horizon of our ordinary Ego, we do not see the spiritual world lying behind this veil. However, the moment we free ourselves of the Ego, the ordinary sense impressions disappear also. We then begin to live in a spiritual world above us, that same world that exists in reality behind the sense impressions, and with which we become one when we lift our nervous system out of our ordinary blood system.

We have already said that our Ego-manifesting blood is like a tablet upon which the nerves acting through the upper blood circulation bring us impressions from the outer world while the nerves acting through the lower circulation provide impressions from those outer world forces that are condensed and compressed into the spleen, liver and gallbladder. Steiner illustrated this by showing the blood as a circle with the arrows pointing from the circumference outward as the upper nervous system and arrows pointing from the center to the circumference as the lower. In other words, the arrows were not both pointing at the blood even though both nervous systems made impressions on the blood. The upper system comprises our enclosed brain and spinal cord. The human being's normal consciousness is aware of the impressions from the upper but not from the lower system.

The lower system is called the "sympathetic nervous system." It passes along the spine and spreads out from there into reticular forms, especially in the abdominal cavity, where one part of it goes by the popular name "solar plexus."

What is interesting is that the physiology of the two nervous systems is analogous to Steiner's drawing, i.e., to the antithetical direction of its arrows. For whereas in the case of the sympathetic nervous system the essential thing is that the ganglia of a certain kind are strong and large, while the connecting filaments radiating out from them are relatively small and of little account (in contrast to these ganglia), exactly the reverse is true in the case of the nervous system of the brain and spinal cord. There the connecting threads are the important thing, whereas the ganglia have a subordinate significance.

Our blood is thus in the center, between the outside and inside worlds, and exposes its two sides to be written upon like a tablet, first by one side and then by the other.

Let us now observe something astounding that is nevertheless completely analogous to what is said above. We have seen that the human being is in position to free its nerves, insofar as these lead to the outside world, from their action upon the blood system. We must now ask whether something similar is possible also in the other direction. And we see that it is possible to practice other exercises of soul that can produce in the other direction the same effect as that just described. There is one difference, however. Whereas we are able, through concentration of thought, concentration of feeling, and esoteric exercises, to free the nerves of our brain and spinal cord from the blood, we are able, on the other hand, through concentrations (called the "mystical life") that go right down into our inner life, our inner world, to penetrate so deep within ourselves that in doing so we most certainly do not ignore our Ego, nor therefore its instrument in the blood. This mystical immersion is not primarily a lifting of oneself out of the Ego; it is rather a positive plunging of oneself down into the Ego, a strengthening or energizing of the Ego feeling. The earlier mystics, in contrast to some today, in looking into their own Ego looked away from everything the outside world could offer.

This inward immersion could truly be said to be the "mystic path" and is in direct contrast to the one leading out into the macrocosm. For whereas we loosen by the process previously described the connection between the nerve and the blood, we here strengthen the connection between the blood and the sympathetic nervous system by true mystic immersion.

This is the physiological counterpart—that the blood is here pressed in more than ever against the sympathetic nervous system, whereas when the wish is to reach the spiritual world the other way the blood is pushed away from the nerve.

There is, however, another and ominous difference. For when one frees oneself from the Ego, the Ego is left behind with all its less desirable qualities. But when one immerses oneself in the Ego it is not at all certain, to begin with, that one is not at the same time pressing down all one's undesirable characteristics into this energized Ego. Let us put aside for now the great spiritual dangers imminent where such undesirable Ego traits of the passionate blood are pressed down into the sympathetic nervous system and assume that the mystic has properly prepared the self through preliminary training and exercises.

The Ego in that case is carried by the instrument of the blood down into the mystic's own inner world. It then comes to pass that the inner nervous system, the sympathetic nervous system, about which the human being in normal consciousness knows nothing, presses its way into the Ego consciousness, so that the person begins to know, "I have within me something that can mediate to me the inner world in a way similar to the way the other nervous system mediates the outer world to me."

But in order to be thus "similar," something quite obvious but at the same time amazing, takes place in our realization. For just as in our becoming conscious of the outer world we do not see the nerves, since no one sees the optic nerve, but rather what is to be seen by means of the nerve, the external world that penetrates our consciousness, so also in the case of the mystic immersion it is not, to begin with, the inner nerves that penetrate the consciousness. It is something quite different that appears. It is truly *our own Self as physical being.*

It is not our spleen, liver and gallbladder. To see these would be the equivalent of seeing the optic nerve in exercising our sense observation of the outer world. This does not happen. Similarly, in observing our inner world we do not see the counterparts of the optic nerve, the materialized digestive organs. To see these would be like looking at the outer world rather than the inner, for in this respect they are also outer world. Instead, what the mystic sees is what caused the seers throughout the ages to choose such strange names as those cited in the second lecture, i.e., Saturn, Jupiter and Mars. The mystic is now aware that in reality, to external sight which uses the brain and the spinal cord, these organs appear in maya, in external illusion, because the aspect they offer outwardly does not show them in their inner essential significance. The mystic becomes aware that what is actually seen are portions of the outside world enclosed within the boundaries of his or her inner organs.

In the balance of this lecture Steiner beautifully illustrates how (at least in one way) the spleen came to be seen by seers as the condensed forces of Saturn. He does so by looking at its function. He notes that it is only one of the ways in which the spleen functions and that it is impossible to explain all of them at once. In a prior lecture he had fleetingly character-ized it as a sieve, a function observed by normal external physiology. And he later shows us why it, in contrast to other organs, can be removed without suffering fatal consequence, i.e., without losing the effect of its function. He goes on to give the spiritual reality underlying that one par-ticular externally observable function.

It has to do with *rhythm*. In this function it is a very significant organ. In fact, to the seer it appears as though it is not even existing of fleshly mat-ter but rather a luminous cosmic body with highly complicated inner life. We immediately recognize the importance of rhythm in the regularity of the pulse beat of the blood. But it is interesting to observe how very notice-ably the spleen's externally observable rhythm differs from other rhythms we perceive. It is far less regular than others due to the fact that it lies near the human nutritive apparatus and has something to do with this.

We know how amazingly regular the rhythm of the blood must be if life is to be properly sustained. But there is another rhythm that is regular only to a very slight degree, namely, the rhythm of eating and drinking. One readily recognizes that such irregularity is probably most extreme in our modern way of life. The worst irregularities must be counterbalanced and to accomplish this an organ must be inserted that reconciles the irreg-ularity of the process of nourishment with the necessary regularity of the rhythm of the blood. This organ is the spleen. It is really a transformer given to counterbalance the irregularities in the digestive canal in order that they may become regularities in the circulation of the blood. This it does by means of a "backward thrust," as we may call it. Only as much is to be conducted into the blood as is useful to it. Outwardly, the only thing that shows itself is that the spleen is to a certain extent inflated for hours at a time after a heavy meal is eaten, and that, if another meal does not follow, it contracts again. One is able to conceive how the rhythmic movements (expansions and contractions) of the spleen, although depen-dent of course upon the outside world (the supply of food), radiate throughout the whole organism and have a counterbalancing influence upon it.

Thus we have in the spleen an organ that is dependent from the aspect of the digestive canal on external human will. But from the aspect of the blood, it is an organ that sets aside to a certain extent human choice, rejects it, and leads back to a rhythm in accordance with the person's being. The human being, insofar as it is the carrier of its own bloodstream,

348 DAVID'S QUESTION, "WHAT IS MAN?"

must be set apart, so to speak, within itself, isolated from what proceeds with irregularity in the outside world, that outside world which it incorporates within itself when it takes in nourishment out of it. Hence this is a process of isolation, of making the human being independent of the outside world. Every such individualizing of any being, making it independent, is called in esotericism *saturnine*, something brought about by the Saturn influence. This as a matter of fact is the original idea associated with Saturn—that a being is individualized in such a way that within itself and of itself it can evolve regularity.

Disregarding the outer planets, Pluto, Neptune and Uranus, never visible to the naked eye (see I-17 & I-27), this is precisely what is brought about by Saturn, our most remote planet, in the relationship between our solar system and the surrounding universe. If we visualize the entire solar system, we might say, "The solar system must be so placed that it can follow its own laws within the orbit of encircling Saturn, and can make itself independent by tearing itself loose, as it were, from the surrounding world and from the formative forces of this surrounding world." For this reason esotericists of all the ages have seen in the Saturn forces what secludes our solar system within itself, thus making it possible for the solar system to develop a rhythm of its own that is not the same as the rhythm outside the world of our solar system.

In a certain way the spleen does something similar within our organism. The forces that are in the spleen isolate the circulation of our blood from all outside influences, and make of it a regular rhythm within itself, a system having its own rhythm.

In the esoteric schools the name *Saturn* was applied to anything that excluded a world outside from a system that took on a rhythmic form within itself. There is always a certain disadvantage for cosmic evolution as a whole when one system shuts itself off and regulates itself within itself, fashions a rhythm of its own. And the esotericists have, consequently, been somewhat concerned about this disadvantage. We might say, indeed, that it is quite comprehensible that all activities in the entire universe have a basic inner relation and are mutually related. The complete separation of any one "world," be it a solar system or the blood system of the human being, from the rest of the universe surrounding it this signifies that it quite independently violates external laws, makes itself independent of them, changes itself and creates its own inner laws, its own rhythm. A contradiction is thus created between what surrounds and what is within the being concerned. This contradiction cannot be compensated for, after it has once appeared, until the inner rhythm set up has again adapted itself completely to the outer rhythm. We shall see that this applies also to the human being, for otherwise, according to what has been said, it would be compelled to adapt itself to irregularity. We shall find, however, that such is not the case. The inner rhythm, although it has established itself, must again strive after doing this to fashion itself in accordance with the entire outside world, which means that it must eliminate itself.[23]

To put it in other words, everything that has made itself independent as a result of a saturnine activity is doomed at the same time, because of that activity, to destroy itself again. Saturn, or Kronos (see I-17), devours his own children, so the myth tells us. Here you see a deeply significant harmony between an esoteric idea, expressed in the name *Kronos* or *Saturn*, and a myth which expresses the same thing in a picture, a symbol: "Kronos devours his own children!'"

How beautifully the Greek myth is paralleled by the Bible! For we note how on the "fourth day," i.e., the Earth Condition of Consciousness (see I-1), this shutting off into our solar system is expressed in Gen 1,14-19, while the return to the outer zodiacal influences is expressed in Rev 22,1-5 when the fruits of Earth evolution are seen as twelvefold and there is no longer a need of the Sun (our solar system).

A little later Steiner observes, without explaining, that the names Cain and Abel embody similar mythological truth (Gen 4,1-16). Etymologically, the name Cain is seen as coming from the Hebrew root *qnh* meaning to create or to acquire (see 1 ABD 806), while Abel is seen as perhaps deriving from the Hebrew root *hbl* meaning "breath" (see 1 ABD 9 at 10). More simply Abel might be seen to arrive at the same spiritual source as "breath" if we say "ab = from and el = god."

4. Man's Inner Cosmic System

Before getting into this lecture proper, it would be helpful to more fully elaborate a concept expressed in direct reference to human blood in *The Riddle of Humanity* (RH, Lect. 4, pp. 48-52). In regard to form, we must stress the difference between force and matter. That force exists is not seriously questionable, but while matter can be seen, force cannot.

---

23. Here is the higher meaning of the Crucifixion and of the Prodigal Son parable, Lk 15,11-32.

The physical body is a body of forces that create the "form" (or "phantom"), which cannot be seen until it is filled with matter. We shall look at the creation of matter in the condensation of *The World of the Senses and the World of the Spirit* (WSWS, Lect. 3) later in this essay.

In *The Riddle of Humanity* (pp. 48-52), Steiner discusses what he calls "physical forces." The parts of the physical body that are actually physical cannot even be directly observed. Here "physical" refers to those parts governed by and subject to physical forces. It is terribly easy to deceive oneself in this regard. Anyone who accepts materialistic criteria will say that breathing is a physical process in the human being. A person takes in air and then, as a consequence of the breath, certain processes occur in the blood, and so on, all of these being physical processes. Of course these all are physical processes, but the forces on which the chemical processes of the blood are based come from the *I* (the Ego or "I Am"). It is precisely in the human body that what is really physical is less involved. For example, physical forces are expressed in the human body when a child begins to crawl and then to assume an upright position. This is a kind of victory over gravity. These extraordinary relationships with balance and with the effects of weight are always present, but they are not physically visible. They are what spiritual science refers to as the physical body. They are physical forces to be sure, but they are, essentially, forces that cannot be observed. It is like having a balance on a stand. In the middle is the support (fulcrum). Forces are acting on one side because of the weight that is there. Other forces are working on the other side where another weight is hanging. The strings by which the weights are attached are not identical with the forces at work there. Even though the forces are physical, they are invisible. This is the sense in which parts of the human body can be called physical—for the most part, they are to be thought of as forces.

By way of further distinction, Steiner adds that aside from physical forces there are forces called "etheric" in the etheric sphere which cause mineral matter to be yoked into a living creature (plant, animal or human), "astral" forces in the astral sphere which involve processes in the nerves of a sensate creature, and finally "Ego" forces which are involved in the circulation of the blood. He then illustrates convincingly how morality for example affects (enters) the human being only through the blood by way of the head. The human kingdom, by virtue of its different head or brain, has morality, whereas the animal kingdom does not. One would never think of judging an animal for an immoral act. The blood's action in rushing to the surface to escape from its embodied Ego when one blushes in shame, or fleeing inward to protect such Ego when one pales from outer danger, are observable manifestations of the spiritual reality of the perceiving Ego's presence in the blood. Shame is the result of a moral judgement by the Ego.

We can now return to *An Occult Physiology,* Lect. 4. Steiner notes that an objection can be made about an apparent contradiction between the importance assigned (in Lect. 3) to the spleen and the reality that, contrary to the situation with certain other "vital" organs, a human being can survive when the spleen is removed. No contradiction exists, for this "reality" is compatible with everything previously discussed. In the spleen as an organism a whole array of supersensible forces and organisms are involved. In addition to a physical force, there are the forces of the etheric and astral bodies and the Ego. But we might say of the physical force alone of the spleen that the more any one of the organs is the direct expression of the spiritual, the less is the organ's physical form, i.e., what we have before us as physical substance (matter), the determining factor. Just as we find in looking at a pendulum that its movement is merely the physical expression of gravity, even so is the physical organ merely the physical expression of the supersensible influences working in force and form—except that in the case of forces like that of gravitation, when we remove the pendulum, which is the physical expression, no inner rhythm due to gravitation can continue. This is the case, of course, in inanimate, inorganic nature; but not in the same way in animate, organic nature. When there are no other causes present in the organism as a whole, it is not necessary that the spiritual influences cease with the removal of the physical organ, for this physical organ, in its physical nature, is only a feeble expression of the nature of the corresponding spiritual activities. On this point we shall have more to say later.

Accordingly when we observe the spleen of the human being we have to do in the first place with that organ only, but beyond that with a system of forces working in it that have only their outward expression in the physical spleen. If one removes the spleen, these forces that are integral to the organism still continue to work. Their activities do not cease in the way in which, let us say, certain spiritual activities in the human being cease when one removes the brain or a portion of it. It may even be, under certain circumstances, that a diseased organ may cause a much greater hindrance to the continuation of the spiritual activities than is brought about by the removal of the organ. This is true, for example, in the case of a serious disease of the spleen.

One who follows these things with patience will see that there is no contradiction between what comes forth from spiritual science and what may be presented by external science. The difficulty is that the field of anthroposophical or spiritual science as a whole is so extensive that it is never possible to present more than a part of it.

The spleen's function in transforming rhythm was used for illustration in Lect. 3 because it is the most easily understood of all the spleen's functions. It is not the most important. Its function as a sort of "sieve" has already been mentioned. Also far more important is the fact of its involvement in the nourishment process whereby the body assimilates external substances having a different composition, form and manner of environmental existence than the human body. The biblical student can find this fundamentally expressed in Genesis in the various passages where each supersensible kingdom, with its descending branches, is said to have been created "after its kind" (Gen 1,11,12,21,24,25; also Gen 6,20; 7,14), including those given the human being for "food" (Gen 1,29; 6,21). Articles of food are after all not just bricks serving as building material for the body. Bricks are used as they are, according to their kind, in constructing a building, but the building belongs to the same essential kind as the bricks, namely, it is governed solely by the spiritual laws that regulate the Physical Condition of Form of the Mineral Kingdom (see I-1). This is not true of nutritive matter in relation to the human being. For all particles of substance in the human being's environment have certain inner forces, their own conformity to law (as clearly implied in Genesis). They do not simply consent to being inserted into the human being's inner activity, so to speak, but attempt first to develop their own laws, rhythms and inner forms of movement. To utilize them, the human being's organism must first destroy their rhythmic life, as it were, that vital activity peculiarly their own.

An illustration Steiner often uses in other lectures to combat the popular assumption that "we are what we eat" seems apt here. If these "laws" applicable to other "kinds" were not first destroyed, then one would, like a structure made solely of bricks, become what one is composed of. He says that if these laws are applicable, then a wolf confined from birth and given only lamb to eat would after a time, through its processes of metabolism, become a lamb in its nature.

We must recognize, therefore, that in those inner human organs that first encounter our food we have the instruments with which to oppose, in the first place, what constitutes the peculiar life of the nutritive substances—"life" here conceived in its wider meaning, so that even the apparently lifeless world of nature, with its laws of movement, is included. The life in our food that contradicts the human rhythm must be modified. And in this work of change the organism of the spleen is the outpost. Other organs also participate, so that in spleen, gallbladder and liver we have a cooperating system of organs whose main function is to repel what constitutes the particular inner nature of food received into the organism.

Thus our food is adapted to the inner rhythm of the human organism. Only when so adapted by the activity of these organs do we have in us something capable of being received into the organic system that is the bearer, the instrument, of our Ego. Before any external nutrition can be assimilated into human blood so that the blood becomes capable of serving as the instrument of our Ego, all those forms of law peculiar to the external world must be set aside, and the blood must receive the nutriment in the form that corresponds to the particular nature of the human organism. We may say, therefore, that in the spleen, liver and gallbladder we have organs that, as they react upon the stomach, adapt the laws of the outside world to the inner rhythm of the human being.

But if only these organs served it, the human being would be shut off completely from the outside world—isolated in itself. The human being must also confront the outside world directly with the help of the instrument of its Ego, i.e., its blood.

Whereas from the nutritional direction the blood connects with the external world only by assimilating that part of the outside world from which all forms of law peculiar to it have been cast aside, from the other side it relates with this external world by coming into direct contact with it. This happens when the blood flows through the lungs and comes into contact with the outer air. Thereby, without weakening the form of the air, the oxygen in it actually meets the instrument of the human being's Ego in a condition that conforms with the air's own essential nature and quality of being.

The human being's noblest instrument, its blood, the instrument of its Ego, thus stands between these two systems of organs that take substance in from the outside world. The human being's outer and inner worlds come into direct contact with each other through the blood that takes air from one side and nutrition from the other. One side provides the carbon and the other the oxygen necessary to combust into body heat (fire), and the meeting of the two sides occurs in the heart.

When two such systems collide they may interact harmoniously. If this were so, then there would be inner equilibrium and a passive result. In reality this is not the case in the human being, for a residue of one or the other always remains for its own inner activity, which is left ultimately to the human being itself to bring into balance or inner equilibrium within its organs. The kidney system brings this about within the human being by disposing of the excess resulting from the inharmonious interaction of the two other systems.

We have now arrived at the point in Lect. 4 where the following figures (copied also in I-86) are found, illustrating the correspondences of the respective planetary forces that over evolutionary periods condensed out of

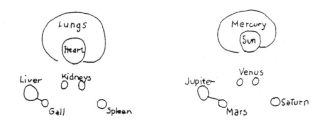

the spiritual world into their human organs—the macrocosm and the microcosm, "As Above, So Below." All seven such forces ("planets") visible to the unaided human eye are included except the Moon, which relates to the reproductive organs not pertinent to this particular analysis. Already above the Saturn/spleen relationship has been shown. The Sun/ heart connection is obvious, the Sun being the heliocentric center of our solar system around which all other planets revolve, just as the heart is the meeting place or center of the human being's outer and inner world organic systems. The planets outside Earth's orbit (Mars, Jupiter and Saturn, in that order) are brought into the human being's "inner cosmic system." Steiner doesn't here elaborate the Jupiter/liver correlation, but it is elsewhere shown. A good, brief discussion is given by Otto Wolff, M.D., in *The Etheric Body* (EB), pp. 9-11. The word "liver" derives from the German *leber* meaning "life" (see also WNWCD). If we look at I-17 and I-27, we see that Jupiter's orbit circumscribed the mass of our solar creation during the Ancient Sun Condition of Consciousness, during which the seed of the human being's etheric (life) body, that component shared with the plant kingdom, was created. Jupiter is the largest planet, and the liver is the human being's largest glandular organ. The Prometheus myth, involving the eagle that each morning comes to eat the liver of the one who brought fire down to Earth expresses exactly this same concept of life. Everyone is aware to some extent of the Mars characteristic (aggressive or warlike), so the Mars/gallbladder likeness is obvious. From the other side, the inner planets, the Mercury/lungs link represents the one closest to the heart and by virtue of the Sun's heat the one involved with the lower density of air, which circulates in and out far more rapidly than the denser nutritional substance, just as Mercury orbits the Sun more rapidly. Finally, inasmuch as Venus is characterized as the goddess of love, or higher harmony, the Venus/kidney tie is clear. If we were to bring in the Moon, its relationship to the more sensual reproductive organs, so often romantically expressed, may be the most widely recognizable of all.

At this point, a particularly astute student might feel that a contradiction is set up between the above planetary correspondences and those illustrated in I-21 for the lotus flowers in the human being. There is no such conflict, but rather than interrupt the flow of thought here, their compatibility will be discussed at the end of this section.

Up to now, we have dealt with how the duality of the inner (nutrition organs) and outer (air organs) worlds are assimilated into the human being's physical body. Both nutrition and air come from the outer world, of course, but they interrelate in the human duality through the blood in producing only a mineral-physical body.

But the human being's Ego as constituted is possible only because it is built up on the foundation of the humanized three bodies, the etheric and astral as well as the physical. We have heretofore dealt with blood primarily as a substance belonging to the physical body. But it does not end there. In this physical aspect, the outer world is contacted through the air, the lung organs. We now come to a different duality, namely, that of the outer world influence as it is taken into the human being through the interworking of the physical and the nonphysical, or in the latter case the etheric and astral bodies.

The human being comes into direct physical contact with the outside world through the air working right into the blood, but it also comes into contact with that world in a nonphysical way through the sense organs and the process of perception unfolded by the soul when it comes into relation with its environment.

The senses too convey their impressions to the tablet of the blood. But how do these two processes, the physical and nonphysical work together?

Though they may not be tangible in the usual sense of the word, perceptions, concepts, feelings, and will impulses, activities of the soul, *exist*. They are a reality, just as are the blood, nerve and organ substance. But as to *how* these things are connected, world conceptions begin to conflict. The very different natures of these two kinds of reality (physical substance and the nonphysical) present people with such difficulties that the most varied answers, offered by the most diverse world conceptions, have come to be associated with them.

There are world conceptions, for instance, that believe in a direct influence upon physical substance of everything connected with the soul, with thought and with feeling, as if thought could work directly upon physical substance. In contrast to these, others assume that thoughts, feelings, and so forth, are simply the products of the processes that take place in physical substance. The dispute between these two world conceptions has long played an important role in the outside world, but not in the field of esotericism, which considers it a dispute over empty words.

Shortly before Steiner's lecture (1911) still another conception had arisen bearing the strange name of "psychophysical parallelism." It seems to still have life.[24] Steiner said then that, to express it rather trivially, we might say that since the disputants no longer had any other resource, not knowing whether spirit works upon the processes of the physical body or whether these bodily processes influence spirit, they concluded that there are two processes running parallel courses. This is a mere expedient, which leads them out of all their difficulties, but only in the sense that it sets these aside, not that it overcomes them. All the disputes result from the fact that people insist upon deciding these questions on a basis that simply cannot be used. If we simply compare these two things, physical and soul activities, and then seek by reflection to find out how each works upon the other, we shall not arrive anywhere. The only way to determine

---

24. See 9 Brit 766, "psychophysical parallelism"; 8 Brit 151-152, "mind-body dualism"; 15 Brit 573-574, "Cartesianism—Later philosophers"; 24 Brit 158, "Mind, The Philosophy of— The mind as immaterial"; and 24 Brit 9, "Metaphysics—The Soul, Mind, and Body—The mind-body relationship."

anything is actually to establish a higher knowledge. We must ascend, on the one hand from the material, and on the other hand from our soul life, to a superphysical (supersensible) world.

The finest element of the human organism is the blood, but it is, externally speaking if we could observe it coursing within the body, merely a physical-sensible thing. We should not confuse this with the fact that it is, along with other bodily organisms, also an impress copy of the etheric body. The first supersensible thing we meet in the human organism is the etheric body. It is only one step away from the physical in the supersensible.[25] And the question now arises, are we able to approach this supersensible also from the other side, from the nonphysical side, the side of the soul life, i.e., sensations, thoughts and feelings based upon impressions of the outside world?

The physical organism cannot be approached directly for substance blocks us. Nor can the ether organism be approached as directly as our soul life. The first event in soul activity is the receipt of external impressions from the outside world working upon our senses. We work these over in our soul, but do more by storing them up in what we call "memory." What happens to cause memory? An impression from direct sensual impression is an entirely different phenomenon from the impression of the same event called up at a later time. When we store up mental pictures in the memory, we are not working with our soul experiences only in our Ego. We must first confront the outside world with our Ego, take impressions from it into our Ego, and work these over in our astral body. But, were we to work them over only in the astral body, we should straightway forget them. When we draw conclusions we are at work in our astral bodies, but when we fix impressions within us so firmly that, after some little time has passed we can again recall them, we have impressed upon our etheric body these impressions received through our Ego and worked over in our astral body.

How does the transfer to the ether body of these impressions taken in through the astral body take place? It takes place through the Ego's activity in the blood. Through the blood the Ego takes in impressions gathered by the astral body from the outside world and condenses them to memory pictures. In this process the blood stirs up the etheric body, so that the true clairvoyant sees currents developing everywhere in the

25. This is reflected in I-9 and I-33, and in many other charts in *The Burning Bush.*

etheric body and taking a very definite course, as if they would join the blood flowing upward from the heart and go up to the head. And in the head these currents come together in about the same way, to use a comparison from the external world, as currents of electricity do when they rush toward a point that is opposed by another point, so as to neutralize the positive and the negative. When we observe with a soul trained in esoteric methods, we see at this point etheric forces compressed as if under a very powerful tension—etheric forces called forth through impressions desiring to become definite concepts, memory pictures, and to stamp themselves upon the etheric body.

Steiner here draws the last out-streamings of these etheric currents, as they flow up toward the brain, and shows their crowding together somewhat as this would actually appear (see his first sketch below). We see here a very powerful tension that concentrates at one point, and announces, "I will now enter the etheric body!" just as when positive and negative electricity are impelled to neutralize each other. We then see how, in opposition to these, other currents flow from that portion of the etheric body that belongs to the rest of the bodily organization. These currents go out for the most part from the lower part of the breast, but also from the lymph vessels and other organs, and come together in such a way that they oppose the other currents. Thus we have in the brain, whenever a memory picture wishes to form itself, two etheric currents, one coming from below and one from above, which oppose each other under the greatest possible tension, just as two electric currents oppose each other.

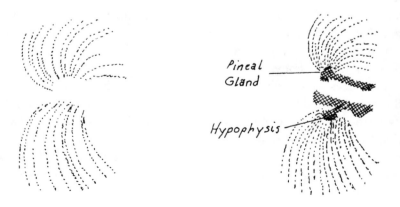

If a balance is brought about between these two currents, then a concept has become a memory picture and has incorporated itself in the etheric body.[26]

Such supersensible currents in the human organism always express themselves by creating also a physical, material organ for themselves, which we must first regard as a materialization. Thus we have within us an organ, situated in the midbrain, that is the physical, material expression for what wishes to take the form of a memory picture, and opposite to this is situated still another organ in the brain. These two organs in the human brain are the physical, material expression of the two currents in the human etheric body. They are, one might say, something like the ultimate indication of the fact that there are such currents in the etheric body. These currents condense with such force that they seize the human bodily substance and consolidate it into these organs. We thus actually get an impression of bright etheric light currents streaming across from one to the other of these organs, and pouring themselves out over the human etheric body. These organs are actually present in the human organism. One of them is the *pineal gland*; the other, the so-called *pituitary body*: the "epiphysis" and the "hypophysis," respectively. We have here, at a definite point in the human physical organism, the external physical expression of the cooperation of soul and body! (See the right sketch above.)

Steiner indicated in 1911 that these two organs are puzzling in the highest degree to physical science, and that we would, therefore, be able to get from external science only inadequate information about them. Still very little is known today about the higher pineal gland. See 9 Brit

---

26. In *Wonders of the World* (WW), Lect. 9, p. 164, Steiner said something that seems also to relate to this difference between the processes of perception and those of memory,

Not only does an etheric current go from the heart to the head, but astral currents are also present in this stream.... Now the brain is a most remarkable instrument.... Owing to the way it has been formed since the last third of the Atlantean epoch, it has acquired one very peculiar quality. It arrests the astrality which rises up ... while it does allow the etheric current to pass.... The brain is permeable for the etheric current, but not for the astral one.... These upward astral currents which are arrested by the brain have a certain power of attraction for the external astral substantialities which are always around us in the astral substance of the Earth. Hence the astral body of man in the region of the head is as though knit together out of two astralities, out of the astrality which continually streams towards us from the cosmos, and the astrality in the human body which comes up from below and is attracted by the outer astrality.

452, "pineal gland" and 18 Brit 326, "Endocrine Systems—The Pineal Gland." In general the same has been true of the pituitary gland, although a relatively greater body of knowledge has come together during the twentieth century on it than on the pineal. See 9 Brit 481, "pituitary gland" and 18 Brit 302, "Endocrine Systems—The Anterior Pituitary."

Before concluding, we return now to the matter mentioned earlier relating to the compatibility of the indicated planetary correspondences with those in I-21.

When we come to discuss the relationship (mentioned in Lect. 2) that esotericism from old has developed between the seven planetary bodies and the human being's organs, certain points should be made.

In these lectures (save for #8), the outer planetary forces (Saturn, Jupiter and Mars) are seen as embedded in the spleen, liver and gallbladder—see I-86. But in I-21 they are seen as embedded in the crown of the head (the pineal, Saturn), forehead (pituitary, Jupiter) and larynx (Mars). It should be noted that in I-21 we are dealing with the direction of spiritualization called the "lotus flowers" (progressive organs—evolution) whereas in I-86 we are dealing with the earthly organs of flesh (retrogressive organs). In OP, Lect. 8, especially at p. 187, Steiner tends to equate the lower retrogressive embodiments of the planetary forces with their counterparts in the development of the higher progressive lotus flowers. According to this, Mars relates to the lower gallbladder and the higher larynx, Jupiter to the lower liver and the higher forehead (or pituitary gland), and Saturn the lower spleen and to the higher crown of the head (or pineal gland).

Steiner here most particularly illustrates the transformation of the Mars forces. The iron elements of the Mars forces relate to the aggressive gall, but also to the larynx, which will become the reproductive organ of the future. In *The Apocalypse of St. John* (ASJ, Lect. 11, p. 189), Steiner graphically portrays the thrust of air from the lungs up through and beyond the larynx, taking the form, whether so intended or not (he does not expressly say so), of the male phallus (but in anatomy the phallus represents both the penis and the clitoris, so that it could symbolize that time when the sexes reunite and spontaneously generate of themselves[27]).

---

27. In *Egyptian Myths and Mysteries* (EMM), Lect. 6, p. 67, Steiner shows how the lungs (relating to air) are female (Isis) while the larynx (relating to iron) is male (Osiris), who, together produced Horus, the future human being. Every person has both, symbolic of the day when they will create through the new word.

This thrust of air represents the time when the reproduction by the human being will be by its "word" in the *image* of its creator (cf. Jn 1,3; Gen 1,26-27). The mouth is thus truly a "sharp sword" (Is 49,2; Rev 1,16; 2,12 and 19,15). The relationship of the iron of Mars to the larynx should help us to perceive a far deeper meaning to the rulership by the redeemed with a "rod of iron"—see Rev 2,27; 12,5 and 19,15.

Not only so, but here again is the illustration of another duality, the activity of the three outer planetary forces (Saturn, Jupiter and Mars; I-86) in the lower human organism being transformed into the higher human organs (I-21, Figure 13). This is what must happen in the transformation of the human being's three bodies into its three higher spiritual states (I-9)—the evolutionary events telescoped so magnificently into the single sentence parable of the three loaves in Mt 13,33. This is the transformation of the three bodies into the festal garments required at the wedding of the bride/bridegroom (see Mt 22,1-14 and Rev 16,15 and 21,2, as well as the essay "Naked" in *The Burning Bush*).

In something of the same way, Mercury, which in I-21 represents the navel or solar plexus region, is shown by Steiner in I-86 as also representing the lung region. He tells us that the metal mercury (quicksilver) has not yet fully attained to its ultimate state. One might so surmise, it being a metal yet in the liquid state. One can see in this immature state the hint of a future relationship between the lungs and the larynx in human reproduction. There is something highly polar about the density of mercury as a metal and the levity of what comes forth as air from the lungs. The planetary forces of Mercury in the human body actually reflect their heavenly position in that these bodily forces (solar plexus and lungs) encircle the heart more closely, both below and above, than any other. This makes the juxtaposition of the "rod of iron" (Mars/larynx) and the "morning star" (Mercury/lungs) in Rev 2,27-28 immensely stirring to the soul, for the "morning star"

Mercury represents the last half of Earth evolution,[28] and the last half of Earth evolution commenced with the Mystery of Golgotha and the dropping of Christ's blood into the Earth. It was with that event that the higher "I Am" could begin to transform the lower Mercury/Mars forces into their higher manna state. Does this not also make Christ's dying refusal of "gall" on the cross (Mt 27,34) highly significant? For he was there initiating what would permit the lower Mars forces to be transformed into the higher.

5. The Systems of Supersensible Forces

It should not be difficult for anyone to believe that forces not visible to the senses can traverse space. We would not get very far, in our day, without the constant application of the invisible forces of electricity and magnetism. They immediately illustrate the point of the reality of invisible forces. Otherwise, one should not for a moment put them in the same category with the creative forces Steiner speaks of in this cycle. Electricity and magnetism are not supersensible forces but are rather subsensible. Electricity, for instance, is the manifestation of the activity of Lucifer (the Devil) while magnetism reflects Ahriman (Satan) (see I-22). That these forces are helpful to us in daily life is not disputed, but so are our arms and legs, which materialized as a result of the Fall of the human being.

A more apt example is fire. The fire that is hot to our touch is the only one of the four elements that comes in contact with the etheric world (force), but in doing so it represents the descending, i.e., materializing, aspect of the duality. Fire was one of humanity's wonderfully helpful discoveries, but it is helpful because it destroys. As one descends further into the subsensible world and comes to electricity, which humanity did not discover until much later, its dual beneficial and malignant aspects become more pronounced. And the same is true of magnetism, which might be seen as the stronger creator of electricity, as in the electromagnetic motor.

---

28. See I-8. Tuesday = Mars Day and Wednesday = Mercury's Day. It is important to note that this "morning star" appears in the message to the angel of the fourth church, the fourth post-Atlantean Cultural Age, the middle one, the Greco-Roman, during which Christ's blood was shed (see I-19 and I-25, as well as pp. 14, 412 and 558 in *The Burning Bush*). Mercury, as well as Venus, is called the "morning star"; see 27 Brit 518 and 524; see also "morning star" under both WNWCD and MWCD.

The modern "observation" of the so-called "black hole" in the universe gives one some concept of the terrifying destructibility of this Satanic principle if it is not indeed "Asuric."[29] Today's wonderful magnetic resonance imaging (MRI) machines nevertheless tend to accomplish Ahrimanically what the human spiritual ear will one day be able to perceive as "the music of the spheres" (Is 6,9-13). Steiner was able to penetrate to this level and beyond to bring back to humanity his gifts of insight such as those in this cycle. Let us, then, use electricity and magnetism only as illustrating the power of the invisible, but attempt to conceive of their supersensible counterparts from the higher etheric and astral worlds, remembering that while there are different levels of etheric force, as I-22 shows, so also are there different levels in the astral force.

In the first paragraph under Lect. 4 above, we discussed the creative triangle of form, force and matter. Steiner points out that the relation between a supersensible system of forces of this sort (e.g., the spleen) and what we see as a physical-sensible organ is such that physical matter, belonging to the physical world fits itself in and, attracted by the force centers, deposits itself within the lines of force. Through the inclusion of physical matter in the supersensible system of forces the organ becomes a physical thing. We may say, therefore, that the reason why, for instance, a physical-sensible organ is visible at the place where the spleen is located is that, at this point, space is filled in a certain definite manner by systems of forces that attract the material substance in such a way that it deposits itself in the form in which we see it in the external organ of the spleen when we study it anatomically.[30]

We should think of the entire human organism as being first planned as supersensible organs, and then, through the most varied sorts of supersensible systems of forces, as being filled with physical matter. The human body is a supersensible organism highly differentiated within itself. We then see not only the assembly of matter in highly varied organ systems, but in regard to the preparation of nutritive substances how each such organism attracts to itself what it needs in the most comprehensive system of nutrition whereby the nutritive substances are absorbed in the greatest variety of ways.

---

29. For the Asuras, see I-22.
30. This seems quite analogous to the lines of force (magnetic field) illustrated when iron filings are scattered over a smooth surface lying on top of a magnet.

Each of the human being's three bodies is thus supersensibly active as a system of forces in first developing and then filling with matter its form so that it becomes sensibly perceptible as we know it. The physical body is directly associated with the assembly of matter. Next to it is the etheric and above that the astral. But it doesn't stop there, for once the three bodies are fully and adequately prepared, the highest of the four forces enters, namely, the Ego forces.

The evolutionary allegiance of any given organ to these different formative forces varies. There are certain organs we have to recognize as being determined principally through the system of forces of the etheric body. Others are determined through the currents or forces coming from the astral body, while others again are to a greater degree determined through the currents of the Ego.

As a result of all that has thus far been presented, one may say that especially that system of organs conveying our blood is essentially dependent upon the radiations going forth from our Ego, and that the human blood, therefore, is connected essentially with the currents and radiations of the human Ego. The other organ systems, with what they contain, are determined in the greatest variety of ways by the supersensible members of the human being's nature.

While all the higher forces work upon the lower ones in regard to virtually every component of the physical body, the process also works in reverse. In other words, the physical organism with its physical system of forces works back upon the etheric, astral and Ego systems. Thus, some of our organic systems are specially requisitioned by the physical system of forces, in which cases it is the physical system of forces that prevails. These are more especially the organ systems that serve in a very comprehensive sense as *organs of secretion and excretion*. Secretion and excretion are processes that have their essential significance purely in the physical world. When this type of organ is diseased or is removed, the organism can no longer continue its normal development or function, as it can when the spleen, for instance, is removed. By way of example, in contrast to the spleen, the thyroid gland performs a physical function absolutely essential to the general economy of the human organism, so its removal (or affliction by disease) may have a very injurious physical effect.

Other organs, such as the liver and kidneys are highly dependent upon the higher supersensible forces, but are nonetheless closely bound to the physical organism and are induced through its forces to secrete physical matter. It is thus of far greater importance for them to be in a healthy condition as physical organs than, for example, the spleen, which is a very spiritual organ in which the physical part is its least significant part.

Having arrived at the concept of the complete human organ, we must now address the question of the full significance of the excretory process in the human being. Immediately after posing this, Steiner insists that without such concepts it will be impossible for us to get any further with our study of the human organism.

To arrive at an answer we must first consider another concept, namely, the becoming aware of our Self. Steiner illustrates this by the example of walking through a room and stumbling against some external object. The impact becomes an inner occurrence through the consciousness of pain—a process (the feeling of pain) that occurs entirely within yourself. The inner process is called forth by the fact that you come into contact with a foreign object which constitutes a hindrance. It is the becoming aware of this hindrance that calls forth the inner process that, in the moment of collision, makes itself known as pain. The inner experience is the effect of the outer object.

Steiner couldn't speak meaningfully of automobiles in 1911. But let us also picture ourselves sitting in a car on a calm and balmy day, windless and seventy degrees Fahrenheit. If we stick our hand out the window, we hardly gain any sensual consciousness that our hand is in any way distinct or differentiated from the ocean of atmosphere surrounding it. If we then commence to drive at a high rate of speed and again stick our hand out the window, we immediately become conscious of it by reason of the hindrance of the air, all the more so to the extent that the temperature varies from its prior comfort zone.

From this you can see that we become aware of our inner being in the *sensing of resistance*. This is the concept we must have—of becoming aware of the consciousness of inner life, being filled with real inner experiences, through the sensing of a resistance. We can then make the transition to another concept—that of the *excretions* in the human organism. Let us suppose that the human organism takes into itself in some way or other, into one of its organ systems, a certain kind of physical substance, and that this organ system is so regulated that through its own activity it eliminates something from the substance taken in, separates it from the substance as a whole, so that through the activity of this organ system the original complete substance falls apart into a finer, filtered portion and a coarser portion, which is excreted. Thus a differentiating of the substance taken in begins, into a substance that is further useful, which can be received by other organs, and another that is first separated and then excreted. The unusable portions of the physical substance are thrust away in contrast with the usable portions, and we have a collision like that of one's running into some outer object.

The stream of physical matter as a whole, when it comes into an organ, runs against a resistance as it were. It cannot remain as it is. It must change itself. It is told by the organ, as we might say, "You cannot remain as you are. You must transform yourself." Let us suppose that such a substance goes into the liver. There it is told, "You must change yourself." A resistance is set up against it. To be further used it must become a different substance, and it must cast off certain portions. Thus it happens in our organism that resistance is perceived. Such resistances are perceived within the most diverse organs. It is only because *secretion* takes place at all in our organism, only because we have organs of secretion, that it is possible for our organism to be secluded within itself, to be a self-experiencing being. For only so can any being become conscious of its own inner life, through the fact that its own life meets with *resistance*. Thus we have in the processes of secretion processes important for human life— processes, in other words, by which the living organism secludes itself within itself. We would not be a being secluded within ourselves if such processes of secretion did not take place.

If air, water or food passed through us as though in a tube or hose, getting no resistance, we would have no consciousness of self as distinct from our surroundings—the situation that existed before the human being descended into material existence. What makes it possible to realize the inner life of the human organism are the processes of *secretion*.

Now let us look at the blood as one of the human organ systems. If it were to go through the human Ego unchanged, it could not be the instrument of the human Ego, what in the very highest sense enables us to be conscious of our own inner life. Only because the blood undergoes changes in its own inner life, and then goes back as something different— in other words, only because something is excreted from the changed blood—is it possible for us not only to *have an Ego*, but to *experience it inwardly* with the help of a physical-sensible instrument.

With the concept of excretion and its function in mind, Steiner then moves to the outermost boundary of our organism, its periphery, in order to carry the concept of self-awareness or self-enclosure to our outer extremity. It is necessary, confronting all the streams of our organism, that there should be one organ connected with this most extensive of all the processes of excretion—the skin. For it presents most directly to the view what we call essential in the *human form*. When we picture to ourselves that our organism can be inwardly conscious of its own life at its outermost periphery only because it has placed the organ of the skin where it confronts all its various streams, we are obliged to see the peculiar formation of our skin as an expression of the innermost force of our organism.

While Steiner does not mention it, there would seem to be in the phenomenon of perspiration an example of the evolutionary development of the earthbound Ego or self-consciousness (9 Brit 313, "perspiration"). While sweat glands are found in the majority of mammals (and apparently not in any lower animals), they constitute the primary means of heat dissipation only in certain hoofed animals and in primates, including humans. The nearer to the human being the animals got in their supersensible-world evolution before descending into materiality, the more they developed this essential tool of self-consciousness, sweat glands. Any dog owner in hot climates should know that a dog can suffer more from heat than a human if its panting is inadequate, because it loses little or no heat through perspiration. The ape is nearer to the human than the horse, but esotericism tells us that it was at the stage when the horse descended that the human, still in the spiritual world, gained by virtue of the horse's loss the possibility for intelligence—thus the human being's affinity for the horse even today. So the horse is about as low as significant perspiration occurs in the animal kingdom.

But in the fashioning of all of our organs of self-consciousness including the most visible, our skin, our own directly voluntary action is completely excluded. One can change the facial expression and, over time, have a certain influence within narrow limits upon the outer form of one's body through one's inner life between birth and death. But the most essential share in the forming of our body is not entrusted to our volition with the help of what reaches us through our consciousness. In this regard, Steiner compares the human being to a machine.

A machine is to be used for some intelligent activity, some activity that has a purpose. In order, however, for the machine to come into existence, it is necessary that activities be carried out which assemble the parts of the machine and give form to the whole. These activities must be similar to those later carried on by the machine itself. We must say, therefore, that when we observe a machine it is wholly and absolutely explicable on mechanical principles. But the fact that the machine is adapted to its purpose requires us to suppose that it came into existence through the activity of a mind which had thought out that purpose beforehand. This spiritual activity has withdrawn, to be sure, and does not need to be brought forward when we wish to explain the machine scientifically. Yet it is there, behind the machine, and first produced it.

So likewise can we say that, for the developing of our capacities and powers as human beings, we need above all those systems of forms lying within the molding of our organism. There must be behind this human form, however, forces that do the forming, which we can as little find in the already fashioned form as we find the builder of the machine in the machine itself. The human physical organism is, indeed, absolutely and entirely explainable out of its own physical laws, just as is the watch. Yet it does not follow from the fact that the watch can be explained by its own laws that the inventor was not behind it.

Therefore, when we think from the point of view of spiritual science, we have first to seek behind the form of the human being as a whole for the form-creative beings.

These beings are those of the hierarchies (see I-6), the Spirits of Will, Wisdom, Motion and Form, and their lower agencies (I-7). We may skip over Steiner's brief illustration of the activity of the Spirits of Form and Movement (Motion), which he concludes by stating the obvious, namely, that the activity of these spirits is not within the range of our normal consciousness. He poses the question, why is it not?

Our brain and spinal cord convey external impressions to the blood, thus inscribing them upon the instrument of the Ego so that the outer impressions are transferred to it. On the other side, the sympathetic nervous system stands guard over the inner cosmic system to keep its processes from approaching as far as the blood. The biblical version describing the hiding of cosmic processes is well stated in the recognition by the Elohim that the Cherubim and the "flaming sword" were positioned between the human being and "the garden" of paradise "to guard the way to the tree of life" (Gen 3,24). The connecting blood then makes its first appearance in the next chapter, Gen 4,10.

In Lect. 4 the contrast between the inner life and the outer is expressed in tensions that finally come to a climax, as we saw, in those organs of the brain called the pineal gland and the pituitary body. Everything that beats in upon us from outside, in order to stand in the closest possible contact with the circulation of the blood, strives to unite with its counterpart, with what is held back by the sympathetic nervous system. For this reason we have in the pineal gland the place where what has been brought to the blood by the brain and spinal cord unites with what approaches from the other direction; and the pituitary body is there as a last outpost to prevent the approach of what has to do with the life of the inner person. Everything that we live through in our inner organization remains *below* our consciousness and would be terribly disturbing if it were otherwise. It is kept back from our consciousness by the sympathetic nervous system. Only when this reciprocal relationship between the two nervous systems, as expressed in the state of tension between the pineal gland and the pituitary body, is not in order does something result that disturbs us on one side or the other. This takes place when some irregularity in the activity of our digestive organs expresses itself in our consciousness in feelings of discomfort. Or it takes place when we have a breaking through from the other direction into the organism, in special emotions such as anger and the like, which originate in our consciousness and have a particularly strong influence on us. It is thus possible for these two sides of human nature to act reciprocally upon each other, the human creature being the duality that it is.

6. The Blood as Manifestation and Instrument of the Human Ego

In all the preceding we see that the blood system is the instrument of the Ego through which it can and does work. From this we must conclude that the whole organization must be active by means of the blood as far as the skin. Moreover, we can find that everything present as a tendency in the force systems of the entire organism is present in the skin itself. The entire organism is a human being because it harbors within itself an Ego that creates, through the instrumentality of its blood, an expression of itself throughout, even to and into its outer boundary. Thus the circulatory, nerve, organ (sweat glands) and nutritional (secretion) systems are all present all the way out to and within the skin.

The blood system is the most immediate instrument of the Ego, but is possible only if all the other systems exist first. The whole human organism must first be built up before the blood as the Ego instrument can come into existence. The animal appears in some ways to be similar, but is not so, for all of the human being's systems have to be built up in precisely their form, manner, structure and function in order to receive the blood that can be the instrument for an indwelling earthly Ego. All the forces must have done their necessary work beforehand in order that the blood system can hold exactly to the form it now takes to be an expression of the Ego. The blood is the most easily controlled element in the human body and has the least stability in itself, pouring out when not fully enclosed, so that, beginning with the nutritive processes, there have to be present in the human organism all the laws that lead ultimately to the formation of the course of the blood, the circulatory system. A human's blood is more determined than any other system by the experiences of the conscious Ego. Thus it blushes from shame or pales from fear or anxiety, rushing outward to hide inner being or rushing inward to flee danger.

The deeper we penetrate into the organ systems, the less they follow our Ego in this way—ultimately to the bones themselves, over which the Ego has almost no power during the earthly life. Thus, the blood, which is most instantly and constantly affected by the Ego's presence, and the bones, which reach their final form with the second dentition and are thereafter beyond the Ego's formative power, merely growing or decaying by virtue of forces already set in motion, represent two extremes in the human organization. The blood is the youngest and the bones the oldest force system in the human being's organization. The structure of a given person's bones, absolutely essential to give the rest of his or her organization its form, must thus be seen as having been formed by the Ego prior to its incarnation. A human being's skeleton, particularly the configuration of its skull which is largely established before its birth, is tangible proof of reincarnation. When one finds a shell, it is proof that something once lived in it. From all that has been said earlier, we know that the shell of an animal is not proof that its Ego lived in it on Earth inasmuch as its group Ego dwells in the astral plane and so does not die with the death of its various animal parts (see I-11). But likewise, from all that has been said, a human skull shows that it was once occupied by a human being who also did not form it during the life it accommodated.

While the foregoing fairly summarizes, I believe, the substance of Lect. 6, let us pause momentarily to consider how, taking into account all that went before, it is reflected in the short passage in Mt 15,10-20, epitomized in its verse 11, "Not what goes into the mouth defiles a man, but what comes out of the mouth, this defiles a man."

We take first the first half, the ingestion as not defiling. We are baffled by the phenomenon that dumb animals know what to eat and what not to eat from the moment of their birth. No animal will eat a poisonous plant, but the human being must be told or else learn from experience what to eat or not to eat. Nor will an animal eat more than it needs, contrary to the vast majority of humans who are given the option of doing so. Thus, the animal is given instinctive knowledge (see 6 Brit 332, "instinct," and 14 Brit 627, "Behaviour, Animal"). Animal instincts have always been a puzzle to us, but anthroposophy shows why they are as they are. The animal's Ego, dwelling in the astral world (I-11), is not limited in earthly knowledge, is not "veiled in flesh," as is the incarnated human Ego.

How is it then that the indwelling human Ego can keep something that goes into it from defiling it? As with all scripture, this passage can have many levels of true meaning.

At the lower level, it can be true that an exalted Ego has more power over the immediate effect of food than a more "normal" person would have. To some extent we see this reflected in the analogous powers in Mk 16,17-18, "And these signs will accompany those who believe: … if they drink any deadly thing, it will not hurt them.…" From this we may reasonably infer, as is indeed in keeping with all the foregoing, that the individual human organism, but most especially its blood, is so built up or constructed by the Ego that only diseases, germs and the like that it sees as befitting its purposes will affect it. One individual will be grievously affected, another but little, and another none at all by ingesting or inhaling certain noxious elements.

At a higher level, one can see that what one ingests or inhales in a given lifetime is done for a purpose, and is handled by the body in keeping with that purpose, so that one will be sick or not according to that purpose. The purpose is tied in with a much longer range goal than that of a single lifetime and is associated with what needs to be learned or experienced in the lifetime. In general, the ingesting thus has only a beneficial consequence to the Ego or entelechy in the long multilived process of its perfection (Mt 5,48). Consequently it does not "defile" but has the tendency toward eventual purification. It comes within the healing consequences of sin, namely, the "pain, toil and death" consequences first introduced in Genesis 3.

If we then take the latter half of Mt 15,11, that what comes out of the mouth defiles, we can also deal with it at different levels, corresponding with the present incarnation or a later one. It is fairly apparent how the character of a person is adversely affected or "defiled" by its words. But beyond character, the soul aspect can be visibly affected in both a short- or long-range manner within the person's lifetime. One does not need to believe in karma and reincarnation to accept this, and indeed this and its consequential effect at a later "judgment" would seem to constitute substantially all of the defilement. On the other hand, the higher meaning, which goes along with the reality of karma and reincarnation, shows us that the words that come out of one's mouth etch themselves into what is carried over into the formation of one's person in subsequent lives, so that in a most direct way there is deep and grievous defilement by each and every unworthy thing that comes from the mouth. When one considers that the organs of speech are in the ascendancy and will one day become the human organs of reproduction, then the progress of the personality in the purification of this organism can be seen as bearing directly upon the eventual salvation of the Individuality.[31] It is this that is most deeply indicated by the brother of Jesus, "And the tongue is a fire. The tongue is an unrighteous world among our members, staining the whole body, setting on fire the *wheel of birth*" (Jas 3,1-12, esp. vs 6; emphasis mine, RSV footnote).

7. The Conscious Life of the Human Being

This lecture presents a dizzying array of dualities, or polar opposites. Most all that have previously been suggested are included along with many others. Together they form a pyramidal base, so to speak, from which Steiner works upward to a summit. That summit is the blood.

The blood embodies within its own nature all of the dualities. It serves as the meeting point for their larger counterparts that work inward from opposite directions within the human organism. And that organism itself reflects the same duality for it represents the embodied meeting place of the sensible and supersensible worlds.

The lecture culminates by illustrating that only in knowing these

---

31. Normal anthroposophical meaning is used here; thus, the "Individuality" is the eternal soul, the "burning bush" that is not consumed, the Ego or "I Am," while the "personality" is its embodiment during the course of a given incarnation. See *The Burning Bush*, esp. pp. 9 and 130.

things can therapeutic treatment be administered to address a disease-causing imbalance somewhere in this maze.

For example, as Steiner points out, one of the most common and serious human ailments is hypertension (high blood pressure), for which doctors almost universally recommend reduction of salt intake. No simple explanation is given for why salt must be reduced in these cases, nor can any be given that is applicable in all cases. However, he does show certain phenomena that would seem to bear on the matter, but in ways that vary widely from person to person.

Let us start with a simple observation. Suppose we add salt to plain tap water that is sufficiently warm to permit full dissolution. By then allowing the water to cool, we note that the salt crystallizes. We may thus say that the cooling process is salt producing, in this sense.

He then looks at the three human activities, thinking, feeling and willing (related to the human nervous, circulatory and metabolic systems). Pure thinking (independent of the senses, as in mathematics) is a cold process, feeling is intermediate, and willing (which includes the limbs) is hot. Blood is fairly high in saline solution. Thus, pure thinking, a cold process, is a salt-producing process, meaning that there is crystallization and thus less salt in the blood solution. Steiner points out that sleep, so essential to one's daytime consciousness (which, as the polar opposite, can be maintained only so long without sleep), dissolves again the crystals. But we must surmise that willing (e.g., exercise), a hot process, also dissolves the salt crystals. And presumably excess crystallization is periodically carried off in the excretory system (sweat or other eliminative processes) so that under certain circumstances salt intake must even be increased to maintain balance in the blood. Whether one must increase or reduce salt intake must surely thus depend upon the interaction of these factors.

But what is also fascinating is how the salt-producing process of pure thinking is the balancing polarity with our bony skeletal system. For as previously explained, our Ego (I Am), which finds its home in our blood, has less effect upon our bones than upon any other part of our body. Our Ego represents pure consciousness, and thinking is life's most conscious activity. But this thinking produces salt deposits, essentially the same thing as our bones. Steiner points out that our bones consist of phosphate of lime and calcium carbonate, that is, salt-deposits.

But our fascination is not yet complete at this point. For what we then notice is that it is the contrast (the duality/polarity) of the Ego's activity *during earthly life* on the one hand (i.e., the consciousness of pure brain thinking) that produces salt deposits, while it is the Ego's activity *between lives* on the other hand that builds up the bony system, composed largely of salt-deposits, over which the earthly Ego has very little control. Consequently, as Steiner asserted in Lect. 6, the human skeleton, particularly the configuration of the skull (the thinking arena) is proof of reincarnation, of the activity of the Ego consciousness before birth corresponding to the supreme exercise of that Ego consciousness (in pure thinking) during earthly life.[32]

---

32. The last two paragraphs of the text suggest that Lot's wife died as the "two men" had foretold (Gen 19,15-25) and that the "pillar of *salt*" was her skeleton (vs 26). Ancient prophets usually spoke metaphorically, as with "branch" (Is 4,2; 11,1; Jer 23,5; 33,15; Dan 11,7; Zech 3,8; 6,12), "root" (Prov 12,3,12; Is 11,10; Rom 15,12; Rev 5,5; 22,16) or "worm" (Job 17,14; 25,6; Is 41,14; 66,24; Mk 9,44,46,48; also fn 36 in the Creation essay).

So it seems with *salt*, not only here but in other passages where deeper spiritual meaning results. Plato spoke of it as "a substance dear to the Gods" (*Timaeus*, 60e, 7 GB 462). The medieval alchemists, searching only for spiritual truth, sought the deeper meaning of *salt, mercury* and *sulfur*. For them, sulfur was metaphorical fire, and so it was also for the Bible writers who used it only in conjunction with fire; see Lk 17,29; Rev 9,17-18; 14,10; 19,20; 20,10; 21,8. Just as they and the biblical writers saw the double meaning of "fire," so also with "salt." Examples of the deeper meaning can be seen in the phrase "covenant of salt" (Num 18,19; 2 Ch 13,5; cf. Lev 2,13) and in Mark's metaphorically cryptic description of the astral world (see I-33) which has been translated as "hell" (Mk 9,48-50, emphasis mine):

[48] "where their *worm* does not die, and the *fire* is not quenched. [49] For every one will be *salted with fire*. [50] *Salt* is good; but if the *salt* has lost its saltness, how will you season it? Have *salt* in yourselves, and be at peace with one another."

Both Steiner and René Schwaller de Lubicz indicate that the *salt* in the more popular Matthean beatitude ("You are the salt of the earth ..."; Mt 5,13; see also Lk 14,34-35) is the same as the *salt* in the medieval triadic contemplation *salt, mercury* and *sulfur*; see Steiner's JTC, Lect. 8, p. 144 and *Rosicrucian Christianity* (ROSC), Lect. 2; also Schwaller's *The Temple of Man* (TOMN), Chap. 1, pp. 34-36; Chap. 34, p. 745, fn 10; Chap. 36, p. 769; *Nature Word* (NW), p. 139; *Sacred Science* (SAC), Chap. 3, p. 74; Chap. 9, pp. 210-211; and VandenBroeck's quotes from him in *Al-Kemi* (AL-KEMI), Chaps. 7 and 9. From all of these we see the dual esoteric meaning of *salt*, or *"fixed salt"* as Schwaller often calls it. Both meanings relate to "form," its lower aspect representing the processes by which earthly creatures return to the mineral state, and the higher representing what is being created as form for a later incarnation. Christ spoke metaphorically of the higher meaning, the "treasures laid up in heaven"(Mt 6,19-20; Lk 12,16-21,33-34) or the "talents" (Mt 13,12; 25,14-30; Mk 4,25; Lk 8,18; 19,12-28). Must one not also contemplate dual meaning where Elisha, in the highly metaphorical second chapter of Second Kings, remedies the "bad" water of Jericho by throwing *salt* in it so that "neither death nor miscarriage shall come from it" (2 K 2,19-22)?

Salt in its higher meaning surely relates to the imperishable "burning bush," the "I Am, the undying Cain and Job in every human being (Ex 3,2-6,14; Gen 4,12-16; Job 2,6), the true "covenant of salt."

8. The Human Form and Its Coordination of Forces

This lecture seems to be primarily one of pulling together what has been said before. For that reason, it will not be further dealt with here.

THE WORLD OF THE SENSES
AND THE WORLD OF THE SPIRIT (WSWS)

Six Lectures at Hanover, December 27, 1911, through January 1, 1912

The information that is crucial for our purposes in the first four and one half lectures of this cycle is abbreviated succinctly below. In spite of its brevity, the student who has considered carefully what has gone before will be able to gather much from contemplating these abstracts. They lay the basis for what follows starting midway through Lect. 5, the subject of blood, which is given in its entirety.

1. Four Essential Moods of Soul

Four moods of soul are essential if one is to progress on the path to clairvoyance:

(a) Wonder

(b) Veneration/reverence

(c) Feeling oneself in wisdom-filled harmony with the laws of the world

(d) Devotion/self-surrender

2. Human Thinking Contrasted with Divine Thinking[33]

Contrast human thinking with divine thinking. When divine thinking thinks correctly, something happens. When it thinks falsely, something is destroyed—annihilated. What follows when this correct thinking is combined with will is Creative Word (Jn 1,1). But when this thinking is incorrect, there is destruction. Consider what happened to the spiritual light of Lucifer as a result of his falsity.[34] Carry these thoughts over into Lects. 3 and 4, especially 4.

---

33. Is 55,8-9: [8] "For my thoughts are not your thoughts, neither are your ways my ways, says the Lord. [9] For as the heavens are higher than the earth, so are my ways higher than your ways and my thoughts than your thoughts." See also 1 Cor 1,18-25.

3. Four Imbalances in the Human Being

Four imbalances in the human being resulting from Luciferic influence are:

(a) Preponderance of physical body over etheric body (the sense world)

(b) Preponderance of etheric body over astral body (the whole feeling of the body)

(c) Preponderance of astral body over etheric body (normal bodily organic processes)

(d) Preponderance of Ego over astral body

Lucifer and Ahriman meet at (b). The order of occurrence in the evolution of the human being is reversed from above; thus (d) came first.

4. The Fourfold Similarity

The fourfold content of soul life is like an expansion/contraction in the succession of the four reigning spirits of the four Conditions of Consciousness, thus:

<Will><Wisdom><Movement><Form
(see **I-1, I-6** & **I-16**)

Steiner sketched them imaginatively as follows (a = shrunk; b = expanded; c = content of soul life):

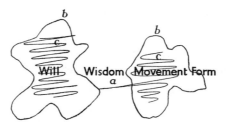

---

34. Lucifer (thought and) spoke falsely in Gen 3,4, "But the serpent said to the woman, 'You will not die.'" As a consequence, in Gen 3,14, "The Lord God said to the serpent, 'Because you have done this, cursed are you ... upon your belly you shall go, and dust you shall eat all the days of your life.'" The name Lucifer means, literally, "light-bearer" (from the Latin, *Lux* = light, and *ferre* = to bear). The woman is the feminine element in each of us that aspires to the higher realm (the light), but because of the Fall that light is clothed in (obscured by) matter (metaphorically, it must crawl in the body of dust that dies).

Form is the outer boundary of movement. Space is created from shattered form. Matter is created from shattered spirit. When form is shattered, space is created but so also is the virginal creation of mineral matter (physical). When movement is shattered it creates plant matter (etheric). The shattering of wisdom creates animal matter (astral). And finally, it would seem to follow, the shattering of will creates the human Ego. The following tabulation results:

Spirits of Form	Imagination	Bones
Spirits of Movement	Inspiration	Muscles
Spirits of Wisdom	Intuition	Nerves

5. Summary Leading to Blood

The following tabulation is developed:

Bones	=	materialized Imagination
Muscles	=	materialized Inspiration
Nerves	=	materialized Intuition

But the human being is a duality as follows:

Senses	vs.	Nerves
Glands	vs.	Muscles
Digestion	vs.	Bones

and the first column is transitory, like a wheel going round and round, with nothing lasting or eternal in it, while the second column represents the three human elements that must be transformed and correspond with the three soul-healing sentences given in Gen 3,16-19, having to do with pain, toil and death.

What follows, almost verbatim, is Steiner's discussion of blood as the special substance that lies between the two "beings" of the human being, the above duality.

And now, in between the two "beings," mediating, as it were, between them, stands the blood—which is in this connection also a "special fluid."[35] For as we have seen, all that we have learned to know as nerve

---

35. As noted earlier, in Goethe's *Faust* Mephistopheles requires Faust to sign their agreement with his blood, saying "Blood is a very special fluid" (see I-32).

substance has only become so in those particular workings of force that were due to the action of the Luciferic influence. But in blood we have something that has directly undergone, as substance itself, the Luciferic influence. You will remember we saw how the manner in which physical body, etheric body and astral body work into one another would be different had it not been for the Luciferic influence. But there we have to do in a certain respect with supersensible things which only afterward take up matter into themselves—which work upon matter with the Luciferic influence they had themselves first undergone, and make it what it is. The substance of nerve and muscle and bone owes its existence to the fact that certain bodies of the human being are irregularly put together. Lucifer has no influence upon the substances as such, for these arise as the result of what he has previously done. They are there because he has already displaced, disarranged, the bodies. Where Lucifer approached the human being he brought about a disarrangement between the bodies (see Lect. 3 above). But he works directly upon the blood—upon the blood as matter, as substance. Blood is the one case—and therefore a "special fluid"— where in the material substance itself we have evidence that the present human being is not as it was really intended to be, is not as it would have been but for the Luciferic influence. For blood has become something quite different from what it should have been.

This may seem a rather grotesque idea but it is true. Recall what was said in Lect. 4 about the origin of matter. We said that matter arises when spiritual form comes to a kind of boundary or limit and there breaks and scatters. This pulverized form then shows itself as matter. That is the actual earthly matter. It really occurs directly in this way only in the mineral world, for the other worlds (plant, animal and human) are taken hold of and changed by other things that intervene. The substance of blood as such, however, is a unique substance.

Blood substance was originally also destined to come first of all to a certain limit. Suppose you have here (a in Diagram 7) purely form-rays of the blood substance, and here (b in Diagram 7) its force is exhausted. Now according to the tendencies originally inherent in it, blood substance was not meant to be dispersed and sprayed into space; instead here at the boundary (b) it was to become just very slightly material and then spray back into itself, spray directly back again into the spiritual. That is how the blood ought to have been. To put it rather crudely, blood ought to have come only so far as to form, as it were, a skin of substance, fine and slight; it ought to have come only to the point of beginning to be material.[36]

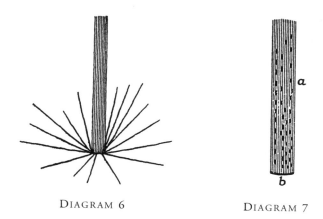

DIAGRAM 6   DIAGRAM 7

It should be forever shooting out of the spiritual for a moment, becoming matter just to the extent of being materially perceptible, then again shooting back into the spiritual and being received up again into it. A perpetual surging forth from the spiritual and shooting back into it again—that is what blood should have been. Its inherent tendencies are directed to this end. Blood was designed to be a perpetual flashing up of light in the material. It was really intended to be something entirely spiritual. And it would have been so if human beings had at the beginning of Earth evolution received their Ego from the Spirits of Form (the Elohim) alone, for then they would experience their Ego through the resistance created by the momentary lighting up in the blood. In the lighting up in the blood the human being would experience the "I Am"; it would be the organ for the human being's Ego perception. That would, however, be the one and only sense perception which human beings would have. The other eleven senses [see I-20] would not be there if everything had happened without the Luciferic influence. The human being would have lived in union together with the ruling Will.

The single sense perception that was designed for humanity was this—to perceive its Ego in the flash of blood substance and in the immediate rush back into the spiritual. Instead of beholding colors and hearing tones and perceiving tastes the human being ought really to live within

---

36. Recall what was said about the upper boundary of the fire ether in the "Fire" essay.

the ruling Will. It ought, as it were, to be swimming in it. What was designed for the human was that it would be placed as a pure Imagination, Inspiration and Intuition into the spiritual World-All, whence it would gaze down upon a being on the Earth or in the environs of the Earth. It would not feel, "I am in that being," but rather, "It belongs to me—the spiritual blood becomes for one moment material, and in what flashes up to me I perceive my I." The one and only sense perception that should have come is the perception of the I or Ego, and the one and only substance that was intended for humanity in the material world is the blood in this form of momentary flashing up. If the human had become like this, if the human had remained the "being" of paradise, it would look down from the World-All upon what was destined to symbolize it on this Earth and to give to it the consciousness of I—a purely spiritual being consisting of Imaginations, Inspirations and Intuitions, within which the I shoots up in the attempt to break through. And in this flash the human being would be able to say, "I am, for through me has come into being what is of me down below" (see Steiner's sketch, Diagram 8).

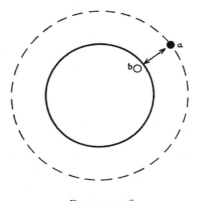

DIAGRAM 8

It is strange but it is a fact. The human was intended to live in the environment of the Earth. Suppose a human being were living here (a in Diagram 8) in the environment of the Earth. It was intended that this human being should produce on the Earth its own reflection, and only through this reflection ray back again its Ego, and then it would say, "There is my sign." It was not intended that this human should carry around with it its being of bones, glands, nerves and all—still less that it should pronounce the grotesque verdict, 'That is I." It should have happened quite differently.

The human should have lived in the environs of the Earth planet, and sunk a sign and symbol into the Earth in the flashing up of form in blood, and it should then have said to itself, "There I drive in my stake—my sign and my seal, which gives me the consciousness of my Ego. For what I have become, in that I have passed through Saturn, Sun and Moon existence—with that I can hover here outside in the World-All. It is the Ego I must now add; and the Ego I perceive by inscribing myself in the Earth below, so that I can always read in the flashing of the blood what I am." We were, therefore, not originally intended to walk the Earth in bodies of flesh and bone as we do, but to circle around the Earth and make records, as it were, down below from which we might recognize and know that we are that—that we are an Ego.

Whoever overlooks this fact has no true knowledge of the nature of the human being.

Then came Lucifer and brought it about that this human should have not merely its Ego for sense perception, but should feel its astral body, too, as its Ego, all that it had acquired on the Moon as astral body—thinking, feeling and willing. The Ego was thus no longer pure. Something else was mixed with it, and this led to the necessity for the human being to fall down into matter. The expulsion from paradise is the Fall into matter. And immediately there followed the change in humanity's blood. For now instead of flashing up for a moment and then being received back again into spirituality, the blood becomes real blood substance. It drives right through and spurts up as blood substance. It receives the tendency to be as we know it today. And so this blood substance, which by rights should return into the spiritual in the very moment when it becomes material, now gushes up into the rest of the human being and fills the human's whole organization, undergoing modification in accordance with the various forces in humanity.

According, for example, as it penetrates into a preponderance of physical over etheric body or of etheric body over astral body, and so on, the blood turns into nerve substance, muscle substance, and the like. Thus Lucifer compels blood to a greater materiality. Whereas blood has been designed to shoot up and immediately disappear again, Lucifer brought it into a coarse materiality (Gen 4,10). That is the one direct deed that Lucifer has performed in matter itself. He made blood into matter, whereas with the other things he at least only brought disorder among them. Were it not for Lucifer, blood would not be as it is at all; it would instead exist in a spirituality that comes only to the edge of materiality, only to the cusp of being born, and then at once returns. Blood as matter is the creation of Lucifer, and since the human being has in blood a physical expression of the Ego, its Ego is bound up here on Earth with a creation of Lucifer (see Gen 3,14-15). And since again Ahriman is only able to approach humanity because Lucifer is there before him, we can say that blood is what Lucifer has thrown down for Ahriman to catch so that both now have an approach to humanity (Steiner's Diagram 9). Can we wonder that an ancient primal feeling makes Lucifer-Ahriman[37] look upon blood as their earthly property? Can we wonder that he has his contracts written in blood, or that he attaches great value to Faust's signing the contract with his blood? For blood belongs entirely to Lucifer. Everything else holds in it something divine. With nothing else is he quite at home. Even ink is for Lucifer more divine than blood. Blood is precisely his element.

DIAGRAM 9

We see, then, that humanity has these two beings in it, the being of senses, glands and digestion, and the being of nerve, muscle and bone. The corresponding forces of both are charged with a coarse materiality, and both are supplied with blood, in the form it has assumed through the action of the Luciferic influence. For it is quite obvious, is it not, even to external science, that the human being, insofar as it is a material

---

37. See I-32 showing that the name Mephistopheles derives from two Hebrew words, *Mephiz* (Corrupter) and *Topel* (Liar). They represent the two thieves on the cross beside Jesus, who is in the middle (see especially Lk 23,32,39-43; also Mt 27,38; Mk 15,27 and Jn 19,18, as well as the discussion of these passages in *The Burning Bush*, pp. 117 and 332, fn 3).

being, is entirely a product of its blood? Everything in the human being that is material is nourished out of blood; it is really all transformed blood. From the point of view of matter, bones, nerves, muscles and glands are all nothing else than transformed blood. *The human being is actually blood, and as such it is a walking Lucifer-Ahriman.* It is because of what is behind matter and is poured into matter through the blood that the human being belongs to the divine world and to a forward-moving evolution, not to an evolution that is a mere relic of the past. Lucifer, and Ahriman, too came into our world through remaining behind at particular stages of evolution.

Bearing in mind all we have said, we can see quite clearly how at the very beginning of Earth evolution humans had something in common, something that united them. They had from the first in their blood something that was common to them all. For if the blood had remained as it was designed to be for humanity, it would have been a pure emanation of the Spirits of Form. In the blood the Spirits of Form would live in us. These Spirits of Form are none other than the seven Elohim of the Bible.[38] Steiner had earlier said in his Munich cycle of lectures on Genesis (GEN), that if the human being had kept its blood in the state it originally was to have had, it would feel in itself the seven Elohim; that is to say, it would feel its Ego within as seven-membered. One of its members would be the chief and would correspond to Jahve or Jehovah ("Yahweh" in English), and the other six would, to begin with, be subordinate. This sevenfoldness that it would feel in its Ego, as it were, a surging up within it of each of the seven Elohim or Spirits of Form, would have produced originally and spontaneously in the human being the sevenfold nature that we now have to acquire with so great toil and trouble. Because human blood has been tainted by Lucifer, humanity has to wait so long. It has to wait until human beings have sent forth sufficient outstreamings of Intuitive and Inspired and Imaginative substance from nerves, muscles

---

38. Scholars seem universally to recognize the plural nature of the Hebrew noun used for "God" in Gen 1. It is especially evident in the fact that almost all translations use the plural pronoun in Gen 1,26, and it is generally under this verse that the plurality of the Gen 1 *Elohim* is discussed. See, for example, 1 NIB 345; 1 Interp 482-483; 1 AB 7; TORAH (Genesis), pp. 12-13; and the translations NJB and NIV. The plural also appears in significant other ancient biblical passages where the multiple nature of the Creator God is either clearly expressed or implied; see Gen 3,22; 11,7; 1 K 22,19; Job 15,8; Is 6,8 and Jer 23,18. See also the discussion of Gen 1,26 in *The Burning Bush*, pp. 135, 402, 609 and 616, as well as in its "Overview" at p. 15.

and bones for them to be ripe to receive once again this sevenfold nature into themselves. This is the meaning also of Is 6,9-13.[39]

As important as it is that we have come to this point, we are now only where we can recognize intellectually how the human nature plays into the sevenfold human being (I-9). But humanity would never have darkened the six other members and illumined so greatly the one, the Ego, had not authority been given to Lucifer to interfere in the course of evolution (see Job 1,12). The real cause of the other members' suffering a darkening at the beginning of Earth evolution, while the Ego grew particularly bright and was made to shine with a light-filled egoness, was the Ego's being hurried into dense matter so that it was able to come to a clear consciousness of its Individuality, of its particular single Individuality, whereas it would otherwise all along have felt its sevenfoldness.

Thus we see on the one hand that if the human being's blood had remained as it was the human would have come to an Ego that would from the outset have had a sevenfold character. Through Lucifer having been given the blood, however, the human being has come to an Ego that is single and unitary in character. The human has come to feel and know its Ego as the center of its being. We can, therefore, understand how the blood in its originally intended form contains something that could work in a social direction, that could bring people together, so that they might feel themselves to be one common race of humanity. This would have been so if the seven Elohim had come to revelation in human Egos, as it was intended they should in the beginning. Lucifer's gift to humanity has meant that people feel themselves as particular Individualities and cut themselves off in their self-dependence from the common race of humanity. Diagrams 6 and 9 show the dispersal of the human being's blood upon the "ground" (Gen 4,10) instead of as intended in Diagram 7, the immediate consequence being the expulsion so that we humans would have to "wander the earth" instead of

---

39. Is 6,9-13: [9]And he said, "Go and say to this people: 'Hear and hear, but do not understand; see and see, but do not perceive.' [10] Make the heart of this people fat, and their ears heavy, and shut their eyes; lest they see with their eyes, and hear with their ears, and understand with their hearts, and turn and be healed." [11] Then I said, "How long, O Lord?" And he said: "Until cities lie waste without inhabitant, and houses without men, and the land is utterly desolate, [12] and the Lord removes men far away, and the forsaken places are many in the midst of the land. [13] And though a tenth remain in it, it will be burned again, like a terebinth or an oak, whose stump remains standing when it is felled." The holy seed is its stump.

paradise and to be cut off from the "face" of the Elohim (Gen 4,14). The world process takes its course on Earth in such a way that through the working of Lucifer the human being is inclined to become more and more independent, while through the working of the seven Elohim it is inclined more and more to feel itself a member and part of the whole of humanity.[40]

THE ETHERIZATION OF THE BLOOD

Before getting to the last of the three major Steiner references under this term blood, let us pause to take note of how they progressively reflect the scheme of the human being's outgoing and return, that is, the descent, redemption and reascent, the "parable" (actually in this sense, the allegory) of the Prodigal Son (Lk 15,11-32). While the boundaries between them are, of course, not completely distinct, overlapping one way or the other from time to time, OP dealt primarily with the aspect of the human being's embodiment (its physiology) and WSWS with its blood as the intermediary or midpoint between its double nature; as we are now to see the "etherization" represents the initiation of the reascent— the beginning of the departure from material embodiment. That Steiner considered the substance of OP, WSWS, and the lectures from *The Reappearance of Christ in the Etheric* (RCE) and *Wonders of the World* (WW) cited in the "etherization" grouping below as being closely related to each other, and to his cycles on the Bible, seems obvious from their timing. As previously mentioned, all the cited OP, WSWS, RCE and WW lectures were given in 1911, and that year falls almost squarely in the middle of the time span (roughly 1908-1914) he devoted specifically, and seemingly primarily, to the Bible message.

The material in this section was also presented in *The Burning Bush* essay "Second Coming." Two preliminary observations should be made that pertain to the first WW quotation below:

1. Steiner speaks of an "impulse" that entered human evolution with the Mystery of Golgotha. He uses the term "impulse" to indicate the planting of the spiritual *seed*, for nothing ever happens on Earth that is not prefigured in the spiritual world ("As Above, So Below"). What is to

---

40. While Lect. 6 is excellent, it moves in a direction that has little direct relevance to our primary concern, blood, and is not included in this summary.

become fruit starting in the twentieth century is based upon the impulse that entered Earth at the "turning point of time."

2. The reference to the human circulatory system as the "ether-world condensed" should not be considered to conflict with the assertion that the blood is also the manifestation and instrument of the Ego. They are two entirely different profiles. In respect to the four elements, the fluid blood (the "water" element) represents the etheric (cf. I-54 & I-80). On the other hand, in respect to the fourfold human being's components (see I-9), the blood represents the Ego (see I-14).

In WW, Lect. 8, Steiner says, "What really do the blood circulation and the heart mean to us? They are the ether-world condensed, they are the densified forces of the etheric world!... The important and mysterious feature of Earth evolution is not only that this densification took place, ... but that as regards each of our systems of organs in Earth evolution an impulse entered [i.e., via the Christ] whereby what was once etheric and had become physical, is once more dissolved, is changed back again into the ether." It is most notable that the etheric, or life, body is represented by the blood, and that Moses saw that blood as being the "life" of all flesh. See Gen 9,4; Lev 17,11,14; see also the topical list of scriptures near the beginning of this essay.

Consider this passage from RCE, Lect. 9:

> When a man stands in front of us today in his waking state and we observe him with the clairvoyant eye, certain rays of light are seen streaming continually from the heart toward the head. If we wish to sketch this schematically, we must draw the region of the heart here and show the continuous streamings from there to the brain, flowing in the head around the organ known in anatomy as the pineal gland.

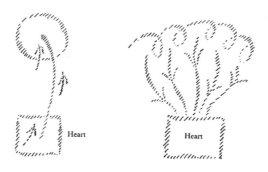

These rays of light stream from the heart to the head and flow around the pineal gland. These streamings arise because human blood, which is a physical substance, is continually dissolving itself into etheric substance. In the region of the heart there is a continual transformation of the blood into this delicate etheric substance that streams upward toward the head and flows glimmeringly around the pineal gland. This process, the etherization of the blood, can be shown in the human being throughout his waking life. It is different now, however, in the sleeping human being. When a human being sleeps, the occult observer is able to see a continual streaming from outside into the brain and also in the reverse direction, from the brain to the heart. These streams, however, which in sleeping man come from outside, from cosmic space, from the macrocosm, and flow into the inner constitution of the physical and etheric bodies … reveal something remarkable when they are investigated. These rays vary greatly in different individuals....

Moral qualities are revealed distinctly in the particular coloring of the streams that flow into human beings during sleep.... At the moment of waking or of going to sleep, a kind of struggle takes place in the region of the pineal gland between what streams down from above and what streams upward from below. When a man is awake, the intellectual element streams upward from below in the form of currents of light, and what is of moral-aesthetic nature streams downward from above. At the moment of waking or of going to sleep, these two currents meet, and in the man of low morality a violent struggle between the two streams takes place in the region of the pineal gland. In the man of high morality and an outstreaming intellectuality, a peaceful expansion of glimmering light appears in the region of the pineal gland. This gland is almost surrounded by a small sea of light in the moment between waking and sleeping. Moral nobility is revealed when a calm glow surrounds the pineal gland at these moments. In this way a man's moral character is reflected in him, and this calm glow of light often extends as far as the region of the heart. Two streams can therefore be perceived in man—one from the macrocosm, the other from the microcosm.

Before we relate this more precisely to the blood of Christ, let us see also the parallel remarks on this process from WW, Lect. 8:

For clairvoyant sight something streams continuously out of our heart—our heart, the outcome of our blood circulation. If you see clairvoyantly the blood pulsating through the human body, then you also see how this blood becomes rarefied again in the heart, how in its finest elements—not in its coarser, but in its finer parts—it is dissolved and returns to the etheric form. Just as the blood has gradually been formed in the ether, so in the human body of the present day we have the reverse process. The blood becomes etherized, and streams of ether flow continuously from the heart towards the head, so that we see the etheric body built up in an opposite direction by way of the blood. Thus what crystallized out from the etheric during the early part of Lemuria to form the human blood circulation [again, Gen 4,10] and the heart we now see returning [see Rev 19,13] to the etheric form and streaming in the human etheric body towards the brain.... [He here relates this process also to our thinking.] These etheric currents are indirectly related to a delicate and important part of the human brain called the pineal gland. They continuously lave the pineal gland, which becomes luminous and its movements as physical brain-organ respond in harmony with these etheric currents emanating from the heart.... So you see we have not only a process within the Earth which leads to solidification, but also a reverse process of rarefaction.

Continuing from RCE, Lect. 9:

Just as in the region of the human heart the blood is continually being transformed into etheric substance, so a similar process takes place in the macrocosm. We understand this when we turn our eyes to the Mystery of Golgotha, to the moment when the blood flowed from the wounds of Jesus Christ. This blood must not be regarded simply as chemical substance, but by reason of all that has been described as the nature of Jesus of Nazareth, it must be recognized as something altogether unique. When it flowed from His wounds and into the earth, a substance was imparted to our earth which, in uniting with it, constituted an event of the greatest possible significance for all future ages of the earth, and it could take place only once. What happened with this blood in the ages that followed? Nothing different from what otherwise takes place in the heart of man. In the course of earthly evolution, this blood passed through a process of "etherization." Just as our blood streams upward from the heart as ether, so, since the Mystery of Golgotha, the etherized blood of Christ Jesus has lived in the ether of the earth. The etheric body of the earth is permeated by what the blood that flowed on Golgotha became. This is important. If what has thus come to pass through Christ Jesus had not taken place, man's condition on the earth could only have been as previously described. Since the Mystery of Golgotha, however, there has existed the continuous possibility for the activity of the etheric blood of Christ to flow together with the streamings from below upward, from heart to head.

Because the etherized blood of Jesus of Nazareth is present in the etheric body of the earth, it accompanies the etherized human blood streaming upward from the heart to the brain, so that not only do these streams that I described earlier meet in man, but the human bloodstream unites with the bloodstream of Christ Jesus. A union of these two streams can come about, however, only if man is able to unfold true understanding of what is contained in the Christ impulse. Otherwise, there can be no union; the two streams then mutually repel each other, thrust each other away. In every age of earthly evolution, we must acquire understanding in the form suitable for that epoch. At the time when Christ Jesus lived on earth, preceding events could be rightly understood by those who came to His forerunner, John, and were baptized by him.... The evolution of humanity progresses, however, and in our present age it is important that man should learn to understand that the knowledge contained in spiritual science must be received and gradually be able so to fire the streams flowing from heart to brain that anthroposophy can be understood. If this comes to pass, individuals will be able to comprehend the event that has its beginning in the twentieth century: the appearance of the etheric Christ in contradistinction to the physical Christ of Palestine.

We have now reached the moment in time when the etheric Christ enters into the life of the earth and will become visible, at first to a small number of people, through a natural clairvoyance. Then in the course of the next 3,000 years, He will become visible to greater and greater numbers of people.

Conclusion

Jesus said, "I am the way, and the truth, and the *life*" (Jn 14,6, emphasis mine). Moses said (see early topical listing herein), "The *life* is in the *blood*." Ritualistically, through Moses Yahweh gave his people a way to remain within their blood family by the sacrifice of animal blood. But as Paul confirmed in Hebrews, this procedure was superceded by the blood of Christ. Steiner has shown us how the human blood, first cast to the "ground" in the fourth chapter of Genesis, can, by a person's coming to an anthroposophical understanding of the Mystery of Golgotha through the taking in of the true "I Am" (Rev 19,12), transform the three bodies through his etherized blood (Rev 19,13). Thereby the unisexual nature will be transformed in time to the bisexual so that the larynx, in the *image* of its Creator, will reproduce through its *word* (Rev 19,13). The larynx will then be the earlier mentioned "rod of iron" (Rev 19,15). That is when one will not want to be "with child" (Mt 24,19; Mk 13,17; Lk 21,23; 23,29), because the age of unisexuality will have ended along with the process of reincarnation (see I-2). But just as in the time of Moses those who did not properly avail themselves of the sacrificial blood were expelled, so now those who remain in the "flesh" (Rev 19,18) face its dire fate.

Then it can be said that the *egoism* that could not see the *fullness*[41] of the seven Elohim (of the sevenfold solar system) is on the way to experiencing itself, its *name*, the "I Am"—the last of the twelve kinds of fruit (Rev 22,2), the true Ego sense, the Ego fully infused by the Christ, the fulfillment and last of the twelve zodiacal senses (see I-20).

Then it can be said that "this poor lisping, stammering tongue lies silent in the grave," for it will have been transformed into the ruling "rod of iron" by virtue of that etheric "fountain filled with blood drawn from Immanuel's veins."

---

41. For the meaning of the *pleroma*, the *fullness* in Jn 1,16, see *The Burning Bush*, pp. 135 and 502.

CHAPTER END NOTE
(Continued from "Topical List" section above; italics mine)

1. **The shedding of another human's blood where it is:**

(a) **Culpable:**

Gen 4,10-11: (to Cain) [10]And the Lord said, What have you done? The voice of your brother's *blood* is crying to me from the ground. [11]And now you are cursed from the ground, which has opened its mouth to receive your brother's *blood* from your hand.

Gen 37,22,26,31; 42,22; **Num** 35,19-21,33; **Deut** 19,11-13; **Josh** 2,19; **Judg** 9,22-24; **1 Sam** 19,4-5; 25,31; **2 Sam** 1,16; 4,11; 14,11; 16,7-8; 20,12; **1 K** 2,5,9,31,33,37; 21,19; 22,35,38; **2 K** 9,7,26,33; 21,16; 24,4

1 Ch 22,6-8: [6]Then he called for Solomon his son, and charged him to build a house for the Lord, the God of Israel. [7]David said to Solomon, "My son, I had it in my heart to build a house to the name of the Lord my God. [8]But the word of the Lord came to me, saying, 'You have shed much *blood* and have waged great wars; you shall not build a house to my name, because you have shed so much *blood* before me upon the earth.'"

1 Ch 28,3; **2 Ch** 24,25; **Ps** 9,12; 55,23; 58,10; 68,23; 79,3,10; 106,38; 139,19; **Prov** 12,6; 28,17; **Jer** 7,6-7; 19,4-6; 22,3,17; 26,15; **Ezek** 3,18,20; 18,10,13; 23,37,45; 24,7-9; 33,4-6,8,25; 35,6; 36,18; **Hos** 1,4; **Joel** 3,19,21; **Jon** 1,14; **Mic** 7,2; **Mt** 23,30,34-35

Mt 27,4,6,8,24-25: [4]saying, "I have sinned in betraying innocent *blood*." They said, "What is that to us? See to it yourself.".... [6]But the chief priests, taking the pieces of silver, said, "It is not lawful to put them into the treasury, since they are *blood* money.".... [24]So when Pilate saw that he was gaining nothing, but rather that a riot was beginning, he took water and washed his hands before the crowd, saying,

"I am innocent of this man's *blood*; see to it yourselves."[25]And all the people answered, "His *blood* be on us and on our children!"

Lk 11,50-51; **Acts** 1,19; 5,28; 18,6; 20,26; 22,20; **Rev** 6,10; 19,2

(b) **Innocent or inadvertent:**

Num 35,22-27: [22]"But if he stabbed him suddenly without enmity, or hurled anything on him without lying in wait, [23]or used a stone, by which a man may die, and without seeing him cast it upon him, so that he died, though he was not his enemy, and did not seek his harm; [24]then the congregation shall judge between the manslayer and the avenger of *blood*, in accordance with these ordinances; [25]and the congregation shall rescue the manslayer from the hand of the avenger of *blood*, and the congregation shall restore him to his city of refuge, to which he has fled, and he shall live in it until the death of the high priest who was anointed with the holy oil. [26]But if the manslayer shall at any time go beyond the bounds of his city of refuge to which he fled, [27]and the avenger of *blood* finds him outside the bounds of his city of refuge, and the avenger of *blood* slays the manslayer, he shall not be guilty of *blood*."

Deut 19,2-10; 21,1-9; 22,8; **Josh** 20; **2 Sam** 3,27-28

2. The express indication that a creature's life is in its blood (whether or not the eating of its blood is prohibited):

Gen 9,3-6: (to Noah) [3]"Every moving thing that lives shall be food for you; and as I gave you the green plants, I give you everything. [4]Only you shall not eat flesh with its life, that is, its *blood*. [5]For your *lifeblood* I will surely require a reckoning; of every beast I will require it and of man; of every man's brother I will require the life of man. [6]Whoever sheds the *blood* of man, by man shall his *blood* be shed; for God made man in his own image."

Lev 17,3-4,6,10-14: [3]"If any man of the house of Israel kills an ox or a lamb or a goat in the camp, or kills it outside the camp, [4]and does not bring it to the door of the tent of meeting, to offer it as a gift to the Lord before the tabernacle of the Lord, *bloodguilt* shall be imputed to that man; he has shed *blood*; and that man shall be cut off from among his people.... [6][A]nd the priest shall sprinkle the *blood* on the altar of the Lord at the door of the tent of meeting, and burn the fat for a pleasing odor to the Lord.... [10]If any man of the house of Israel or of the strangers that sojourn among them eats any *blood*, I will set my face against that person who eats *blood*, and will cut him off from among his people. [11]For the life of the flesh is in the *blood*; and I have given it for you upon the altar to make atonement for your souls; for it is the *blood* that makes atonement, by reason of the life. [12]Therefore I have said to the people of Israel, No person among you shall eat *blood*, neither shall any stranger who sojourns among you eat *blood*. [13]Any man also of the people of Israel, or of the strangers that sojourn among them, who takes in hunting any beast or bird that may be eaten shall pour out its *blood* and cover it with dust. [14]For the life of every creature is the *blood* of it; therefore I have said to the people of Israel, You shall not eat the *blood* of any creature, for the life of every creature is its *blood*; whoever eats it shall be cut off."

Deut 12,16,23,27: [16]"Only you shall not eat the *blood*; you shall pour it out upon the earth like water.... [23]Only be sure that you do not eat the *blood*; for the *blood* is the life, and you shall not eat the life with the flesh.... [27][A]nd offer your burnt offerings, the flesh and the *blood*, on the altar of the Lord your God; the *blood* of your sacrifices shall be poured out on the altar of the Lord your God, but the flesh you may eat."

Job 16,18: "O earth, cover not my *blood*, and let my cry find no resting place." [Note: this usage seems to be more esoteric than exoteric.]

Job 39,30: (speaking of the hawk and eagle) "His young ones suck up *blood*; and where the slain are, there is he" [Note: again this usage may be more esoteric than exoteric.]

3. The prohibition of the eating of blood, while not stating that a creature's life is in its blood:

Lev 7,26-27: [26]"Moreover you shall eat no *blood* whatever, whether of fowl or of animal, in any of your dwellings. [27]Whoever eats any *blood*, that person shall be cut off from his people."

Lev 19,26; Deut 15,23; 1 Sam 14,31-35; 2 Sam 23,17; Ps 50,13; Ezek 44,6-7,15; Acts 15,20,29; 21,25

4. The turning of an object into blood:

Ex 4,9: "If they will not believe even these two signs or heed your voice, you shall take some water from the Nile and pour it upon the dry ground; and the water which you shall take from the Nile will become *blood* upon the dry ground."

Ex 7,17-21; Ps 78,44; 105,29

Joel 2,30-31: [30]"And I will give portents in the heavens and on the earth, *blood* and fire and columns of smoke. [31]The sun shall be turned to darkness, and the moon to *blood*, before the great and terrible day of the Lord comes."

Acts 2,19-20

Rev 6,12b: ... and the sun became black as sackcloth, the full moon became like *blood*...

Rev 8,7-9; 11,6; 16,3-6

5. The effecting of salvation and/or life preservation through animal blood:

Ex 12,7,13,22-23: [7]"Then they shall take some of the *blood*, and put it on the two doorposts and the lintel of the houses in which they eat them.... [13]The *blood* shall be a sign for you, upon the houses where you are; and when I see the *blood*, I will pass over you, and no plague shall fall upon you to destroy you, when I smite the land of Egypt."... [22]"Take a bunch of hyssop and dip it in the *blood* which is in the basin, and touch the lintel and the two doorposts with the *blood* which is in the basin; and none of you shall go out of the door of his house until the morning. [23]For the Lord will pass through to slay the Egyptians; and when he sees the *blood* on the lintel and on the two doorposts, the Lord will pass over the door, and will not allow the destroyer to enter your houses to slay you."

2 Ch 30,16; 35,11

Heb 11,28: By faith he kept the Passover and sprinkled the *blood*, so that the Destroyer of the first-born might not touch them.

6. **The ritual of animal sacrifice as an atonement for sin, peace offering, ordination of priests, etc.:**

Ex 23,18a; 29,12-21; 30,10

Lev 1,3-5: [3]"If his offering is a burnt offering from the herd, he shall offer a male without blemish; he shall offer it at the door of the tent of meeting, that he may be accepted before the Lord; [4]he shall lay his hand upon the head of the burnt offering, and it shall be accepted for him to make atonement for him. [5]Then he shall kill the bull before the Lord; and Aaron's sons the priests shall present the *blood*, and throw the *blood* round about against the altar that is at the door of the tent of meeting."

Lev 1,11,15; 3,2,8,13,17; 4,5-7,16-18,25,30,34; 5,9; 6,27,30; 7,2,14,33; 8,15,19,23-24,30; 9,9,12,18; 10,18; 14,6,14,17,25,28,51-52; 16,14-15,18-19; **Num** 19,4-5; **2 K** 16,13,15; **2 Ch** 29,22,24; **Ps** 16,4; **Ezek** 43,18,20; 45,19

7. **The genital discharge of blood through childbirth (parturition), normal menstruation or longer emission:**

Lev 12,4-5,7 (childbirth); 15,19 (normal menstruation); 15,25 (longer emission). For childbirth and the longer emission, animal sacrifice is required as atonement (see 12,6-8 and 15,29-30) though no mention is made of the animal's blood in these passages.

8. **The sanctity of human blood:**

Ps 72,14: From oppression and violence he redeems their life [i.e., the weak and needy]; and precious is their *blood* in his sight.

9. **The transition away from sacrificing (spilling the blood) of animals:**

Is 1,11c: "I do not delight in the *blood* of bulls, or of lambs, or of he-goats."

Is 66,3

Heb 10,4,19,29: [4]For it is impossible that the *blood* of bulls and goats should take away sins.... [19]Therefore, brethren, since we have confidence to enter the sanctuary by the *blood* of Jesus.... [29]How much worse punishment do you think will be deserved by the man who has spurned the Son of god, and profaned the *blood* of the covenant by which he was sanctified, and outraged the Spirit of grace?

10. Blood as the basis for covenant:

Ex 24,6-8: [6]And Moses took half of the *blood* [of oxen] and put it in basins, and half of the *blood* he threw against the altar. [7]Then he took the book of the covenant, and read it in the hearing of the people; and they said, "All that the Lord has spoken we will do, and we will be obedient." [8]And Moses took the *blood* and threw it upon the people, and said, "Behold the *blood* of the covenant which the Lord has made with you in accordance with all these words."

Ex 34,25; Zech 9,11

Mt 26,28: "for this is my *blood* of the covenant, which is poured out for many for the forgiveness of sins."

Mk 14,24: And he said to them, "This is my *blood* of the covenant, which is poured out for many."

Lk 22,20: And likewise the cup after supper, saying, "This cup which is poured out for you is the new covenant in my *blood.*"

Heb 12,24: and to Jesus, the mediator of a new covenant, and to the sprinkled *blood* that speaks more graciously than the *blood* of Abel.

11. Becoming drunk on human blood, or the wantonness of having shed it:

Deut 32,42-43; Is 1,15; 9,5; 15,9; 26,21; 34,3,6-7

Is 49,26a: "I will make your oppressors eat their own flesh, and they shall be drunk with their own *blood* as with wine."

Is 59,3,7; Jer 46,10; 51,35; Lam 4,13-14; Ezek 9,9; 22,12-13,27; 39,17-19; Hos 6,8; Mic 3,9-10; Hab 2,8,12,17; Zech 9,7; Lk 13,1 Rom 3,15

Rev 17,6: And I saw the woman, drunk with the *blood* of the saints and the *blood* of the martyrs of Jesus.

Rev 18,24

12. The Blood of Christ (ignoring the prophetic aspect of Old Testament sacrifice of lambs):

(a) As a sacrament of remembrance:

1 Cor 11,25,27: [25]In the same way also the cup, after supper, saying, "This cup is the new covenant in my *blood*. Do this, as often as you drink it, in remembrance of me.".... [27]Whoever, therefore, eats the bread or drinks the cup of the Lord in an unworthy manner will be guilty of profaning the body and *blood* of the Lord.

(b) As the agency of human salvation:

Mt 27,49b: And another took a spear and pierced his side, and out came water and *blood*.

Lk 22,44: And being in an agony he prayed more earnestly; and his sweat became like great drops of *blood* falling down upon the ground.

Jn 19,34: But one of the soldiers pierced his side with a spear, and at once there came out *blood* and water.

Acts 20,28; Rom 3,25

Rom 5,9: Since, therefore, we are now justified by his *blood*, much more shall we be saved by him from the wrath of God.

1 Cor 10,16a: The cup of blessing which we bless, is it not a participation in the *blood* of Christ?

Eph 1,7: In him we have redemption through his *blood*, the forgiveness of our trespasses, according to the riches of his grace....

Eph 2,13: But now in Christ Jesus you who once were far off have been brought near in the blood of Christ.

Col 1,19-20: [19]For in him all the fullness of God was pleased to dwell, [20]and through him to reconcile to himself all things, whether on earth or in heaven, making peace by the *blood* of his cross.

Heb 9,6-26: [6]These preparations having thus been made, the priests go continually into the outer tent, performing their ritual duties; [7]but into the second only the high priest goes, and he but once a year, and not without taking *blood* which he offers for himself and for the errors of the people. [8]By this the Holy Spirit indicates that the way into the sanctuary is not yet opened as long as the outer tent is still standing [9](which is symbolic for the present age). According to this arrangement, gifts and sacrifices are offered which cannot perfect the conscience of the worshiper, [10]but deal only with food and drink and various ablutions, regulations for the body imposed until the time of reformation. [11]But when Christ appeared as a high priest of the good things that have come, then through the greater and more perfect tent (not made with hands, that is, not of this creation) [12]he entered once for all into the Holy Place, taking not the *blood* of goats and calves but his own *blood*, thus securing an eternal redemption. [13]For if the sprinkling of defiled persons with the *blood* of goats and bulls and with the ashes of a heifer sanctifies for the purification of the flesh, [14]how much more shall the *blood* of Christ, who through the eternal Spirit offered himself without blemish to God, purify your conscience from dead works to serve the living God. [15]Therefore he is the mediator of a new covenant, so that those who are called may receive the promised eternal inheritance, since a death has occurred which redeems them from the transgressions under the first covenant. [16]For where a will is involved, the death of the one who made it must be established. [17]For a will takes effect only at death, since it is not in force as long as the one who made it is alive. [18]Hence even the first covenant was not ratified without *blood*. [19]For when every commandment of the law had been declared by Moses to all the people, he took the *blood* of calves and goats, with water and scarlet wool and hyssop, and sprinkled both the book itself and all the people, [20]saying, "This is the *blood* of the covenant which God commanded you." [21]And in the same way he sprinkled with the *blood* both the tent and all the vessels used in worship. [22]Indeed, under the law almost everything is purified with *blood*, and without the shedding of *blood* there is no forgiveness of sins. [23]Thus it was necessary for the copies of the heavenly things to be purified with these rites, but the heavenly things themselves with better sacrifices than these. [24]For Christ has entered, not into a sanctuary made with hands, a copy of the true one, but into heaven itself, now to appear in the presence of God on our behalf. [25]Nor was it to offer himself repeatedly, as the high priest enters the Holy Place yearly with *blood* not his own; [26]for then he would have had to suffer repeatedly since the foundation of the world. But as it is, he has appeared once for all at the end of the age to put away sin by the sacrifice of himself.

Heb 13,11-12,20; 1 Pet 1,2,19

1 Jn 1,7: but if we walk in the light, as he is in the light, we have fellowship with one another, and the *blood* of Jesus his Son cleanses us from all sin.

Rev 1,5b: To him who loves us and has freed us from our sins by his *blood* ...

Rev 5,9: and they sang a new song, saying, "Worthy art thou to take the scroll and to open its seals, for thou wast slain and by thy *blood* didst ransom men for God from every tribe and tongue and people and nation..."

Rev 7,14

Rev 12,11: And they have conquered him by the *blood* of the Lamb and by the word of their testimony, for they loved not their lives even unto death.

Rev 19,13: He is clad in a robe dipped in *blood*, and the name by which he is called is The Word of God.

13. Blood as a factor in health, sickness or healing:

Ezek 5,17; 14,19; 28,23

Mk 5,25: And there was a woman who had had a flow of *blood* for twelve years.

Lk 8,43-44: [43]And a woman who had had a flow of *blood* for twelve years and could not be healed by any one, [44]came up behind him, and touched the fringe of his garment; and immediately her flow of *blood* ceased.

14. Blood as a factor in ancestral inheritance or the birth process:

Ezek 16,6-7,9,22,36,38: (To Jerusalem) [6]"And when I passed by you, and saw you weltering in your *blood*, I said to you in your *blood*, 'Live, [7]and grow up like a plant of the field.' And you grew up and became tall and arrived at full maidenhood; your breasts were formed, and your hair had grown; yet you were naked and bare.... [9]Then I bathed you with water and washed off your *blood* from you, and anointed you with oil.... [22]And in all your abominations and your harlotries you did not remember the days of your youth, when you were naked and bare, weltering in your *blood*.... [36]Thus says the Lord God, Because your shame was laid bare and your nakedness uncovered in your harlotries with your lovers, and because of all your idols, and because of the *blood* of your children that you gave to them,... [38]And I will judge you as women who break wedlock and shed *blood* are judged, and bring upon you the *blood* of wrath and jealousy."

Heb 2,14: Since therefore the children share in flesh and *blood*, he himself likewise partook of the same nature, that through death he might destroy him who has the power of death, that is, the devil.

15. The eating, other than sacramentally, of Christ's Blood as a necessity of salvation:

Jn 6,53-56: [53]So Jesus said to them, "Truly, truly, I say to you, unless you eat the flesh of the Son of man and drink his *blood*, you have no life in you; [54]he who eats my flesh and drinks my *blood* has eternal life, and I will raise him up at the last day. [55]For my flesh is food indeed, and my *blood* is drink indeed. [56]He who eats my flesh and drinks my *blood* abides in me, and I in him."

16. Human blood unable physically, i.e., while still in the flesh, to inherit the Kingdom of God:

Mt 16,17: And Jesus answered him, "Blessed are you, Simon Bar-Jona! For flesh and *blood* has not revealed this to you, but my Father who is in heaven."

Jn 1,13: who were born, not of *blood* nor of the will of the flesh nor of the will of man, but of God.

1 Cor 15,50: I tell you this, brethren: flesh and *blood* cannot inherit the kingdom of God, nor does the perishable inherit the imperishable.

Gal 1,16

Eph 6,12: For we are not contending against flesh and *blood*, but against the principalities, against the powers, against the world rulers of this present darkness, against the spiritual hosts of wickedness in the heavenly places.

Heb 2,14: Since therefore the children share in flesh and *blood*, he himself likewise partook of the same nature, that through death he might destroy him who has the power of death, that is, the devil.

17. Other significant usage:

Lev 20,9,11-13,16,18,27: [9]"For every one who curses his father or his mother shall be put to death; he has cursed his father or his mother, his *blood* is upon him.... [11]The man who lies with his father's wife has uncovered his father's nakedness; both of them shall be put to death, their *blood* is upon them. [12]If a man lies with his daughter-in-law, both of them shall be put to death; they have committed incest, their *blood* is upon them. [13]If a man lies with a male as with a woman, both of them have committed an abomination; they shall be put to death, their *blood* is upon them.... [16]If a woman approaches any beast and lies with it, you shall kill the woman and the beast; they shall be put to death, their *blood* is upon them.... [18]If a man lies with a woman having her sickness, and uncovers her nakedness, he has made naked her fountain, and she has uncovered the fountain of her *blood*; both of them shall be cut off from among their people.... [27]A man or a woman who is a medium or a wizard shall be put to death; they shall be stoned with stones, their *blood* shall be upon them."

Num 18,17; 23,24; **1 Sam** 26,20; **2 Sam** 1,22; **1 K** 18,28; **Ezek** 32,6; **Zeph** 1,17; **Zech** 9,15; **Heb** 12,4; **1 Jn** 1,5,6,8; **Rev** 14,20

18. Miscellaneous usages of lesser significance:

Gen 49,11: Binding his foal to the vine and his ass's colt to the choice vine, he washes his garments in wine and his vesture in the *blood* of grapes;

Deut 32,14; **2 K** 3,22-23; **Prov** 30,33; **Ezek** 21,32

APPENDIX TO "BLOOD"

In late February or early March, 1996, an article entitled "The beat goes on" and subtitled "Heart recipients experience traits of donor" appeared in Lubbock's newspaper, the *Avalanche-Journal*. Its source was the Los Angeles Times-Washington Post News Service. It dealt with a book "tentatively called *A Change of Heart*, to be published by Little, Brown & Co. next year," written by the prominent celebrity biographer, William Novak. The editor said that the book, which was later in fact published, speaks of "cellular memory [having] some credibility."

I believe that one with anthroposophical understanding will look upon such a phenomenon, if it in fact exists, as it seems to in this and probably other cases too, as being based upon the use of the donor's etheric body by discarnate spiritual beings who target and manage to invade the consciousness of the recipient. The motivations behind the invasion seem entirely unwholesome in that they tend, as in this case, to emphasize the materialized heart or its cells as carrying a personality's earthly memory. Steiner had much to say about memory, some of it touched upon in this essay (see, for instance, OP, Lect. 4, "Man's Inner Cosmic System"). Perceptions taken in through the astral body are processed with the help of the blood so as to be impressed upon the memory storehouse, the etheric body. It is from that body only that memory can be called up by the Ego.

In the essay "Second Coming," in *The Burning Bush*, p. 223, I point out that one can see in RCE, Lect.10, "how etheric bodies of deceased persons have been inhabited by demonic spirits in such a way as to seemingly demonstrate 'memories' to deceive relatives into thinking there is a communication. And one can see how the use of such bodies could explain memories which certain individuals have which seem to indicate (though falsely) that they are a reincarnation of an earlier personality."

Things aren't what they seem! The "veil of the temple" that Christ rent (Mt 27,51; Mk 15,38; Lk 23,45; Heb 9,8-9; Heb 10,20) is still not open for most of humanity (even within Christendom), which still sees the material illusion (maya) of, rather than the spiritual reality behind, our mineral-physical existence. The "outer tent" is "still standing" (Heb 9,8-9) insofar as humanity fails to come to the insights that are now available through anthroposophical knowledge.

According to those insights, the cells of a transplanted heart can hardly carry the memory embodied in a donor's etheric body over into the consciousness of the recipient. What carries it over would appear to be an unwholesome spirit that utilizes a decedent's etheric body (not yet dispersed into the general Earth ether) by invading the recipient's consciousness in order to deceive humanity. Both nocturnal dreams and waking "cravings" (i.e., habits or addictions) come from what is engraved in the etheric body. Novak's book, allegedly based upon the experiences of his coauthor, Claire Sylvia, fascinating as it is to the imagination of countless thousands, and doubtless very meaningful to her, understandably sells quite well in our time. However, deeper insights into what is behind the phenomenon are urgently needed.

Finally, a word is also needed regarding psychics and psychic revelation. As I write this in the summer of 2000, a psychic has just this week appeared on a prominent evening television talk show, answering questions from the host as well as others who call in with questions about deceased loved ones. The psychic appears to be very sincere and devout and to have spurned offers to utilize the psychic ability for monetary gain. This person purported to tell callers about the status of their loved ones in the afterlife, as well as certain matters pertaining to what happens to suicides, and that sort of thing. The answers seemed uniformly to speak of these deceased souls as though they were in a state that could be explained from our normal earthly standpoint; they all seemed to be about thirty years of age (regardless of age at death) and there was talk about whether they were "happy" or not. Deceased souls were even said to have tried to make communication with living relatives, as evidenced by the fact that telephones had rung without anyone being on the calling end of the line when answered. And as usually happens in these psychic revelations, the persons calling in were convinced that the psychic had communicated with the deceased soul of their loved one because of peculiar facts related by the psychic that clearly pertained to the life of the deceased.[42]

From an anthroposophical standpoint, these revelations are generally considered to be unreliable, at least in the absence of criteria indicating that the psychic, in this life or another, has trod the path necessary to properly develop the spiritual organs essential for genuine investigation in the spiritual world (Mt 7,13-14). That path is nowhere more clearly laid out, to my knowledge, than in Steiner's *How to Know Higher Worlds* (HKHW). The psychic who has not trod that path can hardly be meaningfully distinguished from the mediums and the like who were condemned in the Old Testament.[43] Obviously, however, one soul cannot intuit the spiritual capabilities of another in these matters unless that one has himself or herself trod that higher path. Few have (again, Mt 7,14).

One who studies the life of Rudolf Steiner will see that he was born with immense psychic abilities. Even as a child, he could see spiritual beings above the altar whenever he attended mass (which he did as a youthful companion of certain monks, but never as a member of the confession). In the course of his life path, he became aware of the absolute

---

42. All of this recitation about the television show came from the report made orally to me by a person favorably disposed to these things. I did not witness it and cannot be sure all the relevant facts are fully and properly stated. For that reason I refrain from identifying the program or any of the persons involved, and recite these facts only as being fairly typical of what sincere and recognized psychics in general are able to reveal.

43. See fn 28, p. 65, in "The Nativity" essay in *The Burning Bush*, with citations but distinguishing between these and genuine seers or prophets. Deut 18,21-22 dealt with the question of how to distinguish between the genuine and the false.

necessity of extinguishing that natural clairvoyance (which in some, at least, can be called atavistic, though in his case considerable spiritual development had occurred in previous incarnations[44]). This he did and then, to judge both from his biographical material and his works, followed the steps to higher knowledge set out to some extent in HKHW. To the extent that any human, during earthly incarnation, can attain to these spiritual levels, they are summarized by the three loaves in Mt 13,33 and relate to what Steiner, in reference to earthly existence, calls the development (or attainment) of Imagination, Inspiration and Intuition.

One who considers Steiner's revelations to be true disclosures of the spiritual world and its relation to earthly existence, insofar as earthly language can disclose such matters, must compare the revelations from psychics with what anthroposophy shows. Often, if not usually, there is considerable variance.

That psychics get *real* messages from the spiritual world is readily accepted by anthroposophy. The same is true for mediums and the others proscribed in the Old Testament. What is *real* and what is *true* must, however, be distinguished, for they are not always the same. We ourselves may have real opinions, but they may not be true to the governing facts.

What is clear from anthroposophical insight is that there are many spirits and forces in the supersensible world that are working to mislead and obscure the real nature of the spiritual world, especially in generating within human beings ideas of the spiritual that are in fact materialistic (or overly spiritual so as to play into materialistic hands). To some extent these are discussed in RCE, Lects. 10-13, but they pervade Steiner's works. These are the legions related to as the Luciferic and Ahrimanic forces (see I-32). These beings are in full possession of all knowledge needed to convince, through psychic revelation, survivors that they are the soul of a departed loved one. Edgar Cayce, a leading psychic or medium, prayed earnestly that only the good spirits would speak through him. Implicit was his knowledge that malevolent spirits were only too ready to deceive (Rev 12,9).

In my experience, the lives of most psychics are rather exemplary. For that reason, I do not condemn, but merely alert the reader to the dangers involved in relying upon psychic revelation instead of searching for answers to spiritual questions through the powers of one's own being.

---

44. See "Pillars on the Journey" in *The Burning Bush.*

"What Is Man?"

WHAT SOUL has never gazed up at the night stars and pondered, "What are you to me?" So has shepherd David's cry rung down to us through the centuries:

> When I look at thy heavens, the
> work of thy fingers,
> the moon and the stars which
> thou has established;
>
> *What is man* that thou art mindful
> of him,
> and the son of man that thou
> dost care for him?
>
> Yet thou has made him little less
> than the angels[1]
> and dost crown him with glory
> and honor. (Ps 8,3-5, emphasis mine)[2]

Certainly no writing could fully answer this question. Yet the contemplative soul should by now have begun to sense from what has gone before in this and Volume 1 that it is the *image* of what it looks out upon. It mirrors the starry heavens and *images* the divine Spirit that created it (Gen 1,26-27). The bathroom mirror throws back to it a like question, "Who am I?"

It is entirely appropriate to give credit to modern science for the endless discoveries, in ever accelerating array, that have brought to humanity modern conveniences unthinkable a few generations ago. Unfortunately, neither science nor its accommodating religion have endowed us with the divine wisdom and moral development to bring these benefits to the

---

1. KJV's "angels" and NIV's "heavenly beings" both seem more appropriate here than the RSV's "God." See I-6.
2. See also Job 7,17-18; Ps 144,3 and Heb 2,5-8. Psalm 8 was the Vatican's contribution to the disc deposited by the Apollo 11 mission to the moon; see 4 NIB 711.

broader spectrum of humanity. Indeed, though crumbs sometimes fall ("trickle down") from their table, the benefits have increasingly gone to the haves, thus barring them from the moral high ground while widening the rift between them and the have-nots: spiritual starvation for the haves and bodily deprivation for the have-nots (Lk 16,19-31; Mt 25,31-46; 1 Jn 3,16-18). Nor is modern science and its friendly religion calculated to reverse this trend of declining morality so as to bring peace and goodwill to all God's creatures. Even the sociopolitical economic system we Americans so revere is not calculated to promote that harmony, for it also fails to understand the structure of the human being and the nature of its various needs.[3]

But we can hardly even begin to approach such harmony until we have more seriously and prayerfully pondered this age-old question, *"What is Man?"* A new and higher consciousness, not evident in the scientific, political and religious regimes of our day, must first dawn upon humanity. The Prodigal Son (humanity) has yet to emerge from "the valley of the shadow of death," its "pigpen" in the parable. The times of the Archangel Michael, the bestower of the Holy Spirit's *divine intelligence*, are upon us as we enter the third millennium.[4] The message buried in the Bible and other ancient holy writings must be unveiled at a higher level of spiritual consciousness than is found in the spectrum of modern religious practice.

This is just summation. The reader who has not already felt it to some extent from what has gone before may also miss it here in this final essay. But the last of Steiner's three so-called "scientific lectures" calls forth

---

3. For any social structure to exist in harmony, it must reflect the threefold structure of the human being. At the request of European leaders at the outset of the post-World War I reconstruction period, Steiner idealized and promoted a "threefold social order" that would address the requisites for such a society. It was a responsive, sacrificial endeavor, for he must have known the culture was not then ready for it. It is schematized in chart I-88 in *The Burning Bush,* where its political, economic and spiritual components are also respectively related to the kings, merchants and sailors of the falling Babylon in Rev 18,9-19. A brochure entitled "The Global Social Situation at the End of the 20th Century," by Dr. Y. ben-Aharon, was given me in November, 1999 by the New York Branch of the Anthroposophical Society, 138 W. 15th Street, NY, NY 10011 (212-242-8945). In it Dr. ben-Aharon discusses the work of the anthroposophist Nicanor Perlas, of the Philippines, in the development of the Philippine Agenda 21 and its recent adoption as the "threefold" form of society in that country. For further information, he suggests the Anthroposophical Group in the Philippines, 110 Scout Rallos St., Timog, Quezon City, 1103, Philippines, Tele +63(2)-928-3986, Fax +63(2)-928-7608, E-mail asp@info.com.ph.
4. See the Epilogue "Why Now" in *The Incredible Births of Jesus* (IBJ) and I-19.

astounding new images that can lift the receptive soul to a much higher vantage point whence to resolve our age-old query.

Steiner gave a series of eighteen lectures at Stuttgart from January 1 to 18, 1921, which he called "The Relation of the Diverse Branches of Natural Science to Astronomy."[5] Contrary to his request, they have come to be called "the Astronomy Course," yet they are not such in any usual sense. Parts of it are difficult to comprehend, as one translator (Rick Mansell) has noted at times in his translation.[6] Moreover, sometimes Steiner gives mathematical equations to express the concepts, and these equations are meaningful only to those adequately trained in mathematics. The reader desiring to consider them can find them in the library versions; I spare all others the difficulty of trying to follow this side of Steiner's diverse capabilities. I borrow only those of his penetrating concepts that will, I believe, point us to a higher level of cognition, e.g., "Come up hither, and I will show you ..." (Rev 4,1); cf. also Rev 21,10, "And in the Spirit he carried me away to a great, high mountain, and showed me...."

Combining thorough observation, immeasurable intellect and sublime intuition, he gives us not dogma but pointers—the hallmark of all the great teachers. In Lect. 7, for instance, talking about how the horizontal forms of animals, as distinguished from the vertical orientation of both plants and humans, came into being, he said, "It is in the very nature of these lectures that I can only hint at such things. I have to leave out many of the connecting links ... appeal[ing] to your own intuition and trust that you will think it out." Even if I wanted to, I couldn't reflect all the approaches and nuances he gives in the eighteen lectures, nor would it be appropriate to try.

I shall attempt to express two concepts that seem appropriate for the purpose of this closing essay. The **first** is the existence of and creative

---

5. In my bibliography, the cycle is called *Astronomy: The Relation of the Diverse Branches of Natural Science to Astronomy* (ARNS). Fortuitously I lost the copy of it made from the version identified in the bibliography of *The Burning Bush* (p. 709), which was classified as "U.E.T." (Unpublished English Typescript) and was largely illegible in many places. The copy then provided me by the library (the Mansell translation) appears to have been published in 1989 by The Rudolf Steiner Research Foundation, of Redondo Beach, CA, though apparently in limited printing and now also out of print. A copy of either version can be obtained by loan from the Rudolf Steiner Library, 65 Fern Hill Road, Ghent, NY 12075 (Telephone 518-672-7690).

6. Perhaps these complexities are part of the reason the book has thus far remained out of print in recent times, but even with these it offers the non-technical reader many meaningful insights only a few of which we can illustrate here. Hopefully it will soon again be available in print.

relationship between radial and spherical forces, including their reflection in the lemniscate (figure eight form) and its presence in the human form. The **second** is the so-called "Cassini curve" and what it implies.

The Creative Forces and Forms
(Radial, Spherical and Lemniscatory)

The formation and progressive separation of the Sun, Moon and planets of our solar system as Steiner shows us is given in I-27. The earthly evolution of the four kingdoms in their mineral-physical condition[7] progressed gradually during the course of these separations. The conditions and influences within the system changed from one stage to the next to accommodate the development of each in due course.[8] The plant and human kingdoms have a radial relationship with the Sun, the plant's head being in the ground and the human's head being toward the Sun (see I-78). The intervening animal kingdom is oriented horizontally. While this jumps over a great deal, the general picture of these relative orientations points us toward the vertical and spherical forms and forces that interplay in the creative process.

It might fairly be said that Steiner picked up the work of Goethe and carried it far beyond, always with admiration and gratitude for his conceptual forerunner. In the "Light" essay we saw how he did this with color. Here he takes up Goethe's principle of metamorphosis (morphology). He saw Goethe as a genius in deriving the formation of the bones of the skull from those of the vertebrae. Steiner goes on with his illustration. We've previously seen how the human body (three bodies) comprises three distinct organic functions, thinking, feeling and willing—what we also call the nervous, rhythmic and metabolic systems, respectively.[9] In ever so many ways the radial and spherical forces are reflected in these systems and the interplay between them, and this interplay images relationships in the heavens above us that prompt (and would appear to help answer) the ancient cry, "What is man?"

---

7. The present Conditions of Life and Form reflected in I-1.
8. These changing conditions and influences have largely been beyond the methods of detection practiced by science (as well as the religious establishment, of course), thus raising serious doubt about some of its most fundamental, and even popular, assumptions.
9. Various aspects of these are reflected in the Vol. 1 charts I-40, I-41, I-52, I-70, I-80 and I-84.

The Lord told Job (the archetypal human that is each of us and has no significant meaning otherwise) how ancient he was ("You know, for you were born then, and the number of your days is great!"; Job 38,21) and posed many questions suggesting that Job had lost his (i.e., we have lost our) ancient insights. One of these questions points to the very things Steiner points to in these lectures: "Do you know the ordinances of the heavens? Can you establish their rule on the earth?" (Job 38,33).

In regard to the metamorphosis that permitted Adam to stand erect with a skull encasing a brain that mirrored the spherical heavens above (cf. I-20), Steiner continues his discussion of how the essential bones developed through these respective radial and spherical forces.

We only begin to perceive the principle of metamorphosis applicable to the long bone and skull if we simply compare the inner surface of a long bone (Figure 1) with the outer surface of a skull bone. It is somewhat like turning a glove inside out, but the simile is not perfect, for when the inversion is made certain forces of tension come into play that alter the shape and distribution of the bone surface—accounting for their differences. The bones in between the long bone and the skull, namely, the vertebrae, are intermediary forms between the two opposite extremes. The long tubular bone and skull bone represent a remarkable polarity (Figures 2 and 3). If you think of what envelopes the human skull, you have what corresponds to the central line of the long bone. But how can we draw the counterpart of this line as it applies to the skull? It must be drawn as a circle—a spherical surface—far away at some indeterminate distance (see Figure 4). All the lines that can be drawn from the center line of the long bone toward its inner surface (Figure 3) correspond, for the skull bone, to all the lines that can be drawn from a spherical surface as though to meet in the center of the Earth (Figure 4).

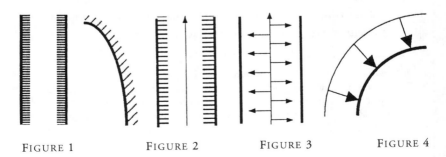

FIGURE 1   FIGURE 2   FIGURE 3   FIGURE 4

In other words, the radius of the Earth has the same cosmic value in regard to the vertical posture of the human organism, perpendicular to the surface of the Earth, as a cosmic spherical surface has in regard to the skull organization. The radial applies to the metabolic/limb system where the will is active but the consciousness is asleep, while the spherical applies to the head/nervous system where the thinking is active in wakeful state.[10] The rhythmic/circular system mediates between the two.

Again and again Steiner relates these principles to the human organism showing in it the interplay between Earth and the heavens. Embryology in particular reflects this interrelationship, and does so most strongly with the spherical where the head formation is the dominant aspect of embryonic life. The cycles of the solar bodies relate to the gestation period and what is being implanted, under karmic necessity, by the incarnating soul in the bodily structure during these ten lunar months (nine calendar months).

While the Moon, to whose cycle the female organism is so finely attuned, clocks the various stages of embryonic development, the other planets also bring their forces to bear during the gestation period. The scope and depth of these matters is beyond adequate treatment in this essay, but we will look at a few examples.[11]

To study embryology only in the context of what happens within the womb is like studying magnetism by looking only at the compass needle. As stated in earlier essays herein, any phenomenon can be properly studied only by considering the whole of which it is a part. The forming of mental images (a spherical or Sun influence) and the life of will (radial or Earth influence) are adequately studied only when the contrast between sphere and radius is considered. So it is with psychology. Just as we take the Earth's magnetism into account in connection with the magnet, so also we must look for the genesis of human embryonic life by finding a resultant between what takes place in the starry world (sphere) and what takes place in the human being as a result of the radial Earth activity. Just as there is a relationship between muscle (radial/unconsciousness) and nerve (spherical/

---

10. See the discussion of how Archimedes' principle applies to the human brain in the "Fire" essay (the section called "The Phenomena of Heat—Heat and the Other Elements") and in the "Light" essay (the section called "Steiner's Light Course").

11. Further references for study, to name but a few, include Powell's *Hermetic Astrology*, Vols. 1 and 2 (HA1 and HA2), *Christian Hermetic Astrology* (CHA) and *Chronicle of the Living Christ* (CLC); Sucher's *Cosmic Christianity* (COSC); Schultz' *Movement and Rhythms of the Stars* (MRS); and Julius' *The Imagery of the Zodiac* (IZOD).

consciousness), so also is there a relationship between what is developing in the embryo and its fading when the human being is born, into the experience of consciousness. In the study of these polarities, we are led out into the life of the cosmos. The metabolic system relates to the radial (Earth) influence while the human head system relates to the spherical (Sun). These two realms of activity and influence fall apart in the human being, as though they represent two Ice Ages, with the rhythmic system in the middle mediating between them, between heaven and Earth.

The human being mirrors this polarity in another way. The genesis of the Earth itself must be distinguished between two phases, one in which active forces work in such a way that the Earth itself is created, and then a later phase of evolution in which the forces work so as to create the human faculty for understanding the realities of the Earth. To understand this deeply is to begin to understand the Bible in its fullness from beginning to end. It is no less a book of science than a book of religion, for what is holy encompasses both. Thus far, neither science nor religion has come to the point of studying the whole. When they do, they will come together.

Only in this way do we really come near an understanding of the universe. It may be complex, but if things are such that we cannot reach the realities with the methods in favor today, then we are faced with the absolute necessity of comprehending the reality with other modes of understanding.

Steiner devotes several lectures at this point to showing again certain relationships between the heavens and Earth, on the one hand, and human consciousness and bodily conditions on the other. To some extent these have already been covered in the earlier essays, especially in "Blood," as well as in charts I-86 (etheric body) and I-21 (astral and physical bodies). We can focus here only upon a few observations that point us in the direction we must go if we are to plumb the depths in our quest.

To assist us in conceptualizing these vital points, we will consider certain geometric figures, particularly the lemniscate and the line involved in the Cassini curve. First, however, let us jump ahead to a most incisive observation Steiner gave illustrating the interplay between Sun and Earth as a mental image of the interplay between the spherical (heavenly) and radial (earthly) forces. We can then transfer it to the similar interplay between these forces in the human being. Here we see a polarity that swings back and forth from one to the other, a sort of rhythmic dance pattern. All three elements, solar/spherical, earthly/radial and mediating/lemniscate, are part of the archetypal pattern for what is being created in the divine image in the human being (see Figure 5). The progressive separation of the Sun and Moon and various planets in the development of our solar system (see I-27) accommodated the progressive development of the Earth's three lower kingdoms as receptacles, so to speak, for the descending human kingdom ("the first shall be last").

FIGURE 5

Steiner shows how both the Ptolemaic and Copernican systems have validity and are merely different ways of describing the relationships within the solar system. It makes no difference which system is used insofar as the relationship between Sun and Earth is concerned, for in a manner of speaking it can be said that each journeys around the other. The portrayal of our solar system in two-dimensional schematic is totally unrealistic, for it is far more complex than that. The concepts brought forward by Kepler are themselves deeply rooted in the ancient mysteries and perceive the planetary interrelationships far differently than commonly thought. These relationships involve incommensurate numbers[12] so that calculations must be made ever anew to bring them in line with reality. The elliptical orbits are constantly changing so that no instant of time involves a pattern precisely like that of any other instant of time either before or after. If it were not so, the system would be fixed and would die. As it is, it constantly renews itself with ever-changing pattern.

Even the zodiac, the "twelve stars" (Rev 12,1) that Abraham was to number so that his descendants would be twelvefold like them (Gen 15,5), is constantly changing, though much more gradually. Steiner illustrates this by showing how the Great Bear (Job 9,9 and 38,32) has and will change through the ages from fifty thousand years ago to the present

12. Incommensurate numbers are those having no common divisor (WNWD).

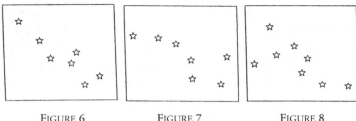

FIGURE 6   FIGURE 7   FIGURE 8

to fifty thousand years in the future (Figures 6, 7 and 8, respectively). The influences from the heavens will differ in the future from what they are today and have been in the past. But in reality neither the Sun nor the Earth revolves around the other. Rather they take turns following each other through space. Steiner portrays this in the form of a moving lemniscate (Figure 9) that moves through the heavenly ecliptic (twelvefold zodiac).[13] But to derive the lemniscate, it is necessary to think of their journey not in plane (two-dimensional) but in solid (three-dimensional) geometrical form, as though the lemniscate rotates on its polar axis as it moves forward through space—like two hot-air balloons joined linearly at their baskets.

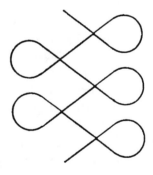

FIGURE 9

As the moving lemniscate evolves, its radial nature appears in line ES in Figure 10, while its spherical (lateral) aspect appears as the cross bar indicating the direction of its movement through space. The radial and spherical are thus brought together by the lemniscate, and portray in their joinder the figure of the Cross. The five-pointed human physical body is

---

13. The "circle upon the face of the waters" (Job 26,10; Prov 8,27); see also Is 40,12,22 and Enoch 80,7 "the entire law of the stars will be closed to the sinners."

brought into that form when its feet are joined together by the placement of Christ on it. All three systems of the human being are reflected in this relationship between the Sun and the Earth, the radial (limb/metabolic), spherical (head/nervous) and lemniscate (rhythmic/circulatory).

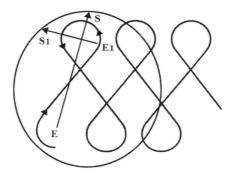

FIGURE 10

While the Sun and Earth reveal this threefold pattern (radial-spherical-rhythmical) in the interrelationship of their movements through the heavens as the structural basis for the human body, the Moon by its monthly cycle divides the gestation period of the human embryo into ten lunar periods. Fetal development is thus exposed during gestation to the forces of the heavenly bodies (both planetary and zodiacal), in segments corresponding to the ten septenaries (seven-year periods) that constitute the allotted human life of seventy years (Ps 90,10).[14] But from within the solar system other patterns bear upon the human bodily structure. One can see the lemniscate pattern being modified in varying ways by the loop patterns of the planets (Mercury, Venus, Mars, Jupiter and Saturn).[15] These patterns are visible to the naked eye. Examples of the loops of Mercury, Venus and Mars were drawn by Steiner (Lect. 11) in Figures 11, 12 and 13, respectively. That these are simple illustrations is obvious when compared with the more precise ones developed by the Mathematical-Astronomical Section

14. Only the first nine are governed by karmic necessity, the number nine corresponding with the ninefold nature and development of the human soul; see I-26 and I-24. The nine months of pregnancy comprise ten lunar months.

15. An elaborate presentation of these loop forms, for each of these five planets, as they progress from one stage to another can be found in Joachim Schultz's *Movement and Rhythms of the Stars* (MRS), Chaps. 20 (for Venus and Mercury) and 25 (for Mars, Jupiter and Saturn).

FIGURE 11   FIGURE 12   FIGURE 13

at the Goetheanum, as reflected in Figure 115 of Joachim Schultz's book[16] showing the progressive loops of the planet Mercury as follows:

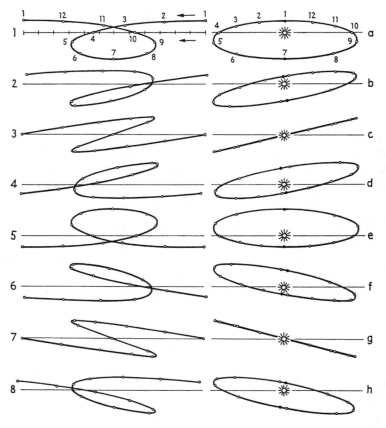

FIGURE 115. The position of Mercury's orbit around the Sun at different times of the year, and the corresponding loop forms. a. Aug 10; b. Sep.26; c. Nov. 11; d. Dec. 25; e. Feb 7; f. March 26; g. May 9; h. June 26.

16. Id.

Steiner then leads us to a recognition of how these forms and figures are reflected in the human structure. Imagine yourself moving in a lemniscate figure, but assume that by variation of the constants the lemniscate form is such that the lower branch does not close but is open (Figure 14).

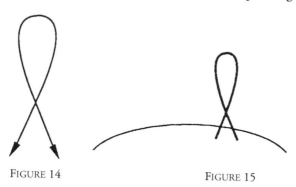

FIGURE 14   FIGURE 15

He assures us this is mathematically feasible. We can then see how the form can be drawn into the human form where, in Figure 15, we see the lemniscate in relationship to what passes through our limb nature and then in some way turns, goes through our head nature and then back again into the Earth. So we would be justified in saying that there is an open lemniscate of this kind in the human form. He then points out that we need only make a deeper morphological study to find the lemniscate, either in this or in some modified form, inscribed in human nature in diverse ways. Investigate, for instance, the curve that arises if you trace the middle line of a left-side rib, then go past the junction into the vertebra, then turn and go back along the right rib (Figure 16). Bear in mind that the vertebra has a very different inner structure from the ribs; both of them are intermediary between the skull bone and the long bone, but the

FIGURE 16

vertebra is closer to the former and the rib to the latter. Think what it must signify that as you go along this line, rib-vertebra-rib, various inner relationships of growth must play their part, not only quantitatively but qualitatively. Then you will find in the lemniscate with its loop formation a morphological key to the whole system. Going upward from thence to the head organization, the farther you go upward the more you will find it necessary to modify the form of the lemniscate. At a certain point you must imagine it transformed—already indicated in the sternum, where the two come together. When you get up into the head there is a far-reaching metamorphosis of the lemniscatory principle.

Study the whole human figure—the contrast, above all, of the nerves and senses organization and the metabolic, and you get a lemniscate tending to open out as you go downward and to close as you go upward. You also get lemniscates, though highly modified, with the one loop extremely small, if you follow the pathway of the centripetal nerves through the nervecenter and outward again to the termination of the centrifugal nerve.

Again and again you will find this lemniscate inscribed in the human body—it above all. In the animal it is far less varied than in the human, and its planes are more parallel.

An interesting play is to take a rod in the form of a lemniscate, holding it in such manner that one loop is near a light source and the other is slanted sufficiently far away. The shadow cast upon an opposite wall will reflect this lemniscate but with one loop open and fading away, just as the human form escapes into the Earth in the above illustration.

If we develop a feeling for morphology in the higher sense, we must assign the human form and figure to the planetary system. You have to think of the total evolution of humanity upon the Earth, bearing in mind the relationship of the great sphere to the human head formation. You will realize there will be some relation between the metamorphosis of the aspect of the starry heavens, the evolution of humanity, and the soul-spiritual evolution of humanity. You have the vault of the great heavenly sphere above us that reveals only that part of the movements corresponding to the *loop* among the planets (Figure 17). In the movement of the fixed stars the rest of the path is omitted. We noted above this great differentiation. The planets must somehow correspond to the total human being, while the fixed stars must correspond only to what forms the human head. For instance, under the dome of the skull our twelve pairs of cranial nerves reflect the twelvefold stars of the heavens (the zodiac), the same twelve Abraham was told to number so that his descendants (the twelve tribes and the twelve apostles) would be like them (Gen 15,5); see I-20 and I-21.

FIGURE 17

What appears to us in projection on the vault of the heavens we relate to the movements we ourselves are making with the Earth. For as we move with the Earth, we must project this backward in time to the embryonic period of life. During that period the heavenly pattern above folds into the fetus the etheric force patterns that manifest during the respective seven-year segments of its earthly life. We have yet to develop adequate studies in embryology giving effect to these realities.[17]

Before leaving our discussion of the lemniscatory form, let us note a further point. Recognizing in the planetary loops the very same principles outside us that are formative within us, let us now follow this loop-forming principle in greater detail. Note that Mercury and Venus form their loops when they are in inferior conjunction, that is, when they are between Earth and Sun. In other words, their loop occurs when the Sun is, so to speak, enhanced by them. As against this, look at Mars, Jupiter and Saturn, whose loops occur when they are in opposition to the Sun. This contrast of oppositions and conjunctions corresponds to a contrast in the human being's building forces.[18] Therefore, in the loop formation of the inner planets something is engaged that bears more *indirectly* (by virtue of the Sun's greater influence) upon the human form, while the

---

17. Robert Powell's *Hermetic Astrology*, Vols. 1 and 2 (HA1 and HA2), particularly Vol. 2, treats of it significantly, but much remains to be done.
18. So many of these contrasts were seen in the numerous dualities in the "Blood" essay.

influence engaged by the loops of the outer planets bears more *directly* (less influenced by the Sun) upon such form.

Thus, it is in connection with the larger loop formation of the outer planets that the sphere-forming process comes into evidence, namely, the forming of the human head. In contrast, their polar opposite is reflected in the movements of the inner planets which, more influenced by the Sun's direct relationship to Earth, deal more with the radial formation. In the outer planets, which make their loop in opposition, it is the loop that matters (and thus it is exaggerated), while with the inner planets, which make their loop in conjunction, their influence is by virtue of what is not in the loop, namely, the more radial open portion of the lemniscate. We see this from ancient times in the assignment of the planets to the human astral organs (see Figure 13 in the "hermetic man" chart, I-21).

Early in this volume we considered the hermetic law "As Above, So Below." Later, we saw in the "Fire" and "Light" essays how the bordering regions of the elements picture, or are pictured by, their neighboring elements. We also saw there the fractal nature of creation, how each stage is a picture of prior stages and is pictured by subsequent ones. Only the totally unimaginative soul could fail to detect in these observations a relationship to the cry of the Spirits of Form, the Elohim, in Gen 1,26-27, "Let us make the human being in our image, after our likeness.... So they created the human being in their own image...." Instead of understanding this passage rightly, classic theology has looked downward instead of upward. It has anthropomorphized the Elohim. That is, it has attributed the human shape to the gods rather than seeking the human from the nature and character of the gods. Our task in ages to come is to reverse this process and see in the human being the reflection of the higher spiritual nature. We must start by placing the human within the larger context of the created heavens if we are to extrapolate from there to the creating Elohim and on to the Christ "I Am," the creative Word itself—for the Elohim reflected the higher light of the Christ. We shall not find that character by telescope, microscope, spaceship or particle smasher, however much these uses might serve other purposes.

There is a remarkable resemblance between the human female sex cell, the egg, and the Earth. And then true to their fractal nature, there is a further remarkable resemblance between the Earth and the far larger Moon. We've lost the meaning of the Moon today. Copernican thinking destroyed it. The Ptolemaic system comprehended it. Let us look briefly at these relationships.

Like the Earth, the unfertilized egg cell has two poles, a so-called animal pole and a vegetal pole, the former being more active and containing the tiny cell nucleus while the latter is less active and contains most of the yolk.[19] After fertilization, when the cell first divides it does so vertically along its axis. Eighty-five percent of the Earth's landmass during the post-Atlantean Epoch is in the northern hemisphere which, by all observation, is clearly the more active hemisphere from a human standpoint, while the oceans lie in the south. When fertilized by the blood of Christ, the Earth also divided along its axis, from a human standpoint, into East and West.

But how is the cell/Earth similarity a reflection of the Moon/Earth relationship? Both the Ptolemaic and Copernican systems were attempts to synthesize what was observed. But the Copernican was based upon what was merely "seen" while the Ptolemaic was based upon what was more deeply "perceived." The Ptolemaic system did not look upon the Moon as being "up yonder." Rather, it considered the Moon to pervade the entire spheroid (or ellipsoid-of-rotation) circumscribed by its path— and the whole Moon was turning. The visible Moon was only a part of the full reality (Figure 18). This idea will not seem so remote if we remember the unfertilized egg cell, either with its nucleus, or later with the germinative area near the periphery (Figure 19).

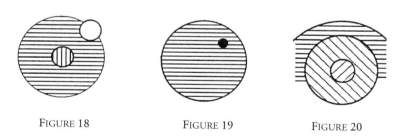

FIGURE 18   FIGURE 19   FIGURE 20

The tiny body of the embryo can be compared with this idea of the Moon that underlay the Ptolemaic system. But in like manner is the embryo, as indeed the human in later life, under the influence of even larger heavenly spheres. Figure 20 shows how we should conceive the Earth as being permeated by both the Moon and the Sun. Spiritually they

19. See 20 Brit 391, "Growth and Development; Animal Development; Preparatory Events."

are their far larger "spheres," not just the visible bodies. It is just such a similar concept that makes the thoughtful person reach out in soul and ask "What is man?" Is the human being to be regarded as no more than its visible body? In the beginning it was not so, nor when the Garden has again been attained will it be so, but in the valley of the shadow of death, where humanity still wanders as archetypal Cain (Gen 4,13-16) and Job (Job 2,6), we are estranged from the character (image) of the Elohim.

The Cassini Curve

In his discussion (Lects. 9, 10 and 15) of the Cassini curve and related geometrical figures, Steiner often goes into the underlying mathematical formulae, which I pass over here. Visual presentation should more readily convey the necessary imagination to most readers. Before going into these images, however, it would be well to look again at the four conic sections as shown in the "Fire" essay.[20] While we saw there four possible conic sections, circle, ellipse, parabola and hyperbola, we also saw that the parabola could be considered as an elongated ellipse with its center and one focus and vertex all coinciding at infinity. This is an interesting observation not only in view of the fact that all celestial orbits are elliptical, but because the Parable of the Prodigal Son is an allegory about the parabolic descent (from infinity) and reascent of humanity. The "elongated ellipse" disappears into infinity, just as one end of the lemniscate disappears through the human metabolic/limb system into the Earth. But if we thus join the parabola with the ellipse, and replace it among this foursome with the Cassini curve, we have the following general description for any point on the curve drawn with respect to its focal points (in the case of the ellipse, hyperbola and Cassini curve we are always dealing with two foci, whereas for the parabola only one):

Figure	Form	Description
21	Ellipse	*sum* of its distances from the two foci
22	Hyperbola	*difference* between its distances from the two foci
23	Cassini curve	*product* of its distances from the two foci
24	Circle	*quotient* of its distances from the two foci

---

20. Drawings illustrating each and all of these can be found in fn 57 of the "Fire" essay.

Steiner then portrays them graphically. The ellipse and hyperbola are shown in Figures 21 and 22.

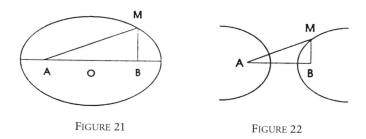

FIGURE 21   FIGURE 22

For the Cassini curve, Steiner takes us through a progressive series of figures (Figure 23) that result from merely changing certain interrelationships within the formula itself, all quite mathematically proper, as he illustrates.

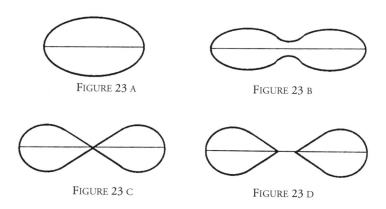

FIGURE 23 A   FIGURE 23 B

FIGURE 23 C   FIGURE 23 D

While we do not have to go out of space to mathematically portray the hyperbola (Figure 22), nor to portray the Cassini curve in Figures 23 a, b and c, we do have to go out of space to portray the one in Figure 23d. This curve is describable in mathematics but cannot be demonstrated within the three dimensions of Euclidean geometry.

Now if we progress to the circle, we note the usual definition of the circle as being a curved line every point on which is a constant distance from a fixed point (its center). But there is another definition for a circle, namely, that curve every point of which fulfills the condition that its distances from two fixed points maintain a constant *quotient* (Figure 24).

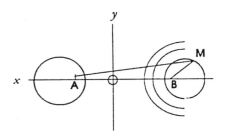

FIGURE 24

Thus, in all of these conic figures we can see the necessity of going out of space, or in the case of the ellipse considering it in the larger dimension of the parabola as an ellipse disappearing into infinity. Moreover, the starting point of the Cassini curve is the ellipse.

Thus we have the hint, even in the field of mathematics, that the human soul appears for a while incarnated in earthly form and then goes out of that into the opposite state, the spiritual state, before returning.[21]

---

21. In the "Prefatory Note" to his classic *On Growth and Form* (OGF), an incomparable treatment of these phenomena, D'Arcy Thompson tells us

> It is not the biologist with an inkling of mathematics, but the skilled and learned mathematician who must ultimately deal with such problems as are sketched and adumbrated here. I pretend to no mathematical skill, but I have made what use I could of what tools I had.

In Chap. IV, "On the Internal Form and Structure of the Cell," Thompson deals with the mysterious forces within the cell that bring about its growth through division. Near the outset he says (p. 286), "There are forms and configurations of matter within the cell which … deserve to be studied with due regard to the forces, known or unknown, of whose resultant they are the visible expression." The mathematics of the Cassini curve may have been beyond Thompson's mathematical skills, but in his Fig. 97 (p. 319) he portrays a "resultant" stage and progression in cell division in a way that would seem to be eminently expressive of Steiner's contemporaneous presentation.

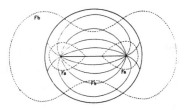

In Thompson's figure we have a picture at the level of the cell of what happens in the evolutionary journey of the human soul between the sensible and supersensible worlds. We will see in our text that it is also a picture of what is happening in the cosmos—our planetary system and beyond. All creation is fractal—image—what is above is like what is below and what is below is like what is above.

But in the imagery of the moving lemniscate, the soul (the Individuality) does not return to the same spot (i.e., the same personality) it occupied in any prior incarnation.[22]

And if we look back again at the illustration of the four conic sections, noting particularly the hyperbola, we see that its parts exist for a while, then go out of existence only to come back into existence in the opposite cone. Recall that the moving lemniscatory relationship between the Sun and the Earth (Figure 10) involved a rotating lemniscate, in other words opposite cones.

Moreover, we saw that what was inside one loop of the lemniscate was outside the opposite loop—how like the radial-spherical poles in the human body.

Now suppose we cause the circle on the right side of Figure 24 to increase in size so that its line of curvature becomes less and less. Thinking thus, eventually it flattens into a straight line, the line in fact shown as the *y* axis. We can even go further and imagine the original circle—which has become now a straight line—moving on further so that it becomes a circle on the left side of the *y* axis. But in the process of moving the circle from the right side to the left, what has happened? The forces of curvature that were on the inside of the circle on the right side flip over and are forces of curvature on the outside of the circle on the left side. See Figure 25. It is quite difficult for us to picture this in our minds. When we pass from the circle on the right to the straight line in the middle, we still have a circle, but with its center in the indefinite distance to the right. The instant we

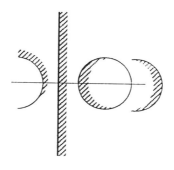

FIGURE 25

---

22. For the meanings of, and distinctions between, the terms "Individuality" and "personality," see fn 31 in the "Blood" essay.

cross to the far side of that line bending it to the left, the forces stay on the right side of the line as it curves into the circle on the left side. If we assume that the forces inside the circle on the right were centripetal forces, then for the circle on the left they become centrifugal forces. On the right they pull or suck inward, while on the left they pull or suck outward.

It is quite legitimate to see in this the relationship between a photograph and its negative, or between matter (flesh) and spirit, or between Sun and Earth, or between spherical and radial, or between thinking (skull/head/consciousness) and willing (metabolism/limb/unconsciousness), or between pressure and suction.

Recall something of the same imagery in the "Light" essay when we were discussing Goethe's theory of color. Goethe wrestled with the problem of how the spectrum is reversed when darkness is allowed to pass through the prism in the same manner that light is made to pass through it. What you get is an inverted spectrum (see Figures 17 and 18 in the "Light" essay). In the ordinary spectrum, green is in the middle between violet on one side and red on the other. In the spectrum obtained by Goethe in applying a strip of darkness to the prism, there is peach blossom in the middle and then again red on one side and violet on the other. Two color bands are obtained whose centers are qualitatively opposite to one another and seem to stretch away, as it were, into infinity (Figure 26).

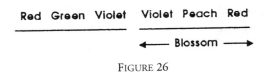

FIGURE 26

Let us apply these thoughts to the human being. Suppose we recognize that there is something in the human organization that is not at all in space but necessitates that we imagine, in a spatial way, separated line systems inherently united by another principle that is outside three-dimensional space (Figure 27). If we think of three dimensions, we can also think of subtracting these to the point that their positives become negatives—a person can have wealth but also debt and can thus be either solvent or insolvent depending upon which is the greater amount. If we apply the concept of forces moving from centripetal to centrifugal as one passes out of space, as illustrated earlier, then we can conceive of the human form somewhat as reflected in Figure 28.

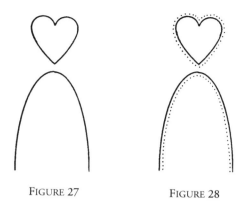

FIGURE 27   FIGURE 28

To further illustrate, let us return to the Cassini curve. It has three essential forms, the ellipse, lemniscate and a third of such nature as to be a single entity from the conceptual and analytical aspect but having two branches. In the last of these, the two branches are really one curve, but in drawing it we have to go out of space and then come back in again. Steiner illustrates all three forms in Figure 29 by asking, "What will be the path of a point that, when illumined from a fixed point, appears with constant intensity when seen from another fixed point?" The answer is a Cassini curve, for it will be the locus of all points through which a point must pass while being illumined with the same intensity of light from another fixed point. It will not be hard to imagine, with respect to the ellipse, that if something shines from A to C and then by reflection from C to B, the

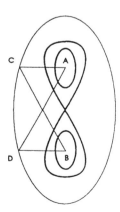

FIGURE 29

intensity of light will be the same as if instead it is reflected from D. It will be rather more difficult to imagine the same with regard to the lemniscate, and still more difficult with the two-branched curve. In the last instance you will have to imagine as you pass from one branch to another that the light goes out of space and then shines into space again.

One must think contemplatively and meditatively upon the ideas that Steiner has been giving us here. They help us to conceive of the relationship between the conscious and unconscious parts of our earthly being, our head and nervous system on the one hand, and our metabolic and limb processes on the other, our thinking versus our willing. And they help us to see how we relate in our incarnated earthly being to our existence while in the spiritual state between incarnations. But let us also think further of how an organ in our body relates to the heavens above and is formed by or out of this relationship. In this thought process, we need to remember that the visible portions of the heavens (the Sun, Moon, planets and fixed stars) are only that and not the full scope of the force fields they represent—any more than our physical body is all there is to our more spiritual forces.

In this endeavor we have to visualize the interaction of two kinds of space. One of them with the ordinary three dimensions may be conceived as issuing radially from a central point (Figure 30); the other, which all the time annuls the first, may not be thought of as issuing from a point at all but must be thought of as emanating from some encompassing sphere infinitely far away (Figure 31). So we have to distinguish two different kinds of points: a point of zero area, which is turned outward and a point within the area of an infinite spherical surface, which is turned inward. In every instance we have to ask the question, is the point's curvature turned inward or is it turned outward? This will affect its field of influence.

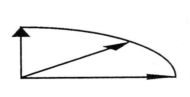

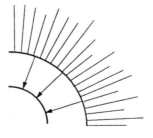

FIGURE 30   FIGURE 31

And yet we must go further. It would seem permissible to see in our etheric organs (our unconscious metabolic processes) the image of forces in the heavens represented by visible bodies of our solar system and to see in our astral organs (our conscious, sensate processes) the image of zodiacal forces represented by the visible fixed stars.[23] But let us imagine that as we go farther and farther out into the universe we come at length to where we no longer find heavenly bodies—yet neither do we find a mere empty Euclidean space. There we must find something whose inherent reality obliges us to recognize its continuation at points within created space. This is simply an extension of the universal law of polarity.

Let us think of this outer inherent reality as the Father from which the Creative Word, the Son (Jn 1,1-3) went forth.[24] Later in John's Gospel Christ speaks of having come from the Father and returning to the Father and drawing all persons to himself (Jn 12,32). In this, he is becoming and acting as this outer inherent reality. And we must then further think of this outer inherent reality as an awesome force of suction (negative space) that pulls the universe outward toward it. Within the universe it is represented by the stars such as our Sun. We've already seen how the suction of the stars in the universe tends to balance out matter (including the black holes).[25] In other words, in the creative process, the creation of light involved suction while darkness involved matter, a process of division one can readily contemplate in the study of chart I-22 so much discussed throughout this volume. This concept obviates the necessity, and thus eradicates the very basis, of the currently popular "big bang" hypothesis.

Steiner, in Lect. 17, shows how something was lost in our comprehension of the universe when the Copernican system superceded the Ptolemaic, and how calculations even today must take their start from the system of Tycho Brahe (the teacher of Johannes Kepler, whose work laid

---

23. While there is an intimate interrelationship between planetary and zodiacal forces in all parts of the human being, it is best to find the illustration of the text statement in **I-20**. The influence of the planetary forces on the etheric body are illustrated in **I-86** while their effect on the astral body is illustrated in **I-21**.

24. The sexist implications of the terms "Father" and "Son" as used here and later in this essay should be considered in the light of what is said about them in the Preface.

25. In the "Light" essay, near the end of the section entitled "Fagg—Light as Electromagnetism" we said that there had to be either unaccounted for mass or suction in the intergalactic spaces to account for what is called "gravitational effects." Science has not yet found or explained any such undiscovered mass.

the foundation for what was to follow in the works of Copernicus and Isaac Newton, but who himself derived his knowledge from the ancient systems and comprehended relationships deeper than what was understood by his followers).

The polarities between the stars and the other "bodies" in the universe, the polarities of matter and negative matter, so to speak, are pictured by Steiner as he begins the last lecture (Lect. 18) as follows:

> If we remember what was said previously about the polar character between the Earth and the Sun, we shall then understand that it is very important to interpret the empirical facts in the correct way. How must we then interpret phenomena that seem on the surface to be similar when we are looking with or without the help of optical instruments towards the Sun? Those empirically observed phenomena on the Sun will reveal themselves in their true light only if we take our start from such an idea as this: An eruption occurring on the surface of the Earth will obviously be interpreted as something which strives upwards and outward. A process on the Sun, such as a Sun spot, for example, must be interpreted as striving from without inward.
>
> With this line of thought, we have to imagine that if we went through and beneath the surface of the Earth, we shall get into dense material substance. We should have to imagine that if we moved from outside the Sun toward the Sun's interior, we should come into an ever less dense state of matter. If you consider the Earth and the whole way in which it is placed in the universe, you find that it manifests as so much ponderable matter in the universe. But with the Sun it is entirely different. With the Sun you have to imagine that as we go from the circumference to the interior we get more into the imponderable matter; we go into negation of matter.
>
> We have exactly the opposite behavior from that which happens as we draw near to the Sun's middle point. The Sun must therefore be conceived as a hollowing out of cosmic matter, a hollow sphere enveloped by more material substance [Figure 32]. In contrast to this, the Earth has a denser material enveloped by more attenuated matter in the atmosphere. As to the Earth, we think of the air outside the Earth. As you go inward from the circumference, the matter becomes denser. Not only is the Sun a more attenuated cosmic body with a materiality much less dense than Earthly matter, but if we call the Earth's materiality

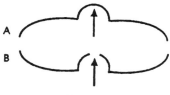

FIGURE 32

positive, then, in a certain sense, in the Sun's interior we shall have to call that negative matter. We can understand the phenomena if we conceive that out there in the inner space of the Sun there exists negative materiality. Now you can say that negative matter exerts a suctional effect while positive matter exerts pressure.[26] If you now conceive the Sun as a collection of suctional forces, then you will not need another explanation for that which we call gravitation.[27]

Think of the movement of the Earth and Sun in such a way that the Earth follows the Sun in the same path and in the same direction.

---

26. We saw in *The Burning Bush* how the Elohim (Exusiai) were the Sun dwellers within our solar system, and Chart I-27 shows how the various lower beings were progressively separated from the Sun in the evolution of the system. The polar nature of the sense-perceptible (e.g., flesh) and the spiritual (e.g., spiritual beings) worlds is reflected in the following passage from *At Home in the Universe* (AHIU), Lect. 3, pp. 56-57:

In the sense-perceptible world, we have certain references to help us describe the spiritual in which we live between death and a new birth. In the realm of the senses we see stars and the planets of our system, and they reveal only their outer nature to our senses. Their inner reality is very different; they are the gathering of spiritual beings who have come together in diverse ways where stars appear in the heavens. When we observe a star with our physical eyes, there is, in fact, a community of spiritual beings at that place in the cosmos. The physical star we see shows us only the direction—a signpost, or chart. Conventional scientific descriptions of stars have very little meaning, because they deal only with those signposts, or charts to orient our vision. When we see a star somewhere in the sky, it indicates the location of a community of spiritual beings.

27. What Steiner is saying here would seem to apply to the scientific concept of celestial gravitation. This concept is used to determine the masses and densities of celestial bodies and thus to investigate the physical constitutions of stars and planets. See 20 Brit 174, "Gravitation, Some Astronomical Aspects of Gravitation." The force called gravity, and its measurement, for bodies of like kind (matter as distinguished from negative matter), is simply a reflection of the principle discussed earlier that the reality of any object can only be understood in the context of the whole of which it is a part. It is the principle of cohesion that causes particles of water to become a globular drop, or the Earth itself as a planet to become spherical. It is like the accumulation of positive charges and negative charges together before these opposites again coalesce by lightning spark. All polarity eventually resolves itself. On the larger scale of creation, this is what the union of all things envisions as eventuality (Eph 1,9-10).

This is the cosmic relationship between the Sun and the Earth. The Sun, as a compendium of suctional forces, proceeds in front, and, as a result of this suctional force, the Earth is dragged after it, moving through cosmic space in the same course and direction in which the Sun pushes itself forward. Thus, you can understand what otherwise would be difficult to conceive. In no other way can you reach an idea which is comprehensive enough to comprise all of the observed phenomena. You have to start by imagining that in the realm of matter, there is material substance of a positive intensity and material substance of a negative intensity. Solar matter has a negative intensity. It is not only empty in relationship to matter-filled space but it is even less than empty. It is hollowing out of space itself.

This may be difficult to imagine, but if you are accustomed to working with mathematical ideas, consider a certain degree of fullness of space as a corresponding magnitude, say $+A$, and empty space would be conceived mathematically as 0, while a space less than empty has to be conceived as $-A$. This will enable you to conceive a relationship analogous to what we employ in mathematics, a relationship between the different intensities of terrestrial and solar matter.

This is essentially the biblical distinction between "flesh" and "spirit" (Jn 3,1-15). Both scientific and theological (religious) thinking has been earthly rather than spiritual. Neither can begin to approach an understanding of the higher kingdoms (plant, animal and human, those above the mineral) until we change our manner of thinking to accommodate this distinction. In the Creation essay, we saw that the human being as an image (Gen 1,26-27) of the Elohim was envisioned by them before the creation in Gen 2 of any matter. In the laws of photography, the image on the film negative is the opposite of the picture that results when the negative is developed, and even an image produced by simple reflection is reversed in appearance. What is visible is the polar opposite of what is invisible. The ancients spoke of the shadow as the spirit of what cast it. "The shadow of each thing shall be its spirit and shall be with it always."[28]

---

28. *Lakota Myth* (LAKM), p. 195. See also its index reference to "shadows."

Let us think for a moment about the forces in the cosmos. Everything that we call the cosmos can be considered to be positive as it relates to the immensity of its balancing negative force, the ultimate Creator God. This gives us the opposite of the "big bang." The awesome force of this one Creator God can be considered to be far stronger than any of the forces in the cosmos (nature) and to encompass the cosmos beyond the farthest reaches of created space.

Gravity is a weak force; electromagnetism is far, far stronger. In Fagg's discussion of the four forces of nature (in the "Light" essay) they were ranked in the following order from strength to weakness: nuclear, electromagnetic, weak and gravitational. Thus gravity is the weakest of the four forces of nature. Think of it in comparison with the illustration of electromagnetic force given in 18 Brit 159, "The absence of only one electron out of every billion molecules in two … 154-pound persons standing two meters … apart would repel them with a 30,000-ton force."

Positive charges repel each other, as do negative; opposite charges attract. This concept alone suffices to pose a concept about the forces between the less-than-empty (materially negative) Sun and the full Earth, especially when we throw in the electromagnetic effects of moving electric charges through magnetic fields. These would seem to bring our solar system into relationship with the fixed stars.

Lightning phenomena suggest that there are forces that bring positive charges or negative charges into association with one another. And when these homogenous aggregations build up enough, there is lightning to equalize the pent up energies of repulsion by the forces of attraction. And this lightning is a destruction of space between the two. The space was created to begin with by the accumulation of like charges. This buildup is similar to what causes the solidification of matter on the one hand and the dissipation of matter in the spirit realm on the other.

The visible light of the Sun is produced when the etheric light of its empty core interacts with the attracted gases from within the solar system, where the two meet on the Sun's surface, and the constant interaction is like lightning—the *sacrifice* of internal power to destroy matter on the surface so that the Sun's "energy" will eventually play out, but only as matter within the solar system is spiritualized.

This concept again obviates the gruesome idea of a "big bang," which is antithetical by its very nature to the manner in which spirit gradually densifies into matter. The expanding universe might simply be a manifestation of the repulsion principle that entered into the universe when a certain stage of densification caused it to become matter rather than spirit. The fugacious or centrifugal force causing the "expansion" of the universe at or near the speed of light is simply the attraction of the Godhead force beyond space (akin to that of the Sun in our solar system) to the matter within the universe, for even the holiness represented by the fixed stars (such as our Sun) is positive compared with the unspeakable holiness of the one Creator God.

The "big bang" theory becomes superfluous since there is a balancing out of matter in the universe by the negative matter in the fixed stars, and both are drawn ever outward to the Father. Thus the Christ, who is one with the Father,[29] told us, "And I, when I am lifted up from the earth, will draw all men to myself" (Jn 12,32).[30]

This concept gives effect also to the fractal nature of all creation. Electromagnetism is simply the *image* of what applies on a far larger scale. Our puny gravitational force is more like what causes positive charges, or negative charges, to congregate in spite of their inherently repulsive nature. This balancing between matter and negative matter in the universe is completely in accordance with Newton's third law, frequently called the law of action and reaction. The creative process envisioned by the descent into matter from the etheric world, so often portrayed in this work by chart I-22, is consistent with, and demands, this balancing. It is the very principle that says there is no spiritual growth without sacrifice.

Recall from the "Blood" essay[31] what the ancient seers called Saturn—Kronos (the root name of "time")[32] who "devours his own children." It is a spiritual reality or law that applies at all levels—the ultimate principle of apocalypse.

Whenever one of the hierarchies (see I-6) sacrificed something, it elevated itself to a higher spiritual level while something came into being in what we call the creative process. The series of sacrifices by the Elohim

---

29. See Jn 10,30,38; 14,10,11,20; and 17,21.
30. And in the light of such passages as Rom 8,19-23 and Eph 1,9-10, we can see that Christ is referring not just to "men" (i.e., human beings) being drawn to himself but to all the lower Kingdoms (animal, plant and mineral) as well, and even the hierarchies (the "heavenly host") themselves.
31. See its fn 23 and related text.
32. See I-17 at p. 568, of *The Burning Bush*, and I-27.

that led to their creating the human being in their own *image* (Gen 1,26-27) is portrayed in chart I-35. The pattern for human elevation, the return of the Prodigal Son, is laid down in the Crucifixion, the essential step whereby the resurrected Christ is called the "first fruits" of those that sleep.[33] All flesh must pass through Crucifixion before the Prodigal can reenter the Garden. It is the removal of the curse of both Cain and Job that inheres in every human being until that Crucifixion (sacrifice) is complete. The pathway is that of sacrificial love, for that is the *image* of God, the heart and core of all Johannine scripture (e.g., Jn 3,16; 1 Jn 4).

---

33. See 1 Cor 15,20,23; Jas 1,18 and Rev 14,4.

CHARTS
AND
TABULATIONS

Preface

AS INDICATED in the preface to this volume, certain charts from Volume 1 are reproduced below for the sake of reader convenience. Only those cited most frequently or otherwise considered most vital are reproduced. Others cited in this volume can be found in Volume 1 or on the website *www.bibleandanthroposophy.com*. All chart designations are in bold type. All Volume 1 charts are identified by the Roman numeral one (**I**) followed by a hyphen and the Arabic number of the chart. Volume 2 charts are indicated by the Roman numeral two (**II**), and start with the Arabic number one (1). Thus, the first chart reproduced from Volume 1 is designated **I-1** and the first chart introduced in this Volume 2 is designated **II-1**.

List of Chart Titles

(The prefix I- is omitted from this enumeration of Volume 1 charts)

Volume One Charts Reproduced:

1. Schematic of human being's creation, descent and reascent per ASJ
2. Schematic of human being's creation, descent and reascent per TL
6. The nine hierarchies
9. The essential nature of the human being
10. The relationship of the Ego to oblivion, sleep and death; and the human being's common relationships with the lower kingdoms
14. The four systems of the human being's physical body as expressions and descendants of Conditions of Consciousness

15. Hierarchical attainment of "human" status in the three former Conditions of Consciousness

16. The ruling hierarchies on Earth and its three former Conditions of Consciousness, respectively

18. Human and other hierarchical and Trinitarian relationships to the zodiac

19. Powell's hermetic astrological charts and tabulations

20. The microcosmic reflections of the zodiacal and planetary natures in the human being (and in the apostolic groupings)

21. Powell's charts and graphs showing "the hermetic man" (planetary relationships of the human being's organs) and "the zodiacal man" (zodiacal relationships of the human being's physical body)

22. The elementary states, the ethers and elements

24. Progressive development of the human being's 9-fold nature charted through the present post-Atlantean Epoch

25. Relationship of the 7 "churches" of the Apocalypse to the 7 Cultural Eras of the post-Atlantean Epoch

27. Steiner's exposition on the organic order and character of the traditional planets; Powell's on the outer three planets

32. Lucifer and Ahriman

33. Course of the Ego between death and rebirth; Regions of soul and spirit worlds

35. The hierarchical sacrifices and the approach and entry of the human being's Ego

86. The reflection of the planets in the human being's physical organs

Volume Two Charts:

II-1   A profile review of creation

II-2   The hierarchical sacrifices and the origin of the four kingdoms

II-3   The four possible worlds

II-4   Planetary influences during the post-Atlantean Epoch

Charts and Tabulations

I-1 ~~Schematic of human being's creation, descent and reascent per ASJ~~

ASJ, fold-out following terminal notes (page 228)

This chart is given primacy. Conceptualizing the creative process is probably the first, most difficult, yet most important, step in anthroposophy. It is not unlike contemplating a chart of the universe. One stretches the mind to comprehend it, yet the moment thinking is relaxed the mind reverts back toward its prior dimension. Constant stretching is required. One should not hesitate to return to this chart again and again.

A different profile of the same concept is also available in I-2, I-3 and I-4.

The Bible, from beginning to end, is an account of the descent of the human being from the spiritual world and its return thereto, encompassing the entire evolutionary process. It assumes added resplendence when seen in the light of anthroposophy. And humanity itself is then seen as the paradigm of the Prodigal Son. Anthroposophy is nothing but that "knowledge of truth" (Jn 8,32) which is vital if the human being is to "come to himself" (Lk 15,17). These three charts portray that same path, which Rudolf Steiner has lighted for the first time since the age of the human being's intellectual maturity.

(While more fully treated later, it may be helpful here to refer to the "twenty-four elders" frequently mentioned in Revelation [e.g., Rev 4,4,10, Rev 5,8, Rev 11,16, Rev 19,4 et al.]. These are identified by Steiner [ASJ Lect. 5] as twenty-four members of the spiritual hierarchies who attained their respective "human" [i.e., consciousness] states in the twenty-four successive Conditions of Life that have preceded our present one, i.e., seven each on Old Saturn, Old Sun and Old Moon plus the first three Elementary Kingdoms of the Earth Condition of Consciousness. All these elders come from the hierarchies [see I-6], but in considering this, one must realize that there are seven levels within each rank of each hierarchy, thus seven "elders" would come from a single rank in the list of nine hierarchies. More is said about the "twenty-four elders in I-12 and I-15.)

I-2 Schematic of human being's creation, descent and reascent per TL

TL, between Notes 3 and 4 of Lecture 11 (page 385)

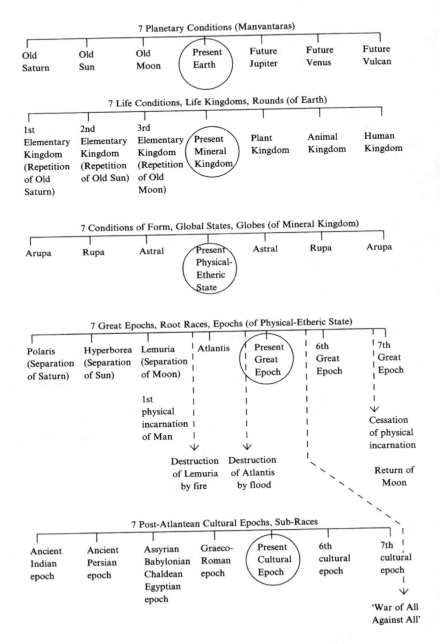

7 Planetary Conditions (Manvantaras)

| Old Saturn | Old Sun | Old Moon | Present Earth | Future Jupiter | Future Venus | Future Vulcan |

7 Life Conditions, Life Kingdoms, Rounds (of Earth)

| 1st Elementary Kingdom (Repetition of Old Saturn) | 2nd Elementary Kingdom (Repetition of Old Sun) | 3rd Elementary Kingdom (Repetition of Old Moon) | Present Mineral Kingdom | Plant Kingdom | Animal Kingdom | Human Kingdom |

7 Conditions of Form, Global States, Globes (of Mineral Kingdom)

| Arupa | Rupa | Astral | Present Physical-Etheric State | Astral | Rupa | Arupa |

7 Great Epochs, Root Races, Epochs (of Physical-Etheric State)

| Polaris (Separation of Saturn) | Hyperborea (Separation of Sun) | Lemuria (Separation of Moon) | Atlantis | Present Great Epoch | 6th Great Epoch | 7th Great Epoch |

1st physical incarnation of Man

Destruction of Lemuria by fire

Destruction of Atlantis by flood

Cessation of physical incarnation

Return of Moon

7 Post-Atlantean Cultural Epochs, Sub-Races

| Ancient Indian epoch | Ancient Persian epoch | Assyrian Babylonian Chaldean Egyptian epoch | Graeco-Roman epoch | Present Cultural Epoch | 6th cultural epoch | 7th cultural epoch |

'War of All Against All'

I-6 <u>The nine hierarchies</u>

OES, Chap. 4 (pp. 122-128); CM, Essay xiv, "The Life of Saturn"; SHPW, Lect. 5; SB, Intro. by Querido (p. 17); UEM, Lect. Aug 7, 1908 (p. 63)

The spiritual hierarchies, of which there are nine between the Trinity (Father-Son-Holy Spirit) and the human being, are as follows:

Name Given by Steiner	Christian Esotericism	Biblical Greek (Heb)
1. Spirits of Love	Seraphim	Seraphime
2. Spirits of Harmony	Cherubim	Cherubime
3. Spirits of Will	Thrones	Thronos
4. Spirits of Wisdom	Dominions	Kyriotetes
5. Spirits of Motion	Mights	Dynamis
6. Spirits of Form	Powers (Authorities)	Exusiai (Elohim)
7. Spirits of Personality	Principalities (Primal Beginnings)	Archai
8. Spirits of Fire (Folk)	Archangels	Archangeloi
9. Sons of Life (or of Twilight)	Angels (Messengers)	Angeloi

It is noted that in the most basic work, OES, Steiner identifies his Spirits of Motion to the Christian esoteric term "Powers," and equates his Spirits of Form to "Authorities." However, in all the other works of his identified above, he conforms to the above listing in this regard.

An excellent article by Jennifer Mellett, entitled "The Spiritual Hierarchies as Depicted in the Florence Baptistry Dome and by Dante," appeared in the informal publication entitled "Anthroposophy in Texas" in recent years, though I do not have the date of the issue. It has a most helpful tabulation entitled, "Different Systems of Ordering the Angelic Hierarchies," which shows the terms used by Dionysius the Areopagite, Dante in *Paradiso* and in *Il Convivio*, Steiner, Brunetto Latini (Dante's teacher) and Gregory the Great in *Moralia* and in *Homilies*. The terminology is generally in line with that above, though with some variations. Others who wrote on these hierarchies, according to Querido's Introduction to SB, include John of Salisbury, Bishop of Chartres, Thomas Aquinas, and Albertus Magnus. As Querido points out, by the sixteenth century, humanity (i.e., materialistic Christianity) had lost this spiritual view of the universe.

I-9 The essential nature of the human being

OES, Chap. 2 (The Essential Nature of the Human Being)

The human being may be described as being composed of 3, 4, 7 or 9 divisions, as follows:

3-Fold	4-Fold	7-Fold	9-Fold
	Physical	Physical	Physical
Body	Etheric	Etheric	Etheric
	Astral	Astral	Astral
			Sentient Soul
			Intellectual Soul
Soul		Ego	Consciousness
			(Spiritual Soul)
	Ego		
		Spirit Self (Manas)	Spirit Self (Manas)
Spirit		Life Spirit (Buddhi)	Life Spirit (Buddhi)
		Spirit Man (Atma)	Spirit Man (Atma)

The essential nature of the body and soul components is as follows:

<u>Component of Human Being</u> <u>Essential Nature of Component</u>

Ego   Lasting or eternal individuality

Astral body   Seat of consciousness, passions & desires

Etheric (Life) body   Seat of life

Physical body   Seat of, or pattern for, mineral
                                 accumulation

I-10 <u>The relationship of the Ego to oblivion, sleep and death; and the</u>
<u>human being's common relationships with the lower kingdoms</u>

   OES, Chap. 2 (p. 30-35); THSY, Chap. 1

Human Being absent Ego   =   Oblivion

Human Being absent Ego and astral body   =   Sleep

Human Being absent Ego, astral & etheric bodies = Death

Or

Ether body   =   Life

Astral body   =   Consciousness

Ego   =   Memory*

Thus

<u>The human being has a(n)</u>   <u>In common with the</u>

Physical body   Mineral

Etheric body   Plant

Astral body   Animal

Ego   —

* What would seem to be memory in an animal is not memory in the
sense that the human being has a memory, but is based upon a function
of the astral body. The cause for what appears to be memory in an animal
always comes from a presently existing circumstance giving rise to need

based upon experience. Absent such a circumstance (such as its master's presence, hunger, etc.), the animal cannot call up from within the same conscious feeling as can a human being.

I-14 The four systems of the human being's physical body as expressions and descendants of Conditions of Consciousness

ISBM, Lect. 8 (pp. 128-129) and Lect. 10 (pp. 163-165); UEM, Lect. 10, Aug 14, 1908 (p. 151); Jn-Rel, Lect. 3 (p. 41)

Body System (i.e., Instrument)	"Body"	Origin
Physical body and organs working purely mechanically	Physical	Saturn
Gland Organs	Etheric	Sun
Nerve Organs	Astral	Moon
Blood (Circulatory) System	Ego	Earth

I-15 Hierarchical attainment of "human" status on the three former Conditions of Consciousness

OES, Chap. 4 (pp. 125-129)

Note again the discussion in **I-1** of the "twenty-four elders." Recall that we are now in the 25th Condition of Life. The human being first attained "human" status (acquired an Ego, consciousness of self, the "I Am" [Ex 3,14]) about midway through the 25th, but all spiritual beings in the 9 hierarchies above the human being also went through the equivalent of a "human" state during a particular Condition of Life, and thus bear the human within themselves. So there are 24 "elders" who passed this way before the human being.

However, one must conclude that there are 7 levels of "elders" within each hierarchical level. Each hierarchical being is, like the human being, a 7-fold being that moves one step higher with each Condition of Life, and thus, like the human being, attains to its self-awareness (human) level in its own 4th evolutionary Condition of Life within its own evolutionary

Condition of Consciousness, which does not coincide with the human being's except once every 7 levels, each group of which is then characterized here as a hierarchical level. Thus, there are in Steiner's description of the hierarchical levels active on *Saturn* several that have as their lowest member the astral body at various descending stages of development. So, just as the human being receives its Ego in its 4th Condition of Consciousness (*Earth*), but more specifically in its 4th Condition of Life (mineral kingdom) thereof, so also during any one of the human being's Conditions of Consciousness there would be 7 elders generally classified during that time as receiving their "human" or "Ego" or "self-awareness" state during that 7-stage Condition. All 7 of these elders would be referred to as a single hierarchical level, but at 7 different stages of development (and each stage, as in the case of the human being itself, would encompass innumerable such spiritual beings within it). Within this framework then, it can be said (see for instance, page 125 where Steiner mentions that the Spirits of Personality reach "human" status on *Saturn*) that one hierarchical level reaches human status during each Condition of Consciousness and specifically as follows:

Spiritual Being	Attains Human Status On
Principalities (Spirits of Personality)	Saturn
Archangels (Spirits of Fire)	Sun
Angels (Sons of Life, Sons of Twilight)	Moon
Human Being	Earth

Those hierarchical beings higher than Principalities thus attained human status prior to *Saturn*. While they continue to advance, such levels are beyond those we need here discuss.

I-16   The ruling hierarchies on Earth and its three former Conditions of Consciousness, respectively

UEM, Lect. 4 (pp. 52-53)

In the same way that Elohim (Gen 1,1), or Exusiai, ruled the Earth evolution, so also did higher hierarchies rule prior incarnations of the Earth.

Ruling Hierarchical Level	Condition of Consciousness
Exusiai (Elohim), Authorities	Earth
Dynamis, Powers or Mights	Moon
Kyriotetes, Dominions	Sun
Thronos, Thrones	Saturn

It was the sacrifice by the ruling hierarchy during each such period that made the development of the human being possible during that period, i.e., physical (Saturn), etheric (Sun), astral (Moon) and Ego (Earth), respectively.

I-18 Human and other hierarchical and Trinitarian relationships to the zodiac

Steiner spoke often about the "Zodiac," about how consciousness of its influence had gradually been lost as the human being descended from spiritual consciousness into materialistic consciousness, about how modern astrology was merely dilettantism, and about how the former consciousness would one day again be regained as knowledge. And he left many guideposts in that direction, so that now, after many decades of dedicated research by his disciples, we have the recent, amazing works of Robert Powell on "hermetic astrology." The substance of these will be touched upon later. The foregoing is mentioned here only to awaken the reader to the fact of the influence of the Zodiac (the "fixed stars" beyond our Solar System) upon the human being. The truth of this is strewn through the Bible when the meaning of its passages is understood. We get an inkling of it when Yahweh tells Abram, in Gen 15,5 (according to a modern translation), "'Look toward heaven, and number the stars, if you are able to number them.' Then he said to him, 'So shall your descendants be.'"

From what follows, one can see that Christ, the "Mystical Lamb," represents the highest of the twelve "animals" of the "Zodiac," and as such is also called, "the Son." Above him is the Father, so that the macrocosmic Word behind the Zodiac had 12 sons, and thus microcosmically Jacob had 12 sons, as also did Ishmael, and Christ had 12 disciples. None of these are mere coincidence, but represent truth inscribed into all that we call "creation."

"In the same way that Christ has *the Constellation of the Ram* as the source of His spiritual emanations in our cosmos [citing ISBM, Lect. 2] ... so does the Sophia have *the Constellation of the Virgin* as the source of her spiritual emanations in the macrocosm ..." (Prokofieff, THNS, Sec. 2, Chap. 1, p. 86). In the ancient Mysteries, known to the Magi, "there was a prophetic indication of the event that would take place when the sun stood at midnight between December 24 and 25 in the *sign of the Virgin* ..." (EIE). Inasmuch as all spiritual beings are 7-fold (ISBM, Lect. 2 and Prov 9,1), Christ could only become an incarnated human being (i.e., descend to the physical state) by entering therein *through the Constellation of the Virgin.*

For now, it must suffice merely to set out certain tabulations from ISBM, Lect. 2 (esp. p. 32); SIS, Lect. 2; EIE; THNS, Sec. 1, Chaps. 1 and 2, Sec. 2., Chap. 1 (esp. p. 86).

7-Fold Human Being	Hierarchy	Zodiacal Symbol Animal (Latin)	Animal (English)	7-fold "Mystical Lamb"
	Son/Christ	Aries	Ram (Lamb)	12th member
	Holy Spirit	Taurus	Bull	11th member
	Seraphim	Gemini	Twins	10th member
	Cherubim	Cancer	Crab	9th member
	Thrones	Leo	Lion	8th member
7th Spirit Man	Kyriotetes	Virgo	Virgin	7th member
6th Life Spirit	Dynamis	Libra	Scales	6th member
5th Spirit Self	Exusiai	Scorpio	Scorpion	
4th Ego	Archai	Sagittarius	Archer	
3rd Astral Body	Archangels	Capricorn	Goat	
2nd Etheric Body	Angels	Aquarius	Waterman	
1st Physical Body	Human	Pisces	Fishes	

The human being's highest "fold" is represented by the cosmic sign of the Virgin, to be attained at the conclusion of the Venus Condition of Consciousness. The human being will then have attained to the state of the Cosmic Virgin "Sophia"—thus, "Anthropo-Sophia," the Holy Virgin who gave birth to the Christ in the physical state.

I-19 Powell's hermetic astrological charts and tabulations

HA1, Chap. 3

The length of time required for the Sun to travel its complete cycle through the 12 constellations of the "Zodiac" is 25,920 years (an astronomical fact). The average length of time allocable to each constellation is thus 25,920/12, or 2160 years.

In *Sidereal Zodiac* (SZ), Robert Powell updates "the original definition of the zodiac by Babylonian astronomers" to our own time by formally defining it "for the epoch 1950.0, in line with conventional astronomical practice" (p. 12). That practice, however, appears to involve some other changes from Babylonian practice, changes made by the Greek Hipparchus by the second century B.C. One of these is the use of the "ecliptic" rather than the "zodiacal belt" as a frame of reference. In SZ, p. 1, Powell states:

> In modern astronomy the zodiacal belt is defined in relation to the path of the Sun through the fixed stars, which path is taken as the middle of the belt, so that the zodiacal belt, usually taken to be 16 degrees wide, by this definition extends 8 degrees north and 8 degrees south of the path of the Sun. The zodiacal belt is thus a belt of fixed stars along the middle of which runs the path of the Sun and contains also the paths of the Moon and the five planets known to the ancients through naked eye observation--Mercury, Venus, Mars, Jupiter, and Saturn.

Another is given by Powell as follows (SZ, pp. 9-10):

> The vernal point, i.e., the location of the Sun in the ecliptic at the time of vernal equinox, was adopted in Greek astronomy as the beginning of the ecliptic, apparently because the vernal equinox was considered by Greek astronomers as the start of the year. This represents another point of difference between Greek and Babylonian astronomy.

Since the Babylonian year consisted of twelve or thirteen lunar months, the start of the year was related to a lunar phenomenon, namely the appearance of the first new Moon of the year, which was, generally speaking (at least in later Babylonian times), the new Moon falling nearest to the vernal equinox. However, as early as the fifth century B.C., the Greek astronomer Euctemon defined a seasonal calendar, consisting of twelve (approximately) equal solar months, related to the solar phenomena of equinoxes and solstices. The months in Euctemon's calendar have the same names--the equivalent Greek names--as the signs of the zodiac in Babylonian astronomy. Thus the solar month commencing on the day of the vernal equinox was called by Euctemon the month of Aries. Similarly, the solar month commencing on the day of the summer solstice was called the month of Cancer..... This calendrical system is still in vogue today in astrology.

Christians will readily recognize the lunar nature of the Yahweh faith, since the Passover, and the Christian Easter celebration, are both related to the vernal equinox in terms of its proximity to the new Moon. At the time these systems were established, it was Aries that was arising at sunrise on the eastern horizon at the vernal equinox, but today this is no longer true due to the precession of the equinoxes (an astronomical fact that conventional astrology ignores). See 4 Brit 534, "equinox" and "equinoxes, precession of the," and 1 Brit 551, "Aries."

Because humanity must come to recognize the "ages" preordained by its relationship to the heavenly bodies (as the outward manifestation of spiritual beings and their forces), it is important to understand that it is the "vernal point" that determines the dates of the "ages." It is based upon the zodiacal sign rising in the eastern sky at sunrise at the vernal (spring) equinox. Due to the "precession of the equinoxes," this point retrogresses one degree each 72 years so that an "age" consists of 2,160 years and a "zodiacal year" of twelve ages consists of 25,920 years.

In order to relate to the reality of the changing relationship of the heavenly bodies to the Earth by taking the precession of the equinoxes into account, Powell defines the "sidereal zodiac" by fixing it in relation to the brightest star in the zodiacal belt, Aldebaran, located approximately in the middle of the constellation Taurus (as the eye of the bull), placing the zero point exactly 45 degrees west of Aldebaran on that date, i.e., 1950 (pp. 27 and 32). His portrayal of the sidereal zodiac, so defined, is shown below:

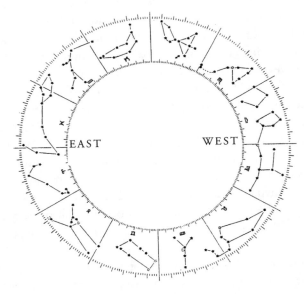

Based upon such chart, the dates of the "Astrological Ages" are as follows:

Aquarius	23,546–21,386 B.C.
Capricorn	21,386–19,226
Sagittarius	19,226–17,066
Scorpio	17,066–14,906
Libra	14,906–12,746
Virgo	12,746–10,586
Leo	10,586–8,426
Cancer	8,426–6,266
Gemini	6,266–4,106
Taurus	4,106–1,946 B.C.
Aries	B.C. 1,946–215 A.D.
Pisces	A.D. 215–2,375
Aquarius	2,375–4,535

However, there is a time lag of approximately 1,200 years (1,199 to be exact) between each "Astrological Age" in the heavens and its respective Cultural Age on Earth, so that the seven respective Cultural Ages of the post-Atlantean Epoch are as follows:

Cultural Age	Dates	Civilization
Cancer	7227–5067	Indian
Gemini	5067–2907	Persian
Taurus	2907–747 B.C.	Chaldo-Egyptian
Aries	747–1414 A.D.	Greco-Roman
Pisces	1414–3574	European
Aquarius	3574–5734	Russian-Slavonic
Capricorn	5734–7894	American

This time lag is explained by the fact that transformation to a new state of consciousness is not effected instantaneously. Rather, it proceeds initially in subconscious strata as a cultural impulse which manifests in a new Cultural Age only when it has reached a certain level. The time lag is an expression of the time taken for the transformation of consciousness to take effect.

This time lag is determined by a remarkable phenomenon in the heavens that Powell identifies as "the Venus Pentagram," which makes a complete rotation of the sidereal zodiac in 1,199 years. It is explained in HA1, pp. 58-63 and pictured below:

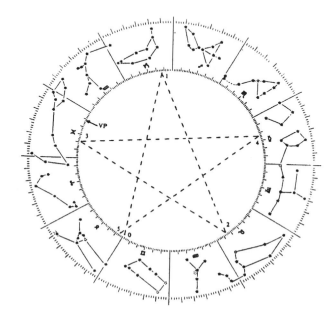

While each Cultural Age is ruled over by a Time Spirit (Archai),[1] the Archangels rule over shorter periods. The succession of the seven Archangels is: Oriphiel, Aneal, Zachariel, Raphael, Samael, Gabriel and Michael. Johannes Trithemius (1462-1516), Abbot of Sponheim, assigned 354.33 years to each archangelic regency (see ARCHM, App.).[2] Steiner described the successive regencies in KR-6, Lect. 8, but in such manner that I originally inferred that the seven always fell within a Cultural Age (2,160 years, averaging 308.57 years). However, Steiner later identified specific dates in an Aug. 18, 1924 notebook entry editorially footnoted in TFP, Lect. 7. These dates corresponded more closely to the 354.33-year periods given by Trithemius. The differences might be compared to those determined for the Astrological or Cultural Ages themselves, for the twelve zodiacal signs in the sky are not of equal 2,160-year spans. The two archangelic tabulations are compared below, working backward from the 1879 period given by Steiner for the start of the current Michaelic Age:[3]

	TFP, Lect. 7	354.33 Year
Gabriel	1879–1510	1879–1524
Samael	1510–1190	1524–1170
Raphael	1190–850	1170–816
Zachariel	850–500	816–461
Anael	500–150	461–107
Oriphiel	A.D. 150–200 B.C.	107–248
Michael	200–	248–602

Tradition also assigns (see KR-3, Lect. 11; RSMW, Chap. 11, p. 96; MOT, Letter 13, p. 367) to each Archangel a special relationship to one

---

1. The special connection of the Archai to Venus is explained by Steiner in *The Spiritual Hierarchies and the Physical World* (SHPW), Lect. 7, April 16, 1909.
2. Interestingly, Robert Powell points out that the lunar year of twelve synodic months is 354.33 days, suggesting a clear correspondence with Trithemius' calculations.
3. Notably, the present Michaelic Age is the first since Christ's blood was shed so that the Divine Intelligence could be brought down to Earth, while his previous Age included the lives of the great Greek philosophers Solon, Heraclitus, Socrates and Plato, whose youthful student, Alexander (356–323 B.C.), spread Greek civilization over the area Paul was to evangelize.

of the chief planets, so that the order of the Archangels is also the order
of the days of the week (see **I-8**):

Oriphiel	Saturn	Saturday
Anael	Venus	Friday
Zachariel	Jupiter	Thursday
Raphael	Mercury	Wednesday
Samael	Mars	Tuesday
Gabriel	Moon	Monday
Michael	Sun	Sunday

I-20 The microcosmic reflections of the zodiacal and planetary natures
in the human being (and in the apostolic groupings)

RH, Lect. 13 (pp. 178-179) and Lect. 7; SSFS, Lect. 3; SM, Lect. 8;
MBSP; MLO, Lects. 5 and 6; HA1, Figs. 13 and 23, Tab. 16; MSZ; TI,
Lects. 3 and 7; OH, Lect. 5

The zodiacal nature is microcosmically reflected (e.g., Gen 15,5; Ezek
1,22) in the human being in multifarious ways. The 12 constellations
seen under the dome of the firmament are reflected under the dome of
the human being's skull. As Steiner has said (e.g., RH, Lect. 13, pp. 178-
179) there are 12 principal nerves that originate in the head. This is true,
but only as part of the picture. One can confirm (e.g., 24 Brit 811-821,
"Nerves and Nervous Systems") that the peripheral nervous system is
made up of 3 parts, namely, the cranial nerves, the spinal nerves and that
part of the autonomic (involuntary) nervous system that is outside the
brain and spinal cord. These three are the "Trinity" above the zodiac. The
highest of these three are the cranial nerves, of which there are indeed 12
pairs as follows:

1. Olfactory
2. Optic
3. Oculomotor
4. Trochlear
5. Trigeminal

6. Abducens
7. Facial
8. Vestibulocochlear
9. Glossopharyngeal
10. Vagus
11. Accessory
12. Hypoglossal

Next are the 31 pairs of the spinal nerves (cf. **I-86** re vertebrae), roughly reflective of the division of each of the 12 constellations into degrees, or months into days. The greater consciousness (in an earthly sense) is located in the cranial nerves, the middle consciousness in the spinal nerves, and the unconscious (involuntary) in the autonomic nerves.

In quite another way the 12-fold zodiacal nature is reflected in the number of senses in the human being. Typically thought to be five in number (sight, hearing, smell, taste and touch), in reality there are 12 senses (the order, for now, listed in RH, Lect. 7):

1. Touch
2. Life
3. Movement
4. Balance
5. Smell
6. Taste
7. Sight
8. Warmth
9. Hearing
10. Word (Speech)
11. Thought
12. Ego

That there are 12 is a microcosmic reflection of the 12 macrocosmic (zodiacal) forces. One may get the idea there is a correspondence between a particular zodiacal constellation and a particular human sense. Initially this idea could come from the fact that on occasion Steiner himself makes such an identification for a particular purpose (e.g., see MLO and MBSP). One could be thrown into quite a state of confusion by Steiner's apparent inconsistency from one lecture series to another. Davidson adverts to this potential conflict in MSZ, and seems to explain it by suggesting that one must seek the macrocosmic-microcosmic connection on an individualized basis. It would seem, however, that Steiner, himself, has given us a more precise explanation, or at least a complementary one, in RH, Lect. 7. There he first draws a circle on which he lists, in the above order the 12 senses around the periphery, as follows:

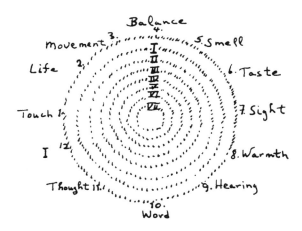

He then asserts that there are 7, and only 7, life processes:

1. Breathing
2. Warming
3. Nourishing
4. Secreting
5. Maintaining
6. Growing
7. Reproducing

which he portrays by 7 successively interior, concentric circular paths within the initial (zodiacal) circle, as follows:

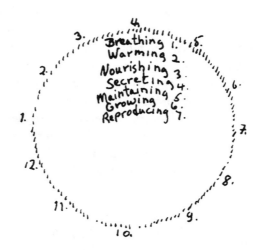

Prior to drawing either diagram, Steiner had pointed out that each of the 12 senses flows through each of the life processes, and that no one such sense could manifest in an organ (such as the ear) without the presence of all of these forces. Thus, we see that not only are our 12 senses a reflection of the 12 zodiacal constellations, but also of the 7 planetary forces, and that all of these interact in a manner reflective of the way the bodies of our solar system travel through the forces of the constellations.

That the rhythm of the zodiac is reflected in the human being is indicated by the following (see MK, Lect 2, p. 36 et al.; HI-2, Lect. 7; PM, Lect. 10; TIEC, Lects. 1 and 4; EVC, Lects. 11 and 12; EVEM, Lects. 10 and 14; CHM, Lect. 2; MSCW, Lect. 10): A solar year, time required for Sun to travel its complete cycle through the 12 constellations of the zodiac is *25,920 years* (see I-19); the length of human life at approximately age 70 (Ps 90,10) is *25,920 days*; and the average number of times a human breathes in a day is *25,920 breaths*.

Nor does the microcosmic reflection even stop there, for in MLO, Lect. 6, Steiner shows how the human being's 3 systems, thinking, feeling and willing, are a trinity reflective of the 12 zodiacal forces, as follows:

UPPER MAN

1	Upright Position	♈
2	Direction forwards	♉
3	Symmetry	♊
4	Upper Arm	♐
5	Elbow	♑
6	Lower Arm	♒
7	Hands	♓

MIDDLE MAN

1	Head and Feet, Twins	♊
2	Breast enclosure	♋
3	Interior, Heart	♌
4	The second Interior part of man	♍
5	Balance	♎
6	Organs of Reproduction	♏
7	Thigh	♐

LOWER MAN

7	Feet	♓
6	Leg	♒
5	Knee	♑
4	Thigh	♐
3	Organs of Reproduction	♏
2	Balance	♎
1	Kidneys, Solar Plexus	♍

And in SM, Lect. 8, he illustrates how each of the human being's senses, though active in all 3 soul forces (thinking, feeling and willing), is predominantly related to one of them, as follows:

Thinking	Feeling	Willing
Ego	Warmth	Balance
Thought	Sight	Movement
Speech	Taste	Life
Hearing	Smell	Touch

Not only is this 12-fold, 7-fold and 3-fold macrocosmic nature reflected in the microcosm of the human being's physical makeup, but Steiner tells us (HCT, Lect. 3) that it is also reflected in humanity's thinking through 12 World Outlook Shades (Zodiac), 7 World Outlook Moods (Planets) and 3 World Outlook Tones. (He adds that one additional Tone, namely, "Anthropomorphism," is in reality a harmony of these 3, as they are reflected within the human being itself.) The Tones are reflective as follows:

Sun	Theism
Moon	Intuitionism
Earth	Naturalism

The Shades and Moods are portrayed in the following diagram:

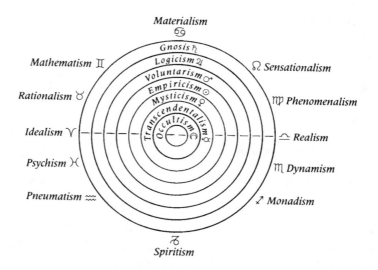

We can then see the same 12-fold, 7-fold, 3-fold and even 1-fold nature reflected in the 12 apostles, as follows:

12-fold	Matthew, Mark and Luke Gospels
7-fold	John 21,2
3-fold	Peter, James and John (at Transfiguration, Gethsemane, etc.,)
1-fold	Evangelist John

I-21   Powell's charts and graphs showing "the hermetic man" (planetary relationships of the human being's organs) and "the zodiacal man" (zodiacal relationships of the human being's physical body)

HA1, Figs. 13 and 23 and Tab. 16

In his HA1, Robert Powell shows how ancient tradition has associated the human being's soul organs ("lotus flowers," "chakras" or "wheels") with the planets and its physical body with the Zodiac, in what are referred to as "the hermetic man" and "the zodiacal man." The former is portrayed in his Figure 13 and the latter in Table 16 and Figure 23.

TABLE 16

The zodiacal melothesia

Early in the hermetical-astrological tradition the twelve signs of the zodiac were placed in correspondence with various parts of the human body, as indicated in the following tabulation:

ZODIACAL SIGN	PART OF THE BODY
Aries	head
Taurus	larynx region
Gemini	shoulders and arms
Cancer	breast region
Leo	heart and back
Virgo	solar plexus and stomach region
Libra	hips and pelvic region
Scorpio	region of reproductive organs
Sagittarius	thighs
Capricorn	knees
Aquarius	calves and ankles
Pisces	feet

FIGURE 13
The hermetic man

The hermetic man—the planetary archetype of the human being—
shows the correspondance between the planets and the lotus flowers.

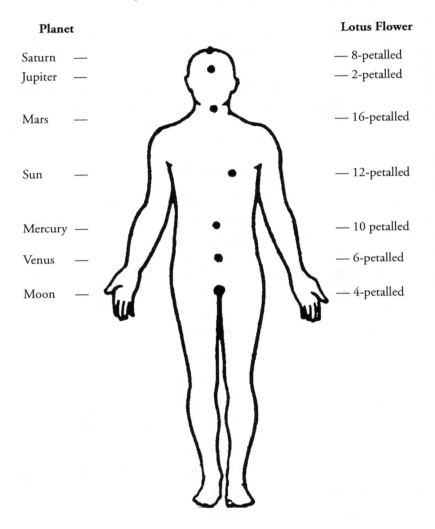

Planet		Lotus Flower
Saturn —		— 8-petalled
Jupiter —		— 2-petalled
Mars —		— 16-petalled
Sun —		— 12-petalled
Mercury —		— 10 petalled
Venus —		— 6-petalled
Moon —		— 4-petalled

[The glands represented by these seven stages from top to bottom represent the human astral body. For a portrayal of their counterparts in the
etheric and physical bodies, see **I-86.**]

FIGURE 23
The zodiacal man

The zodiacal man, from a fifteenth century Shepherd's Calendar, showing the correspondence between the twelve signs of the zodiac and parts of the body—see Table 16 for a tabulation of this correspondence.

(Reproduced from Fred Gettings, *The Hidden Art*, London, 1912, p. 24.)

I-22 The elementary states, the ethers and elements

GEN, Lects. 2, 4 and 7; FE, Lects. 5, 6, 9 and 28; EoB; NEOA

The elementary states within our Earth existence (i.e., Earth Consciousness-Mineral Kingdom-Physical Form, as per I-1) are as follows:

Solid (Earth)

Watery

Gaseous

Warmth

Light (ether)

Chemical or Sound (ether)

Life (ether)

Steiner indicates that it is in the Earth that we have to look mainly for solid, fluid and gas, that warmth is shared by Earth and Sun, and that the three ethers are of Sun nature (GEN, Lect. 7). Lect. 4 ends with the following tabulation:

Saturn	Sun	Moon	Earth
Warmth or Fire	Light	Sound	Life
	Warmth	Light	Sound
	Air	Warmth	Light
		Air	Warmth
		Water	Air
			Water
			Earth

The form of the chart seems difficult to fathom. In Lect. 2, Steiner, speaking of the human being's descent from the spiritual to the material world in a process of densification, points out that whenever there is a descent there is a corresponding ascent. "Thus, when we descend from warmth into the denser, we come to the gaseous condition; if we ascend, we come to light. Ascending still further, beyond the light we come to a yet finer etheric condition, . . . something which is not really recognizable in the ordinary sense-world. We get only a kind of external reflection of it." He then discusses how the chemical/sound ether manifests in the "Chladni" sound-figure experiment, when fine powder is placed on a metal plate and the bow of a violin is then drawn across the plate.

This process of descent and offsetting ascent would seem to illustrate the principle of "Fission," which is so amply demonstrated in scripture. I have constructed the following chart in an effort to more clearly illustrate the process:

Saturn	Sun	Moon	Earth
			Life
			/
		Sound	
		/	\
	Light		Light
	/	\	/
Warmth (Fire)		Warmth	
	\	/	\
	Air		Air
		\	/
		Water	
			\
			Earth

As can be seen, the process from Saturn to Earth is one of descent from a state of warmth, which has required "Fission." It would seem that the reascent of the human being will require "Fusion," a principle also demonstrated in scripture.

But just as there are (invisible) elemental spirits below, as well as spiritual hierarchies above, the human being, so also there are (invisible) conditions of matter below, as well as above, those we call gas, fluid and solid. Steiner refers to them (in EoB) as constituting the "sub-physical" world, which he sets out as follows:

Astral World . . . . the province of Lucifer
Lower Devachan . . . . the province of Ahriman
Higher Devachan . . . . the province of Asuras

Life Ether _____

Chemical Ether _____

Light Ether _____

sub-physical Astral World
                    electricity _____

sub-physical Lower Devachan
                    magnetism _____

sub-physical Higher Devachan
            terrible forces of destruction _____

In the lecture he had pointed out that, just as a human being is in a state of growth until the 35th year and thereafter is in a state of decay, so also is matter in the same pattern. Up until the Atlantean Epoch, matter was in a progressive process, but decay has set in with the post-Atlantean Epoch. "Light is being destroyed in this post-Atlantean age of the Earth's existence, which until the time of Atlantis was a progressive process. Since then it has been a process of decay. What is light? Light decays and the decaying light is *electricity*. What we know as electricity is light that is being destroyed in matter. And the chemical force that undergoes a transformation in the process of Earth evolution is *magnetism*. Yet a third force will become active and if electricity seems to work wonders today, this third force will affect civilization in a still more miraculous way. The more of this force we employ, the faster will the Earth tend to become a corpse and its spiritual part prepare for the Jupiter embodiment. . . . [I]t is necessary for the Earth to be destroyed, for otherwise the spiritual could not become free."

In NEOA, Lect. 1, Unger, keying off Steiner's EoB lecture, gives the following schematic of how the subsensible world is constituted:

                                                    Life Ether
                              Chemical Ether
            Light Ether

Warmth   Gaseous   Fluid
Ether   Condition   Condition   Solid Condition
            Electricity
            (Lucifer)

                              Magnetism
                              (Ahriman)

                                                  Third Force
                                                  (Asuras)

Steiner's EoB lecture was in 1911. Unger's were between 1968 and 1978. In his Lect. 2, Unger expresses the view that nuclear energy, of itself, is not yet the "Third Force." Rather, "there is embodied [in it], somewhat prematurely, some small part of the future forces which have been spoken of . . . the 'tip of the iceberg.'"

I-24 Progressive development of the human being's 9-fold nature charted through the present post-Atlantean Epoch

OH, Lect. 3; GSMk, Lect. 4; MTA, Lect. 11

As to the Mineral Physical Conditions of Earth evolution, we are now in the 5th "Evolutionary Epoch," namely, the post-Atlantean (see **I-1**), which is in turn divided into 7 Cultural Eras, of which we are also in the 5th, the one following the Greco-Roman (see **I-19**). Each aspect ("fold") of the 9-fold nature of the human being is the primary target for humanity's development through the post-Atlantean Epoch, as follows:

Atlantis	=	Physical body
Post-Atlantean:		
Indian	=	Etheric body
Persian	=	Sentient or Astral body
Chaldo-Egyptian	=	Sentient Soul
Greco-Roman	=	Intellectual or Mind Soul

Present	=	Spiritual or Consciousness Soul
6th Cultural Era	=	Manas or Spirit Self
7th Cultural Era	=	Buddhi or Life Spirit
After Catastrophe	=	Atma or Spirit Man

This is not to say that the development is completed during the indicated Cultural Era, for the human being will not attain to the state of manas or Spirit Self, proper, prior to the Jupiter Condition of Consciousness (see I-1), which is far in the future. Prior to the commencement of the Ego (soul) state in the Chaldo-Egyptian period, higher spiritual beings in the state of atma (during the Indian Era) worked on the Etheric Body, and in the state of buddhi (during the Persian Era) worked on the astral body, and in the state of manas or "Manna" (during the Chaldo-Egyptian era, e.g., Ex 16,31; Num 11,7; Jn 6,31; 1 Cor 10,3; cf. Rev 2,17) worked on the Sentient Soul, for the Ego was not yet then strong enough to make itself felt independently, which became possible only during the Greco-Roman Era (the Christ era).

I-25 Relationship of the 7 "churches" of the Apocalypse to the 7 Cultural Eras of the post-Atlantean Epoch

ASJ, Lect. 3

The 7 "churches" of the Apocalypse are identified with the 7 Cultural Eras of the post-Atlantean Evolutionary Epoch (see I-1 and I-19) as follows:

	"Church"	Cultural Era	Rev Ref.
1.	Ephesus	Indian	2,1-7
2.	Smyrna	Persian	2,8-11
3.	Pergamum	Chaldo-Egyptian	2,12-17
4.	Thyatira	Greco-Roman	2,18-29
5.	Sardis	Present (European)	3,1-6
6.	Philadelphia	6th (Slavic-Russian)	3,7-13
7.	Laodicea	7th (American)	3,14-22

I-27 Steiner's exposition on the organic order and character of the traditional planets; Powell's on the outer three planets

HA2, Chap. 8; ISBM, Lect. 3

Modern minds will require us to treat of the outer planets, Uranus, Neptune and Pluto, which were not a part of the ancient cosmology in the same way as those within the orbit of Saturn. Steiner (ISBM, Lect. 3) said,

In the numerous popular accounts of the origin of our planetary system one is first led back to a kind of original mist, to a vast fog-like structure, a nebula, out of which our sun and its planets have somehow agglomerated, although for the driving force in this process only physical forces, as a rule, are taken into account. This is called the "Kant-Laplace theory," though it is somewhat modified today. . . . The modified Kant-Laplace theory may definitely hold good as an external event, but within the whole forming of globes, within this whole crystallizing of the separate cosmic globes, spiritual forces and spiritual beings were at work. . . .

When our Earth came forth from the purely spiritual devachanic state and received for the first time a kind of externally perceptible existence, it was not like it is today. In fact, seen externally, it could really be pictured as a kind of great primordial nebula, as our physical science describes. Only we must think of this primordial mist as immense, far greater than the present earth, extending far beyond the outermost planets now belonging to our solar system--far beyond Uranus. To spiritual science what is seen coming forth from a spiritual condition is not merely a kind of physical mist. To describe it as a kind of mist and nothing more is about as sensible as if a man who has seen another should reply to a question as to what he saw: I saw muscles which are attached to bones and blood--simply describing the physical aspect. For in the primordial mist there were a multitude of spiritual forces and spiritual beings. . . .

When you add the fact that not only these various beings were united with the original nebula, but a whole series more, standing at very varied stages of evolution, then you will understand that not only these cosmic bodies, earth, sun, moon, separated from the nebula, but other cosmic bodies too. Indeed they all agglomerated as separate globes because scenes of action had to be found for the varying stages of evolution of the different beings.

Thus there were beings at the very beginning of our Earth who were scarcely fitted to take part in further development, who were still so young in their whole evolution that any further step would have destroyed them. They had to receive a sphere of action, so to speak, on which they could preserve their complete youthfulness. All other fields of action existed to give dwelling-places to those who were already more advanced. For the beings who arose last of all during the Moon existence, and who therefore had stayed behind at a very early evolutionary stage, a field of action had to be separated out. This scene of action was the cosmic body which we call "Uranus," and which therefore has but slight connection with our earthly existence. Uranus has become the theater for beings which had to remain at a very backward stage.

Then evolution proceeded. Apart from Uranus, all that forms our universe [Ed., solar system] was contained in an original pap-like mass. Greek mythology calls this condition "Chaos." Then Uranus separated out, the rest remaining still in the Chaos.

The Kant-LaPlace theory still has considerable "scientific" validity. See 10 Brit 941, "solar nebula." Steiner does not mention Pluto, which was "scientifically" discovered in 1930. His above remarks leave room for it to have been in a pre-evolutionary mass in similar manner to Uranus (see AM, Lect. 1) and Neptune, a matter to which we shall return momentarily.

Steiner then says that the other "planets" separated out in the following order and character:

1. Saturn, for those beings who stood in their development at the stage we human beings stood at during Old Saturn (our present Saturn thus being the only planet to have any nominal connection with an earlier Condition of Consciousness);

2. Jupiter, for beings of "a certain stage of development";

3. Sun, for the most advanced beings, taking with it all but Earth and Moon (which remained together);

4. Mars, whose spiritual beings pulled away from the Sun and, in the process of reaching its outer orbit, passed through the (still joined) Earth and Moon, leaving behind what later developed into iron (a necessary component of human blood, which then came into existence, the fluid sap of living beings having theretofore been chlorophyll which contains no iron);

5. Moon, separating from Earth to remove retarded beings and permit the evolution of those beings (human) who remained, leaving Earth alone as it now is;

6. Venus and Mercury, for those Fire-Spirits (Archangels) who, though far above human beings, had not advanced far enough to endure the Sun existence, Mercury in the neighborhood of the Sun being the more advanced of the two and Venus between Mercury and Earth.

For the sake of visual clarification, Figure 20 from HA2 presents the heliocentric (Sun-centered) view of our solar system:

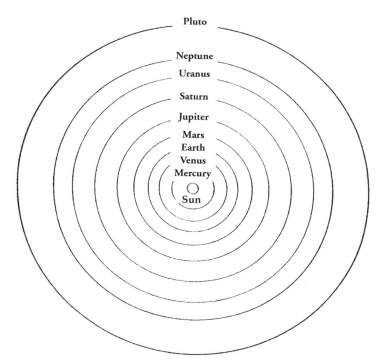

Returning to the 3 outer planets, Steiner clearly indicates that Uranus separated and that, as of that point, "all that forms our [solar system] was contained in an original pap-like mass." Assuming that Neptune had previously separated, it need not have been mentioned for the purposes of the human being's evolution through the 7 classical planetary states. As of the time he spoke (1908), Pluto had not been "scientifically" discovered, and the state of his teachings was still too preliminary to go into the detail of any outer planets. For this, however, we are beholden to his disciples whose teachings have, to a considerable extent, culminated in the works of Robert Powell.

Powell tells us, "According to Orphic cosmogony, a divine dynasty of six generations [of gods] are said to have held in turn the rule of the universe. These six are: Phanes, Night, Ouranos, Kronos, Zeus and Dionysos. . . . A series of *manvantaras*, or planetary periods [occurred], each drawing successively closer towards the Sun. The first . . ., Phanes, took place within the orbit of Pluto . . . the second . . ., Night, . . . within the orbit of Neptune," the third within the orbit of Uranus. In between each such manvantara, a period of cosmic rest (*pralaya*) occurred. During these 3 early manvantaras there were laid down the following respective elements:

Pluto	Life	(primal love/will)
Neptune	Sound	(cosmic harmony)
Uranus	Light	(cosmic intelligence)

During these three manvantaras, however, the human being did not exist, not even in a rudimentary form. For this reason, [these] planets . . . represent qualities that are superhuman . . ., but which nevertheless pervade the cosmic existence in which the human being is embedded.

Powell described these 3 higher stages of consciousness in HA1, Chap. 4:

Lunar consciousness	Illumination
Solar consciousness	Inspiration
Zodiacal consciousness	Union (Intuition)

The fact that these states of consciousness are beyond the human being's present evolution is reflected in the physical sphere by the fact that these 3 planets are not visible to the naked eye, as are all the others.

In his Table 19 (see I-17), Powell gives the manvantaras of Orphic cosmology and the stages of human evolution:

Orbit of	Condition of Consciousness
1. Pluto (Phanes)	
2. Neptune (Night)	
3. Uranus (Ouranos)	
4. Saturn (Kronos)	Old Saturn
5. Jupiter (Zeus)	Old Sun
6. Mars (Dionysos)	Old Moon
7. Earth	Earth
8. Venus	(Future) Jupiter
9. Mercury	(Future) Venus
10. Sun	(Future) Vulcan

What, then, if anything, do Uranus, Neptune and Pluto have to do with the human being?

Whereas the Sun, Moon and 5 planets are incorporated into the human being's astral and etheric bodies via the lotus flowers and organs, respectively, Uranus, Neptune and Pluto work from beyond, at a level transcending normal human behavior. Just as there is an inherent polarity in all creation, so do these outer forces call the human being's higher self as follows:

Uranus	cosmic intelligence
Neptune	cosmic harmony
Pluto	cosmic life

But at the same time these represent forces of hindrance, for they have become *trapped* as negative forces within the interior of the Earth, and are now being released through technology for technological progress, posing grave dangers to the future of humanity and planet Earth through their release. The discoveries of these 3 planets are linked in a remarkable way with the discoveries of forces (see **I-22**) connected with them:

Uranus discovered in 1781–Galvani in 1780 began experiments leading to discovery of *electricity*, which is essentially *trapped light*;

Neptune discovered in 1846–Faraday in 1845 concluded that all matter must contain *magnetism*, which is essentially *trapped sound*;

Pluto discovered in 1930–in 1932 came artificial splitting of the lithium nucleus by neutron bombardment, leading to discovery of *atomic power*, which is essentially *trapped life*.

The classical planets are connected with cosmic forces that have densified in the Earth to become the following metals (see also HI-2, Lect. 9, OP, Lect. 8 and AOMR, p. 30):

Saturn	Lead
Jupiter	Tin
Mars	Iron
Venus	Copper
Mercury	Quicksilver (Mercury)
Sun	Gold
Moon	Silver

In the same way, the transcendental planets that have densified have become trapped within the interior of the Earth as follows:

Uranus	Electricity
Neptune	Magnetism
Pluto	Atomic Power

The polarities involved, depending upon the human being's moral development, or lack thereof, are:

Trapped Light (Electricity)	Illumination
Trapped Sound (Magnetism)	Inspiration
Trapped Life (Atomic Power?)	Intuition (Union)

I-32   Lucifer and Ahriman

LA; Jn-Rel, Lect. 5; AD; BWM; DCOSP

Two biblical terms, "Devil" (diabolos) and "Satan" (satan), are generally considered virtually interchangeable, and not without some superficial justification in scripture itself, but in esotericism they have quite different meanings, which are polar opposites but which work together for an evil result so that in the popular mind (as well, perhaps, as in that of the scribes preceding even our earliest extant manuscripts) they are indistinguishable. Ahriman was first recognized by Zarathustra (1 Brit 168, "Ahriman"). In Goethe's *Faust* he is known as "Mephistopheles." Steiner says this is a term derived from two Hebrew words, "Mephiz" (Corrupter) and "Topel" (Liar). Anthroposophy makes a clear distinction: "Devil" equals "Lucifer" and "Satan" equals "Ahriman." Hardly any anthroposophical work can be found that has no reference to a "Luciferic" or an "Ahrimanic" influence. Consequently, neither the references cited above nor the illustrative characteristics of each listed below can be considered all-inclusive. They are given only as a bare indication of the influence or reflection of each:

Lucifer	Ahriman	Ref.
Tendency to spiritualize Force	Tendency to materialize Matter	KM
Fallen Archangels	Fallen Archai	See below
Electricity, or fallen light ether	Magnetism, or fallen chemical ether	I-22
False motive	Belief in chance	MK
Serpent	Beast	Gen, Rev
False spiritualization	Reliance upon physical world	
Inner conceit	Illusions about external world	MK
Circulatory System	Nervous System	BWM

It has been deceptively difficult to characterize these beings as to the hierarchy from which each "fell." It seems clear that Lucifer fell during

Ancient Moon and Ahriman during Ancient Sun, but their actual rank, the Condition of Consciousness during which they had attained the "human" stage (see I-15), is deemed to be the preceding Condition in each case. Thus, Ahriman is from the rank of the Archai (see *The Book of Revelation and the Work of the Priest* [REVP], Lects. 11 and 18), which attained this status on Ancient Saturn though he appears to have fallen during Ancient Sun (*Manifestations of Karma* [MK], Lect. 7, pp. 166-167). Since Lucifer appears (MK) to have fallen during Ancient Moon, it would seem that he belongs to the rank of Archangels, which attained "human" status during Ancient Sun (I-15). This would accord with his desire to implant "Light," for the controlling hierarchy of the Sun Condition was the Spirits of Wisdom (I-16), and he was able to fight on somewhat the same plateau as the Archangel Michael.

I-33   Course of the Ego between death and rebirth; Regions of soul and spirit worlds

OES; THSY; LBDR; RE, Lects 4 and 5; TIEC, Lect. 5; MTA, Lect. 13; MM, Lect. Two; DCOM; HoP, Sec. 5; BDR, Lect. Ten; PSI, Lect. 6; EVC, Lect. 10; HSBA, App. 5; CTK; ORL, Lect. 1

To understand the hidden reflection (as we shall see elsewhere herein) in numerous biblical passages of the course taken by a human being between death and rebirth, a tabulation is given here of the progressive stages of that journey. First a brief recap of fundamentals is set out.

Component of Human Being	Essential Nature of Component
Ego	Lasting or eternal Individuality
Astral body	Seat of consciousness, passions and desires
Etheric (Life) Body	Seat of life
Physical Body	Seat of, or pattern for, mineral accumulation

State of Consciousness | Components Joined

Waking | Ego and all 3 bodies, i.e., astral, etheric (life) & physical

Sleeping | Etheric (life) and physical (the astral & Ego separating therefrom)

Death | Physical, the minerals of which, absent life body, proceed to disintegrate (the Ego and astral & etheric bodies having separated)

Course of the Ego between Death and Rebirth

1. Etheric world, for approximately 3 days, during which the etheric body remains attached with the astral body and Ego permitting a panoramic review, in reverse, of the life just past.

2. Astral world, for approximately 1/3 the length of the person's life (equal to the time spent sleeping), during which the Ego remains attached with the astral body. This is the period of purification, or burning fire, known in the Roman Church as Purgatory, also sometimes in anthroposophy as "the soul world," and in Eastern religions as "kamaloca." The attachment of the Ego and astral body permits a review, also in reverse, of the life just past, actually of what is experienced during sleeping periods (nightly reviews beyond waking consciousness) by the Ego and astral bodies during that life; characteristic of this review is placement in the position of those with whom one dealt, in the sense of Mt 7,12 (the Golden Rule).

3. Spiritland, or "Devachan" as it is known in Eastern terminology, which can be entered only after all desires and passions have been eliminated in the astral world. The only component that can enter here is the Ego itself, along with the part of its 3 "bodies" (astral, etheric and physical) that the Ego has been able to convert to the respective higher 3 spiritual components of the future, i.e., manas (Spirit Self), buddhi (Life Spirit) and atma (Spirit Man). The Ego's consciousness during its sojourn in Spiritland is dependent upon the extent to which it has perfected its "Three Bodies," but only manas (the purified astral body) can meaningfully be developed during Earth evolution; consider here the

parable in Mt 13,33, "The kingdom of heaven (is) like leaven which a woman hid in three measures of flour, till it was all leavened."

4. "Cosmic midnight" when the Ego has ended its spiritual ascent and begins its descent to another incarnation for the purpose of, and resolved toward, further perfection (Mt 5,48).

5. The Descent, which retraces the stages of the ascent, during which the elements of one's "Three Bodies" are formed, including finally the choice of time, place and parentage, from what is then available on Earth.

Pathway of the Ego's Course Through the Heavens

Stage of Ego's Journey	Space Into which Ego Expands
1. Etheric World	Proximity of Earth and Physical Body
2. Astral World	Orbit of Moon (though Mercury and Venus orbits have both astral and spiritual character)
3. Lower Devachan	Successive spheres reaching out to the "planets" in the order of their distance from the Earth (remembering that in times past esotericism reversed the order of Venus and Mercury), thus, the Mercury sphere, Venus sphere, Sun sphere, Mars sphere, Jupiter sphere and Saturn sphere
4. Higher Devachan	Zodiacal sphere, among the stars of the 12 formative constellations.

Nature of the 7 Regions of the Astral (Soul) World

Soul World Region	Earthly Counterpart
1. Burning Desire	Solid physical bodies
2. Mobile Sensitivity	Liquids
3. Wishes	Gases
4. Liking and Disliking	Warmth

5. Soul Light   Light (Ether)
6. Active Soul Force   Sound (or Chemical, Ether)
7. Soul Life   Life (Ether)

Nature of the 7 Regions of Devachan (Spiritland)

Spiritland Region	Form it Assumes on Earth
1. "Solid Land"	Physical
2. "Oceans & Rivers & Blood Circulation"	Life
3. "Atmosphere"	Sensation--Raging Tempest/Battlefield
4. "Warmth"	Thought
5. "Light"	Wisdom
6. & 7. See Note immediately below	

Note--In OES, Chap. 3, where the above is related, Steiner says of Regions 6 and 7, "descriptions will be found in a later part of this work." It is not totally clear to what he was referring, but presumably it was to what is implied in Chap. 6 dealing with the future Jupiter and Venus Conditions of Consciousness. Inasmuch as they will not mature during Earth evolution, it would have been inappropriate for him to designate a form for their earthly manifestation. Inasmuch, however, as Region 5 ("Light") dealt with the first ether, it would seem that Regions 6 and 7 would deal with Sound and Life Ether, respectively. We shall see, indeed, that the biblical passages first referred to appear only to go through these first 5 stages applicable to Earth evolution.

I-35 The hierarchical sacrifices and the approach and entry of the human being's Ego

ISBM, Lects. 3 and 4

We have already seen, in I-27, the order in which the "planets" of our solar system separated from the original "pap-like mass." When the Sun separated (along with what later became Mars, Venus and Mercury) from the Earth-Moon mass, the exalted spiritual beings who led the Sun

(Sun-beings) were the Exusiai (Gk) or Elohim (Heb) or Spirits of Form (Steiner). They were 7 in number (or groups), of whom Yahweh was the most exalted. When needed by humanity later, spiritual forces caused the Moon to separate from the Earth, at which time Yahweh left the domain of the Sun and took abode on the Moon. The Moon-forces, under Yahweh's leadership, as a Spirit of Form, give the human being form; forces that give form proceed from the Moon, while those that continually alter the form proceed from the Sun; thus, the development of the Ego-human being had to proceed from the Moon (Yahweh) because it involves consciousness of self which can only come from separation, which in turn can only come from the development of form. Hence, one begins to come to an understanding of how compelling is the interpretation and meaning of Ex 3,14, "I AM the I AM."

These Spirits of Form (Exusiai or Elohim) have played an important part from the beginning of the human being's evolution. They stand 4 levels above the human being in the hierarchies. This means that during Earth evolution the lowest element of their 7-fold being would be Spirit Self in the human being, the stage just higher than the Ego. We saw, in I-15 the evolutionary stage at which the 3 intervening hierarchies (Angels, Archangels and Archai) attained their "human" or Ego status. Consistent with this pattern, we can thus see from an inspection of the I-18 chart that on Old Saturn the Spirits of Form (Elohim) had no physical body, their lowest being the etheric. On Saturn, they "rayed in fructifying life-saps" and the warmth substance rayed these back again, giving "mirror-pictures," thus even then giving the human being a "likeness" (Gen 1,26) of its Godhead.

On Old Sun the Elohim no longer need the etheric body, which they relinquish to the human being, endowing its physical body with an etheric body, a portion of that given up by the Elohim. This advance from Saturn to Sun is portrayed by the ancient Greek myth of Gaea (Saturn) and atmosphere Chronos. The lowest member of the Elohim on Old Sun is now the astral body, which manifests through the raying of instincts, desires and passions (of a higher nature). The myth of the Titans relates to this astral event.

On Old Moon, the Elohim lay aside their astral body, relinquishing it to the human being, so that their Ego is their lowest member. On Old Moon these Elohim have only pure Egos. On Old Moon, all that we call "human being" has gradually flowed down out of its environment, from the outside, not from within it.

In Earth evolution, the Elohim sacrifice the lowest body they had on Old Moon, their Ego, to the human being, and thus the human being is able for the first time to take within itself something for further development, its own Ego. The lowest member the Elohim, namely Yahweh at this point, have is Spirit Self, or manas (which in the Bible is called Manna). From this we see the significance not only of the bringing and giving of "the I Am" in Ex 3,14, but also of the coming of the scriptural Manna (Ex 16, Num 11, et al.) and of the statement by Christ that the kingdom is now to be found "within" the human being (Lk 17,21).

The approach and entry of this Ego into the human being during Earth evolution is shown in the following table (see diagram in "Naked"):

Period	Ego Penetrates	Creating
Lemuria	Astral body	Sentient Soul
1st 2/3 Atlantis	Etheric body	Intellectual Soul
Last 1/3 Atlantis	Physical body	Consciousness Soul
Golgotha Deed	Works on Astral	Manas
Golgotha Deed	Works on Etheric	Buddhi

While Christ's Deed on Golgotha made it possible for the human being to develop both its manas and buddhi, the wisdom that is all around us, e.g., in a piece of the thigh bone, manifests the manasic nature of the lowest member of the Yahweh being.

I-86 The reflection of the planets in the human being's physical organs

OP, Lects. 4 and 8; see also BMFE, Lect. 2, p. 32

One significant way the human being reflects its planetary system within his body is shown by the following Steiner sketches:

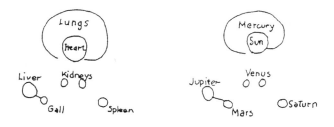

The related lecture text explains the correlation. The noblest instrument possessed by the human being is said to be its "Blood," which is the instrument of its Ego. Before any sort of nutrient can be taken in from the plant or animal kingdoms, which have their own rhythms, its rhythm must be modified to correspond with the human rhythm. The digestive organs involved in this process are the spleen, gall bladder and liver, whose main collective function is to repel what constitutes the particular inner nature of this food. These organs thus adapt the laws of the outside world, from which we take our food, to the inner organization or rhythm of the human being. There must, however, be a continual living reciprocal activity of the human being with the outside world, though these three organs are placed in opposition to it. What is thus fed into the "Blood" (Ego) system must be balanced by what represents the outside world. This is accomplished by the lung system through which oxygen enters the "Blood" directly from the outer world, assisted by the kidney system. Thus, we have the spleen-liver-gallbladder (inner) system balanced by the lung-kidney (outer) system. The blood system (Ego) with the heart as its central point is placed in the middle where these two opposing systems are brought into balance for the sustenance of the human being.

It can be seen that the outer planets are associated with what comes from food and the inner two planets with what comes from air and "Blood" purification. Just as the Ego, in its spiritual connection, presupposes the physical, etheric and astral bodies, so also the physical blood-system (Ego), in its physical side, presupposes these two counterbalancing systems, portrayed as follows:

Spiritual	Physical
Physical	Blood-heart
Etheric	Spleen-liver-gallbladder system
Astral	Lung-kidney system

There is a further powerful indication of these relationships. In I-27 we saw the relationships of the various metals to the planet from which they originated. We now see that where one of the above organisms manifests too strong an inner vitality, it must be counterbalanced, which can be brought about by a proper application of these metals (which is beyond our present scope). We thus see the outer cosmic system duplicated in our inner cosmic system.

This is not the only manifestation of the planetary system in our earthly being. Another one, for instance, is that set out in I-21 where the planets are shown to have a relationship to the seven "lotus flowers" (Pineal, Pituitary, Larynx, Heart, Solar Plexus, Kidney, Reproductive). Another is the relationship between the number of spinal vertebrae and days in the monthly cycle of the Moon. In RMI, Lect. 5, Steiner numbers the vertebrae at 28 to 30. While trying to get a better fix on the number, it is also fascinating to distinguish (see 24 Brit 810, "The Spinal Cord," and 815, "Spinal Nerves," "Nerves and Nervous Systems") between vertebrae and spinal nerves (see I-20), as follows:

Type	Number Vertebrae	Nerves
Cervical	7	8
Thoracic	12	12
Lumbar	5	5
Sacral	5	5
Coccygeal	3	1
Total	32	31

However, the Coccygeal vertebrae are described as "vestigial" and as "rudimentary and occasionally absent," so they would not seem to be of significance in this count. If they are eliminated, the total vertebrae count is 29, which corresponds approximately to the 27 1/2 days in the lunar month, the median (between 29 and 27 1/2) being close to 28, a number divisible by the planetary seven. Thus our bony skeleton relates primarily to the Moon forces, while the higher nervous system relates more closely to the 30+ days derived by dividing the year by the zodiacal Twelve. Steiner sketched (RMI, Lect. 5) the following illustration of how the ancient initiates saw in the formation of the human spine a copy of the monthly movement of the Moon, "of the streams that the Moon sends down continually upon the Earth":

The editor/translator of RMI notes that in German the same word is used for "rotations" and "vertebrae," and even our English word is taken from the Latin *vertere* (to turn). The relationship of the lunar month to human embryology is amazing. Only a hint of it is given in the fact that the human gestation period of approximately 275 days comprises ten lunar months (**I-20**).

II-1   A profile review of creation

Cited charts and OES, Chap. 4

From the description in **I-27** of the separation of the various bodies of our solar system from its original nebula during Earth evolution (i.e., the Earth Condition of Consciousness; **I-1**), we see a process of segregation that recognizes different levels of spiritual development among its beings, each level being drawn into its own appropriate sphere for further development. Starting from **I-16**, we must recognize that the Exusiai (Elohim) were the highest of the nine hierarchical ranks (see **I-6**) to *dwell* as spiritual beings within our solar system, while higher ranks (up through the Thrones) were represented in it through having sacrificed their being during earlier Conditions of Consciousness in order to provide the Exusiai with the spiritual substance for creation during Earth evolution. Some concept of this process can be gathered by contemplating charts **I-35** and **I-15** (as well as **II-2** below). While **I-35** shows the progressive sacrifices by the Exusiai that made the fourfold human being possible (**I-9**, column two), if we go all the way to the lowest kingdom, the mineral kingdom, we find that it was the Thrones' sacrifice of their will during the Ancient Saturn Condition of Consciousness (**I-16**) that made the stones (our present mineral kingdom) possible (**II-2**). Spiritual advancement, as described in **I-16**, was only possible through sacrifice, a principle applicable also to human beings, demonstrated for them by the Crucifixion of the Christ. To consider Christ's death as vicarious is to miss its meaning, its implication and efficacy relating to our own resurrection. It was exemplary, not substitutional; it enabled and empowered (Jn 1,12), not relieved; it was the "first fruits," not the only ones. It telescoped into one human being what would eventually be required in each through the course of human evolution (cf. Mk 10,39-40; Lk 20,34-38; Rev 7,3-4; 14,3-5; and the essay "Fire" on the meaning of the "hundred and forty-four thousand").

To say that the Exusiai were the highest rank to *dwell* within our solar system is not to say that higher ranks were not active within it, only that the locus, so to speak, of their spiritual *dwelling* was not there. Nor is it to say that the Exusiai had no presence higher than our solar system, but again only that it was their primary *dwelling*. At all times there is an inter-relationship and cooperative activity between all the hierarchies; see for instance I-7 and I-29.

II-2 The hierarchical sacrifices and the origin of the four kingdoms

SHPW, Part Two, All Lects.; OES, Chap. 4

This chart is closely related to I-16 and I-35. It is skeletal and ultrasche-matic. To put flesh on it and spirit in it, reference to Steiner's explanation in SHPW is needed. A few of his remarks are paraphrased following the tabulation. What is sacrificed in column one below is the spiritual charac-teristic by which Steiner named that hierarchical level in I-6 (thus *will* in the case of the Thrones, *wisdom* of the Kyriotetes, etc.). The last column can be seen as identical to the tabulation in I-15 (but in the case of the Luciferic spirits during Ancient Sun, note the last paragraph of I-32).

Sacrificing Hierarchy	Condition of Consciousness	Element Created	Resulting Product	Spirits Created
Thrones	Ancient Saturn	Fire	Time	Archai
Kyriotetes	Ancient Sun	Air	Light/Eternity	Archangels/ Luciferic Spirits
Dynamis	Ancient Moon	Water	Dreamlike imag-ination/Longing	Angels
Exusiai	Earth	Earth	Death/Redemption	Human Being

Column four (Product) is the unique contribution of this chart. The time created by the Throne's sacrifice *to the Cherubim* of their will during Ancient Saturn is not an "abstract time" but rather "an independent being." The beings thus born are the Spirits of Personality, known as Archai (meaning time beings), the beings who order time. "What we call … warmth [see "Fire"] in Saturn is the sacrificial smoke of the Thrones, which generates time."

Steiner calls the Kyriotetes, the Spirits of Wisdom, "the great Givers of the Cosmos … for they themselves streamed out into the cosmos and first created order" during Ancient Sun. The Archangels (literally, from "arch" and "angel" we have the "Messengers of Beginning") came into being and mirrored back, in time, so as to become light (see "Light"). But here we have the real archetype of the Cain and Abel sacrifices, one being accepted and one rejected (Gen 4,3-5). For the Thrones continue to sacrifice to the Cherubim in the Sun period also. It is then that some Cherubim accept the sacrifice and some do not. In those Cherubim who reject the sacrifice, the creation of time, "lies a capacity … to grow beyond the conditions of time," and this we call "eternity," having "come to the point in the development of the ancient Sun when time and eternity become separated." (The inability of Cain to die [Gen 4,12-15] is the earthly reflection of this higher eternity created by the Cherubim.) But by their rejection the "sacrificial substance no longer needs to follow the inclinations and impulses of the Cherubim, for [they] have released it" with the consequence that other beings are able to become independent of the desires of the Cherubim (cf. Gen 4,7, the freedom to "do well" or "not," the earthly reflection of this higher independence). These independent beings are the "Luciferic spirits" who are born on Ancient Sun (see I-32).

The sacrifice by the Spirits of Motion (Dynamis) during Ancient Moon creates movement, but it is not movement in space. Rather it is "related to the process of thinking." But it is not thinking as we conceive of it, but a form of picturing as in our dreams. The consequence of these dreamlike images is a sense of "longing." It cannot be alleviated without the entrance of the "I Am," which must await the Earth Condition of Consciousness. So the Moon existence may be called the "Planet of Longing" while Earth existence may be called the "Planet of Redemption." But death, which can be experienced only by incarnated beings, human beings on Earth, is a necessary pre-condition to that redemption; for *"within the world of maya [illusion] the only thing that shows itself in its reality is death!"*

II-3   The four possible worlds

AHIU, Lect. 2

The present chart relates in some respects to I-33, which describes the journey of the human soul between death and rebirth.

The four different worlds are as follows:

World	Characteristics	Human Element	Inhabitants
Earth	Perceptible and physical	Physical body	Human beings
Etheric	Imperceptible and supraphysical	Etheric body	Third hierarchy
Astral/Lower Devachan	Perceptible and supraphysical	Astral body/Ego	Second hierarchy
Higher Devachan	Imperceptible and physical	Ego/Spirit	First hierarchy

Columns two and four are those explicitly given by Steiner; columns one and three are partially explicit and partially inferred. It might help to comprehend how the third "world" is "perceptible," and Steiner gives light as an example of what we can perceive here on Earth while it remains supraphysical—to the mystification of science (see "Light"). Actually he speaks of "the spirit beings who populate the Sun" as being supraphysical but perceptible (see the discussion of the interior of the Sun and outer stars in the essay "What Is Man?"). The "physical" in the fourth world relates to the perfection of the physical body when it is transformed into Atma at the end of the Venus Condition of Consciousness (see the essay "Three Bodies" in *The Burning Bush*, at pp. 413-415). It is then the ultimate resurrection body.

II-4   Planetary influences during the post-Atlantean Epoch

AHIU, Lect. 3

The predominant planetary influence during each post-Atlantean Cultural Age is given as follows:

| | | | | Mars | | |
Moon	Mercury	Venus	Sun	(Iron)	Jupiter	Saturn
Ancient	Ancient	Egypto-	Greco-	Fifth post-	Sixth post-	Seventh post-
Indian	Persian	Chaldean	Roman	Atlantean	Atlantean	Atlantean

During our fifth post-Atlantean Cultural Age, the element of iron in our blood is complemented by what Steiner calls cosmic iron, which becomes Michael's armor in his task in the cosmic battle to help humanity progress in the face of strife and war. Iron is the polarity of our age. Now is the age when humanity must begin to develop the Psalmist's "rod of iron" enabled during the Cultural Age of Christ. (See Ps 2,9 and Rev 2,27 in connection with I-25; the ultimate maturity then reflected in Rev 12,5 and 19,15; see the discussion of the "rod of iron" in the "Blood" essay.)

Other charts that relate different aspects of the Cultural Ages include I-24, I-26 and part of I-19.

ABBREVIATIONS AND BIBLIOGRAPHY

The bibliography in Volume 1 is a research tool by itself, listing chronologically and by lecture location all Steiner titles then available in the English language, insofar as I was able to acquire them. The bibliography below lists only works that either were not included in the first volume or are cited in this volume. Because of the limited nature of the Steiner portion of this bibliography, its titles are listed alphabetically by abbreviation rather than chronologically. The relatively few Steiner titles listed below that have been added since Volume 1 are identified by an asterisk in front of the abbreviation. Several titles listed in Volume 1 have come out in new editions since the list in that volume was prepared, sometimes with new titles; in these cases, proper identification is given below, but the work is not identified as a new one added since Volume 1. Anthologies added since Volume 1 are identified only by their later dates of publication.

Abbreviations used for Anthroposophical publishers are as follows:

AM	Anthroposophical Movement Weekly News
ANS	Anthroposophic News Sheet, Dornach, Switzerland
AP	Anthroposophic Press, Great Barrington, MA
APC	Anthroposophic Publishing Co., London
AR	Anthroposophic Review
FB	Floris Books, Edinburgh, Scotland
GBR	Garber Communications, Blauvelt, NY
MP	Mercury Press, Chestnut Ridge, NY
RSP	Rudolf Steiner Press, London
RSPB	Rudolf Steiner Publications, Blauvelt, NY
RSPC	Rudolf Steiner Publishing Co., London
SBC	Steiner Book Centre, North Vancouver, Canada
TLP	Temple Lodge Press, London
U.E.T.	See next paragraph

Publication dates are for English editions only. Many of the Steiner titles below were not in print during my own library accumulation. Loan copies of these were provided by the Rudolf Steiner Library. In some instances these copies contained no publication data, nor was it available on the Library's catalogue listings. In these instances, if the document was in typescript form I usually assumed it was unpublished. In the most common of these situations, the publication data is given as "unpublished English typescript" and abbreviated U.E.T. Where publication data uses one of the publishing company abbreviations above or is otherwise shown in the normal format (city, publisher name, year), it is believed to be reliable. In all other cases, the data is simply the best practically available to me in compiling this list and cannot be deemed fully reliable.

Steiner Writings and Lectures:

Abbre- viation	Earliest Date	No. & Location of Lectures	Title
AGSS	08-22-06	14-Stuttgart	*At the Gates of Spiritual Science*, 2d Ed., RSP and AP, 1986
*AHIU	11-13-23	5-The Hague	*At Home in the Universe*, AP, 2000
ALPH	12-18-21	1-Dornach	*The Alphabet*, MP, 1982
AM	01-04-18	7-Dornach	*Ancient Myths/Their Meaning and Connection with Evolution*, SBC, 1971
APOC	01-16-05	2-Cologne	*The Apocalypse*, U.E.T.
ARNS	01-01-21	18-Stuttgart	*Astronomy: The Relation of the Diverse Branches of Natural Science to Astronomy* (Mansell translation; in Vol. 1, a different translation was described as U.E.T.)
ASJ	06-15-08	13-Nuremburg	*The Apocalypse of St. John*, 4th Ed., RSP & AP, 1977
AUTO	Dec 1923	Weekly	*Autobiography*, AP, 1999 (New translation and much improved edition of what appeared in Vol. 1 under the title *The Course of My Life* [CML])
AWASJ	10-10-04	3-Berlin	*On Apocalyptic Writings, with special reference to the Apocalypse of St. John*, U.E.T.
BBUS	12-17-20	3-Dornach	*The Bridge Between Universal Spirituality and the Physical Constitution of Man*, AP, 1958
BDR	11-05-12	10-Berlin	*Between Death and Rebirth*, 2nd Ed., RSP, 1975
BG	05-28-13	9-Helsingfors	*The Occult Significance of the Bhagavad Gita*, AP, 1968
BKM	10-17-10	13-Various	*Background to the Gospel of St. Mark*, 3rd Ed., RSP & AP, 1968

BMFE	11-02-08	9-Berlin	*The Being of Man and His Future Evolution,* RSP, 1981
BWM	11-20-14	3-Dornach	*The Balance in the World and Man/Lucifer and Ahriman,* SBC,1948
CBRel	03-17-07	2-Munich	*Christianity Began as a Religion but is Greater than all Religions,* APC, 1959
CCWL	12-13-07	1-Berlin	*Christmas/A Contemplation out of the Wisdom of Life/Vitaesophia,* MP, 1982
CHM	02-06-17	7-Berlin	*Cosmic and Human Metamorphosis,* GBR, 1989
CHS	07-12-14	4-Norrkoping	*Christ and the Human Soul,* 4th Ed., RSP, 1984
CIDE	10-25-09	7-Berlin	*The Christ Impulse and the Development of Ego Consciousness,* AP, 1976
CM	1904	Book	*Cosmic Memory,* RSPB, 1959
CMF	1902	Book	*Christianity as Mystical Fact,* 3rd Ed., AP, 1997
CSW	12-28-13	6-Leipzig	*Christ and the Spiritual World/The Search for the Holy Grail,* RSP, 1963
CTK	12-15-12	1-Bern	*Concerning the Technique of Karma in the Life after death and the Secret of the Human Brain,* no pub. data given
CWCR	1917	Article	*The Chymical Wedding of Christian Rosenkreutz,* RSPB, no pub. date given
CY	03-31-23	5-Dornach	*The Cycle of the Year as Breathing-Process of the Earth,* AP, 1984
DCOSP	01-01-09	2-Berlin	*The Deed of Christ and the Opposing Spiritual Powers/Mephistopheles and Earthquakes,* SBC, 1954
EAR	10-23-11	6-Berlin	*Evolution in the Aspect of Realities,* GBR, 1989
ECMCR	09-17-11	13-Various	*Esoteric Christianity and the Mission of Christian Rosenkreutz,* 2d Ed., RSP, 1984
EIE	12-23-17	1-Basel	*Et Incarnatus Est: The Time-Cycle in Historic Events,* MP,1983
ELW	Sep 1922	Book	*The East in the Light of the West,* 2d. Ed., RSPC & AP, 1940
EMM	09-02-08	12-Leipzig	*Egyptian Myths and Mysteries,* AP, 1971
EoB	10-01-11	1-Basle	*The Etherization of the Blood,* 4th Ed., RSP, 1971
EVC	08-19-23	13-Penmenmawr	*The Evolution of Consciousness* (this is the same cycle as *The Evolution of the World and of Humanity,* but a different translation), GBR, 1989

EVEM	06-30-24	14-Dornach	*The Evolution of the Earth and Man,* AP & RSP, 1987
FE	09-26-05	31-Berlin	*Foundations of Esotericism,* RSP, 1983
FM	12-14-05	29-Various	*The Festivals and their Meaning,* RSP, 1992
*FMEET-1	09-16-19	35-Stuttgart	*Faculty Meetings With Rudolf Steiner,* AP, 1998
*FMEET-2	10-02-22	36-Stuttgart	*Faculty Meetings With Rudolf Steiner,* AP, 1998
FSC	06-01-14	1-Basel	*The Four Sacrifices of Christ,* AP, 1944
GEN	08-17-10	10-Munich	*Genesis,* RSP, 1982
GOSP	11-14-09	1-Stuttgart	*The Gospels,* Eng. typescript; unclear if otherwise published
GOSPSJ	11-16-07	8-Basel	*The Gospel of St. John,* U.E.T.
GS	1883	Book	*Goethean Science,* MP, 1988
GSJ	05-18-08	12-Hamburg	*The Gospel of St. John,* Rev. Ed., AP, 1962
GSL	09-15-09	10-Basel	*The Gospel of St. Luke,* Rev. Ed., AP, 1962. The new translation of this 10-lecture cycle currently being published by AP under the title *According to Luke* is not timely for citation in this volume.
GSMk	09-15-12	10-Basel	*The Gospel of St. Mark,* AP & RSP, 1986
GSMt	09-01-10	12-Berne	*The Gospel of St. Matthew,* 4th Ed., RSP & AP, 1965
HBBSS	08-02-22	10-Dornach	*The Human Being in Body, Soul and Spirit/Our Relationship to the Earth,* ANS, 10-29-39
HCMF	12-22-18	8-Dornach	*How Can Mankind Find the Christ Again?,* 2d Ed., AP, 1984
HCT	01-20-14	4-Berlin	*Human and Cosmic Thought,* RSP, 1961
HI-2	12-30-22	9-Dornach	*Health and Illness,* Vol 2, AP, 1983
HKHW	1904	Book	*How to Know Higher Worlds,* AP, 1994 (New edition of what appeared in Vol. 1 under the title *Knowledge of Higher Worlds and its Attainment* [KHW])
HUHT	05-26-22	1-Dornach	*The Human Heart,* MP, 1985
*ILPB	09-08-18	1-Dornach	Excerpt from *Polarity in Human Life,* entitled *On the Importance of Life in the Physical Body.* Available from the Rudolf Steiner Library, it is identified simply as "Pages 63-4" from GA-184 (its identification in the Steiner archives in Dornach), being a single paragraph translated in Nov. 1997 by one M.S.

ISBM   01-06-08   11-Berlin   *The Influence of Spiritual Beings Upon Man,* AP, 1961

ITSP   1894   Book   *Intuitive Thinking as a Spiritual Path,* AP, 1995 (New edition of what appeared in Vol. 1 under the title *Philosophy of Spiritual Activity* [PSA])

Jn-Rel   06-24-09   14-Kassel   *The Gospel of St. John and Its Relation to the Other Gospels,* 2d Ed., AP, 1982

JTC   10-05-11   10-Karlsruhe   *From Jesus to Christ,* RSP, 1973

KC   8-12-24   7-Torquay   *The Kingdom of Childhood,* 2d Ed., AP, 1988

KM   07-31-17   9-Berlin   *The Karma of Materialism,* AP & RSP, 1985

KR-1   02-16-24   12-Dornach   *Karmic Relationships,* Vol. 1, 2d Ed., RSP, 1972

KR-2   04-06-24   16-Dornach   *Karmic Relationships,* Vol. 2, 2d Ed., RSP, 1974

KR-3   07-01-24   11-Dornach   *Karmic Relationships,* Vol. 3, 2d Ed., RSP, 1957

KR-4   09-05-24   10-Dornach   *Karmic Relationships,* Vol. 4, 2d Ed., RSP, 1983

KR-5   03-29-24   7-Various   *Karmic Relationships,* Vol. 5, 2d Ed., RSP, 1984

KR-6   01-25-24   9-Various   *Karmic Relationships,* Vol. 6, 2d Ed., RSP, 1989

KR-7   06-07-24   9-Breslau   *Karmic Relationships,* Vol. 7, RSP, 1973

KR-8   08-12-24   6-England   *Karmic Relationships,* Vol. 8, RSP, 1975

LA   04-01-19   5-Various   *Lucifer and Ahriman, The Influences of,* SBC, 1976

LAI   12-03-16   1-Zurich   *Luciferic and Ahrimanic Influences/Influences of the Dead,* AM, 5-22-27

LBDR   10-26-12   16-Various   *Life Between Death & Rebirth,* AP, 1968

LC   12-23-19   10-Stuttgart   *Light Course,* MP, no date

MBSP   07-22-21   3-Dornach   *Man as a Being of Sense and Perception,* SBC, 1981

MCR   11-18-11   8-Various   *The Mission of Christian Rosenkreutz,* RSPC, 1950

MK   05-16-10   11-Hamburg   *The Manifestations of Karma,* 3rd Ed., RSP, 1984

MLO   06-02-12   10-Oslo   *Man in the Light of Occultism, Theosophy and Philosophy,* GBR, 1989

MM   03-21-10   11-Vienna   *Macrocosm and Microcosm,* Rev. Ed., RSP & AP, 1985

MS-1   12-09-09   9-Berlin   *Metamorphoses of the Soul/Paths of Experience,* Vol. 1, 2d Ed., RSP, 1983

MS-2   01-20-10   9-Berlin   *Metamorphoses of the Soul/Paths of Experience,* Vol. 2, 2d Ed., RSP, 1983

MSCW   10-19-23   12-Dornach   *Man as Symphony of the Creative Word,* RSP, 1991

MSF   09-27-23   4-Vienna   *Michaelmas and the Soul-Forces of Man,* AP, 1946

MT   07-23-22   8-Various   *The Mystery of the Trinity/The Mission of the Spirit,* AP, 1991

MTA   04-02-21   17-Dornach   *Materialism and the Task of Anthroposophy,* AP & RSP, 1987

MWLSS 03-18-08   1-Munich   *Man and Woman in the Light of Spiritual Science,* AR, #2

MWS   11-26-22   12-Dornach *Man and the World of Stars,* AP, 1963

MYST   12-25-07   1-Cologne   *The Mysteries, a Poem by Goethe,* MP, 1987

MYSTG 12-02-06   1-Cologne   *The Mystery of Golgotha,* U.E.T.

NEWSS 1924   Dornach   *The Newssheet and the Members,* Ghent, NY, Rudolf Steiner Library Newsletter #24, June, 2000, p. 4

OES   1909   Book   *Outline of Esoteric Science,* AP, 1997 (New edition of what appeared in Vol. 1 under the title *Occult Science—An Outline* [OS])

OH   12-27-10   6-Stuttgart   *Occult History,* RSP, 1982

OP   03-20-11   8-The Prague *An Occult Physiology,* 3rd Ed., RSP, 1983

ORL   02-17-13   2-Stuttgart   *Occult Research into Life Between Death and a New Birth,* AP, 1949

OSC   05-18-07   1-Munich   *Occult Seals and Columns,* U.E.T.

OSG   05-03-11   1-Munich   *The Concepts of Original Sin and Grace,* RSP, 1973

OSOE   11-08-06   3-Berlin   *The Origin of Suffering/The Origin of Evil, Illness and Death,* SBC, 1980

PCR   09-06-22   10-Dornach   *Philosophy, Cosmology & Religion,* AP, 1984

PM   09-08-24   11-Dornach   *Pastoral Medicine,* AP, 1987

PSI   04-24-24   6-London   *Planetary Spheres and Their Influence on Man's Life on Earth and in Spiritual Worlds,* RSP, 1982

RCE   01-25-10   13-Various   *The Reappearance of Christ in the Etheric,* AP, 1983

RE   06-03-09   10-Budapest *Rosicrucian Esotericism,* AP, 1978

REVP   09-05-24   18-Dornach   *The Book of Revelation and the work of the priest,* RSP, 1998 (Published version of the unpublished English typescript that appeared under the abbreviation APOC-CC in Vol. 1)

RH   07-29-16   15-Dornach   *The Riddle of Humanity,* RSP, 1990

RMI   01-04-24   6-Dornach   *Rosicrucianism and Modern Initiation,* RSP, 1982

ROSC   09-27-11   2-Neuchatel *Rosicrucian Christianity,* MP, 1989

RP   1914   Book   *Riddles of Philosophy,* AP, 1973

RPA   04-22-07   4-Munich   *Reading the Pictures of the Apocalypse—Part I,* AP, 1991

*RR	12-23-22	5-Dornach	Included in RR in Anthologies
*RR	06-15-15	1-Dusseldorf	Included in RR in Anthologies
RT	05-22-20	3-Dornach	*The Redemption of Thinking*, AP, 1956
RWI	05-22-07	14-Munich	*Rosicrucian Wisdom: An Introduction*, RSP, 2000, this is a new edition of the title listed as *Theosophy of the Rosicrucian* (TR) in Vol. 1
SE	01-21-09	11-Various	*The Principle of Spiritual Economy*, AP & RSP, 1986
SFM	05-28-12	3-Norrkoping	*The Spiritual Foundation of Morality*, AP, 1995
SGM	06-06-11	3-Copenhagen	*The Spiritual Guidance of Man*, AP, 1950
SGSM	02-11-11	1-Munich	*The "Son of God" and the "Son of Man,"* U.E.T.
SHPW	04-12-09	10-Dusseldorf Part 1 5-Berlin Part 2	*The Spiritual Hierarchies and the Physical World/Reality and Illusion*, AP, 1996 (Part 1 is a new translation of what was called *The Spiritual Hierarchies* [SH] in Vol. 1; Part 2 was not in SH)
SIS	12-23-20	4-Dornach	*The Search for the New Isis, Divine Sophia*, MP, 1983
SKN	10-11-06	13-Berlin	*Supersensible Knowledge*, MP, 1988
SM	08-21-19	14-Stuttgart	*Study of Man*, 2d Ed., RSP, 1966
SMRC	02-20-10	1-Dusseldorf	*The Sermon on the Mount and the Return of Christ*, U.E.T.
SSFS	08-06-20	16-Dornach	*Spiritual Science as a Foundation for Social Forms*, AP & RSP, 1986
SSSAS	01-30-24	1-Dornach	*About the School of Spiritual Science and its Arrangement into Sections*, extract of lecture in *The Constitution of the School of Spiritual Science*, pub. by Anthrop. Soc. in Great Britain, 1964, p. 24
ST	08-24-13	8-Munich	*Secrets of the Threshold*, AP & RSP, 1987
TCR	04-13-22	1-The Hague	*The Teachings of Christ, The Resurrected/Reflections on the Mystery of Golgotha*, AP & RSPC, 1940
TFP	08-11-24	11-Torquay	*True and False Paths in Spiritual Investigation*, 3rd Ed., RSP & AP, 1985
THSY	1904	Book	*Theosophy*, AP, 1994 (New edition of same title in Vol. 1)
TI	06-06-16	7-Berlin	*Toward Imagination*, AP, 1990

TIEC	06-24-21	5-Dornach	*Therapeutic Insights/Earthly and Cosmic Laws,* MP, 1984
TIG	01-19-05	1-Dusseldorf	*The Idea of God* (Extracts), U.E.T.
TR	05-22-07	14-Munich	*Theosophy of the Rosicrucian,* 2d Ed., RSP, 1966
UEM	08-04-08	11-Stuttgart	*Universe, Earth, and Man,* RSP, 1987
WC	03-01-20	14-Stuttgart	*Warmth Course,* 2d Ed., MP, 1988
WH	12-24-23	9-Dornach	*World History in the Light of Anthroposophy,* 2d Ed., RSP, 1997
WHA	03-16-11	1-Berlin	*What Has Astronomy to Say about the Origin of the World?,* U.E.T.
WSK	1912	Book	*A Way of Self-Knowledge/The Threshold of the Spiritual World,* AP, 1999 (New edition of what was called *A Road to Self Knowledge/The Threshold of the Spiritual World* [RSK] in Vol. 1)
WSWS	12-27-11	6-Hanover	*The World of the Senses and the World of the Spirit,* SBC, 1979
WW	08-18-11	10-Munich	*Wonders of the World, Ordeals of the Soul, Revelations of the Spirit,* RSP, 1963
YG	10-03-22	13-Stuttgart	*The Younger Generation,* AP, 1967

Anthologies:

ANGELS	*Angels,* RSP, 1996
ARCHM	*The Archangel Michael/His Mission and Ours,* AP, 1994
ASA	*Art as Spiritual Activity,* AP, Ed. Howard, 1998
BEET	*From Beetroot to Buddhism,* RSP, 1999
CRA	*A Christian Rosenkreutz Anthology,* GBR, 1981
EVL	*Evil,* RSP, 1997
FD	*The Fourth Dimension,* AP, 2001
FJSP	*Freud, Jung & Spiritual Psychology,* AP, 2001 (New translation of what appeared in Vol. 1 under the title *Psychoanalysis and Spiritual Psychology* [PSP]
FLTL	*From Limestone to Lucifer,* RSP, 1999
GDNA	*Guardian Angels,* RSP, 2000
HEAL	*The Healing Process,* AP, 2000
HCES	*From the History & Contents of the First Section of the Esoteric School 1904-1914,* AP, 1998
LMIW	*Love & Its Meaning in the World,* AP, 1998

LNM	*Light for the New Millennium, Rudolf Steiner's Association with Helmuth and Eliza von Moltke, Letters, Documents and After-Death Communications*, RSP, 1997
MAMED	*From Mammoths to Mediums*, RSP, 2000
MEANL	*The Meaning of Life*, RSP, 1999
NATS	*Nature Spirits*, RSP, 1995
RR	*Reverse Ritual/Spiritual Knowledge Is True Communion*, AP, 2001
RSEC	*Rudolf Steiner, Economist*, Canterbury, Eng., New Economy Publications, Ed. Budd, 1996
RSSB	*Rudolf Steiner Speaks to the British*, RSP, 1998
SSCRR	*The Secret Stream: Christian Rosenkreutz and Rosicrucianism*, AP, 2000
STACON	*Staying Connected*, AP, 1999
VMIL	*A Vision for the Millennium*, RSP, Ed. Welburn, 1999
WEEB	*World Ether/Elemental Beings/Kingdoms of Nature*, MP, 1993

Steiner Biographies:

Barfield	*Introducing Rudolf Steiner*, Ann Arbor, Anthroposophical Society in America (IRS)
Barnes,	*A Life for the Spirit*, AP, 1997 (LFS)
Hemleben	*Rudolf Steiner, An Illustrated Biography*, London, Sophia Books, 2000 (RSIB)
Steiner	*Autobiography*, AP, 1999 (AUTO)

Other Anthroposophical Writers:

AFEM	Schmidt-Brabant/Sease, *The Archetypal Feminine*, TLP, 1999
ANAS	Vreede, *Anthroposophy & Astrology*, AP, 2001
AOMR	Wolff, *Anthroposophically-Oriented Medicine and Its Remedies*, MP, 1991
ApSJn	Bock, *The Apocalypse of Saint John*, FB, 1957
ASOT	Tomberg, *Anthroposophical Studies of the Old Testament*, 2d Ed., Spring Valley, NY, Candeur Manuscripts, 1985
BAL	Kuhlewind, *Becoming Aware of the Logos*, Great Barrington, MA, Lindisfarne Press, 1985, orig. pub. Germany, 1979
BB	Smith, *The Burning Bush*, AP, 1997
BC	Welburn, *The Beginnings of Christianity*, FB, 1991
BFS	Welburn, *The Book with Fourteen Seals*, RSP, 1991
CaA	Bock, *Caesars and Apostles*, FB, 1998

CEWA   Querido, *Creativity in Education: The Waldorf Approach*, San Francisco, H. S. Dakin Co., 1982

CHA   Powell, *Christian Hermetic Astrology*, Great Barrington, MA, Golden Stone Press, 1990

CJ   Bock, *The Childhood of Jesus*, FB, 1997

CLC   Powell, *Chronicle of the Living Christ*, AP, 1996

CLT   Zajonc, *Catching the Light*, NY, Oxford Univ. Press paperback edition, 1995; Bantam Books, 1993

COSC   Sucher, *Cosmic Christianity/The Changing Countenance of Cosmology*, AP, 1985

CRRS   Roboz, *Christian Rosenkreutz; From the works of Rudolf Steiner*, SBC, 1982

CSM   Kelber, *Christ and the Son of Man*, FB, 1997

CVT   Prokofieff, *The Case of Valentin Tomberg*, TLP, 1997

DR   Macbeth, *Darwinism Retried: An Appeal to Reason*, Boston, The Harvard Common Press, 1971

DTF   Macbeth, *Darwinism: A Time for Funerals*, Mill Valley, CA, Robert Briggs Associates, 1982

DWJL   Smith, *The Disciple Whom Jesus Loved*, AP, 2000

EB   Wolff, *The Etheric Body*, MP, 1990

EI   Prokofieff, *Eternal Individuality*, TLP, 1992

EVM   Wachsmuth, *The Evolution of Mankind*, Dornach, Philosophic-Anthroposophic Press, 1961

EWE   Prokofieff, *The Encounter With Evil, TLP, 1999*

GJC   Archiati, *Giving Judas a Chance*, Birmingham, AL, Spiritual Science Publications, 1999

GSPS   Weisshaar, *A Guide To Spiritual Science*, Spring Valley, NY, Proteus Press, 1951

HA1   Powell, *Hermetic Astrology I*, Kinsau, Germany, Hermetika, 1987

HA2   Powell, *Hermetic Astrology II*, Kinsau, Germany, Hermetika, 1989

HOE   Bosse, "How Old is the Earth?", *Jr. of Anthrop. Medicine*, Vol. 11, No. 1, Spring, 1994

HSBA   Prokofieff, *The Heavenly Sophia and the Being Anthroposophia*, TLP, 1996

IBJ   Smith, *The Incredible Births of Jesus*, AP, 1998

IPENT   Leviton, *The Imagination of Pentecost*, AP, 1994

IZOD   Julius, *The Imagery of the Zodiac*, FB, 1994

MAA   Poppelbaum, *Man and Animal*, London, APC & AP, 1931

MHT   Powell, *Most Holy Trinosophia*, Great Barrington, MA, Golden Stone Press, 1994

MHTNR   Powell, *The Most Holy Trinosophia and the New Revelation of the Divine Feminine*, AP, 2000

MJ   König, The Mystery of John/& the Cycle of the Year, Aberdeen, Scot., Camphill Books, 2001

MOT   Anonymous (V.T.), *Meditations on the Tarot*, Rockport, MA, Element, 1985

MRS   Schultz, *Movement and Rhythms of the Stars*, FB and AP, 1963

MSZ   Davidson, *Making Sense of the Zodiac*, NEWS, Winter, 1992

MYSTE   Welburn, *The Mysteries*, FB, 1997

NCHG   Stein, *The Ninth Century and the Holy Grail*, 3rd Ed., TLP, 2001

NEOA   Unger, *On Nuclear Energy and the Occult Atom*, AP, 1982

PLATOP Settegast, *Plato Prehistorian*, Great Barrington, Lindisfarne Press, 1990

RML   Archiati, *Reincarnation in Modern Life*, TLP, 1997

RSAI   Schiller, *Rudolf Steiner and Initiation*, AP, 1981

RSMW   Kirchner-Bockholt, *Rudolf Steiner's Mission and Ita Wegman*, RSP, 1977

SAPP   Barfield, *Saving the Appearances*, 2nd Ed., Hanover, NH, University Press of New England, 1988

SBSC   Thomas, *Science Between Space and Counterspace*, TLP, 1999

SZ   Powell, *The Sidereal Zodiac*, Tempe, AZ, American Federation of Astrologers, 1979

TBD   Kranich, *Thinking Beyond Darwin*, Hudson, NY, Lindisfarne Press, 1999, orig. German Ed. published in 1989

THNS   Prokofieff, *The Twelve Holy Nights and the Spiritual Hierarchies*, TLP, 1988

Non-Anthroposophical Writers:

AL-KEMI VandenBroeck, *Al-Kemi*, Great Barrington, MA, Lindisfarne Press, 1987

ANGAZ   Lewis/Oliver, *Angels A to Z*, Detroit, Visible Ink, 1996

Bede   Marsden, *The Illustrated Bede*, FB, 1996

BONES   Lewin, *Bones of Contention*, Chicago, Univ. of Chicago Press, 1987, 1997

Columba Marsden, *The Illustrated Columba*, FB, 1995

CURV   Cook, *The Curves of Life*, NY, Dover, 1979, orig. pub. London, Constable, 1914

DCOM   Dante, *Divine Comedy*, see 21 GB under "Treatises and other reference Materials" Below

DDOM   Johnson, *Defeating Darwinism by Opening Minds*, Downers Grove, IL, InterVarsity Press, 1997

DOT   Johnson, *Darwin on Trial*, 2^d Ed., Downers Grove, IL, InterVarsity Press, 1993

DP   Huntley, *The Divine Proportion*, NY, Dover, 1970
       Bodanis, $E = mc^2$, NY, Walker & Co., 2000

EM   Schwaller de Lubicz, *The Egyptian Miracle*, Rochester, VT, Inner Traditions International, 1985, orig. pub. France as *Le Miracle Egyptien*, 1963

EMS   Fagg, *Electromagnetism and the Sacred*, NY, Continuum, 1999

EMST   Geldard, *The Spiritual Teachings of Ralph Waldo Emerson*, Great Barrington, MA, Lindisfarne Books, 2001

ESOTS Schwaller de Lubicz, *Esoterism & Symbol*, Rochester, VT, Inner Traditions International, 1985, orig. pub. France as *Propos sur Esoterisme et Symbole*, 1960

ETR   Born, *Einstein's Theory of Relativity*, Rev. Ed., NY, Dover Publications, 1962

EVED   Korsmeyer, *Evolution & Eden*, NY, Paulist Press, 1998

EWP   Frost & Prechter, *Elliott Wave Principle*, 6th Ed., Gainesville, GA, New Classics Library, 1990

FACC   Allen/Allen, *Francis of Assisi's Canticle of the Creatures*, NY, Continuum, 1996

Fld   Abbott, *Flatland*, Princeton, NJ, Princeton Univ. Press, 1991

FOSSIL Tattersall, *The Fossil Trail*, NY, Oxford Univ. Press, 1995

FRAC   Lauwerier, *Fractals*, Princeton, NJ, Princeton Univ. Press, 1991

FTSL   Goethe, *Fairy Tale of the Green Snake and the Beautiful Lily*, Garber, 1991

GAL   Ghyka, *The Geometry of Art and Life*, NY, Dover, 1977

GODEV Edwards, *The God of Evolution*, NY, Paulist Press, 1999

GRS   Trible, *God and the Rhetoric of Sexuality*, Philadelphia, Fortress Press, 1978

HISC   Cahill, *How the Irish Saved Civilization*, NY, Doubleday, 1995

HNSS   Novalis, *Hymns to the Night/Spiritual Songs*, TLP, 1992

HOR   Borgman, *Holding On To Reality*, Chicago, Univ. of Chicago Press, 1999

HP   Bamford, ed., *Homage to Pythagoras*, Hudson, NY, Lindisfarne Press, 1994

IQM   Pauling and Wilson, *Introduction to Quantum Mechanics*, Dover Ed., NY, Dover, 1985

LAKM   Walker/Jahner, *Lakota Myth*, Lincoln, University of Nebraska Press, 1983

MTE   Assman, *Moses the Egyptian*, Cambridge, MA, Harvard Univ. Press, 1998

NSEB   Marko Pogacnik, *Nature Spirits & Elemental Beings*, Forres, Scotland, The Findhorn Press, 1995

NU   Liderbach, *The Numinous Universe*, NY, Paulist Press, 1989

NW   Schwaller de Lubicz, *Nature Word*, West Stockbridge, MA, Lindis-
          farne Press, 1982

OGF   Thompson, *On Growth and Form*, Dover Ed., NY, 1992

PARZ   Wolfram von Eschenbach, *Parzival*, NY, Vintage (Random House),
          1961

PaSin   Wills, *Papal Sin*, NY, Doubleday, 2000

PHEN   Teilhard de Chardin, *The Phenomenon of Man*, NY, Harper & Row,
          1965

PPQT   Heisenberg, *The Physical Principles of the Quantum Theory*, Dover
          Ed., NY, Dover, 1949

REL   Einstein, *Relativity*, 15th Ed., NY, Three Rivers, 1961

RIB   Johnson, *Reason in the Balance; The Case Against Naturalism in Sci-
          ence, Law & Education*, Downers Grove, IL, InterVarsity Press,
          1995

SA   Wills, *Saint Augustine*, NY, Penguin Group, 1999

SAC   Schwaller de Lubicz, *Sacred Science*, Rochester, VT, Inner Tradi-
          tions International, 1988, orig. pub. France as *Le Roi de la
          theocratie Pharaonique*, 1961

SCAL   Carolan, *The Spiral Calendar*, Gainesville, GA, New Classics Library,
          1992

SGP   Tompkins, *Secrets of the Great Pyramid*, NY, Galahad, 1997 (under
          arr. with HarperCollins, 1971)

SHAD   Penrose, *Shadows of the Mind*, NY, Oxford Univ. Press, 1994

SOPH   Thomas Schipflinger, *Sophia-Maria*, York Beach, ME, Samuel
          Weiser, Inc., 1998

SYMB   Schwaller de Lubicz, *Symbol and the Symbolic*, Rochester, VT, Inner
          Traditions International, 1978, orig. pub. France as *Symbol et
          Symbolique*, 1949

TCI   Collin, *The Theory of Celestial Influence*, London, Arkana (Penguin),
          1993, orig. pub. England by Vincent Stuart Pub., 1954

TIM   Plato, *Timaeus*, see GB

TIMN   Schwaller de Lubicz, *The Temple In Man*, Rochester, VT, Inner Tra-
          ditions International, 1977, orig. pub. France as *Le Temple
          dans l'Homme*, 1949

TOMN   Schwaller de Lubicz, *The Temple Of Man*, Vol. 1 and 2, Inner Tra-
          ditions International, 1998, orig. pub. France as *Le Temple de
          l'Homme*, 1957

WWNT   Mack, *Who Wrote the New Testament*, NY, HarperCollins, 1996

Treatises and Other Reference Materials:

AB	*Anchor Bible*, NY, Doubleday, dates for individual volumes vary
ABD	*Anchor Bible Dictionary*, NY, Doubleday, 1992
ABRL	*Anchor Bible Reference Library*, NY, Doubleday, dates for individual volumes vary; some volumes individually listed
ALB	*Archaeology of the Land of the Bible*, NY, Doubleday, 1990 (part of ABRL)
ALB-2	Archaeology of the Land of the Bible, Vol. 2, NY, Doubleday, 2001 (part of ABRL)
AMPB	*Amplified Bible*, Grand Rapids, Zondervan Pub. Co., 1965
Barc	Barclay, Philadelphia, Westminster Press, N.T. volumes are rev. eds., dates vary for different volumes, N.T. being generally in 1975-1976
	Bible Review, Vol. XVI, No. 2, April 2000, "Mt Sinai—in Arabia?", pp. 32-39,52, Washington, D.C., Biblical Archaeology Society
Brit	*Encyclopaedia Britannica*, Chicago, Encyclopaedia Britannica, 1992
CDGRM	Burr (trans.), *The Chiron Dictionary of Greek & Roman Mythology*, Wilmette, IL, Chiron Publications, 1994, orig. pub. Germany, 1981
CGOS	Miller, ed., *The Complete Gospels*, NY, HarperCollins, 1994
DSS	Wise/Abegg/Cook, *The Dead Sea Scrolls*, NY, HarperCollins, 1996
GB	*Britannica Great Books*, Vol. 7, Plato (*Timaeus* and *Republic*), Chicago Encyclopaedia Britannica, 1952
GEL	Liddell and Scott, *Greek-English Lexicon*, 9th Ed., Oxford Univ. Press, 1940, with Rev. Supp., 1996
HC1	Latourette, *A History of Christianity, Beginnings to 1500*, Vol. 1, Prince, Peabody, MA, 1953, 1997
HC2	Latourette, *A History of Christianity, Reformation to the Present*, Vol. 2, Prince, Peabody, MA, 1953, 1997
HEL	Brown-Driver-Briggs, *Hebrew and English Lexicon*, Peabody, MA, Hendrickson, 1906
HSP	Dungan, *A History of the Synoptic Problem*, 1999 (part of ABRL)
Interp	*Interpreter's Bible*, Nashville, Abingdon Press, 1951-1957
INTPN	*Interpretation*, A Bible Commentary for Teaching and Preaching, Atlanta, John Knox Press, dates for individual volumes vary
IS-OTL	Childs, *Isaiah*, Louisville, Westminster John Knox Press, 2001 (part of The Old Testament Library)
IS-WBC1	Brueggemann, *Isaiah 1-39*, Westminster John Knox Press, 1998 (part of Westminster Bible Companion)

IS-WBC2   Brueggemann, *Isaiah 40-66*, Westminster John Knox Press, 1998 (part of Westminster Bible Companion)

JEROME   Kelly, *JEROME, His Life, Writings, and Controversies*, Peabody, MA, Hendrickson, 1975, 1998

Jr AAR   *Journal of the American Academy of Religion*, Cary, NC, Oxford Univ. Press

Jr Bib Lit   *Journal of Biblical Literature*, Atlanta, Society of Biblical Literature

KJV   *King James Version* (of the Bible), Nashville, Thomas Nelson Pub., 1984

KJV/NIV–INT   Marshall, *The Interlinear KJV-NIV Parallel New Testament in Greek and English*, Grand Rapids, Zondervan Pub. House, 1975

LB   *Living Bible*, Wheaton, IL, Tyndale House Pub., 1971

MWCD   *Merriam-Webster's Collegiate Dictionary*, 10th Ed., Springfield, MA, Merriam-Webster, Inc., 1996

NAB   *New American Bible*, Washington, D. C., Confraternity of Christian Doctrine (1991)

NACB   *New American Catholic Bible*, Nashville, Thomas Nelson Pub., 1971

NCC-RSV   *Nelson's Complete Concordance of the Revised Standard Version, Bible*, 2d Ed., Nashville, Thomas Nelson Pub., 1984

NEB   *New English Bible*, NY, Oxford/Cambridge, 1961 (in Vol. 1, identified as being in "The New Testament in Four Versions," NY, Iversen-Ford Associates, 1963)

NHL   Robinson, *The Nag Hammadi Library*, NY, Harper & Row, 1978

NIB   *The New Interpreter's Bible*, Nashville, Abindon, dates for individual volumes vary from 1994 et seq.

NICENE-1   *Ante-Nicene Fathers*, Vols. 1-10, Peabody, MA, Hendrickson, 1994

NICENE-3   *Nicene and Post-Nicene Fathers*, Series 2, Vols. 1-14, Peabody, MA, Hendrickson, 1994

NIV   *The New NIV (New International Version) Study Bible*, Grand Rapids, Zondervan Pub. House, 1985

NJB   *New Jerusalem Bible*, NY, Doubleday, 1985

NKJV   *New King James Version* (of the Bible), Nashville, Thomas Nelson Pub., 1982

NRSV   *New Revised Standard Version* (of the Bible), Nashville, Thomas Nelson Pub. for Cokesbury, 1990

NTINT   Brown, *An Introduction to the New Testament*, 1997 (part of ABRL)

OTP1   Charlesworth, *The Old Testament Pseudepigrapha*, Vol. 1, 1983 (part of ABRL)

OTP2   Charlesworth, *The Old Testament Pseudepigrapha*, Vol. 2, 1983 (part of ABRL)

PENTA   Blenkinsopp, *The Pentateuch*, NY, Doubleday, 1992 (part of ABRL)

PHILO   *The Works of Philo*, Complete and Unabridged, New Updated Ed., Peabody, MA, Hendrickson, 1993

PSEUD   Luibheid (Trans), *Pseudo-Dionysius*, Mahwah, NJ, Paulist Press, 1987

RC-JON   Trible, *Rhetorical Criticism/Context, Method, and the Book of Jonah*, Minneapolis, Fortress, 1994

REB   *Revised English Bible*, NY, Oxford Univ. Press, 1989

RSV   *Revised Standard Version* (of the Bible), Nashville, Thomas Nelson Pub., 1972

RULE   Charlesworth, *The Dead Sea Scrolls: Rule of the Community*, NY, Continuum Pub. Co., 1996

TIOT   Birch, Brueggemann, Fretheim & Petersen, *A Theological Introduction to the Old Testament*, Nashville, Abingdon, 1999

TORAH   *The JPS Torah Commentary*, Philadelphia, Jewish Publication Society, dates for   individual volumes vary from 1989 to 1996

TOT   Brueggemann, *Theology of the Old Testament*, Minneapolis, Fortress, 1997

WNWCD   Webster's New World College Dictionary, 4th Ed., NY, Macmillan, 1999

WNWD   *Webster's New World Dictionary*, 2d Coll. Ed., NY, Simon & Schuster, NY, 1982

Index 1

Index of Scriptures Cited

1,1-3	102,142,174,186,225,269,290,305,429
1,1-4	82
1,1-10	292,293
1,1-18	28
1,3	9,98,113,310,361
1,4-9	301
1,5	241,289,299,304,307,311
1,5b	292
1,12	483
1,13	401
1,14	103
1,15	83
1,16	190,247,307,390
1,33	121
1,45-51	109
2,1	109
2,1-11	199,231,323
2,4	114
2,19	27
2,19,21	21
2,21	104
3,1-15	432
3,2	339
3,5,6,8	77
3,6	103,302
3,6-8	31
3,6,8	164
3,7-9	77
3,8	77,164,224,288
3,14	299
3,14-15	334
3,16	316,435
4,7-42	323
4,10-11	208
6,1-14	179
6,9	206
6,14	206
6,16-21	107
6,31	466
6,31,49	183
6,53-56	400
7,38	208
8,6	102
8,6,8	26,101
8,12	292,293,301
8,23	294
8,28	299
8,32	183,438

INDEX 2

Index of Subjects

revelations, 17, 18, 20–21, 32, 37,
  42–44, 188, 238, 316, 331,
  405
on science, 70, 71, 119, 130, 132,
  135–39, 141, 143, 146, 149,
  153, 160, 165, 223, 224, 228,
  236, 286, 331
  astronomy, 134, 142–43, 163,
    331, 346, 360–62, 411,
    413–14, 429–32
  fire, heat, and light, 125–26,
    126n, 129–32, 134, 151,
    153, 155, 165, 223, 229,
    236. *See also Light Course*
on shadow, 108
on social conflict, 326
on social order, 407n
on thought, 108
Wachsmuth and, 18
*The World of the Senses and the World
  of the Spirit* (WSWS), 375–85
stones, 201–2
suction, 152, 163, 164, 315, 316, 429
Sun, 65, 354, 477–78. *See also* planets
  and planetary system
"Sun-demon," 65, 66
sunset, 303
symbolic meaning, 115
sympathetic nervous system, 344, 368,
  369

T
Tattersall, Ian, 16
Teilhard de Chardin, 11, 30, 210, 218,
  295
temperature. *See* heat
Ten Commandments, 25, 99–101, 103–
  4, 328–29
Tertullian, 193–95
Thales, 92, 94–95
thermodynamics, second law of, 159–60
thinking, human *vs.* divine, 375
"third day," 109–11
"third element," 117n
Thomas, Nick, 259n, 292, 293
Thompson, D'Arcy, 424n
time, 160, 174

and space, 62–63, 131, 138, 292
  transcending/eliminating, 25
  velocity, color, and, 263–69
and timelessness, 57, 62
Tomberg, Valentine, 280n, 309, 310
Tompkins, Peter, 187
transplants, organ, 403
truth, 183
  perception of, 183

U
uncertainty principle, Heisenberg, 229,
  232, 234, 239
unity, 30, 305
universe, expanding, 433–34
ur-phenomenon of color, 243, 255

V
vacuum, 228
veil, 301
velocity, 263–64, 279, 292
Venus, 355
  evolution, 298n
vertebrae, 339
vibrations, 272. *See also* sound/tone
  effects
virtual particles, 209, 227
vision. *See* eye; light; "seeing"
vitreous humor, 251, 252
vocal chords, 277–78

W
Wachsmuth, Guenther, 18
Waldorf Schools, 238, 242
  at Stuttgart, Germany, 134, 238–39
warm-bloodedness, 329–32
water, 50
  as the basic element, 95
water prism, 243–44
wave theory of light, 256–59. *See also*
  light, wave-particle duality
"What is man?", 2, 4, 5, 20, 23, 24, 147,
  409, 422
whirlwind, 198–201, 203–4
Will, 137–38, 152, 153, 242, 379–80
will, 377
women, 306n. *See also* male and female